STAMPING OUT THE VIRUS

STAMPING OUT THE VIRUS

ALLIED INTERVENTION IN THE RUSSIAN CIVIL WAR 1918-1920

Perry Moore

Schiffer Military History
Atglen, PA

DEDICATION

This book is dedicated to the usual suspects in one's life: My deceased father, Col. Lowell Moore, and mother, Priscilla. A few months prior to her death, I had told her about the book. She gave me this astonished look, then said, "A book?! On what?" I told her, then she said, "I've never heard about that." She was 79. My father thought my wargame designs were complex and resembled what he saw at the War College.

My wife Marianne for all the support and understanding regarding this project. Sons, Lennon and Shon. Shon had the same reaction as his Grandmother did. Lennon said "Cool." Daughter Natasha, who is truly a princess, even at the age of 3.5 years (and a huge Beatle fan). And Nicole, for inspirational purposes.

Lastly, to Bob O'Hara, whose diligence and keen research abilities made this book possible. To author David Glantz, who provided inspiration and made suggestions via email as the book manuscript developed. To Capt.Craig Martelle, for help with some of the Russian sources and translations.

Book Design by Ian Robertson.

Library of Congress Control Number: 2002109119

Printed in China
ISBN: 0-7643-1625-7

We are interested in hearing from authors with book ideas on related topics.

Published by Schiffer Publishing Ltd.
4880 Lower Valley Road
Atglen, PA 19310
Phone: (610) 593-1777
FAX: (610) 593-2002
E-mail: Schifferbk@aol.com.
Visit our web site at: www.schifferbooks.com
Please write for a free catalog.
This book may be purchased from the publisher.
Please include $3.95 postage.
Try your bookstore first.

In Europe, Schiffer books are distributed by:
Bushwood Books
6 Marksbury Avenue
Kew Gardens
Surrey TW9 4JF
England
Phone: 44 (0) 20 8392-8585
FAX: 44 (0) 20 8392-9876
E-mail: Bushwd@aol.com.
Free postage in the UK. Europe: air mail at cost.
Try your bookstore first.

North Russia

South Russia

Preface

Like most Americans, I was in a state of disbelief upon reading about how U.S. troops were sent to North Russia to help the British and French troops who were trying to stop Bolshevism. This was in an email I had received. This email arrived to my computer since I had belonged to a wargame discussion group. I thought the email was a joke. I had never heard nor read anything on this; after all, my life began long after WWII. History schoolbooks failed to mention this. This event was the seed that drove me. This was in 1997.

The Internet was firmly established by then, and I immediately surfed the net for information. Once finding out it was true, the research began. I have read nearly all the books on the topic, many long out of publication and written from 1919-1940. Nearly all of the books were vague and abstract as to military operations, and their maps failed to even note unit locations. As a wargame designer since 1980 (http://pweb.jps.net/~perrya), the lack of these details seemed to me as incredible research negligence on the part of the authors. How odd I thought, because the information was always there.

Using the Net I found a researcher in the UK, and together we found the missing military information, mainly in the PRO, London (similar to the U.S. National Archives). The Net provided a vital communication link that shortened what would have been a very time consuming and long period. After several months and a thousand dollars, I had gathered several boxes of military records.

Now began writing the book, it was divided into the Northern and Southern theatres. Within six months or so, the first draft was completed. During 1998, I had also designed a wargame on the topic (Operation Elope) bought by Decision Games (published in the summer of 2002). This covers the French, English, and U.S. advance from Archangel in 1918-1919.

Research continued using the Wrangel archives at the Hoover Institution, Stanford University. It was fascinating to hold documents and reports that General Wrangel (he was on the southern front) handled. Many Russian books and other material also were used, many never being available in the West.

Real life intervened, and the book manuscript sat collecting dust. Another draft was completed in 2000. Research using the Net supplemented the existing material as time went on.

That is how the book you now hold came to be. It is, bar none, the most comprehensive on the topic, providing such details as the military operations, battles, maps (many of which I did), and orders of battles. One could call it the source book on the allied intervention in the Russian Civil war.

Then, in 2001, another email arrived from a Mr. Prouse in Canada. His Grandfather (John) was a Captain in the RAF, and had actually served in the Archangel area. His grandson had found many old photos of the event. These photos had been taken by his grandfather and were lost in an old box (yes, stored in an attic for many years), and here for the first time are published.

Also, noted author Col. David Glantz (several WWII East Front books) agreed to read an early draft of the manuscript. He found the book quite detailed and interesting.

Feel free to contact the author at Perrya@jps.net.

Lastly, thanks to Eugene Pinak, an attorney in Kiev, Ukraine, for providing some rare research material on Wrangel.

North Russia

1

The Gradual Escalation into Confusion

The Allied Military Intervention in the Russian Civil War was an anomaly in history. For it was the best chance to prevent the birth of Communism. What happened in 1919, happened more recently in Vietnam during the 1960's. Namely, an outside nation intervened militarily in another nation's internal situation. In Vietnam, the intervening nation was indecisive militarily and politically, the military forces sent were too few for any positive outcome and the war was not popular at home. This was the same scenario confronting the British by 1918-19. The Russian revolution had caused great concern in Britain and France, many of the lucrative markets had vanished and Bolshevism was looked upon as a virus that had befallen upon a war torn Russia. The old saying that "History often repeats itself" is true.

The seeds of the allied intervention into Russia's Civil War began to germinate in the first quarter of 1918. The original Allied intent was valid, as the British proposed sending a small group of men to Murmansk (where 450,000 tons of war supplies were stockpiled) to defend the vital railroad that was the sole transportation line from the small port on the White Sea (oddly enough, it was at the British instigation that Murmansk was built in 1916). This port had a capacity of 3500 tons daily, however, due to poor upkeep, had a real capacity of only 500 tons daily. By Dec. 1917, the British had a naval squadron stationed there under Rear Adm. Kemp consisting of the BB Glory, CA Iphigenia and 12 trawlers. On Feb.13th, 1918, Kemp requested 6,000 troops to defend the port. By Mid-March, the CA Cochrane and French BB Amiral Aube had also arrived.[1]

Reports had been received and confirmed that German and Finnish troops would be moving toward this port from Finland (this was erroneous at this time). The other fear of the British concerned the large stockpile of allied supplies sent to the Allied Russian army (in 1917) via Archangel. These supplies (amounting to 160-200,000 tons) were substantial and had remained sitting along the dock piers (by some accounts, the actual military items there considered of value were: 50,000 cases of rifle cartridges, three million 3" detonating Shrapnel and HE fuses, eight 12" naval guns, 110 3" artillery guns, and 300,000 3" shells) for up to a year. Their fear was that the Bolsheviks might take them and use them (actually, the Reds had already took what was of value in February!). Of the two reasons, the Murmansk situation "appeared" to be the more critical. Adding to all this was the fact that German submarines were still active in the North Russian waters until Summer and the direct German intervention in Finland (to thwart the Red attacks) appeared real. Thus, on April 3rd, 1918, the Allies adopted a Resolution of Intervention in not only North and South Russia but also Siberia. This resolution was firmly agreed to by Britain and France at the behest of the Russian Ambassador, which opposed Communism. These telegrams arrived to the French Ambassador, Mssr. Noulens, at the French mission in Moscow. In June, Noulens advocated that the Allies should send a sufficient force to halt Bolshevism and that Archangel could be a military base (provided the British provided the money to organize a counter revolution).

This need increased dramatically when the German's last offensive of WW1, *OPERATION MICHAEL*, began in March 1918, and broke through the British lines. In essence, the German success played upon the allied fears creating a sort of abnormal paranoia regarding to the German military capabilities. During this time, reports filtered in stating that the Germans had moved up to 15,000 men into Finland and that much of the Finnish Army was pro German. The reality was that the Germans had planned to intervene in Finland and the plans were in fact drawn up by mid-February. The troops to be used were from a variety of units on the eastern front. Together, they would form the Baltic Division under Gen.Von Goltz. This division comprised of the:

> 2nd Gds Cavalry brigade, 1st and 3rd Uhlan regiments, 95th Infantry brigade, 3rd, 4th and 5th Jager battalions, one light and two heavy artillery batteries, five cycle companies, two machine gun detachments, a armor car detachment and one recon company totaling 9,000 men. The staff came from the 12th division and concentrated near Danzig by March 1. Another German group under Captain Karmann consisting of the 225th regiment, 5th Cycle battalion, a cavalry company and two artillery batteries gathered at Tallinn.

Unbeknownst to the British, the Germans only interest upon their arrival in April, in Finland was ironically to defeat the Bolshevik! This was accomplished by May. The White Finnish forces along the Karelian were not under German control and it was their attack toward Kem (hence the Murmansk Railroad line) in mid March (it reached the railroad by April 9th) that had caused the British paranoia to elevate. Red Finnish forces under British control repelled this advance. Another White Finn detachment of 550 men was sent to seize Kestenga but this failed. Further to the north, the White Finn "Kuolajarvi Bn" poised the most serious threat near Kandalahti. The Bolshevik considered these attacks serious and this led them to allow the British and French forces to land at Murmansk. For the Reds, that was their only reason to allow capitalist troops on their soil. Then, when the danger was over, repel them.

On May 23rd, the British War Cabinet decided on a plan of action that called for a 560 man force to be sent to Archangel and another 600 man force to Murmansk. The German threat did happen, when on June 7th, the German Finnish Army attacked into East Karelia towards Kem. This force was based on the Baltic Division and included two other divisions and a special Arctic Warfare brigade. In total, some 25,000 men .

By the 17th, another Russian-German pact was signed stating that the Russians must kick out the Allies; in return, the Germans would withdraw from Russian occupied territory. Nevertheless, the British forces advanced toward Kem on June 9th, as 150 U.S. sailors arrived at Murmansk. Things were spinning out of control, as Messrs. Lenin and Trotsky tried to "walk the wire" between the Germans and Allies. Attempting to obtain what they wanted (not known by the Allies at the time was the fact that Germans did have plans to seize Murmansk and Archangel in late September, 1918, using Finnish troops. This was stated in the secret German-Russian pact of August 27th, 1918).

Upon the arrival of General Maynard in mid-June to take command of Allied forces, the following forces had already deployed:

> 150 Marines in Penchanga, 150 Marines, 400 Serbs, and 150 Poles in Murmansk. At Kandalaksha were a few hundred French artillery men, Red Finns and more Serbs. At Kem, 250 Marines, 250 Serbs and one armor train. Some 2000 men to defend the port and 350 miles of railroad.

From the start, the intervention was a pure British show. The Americans, at first, chose the correct course, stay out of Russia. The French, who had lost millions of dollars when the Russian Revolution occurred, sided with the British because of this sole reason. The French hoped to "get something back". It was during the second quarter of 1918 that the second reason to intervene became increasingly the excuse. By this time, even the British knew that the supplies stockpiled at Archangel had been pilfered by the Reds and what remained along the docks was not of military value. Thus, the British sent 150 Royal Marines to secure Murmansk on March 6th, on April 18th, another 150 Royal Marines of the 1st Co\29th London Regiment, 600 French, one Serbian unit, 253rd Machine Gun Company and two artillery sections from the 584th Field Artillery landed. On May 17th, another 500 men landed and again on June 23rd, another 600 men and a Machine Gun company.

The Bolsheviks did not actually oppose this arrival and the Red garrison of 1000 men was disarmed. By July, the small force at Kem had advanced further south to Soroka. The opposing 3000 man Red force sent by Lenin retreated burning bridges instead of fighting. The Soviet men in charge at Murmansk now signed an agreement with the British on July 7th, making the British responsible for it's defense! Lenin and Trotsky were beside themselves. Suffice to say all parties on both sides were confused about the overall military situation.

A Call to Arms

The call for pilots for North Russia was sent out to various units in May 1918. It was labeled Top Secret. Those interested in flying in the "stunt" were asked to report to Blandford, England. Upon the arrival of volunteers, these men waited for the medical examination. The men were examined and passed and instructed to take supplies of everything they would need for six months; take clothing that could withstand summers "like those on the Riviera and winters like those north of Scotland", and swore to say nothing about the stunt to anyone but cameras are permitted. On June 14th, the midnight train to Newcastle left with the pilots and observers in addition to the artillery and infantry. No one knew of the destination. Once at Newcastle, the men boarded the Transport *City of Marseilles* and left the port on the 15th escorted by several destroyers. It was out at sea the men found out that the destination was Russia.

The first RAF contingent comprised of: one colonel, four pilots, 4 observers, and 57 NCOs and others. Upon arriving at Murmansk, the RAF began to recruit ex-pilots of the Russian Imperial Air force to form the Slavo-British allied legion (SBAC). A school was started headed by Lt.Col. Maund and Col. Valentine. Most of the Russian pilots had not flown for over a year and most never had conducted strafing or patrolling missions. The HMS Nairana arrived with seven Short 184 seaplanes. These were used during the training period in the Murmansk environs. The local populace was extremely frightened of the airplane having never seen any before.

With the German Offensive failing, the British wanted to enter North Russia at Archangel. By early July, the Supreme War Council had approved to send 1,200 troops to Archangel (the 21st French Colonial Battalion and 2nd line/10th battalion of the Royal Scot Regiment.) and a new commanding officer, General Poole.

The British government would not go into Russia alone, so again, they asked the Americans and French, and again President Wilson refused. However, the French agreed. After some more arm twisting and some questionable activities of the U.S. Ambassador in Russia, President Wilson agreed to send U.S. troops on July 17th, 1918 (the 339th regiment of the 85th division) .Oddly enough, on the 16th, Czar Nicholas II and his family were murdered by the Reds in Ekaterinburg !

The Americans agreed on the sole condition that the troops would only be used to defend the immediate area around Archangel. The supplies stockpiled there now amounted to the following: 15,000 tons of general cargo, 73,600 tons of military (shells, artillery guns, trucks, barb wire, small arms) 52,700 tons of coal, and 6,300 tons of admiralty stores, all occupying acres and acres of land. The British agreed to the U.S. terms

OPERATION ELOPE

The plan to enter Archangel (a city of 50,000) went under the name OPERATION ELOPE. To insure success, British intelligence had contacted many former Imperial Russian Officers working underground to overthrow the Bolshevik regime. Much of the military present was still in Imperialist control since the Red garrison (800 men and one machine gun company) did not have sufficient men to control the entire city. Commander George Chaplin, a 35 yr. old man and a local attorney, Nicholas Startsev, created a planned uprising (with 500 men). The attorney ran an arms distribution ring to certain opposition groups in the area. Chaplin went under the disguise as "Commander Thomson, RN" and spoke perfect English. He had been in the employ of the British Mission since May planning the uprising. The plan comprised of illusions: rumors were started days before the Allies landed indicating a large scale invasion (not true) and it was hoped that the 800 man Red force with poor morale would run. To heighten the impact, Poole flew two Short 184 seaplanes from the Seaplane CV Nairana circling Archangel for 30 minutes, as though preparing an attack. To draw this large Red force away from the city, Chaplin also created a diversion in Shenkursk, a city of 10,000 , some 150 miles south of Archangel in late July.

The Bolo (slang for Bolshevik) took the bait and sent several hundred men to squelch the uprising in Shenkursk. This left only a few hundred men under Commissar Kedrov to defend Archangel and its anti-Bolshevik populace (more concerned with food instead of the Allied invasion). Of course, the coming Allied invasion was not a surprise to Kedrov who had declared martial law and began to build defenses on Mudyug Island (despite large swarms of mosquitoes plaguing the Reds). This defense consisted of a battery of four six-inch guns on the north and south ends of the island. The Allied ships had to pass this island (the narrows being 500 yards wide).

Fleeing from Vologda on July 24th to Archangel were Allied Ambassadors and other diplomats fearing imprisonment or reprisals (they had been told to leave Moscow). Since the Archangel to Vologda railroad could only support one train in either direction, the fleeing Ambassadors and Kedrov ran into each other midway! Kedrov was on his way to Moscow to report to Lenin about the coup led by Chaplin. The two trains met and halted. Kedrov and the allied ambassadors chatted, after which, one of the trains moved to the side rail, allowing the other to pass. When the fleeing Ambassadors reached Archangel they contacted General Poole who was with the invasion forces out at sea. The ambassadors told Poole what had happened. Poole then landed immediately not waiting for the original date of August 3rd.

Sources

1. U.S. National Archives, Microfilm 925.
2. Goldhurst, Richard. 1978. *The Midnight War*
3. Strathovsky, Leonid. 1971. *Intervention in Archangel.*
4. Warth, Robert. 1973. *The Allies and the Russian Revolution*
5. "The RAF in North Russia." 1919. The Aeroplane Magazine.
6. Quanitan, Antony. 1959. *The French in South Russia.*
7. Various records from the Public Records Office, London.

2

Invasion!

General Poole did not wait to invade until the 3rd and ordered the invasion fleet near Murmansk to begin sailing on the evening of July 30th. This invasion fleet consisted of the following:

> CL *Attentive* (carried 100 French troops), CA *Amiral Aube* (carried 300 troops) Seaplane CV *Nairana* (with 8 Short 184 planes and 200 troops), Merchant ships *Tay and Tyne*, six armed trawlers and two gunboats, *Advokat and Oypt*. General Poole was aboard the *Salvator* Yacht. Following were four transports, the *Stephans, Asurian, Westbourough and Kassala* filled with troops escorted by four armed trawlers and the expropriated Russian DD *Sergeyev*.

Several hours before the main invasion force landed, the first British contingent was already ashore. This was a company of men some fifty miles from Archangel at Onega. The small force had crossed the White Sea from the port of Kem aboard the steamer *Archangel Michael*. There was little problem seizing Onega defended by only 13 Bolos, but as Colonel Thornhill and his men moved east towards Oberskaya to cut off Kedrov's men , the British met with stiff resistance from the Red 159th regiment (700 men, 24 MG, 2 guns) and fell back to Onega. The unplanned result did have the effect of drawing more of Kedrov's men away from Archangel.

Four transports carried 849 French soldiers of the 21st Colonial Battalion (trained in the tropics), 100 Royal Marines, 64 U.S. Soldiers from the 339 regiment/85th Division, and 50 Poles (another 200 British soldiers would arrive on August 2nd). As this convoy drew closer to Archangel, the captured Russian DD *Sergueyev* acted as an escort. In Archangel, the small-armed militia began their coup resulting in most of the Reds fleeing.

However, not all of the Reds had fled Archangel, some 180 remained in the city led by Alexandrov. Another 20 Reds held the main wharf area but fled when the *Aube and Attentive* began a brief bombardment. The only resistance from the Reds came from Mudyugski Island which contained two six inch shore batteries in forts. On August 1st, when the flotilla approached, these guns opened up. The British began to fire from a position 5000 yds away using their two six inch and three four inch guns.

Both the *Attentive and Nairana* were sent to deal with this defense. One battery on the north end of the island was silenced with the landing of 150 British soldiers, however, the battery in the southern part continued to fire. The *Attentive* fired some 30 rounds and the shore battery returned it at a distance of 5000 yards. The Reds scored a damaging hit on the *Attentive's* funnel (which knocked out two boilers) this prompted the *Nairana* to send in the Short airplanes (piloted by Lt. .Macdonald, Capt. Simpson and Maj. Moller). They swooped down on the battery dropping their small bomb loads (most missed their target). The Reds finally surrendered when another 100 British troops landed. By 8 p.m. the remaining Reds had fled the island. Thus, ended the first naval and air to ground combined operation in history. The French CA *Aube* ran aground in the foggy approach but was able to continue.

As the flotilla continued to Archangel, maneuvering grew difficult as the route went through an enemy minefield. The Reds had also sunk their icebreaker ships the *Svyatagor and Mikoula*, as well as the ML *Oussurin* in the channel southwest of Pt. Lapeminiski, which partially blocked the channel. The actual port where the tons of supplies were stored and unloaded was at Ekonomia, a few miles north of Archangel. Most of the allied troops would actually land in Archangel, and the Reds retreated to Bakaritza as the Allied troops landed. The *Attentive*, although damaged, continued up the Dvina River in pursuit of the Reds. The airplanes from the CV *Nairana* swooped down on the Reds led by Ber, machine gunning and bombing with impunity. The 800 men of Kedrov resisted as the British and French troops approached across the Railroad bridges spanning the Dvina Channel.

The populace in Archangel welcomed the Allies as liberators. Large crowds lined up along the dirt streets and cheering. The allies had entered a vast territory of 330,000 square miles of marsh, forest and tundra intersected by six rivers, the largest being the Dvina. Few roads existed.

The Reds scattered from Bakaritza fleeing south to the main Red base at Plesetskaya. Thus, on August 1st, Archangel had been seized with only 600 men (had the Reds known this, their 800-1000 man force could have resisted quite nicely). Knowing that the English were landing in the Archangel region and that the urban garrison was small and unreliable, Lenin proposed to urgently dispatch a bomber detachment to destroy the English naval squadron. From Archangel, the nearest Red airbase was in Vologda almost 600 kilometers away with not one airfield in between, he ignorantly exclaimed: "But there are some airfields in the Archangel province and why not make use of them as airfields?" Lenin did not consider aircraft fuel, ammunitions, repair parts and maintenance requirements. Luckily, the seasoned pilot, A.V.Sergeev, called in an expert, who with difficulty argued Lenin out of this silly idea!

With Archangel in the hands of the Allies, the main base was set up. The coup had succeeded, its leader was Nikolai Chaikovsky. Oddly enough, he spoke perfect english and had lived in London for 20 years, and in Independence, Kansas for four years. After the commotion died down, General Poole informed him that Archangel was under martial law and he (Poole) was in charge. One of the first items set up was a military training base for the Russians who opposed the Reds. This base was set up under the British system and all Russians enlisting were armed and paid by the British. Also trained here were Finns and Poles. Each company and section was to be led by a Russian and the unit would be subordinated to a British, French or U.S. unit. Even an Officer Candidate School was opened.

Upon the arrival in Archangel with the invasion force, the RAF (commanded by Lt.Col. Van der Spuy, a South African) aircraft was based on the small 400 yard long x 150 yard wide airfield at Bakaritza, along the Dvina river. This location was near the railroad so the RAF members used old railroad cars for accommodations. Construction began on hangar towers and by mid- August, the airplanes from the HMS Nairana landed.

The first RAF flights were orientation to familiarize the pilots with the vast landscape of forests and marsh with little clearings for emergency landings. The flight to the front was 70 miles. The Russian pilots , likewise, began to fly their 18 Sopwith Strutters, two Nieuports (a 17 and 24). These were found in their crates at Bakaritza ,which the Bolshevik Mozhaev commission did not have time to build. Some of them had already become unfit. However, students from the Archangel Polytechnic University were able to repair 16 engines. Six of the airplanes were armed and formed the first air-detachment of the White North Army. This detachment under the command of Kazakov with pilots Modrakhs, Shebalin, Kossovsk, Kropinovs and Sveshnikov. On August 15th, the unit arrived at the airfield in the village of Obozerskaya, 123 versts (80 miles) from Archangel. On September 11th, the Second Russian Air-Detachment was created and led by Captain Belousovich. In this detachment contained the pilots Kravets, Tolstovs, Slyasarenko, Baidak, and Tumanov.

During September, these detachments were in two different locations in order to stabilize the front. The first was located on the Archangelsk-Vologda "railway front" north of the Emtsa River (*Obozerskaya)*, the other along the "Dvinsk" or " Vaga" rivers near the confluence to the North Dvinsk region. In this more remote area, the 2nd Air detachment of Belousovich was sent. On 17 September Kazakov's detachment was relocated to the 2nd Dvinsk airfield near Bereznik. Soon both detachments were at Bereznik. The British Squadron remained at Obozerskaya only 30 miles north of Emtsa and 60 miles South of Archangel.

The composition of the Red 6th Army contained several Red Aviation detachments. The very reliable Kostromsk Air Group (10 aircraft, mainly – "Farmans-30" and "Sopwith 1 _"), which broke down into two detachments and almost wholly manned by communists. At the close of August they arrived at the front airfield in the village of Plesetskaya (today – City of Plesetsk). On 31 August pilot, Lavrov, of the 1st Detachment of Kostromsk Air Group and pilot, Malinovsk, in a Sopwith Strutter conducted the first Red combat flight. On September 2nd, the Air Group had its first loss. A "Farman-30" piloted by Kudryavtsev and Malinovsk bombed the village of Kholmogorsk. They were hit by machine-gun fire from allied troops. On September 15th, a "Sopwith" piloted by Lavrov and flier Skroyak was also hit by anti-aircraft fire over Obozerskaya on their final pass, again the flier was required to land on the railway!

This "No.2 squadron" was sent up the Dvina River to another new airbase at Siskoe and Beresnik. The RAF contingent contained 14 Canadian, 16 British and 27 Russian pilots . The most experienced were the Russians (Colonel A.A.Kazakov the best Russian ace of the First World War, shooting down 17 German aircraft, as well as Staff-Captain Shebalin,

Captains Modrakhs, Kossovsk, Sveshnikov and Esaul Kachurin, to name a few). The Canadians had less than twenty hours of flight time (The reader should be aware that enormous Russian aircraft supplies were kept on territory in the Central air-park facility. This was the largest in Russia at Khodin. By 1918, there were 70 Nieuport-23, 23 Nieuport-17, 4 SPADs, 12 Farman-40 recon, 15 Kodronovs, and 72 English aircraft of diverse makes, mainly Sopwiths. So, the Russians did have many aircraft left over from WW1. However, most were non-operational for a variety or reasons. Through the winter and spring of 1918, in storage around Moscow, Yarospavlya, Smolensk, Ribinsk, and other cities, some 502 aircraft and 1320 motors existed, as well as a mass of other aircraft property that had been found. A total of 250 engines of English and French origin were stockpiled in Murmansk and Archangel. By May 15, 1918, Trotsky had established the regular composition of the Red air-detachment: 6 aircraft, 4 cars, 5 vehicles, and 113 men. In practice these numbers strongly varied. In the civil war, it was ordinary to see detachments with three-four aircraft, and at times only one that could get into the air. An air group consisted of 2-10 air detachments. A "Divizion" was like a British Squadron consisting of three detachments or flights. Usually a Divizion would comprise three detachments each with 6 aircraft for a total of 18.)

Unlike the allied aircraft, the Reds aircraft while numerous lacked faithful pilots and fuel. The supply of aircraft fuel available to them was no more than 32 tons and front air-detachments were limited to 640 kilograms of fuel a month. This is about how much was burned by one «Rotary» motor after 20 hours and about as much was used by Commander Yurovsk to burn the executed corpses of the Tsar's family!

But as October closed other fuel additives came about. At first the Reds made attempted to create a different type of a aircraft fuel, and soon diverse mixtures began to appear. One was called the "Kazan mixture." This mixture comprised of kerosene, gasoline, alcohol and ether. Barrels of this fuel always were printed with warnings: "before using, shake up" because over time the liquid separated and the more heavy elements fell to bottom. Flights using "Kazan," peculiarly in cold weather, were very risky. The mucous sedimented particles could clog the carburetor jets causing the motor to stop, which forced the aircraft to land.

Besides "Kazan," there was a wide variety of spirit mixtures, bearing a generalized nickname of "aviation cocktail." These consisted of alcohol Ethyl , Methyl and also Sulfur in diverse proportions. The rotary motors could work on clean alcohol-refined products; however, in winter the engine was required to be warmed up . In a one case, when Commander Knyagintski of the 9th Army of the South Front took the Tsimlyanski Spirits factory, he fueled to the aircraft with this alcohol so they could run their motors!

In the memoirs of some airmen (A.K.Petrenko, A.K.Tomanski) wrote that while assigned to flights using the fuel substitute, these pilots got poisoning from the by-products of the combustion resulting in head pain, weakness and dizziness. The greatest harm from the ersatz-fuel was in that it brought about power shortage and premature motor wear. Each «petrol substitute» did harm in its own way. The Kazan mixture formed carbon in the combustion chambers and on cylinder valves, which was difficult to remove. Alcohol motors unsteadily held small turnovers and lightly super-cooled in flight, on Benzol and Toluene it was the reverse, which caused the motors to rapidly overheat.

The main RAF HQ was at Archangel. It contained two wooden hangars insulated with double walls of sawdust, wooden floors, and had electric lights. Here, the 130-man crew maintained the airplanes. The Bakaritsa airfield was a seaplane base for winter use. It, too, had two wooden hangars and a crane. On August 9th, the Red command dispatched to the Archangel Front six M-9 flying boats of the newly created White Sea Hydro-Detachment. Naturally, with six small engines and a pair of 1-pood bombs these planes could hardly change the situation, but Lenin persistently held on to the idea to attack the interventionists from the air. By August 12th, the first three seaplanes and crews were sent by rail from Petrograd to Vologda. On the next day, the remaining three followed. But the hydro-detachment did not fulfill the hopes of Lenin. Upon arrival on the 14th, the front the detachment Commander Peterr Babanenko and pilot Aleksander Serov (son of reputed Balentin artist Serov) defected and flew their M-9 seaplanes to the Whites in Obozerskaya (Obozersk)! This kind of action was typical and created a large distrust regarding aircraft and pilots from the Bolshevik leaders.

Thus, by September, the French and American troops were supported by the RAF and their Short 184's, DH4's, while the Royal Scots (which had formed in mid-July and arrived on August 25th) were supported by mostly White Russian pilots. In both cases, most of the flying was strafing, photography and bombing.

The RAF now found a spot to create another airfield, 50 yds wide x 250 yds long, barely enough space to land the eight DH4's of Flight A, which had just arrived. From this base (with only canvas hangars) the enemy at Emtsa was only 40 miles and their main base at Plesetskaya, some 60 miles (the Reds had an airbase here with perhaps three Nieuports. These seldom flew and usually ran when allied planes were spotted). Next to Archangel, the Beresnik airbase at the confluence of the Vaga and Dvina Rivers was the most important. This was the home of Flight B (five Re-8's, Nieuport 17 and Sopwith Strutter) and many daring Russian pilots.

The commander of the Allied forces was the unimaginative Major General Poole. Born in 1869, he entered the Army in 1889. He became a Captain in 1898. His combat experience was derived from Somaliland and South Africa in 1903-4. By 1909, he had become a major, and a Lt. Col. by 1915. During WW1, he earned his accolades as an artillery officer and by 1918 was a Colonel.

The ports of Murmansk and Archangel contained many Russian ships in various states of disrepair. Most of these were not useable. At Murmansk, the BB *Poltava* was used as a prison, while the *Braemer Castle* was used as a Hospital ship. The British HMS BB *Glory* and HMS *Josephine, Alvina, Sviatogor*, and *Alexander* remained on station. At Archangel, the French CA *Amiral Gueyon* arrived, while the Russian *Kalyan* was used as a hospital ship. The Russian icebreakers *Kozma, Pozharsky, Kanada, Susanin, Gor and Milner* were used and operational

The first troops to see combat on August 3rd were 25 U.S. Navy sailors from the U.S.S Olympia. These men, led my Ensign Hicks, were detailed to the railroad area. Hicks had found a ready to go locomotive and ordered two vacant flatcars to be attached to which a heavy machine gun was positioned. Now began the Bolo chase along the rail line to catch the fleeing Reds. This chase continued for 30 miles until the railroad bridge (which had been blown) crossing at the river. On the other side of the river, the Reds had entrenched and produced withering machine gun fire. Hicks got hit in the leg. Many sailors wanted to advance on foot, wisely, this did not occur. Unbeknownst to the American sailors, they had established the "Railroad" front out of zeal. This position would be held for another month with most of the French 21st battalion.

By mid-August, a small force(known as Force B) consisting of 100 French, 25 American Sailor, 35 Russian and 27 Poles led by Col. Haselton were dispatched up the river to Siskoe and then ordered to Plesetskaya in order to get behind the Bolos at Oberskaya. Another force, under Col. Josselyn traveled up the Dvina. According to the war diary, the Allies had only one effective airplane due to crashes and lack of parts. It is more interesting to note, that on the 16th, the diary notes an Allied force of 21 men (Force A, moving up the railroad) battled a Red group of 88 men. Among the enemy killed was a German officer. Force B, met a Red unit consisting of 250 men , one armor car, field and MG guns near Seletskoe, which was beaten back. Force B was reinforced with 100 Russians and 10 Lewis Guns, and two Vickers MG. Force C, which had sailed up the Dvina met a few Bolo gunboats near Borok. By the 18th, Force C had reached Troitsa just as a Bolo steamer was sunk from dive bombing airplanes. To help Force A advance along the railroad, an armor train (consisting of one 77mm , one truck mounted 55mm, two trucks mounting a French 75mm each and one truck with two 77mm howitzers) was being prepared to support them. This arrived on the 22nd. To help force C, two 18 pdrs were sent up the Dvina. Force B's deployment changed from marching on Peletskaya to Oberskaya from Seletskoe. It was then held up due to a blown bridge. On the 30th, the Reds seemed to be pushing the weak Allied units around forcing Force B to fall back to Fedorovskaya. The 150 Bolos were now moving on Siskoe. Quickly, a platoon of the Royal Scots and 35 Royal Marines were dispatched there. Likewise, Force C, had to also withdraw to Beresnik when Reds and mounted cavalry units were moving in on their flanks. Force A on the 31st, attacked at 6:30 a.m after an one hour artillery barrage. Air support was not available due the low cloud ceiling. The Reds quickly counterattack and then routed.

British troops march down the main street in Archangel, June 1919. Photo: IWM

Most of August consisted of establishing the Allied base and the organization of troops. The troops landed were: British 2nd line /10th Bn /Royal Scot Regiment arrived on Aug.25th, 21st French Colonial Battalion (870 men), 41st Field Artillery battery (two 4.5 howitzers, two 75mm), one Serb and Italian company, HMS Monitor 25, 63rd French Artillery battery (4-6 75mm), 87th Depot base, and 8 DH4 aircraft. The Allies had also gathered a few abandoned steamers.

The French were immediately sent south along the Railroad after a few days, advancing 30 miles (Poole's objective was Vologda, some 400 miles south!) while a mix of British/French units traveled by steamer down the Dvina. Red resistance was nil but as the French moved closer to Oberskaya, 75 miles south of Archangel, the resistance was solid. So much so, that General Poole attributed it to German troops, which Poole felt surely were directing the Reds (the Germans were never helping the Reds in North Russia). On August 6th, a combined British/French/Polish force was sent down the Dvina River in three steamers. Their objective: Kotlas. A town 400 miles away! By the 8th, the "Dvina" force had traveled 140 miles arriving at Beresnik with no opposition. However, waiting there was the absent resistance: four well armed Red gunboats. The gunboats and Red soldiers on the shore pinned the advancing force, halting the voyage until the allied gunboats, *Opyt and Advokat* arrived. Also arriving was the *M25* monitor (with one 7.5" gun). After a brief battle, the Bolo continued to fall back. However, allied logistical problems began to arise, supplies had to be transported along the 200 mile Dvina River. In places it was two miles wide and 8 feet deep, while in other zones, 3 feet deep and 10 yards wide. Adding to this problem was rapidly changing current directions (even the *M25* monitor was plagued by the river currents and draft). With the *M25* in the lead, the river force meandered down the Dvina until August 28th, when a Bolo artillery ambush occurred. The *M25* battled with the onshore batteries effectively silencing them but not before 11 of the M25's crew were killed or injured. General Poole in his report of the 17th, remained hopeful that Kotlas could be reached by September 20th, if first class type reinforcements arrive. Also occurring on the 17th was the Russian air detachment flying to support the allies along the Dvina.

It was during the last week of August that the Russian airbase at Siskoe came under attack. The local populace had fled and the Russian pilots (Shebalin, Modrack, Kropinov, Abramovich, Katchurin, Sveshnikov, Bielousovich, Baidek, Tolstov, Belousov, Lutz,and Lvov) suddenly became an infantry squad taking up defensive positions, among them was Kazakov. Armed with their Lewis guns (taken off their planes and the aircraft hidden behind forests) and rifles they repelled repeated Red attacks. Kazakov after this operation was awarded by the British the D.S.O. (Distinguished Service Order for Excellent Service).

The plan of General Poole was simple: move south along the railroad and the Dvina and Vaga Rivers. The ultimate goal would be to take Vologda. Poole was no fool and he knew that without more forces even this was a dream. Thus, his operational objectives were modest, take Plesetskaya, a main Red base. In the bigger scheme of plans, the allied objective was to divert the Red forces, create a White Russian army, which could move on Moscow, and to strike for Kotlas to meet with the White Russian forces under Admiral Kolchak (also supplied and armed by the British) who would, in the Spring of 1919, advance past Perm.

During this time, the average monthly food rations for the local population was as follows:

Women and children = 14 lbs of flour, 1.8 lbs of rice, 1/4 lb of tea, 1 lb of sugar.

For the Allied soldier:

27 lbs of flour, 15lbs of meat, 4 lbs of rice, 1/2 lb of tea, 2 lbs of sugar, 12 lbs of fish

By September 1918, the force disposition in the *Murmansk District* was as follows:

British HQ: Maj.Gen. Maynard; French HQ: Col. Begou; Italian HQ: Col. Sifola.

	120 RR btty (six 18pdr)150 men
	Sec.1 (155mm) 60 men
	Two Royal Marine Sect. 60 men
	492nd Royal Engineers Co. 200men
	Co 1/13th Yorkshire bn 180men
	No.1 Stokes Mortar btty 131 men
	Armor train 60 men
AT KOLA:	236th Brig (Lt.Col. Rowlandson)
	6th Brigade RFA (Col.Sawins)
	420th btty(six 4.5 howitzer 480 men)
	434th btty (four 18 pdr 120 men)
	(2 66mm sections mountain guns 60 men)
	Co.2/13th Yorkshire bn 180men
	One Italian Bn (1100 men)
	One Reserve Italian Co. (160 men)
	One section Carabinieri 30 men
	28th MG Co. 60 men.
AT DROVIANOI:	Co 3/13th Yorkshire 180 men
AT LOPARSKAYA:	1 section of two 12pdr 60 men
	1 section of infantry 25 men
	Co 1./French Ski Bn 140 men
AT IMANDRA:	Co.4/13th Yorkshires 180 en
AT KANDALASKSHA:	238th brigade (Col Burton)
	61st French artillery battery (four 75mm, 130 men)
	one section of two 3" guns 130 men
	one Finnish arty btty, (four 75mm 120 men)
	Two sections/548 Royal engineers
	Two companies/ 11th Sussex Bn (360 men)
	Co.1/29th bn (180 men)
	No.3 Stokes mtr btty (120 men)
	Two MG sections (60 men)
	One Finnish Bn (800 men)

AT KEM (Gen. Turner):	62 French artillery btty (four 75mm)
	1 old armor train (two 18pdr)
	1 section of engineers
	1 Demolition platoon
	1st Bn/13th Yorkshire (720 men)
	One Bn of Karelians (2000 men)
	One RAF detachment(6 Re8 planes)
	One Russian company (300 men)
AT SOROKA (Col Leckie)	One Canadian Company (50 men)
	One Serbian Bn (Col. Mareukovitch) 500 men
	235 MG Co. (120 men)
	One Co. of Russians (100 men)
	One Co. of russians (200 men)
AT OLYMPIA:	One Serb Co (250 men, one MG section)
AT ALEXANDROVSK:	One Italian and French section (80 men)
AT PETCHENGA:	Two Cos./ Royal Sussex Bn
(Lt Col Elliott)	one Serb Co (200 men)
	one Serb arty btty (four 75mm)
	one btty/435th Howitzer (130 men)

The total number of men was 13,090, of which 6330 were British, 590 French, 1520 Italian, 1070 Serb, 600 Russian, and 2980 Finn.

Leaving Ireland on July 31st, was the 1000 man 2nd line/10th battalion of the Royal Scot regiment. It headed for Newcastle and boarded the SS *City of Cairo* on August 8th. It would be the first major troop deployment of the British. It landed in Archangel on August 25th. Poole did not waste time, on the 26th, he ordered companies A, B and C to travel down the Dvina to Beresnik. D Company remained in Archangel. This would soon become known as "C Force" along with other troops sent earlier (M25 monitor, two 18 pdr guns, 50 Pole, 100 French). It's first attack was on the 500 Red manned area five miles south of Beresnik.

The U.S. 339th regiment, 310th Engineers (788 men), and 337th Field Hospital had originally been slated for France. After the 339th had its one month training it sailed to England. The troops of the regiment while in England suddenly had their Enfield rifles taken away and issued much older Russian rifles. Then, the troops were issued heavy winter coats, boots, skis and snowshoes of which most of the men had no training with. Each man was issued ten ammo rounds. Naturally, the troops asked, "What the fuck is going on"? Their commander, Col. George Stewart, was ordered to say nothing. By the last week of August, the U.S. would be sending all three battalions of the regiment, 1st Bn/310 Engineers, 337th field hospital and Ambulance companies; this totaled 5,710 men to Archangel. The regiment was armed with 24 Lewis Guns, 50 Colt Machine Guns, 1000 skis, 5,500 snowshoes, 7,500 moccasins, 8 3" Stokes Mortars and 50 Ice tongs. The remaining units of the 310th Engineers would arrive later. The Americans sailed from England aboard the SS *Tydeus, Nagoya and Somali* on August 27th. Their original destination had been Murmansk (a quiet, secure area). However, without the U.S. knowledge, the ships were diverted to Archangel where they arrived to their surprise on September 4th at 10 a.m. The Americans immediately sent 378 to sickbay due to influenza that had broke out during the cruise. The

Americans were also subordinate to the British and this rubbed the Americans the wrong way, in every way.

American officers reported to British officers of the same rank. Thus, discord amongst the allies was on automatic. General Poole then ordered American troops to man and operate the Archangel power plant, waterworks, sawmill and local streetcar system for security reasons! When the U.S. chief medical officer, Major Longley, created an American hospital in Archangel and hoisted the American flag, General Poole ordered it removed. When Longley heard of this, he stationed men at the flag post to prevent this. Other British oddities occurred: in North Russia, a sergeant was made a Major and Captains would become Colonels. These ranks were only temporary while in North Russia.

While the American troops were inexperienced, they were Class A, not the Class B or C (former sick, injured ,old) that the British sent. Except for the engineer battalion, General Ironside and Poole had mostly negative comments (in internal correspondence and reports) regarding the Americans. In public, they, however, praised them. However, it is clear that without the Americans, there would be very little success. It was the American troops that moved and defended the most remote outposts (some over 200 miles from Archangel) against overwhelming odds during the coming winter. For the Americans, it was a crash course in combat and one they learned exceedingly well.

The situation, which existed up to now, was as follows: A French company and artillery took Obozerskaya on September 4th**.** The attack upon Oberskaya by the French was supported at first by only single airplane sorties. The advance was slowed due to enemy resistance and the Reds blew each bridge as they fell back. The advance of the armor train that carried the artillery support set the pace. When the French had moved to within four miles of the town, the Reds received six Anti-aircraft guns operated by German personnel. This increased to a total of 11 AA guns just prior to the town falling. The AA fire was accurate but no planes were lost. The main assault on the town was supported by three Short 184's, each carrying two 112 lbs, two 40 lbs. and one 20 lb bomb. The observer would simply hand drop these over the side of the airplane. Once the bombs were dropped, it was the strafing that caused the Bolo to panic and yield Oberskaya to the French. Had the Reds morale not been so flimsy, the defenses in the town would have been formidable. The force was held up due to blown bridges. Between Oberskaya and Vologda, another 262 bridges existed! Poole , then created "B Force" consisting of another French company under Col. Hazelton, which moved up the Dvina River to Seleskoe and advance to the rear of Obozerskaya but was still about nine miles east. Force D began at Siskoe and consisted of one British company from the Royal Marines, one MG section and a platoon from Co.1/Royal Scots. However, no sooner had it left Siskoe was it delayed by the Reds at Tiogra, its job was to secure the communication lines to Kodish.

The RAF went to extraordinary lengths to recover downed airplanes (usually due to engine failure). It was not unordinary for a DH4 plane to be recovered by 30-50 Russian laborers and dragged through five miles of forest to the railroad. All the detachable items would be taken off and carried or dragged while the fuselage put on sleigh and dragged. To travel took five days. However, as time went on, this recovery detail was less important due to sufficient airplanes. Because the airplanes sent with the invasion force and those found at Archangel were in poor shape, engine failure during flight was always possible. Thus, pilots were instructed to always remain in sight of either the railroad or the river. Pilots hesitated about flying either the DH4 or RE 8 airplane due to engine failure. The RAF's other problems were with the inexperienced ground crews that often caused aircraft crashes due to overloading. In one case, an RE 8 was loaded with eight 24 lb bombs, four drums of MG ammo, and a 200 lb. bomb. The plane barely was able to get airborne when its wheel hit a stump, which caused subsequent damage. Soon, the plane was uncontrollable and crashed.

Most of the Russian pilots that volunteered came from the Old Imperial Airforce. The most famous of them were Capt. Babanenko and the renowned, Major Kazakov. Kazakov (30 years old) had reached the rank of Colonel by November 1917, but lost the rank to the revolution. By June, 1918, he and many of his followers had reached Murmansk. The British RAF offered him a rank of Major on July 19th, and put him in charge of the British-Salvo air corps (Nos. 1 and 2). This unit eventually had 34 former Russian pilots . The No.1 group moved from Yemetskoe to Beresnik on Oct. 23rd, while No.2 group moved from Yakovlevskoe to Chamovo on Oct. 15th. This unit arrived at Bereznik on Oct. 22nd. These gallant units were strafing and bombing the Reds along the Dvina River. Unlike the Allied pilots, who were green, the Russians were experienced. They flew at very low strafing altitudes, in one case, enabling the pilot to see ex-German POW uniforms. Thus, by November, the allies had the No 2 squadron, commanded by Kazakov (and mostly Russian), and No.3 commanded by Major Carr RAF.

Sources:

Haliday, E. *The Ignorant Armies*
Bradley, John. *Allied Intervention in Russia.* 1984
Fogelsong, David. *America's Secret War Against Bolshevism.* 1995
Kettle,Michael. 1992. *Churchill and the Archangel Fiasco.*
Ironside,Edmund.1953. *Archangel 1918-19.*
Various Records. Public Record Office. London.
Regimental History, PRO.London.
Microfilm Roll 925, U.S. National Archives.
Americans in North Russia, Bently Historical Library, Michigan.
Altham, Capt.1923. *The Dvina River Campaign*
Cross and Cockade Magazine. Vols 18, 28.
Carey, Donald. 1997. *Fighting the Bolshviks.*
The Russian Civil War Encyclopedia.1985. Moscow Press.
Strathovsky, Leonid. 1972. *The Origins of American Intervention in North Russia.*
Footman, David. 1957. *Murmansk and Archangel.*
Iakushkin, Everginei. 1928. *English Intervention 1918-20.* Moscow Press.
Kondratev, C. *Aircraft of the Russian Civil War.* Moscow. 2000.

3

Combat in September

August had been relatively calm combat wise. Most of the action had been small skirmishes between the French, Royal Scots (Cos. A,B,C) and the Bolo. Clearly, the Reds were not interested in any major confrontations. Trotsky was satisfied to keep the allied forces at bay and realized what plans and objectives Poole had. Thus, he would oppose the whole invasion for one year with his 18th division (General Oubarevish) of the 6th Red Army (General Samolio). The division had 19,460 men and well armed with 283 allied machine guns, 90 artillery howitzers and a few planes (by April 1919). The 18th division had three brigades, each brigade having 2-3 regiments (each regiment had 33 officers, 27 platoon leaders, 81 section leaders, 72 drivers, 9 foragers, 18 cooks, 3 doctors and 800-1250 men). The main heavy infantry weapon was the Maxim machine gun, there were between 12-18 per regiment. These were further subdivided into MG sections consisting of 6 MG per battalion or 2 MG per company. The MG section contained 120 men, 32 horses and 6 carts. Further, each Battalion had 20 scouts and there were 50 sappers in each regiment. For communication, there was one telephone/wireless at the battalion HQ and none at the company or platoon level, which used messengers. Trotsky's problems stemmed from the poor morale of the Bolo soldier that fluctuated like wild fire, depending on whether they were well led and fed. The soldiers were peasants or remnants of the old Imperial Army. Their skill in operations improved as the war went on but their morale always was unpredictable. Many times they would flee at the sight of American troops or the least resistance, yet other times, they fought with the same tenacity as the Americans did until their unit leader was killed, then the morale would plummet. The supreme leader of the operations was Trotsky, who personally planned many of the operations for the army. Much of the equipment was either German or British left over from WW1. Trotsky was not overly concerned with the intervention militarily. He felt that the Allies were not strong enough to advance 300 miles and that the 6th Army simply had to impede any advance and contain it. He would allow the allies to attack, give ground but no breakthroughs. Naturally, he used the intervention to the benefit of the revolution politically, which allowed him to recruit more soldiers. He never entertained the thought of trying to retake Archangel until after the Allies evacuated in the fall of 1919.

The other problem was that the division was scattered and only a few token units near Archangel. It's divisional HQ, the 48th rail repair regiment, three Nieuport 17s, two armor trains and an artillery battery were at Plesetskaya over 200 miles from Archangel. At Emtsa, the 4th and 5th battalions(400 men total); in Kodish, the 1st Bn/83rd regiment and the 1st Brigade HQ; in Siskoe, the 2 Bn/83rd regiment and at Toulgas, the 8th Bn and a cavalry company (the terms battalion and regiment are in name only, on average, the Red Bn had 300-500 men, most regiments had 1000-1700). At Vologda, the base for the 6th Army, the remainder of the division's artillery (15-20 guns), 2500 men, 23 Ford trucks and 13 Cars. In Kotlas, 400 miles away, gunboats *Jalyaboff, Pavlin, Karl Liebknecht, Rosa Luxemburg, Femk, Chernophrye, Uritskey, Bobets, Caxton, Sverdiloff,* and many steamers (armed with one 30mm gun), three armed barges (each with two six inch howitzer) and the 3rd brigade HQ, 1st and 2nd Bns/161 regiment (2000 men total) 50 MG and M9 seaplanes. The Bolo had mined the railroad south of Plesetskaya.

The base pay the for a private Bolshevik soldier was 250 rubles a day, a company commander earned 1000 rubles and the battalion commander, 1200 (in 1918, the ruble was worth 10 cents each) plus free food (1 lb. of black bread and .75 lbs. of fish or horsemeat twice a week). When the Lenin and Trotsky took over with the revolution, their hope was to get rid of classes. But in reality, they simply recreated different classes. One example was the food rations that certain classes received:

> Soviet Official and factory workers received 1/2 lb. of bread, 3 lbs. of fish and potatoes daily; Students received 1/2 lb. of bread, 3 lbs. of potatoes and 2 pounds of fish and all non communists received only 2 Herrings a week! To give an example of buying power in 1918 in Russia, the following items cost: a pound of bread = 68 rubles, a pound of butter=250 rubles, one egg= 25 rubles ($2.50), a new man's suit= 1800 rubles. The battalion commander had servants.

Besides the 18th division, the 6th division (46th reg(1000), 47th reg(2400) 48th reg(840), 16th Yuriev reg and 49th reg (1400, 17MG) held the area between Lake Onega and Lake Ladoga. The 4th Division (1st Finn.reg (2000) 164th Finn (500), 41st Urozero (300), 300 Cavalry and 16 artillery guns, 42nd air squadron) held the area between the Gulf of Finland and Lake Ladoga.

The U.S. 3rd battalion, which had just disembarked was ordered to entrain, which brought them to the front to help the French (the French soon refused to take orders from the British and only from the Americans) arriving on September 6th. The U.S. 1st battalion (along with a French company) was immediately loaded onto steamers and barges to sail down the Dvina River on the 6th. It arrived at Bereznik on the 11th, some 130 miles from its garrison duty: Archangel. These forces augmented the British troops, the Royal Scots.

Poole decided to attempt an encircling movement on the Bolos located near the railroad. Company K/1st Bn led by Capt. Donohue left on September 7th. On the first day, they advanced five miles, by the second day, 13 miles. When the third day arrived, Donohue admitted he was lost. One the 4th day, the men did nothing until Donohue got his bearings.

Luckily, on the 5th day, a search party was sent and located the lost Company K. The company did make it to there designated area and opened a withering gunfire on the Reds at Seletskoe. The Red commander was ordered to hold at all costs and when Reds wanted to fall back only their commander prevented this. So, they killed him and fled to Kodish!

On the 11th, Co. M fought the first engagement with Red troops near Obozerskaya for an important bridge. On the 16th, Cos. L, I, repulsed a savage Red attack which tried to encircle them. In this attack, Red airplanes strafed and bombed to the amazement of U.S. troops. Co.K arrived to reinforce D force and tried to advance on Kodish, which gained little. On 9/23, D force was augmented with a U.S. MG platoon and two days later, Co.L. Poole's plan called for D force to move along the road to Kodish as B Force advanced along the RR. On the 26th, the U.S. Cos. K and L began their advance, crossing the river on rafts and quickly established a bridgehead on the left bank of the Emsta River opposite Red trenches. Here, the advance stalled for a week, finally some artillery and British Royal Marines arrived to support. Weakened from exposure, the small bridgehead was pulled back.

Located some ten miles south of Verst 455, a Red armor train sat pounding the French and Americans. So, by September 28, a plan was called up to seize the Bolo train. This attack, led by an American company was directed to advance to the rear of the Bolo position through a bog! Supporting the attack was the British armor train consisting of one 18 pdr gun, one 75mm gun, two 3 inch Naval guns.

The British salvaging a downed aircraft from the Dvina. Note the steep banks of the river near Troitsa, 1919. Photo: IWM

The Americans moved out during the night through the waist deep swamp and became lost. However, the advance continued along with the French and ran into the Bolo conducting an attack of their own. The attack was furthered plagued by machine guns jamming and inaccurate shelling by the British, which destroyed a bridge, held by the Americans. Not all the attack snafus were American. As Co.A advanced towards Pless on September 15th, it was found that the town was strongly held. So, Co. A /Royal Scots was detailed to make a flanking march through the forest. During the march, the rained poured turning the ground into knee deep mud, torrents of water crossed the path. Shivering from the cold, after a six hour march it was noted they had gone too far. Turning, the company then ran into an impenetrable swamp and this was the last blow to their morale. Instead of continuing, the men took cover and rested for several hours.

These early attacks were typical.

Most of the fighting along the Dvina River was conducted by Cos. A,B, C of the Royal Scots (Cos .A,B.C had advanced along the left bank of the Dvina reaching Kurgomin on 9/17, and pushed back to Borok by Red forces near Nizhe-Toimski by the 27th.) The American 1st Bn (Cos. A,B,C, D) arrived at Beresnik after a five day, 140 mile journey in a coal barge. By the time they arrived there on Sept 13th, three men had died due to the horrible conditions (no heat, wet). Cos. B,C,D began to advance to Chamova to relieve the exhausted Royal Scot. The U.S managed to advance to Seltzo before being halted by accurate Red gunboat and artillery fire.

Part of Poole's plan was to send troops down the steeply banked Vaga River to prevent a possible Red avenue for an advance. Thus, most of Co.A of the U.S. battalion, two gunboats and the steamer Tolstoy moved down the windy river on September 16th. Besides a few Red snipers, no enemy was seen and on the 17th, the town of Shenkurst (7,000) welcomed the allied troops. Shenkurst was anti-Bolshevik since it was a summer like resort for the Moscow aristocrats. Unlike the other towns, this one had brick buildings, six schools, a monastery, sawmill and shipyard. With the town in allied control, the Americans continued to advance on the 19th, looking for a fight. At the village of Rodvino, a Red AA gun fired and hit the steamer causing it to turn toward the firing gun. Like an amphibious assault, the

The RAF adaptation for winter flying: skis.

Americans jumped off the steamer and waded ashore, easily taking the village and quickly seized Ust Padenga and Puya. At Puya, the Reds stood and tried to encircle the Americans but failing, they retreated. Now, Co. A halted.

The British suffered an embarrassing event when a company of the Royal Scot regiment together with a company of Russians and Poles attacked Kuliga on Sept. 27th. Because of a leak or spy, the Reds knew and where. The attacked proceeded under withering fire. First to panic and run were the Russians. However, when two of the British officers had been killed, two platoons of the Royal Scot panicked and ran. Many simply tossed their weapons aside to run faster! The only covering force holding back the Reds were eight Canadians and the British artillery. In all, the unit lost 77 men. This is a staggering amount for such a small battle. The Royal Scot unit was Class B, meaning, unfit for combat. Most of the men had been promised a "cushy holiday" in Russia. Only 10% had seen combat in France and many were not ashamed for fleeing the battle.

During the month of September, the American President Wilson and the U.S. Ambassador because of communication delays and different interpretations of U.S. policy, were at odds as to how the U.S. troops were being used. These reports, often weeks late, showed the troops in offensive operations. Wilson became irate and by the 26th, sent a clarification as to the conditions of the use of American troops. The language in this was clear; " all military efforts in North Russia must be given up except for guarding of the ports". The Ambassador conveyed this to General Poole but then encouraged his actions rather than censoring, stating, " it has the entire admiration of the President". As for Poole, he knew little of the conditions regarding use of American troops. He simply followed the orders given to him to advance down the Dvina towards Kotlas and secure the railroad. Finally, on October 2nd, the U.S. Ambassador and Poole met. The Ambassador produced the cables and papers regarding the use of American troops. Poole was dumbfounded, since out of the five battalions there, three were American and his orders could not be fulfilled. Immediately, Poole requested four British battalions to replace the Americans. None came and the Americans were not withdrawn.

The troop dispositions by this date is as follows:

VOLOGDA FORCE:

A.	Railroad (Lt. Colonel Lucas/ 21st French Colonial bn)
	Two U.S. companies/339th regiment
	One French Company/ 21st Bn
	One French MG company
	One armor train
	One artillery battery
B	**SELETSKOE (Lt. Col. Haselton)**
	Two U.S. Companies
	One detachment Russian SBAL
	Two 18 pdr guns
C	**ONEGA RIVER (Lt. Col Edwards)**
	One platoon/ 21st French Bn.
	One Russian Naval brigade
	One U.S. Company arriving.

D **LINES OF COMMUNICATION (Lt.Col. Musgrave)**
The Railroad up to Obozerskaya.
One company/ 21st French Bn.
Two Armor trains
Russian troops holding the bridges.

1. VAGA COLUMN (Lt.Col Graham)

A **U.S.T PADENGA (Capt. Simon, U.S. Army)**
C Company/ 1st Bn/339th U.S.
50 SBAL Russian
Two 18 pdrs w/ Russian crews
Two AA guns w/ Russian crews

B **SHENKURSK**
A company/3rd Bn/339th U.S. Reg.
120 Russian SBAL
Two 18 pdrs/Canadian 16th Brig.
One 3" Field gun w/ Russian crew.
40 SBAL recruits
175 Mounted Cavalry (Russian).

Total Strength on the Vaga Column

	Officer	**Other Ranks**
British Troops	10	36
Canadian 16th Artillery brigade	3	107
U.S. 1st Bn/339th	15	531
310th Engineer Bn	3	94
337th U.S. Ambulance	3	36
North Russian Troops	29	419
Slavo-British Legion	5	70
One Section Russian Artillery	6	50
1st Russian Cavalry	1	19
1st Russian Lt. Battery		7
Mounted Russian troops	32	143

2. RIVER COLUMN (Lt.Col Skiel)

A **RIGHT BANK (at Kurgoman)**
Two Cos./2nd line/10th Bn/Royal Scots
Two artillery sections/16th Canadian Arty Brigade HQ

B **LEFT BANK (Lower and Upper Toulgas)**
One U.S. Company
One Royal Scot Company
One section Canadian Artillery

Total MGs: 9 Vicker HMG, 31 Lewis Guns.

RIVER COLUMN STRENGTH

	Officer	**Other**
British Troops	21	644
U.S. Troops	7	288
Supply	5	60

Lastly, another 515 American soldiers and 700 French troops arrived .

The Red Forces Opposing the Allied Forces

On October 1, 1918, the 6th army became part of the Northern Front. By February 1919, it was placed under the High Command as an Independent Army.

The 6th Army contained:
18th Rifle Division (November 1918-April 1920)
19th Rifle Division (December 1918-January 1919)
1st Kamishinskaya Rifle Division (March-April 1919)
1st Rifle Division (August 1919-April 1920)
54th Rifle Division (August 1919-April 1920)
Subordinate to the 6th Army was the North-Dvinsk Flotilla.

The operations of the 6th Army developed along established communication lines of rivers and roads. The headquarters of units of the 6th Army were divided into combat regions. In 1918 they were: Archangel, Velsko-Shenkursk, Kotlas, and Vyatki. From September to December 1918, the 6th Army operated in the sector from Archangel to Vologda, along the North Dvina river, to Kotlas and Vyatki. Its mission was to stop the units of Northern and Eastern White forces from making a connection, and therefore, a solid front.

The 6th Army launched *Operation Shenkursk* in 1919, and conducted battles to liberate the Vologda-Arkchangel railroad line, as well as the rivers of Pechora, Northern Dvina, Pinega, and Mezen. The army was then split up; its headquarters re-formed to the District Military White Sea Military District, and most troops were transferred to the 7th Army.

The 18th Division was formed November 26, 1918, from forces around Archangel and Velskaya, as well as units from the Kotlas region. From December 1918 to January 1919, it conducted an active defense in the Archangel and Kotlas sector, and then participated in *Operation Shenkursk*. In February 1920, the 18th fought to liberate Archangel and Onega.

The 18th Rifle Division comprised:
52nd Rifle Brigade with the 154th, 155th, and 156th Rifle regiments.
53rd Rifle Brigade with the 157th, 158th, and 159th Rifle Regiments.
54th Rifle Brigade with the 160th, 161st, and 162nd Rifle Regiment.

The 19th Division was under 6th Army command for only a short time. Before and afterwards it was with the 7th Army, and fought along the Murmansk railway.

1st Kaminishin Division was formed in the City of Kamishin in October 1918. It became part of the 10th Army (October 1918-March 1919) and 6th Army (March to April 1919). Later it was transferred to the Northern Front to fight against the White forces of General Miller in the region of Plesetskaya and the River Onega after the British had evacuated. On April 12, 1919, the division was disbanded and its units turned over for the forming of the 35th and 40th Rifle Divisions. The Division was brought in to cover losses of the 18th division.

The 54th Division was formed in August 1919, with a composition of two brigades from troops in the Mezenskaya, Pinezhskaya, and Kotlas regions (the 3rd brigade was formed in November 1919, with the arrival to the front of the Kaluzhsk Brigade). It was with the 6th Army from August 1919 to April 1920. In 1919, it conducted battles in the North Dvina, Dvina, and Pinega river region. From January-February 1920 it participated in liberation Zholmogor, Archangel, and Pinega. In April 1920 it fought in the region between Padozhski and Lake Onezhski.

54th Rifle Division comprised:
Rifle Brigade with the 478th, 479th, and 480th Rifle Regiments.
161st Rifle Brigade with the 481st, 482nd, and 483rd Rifle Regiments.
163rd Rifle Brigade with the 484th, 485th, and 486th Rifle Regiments.

The Ist Division also was under the 6th Army and fought along the Murmansk railway.

The **North Dvinsk Flotilla** was created in the basin of the North Dvina in August 1918 to prevent allied troops from advancing into the Russian interior, and to give support to Red Army units defending the North Dvinsk sector. In Kotlas, the North Dvina Flotilla was formed from seamen of the Northern Ledovitaya Flotilla. On August 10, 1918, in the region of Bereznik it entered into its first river battle with allied ships, ending in a defeat for the Whites. From August-November 1918, the flotilla conducted bombardments on the allied troops along the river. On October 30, 1918, the flotilla's composition contained five armed steamers and two floating batteries.

At the commencement of the campaign in 1919, the flotilla's composition was three combat detachments totaling six gunboats, seven tugboats, six guard vessels, 11 patrol boats, 15 transport barges, and three messenger boats. During much of 1919, the flotilla was assigned to the 54th Rifle Division and participated in the Kurgoman and Troitski operations along the Rivers Vaga and Shipilikh. On October 23, 1919, the flotilla retired up\river to Kotlas for the winter. Some 500 sailors participated in battles with the Whites in the region of Yarensk.

4

More Combat in October

The Reds conducted a steady attack upon the outposts of Co.B/Royal Scots near Borok from the 5th to 10th. Elements of the U.S. Company A arrived to hold off the savage attacks. These attacks were far worse being supported by numerous Red gunboats, many with naval guns. The M25 had been withdrawn due to an early freeze in the lower Dvina.

The Canadian 16th artillery brigade (67th and 68th batteries), with the (6) 18 pdrs and about 487 men arrived . This, unlike, all the other troops that had been sent was a veteran combat unit from the Western Front. These were the best troops.

Also reinforcing the Dvina river column was Co. H of the U.S. 1st battalion, moving from Onega to Chekuvo. The Americans were stiffened with a machine gun platoon and 93 Cossacks (totaling 350 men) . The unit repaired the telephone/telegraph lines along the way and when they reached Kaska, ten miles south of Chekuvo, the met 700 entrenched Red soldiers. The first to desert were the Cossacks and the Americans dug in as withering MG fire forced everyone prone. The Reds had checkmated them.

On Oct.12, Cos.K and L managed to advance to 1000 yards of the Red lines to their flank. On the 13th, Co.L moved south to attack Kodish from the Red rear as Co.K attacked frontally. Despite the artillery and MG fire, Co.L ran into swamps during the night impeding them. The British Marines crossed the river turning the Red positions by moving through the woods. The Reds reinforced their position and failed when they counterattacked, fleeing Kodish and reestablishing a defense at Kockmas. While this occurred, a White Russian unit armed with 40 Lewis guns and a platoon from the Royal Scots took Shred Mekrenga and Tarasovo. Just when the Red base at Plesetskaya was being threatened, General Ironsides (who had arrived to replace Gen. Poole) orders the advance to halt! He transfers Co.L, the Marines and Canadian artillery to the Dvina River leaving D force with only 180 men (mostly the U.S. Co.K). Company K was strung out along it's LOC back to Kodish. In Kodish, 70 men with 4 Mgs defended (only 40 men were combat ready). The nearest allied troops and artillery were now 10 miles away at Seleskoe.

Only the 2nd Battalion actually garrisoned the Archangel area. The protests of President Wilson fell of deft ears. The American public knew nothing about this action.

Upon the arrival of the 3rd Bn, Major Young, was ordered to prepare an attack to commence on the 29th! Young followed orders and for companies I,L,M it would be their baptism of fire. The plan simply called for the U.S. to take the Red base at Plesetskaya, 50 miles from the front. The French with artillery support would attack along the railroad, while the U.S. companies would circle through a nearby forest and attack from the east—a flanking movement. To further augment the attack, an armor train was used and three Stokes mortars. No maps had been given to the Americans and thus, the companies moved through the woods only to stumble on swamps in the night that forced the Americans to turn back but not before they had got lost. Meanwhile, the French had attacked and took a key bridge across the Emtsa River and held it against the Red counterattacks. British artillery firing with poor intelligence, barraged the French and two U.S. platoons (led by Lt. Donovan) holding this bridge, killing two U.S. men. Major Nichols was avid and screamed at the British Colonel Sutherland to adjust the artillery fire. Col. Sutherland telephoned for another quart of Whiskey before changing the coordinates. Fearful that he might lose control, Sutherland ordered a withdrawal. Both the American Maj. Nichols and French commander immediately countermanded. The three men coldly stared at one another. Sutherland then left. The Reds counterattacked with their own armor train and were just stopped short of the bridge. The attack failed and the Allied advance to Vologda ended.

On the river front, the 1st battalion reached Bereznik and split Company A. Two platoons remained here with the rest of the force moving 30 miles further south to join the British Royal Scots by the 17th and under attacks from Red gunboats. The battalion moved to Seltso where it met stiff Red resistance. Cos. B,C and D attacked advancing 1500 yards before Red MG fire halted them. It was the arrival of an artillery battery, which laid down accurate fire, which allowed the Americans to seize the town and which now was nearly out of ammo.

However, some 20 Red gunboats pounded the Americans as 1700 Bolos assaulted the U.S. positions which completely overpowered the defending unit. They withdrew to Toulgas by the 20th. As General Ironside noted, " the Red attack completely outclassed us". In the course of this, four precious 18 pdrs were lost.

By this time, winter in North Russia was made known. Freezing temps, snow made the life of the infantry and pilots intolerable.

With the sub-zero temps as the norm, the ground crews prepping the airplanes had a very time consuming task. The runways had to be clear or ice or snow, if possible. The machine guns, bombs and ammunitions or any metal object had to be either warmed or kept warm before handling it. Using heavy gloves slowed the process further as loading the weaponry with heavy gloves was extremely difficult. Even tools could not be touched with bare hands. What would normally take a few minutes in the summer, now took up to an hour. The aircraft engines had to be insulated with thick padded covers and further augmented by six or more lamps to prevent the radiator from freezing. An example is trying to get the DH4 with a water-cooled engine flying:

The engine was kept warm day and night by the flameless lamps. When the call for air operations came, some five gallons of hot water were poured though the radiator, even before two gallons had passed through, the drain plug froze. This had to be removed. The engine was then filled with warm oil and water and cranked over at 1500 revolutions for three minutes. The throttle barrel that controlled the speed froze and the air intake and mixing chambers had 1/8th of an inch of ice covering them. Then the exhaust gas release became frozen solid with 3/4" ice. The controls to the throttle barrel had frozen due to the freezing of the oil. Finally, it took 20 minutes to taxi the plane due to ice and snow. In flight, if was frequent that the throttle and control rods would freeze again. Also, the air intake pipe and the induction pipes also were covered with ice. Many times the plane would finally get airborne and then catch on fire. The only plane that was reliable in the winter was the Sopwith with the rotary engines. The Re-8's were too heavy.

Besides the weather making life miserable, the bitterest complaint was the British field ration that nearly all the troops had to consume. This comprised of:

Bully meat (corned beef from Argentina)
Vegetables with a gob of fat
Dehydrated vegetables,
Cement like biscuits
Black tea
Tinned butter and jam.

The Americans missed the coffee and the biscuits (which were four inches by two inches and 1/4" thick) were impossible to break or even soften! The dehydrated vegetables took 1-2 days of soaking and even then they were very unpalatable.

When these were given to a Russian peasant, even she refused to eat them who then gave to her horse!

By October 23rd, the British had established themselves at Kurgomin-Tulgas area when Co.A of the Royal Scots came under another heavy red attack on their left flank. Again, on the 27th, the British attacked in a blinding snowstorm with two platoons of Co.B and Company C of the Royal Scots together with 30 Poles. The town of Topsa was the objective, however, when the advance moved through the forests the snowstorm increased. Lt. Penman who the led the attack thought this low visibility would provide the British with the element of surprise. This was true but upon the British troops which met a wall of MG and rifle fire from the Bolos. The attack force was ripped apart, some eight men were killed and many vanished into the blizzard.

On Oct. 14th, Co D of the Scots arrived at Oberskaya to hold verst 444 where an expected Red attack in waiting. The Reds began with an intense artillery barrage on the dug in Scots, yet, no infantry assault. The British armor train returned the fire and then retreated when it ran out of ammo. As soon as it disappeared, the Bolo armor train opened up with a massive artillery barrage which was followed by charging infantry. The Scots opened up with MG fire. Now the second wave of Reds came, and soon, some Reds were able to penetrate. Hand to hand combat ensued until the Bolo had had enough. A French infantry company then replaced Co. D on Oct 20th.

Also occurring on the 14th, was the last free election in Russia at Archangel. Of the eligible 21,000 voters there, some 8,000 voted in 32 Socialists, 26 Bourgeoisie and two

Jews to the local government. It was also the day General Poole was replaced officially by General Ironside. General Ironsides stood out being 6 ft. 4 inches, 270 lbs and only 37 yrs.old with curly brown hair, blue eyes. Ironsides was tough and had been the leader of the 99th brigade in France. Born on May 7th, 1880, he was the son of an Army surgeon and entered the Army in 1899, first going to South Africa until 1902. By 1908, he was a Captain, by 1914, a Major and a staff officer 1st Grade by 1916. In 1918, he was a Brig. General. He clearly had fast promotions and was looked upon well. He spoke six different languages. He was a man well liked by everyone under his command but he arrived with many mixed feelings, just as Poole had. He, like Poole, questioned what was the real purpose for the military action and wondered how it could be done with so few troops; yet, he carried out what he was ordered to do.

Poole was replaced when the U.S. State department cabled the British Foreign office threatening to withdraw the U.S. troops if the agreement was not complied with.

During October, the U.S. 310th Engineering units built blockhouses along the fronts since the troops could not dig trenches in the frozen tundra. These houses were "redoubts" with double logged walls and clear fields of fire. On the railroad front, the engineers used 40,000 rolls of barbwire and built 316 shellproof blockhouses, 273 MG emplacements, and 167 infantry outposts

One of the main administrative functions Ironside had was trying to create a volunteer White Russian army. Its purpose would be to take over the front and continue to uprising after the Allies had left. The British Slavo unit created had about 3000 motley volunteers, out of which, 500 were actually fit for service. The quality of the Russians for the most part was pathetic. The Americans and British privately thought they were a bunch of cowards and only volunteering to get free food and always totally unpredictable in combat. By October 1st, the 1st Archangel Regiment, 1st Field battery, 1st Archangel cavalry, the Light Artillery division consisting of 1st and 2nd batteries, and the Heavy Artillery battery had been formed for the new National North Russian Army. Most were former POW's and old men. Even the Russian officers who were to lead the men were of the same quality. To make matters worse, the British instructors were, as Ironside stated, " the scum of the officers in England" and " sending officers who are drunk is the worst kind to send to this sideshow, an isolated post under no supervision". Thus, the Archangel regiment of the newly created army refused to parade on October 29th. The men refused to salute and demanded increased meat and bread rations. They wanted better hours and conditions equal to the allied troops. This was simply the tip of the iceberg of forthcoming problems.

By the start of 1919, the following 4,358 men had been added:

3rd Battery, Lt Arty division
1st Engineer Company
2nd North Russian regiment
2nd Artillery division (two light arty batteries)
2nd Heavy artillery battery
1st Shenkursk Bn (became the 3rd NRR)
2nd Kolmogori Bn (became the 4th NRR)
3rd Onega Bn (became the 5th NRR).

Ironside continued to have faith in this attempt to create a new army that would continue on the fight once the Allies left . The army only had a few reliable and good units that could be counted on during a battle. By May 1919, the army was about the strength of an Allied division, 18,000 men and consisted of:

1st Squadron, Northern Dragoons (Archangel)
2nd Squadron, Northern dragoons (Vaga)
1st Russian Field Artillery division:
    1st Battery (18pdr and 75mm)
    2nd Battery (18pdr)
    3rd Battery (60 pdr)
    4th Battery (3" Russian guns)
2nd Russian Field Artillery division:
    1st and 2nd Batteries (75mm)
North Russian Howitzer Division:
    1st Battery (155mm and 4.5" guns)
    2nd Battery (155mm and 6" guns)
1st and 2nd Cos. Engineers
1st North Russian Regiment (Archangel)
2nd North Russian Regiment (Murmansk)
3rd North Russian Regiment (Shenkursk) This had three battalions, each with three companies and one MG company. One of the best.
4th North Russian Regiment (Kholmogori) This had eight companies and two MG companies. Very good.
5th North Russian Regiment (Onega) Composed of two battalions.
6th North Russian Regiment (Obozerskaya)
7th North Russian Regiment (Tarasevo) Two Battalions.
8th North Russian Regiment (Pinega) Eight companies.
1st and 2nd Trench Mortar Batteries.
1st Automobile Division.

The other British attempt to create a local force was the Slavo-British Legion. It's purpose was the same but on a smaller scale. By November, it had grown to 3000 but only 500 or less were considered "combat ready". The balance of the force was used on the lines of communications, supply, depot etc. It's composition by November was:

1st Regiment (Lt.Col. Carroll)
Battalion 1 (aka Edwards Bn, Lt.Col Edwards)
        Four infantry Companies, two MG sections
    Dvina Bn (aka No.2)
        Four infantry Companies, two MG sections
    Dyer's Bn (aka No.3, Lt.Col Wells)
        Four companies, two MG sections.

Artillery (Major Body)
Four sections of Mountain Howitzers
One section of Lt. AA guns
Signal Section (45 men)
Headquarters (80 men)
8 British officers, 2 Russian Officers, 9 Russian Sgt., 9 British troops and 56 Russian troops.
The unit was staffed with 50% British officers.

New British troops arrived, the 2nd line/7th Battalion Durham Light Infantry regiment. The unit containing 170 officers and 576 men arrived on October 25th, aboard the SS Goentoer and like the others, quickly sent on down the river for winter. Also arriving, on the 23rd, was the 17th Bn/Kings Liverpool/ 236th Brigade(formerly known in WW1 as 75th Brigade/25th division) regiment from Murmansk. This unit added another 29 officers and 808 men. The unit arrived at Murmansk on October 19th from Glasgow aboard the SS Keemun. Apparently, the British had selected this unit and told very few officers. Prior to leaving Glasgow, rumor had it the battalion was headed for India. On the train to Glasgow, the men were locked in their cars and not allowed to get off. When the unit reached Murmansk, they were not allowed off the ship. Although the unit arrived at Archangel on the 23rd, it would not be sent down to the fronts until November.

Along the Vaga River, by 10/18, the most advanced troops withdrew back to Ust Padenga. The company HQ was at Netsvetskaya and main U.S. position, one mile from Ust Padenga. By 10/31, Co. A was replaced by Co.C and Canadian artillery. Co. A returned here on 12/1. So much for the promise of "only garrison duty". According to the Americans, their impression of the Bolsheviks were nothing more than armed peasants who knew nothing of military operations.

The advance of Co.K/3rd Bn started from Seleskoe along with British and French troops. The Reds did not resist and fell back to Kodish. Now, Co.L reinforced and the allied troops were ordered to take the town and then Plesetskaya. The only barrier was the Emsta River. The attack began with some 350 men crossing on rafts under the withering MG fire from the Reds. The crossing failed. The American soldiers of Co.H/2nd Bn were ordered to advance to Onega. Their arrival met no opposition but on the 24th, some 300 Reds with many MG's attacked the 115 Americans and successfully engaged the U.S. for five hours until the Red leader,Siskin, was killed. Once this occurred, the Reds fled. A week later, Co.H was ordered to attack toward Kaska along the Onega River, held by 700 Reds. The American attack succeeded when the company was deployed along both sides of the Onega River. The Reds, startled, fell back to Turchasova and the U.S. advanced to Kyvalanda. The Americans were ordered once again to take Kodish with Cos. K and L supported by two artillery guns. This time, the two companies successfully crossed the Emsta River and assaulted the Red positions seizing the small town (which would be retaken by the Reds by late October).

In October, the Allies held Pinega, Shenkursk, Seletskoe, Obozerskaya and Onega. Some 14000 troops were present including some 4500 White Russians on the front lines.

The bulk of the 21st French Bn and two U.S. companies held the Railroad front near Emtsa. During October, influenza severely hit the Allies, some 10000 cases and resulting in an daily average of 30 deaths. Some 700 U.S. and 700 British troops remained in Archangel as garrison units. The first Russian regiment was formed and trained, the 1st Archangel (some 1500 men) led by Col. Durov.

The main foe to the Allied intervention was the Russian Red 6th Army based at Vologda. By October, this 18th division had grown to 8000-13000 men with many artillery guns. The division contained many ad hoc units with names like Petrograd, Lenin, 96th Saratov, 2nd Moscow, 2nd Kasan, 154th, 2nd Ski. By March 1919, the army had some 15000 men, 66 artillery guns, 9 heavy guns, 150 MG. Rifle strength was 18,300 men and most were on the front. Another 10000 were held in reserve in Moscow. Vologda itself only had a garrison of 4800 men.

The Reds desperately wanted to retake Kodish and their attack began on 10/29.

5

The Winter Battles in November and December

By 11/1, the Reds were attacking the American rear there and the bridge crossing the Emsta River at Emsta. The garrison at Kodish (40 combat ready men) held off a Red battalion (400-700 men) with 4 MG's and several Lewis Guns as they fell back across the river across the bridge covered by rest of Co.K. Once back across, Co.E replaced Co.K near Kodish. Co.K returned to Seleskoe and then to Archangel for rest.

On the 9th, Company B (200 men) of the 17th Kings Liverpools moved down the railroad to Oberskaya, and on the 14th, Co.C (200 men)traveled down the Dvina to Beresnik. Further, on the 21st, it's D Company (160 men) also moved down the rail. Company A remained at Archangel. For this new unit, the Liverpools were a nervous lot. The unit had no clue who was or was not the enemy, unlike the Western Front..

On November 11th, the first of many strong Red attacks began. Planned by Trotsky, the attack called for 600 Reds with the support of five gunboats, to cross the Dvina river and take Toulgas. The 150 Americans of Co.B, Canadian artillery battery (two 3" guns, 57 men), and two platoons of Co.A/ British Royal Scots held both sides of the river in a series of blockhouses. While the main attack occurred, another 300 Reds appeared (led by Melochofski) to the rear from nearby woods to complete the encirclement. The Canadians were in the rear along with 7 U.S. soldiers with one Lewis gun. The Canadian artillery men swung their guns around just as the Reds were 50 yards away and fired using shrapnel rounds on the 1st wave, ripping the Reds apart. Many of the Reds in the frontal attack managed to come between the block houses and hand to hand combat ensued. The platoons of the Royal Scots fought a heroic defense firing MG's and Lewis guns at bayonet range. One of the blockhouses was destroyed near the bridge. The Red soldiers began to charge across only to be mowed down by one MG and one Lewis Gun. On the 12th, five Red gunboats (each with 4 6" guns) arrived out of range of the Canadian 3" guns, and pounded the Americans with 4000 rounds with 8 long range guns (four were howitzers). The Reds continued to shell the blockhouses until the 14th (many of the shell casings found later indicated they had been made in the U.S.A). Many of the blockhouses were missed and the Americans counterattacked (led by Capt.Cudahy) reaching the Red trenches through the forest. The Reds, not suspecting the Americans would leave the blockhouses, routed when fired upon. During the battle several key Red leaders were killed: Melochofski, Murafski and Foukes which weakened the morale. By the 15th, the Red attack was over and being harassed by the Allies planes. The Reds lost 400 Kia to the Allied 28 Kia,70 Wia. To date, this had been the most fierce battle encountered by the allies. As Ironside noted, "it was the exceedingly gallant behavior of the Canadian artillery that saved the show, turning their guns and firing at point blank range."

On the 14th, another "bad show" occurred again with the British Royal Scot Unit. The town of Kuliga was held by some 30 Royal Scots led by Lt. Dalziel. The Bolos attacked with 140 men hoping to penetrate the outer defenses on the west bank of the Dvina. During the attack, the officer received a bullet through the neck. Panic set in and the remaining men fled the battle leaving Lt. Dalziel behind. With no resistance, the Bolos entered and found Dalziel trying to prop himself up and aim his revolver unsuccessfully. Dalziel was later found clubbed in the head from rifle butts. General Finlayson, in a confidential report wrote:

"British prestige is suffering very greatly, not only in the eyes of the Poles, Americans and the few Russians, we are descending without any doubt in the eyes of even the Bolsheviks."

By now, the harsh winter set in. Common temperatures dropped to -10 F, and snow covered everything. Ice formed in the Dvina forcing the Gunboats to withdraw and the bogs became ice lakes. The sun rarely shown and when it did it was for only a few hours. This had an insidious effect on the troops whose nerves were already frayed. Sentries saw "ghosts," and if injured, even minor injuries would likely cause one to freeze to death. In fact, one was likely to die within minutes of being hit. Inside the blockhouses, the front line men were warm having a stove inside and well protected. Life on the front line was either horribly boring or buzzing. There would be long periods of sentry watch, peering out the slits in the blockhouses. Firing at ghosts or Bolos dressed in white smocks. The weather also severely hampered the ability of airplanes to operate. In fact, it was quite an effort just to get them operational. The pilots wore silk gloves, socks and underwear. Layered over were wool winter clothing and an electrically heated suit consisting of gloves, insoles and waistcoat. Once in the airplane, these suits were plugged in with the power being supplied by a wing mounted generator. These precautions did not prevent frostbite.

The U.S. troop deployment at this time was as follows: Co.C at Ust Padenga, Company A at Shenkursk, Co.L and MG platoon near Kodish, Co.K at Seletskoe, Co E, I at Obozerskaya, Co.G at Pinega, Co.H at Onega area. Elements of the U.S. Engineers along the RR. Co.M near Archangel on RR, Co.F near Yemetskoe on Dvina River. Near Toulgas, Co.B.

The weapons and composition of the U.S. companies in North Russia had each company with 4 platoons. A company ranged from 120 to 160 men, each having 8 Lewis Guns. Machine guns used included Vickers, French Chauchat LMG, 1 pdr guns, 2-3 stokes mortars and ample rifle grenades. The 339th also arrived with a trench mortar platoon.Each Company HQ contained 3 stokes mortars and 21 men. Each battalion contained four companies. A Vickers MG took up to 7 men to man and carry, while two Stokes mortars required 10 men. Troop movement was tedious. In deep snow, troops were exhausted after advancing only 500 yards. The allies had very few horses which were used to pull a sleigh. Average movement rates ran from 1-2 miles an hour,and in nine days, a march could move some 150 miles. The Americans had no training with the skis which were sent, even snowshoes took time to get use to. The French sent a ski company as did the Italians. In February 1919, the Reds had the 2nd Ski Bn of 400 men. Communications was provided by the telegraph between command posts but between lower level units it was with "runners." The few trucks there were used only during the summer months. It has been said that the Americans were an unfit bunch. While it is true they were inexperienced, under fire, they became respected by all except for the British. The troops the British sent truly were unfit units in the beginning. It was not until 1919, did the Brits send some good experienced soldiers. It was the Americans who were always on the front.

The Bolshevik Operations from October to December mainly focused on the Dvina River. This was because they knew that Kotlas was the objective and if the Allies could reach it they may be able to link with Kolchaks forces attacking from Siberia. Of course, at this time, it was not possible. But in April, 1919, when Kolchaks forces had advanced past Perm, there was a slim chance, at best. The Bolo was content to remain on the defensive along the Railroad. The Allies had tried several times and each time, failed.

By December, 1918, the Allied rifle strength on the Archangel front consisted of: 3121 British, 1400 French, 4200 American and 1700 White Russian totaling 10,421. The Americans had 450 men holding the RR, 1400 along the Vaga River, 500 along the North Dvina, 200 at Pinega and 900 in Archangel. The British had 2700 in Archangel, 1200 along the North Dvina and 300 on the Vaga. The French had 100 in Archangel and 120 along the RR.

December was relatively calm. After the Americans arrived at Pinega with Company G, a platoon of U.S. troops and 210 White Russians advanced to seize the port of Karpogora. On the 5th, the Reds attacked and repelled. Taking the port was a walk in and the locals were told that the 210 White Soldiers would garrison the town for protection. The American platoon left and not having moved ten miles away, the white Russian soldiers left as the garrison soon caught up after abandoning their posts!

On December 5th, D Company /17th Bn/ Liverpool regiment had just arrived at Tarasovo. A Red defector informed them that an attack was planned to begin at 7 a.m. on the 6th. In the early morning hours, D company (80 men) together with 30 NRR had moved through the woods without any tracks or roads for some 11 miles. It's purpose was to conduct a pre-emptive attack on the Bolos while they were still assembling. By 6:25 am they were in position. In a flash, the men seized four blockhouses. At 8 a.m., they spotted a Bolo artillery column with some several guns and two Maxim MG. This, too, was seized. Company D continued to advance through the woods. Resistance stiffened near the supply dump, but after a firefight, it, too, was seized. By now, the company was within a mile of the main base containing 600 Red troops. Here a real battle brewed for some time until the British troops ran low on ammo and their Lewis guns were jamming due to the snow. They returned to Tarasavo by 4 p.m.

The first of several defections by White Russian units occurred on 12/11, when two companies from the 1st Archangel regiment were deployed along the RR front. Each company had 10 officers and one MG platoon. The units upon receiving orders refused and stayed in their warm barracks. The barracks were surrounded and those which did not surrender came under attack. The 13 instigators were executed by two British platoons.

General Ironside now planned a new offensive with the limited objective of seizing Emtsa, a large village between Verst 455 and Plesetskaya. The plan called for an ambitious three pronged attack. One force would attack down the Onega River and attack the Western flank. Attacking from the East, a force would retake Kodish and advance through Avda and Kochmas to attack Emtsa. This was the same plan that General Poole had tried, and failed. So secret were the plans, not event he commanders of the units involved were not told until the 29th.

The Allies conducted another attack to retake Kodish on Dec.29th. The U.S. Cos. E,K and part of L were used in addition to a mortar section and MG platoon. The plan called for the Americans to attack frontally, while the British MG company lie in wait to ambush the expected retreat under the pursuit from a company from the 1st Archangel regiment. In Kodish, a strong the 1st Onega regiment of 1200 Reds and 4 artillery guns waited (another 700 were further back in reserve). The plan called for the U.S. to penetrate to Kochmas and then Plesetskaya by the 31st! The attack began at 6 a.m. in -20 F,snowy weather with a rolling barrage conducted by 7 stokes mortars and a few artillery guns for 15 minutes. Cos.E and K (with 20 Lewis guns)followed the barrage as over 1000 rounds fell on the Reds. The Reds pulled back but provided stout resistance to the Americans. The White Russian unit never deployed because the commander did not like weather conditions! And for the British, the MG company never deployed because it's commander was still recovering from the previous nights drunk (Ironside subsequently called the British leader and men, " disgraceful"). The Reds, in spite of outnumbering the U.S. 1200 to 450 men, pulled

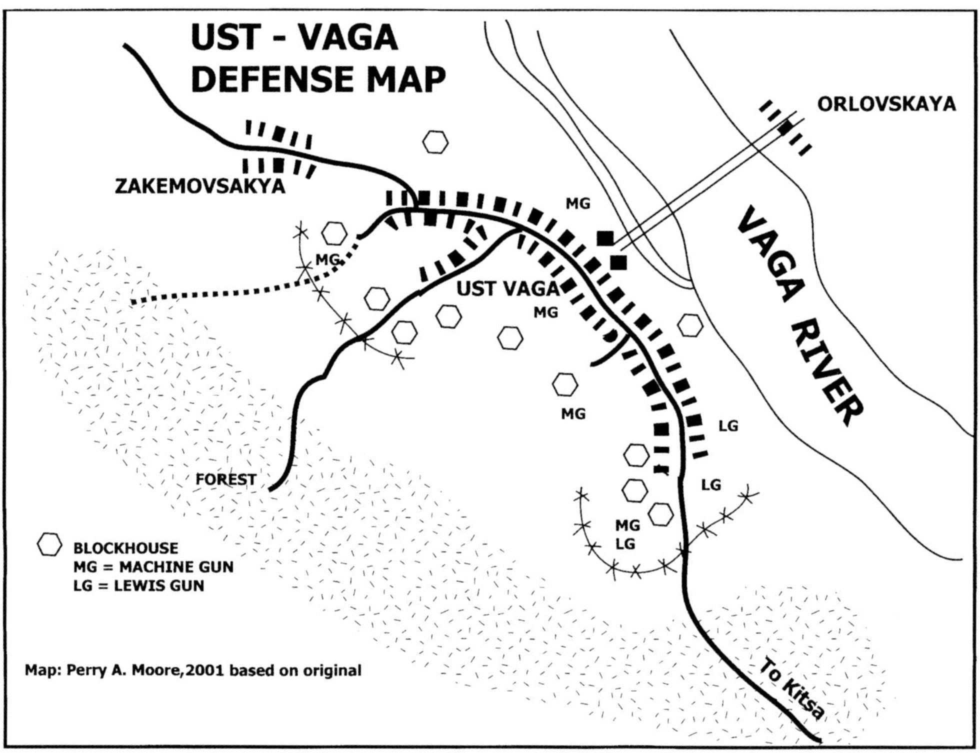

back in good order allowing the Americans to take Kodish! But any advance past Kodish was stopped cold by the MG fire zones of the Reds. The French were also suppose to attack along the RR, like all of the rest of the allies, they cancelled their attack when their ski detachment failed to make much progress (this was ski unit "Courier de Bois." It left at 2 PM and due to snow, had advanced only two miles in four hours. By 6 PM, the unit was exhausted. By the evening of the 30th, it still was 10 miles from its objective, Emtsa.) However, luck had been with the Americans who literally walked into Kodish at 1 p.m. The Americans attempted to move onto Avda. Here, the U.S. met withering fire from the Reds from prepared defenses. During the night, the Reds counterattacked and out of four American platoons, only 100 men remained, of which 35 were Wia, and 7 Kia. In one battle, one U.S. platoon was surrounded and armed with only one stokes mortar. This mortar fired 250 rounds directly hitting the Red MG nests, allowing the platoon to escape. The advance was halted at 11 p.m. Cos.E,L had been shattered replaced by Co.D/ Kings Liverpools Bn and some White Russian units which held Kodish for a time until retreating back across the Emtsa River by January 15, 1919.

Ironside's main attacking column, the Railroad units, which were to strike toward Plesetskaya, did not even become involved. Their planned attack continued to be postponed until the French ski unit was in place. Finally, at 11:30 PM on the 30th, Major Brooks (U.S. 339th) received orders postponing the attack, "until further notice." This was to have been a key asset . The failed advance of the U.S. companies to reach Kochmas (miles south of Kodish) and the failed west flank attack with a company down the Onega valley that only reached Turchasova, happened before the center attacking group (the railroad) was activated. Ironside was willing to order the center group to attack had the Americans reached Kochmas. But he was unwilling to send the railroad force into frontal attacks if the Red flanks were not in danger.

Despite the poor reputation, the Red fighter proved to be a dangerous foe at times. The Red forces at Emtsa amounted to 900 men of the Gatchina Regiment.

Opposing the railway forces at Verst 443 were about 200 men and 6 Maxims HMG defending in trenches. At Verst 441, an armor train stood mounting two 75mm guns and several Machine Guns. Another armor train was near Emtsa mounting two 75mm guns and six Maxim MG's. According to the intelligence reports, once the first line was penetrated, no opposition was present until Emtsa.

The Railroad force was the strongest of all the attacking forces, and in view of the intelligence reports, it appears this force could have easily reached Emtsa by itself. And if the variable morale of the Bolo came into play, there would've been a good chance the town could've been taken without any flanking movements.

The composition of the Railroad column was as follows:

INFANTRY
Co. B/ 17th Bn/ Liverpools
Co. G/ U.S. 1st Bn/339th
Co.1 and 3/ French 21st Bn
One French MG company
One Co. / Russian
Reserve: Co 2/French 21st and Co. I/U.S. 339th
ARTILLERY
Three 155mm guns, two 75mm, 1 75mm Naval.
Armor train No.1 (one 18pdr, two 77mm howitzer, 8 lewis guns)
Armor train No.2 (two 75mm, 2 lewis guns)

The orders instructed that by the end of the first day Emtsa and Emtsa bridge (to the south) shall be taken. On Day 2, to continue the advance onto Plesetskaya.

It was Co.B (200 men) that had the task of taking Emtsa and the U.S. Co.G to continue the advance to Plesetskaya on Day 2. Co. 1 of the French would support the Liverpools, while Co.3, would provide flank protection for the Liverpools (oddly, no flank protection for the American troops!).

The rate of march of the advancing troops was ordered 30 meters a minute. This means it would take 15 minutes for B company to reach the first enemy line. Once storming the trenches, move at the same rate and not less than 200 meters to the rolling barrage which will extend its fire in 100 meter bounded every two minutes. The second enemy position was to be shelled for 10 minutes. The plan called for half of Company B to continue advancing to the Emtsa bridge once the town fell, reaching it by 1800. The U.S. Co.G would then ride on the armor train as close the Emsta Bridge before dismounting and continue advancing to Plesetskaya. On a more humorous note, the detailed attack plans called for a MG gun mounted on an armored "hand" car which would roll down the Railroad preceding the armor train. As far as other factors, the armor train carried 2800 rounds of 75mm and 200 155mm. For communications, the orders stated that a party of signalman would follow the attacking waves carrying 15km of telephone cable. Also, the train would lay the cable down as it went toward Emtsa. The train carried 30km of rolled cable. Once Emtsa was taken, two red rockets should be shot into the air. Further, each man carried 120 rounds and two hand grenades. For food, each man carried two days rations. The attacking company also had 32 wire cutters, 16 axes and 12 VB grenades. Aboard the trains, a reserve of 100,000 rds existed, 100,000 French, 2000 grenades, 4000 VB grenades.

Finally, at the end of the 11 page attack plan, it's author, Major Alabernarde warns the reader, " Pay careful attention to the uniform of the opposing forces in order to avoid firing on friends." More succinctly, " Beware of friendly fire." This attack plan is incredibly detailed in what actions and times are to take place making for little room for the unexpected. But it was your typical WW1 attack plan. Up to now, it was the biggest offensive in North Russia.

Ironside's purpose of advancing along the Dvina River was to reach Kotlas, which lay several hundred miles away, in hopes of forming a solid front with the Kolchak forces. At this time, the forces opposing Kolchak were as follows:

Red Order of Battle Opposing Kolchak

1st Army near Simbirsk with 30,000 men (24th xx, 1st xx), 20 guns, 500 cavalry.

2nd Army near Glazov to Sarapol with 12,800 men (2nd xx, 28xx) 1120 cavalry.

3rd Army at Perm to Osa with 30-40,000 men (7th xx,5th xx, 30th xx, 29th xx) and 50 guns, 4350 cavalry. This army blocked the way of Kolchaks Northern Army led by the young Czech, Gadja. As time went on, the army would retreat after losing 25,000 men.

4th Army near Samara with 19,000 men, 1000 cavalry and 30 guns.

5th Army west of Ufa with 45,000 men (26th xx, 27th xx, 4th xx) 30 Heavy guns, 50 Lt. Guns

6th Army at Vologda with 10,000 men (18th xx) 250 cavalry, 189 MG, 75 guns [Note: this was the strength of the division in Dec, 1918; the previously mentioned strengths are as of May 1919].

7th Army at Petrograd with 10,000 men (6th xx, 10th xx, 19th xx, 85thxx, 86th xx) 300 cavalry, 90 MG, 16 3 inch guns. The 86th and 85th both both had become demoralized and withdrawn, replaced by the 10th xx (82,83,84,87th regiments) at Gatchina. The 19th division was comprised of: 183rd reg (500 men, 620 rifles, 73,600 cartridges, 25 Maxim MG, 71 carts); the 186th reg (450 men, 580 rifles, 8 Maxim MG and 41 horses; the 169th reg (110 men, 279 rifles, 8 Maxim MG and 20,000 cartridges); the Finnish reg (500 men and 8 Maxim MG), 1st Artillery division with 8 guns and 50 men and 2nd artillery division with 10 guns.

These were the Red forces opposing the Allies and Kolchak's forces.

Kolchak's Siberian Army at this time consisted of:

The Northern Army (Gaida) from Ekaterinburg to Perm with 28,000 men (5th xx, 1st xx, 4th xx, 7th Ural xx, 3rd xx and Votkin xx, of these, 17,000 were the elite 1st Siberian Corps which acted as a spearhead in the attack) 2700 cavalry, 56 guns, 268 MG.

Thc Central Army at Sarapol with 8000 men, the 14,000 man 2nd Siberian Corps, 500 cavalry, 50 guns and 67 MG.

The Southern Army at Ufa to Boulgma with 24,000 men, 2200 cavalry and the 3rd Siberian Corps (8,000 men), 459 guns and 71 MG.

Dutov's Army at Orenburg contained 3000 men and 5000 cavalry.

Kolchak's reserves at Ufa contained another 7200 men and at Ekaterinburg, some 4300 infantry and 1100 cavalry. Most of the Czech forces (9800 men) fought with the Northern Army. Many others had been moving by rail to Vladiostock.

While the standard Red divison at this time was supposed to contain 927 officers, 24,867 enlisted, 4284 cavalry, and 28 guns, in reality, the average Red division might consist of 5000 enlisted, 200 officers, 3000 rifles, 40 MG, and 30 guns.

6

The New Year Arrives 1919

Assuming control of the North Russian Army in January, 1919, was Lt. General Eugene Miller. He was a character with a blonde mustache and moderate build. Born in 1867, he became a 2nd Lt. in the Tsarist Army, a Lt. by 1890, a Lt. Col. in 1896 and by age 34, a full Colonel in 1901. He served as military attaché in the Netherlands and Italy. In 1914, he commanded a regiment and later became Chief of Staff of the 5th Army and 26th Corps. When he assumed leadership of the North Russian Army he was 51.

As January 1919 dawned, the Americans had advanced into the outer limits of an abyss like a prong down the Vaga River. Near Ust Padenga (200 hundred miles from Archangel) this intrusion force consisted of:

Company A/ U.S. 339th
80 Cossacks
One Russian artillery detachment (two 47mm)
48 Canadian and two 18 pdr.
4th Russian Company
One detachment/310th U.S. engineers.
In total, some 450 men, 18 MG, 2 18pdr, 2 47mm.

The main position was at Netsvetiaskaya, which overlooked Ust Padenga. A mile further, they held Niji Gora. The White Russians held Ust Padenga (with 2 arty guns, 1 AA gun), while one platoon of 45 Americans, 3 MG's (led by Lt.Mead) at Niji Gora. The White Russians had refused to occupy Ninji Gora stating it was a too dangerous position. But the British High command had ordered the Americans there. At Shenkursk, Co C, and the 68th

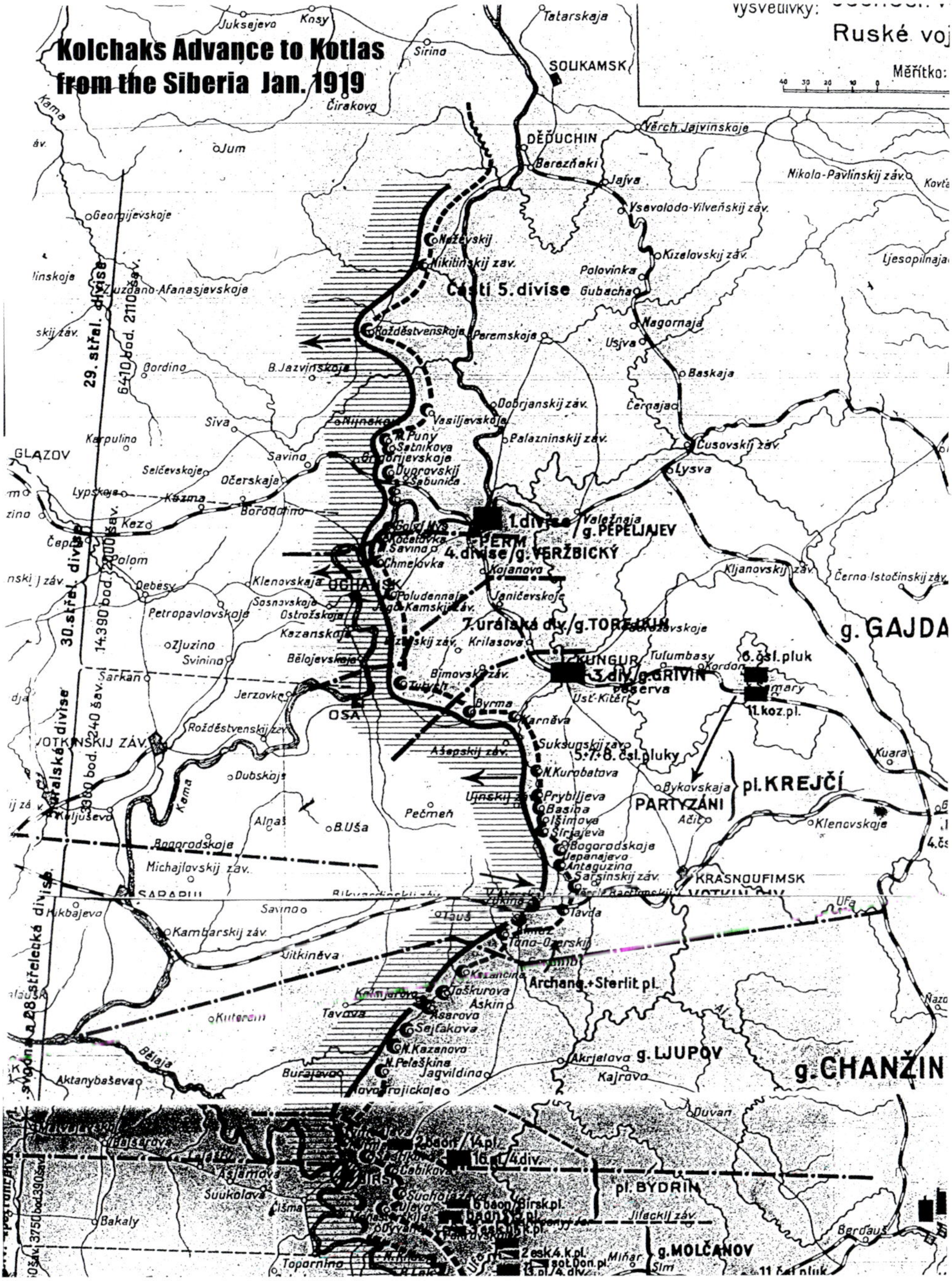
Kolchaks Advance to Kotlas
from the Siberia Jan. 1919
Ruské voj
Měřítko:
SOLIKAMSK
DĚDUCHIN
Části 5. divise
1.divise
g. PEPELJAJEV
PERM
4.divise/g.VERŽBICKÝ
7.uralská div./g.TOREJKIN
KUNGUR
3.div./g.GRIVIN
g. GAJDA
6.čsl.pluk
11.koz.pl.
pl.KREJČÍ
PARTYZÁNI
KRASNOUFIMSK
GLAZOV
OCHANSK
OSA
VOTKINSKIJ ZÁV.
29. střel. divise
30.střel. divise
Archang.+Sterlit.pl.
g. LJUPOV
g.CHANŽIN
pl. BYDRIN
g.MOLČANOV
Kama
Bělaja

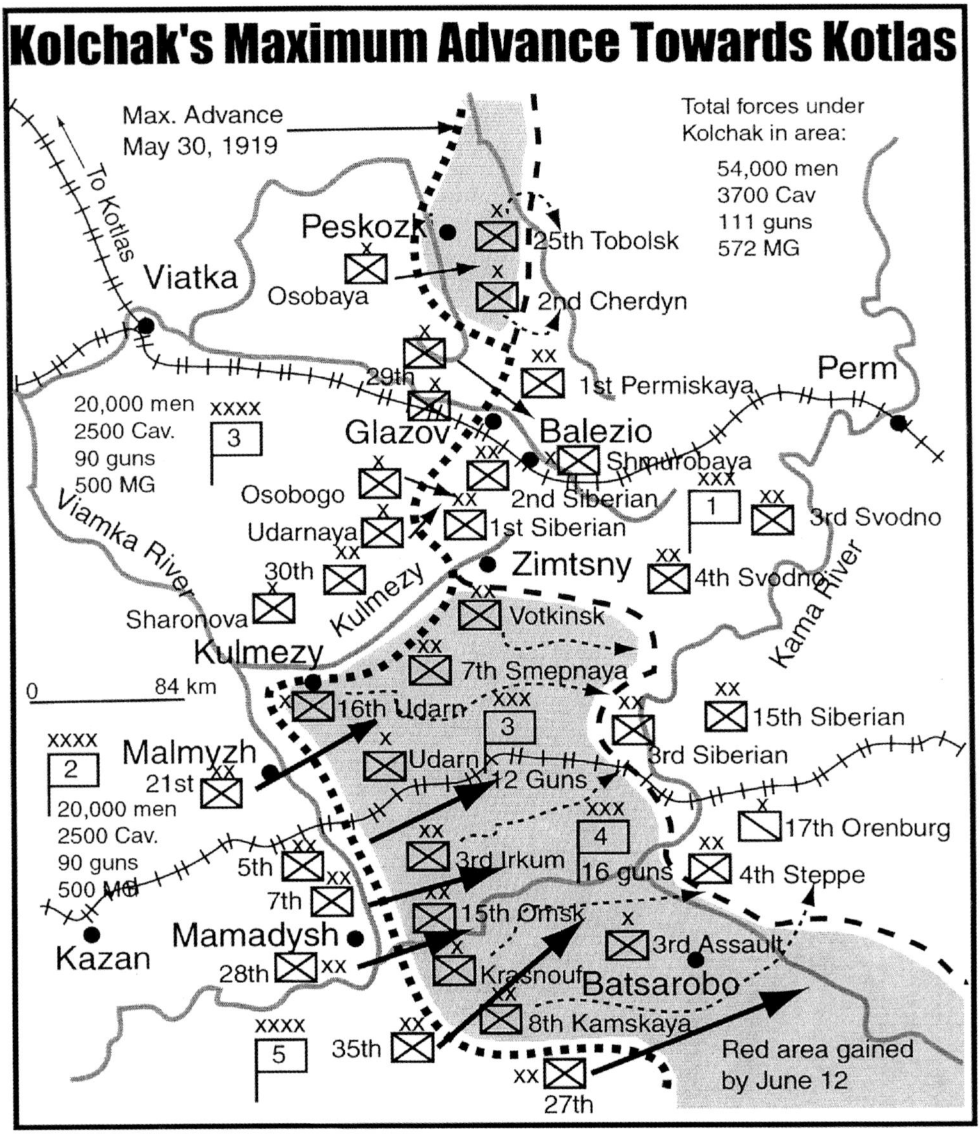

FA Canadian btty occupied. Some 23 men/Co.A and 20 men of the 310th engineers furthered augmented Ninji Gora. Just outside the village, on a hill, another 22 men with Lt. Harry Mead withstood the harsh climatic conditions. Militarily, it was an exposed position in shape of a "V." The snow was 30 inches deep, the temperature, minus 45°F. The Reds once again massed their troops (now dressed in white smocks) and on the 19th began an intense shelling upon the Americans (the Red guns were out of range of the four Canadian 3" pdr guns and 3 trench mortars). The Americans seemed to be untouched by the intense barrage, which when lifted revealed some 1500 Reds advancing from a concealed ravine from three sides and into the town!

One eyewitness survivor described it in this manner:

> " All at once, around to the left, a new attack developed. Out of a hollow concealed strip of forest less than 400 yards, another Bolo column appeared. The other enemy force to the right was 200 yards away. Their shots were hitting the blockhouse. Empty cartridge cases, clips and Lewis gun pans littered the floor as we fired. The air was filled with acrid powder fumes, our faces grimy and despite the cold, we were sweating. One squad fought it's way across the street despite the furious fire of machine guns from the edge of village. An officer yelled, "where's the telephone?" and "call in the artillery," The soldier listened and attempted to dial. The Russian guns were firing and their shells landed all over. The soldier looked up, " the line is dead." The officer groaned, "oh my God." After a moment, the officer yelled, "Get out."

Out of the 43 men of 4th platoon, 32 were either killed or wounded. The Red artillery had fired some 1800 rounds.

The Reds had secured many Lewis guns and MG's and were camouflaged wearing white smocks. One company of North Russians arrived to reinforce but ran upon seeing the Reds. The Americans had no choice but to retreat in waist deep snow across flat, clear terrain. Every man was now for himself. Matters became worse when the artillery manned by North Russians abandoned the guns. When the platoon finally made it back near Ust Padenga (held by rest of Co.A at Visorka Gora) only 7 men remained! The Red artillery (two 4.2" and two 3" howitzers) continued to barrage on the 20th, consuming thousands of shells and turning Shenkursk into rubble. The Canadian artillery (Capt. Mowat) continued to hold Nikolofskia but lost one gun. By the 22nd, Ust Padenga was evacuated. The Reds had taken two villages, the last one before Shenkursk, was Visorka Gora. This line contained five blockhouses each with a MG. Also present were seven Stokes mortars and more importantly, 300 men. The Reds, while losing many men, could afford the war of attrition and began to send ski units gliding through the forests to attack the town of Shenkurst directly. This, while Visorka Gora, which shielded the town, also was attacked. The RAF flew a few bombing missions. The planes carried eight 20lb Cooper bombs dropped by the observer (the bomb release gear was frozen). This would slow down the 700 fresh Red troops which suddenly appeared.

The Line of Communications from Shenkursk and the river base at Bereznik was 120 miles. Between these points, one allied position existed at Shegovari (44 miles from Shenkursk) with two White Russian platoons and at Kitsa (60 miles away) with one platoon. The British command had sent the Americans out on a very frail, dangerous limb, which was about to snap.

American Cos. A and C were in Shenkursk on the 24th, travelling five miles. By now, the town was under attack from all sides. The town of Shenkursk had been prepared defensively to repel any Red attacks (akin to the French and Dien Bien Phu in 1954). It had a series of formidable trenches and blockhouses that encircled the town. Each of these had a cleared firing lane into the thick forests surrounding it. The trenches had miles of wire laid before them making them impenetrable. The men present felt that the defenses could be held with a few hundred soldiers and repel a divisional size attack. There were also two months of supplies stockpiled.

Company A stragglers finally reached the town at 1600 on the 24th, all totally exhausted from their narrow escape. To the British Command at Beresnik, there were two choices: stand and be destroyed eventually or run. The Red artillery now honed in on the town with a barrage similar to those on the Western Front. By midnight, the order (this arrived via airplane in a near crash landing on the frozen Vaga) was given to evacuate from the town via the only trail not blocked by the surrounding Reds (an unused logging path that the Reds had missed to block). The artillery guns were destroyed and all unnecessary baggage left behind. The 100 wounded were put on sleighs and pulled. The caravan had food for only three days. The bulk of the caravan left as Cos. A and B/U.S. 339th held the perimiter. A one mile long caravan then slowly disappeared into the forest.

For the Reds, unaware that the city was defenseless, continued barrage using their one 9" gun, two 6" guns and four 4.7" guns while the Americans, Canadians and North Russians totaling 1000 slipped by (instead of being surrounded) to Shegovari. They arrived at 5 p.m. and at Vistavka (3 miles from Kitsa) by 12:30 a.m. on the 26th. Eventually, the Americans made a stand at Visorka Gora from inside five blockhouses. For two days, all Red attacks were repelled with the help of the Canadian artillery (two 18 pdrs) using shrapnel fuses. The impact was devastating. The Americans reached Spasskoe after a six hour march. By the 27th, the Americans were exhausted. Co.A had had no rest in six days. The Canadians had lost 4 guns. The Reds pursuing the allies eventually totaled 3000 men but were never able to destroy them. In the end, the Red losses were 500 men and General Ironside commented on the Red leadership of General Samoilo, who led the Red attack. It showed that the Red force was becoming a real military unit.

It was a narrow 60 mile escape some 200 miles from Archangel. It was a miracle. Had the Reds pursued it vigorously, they could have continued to expel the Allied forces. However, the main reason the Reds had conducted this offensive was that Kolchak's Northern Army under Gaida had taken Perm in the East. Now, Kolchak and the Allied forces were much closer to Kotlas. In the Archangel theatre, the totals now amounted to:

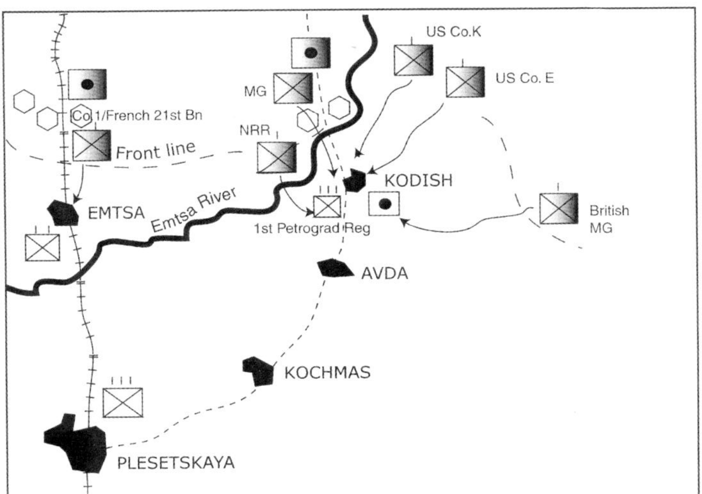

The Allied Offensive on Kodish & Emtsa Dec.29,1918

Map: Perry A. Moore, 2001 from original sketch.

British:	6220 men	2000 in reserve
French:	1680 men	1200 to defend the LOC
U.S.:	5100 men	35 artillery guns (17 in reserve)
North Russ:	5300	10 heavy guns (5 in reserve)

According to Allied intelligence the Red troop disposition were as follows:

Along the Railroad:	The Riazen reg (1000 men) Artillery with 450 men and sixteen 3" guns, four 4.2" guns and two 6" guns.
At Sheleksa:	Gatchina regiment (1000 men)
At Plesetskaya:	Cavalry (150 men) One infantry Bn (300 men)
At Kodish:	1st Bn/159th reg (500 men), one ind. Company (200 men), Cavalry (80), four 3" guns, four trench mortars, 12 MG.
At Tarasevo:	2nd Bn/159th regiment (500), a guerilla force (400 men), two 3" guns, 11 MG and two mortars
At Kochmas:	One battalion with 500 men.
	Shenkursk: 2000 men.

The Red offensive was not over. Starting on the 26th, large attacks were conducted toward the allied base located at Toulgas and the Reds had managed to overrun one of the positions. The allied forces counterattacked and for the next several days the battle went back and forth until the 30th, when the Allied position was untenable. The Allied troops withdrew. Thus, by the end of January, the Reds had caused a major blow to the Allies. In terms of manpower, there was some parity but in terms of artillery, the Reds had many more guns.

The month of February was relatively quiet. The French had finished training a Russian ski company and on the 7th, attacked the Reds at Avdah near Seleskoe. The Reds were surrounded but too strong. The North Russian Army had grown to 11570 men of dubious worth. Ironsides now demanded additional reinforcements from Murmansk..

The Reds, too, had received the following additional units:

The 161st, 160th, and 162nd regiments had been formed at Vologda. The 159th (1300 men), 154th (1400 men, 12 MG, 3 trench mortars), and 155th regiments were beginning to arrive. Arriving on the Vaga River front was the 156th Regiment (1300 men), and on the Railroad front, the 158th adn 157th regiments (1500 men), including two 4.5" howitzer.

The number of Bolos on the various fronts were as follows:

Railroad:	4500 men
Kodish:	6500 men
Vaga:	4000 men
Dvina:	4500 men
Onega:	1500 men
Vologda:	3,000 men
Kotlas:	5000 men
Viatka:	9000 men

As for the Allies, their troop dispositions for the Dvina Force ran as follows:

KURGOMIN	4 platoons/Co C/17th bn	185
	4 platoons/Co B/2nd Bn Royal Scot	224
	Russian Cavalry	42
	2 sections (4 18 pdr guns)/67th Canadian btty	128
PLESS	3 platoons/Co.D/2nd Bn Royal Scot	127
	Others	47
TOULGAS	4 platoons/Co.C/2nd Bn Royal Scot	188
	4 platoons/Co.B/1st Bn/U.S. 339th	222
	Misc.	63
	1 Section/67th Canadian Btty (2 18pdrs)	63
	1 section/421st Btty (2 4.5" How)	49
SHUSHUGA	1 platoon/Co.D/2nd Bn Royal Scot	50
IGNATOVSKAYA	1 Russian Company	200
	Cavalry	110
KITSA	4 platoons/Co.A/1st Bn/U.S. 339th	210
MAXIMOVSKAYA	1 Cossack Cavalry Det.	97
EVIEVSKA	2 Russian companies	350
	Cavalry Det.	35
	1 section/2nd Russian Btty (2 18 pdr)	31
VISTAVKA	4 platoons/Co.C/U.S. 339th	210
	2 platoons/Co.A/2nd Royal Scot	75
	Misc.	39
	Half section/67th Canadian Btty (3 18 pdrs)	98
PIANDA	HQ 16th Arty Brigade, Canadian	63
	1 section/1st Heavy Russian Btty (3 155mm)	112
OSSINSOVO	1 platoon/Co.A/2nd Bn/Royal Scot	63
	Russian Bn	200
BERESNIK	1 platoon/Co.A/2nd Bn/Royal Scot	39
	1 platoon/Co.D/U.S.339th	47
	2 platoons/Slavo-British	92
	Misc.	183
	3 18 pdrs.	
MONITOR ISLAND	2 3" naval guns	
CHAMOVO	3 platoons/Co.D/U.S. 339th	139
U.S.T VAGA	1 18 pdr w/Russian crew	35
	Misc.	123

Two platoons from Company A /Royal Scots were finally sent to reinforce the river column. But this was not enough as the Reds succeeded in taking Tarasova.

The Allied forces attempted another attack on the 7th using Company B/Liverpools, an American trench mortar unit and the French ski unit, Coureurs des Bois. The attack called for the retaking of Avda. Kodish fell at 0820 but the resistance at Avda was so strong, the attack was aborted. On the 9th, the Reds resumed their fierce artillery barrages upon the Liverpools at Kodish. The Reds had quickly overran the outposts and threatened the town.

The Allies frequently used patrols to determine the enemy's strength, they usually consisted of the following:

> 6 officers, 70 men, 4 Lewis Guns, 250 Ammo pans, 96 Mills bombs, 1 trench mortar, 200 trench shells. Each man carried 100 rounds and 12 days of rations.
> The total weight of the equipment: 9010 lbs in 35 sleighs.

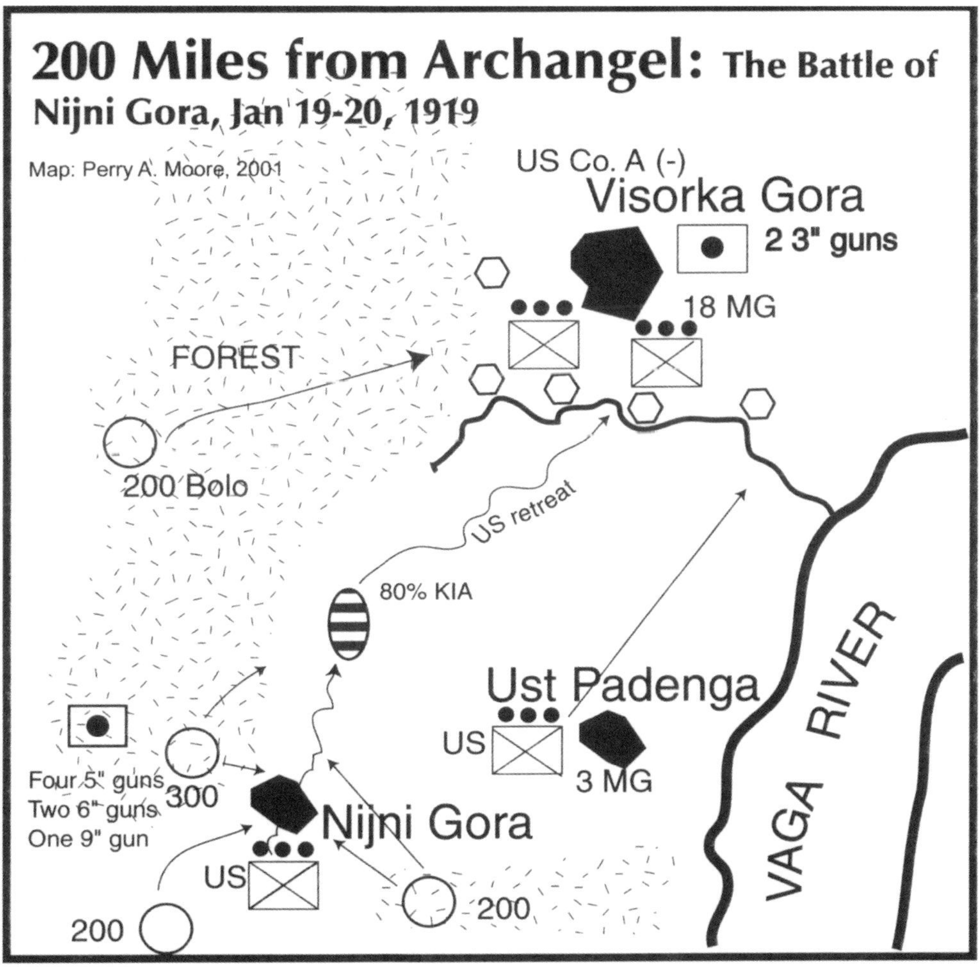

Throughout the allied intervention, the only means of intelligence gathering on the enemy came from deserters, prisoners or air observation. Thus, it was highly susceptible to inaccuracy. These reports usually were written in two week periods. Despite their inaccuracy, they did provide a picture of the enemy, which was often correct.

The following report was for the Murmansk Front, dated February 9-23,1919:

> The composition of the newly created 19th Red Division of 7th Army comprised of:

Divisional HQ	Petrozavodsk	Gen. Solodoukhin
55th Brigade (the 164th,165th reg. Being formed	Petrozavodsk	163rd Reg (Ivanoff) 56 officer, 500 men, 620 rifles, 73700 cartridges, 25 Maxim MG, 71 carts, 77 horses, 12 two horse carts.
56th Brigade (the 167, 168th regiments being formed) Located at Povienets.	No staff yet.	Cmdr. Zuevich 186th Regiment has 24 officers, 450 men, 580 rifles, 17700 cartridges, 8 Maxim MG, 41 horses
57th brigade (the 170,171 regs. Being formed) Located at Olonets.	No staff yet.	Cmdr. Kozgevnikoff 169th regiment has 112 men, 279 rifles, 20000 cartridges, 8 Maxim MG
1st Artillery Division Located at Mediezy Gora	Cmdr. Allafusoff	Comprised of 4 officers, 20 men. Consists of three batteries totaling eight guns, 9 ammo boxes, 36 artillery horses, 14 baggage horses, 20 riding horses.
2nd Artillery Division Located at Alexandro Svir.	Cmdr. Yevtukhovich	Comprised of 11 officers, 84 men in three batteries with total of 10 guns
Communications	Cmdr Baranoff	65 men, 2 motorcycles, 4 cars, 6 trucks.
Lake Onega Flotilla	Cmdr. Pantzerzhansky	146 men, 125 rifles, 22 Maxim MG, (3) 75mm (1) 47mm, (4)35mmm 350 75mm shells, 100 47mm shells, 800 35mm, 4 steamers, 4 floating batteries, 2 minelayers. Seaplane unit consists of: 20 men, 5 Lewis Guns, 50 5 lb bombs, 25 10lb bombs, 2-4 M9 airplanes.
164th Finnish reg	41st Urososero reg	40th Petrozavodsk reg

The request by Ironside's for more troops was answered. The 13th Bn/Yorkshire "Green Hornet" regiment was sent from Murmansk on the 6th. The battalion had 23 officers and 684 men. The unit began moving from Popov to Soroka. They loaded upon sleighs for the march across the tundra to Koleshima, Ruiga, Nuksha, Unejma,Malashika. It reached Onega at 1930 on the 13th. The march continued reaching Bolshie-Ozerki at 1800 on the 16th. Cos.A (123 men) and D arrived at Seletskoe by 1300 on the 22nd. Company B arrived on the 24th. Company C (105 men) was sent to Archangel. From there, A Company replaced Co.C/17th Liverpools at Shred Mekhrenga. B Company replaced D Company/17th Liverpools. It was an amazing journey in –40°F temperatures covering around 175 miles and using over 200 sleighs!

The Red forces began a reorganization of their own military. Oddly enough, the scheme of a division was based on the European model. Soldiers were drafted and trained officers were put in command instead of untrained party members. At the head of the Red Army Revolutionary committee was Leon Trotsky. Within the committee were the following: Votzeitis, an ex Colonel of the General Staff; Velitchenko, an ex professor of engineering; Scheidman, an ex. General of the 2nd Corps and later, 3rd Army during WW1; Martinoff, an ex Lt. General; Batel an ex-General and Svetchin, an ex Major General who commanded the 7th Finnish regiment. This group controlled all military matters.

The new Red divisions comprised of three companies to a battalion, three battalions to a regiment, three regiments to a brigade and three briagdes to a division. In theory, it was hoped that 250 men would make a company, most only had 150 men due to the shortage of manpower. According to the new plan, an infantry division would look like this:

Infantry	927 Officer	24867 men	4284 horses	
Artillery	154 officers	4668 men	4152 horses	28 guns
Cavalry	46 officers	878 men	954 horses	
Technical	110 officers	2399 men	1061 horses	
HQ	50 officers	1543 men	1057 horses	

However, the model hoped for never or seldom materialized. Below are the actual strengths of some Red infantry divisions:

1st Rifle	216 officer	3025 men	64 horses	1185 rifles	3 guns
3rd Rifle	233 officer	1038 men	181 horses	370 rifles	28 guns
11th Rifle	275 officer	9004 men	268 horses	3749 rifles	12MG 44 gun
8th Rifle	299 officer	4328 men	824 horse	4879 rifles	50MG 74gun

Basically, the full strength model division set as a standard only happened when a sector was threatened, to wit, the 18th division that opposed the allied forces, which slowly grew from 7000 men to 14,000 by this time. Allied forces by the beginning of March 1919 consisted of 11,000 men on the front lines: 4500 U.S.; 5000 British; 700 French; and 700 Pole. In addition, he had 5000 dubious Russian.

The Red strength had increased to 16,800 men. At Kotlas, there were 8000 men, and 9000 at Vologda (including 66 guns and 150 MG's).

Unbeknownst to General Ironside, on March 4th, the British War Cabinet had decided once and for all to evacuate and abandon this "North Russian Stunt." This was to be done as soon as possible but not before two more full size Class A, experienced brigades were to arrive in June and July. Their purpose was to simply give the Reds a "real bloody nose" in one last offensive before withdrawing in September. Thus, regardless of the success of Kolchak advancing past Perm and towards Kotlas, it had been decided to "get out." Kolchak was not told.

On March 11th, Col.Van Spuy, the air commander was on a reconnaissance flight along the Vaga River when his motor of his aircraft went dead. The Colonel was required to land on the shore among numerous Red soldiers. He was captured by two Red army soldiers, which dragged him by the collar from the cockpit and lead him off driven by rifles butts.

The new commander of aviation to be appointed was a Colonel Grey, an elderly 55-year-old flier and veteran of the First World War, with which the Russian airmen rapidly had good relations.

At Archangel, the allies received a large shipment of new English aircraft. In general, th there were 21 D.H.9 bombers, 12 D.H.9a bombers, 15 "Sopwith Snipe," a few "RE 8s" and 6 educational-training "Avro-504" destined for the archangel flying school. However, the "Avros" were armed and sent to the "river front" instead. Together with the aircraft arrived more English pilots. The White Russians pilots received from the new aircraft four "DH 9" and three "Snipes." These aircraft allowed them to replace the worn out "Sopwith"s. As the numbers in the air-corp's composition grew, its organizational structure changed. The Air-corps was divided into three squadrons. First squadron commanded by A.A.Kazakov, given the rank of a British Major, RAF, second and third squadrons to Majors Kerr and Boumen.

The forces under Kolchak also went to the offensive along a 1000 mile front from Perm to Orenburg. The main focus of the attack fell on the 5th and 2nd Red Armies in the center. The Red Armies were unable to regroup quickly and Kolchak's forces were pursuing rapidly.

On the 7th, the best North Russian unit, the 3rd regiment defended the Onega valley. Some 1000 men defected to the Reds, which allowed the Reds move untouched through a gap. This Red exploitation threatened the 6th Russian regiment near the RR and forced to retreat.

A series of mutinies from allied troops now began: The 13th Bn, which had only just arrived, refused to take their positions. It was only the presence of General Ironside that the men agreed to replace the Americans. On the railroad front, a French company refused to leave their barracks. Then the Poles refused to return to the front until their priest had blessed them. The British colonel placed the priest under arrest. Even the American Co. I refused to return to the front when it was ordered. An American officer, Lt. Moore, wrote a paper questioning why American troops were more than 20 miles from Archangel. In Archangel itself, the unions staged a pro-Red rally! Some 30 men were shot by firing squads after being arrested.

The allies received two 60 pdrs in March. These huge guns were towed to the front, each requiring 46 horses just to tow the guns, another 10 horses towed 50 rounds of ammo. The allied forces along the Dvina River now reached 6000 men but 75% were Russian. Luckily for Ironside, another battalion, the 6th Bn/Yorkshire, was sent from Murmansk.

This unit left in the first week of March in the same manner the 13th Bn had. Cos. A.B and C arrived just in time to counter the upcoming Red offensive. D Company move to Kholmogori for an attack on Zempzova. The battalion had 673 men. Also arriving was the 280 Machine Gun battalion. This unit contained two Vicker HMG companies and two Lewis Gun companies bristling with 16 HMG, 32 Lewis Guns, 16 carts and 118 pack animals.

The next major attack again came from the Reds led by Gen. Kuropatkin who sent a force of 1200 men (2nd Ski Bn) to divide the allies along the Onega river and those on the RR. This swift flanking action (the Reds were on skis) caught the defending French company off guard at Bolsherzerski (16 miles west of Oberzerskaya) on the 17th. The French were decimated and fell back towards Oberzerskaya. This move split up the allied units on the Railroad and those along the Onega. The Red 6th Army now could fall on Oberzerskaya and then attack the Allied rear. Through defectors, Ironside learned of the coming major offensive of the Reds. With the limited manpower, he culled all the units for the most fit men in Archangel and elsewhere eventually creating an "ad Hoc" group of 500 men to defend Verst 18, some 12 miles west of Oberzerskaya. If this fell, the RR line to Archangel would be cut.

In the spring offensive, Soviet aviation became more active. At that point on the "river front" there was the Red 18th Reconnaissance Detachment with pilots (Dyachkov, Kovalev, Kudryavtsev, Lavrov. Smirnov and Sovorov) and also units of the Naval Aviation consisting of the 1st Naval Fighter Detachment, White Sea Hydro-Detachment and 3rd section Sea Naval Hydro-Detachments (Kamsk). These had been combined together and created the Northern Aerial Squadron subordinate to the Severodvinsk Flotilla Command.

The airfield of the 18th Detachment was located near the Vaga River, to the North of Shenkursk. The naval fighters were based on the field in Puchga Village along the shore of Dvinsk. Also at this location were aerial-barge-transports with seaplanes hangers. Floating workshops, barracks and staff quarters were also the steamer *Pugachev (*there was no communication between the army and sea aviation units. Although their airfields were divided by not more than 25 miles, the land and sea squadrons never flew joint operations and frequently did not know what the other was planning or doing).

At Pinega, the North Russian 8th regiment revolted and the unit fought amongst themselves. When the French collapsed, the American Co.H (- 2 platoons), and one Russian Company (200 men) and 8 howitzers deployed to support the French (one company had been cut off at Chinova). The British tossed in Cos.A and C /6th Yorkshire Bn, and a Polish Company. The Americans and British began their advance from near Chinova.

Opposing the Allied troops in Murmansk area, the Red 19th division under General Solodoukine. The unit was quite strong containing the 55th brigade (163,164,165 reg), 56th brigade (166, 167,168 regs), 57th brigade (169,170, 171 regs). Added to this were the following independent units: 41st,1st, 1st Finnish regs.

The allied forces plan was to counterattack using a flank attack. This began on the 23rd with the U.S. Co. H and the 6th Bn/Yorkshires from the Chekuevo area, west of Bolshi-Ozerki. The Russian troops were easily routed from Red artillery fire. The Red repelled the attack but caused the Red commander concern and under pressure from two fronts. To ensure success, the Red commander brought up the 2nd Moscow reg (48 MG,1900 men), 96th Saratov reg (18MG,1420 men) and 2nd Kazan reg . On the Railroad front, the Americans in Co. E (2 platoons) advanced through five feet of snow to near Bolsheozerki just as

French were pulling back. It was ordered simply to dig in, which did nothing to help the French. Allied airplanes frequently flew as artillery spotters. Two platoons/Co. H quickly occupied the blockhouses (these were constructed by the engineers. Each one had two walls separated by six inches of sawdust or dirt. The walls were akin to log cabins and HE fire, unless a direct impact was achieved, were impenetrable) built by Co.C/310 engineers. The U.S. Co. M was moved closest to the Reds.The allies quickly fortified Obozerskaya with wire, machine guns and artillery.

Several hundreds of miles away at Perm, Kolchak's Northern Siberian Army commanded by the young Czech, Gadja, had attacked and advanced on the 19th to within 160 km of Viatka. This was the first objective of Gadja as the railroad connected from here to Kotlas (the whole objective of the Allied forces). The furthest his forces would ever advance toward the Allies was halted at the town of Glazov. Gadja's forces at this time consisted of : 25th regiment, 2nd regiment, 1st Perm division, and the first Siberian Corps comprising of the 1st and 2nd Siberian divisions. The 25th regiment had advanced to Kausopodok opposite little resistance of a Red Special detachment by the 24th, while the 2nd regiment and 1st Perm division had crossed the Vamka river. At one point it was within 140 km of Viatka by the 30th. The 1st Siberian Corps stuggled to advance south of the railroad. The Red 3rd Army opposing this offensive contained only the 29th and 30th divisions, which were placed to oppose the 1st Siberian Corps.

The other Red army opposing Gadja was the 2nd Army. When combined, the 2nd and 3rd Armies had 41,200 men, 5100 cavalry, 189 guns and 1000 MG. The 2nd Army held the line along the southern prong of the Vamka river with the 28th, 21st, 7th and 5th divisions, a front some 160 km long.

Gadja's problem was that his 3rd Siberian Corps with the 7th, Bomkunkau divisions, 16th regiment and a special brigade had advanced in a southerly instead of a westerly direction. This created a protruding flank held by the 7th division and 16th reg.

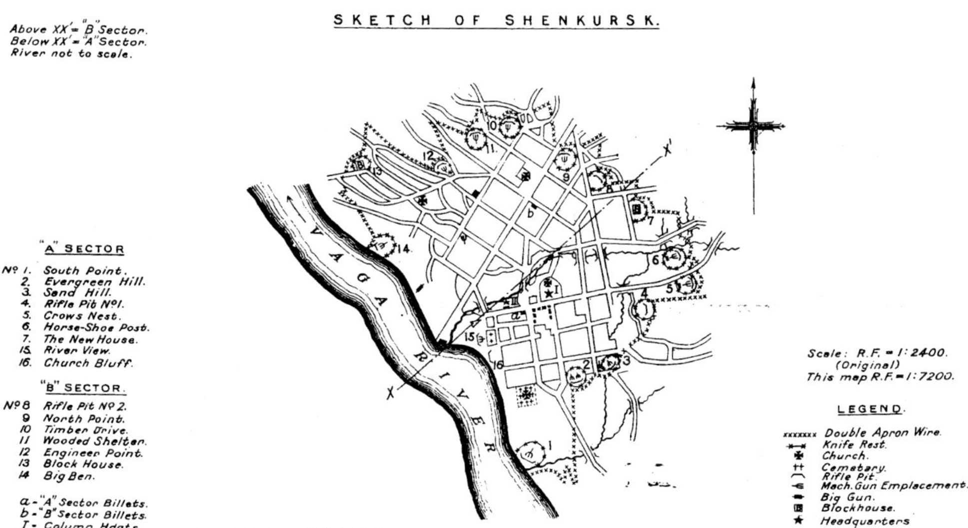

Map: Univ. of Michigan

The Red 2nd Army began the counterattack on the 25th attacking the 4th Siberian Corps (consisting of the 3rd, 15th Omsk and 8th Kama divisions). This corps held the line along the Vamka river. The Red 28th division easily ripped through the 15th Omsk division and by the 30th, had advanced 85 km. Gadja's 3rd division offered more resistance but it was attacked by the 5th and 7th Red divisions and forced to pull back when the 15th Omsk broke. Part of the Red 30th division (3rd Army) now conducted a flank attack on the 7th division, while the reserves at Viatka went to the attack hitting the 16th Regiment. The lines now stablized. Gadja's men were in such poor condition he knew he could not take the offensive. His men lacked clothing and food making defections to the Reds frequent. The conditions of winter and sub-zero temperatures and then mud, slowed both side down. The Red airforces in this area consisted of the following:

5th Socialist det.
1st and 2nd Irkutsk dets.
1st Tversk airgroup
2nd Olonetski det.

The White airforce consisted of:

1st, 2nd and 3rd Siberian det.
33rd Siberian air corps

Back in the Obezerskaya area, the main Red attack consisting of 7000 men and artillery began on the 31st. The allies numbered 200 Americans and 300 British/French. First, the Reds cut off the town from Archangel, which also destroyed two allied artillery guns. The Reds then attacked Company M in a frontal attack, the flanks held by the British and French. The Red attacks were repelled with heavy losses to three battalions. On April 1st, the Reds, in three waves, assaulted from opposite directions coming to within 200 yards. At this range, the Americans employed their rifle grenades as artillery fired shrapnel, all well placed and forcing the Reds to fall back. They lost another 2000 men. Many wounded crawled to the American lines to escape the harsh bitter cold. On the 2nd, Co.H and the British 6th bn attacked with two stokes mortars from the Chekhuvo area (600 men) Co.A/6th Yorkshire attempted a surprise attack on the Reds, only to be given away by guard dogs barking. The Polish company assaulted frontally, which failed due to intense Red MG fire. Co.C/6th Yorkshire attempted a night attack through the forests, but got lost. Co.A was subsequently attacked by the Reds which was beaten off, while Co.C saved the platoons of U.S. Co. H from an overwhelming Red assault. The Reds, then changed the direction of attack on the 4th and ended the attack on the 5th. The battle had lasted a grueling 60 hours and cost them 2000 KIA.

Tension between the allies increased, to wit, in mid April, Capt.Ramsey of the U.S. Co. F was at Kitsa. Ramsey informed the British Colonel in charge of all troops there, that the Americans were going to cross the river to the other side. The Colonel politely told the American that if his troops went over to the other side, he would order the Canadian artillery to open fire on the Americans for insubordination. Captain Ramsey gladly issued orders and the Americans crossed the Vaga River. The British Colonel then ordered the Canadians to fire. The Canadians refused. So much for old colonialism sores. In another incident, the Poles refused to enter the forests while pursing the Reds, an American officer, Capt. Ballensinger of Co. H drew his handgun and ordered the Poles at gunpoint. Worse, were the totally unreliable North Russians. On the 25th, the 2nd Bn/3rd Regiment of 400 men and six artillery gun mutinied and killed 7 of their officers at Toulgas. About 100 remained allied and fought the other 300 men until the 100 men retreated back to Shusuga. They were pursued by the 300 men and surrounded. A Canadian artillery battery forced the Reds back.

In the beginning of April, the troops' dispositions and strengths on all fronts comprised the following:

TOULGAS to KURGOMIN	1.5 Cos./Royal Scot	268
(total : 1141 men)	3 U.S. Companies	541
The Dvina column HQ in Pless,	1 Slavo-British platoon	26
commanded by Lt.Col. Montford.	67th Arty Btty/16th Canadian (6 18 pdr)	194
	Det.421 Arty Btty (2 4.5" How, 2 18 pdr)	111
VAGA COLUMN		
KITSA to MAXIMOVSKAYA	1 Co/17th Bn/Liverpools	133
Commanded by Lt.Col. Poignant.	2 Companies/2nd Bn/R.Scots	310
Total men: 1132.	1 Co/U.S. 339th	218
	U.S. Engineers	83
	Russian Infantry	170
	Russian Cavalry	69
	2 sections/68th Btty/Canadian (4 18 pdr, 1 4.5" How)	91
	Russian artillery (1 18 pdr)	55
MORJEGORSKAYA	Two platoons/280MG	80
Total: 1314	Russian Infantry	910
	U.S. Engineers	30
	Slavo-Legion	204
	1 section/68th Btty/16th Can (3 18 pdrs)	63
BERESNIK	One U.S. Company	156
Total: 700 men	2 platoons/2nd bn/Royal Scot	63
	HQ/16th Canadian Brig.	66
	Russian artillery (1 18pdr, 1 75mm, 2 155mm, 1 4.5" how, 4 60 pdrs, 2 3" Naval guns, 1 6 pdr)	385

VOLOGDA FORCE	SHREDMEKRENDIZM	
HQ at Obozerskaya	2 sec/280 MG	68
Lt.Col Lucas	2 companies/13th Bn/Yorks	286
	Seletskoe Russian Reg.	374
	Archangel Company	155
	Russian Cavalry	25
	Sec/421st btty (1 4.5 " How)	22
	SBAL (1 4.5" How, 2 3" Guns)	48
EMTSA RIVER.KODISH AREA	1 Co./17th Bn/Liverpool	202
Total: 477 men	1 Co Russian	123
	2 platoons/Dyers SBAL	84
	2 sec/252 MG Co. (1 4.5" How)	45
VOLOGDA FORCE RESERVE	3 platoons/13th bn/ York	210
Total: 704	1 Co/17th Bn/Liverpools	119
	252 MG Co.	50
	1 Russian Co	282
	1 Co/Dyers SBAL	50
RAILWAY COLUMN verst 445	3 U.S. Companies	645
Major Nichols, U.S. Army	U.S. MG Co	100
	Armor Train (1 18pdr, 2 3" Naval guns)	18
	2 sec/63rd French Btty	50
	(2 155mm, 2 75mm)	
	SBAL Heavy Gun sec. (1 6" How)	12
	Russian Arty Det.	30
	(1 6" How, 2 6" Naval guns)	
	1 Co/Archangel Reg NRR	
OBOZERSKAYA	2 Cos/French Foreign legion	210
	1 sec/63rd French Btty (2 75mm)	342
	Russian Artillery (4 75mm, 1 155mm	20
	on trucks; 1 75mm and 1 155mm)	175
BOLSHOI-OZERKE	1 U.S. Company	2
	1 Co/Archange	11
	l Reg NRR	176
	1 pla/French Foreign Legion	41
	1 pla/13th Bn/Yorks	50
	MG Section	20
	Russian Artillery	40
	(1 76mm, 4 75mm, 1 155mm)	

ONEGA HQ at Chekuevo	2 pla/U.S. Company	113
Lt Col. Laurie	Onega Russ.Bn	718
Along River	3 Cos/6th Bn/Yorks	600
	2 pla/U.S. Company	80
	2 Cos/Archangel Ren NRR	439
	2 MG sec	92
	Russ.Cavalry	17
	1 Polish Co.	200
	Russian Arty (2 75mm)	23
PINEGA HQ at Leunovo	TOROMSKAYA	
	2 pla/U.S. Company	80
	3 Russian Companies	
	sec/280 MG	30
	1 Co/6th Bn/Yorks	200
	Russian Artillery	
	(2 18pdrs, 1 47mm, 3 3"guns)	
LINE OF COMMUNICATIONS	LAVLA	
	French MG Bn	100
	U.S. Engineers	42
	MERCHA	
	1 Co/French 21st Bn	112
	U.S. Engineers	42
	ISAKOGORKA	
	6 pla/Dyers SBAL	390
	Chinese Labor Co.	158
	2 pla/Archangel NRR	89
	TUNDRAS	
	1 pla/Archangel Reg	38
	1 Co/21st French Bn	94
	1 Armor train (2 47mm)	
	KHOLMOGORSKIA	
	1 Co/21st French Bn	74
	1 Armor train (1 6pdr, 1 75mm)	18
	1 pla/Archangel Reg	38

ALONG THE DVINA RIVER	KHOSPIRMOGORI	
	2 pla/U.S. Company	100
	Russian	968
	YEMETSKOE	
	2 pla/U.S. Company	100
	Russian	245
MAIN BASE		530
ARCHANGEL, BAKHARITSA,		200
ECONOMIE		100

Total fighting strength along the fronts: 6577 men. Artillery lacking trained personnel: 4 8" Howitzer, 2 6" Howitzer, 5 75mm, 2 6pdrs, 16 4.2" guns, 3 3" Naval guns, 1 155mm.

In April, Co. F reinforced Cos. A and D, it was then sent to the Kitsa area along the Vaga to defend. Cos. B and C held Toulgas and Kurgomin along with four 6" guns. The Reds by this time had 66 artillery guns and 10 heavy guns (6 and 9" guns).

The Bolos were not finished yet. On the 5th, they attacked the British base at Shed Mekhrenga. This base was held by Companies A and B/6th Bn, two artillery batteries, one MG company and two North Russian battalions. The Reds attacked with yet another powerful force and for 13 hours, the battle see-sawed with the favor tipping to the Reds. The British finally summoned it's Co.D at Seletskoe, which arrived just in time thwarting the enemy attack back. By the 7th, over 200 Bolos were lying dead around the blockhouses.

The Reds added several new units: 6th Kamishin reg, 157th, 6th reg, 155th reg, 161st and 162nd regs, The Syren Force dispositions leading from Mumansk was as follows:

ALEXANDROVSK	Engineers	15
	Italian	50
	Sussex	28
MURMANSK	1203 Arty Btty	114
	492 Eng.Co.	126
	Railway	145
	29th London Reg	96
	Marines	92
	Supply	320
	Italians, French	515
	11th Bn/Sussex	355
	Admin/Misc	450
KOLA	420 Arty Btty	133
	236 Trench Mortar Btty	13
	Italian	966
	Sussex infantry	31
	Admin/Supply	200
	North Russian	93
LOPARSKAYA	Det 29th Bn/London	19
IMANDRA	Det.29th Bn/London	17
	Others	6
KANDALAKSHA	434 Arty Btty	72
	Det 29th Bn/London	55
	Marines	125
	6th Brigade HQ	25
	Det. 11th Sussex	30
	Supply	70
KANAJAYA GUBA	Finnish	1279
KEM	Det 13th Bn/Yorkshire	28
	French Artillery	213
	Karelians	3788
	Marines	33
	253 MG Company	5
	RAF	68
	Russians	202
	Armor trains	9
	Supply/Admin	230

SOROKA	1 platoon/13th bn/York	41
	253 MG Company	122
	Serbs	763
	Russian	229
	French	190
	Slavo-British Bn	452
	Canadians	49
	Supply	100
ONDA RIVER BRIDGE	Russian	27
HALTE	Serb	31
SEGEJA	237 Trench Mortar btty	8
	French (incl. 3 arty guns)	77
	253 MG Co. Det.	22
	Russian	54
	Serbs	76
PETCHENGA	435 arty btty	39
	A Co,HQ/11th Sussex	504
	236 Trench Mtr Det.	15
	Serbs	186
	Supply/Misc	96

By early May, the Syren Force was sent additional reinforcements: Co. 1 of the Kings Royal Rifle and Co.1 of the Middlesex regiment. Both contained about 200 men and proceeded to build an airfield between Lakes Vigozero and Segozero. This force totaled about 3000 men.

Sources:

1. Kondratev, C. *Aircraft of the Russian Civil War* Moscow Press, 2000.
2. WO 95/5430, WO 95/5419, WO 106/1153, WO 161/5, WO 158/5430, WO 106/1148, ADM 173/1695.
3. U.S. National Archives, Microfilm 925.
4. Goldhurst, Richard. *The Midnight War.* 1978.

7

The Buildup, Summer Offensive, and Fade Out

In May, the British Syren Force conducted their Lake Onega attack which was a big operation from Urosozero to Maselga and Medvyeja Gora. The offensive called for a total of 3000 men (2000 allied and 1000 Russian), one artillery batty, another battery mounted on trucks (4.5" howitzers), one armor train, six Re 8 planes. Basically, the shores of the lake were to be cleared by the 21st. All objectives were taken. The British controlled this lake with one gunboat, 3 monitors and 12 motorboats.

As a result of local offensive operation, the Karelian group of British forces held of the North shore of Lake Onega with the settlements of Povenets and Medvezh. In Medvezh, the British established a seaplane base. On June 6th, the forward wing arrived with four Fairey IIIC seaplanes with crews and ground personnel (the wing had a total of 18 aircraft and operated for many water locations in N. Russia). On that same day, Lieutenant Yang with observer Ross-Smith accomplished the first photo-recon flight over Red positions along the Suna river region.

The missions of the naval pilots on this backwater front were combat air control over the British Onega flotilla, attacking against the Red flotilla at Red ports and observation flights. This lake west of the Archangel was important because it bordered the Murmansk-Petrograd Railroad.

Frequent targets bombed were, in particular, a wooden railway bridge over the Suna river but even after direct hits, the Reds always repaired it after a couple of days. The British Naval airforce dropped, in addition the high-explosives, mustard gas bombs. A large supply of such bombs were supplied to Russia from Great Britain on the eve of the revolution, the British employed them along the Dvina during the upcoming summer offensive.

A few dozen Red soldiers were poisoned, but overall the gas did not bring the expected success for three reasons:

1) the environmental conditions of the North were not compatible with using chemicals,
2) employing them by aircraft did not create an effective concentration. During the attack to cover the evacuation they dropped a new "nerve gas," which proved effective. This "nerve gas" was not directly called this in the documentation, but various after action reports noted severe vomiting and convulsions from some witnesses,
3) the British simply employed these weapons much too late to do any good (Summer 1919).

The various raid results on the ships of the Onega Red Flotillas accorded some damage. The most effective raid took place on August 3rd, when the Reds Gunboat No.2 was made non-operational This three hundred ton paddle-boat with four 3"-inch field guns was captured during the Whites landing. The boat was repaired and included in the composition of the White flotilla under the name Silny or Strong.

On August 12th, from Petrograd to Petrozavodsk the Red 4th hydro-detachment, 2nd battalion of the Baltic air brigade arrived with 4 M-9 aircraft under the command of naval pilot Kovalevsk. This was the entire Red aviation in the Onega region. The Red naval pilots flew extremely few missions. Their first battle took place on September 7th, when one of their hydro-airplanes dropped bombs on a small river village with White soldiers.

There was no air to air combat over the lake. The only threat to British "Shorts" was disorderly firing from the ground. In all that time, the Reds were only able to hit one British airplane flown by Lieutenants Blempaid and Carvey. The pilots were able to fly over the line of contact but unable to make it to the water and crashed into the forest. Upon hitting the ground the aircraft literally broke into pieces, however the crew, as odd as it may sound, survived. Another two British aircraft suffered technical failures due to some cause. The machines were written off and replaced with new ones and the number in the air unit remained roughly the same.

RAF DH9A bombers based at Beresnik in 1919. Photo: IWM

At the close of April 1919, British seaplanes made an appearance on North Dvina river This unit comprised of 12 Fairey IIIC's and 12 out of date Short 184's. These were delivered to Archangel by the British sea-plane-carrier "HMS Pegasus."

To the North of Onega Lake, in the settlement of Lumbush from mid August to the end of September 1919, the British established another airbase. This air unit contained five Camels (naval 2F1 types), four RE.8 and two Avro 504. The Fliers of this detachment did the same tasks as their colleagues in the seaplanes.

The Bolsheviks used POWs as a hostage. In September, a soviet hydro-airplane dropped over a British airfield a pennant with a message, in which said, if the Petrozabodsk bombardments do not cease, then the captive pilot will be shot. On September 25th, the last air sortie by British aircraft over the Red hydrodrome at Medvezh.

By then the British aviation had already abandoned the Archangel region. On the 26th, the Onega air group also evacuated.

In Ironside's telegrams sent to the War office at 2 PM on April 30, 1919, he listed the following strengths:

BRITISH	
RAF	30 Off. 246 men
MG Corps	27 Off, 390 men
Engineers	44 Off, 205 men
Signals	19 Off, 174
Supply	70 Off, 741 men
Artillery	28 Off, 665 men
Infantry	124 Off, 3912 men
Admin	50 off, 340 men
MT drivers	4 Off, 14 men
Mappers	32 men
Interpreter	14 Off, 63 men
French	39 Off,1161 men
Italian	3 Off, 30 men
U.S.A	188 Off,4716 mn
Polish	15 Off, 259 men
Japanese	1 Off.
Partisans	354 men
Dyers reg	536 men
NNR army	689 Off, 16,140 men
SBAL	118 men
French Foreign Legion	14 off. 392 men

The British build up now began. The troops now being sent were combat experience men. Departing Southampton on May 12th, was the *1st Bn/Ox and Bucks Light Infantry*. A unit with 34 officers and 801 men. It arrived at Murmansk on the 19th, unloaded for exercise. It sailed for Archangel with other units from the 238th Brigade (Commanded by Gen

Grogan) on the 24th and berthed the 26th. By the 31st, it was ready to be sent to the front lines.

Another battalion. The *2nd Bn/ Hampshire Regiment*, arrived on the 27th with another 650+ men in companies W,X,Y and Z. This unit was polyglot of men from some 27 other units. These two battalions in addition to the *55th Artillery Battery, 238th and 239th Trench Mortar Btty, 8th MG Bn, 1152nd Supply Co and 384th Engineer Company comprised of Grogan's Brigade.*

On the Dvina River, the additional river monitors appeared to augment the M23 and 25 (these had one 7.5" gun): *M27, M29, M33, M31*. These monitors were like "dreadnoughts" for the Dvina River. They began service in 1915, were 177 ft long and a draft 6 ft. This made the Dvina accessible. They had a speed of 11 kts. The M27 was armed with the triple 4 " Mk IX gun and 2 3pdr AA. The M29, M31 and M33 types had a draft of 4 ft, had a speed of 9 kts and carried two six inch guns. The worst feature of the monitors was the fact the platforms were unstable and severely affected the accuracy of their big guns.

Also arriving was *Kite Balloon No.1* detachment containing 7 officers and 93 men with a balloon to be used along the Dvina for observation. This unit was requested on March 7th along with 12 Fairey 3C airplanes to carried aboard the Seaplane carrier, *Pegasus* and cargo ships. In order for the seaplanes and kite balloon to operate hundreds of miles upstream on the Dvina, the British shipped 3-4 large Rhine barges from Europe. These would be used to house the crew and pilots, supply and maintenance. The barges, A17, 21, No.2 Hydrogen, Francois and Scaldes all were towed to Archangel in April. The barges were renumbered, and Nos.3 and 4 contained hoists to lift the aircraft for repairs. These "floating" airbases were essential as the closest ground based aircraft were 30-50 miles from the front making for coordination impossible. Thus, in this manner, the seaplanes were vital. They could react within 15-20 minutes or sooner for emergencies.

As for the Americans, their troop disposition was as follows:

1st Bn	HQ, Cos. A,B at Morjegoraskaya on Dvina River Cos. C, D along right bank of Dvina River.
2nd Bn	HQ in Archangel Co.E on the railway Co.F along the Vaga River 2 pla/Co.G along the railway and 2 platoons in Archangel Co.H at Onega
3rd Bn	HQ at Verst 455 on railway Co.I along railway 1 pla/Co.K at Kholmogorskya 3 pla/Co.K at Yemetskoe Co.L and Co.M along the railway
310th Eng.Bn.	HQ in Archangel Co.A: 1 pla at Bakaritza, Railway, Pinega,Obozerskaya Co.B along the Dvina at: Bereznik, Mala Bereznik, Vaga river. Co.C : 1 platoon at Solombala, Pinega, Seletskoe,Onega.
Misc.	Trench Mortar platoon, signals,MG company along the railway. HQ 339th Regiment at Archangel

It seemed that the month of May was the adjust and buildup month for both sides. Very little combat occurred. Both sides added to their arsenal. The Reds knew the Allied forces would strike again when the weather turned near tropical and mosquito ridden. At this time, the Reds were simply conducting an elastic defense to contain any allied attack. For Messrs. Trotsky and Lenin knew the Armies of Kolchak had shot their bolt, in fact, they were now retreating and any chance of a link up with the British at Kotlas was a pipe dream. Thus, their strategy was let the allies attack. They knew they would evacuate within a few months. Oddly, what the British were now doing was indeed odd. The buildup with combat experienced men from the West Front, the many monitors and gunboats, planes, which would arrive in June and July, all should have been arrived in August/September 1918, not after a decision to withdraw. How insane!

Part of the problem was with the hydrology of the Dvina River, which in the Summer of 1919, the water depth rose and dropped. In May/June, Ironside had decided to conduct a limited offensive attempting to reach Kotlas, if feasible (even though Kolchaks men were retreating). Thus, the buildup was carried on. And if Kotlas was not possible, then, "give the Bolo a real bloody nose" in order that the North Russian army had a chance once the British left in September.

But when July arrived, the Dvina river water level dropped and continued to drop, which cancelled the plans to use the monitors and gunboats so vital for artillery support as the infantry advanced along the banks of the river. The RAF could not make up for this due to maintenance and weather curtailing many sorties. But, when the big attack began on August, it was limited, but highly successful. It was all simply too late. It was a year too late. The War Cabinet's indecision is largely to blame, as they wanted to get involved but only use token force and low quality troops at that. The desire was not there (the identical situation arose in Vietnam, first with the French and then the Americans).

The world's first true aircraft carrier, *Argus*, arrived at Archangel in late July 1919, delivering 20 aircraft. Photo: CPL

The Red force dispositions for late April 1919 are as follows:

1st & 2nd Bns/159th reg	Gorodok area, Onega	350 men, 15 MG ea.
3rd Bn/6th Kamishin reg	Emtsa	400 men, 12 MG
Mining detachment	Emtsa	80 minelayers
1st & 2nd Bns/Kamishin	Emtsa	800 men, 24MG
97th Saratoff Reg	Betw.Emtsa-Plesetskaya	1400 men, 18MG
2nd Moscow Reg	Plesetskaya	1900 men, 48MG
Cavalry/ 18th division	Plesetskaya	100 men
18th Division HQ	Plesetskaya	300 men
2nd, 3rd Bns/157th reg	Kodish	800 men, 20 MG
Cavalry	Kodish	80 men
1st Bn/157th reg	Kochmas	400 men, 10 MG
1st Bn/155th reg	Aleksandrovo	350 men,8 MG
2nd Bn/ 155th reg	Aleksandrovo	200 men, 9 MG
3rd Bn/155th reg	Tarasovo	350 men, 8 MG
2nd, 3rd Bns/6th reg	Beresnik area	1400 men, 14MG
Cavalry	Beresnik area	50 men
2nd brigade HQ/18th xx	Shegovary	150 men
156th reg	Rt.bank of Vaga River	1500 men,38MG
161st reg, Pechorski reg, 1st Naval Bn	Near Toulgas	4630 men, 72 MG
Cavalry+ Engineers	Toulgas area	150 men
162nd Reg	Troitsa	1700 men, 27MG
Sailor Bn	Troitsa	300 men
3rd Brigade HQ/18xx	Petropavsky	100 men
Red Artillery	Onega	Two 3" guns
	Railroad front (450 men)	Seventeen 3" guns
		Four 4.5" howitzer
		One 4.8" gun
		Six AA guns
		Two 1" guns
	Emtsa	Eleven 3" guns
		Two 4.5" howitzer
		Four AA guns
		Two 1.5" guns
		Two 4.8 " guns
		Two 4.2" guns
		Two armor trains
	Kodish	Four 3" guns
		Two AA guns
	Kochmas	Six 3" guns
		Two AA
	Aleksanrovo	Two 3" guns
		Two AA

	Beresnik	Six 3" guns Four 4.2" guns
	Toulgas to Seltso	Eight 3" guns
	Troitsa	Four 3" guns Two 6" guns Two 4.2 guns Two AA guns
	Pinega	Four 3" guns Two 2" guns

According to the intelligence reports, the 18th division contained 13,230 men with another 10,000 in reserve. A total of 265 MG, Cavalry at 230 men, 1800 men in non-combat roles, another 2050 men with 18 MG and 2000 men manning the following artillery :

(4) 8" guns
(2) 4.8" guns
(2) 4.5" guns
(8) 4.2" guns
(50) 3" guns
(8) 1.5" guns
(14) AA guns

It was thought a squadron of 22 airplanes supported it.

The first and second brigades of the Red 18th division covered three main avenues of approach: Onega, Railroad and North Dvina. The Onega force was commanded by Strievski, and had 1060 men, 34 MG and 2 artillery guns. The Railroad front near Emtsa was under Murin with 3,140 men, 54MG, 25 guns. The North Dvina force, under Ananyin, held near Kochmas with 4000 men, 68MG 25 guns. At Plesetskaya, another 1500 men and 19 MG. The third brigade had forces covering the Vaga River (Raudmetz) with 3250 men, 44 MG,

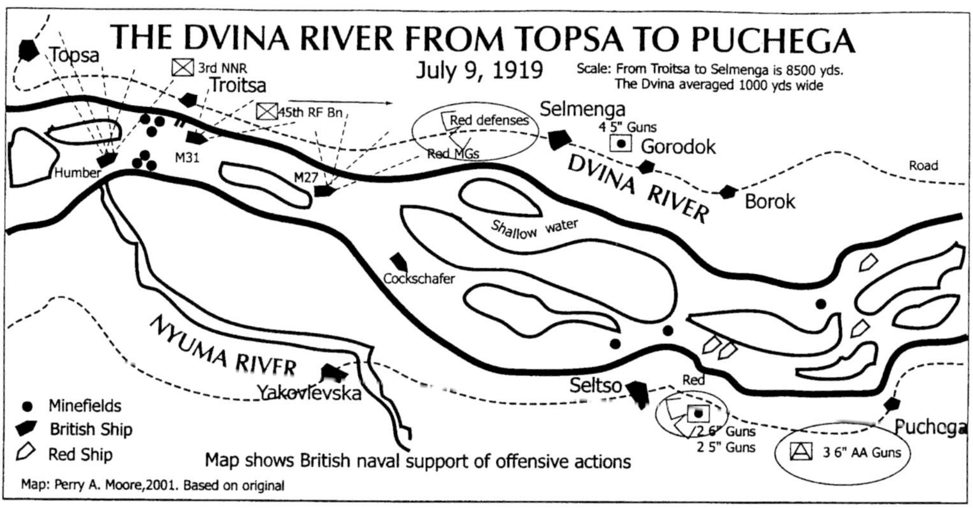

11 Guns; the Upper Dvina at Seltso (Borgdoulin) with 4100 men, 61 MG and 23 guns, and at Karpogorvi (Shennkov) with 2500 men, 15 MG and 6 guns.

Through defectors and intelligence, the Allied forces knew the composition of the Red flotilla along the Dvina and Vaga River:

Vinogradoff GB	2 105mm, 1 AA,1 wireless
Liebknecht	2 105mm, 1 AA
Luxemborg	???
Fenik	1 3" gun, 1 2" AA
Chesnoreye	1 3" gun
Oritzky	1 3" guns
Caxton	2 75mm guns
Bobets	1 4" naval gun
Sverdloff	1 75mm gun, 1 MG
Jelyaboff	2 MGs and wireless
Gogol	Hospital ship
Shegovari	Hospital ship
Barge 1	4 3" guns
Barge 2	2 6" howitzers
Barge 3 9	2 105mm
Steamers	ea. With 2 130mm guns and 2 6" guns
11 Tugs	Unarmed: Solvichegodsk, Goncharoviski, Kommunist, Mihail, Archangel, Elena
VAGA RIVER	1 Barge with two 4.2" howitzers, 3 unarmed steamers: Shenkursk, Yarensk and Tolstoy
LAKE ONEGA	3 gunboats, 5 steamers, 40 tugs, 2 submarines, 1 torpedo boat, 1 seaplane unit. These were based at Voznesenie. The following had a 600 man transport capacity: SS Petrograd, Kivach, Karia and Petrozavodsk. The following had a 200 man capacity: SS Emperor, Tsar, and Voznesenie.

The boats on the Dvina were all based at Kotlas where a 2000 man, 50 MG and 90 guns stood to defend. The Reds also employed 12 engineer companies to build fortifications. The railroad from Emtsa to Plesetskaya was mined to just north of the Emtsa bridge. New trenches, some 300 yds long were dug on both sides of the line at Verst 443. Use of barb wire also was extensively used. The Reds also had a number of armor trains: Train 1 was at Emtsa with

The *HMS Cock-shafer* arrived in North Russia and was used along the Dvina River during the summer of 1919. Photo: IWM

two 3" guns and 10 MGs; further back, Train 2, with two 3" guns. Also present were two AA trains, armed with a total of four AA guns and three MGs.

The intelligence regarding the Red 18th division varied. As another report issued during May, 1919, show the composition and dispositions as follows:

18th division HQ	Plesetskaya	300 men
1st Brigade	HQ at Kochmas	150 men
154th regiment (Kiselev)	Moved to East Front	1200 men
155th regiment (incl. The Battalion of Death)	Alexandrovo	900 men, 24 MG
156th regiment (Bougov)	Left bank of Vaga	1500 men, 24MG
2nd Brigade		
157th Regiment (Lepin)	HQ at Shegovaru	140 men
158th Regiment (Mironof)	Kodish	1200 men,30 MG
159th Regiment (Strievsk)	Moved to East front	
	Turchasevo, Onega	700 men, 27MG
3rd Brigade	HQ on SS Jelyabov	100 men
160 Regiment (Koudrin)	Trufanagora. Pinega	2500 men, 15 MG
161 Regiment (Gorodek)	Left bank, Dvina	1080 men, 32 MG
162 Regiment (Oerke)	Right bank, Dvina	1700 men, 27 MG
Other units attached:	1st Kamishin reg	Left front
	2nd Moscow Reg	1000 men, 18MG
	4th Tsaritsyn Reg	left front
	6th Kamshin Reg	1200 men,36MG at Emtsa area
	97th Saratoff Reg	900 men,18MG at Sheleska
		400 men,14MG left bank Vaga.
	6th Soviet Regiment	370 men
	Partisan groups	300 men
	Sailor Bn	100 men on Dvina
	Engineer Company	200 men on Vaga
	Scout Detachment	150 men at Seltso
	Chinese Punitive Unit	80 men at Emtsa
	Petrograd Mining Det.	50 men
Cavalry	One platoon at Sheleksa	100 men
	One Det at Plesetskaya	80 men
	One Det at Kodish	50 men
	One Det at Shegovari	50 men
	One Det at Seltso	200 men at Plesetskaya
Non Combat Troops	Chinese Labor Co.	200 men at Emtsa
	Russian Labor Co	100 men at Emtsa
	No.1 Armor train Train	100 men at Emtsa
	No.2 Sebejsky armor train	100 men Plesetskaya
	Fighting Train No.2	100 men Plesetskaya
	Transport and Misc	1000 men Plesetskaya
	Total:	17,180, 263 MG

ARTILLERY	1st Lt Btty, Onega	Four 3” guns, 100 men
	2nd Lt Btty, Vaga	“
	3rd Lt Btty, Vaga	“
	4th Lt Btty, Tarasovo	“
	5th Lt Btty, Kotlas	Four 3 “ guns, 175 men
	6th Lt Btty, L.bank Dvina	“
	1st Lt Btty/1st Kamishin at Kochmas	Four 3” gun, 100 men
	2nd Lt Btty/ 1st Kamishin at Kodish	“
	3rd Lt Btty/1st Kamishin at Railway	“
	One Field Btty on Vaga	Two 3” guns, 50 men
	One Field Btty at Pinega	Four 3” guns,100 men
	Two 4.2: How at Railway	50 men
	Two 4.2” How at Vaga	“
	Two 4.2” How on barges	“
	Two 4.2 “ How at Dvina	“
	One 4.8” at Railway	25 men
	One 4.8” gun at Kodish	“
	Two 6” gun at Shenkursk	50 men
	Two 6” guns on Dvina	50 men
AVIATION	3 airplanes, 30 men	Plesetskaya
(nearly all planes	2 airplanes, 1 Ballloon	50 men, Emtsa
seldom flew due	1 airplane,10 men	Tarasovo
to lack of trust,	6 airplanes, 60 men	Shenkursk
fuel, and spare	2 airplanes, 20 men	Seltso
parts)	2 airplanes, 20 men	Borck
	6 airplanes, 60 men	Dvina River
ENGINEERS	12 Cos. Mezen Partisans, 900 men	Mezen
	Pechora Partisans,1000 men	Pechora
	Grand Total: 19310 men, 303 MG	
AA GUNS	Two 3” guns, 50 men	Railway
	Two 3” guns, 50 men	Kochmas
	Two 3” guns, 50 men	Tarasovo
	Four 3” guns, 175 men	L/Bank of Dvina
POM-POMS	Two 1.5” guns, 50 men	Railway
	“	Tarasovo
	“	R.Bank of Dvina
	“	Pinega
ARMOR TRAINS	Eleven 3”, two 4.2” How, 4 AA guns	

The report gives a very clear idea of the force that was opposing the allies. Further, the report broke down the actual number of combat troops that were on the front line (in many previous books, an author would cite a figure and the reader assumed this was the number of men on the front, which is incorrect). In this case, the report states a total of 32,160 men. But the actual combat troops on or near the front was as follows:

18th Rifle Division: 13,230, 265 MG
Artillery: 90 guns, 2050 men
Cavalry: 330 sabre
Reserves (Vologda,Moscow): 10,000 men, 50MG
Non-Combat and Misc: 3850 men, 18MG
Outside Archangel District: 1900 men, 20MG.

Opposing the Syren Force south of Murmansk was the Red 6th Division with the 49th and 50th regiments. In the Karelian area, the Red 90th, 170th, 169th,154th,158th, and 4th regiments defended.

The Syren Force now consisted of the following:

British	46 guns, 81MG,1957 men
French	300 men, 18 guns
Serbian	1036 men, 34MG,2 guns
Canadian	24 guns, 105 men
Italian	1248 men, 18 MG
N.Russian	2500 men, 12MG,2 guns
Finnish	1279 men,12 Mg, 4 guns
Karelians	3798 men, 26 MG
	5 subschasers, 3 MB

In June, the French 21st battalion evacuated and returned to France, along with two U.S. battalions (aboard the TRs Kailen, Tsar,Porto and Menominee).When the Reds found out about the U.S. withdrawal, the propaganda used was that America had disapproved of the White Russian government. This type of propaganda was effective to the North Russians.

The front lines near Viatka to the east had remained stabled during most of April. However, the Reds attacked again with the 2nd Army and the result being that by June 5th, another 45 km had been gained. Gadja's 3rd and 4th Siberian Corps were no match and by the 12th, the 1st Siberian Corps along the railway became aware that their position was not secure and diverted forces. The Red 3rd Army also conducted another attack. This attack was a success with the only counterattack by Gadja's 1st division, which stabilized the tenuous line. By the 12th, the 3rd Army had advanced about 50 km reaching Kau with the 25th regiment. There would be only retreats left for all of Kolchak's men. The beginning of the end began for Kolchak.

The 2nd bn/Hampshires arrived at Kurgomin on the 6th. Its W and Y Companies relieved the Royal Scots on the left bank of the Dvina and X and Z companies did the same on the right bank. Thus, finally, the battle proven 2nd line/10th Bn/Royal Scot unit was withdrawn. The Reds continually barraged the new unit, but their aim was so poor, the closest shells hit 400 yards away.

PLACE
STAMP
HERE

SCHIFFER PUBLISHING LTD
4880 LOWER VALLEY ROAD
ATGLEN, PA 19310-9717 USA

Off the battlefield, a series of rather optimistic telegrams went to and fro from the War Cabinet and General Ironside. On the 6th, Ironside replied to the War Cabinet's inquiry as to what the plans were, and despite the desertions and low morale Ironside was unduly optimistic :

> "...if a chance of junction appears, operations on the Dvina will be extended to a point about 30 miles south of Kotlas to ensure cutting of railway and capturing enemy material and to block the Suchona River, but in no case any further. Grahams brigade will be employed at Kotlas to prepare a base and send down tugs and barges, the British brigade (Sadlier-Jackson) will be employed to clear of the Witchegda River and to connect with the Siberians (Kolchaks men) at Shaposhnikoff. If this is not possible, we will seize Kotlas and destroy it."

Ironside was dreaming and deep in wishful thinking. Kotlas was over 300 miles away, and he was talking of moving even further! And to suggest that two brigades could cover this front and not be trapped and cut off was insane.

A week later, Ironside received a telegram from the War Cabinet, in effect, saying that because of Kolchak's reverses any real prospect in joining with him are questionable and to only plan for his proposed operation and to wait until the 27th for their final decision.

Ironside again writes over-optimistically, stating:

> "...that in any case, I should be able to pull in Kolchaks right wing from the direction of Yarensk on the Witchegda and make a large reinforcement to the Russian force detailed from ours to move just south of Kotlas by arming the badly armed....in no case do I think that any advance less than to Kotlas will have the desired effect and will halt if the enemy really puts up a stubborn resistance."

The cap that General Ironside was wearing was that of a salesman.

The British using their huge 60 pdr guns. Three of these monsters were sent to North Russia. Moving them to the front was a difficult matter! Photo: IWM

On the 25th, Ironside received a telegram from the War Cabinet where it is clear that second thoughts about Ironside's proposal are being created:

> "...if it is clear that offensive operations of some kind are an essential preliminary to withdrawal, it only remains to consider what their scope should be and whether, on the Dvina, it is really necessary to push the offensive as far as Kotlas."

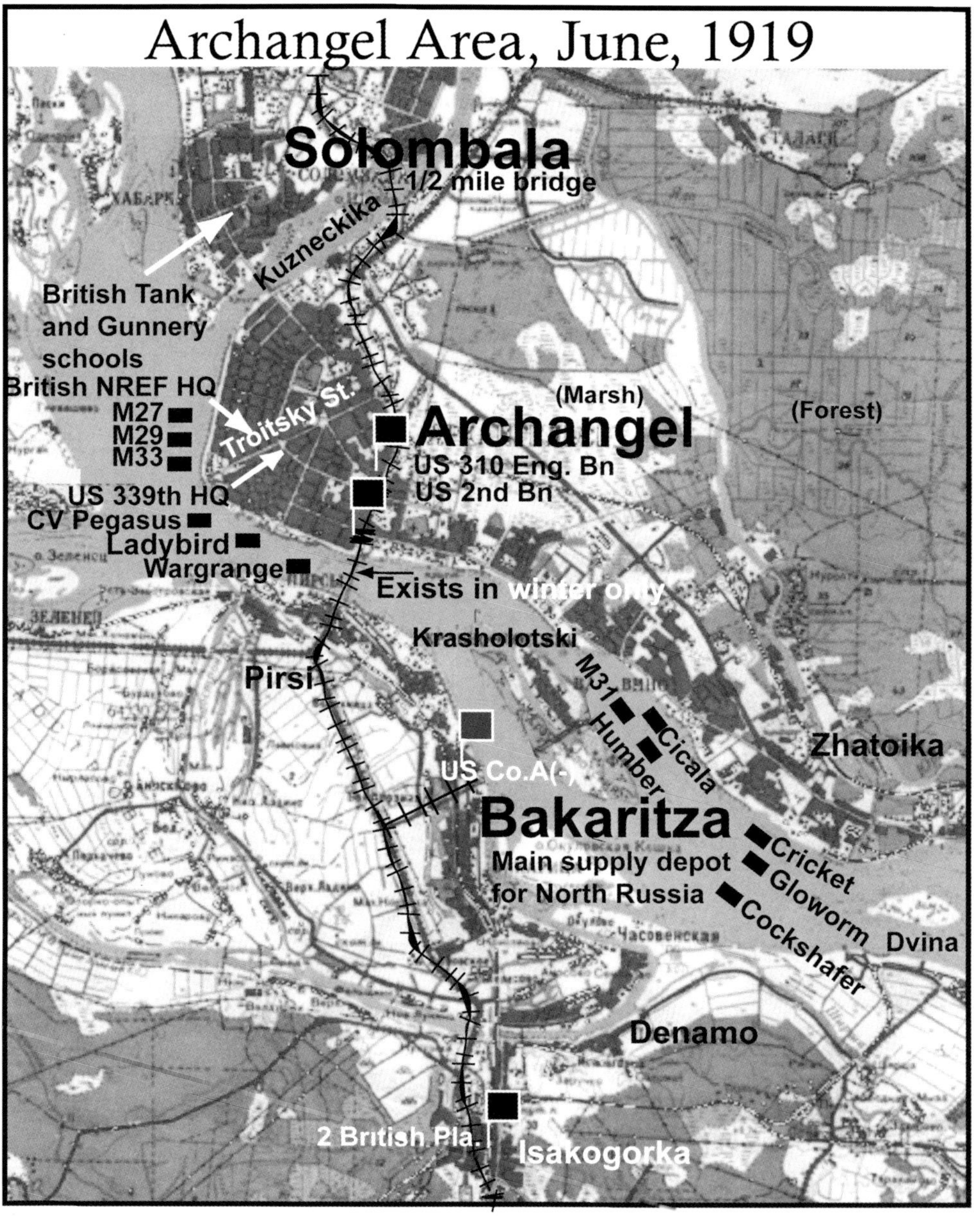

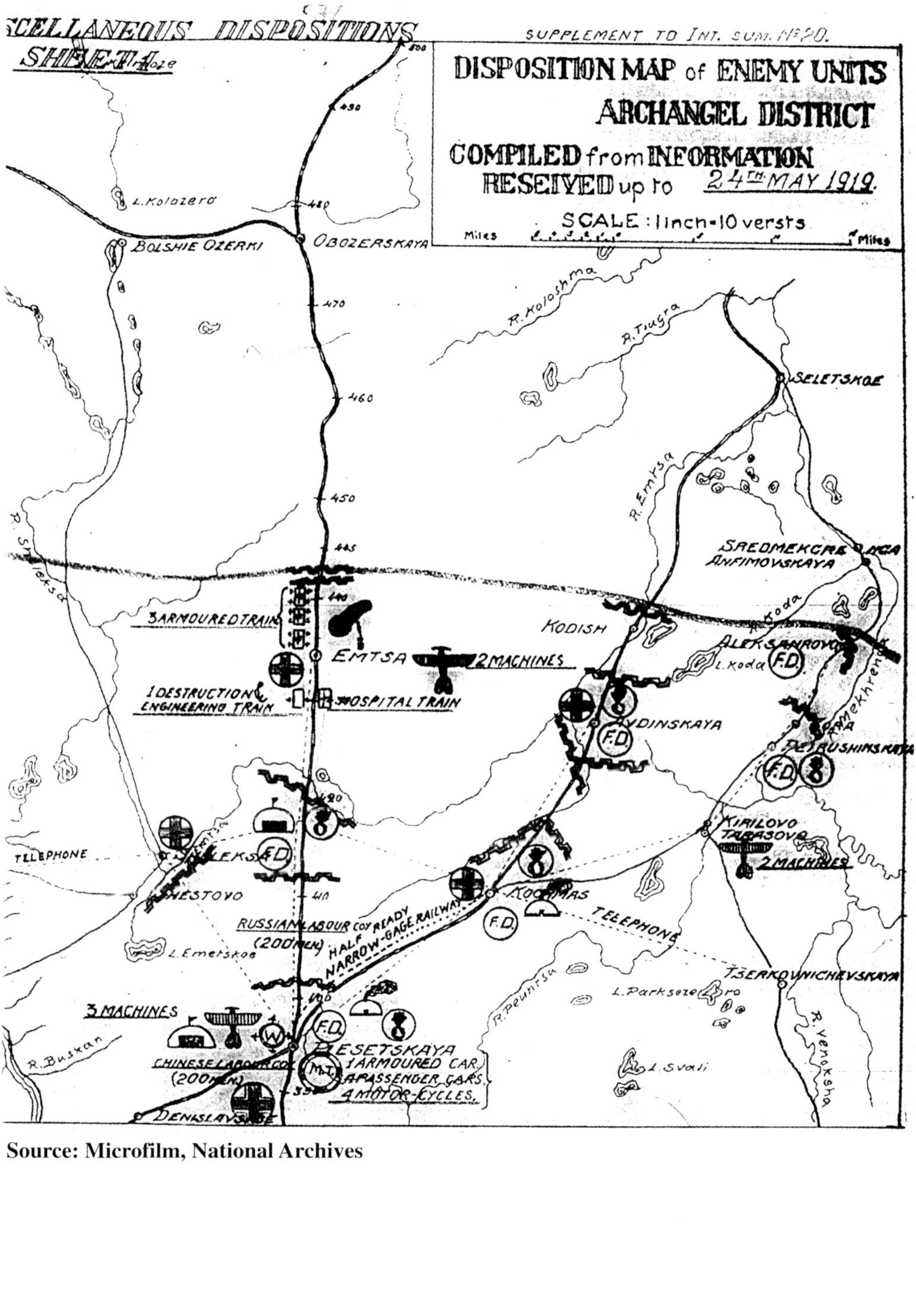

Source: Microfilm, National Archives

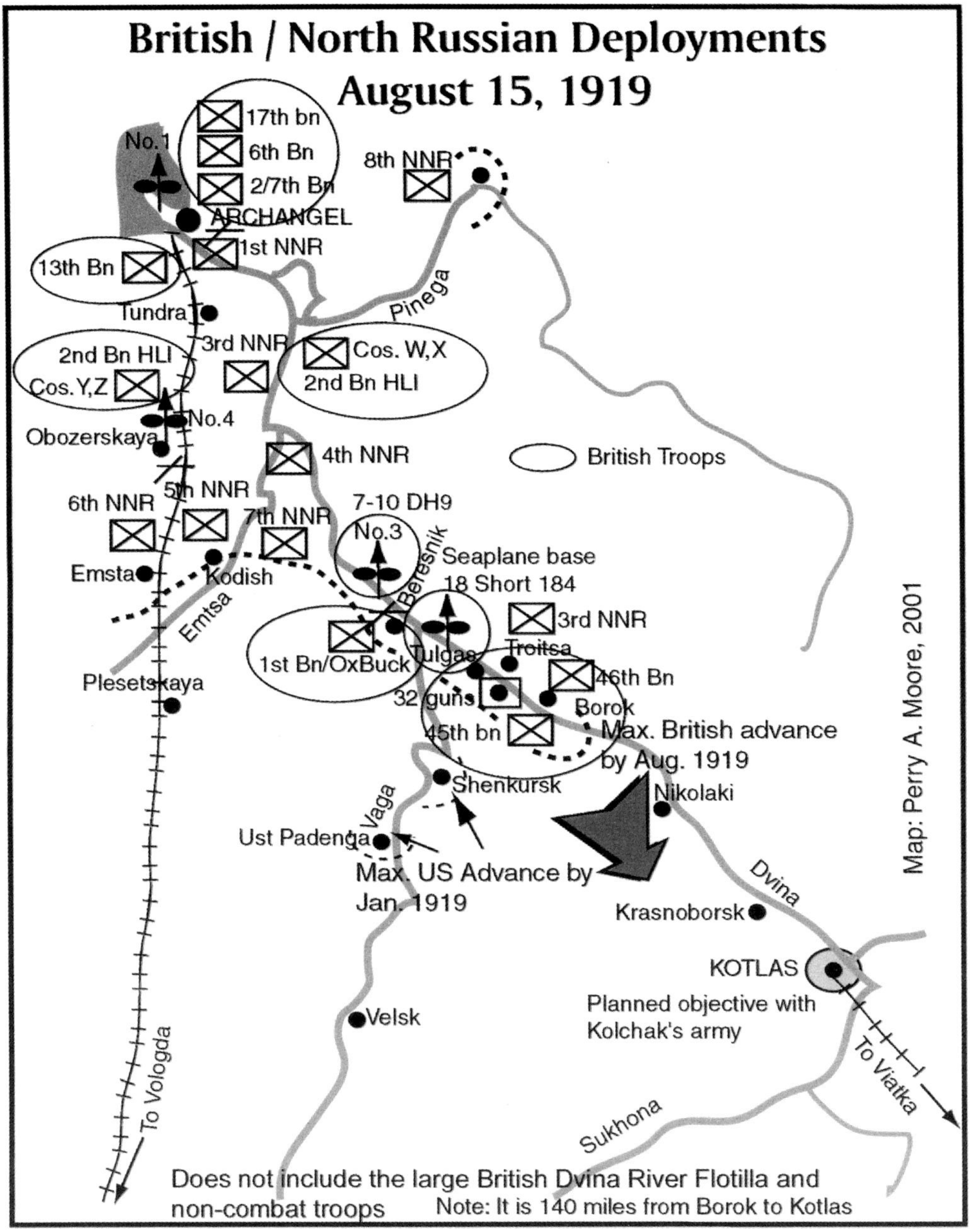
British / North Russian Deployments
August 15, 1919
17th bn
6th Bn
2/7th Bn
No.1
ARCHANGEL
8th NNR
1st NNR
13th Bn
Pinega
Tundra
3rd NNR
Cos. W,X
2nd Bn HLI
2nd Bn HLI
Cos. Y,Z
No.4
Obozerskaya
4th NNR
British Troops
6th NNR
5th NNR
7th NNR
7-10 DH9
No.3
Beresnik
Seaplane base
18 Short 184
Emsta
Kodish
Emtsa
3rd NNR
1st Bn/OxBuck
Tulgas
Troitsa
46th Bn
Plesetskaya
32 guns
Borok
45th bn
Max. British advance
by Aug. 1919
Shenkursk
Nikolaki
Vaga
Ust Padenga
Max. US Advance by
Jan. 1919
Dvina
Krasnoborsk
KOTLAS
Planned objective with
Kolchak's army
Velsk
To Vologda
To Viatka
Sukhona
Does not include the large British Dvina River Flotilla and
non-combat troops
Note: It is 140 miles from Borok to Kotlas
Map: Perry A. Moore, 2001

Meanwhile, the Nieuports of the Red 1st Naval Fighter Detachment repeatedly attempted to intercept the Sopwiths and RE.8s of the Slavic-British Air Corps. Neither type of aircraft was ever shot down, but one day a Red did his best to damage Lieutenant Babanenko's "Sopwith."

Also, there were a few uneventful aerial battles with aircraft of the Red 18th Recon. detachment on May 31st. Pilot, Smirnov, at a height of 3200 meters attacked a British two-seater aircraft, but was himself hit by fire from the aerial gunner. A few bullets put holes in the engine cylinders and damaged the machine-gun. He made a forced landing. Red propaganda did this with Smirnov to build him up as a prominent fighter ace. The propaganda served to create a legend that was believed within the White pilots. This propaganda caused panic and fear within White pilots and they even nicknamed him the *Red Devil*. The reality was, in fact, he had no more than a few kills.. Smirnov lived to fight Japanese zeros in the pacific in 1942 with the Dutch.

In the middle of June, in connection with planned offensive prior to the withdrawal along the Dvina front, the British decided to neutralize the Red air strength in this region. So far, the Red Naval aviation supplied the most trouble for the White Army. Thus, the attack was selected for the airfield at Puchuga. Colonel Kazakov worked up a plan, which was a daring plan. Because he had little faith in making bombing runs, he proposed to perform, under fighter cover, a landing of three Sopwiths onto the Red airfield! The crews would then run to the tent-hangars and set fire to them using torches and cans of benzene. After this was completed, another flight of the Sopwiths, and DH 9s would drop 250-pounds bombs on any standing buildings.

In spite of the high risk, the British accepted the plan. The raid occurred on the evening of June 17th. The mission had a force of 13 aircraft, however, once into the flight engine trouble required the return of Lieutenant Beresnevich's "Nieuport" and British pilots' Nayts Snipe. Because of this, there was a change in the plan. In exchange for landing on the flying field, the Sopwiths would strafed the hangars, firing incendiary bullets. A few DH 9As their dropped bombs on the airfield while others bombed the aircraft carriers/barges. But, as Kazakov feared, the bombs were not very accurate.

Nevertheless, from the air it was visible that the incendiary bullets lit up a Nieuport standing on the strip and set fire to some fuel barrels on the airfield. Also, bullets and bombs splinters incapacitated another Nieuport and a SPAD inside their tents. Two M-20 seaplanes were damaged on their barges. The Reds lost two killed and six wounded. On the following day, the Red 1st Fighter detachment, now without aircraft, was sent to the rear to reform.

This may have been the first operation in the Civil War for air superiority that had been successful. The Commander of the Dvinia Red Flotilla, V.N.Varvatsi, in a report of the battle called the bombardment of Puchugi a "defeat of our aviation" and a "sign of coming failures and defeat."

On June 19th, the British, inspired by success, undertook a powerful air raid on the ships of the Red Dvinia flotilla. In 20 hours five DH9s attacked the armed steamers, tugs and barges near Seletso Island. Many hits from 250-pound bombs sunk the "Plavbatareya No.5," a large river barge with two naval six-inch guns. On the following day another raid, supported by artillery of English gunboats. The armed steamer «Communist» was hit with six 20 lb bombs but remained afloat. Less serious damage from bombs fell to four big and five smaller tugs in the composition of the Red Flotilla. Still another four armed steamers were hit by artillery fire. The Flotilla lost 10 killed and 23 injured. This British success prevented the Reds from placing floating mines on the Dvina and Vaga rivers. By the end of June the front stabilized near the area around the villages of Sluda and Selmenga.

General Grogan now planned his first offensive that called for two columns to advance. One column attacking Topsa and one Troitsa. The North Russian unit was ordered to take Topsa while the 2nd Bn, Troitsa. The plan called for Cos. W and Y, a battery of mortars and a section from Co.C/8th MG, 60 pack mules to plunge some 18 miles through the mosquito infested forests to their objective. The Red forces at Troitsa and Topsa had built a semi circle of blockhouses. The end reaching the banks of the Dvina. The perimeter of this line ran some eight miles. Topsa was a town perched on a high hill overlooking the swift moving river some six feet deep and 50 ft wide. Troitsa was in the thick forests.

The 2nd Bn began it's advance at 0400 on the 19th, the track vanished into a series of bogs forcing all of the mules to be unloaded. The men then carried all of the weapons and ammo across the bogs. There were a never ending series of marshes and deep gullies which tired the men. The heat and insects became unbearable, but by Noon, the force reached the Topsa river. So exhausted were the men, they slept for hours along the wooded banks. The trek continued at 1400 and by 2300, the force finally arrived at it's "assembly" site, two miles east of Troitsa. After a rest, the men were in attack position at 0445, June 20th.

The attack began and Co.Y assaulted the trenches east of the village, while Co.W, attacked the town. It became apparent that the Reds in Troitsa were much stronger than intelligence had indicated. Company W 's advance stopped and soon the Reds were trying to flank and surround it. The unit was pinned. The attack by the 3rd North Russian Reg at Topsa failed to occur. It was critical for British and now it was possible that the British may become cut off. By 0900, company W was almost surrounded, the order to retreat was given and both companies slipped through the Red pincers. The men, exhausted, retreated to Topsa, where the North Russians had seized the village! The attack had failed partially, and by the 26th, all of the 2nd Bn/Hampshires occupied the area just north of Troista. The Reds lost about 600 men.

The *HMS Humber* was one of several river boats used on the Dvina. Photo: R.A. Burt.

Supporting the offensive was the Royal Navy River Flotilla under Capt.Altham. In early June, the flotilla was further strengthen with the China Class gunboats, these consisted of: *Humber, Cicala, Ladybird, Cricket, Cockshafer and Glow-worm.* These were originally built for the Danube River. They had two 6" guns, two 12pdr, six MG and a speed of 14 knots. More important for river operations was their draft of only 4 feet. This allowed them to move further upstream than the monitors with a 6 foot draft. The *Humber*, built in 1913, had three six inch guns, two 4.7 howitzers and 2" thick armor sides. It originally was a Brazilian monitor named, Javary. Many of them continued to be useful into WW2.

Supporting this particular attack were the *Cockshafer,Glow-worm, Humber and Cricket.* When the Cockshafer and Glow-worm arrived and bombarded, the Red gunboats appeared. A brief volley of gunboat to gunboat fire resulted (the Cockshafer alone fired 131 HE, 51 6" shrapnel, and 47 3" rounds). The situation was made worse with the many mines the Reds had floated down the river. As the ships dodged the mines, Reds fired from the banks making any advance slow and dangerous. At Troitsa, the flotilla anchored due to it's deep water. A sandy, nearby island provided a base for the many seaplanes and the Kite Balloon detachment. The Rhine barges to house the RAF were brought up. Because of the river width and current/depth, the whole flotilla could not operate at the same time in one combined unit.

Also supporting the attack was one Fairey IIIC and three Short 184's observing and attacking the Red troops. While the attack occurred, many more units were arriving:

The Sadlier-Jackson Brigade
45th Bn/Royal Fusiliers (930 men)
46th Bn/Royal Fusiliers (938 men)
443rd Artillery Btty
444th Artillery Btty
240 and 241 Trench Mortar Btty
385th Engineer Co
250 the Signal Co.
201st MG battalion
1153rd Supply transport Co.

And more aircraft arrived:

7 FaireyIIIC
6 Short 184
12 DH9A bombers
6 Strutter
9 DH9s
2 RE8

These arrived aboard the *Wargrange, Nascopie and Pegasus.* The 6 strutters were in such poor condition their engines had to be replaced. However, no bombing sights were received!

The large Rhine barges finally made it down the Dvina river by June 7th. The RAF "S" flight consisting of 2 Fairey IIIC and one Short 184 flew to Kourgomin, during the flight, one of the modern Fairey's crashed. During the support of the attack, one Short 184 also crashed. The Seaplane Storage Barge No.2 and 1 (SSB) both were towed by the *Fandango* minesweeper up the Dvina, Now, "S" flight turned into "B" flight and began bombing on the 25th. Three more airplanes arrived for the flight and on the 28th, they were bombing the Red gunboats at least twice a day. On June 30th, five sorties were flown attacking the Red gunboats. One of the planes acted as a spotter using a 52M transmitting set, a wireless with a short range. Only one of the gunboats received a direct hit, crippling it. The RAF flew 79 hours in various operations in June, dropping some four tons of bombs. During June, the average daily flight time amounted to 5 1/2 hours. By June, the RAF in the Archangel consisted of: 81 officers and 246 men. Beresnik, home of No.3 Squadron, had 40 officers and 60 men. At Obozerskaya, where No.4 Squadron was, 7 officers and 22 men. More pilots and ground crews would arrive in July.

Arriving on Lake Oneda were six 40 ft chasers and six 35ft motorboats armed with one 3 Pdr and MG.

The most important event in June was that the British government finally had approved (albeit much too late) of a British offensive towards Kotlas to meet the White Russian army under Admiral Kolchak (which by now was retreating further and further). Approval arrived on the 27th, two months late! In other political developments, the Finnish troops (100,000) under General Mannerhiem sought to make a deal with Kolchak. His offer was to attack Petrograd if Kolchak would agree to make Finland a separate state independent of Russia. Kolchak declined. The White Finns had succeeded in seizing all of the Karelian peninsula.

The Reds made a rare appearance on Lake Onega with four armed ships on June 8th. The British flotilla of six motorboats and two launches intercepted and a brief sea battle ensued. The main difference is that the Reds were also torpedoed and strafed by the RAF planes. This was too much for the Reds who fled. The air units on Lake Onega at Medvejda Gora comprised of 4 Fairey IIIC and a crew of 7 officers and 30 men. The planes were put on trains and moved from the port to Lake Onega, a journey of 3-4 days. The Red front was about 5 miles from Medvejda Gora. The first plane, the N9235, flown by a 19 yr. old Lt. Young, took off and nearly got riddled from Red gunfire. The flagship on the lake was the *Jolly Roger*, a sub-chaser with a speed of 30 knots and a 3 pdr, 37mm and a MG. However, without the RAF, this small flotilla was outclassed by the several Destroyers the Reds manned.

The RAF on Lake Onega with Short 184s and Faireys in 1919. Photo: G. Blamied

On June 7th, the RAF attacked a small Red convoy with N9241 at midnight. The Fairey dropped one 112 lb and three 20 lb bombs on two steamers. At 0200, Faireys N9236 and N9235 took off, followed by N9241, attacking the same convoy in waves dropping their bombs and raking the steamers with MG fire. Over 1700 MG rounds were fired. Then, the naval flotilla intercepted adding to the confusion. The Red convoy fled after changing direction. The RAF then began strafing and bombing runs on the Red trains operating. Most of the bombing was done with 230 lb or 112 lb bombs.

By late June, the RAF at Kem (Murmansk Front) contained the following:

5 Fairey IIIC (Nos. 9230,9321,9234, 9238,9241)
5 Sopwith Camels (Nos. 4054, 4065,6479, 4061, 4068)
5 Short 184 Seaplanes (Nos. 9024,9045,9021,9119,9193)
2 Avros (Nos. E3548,3783)
2 Re 8 (N4952,N4959)

By the end of June, the U.S. 1st and 3rd Bns/339th Reg, 21st French Bn and Foreign Legion, Cos. A and B/13th Bn/Yorks and Cos.A,B/7th Bn/Lt Durham, and all of the 2nd Bn/Royal Scots had left North Russia. What remained were mostly British and Polish troops and the North Russian Army that had been created. By now, the North Russian Army consisted of the following units:

1st Archangel Reg.	111 Officers, 3700 men
2nd North Riflle Reg.	80 Officer, 850 men
3rd North Rifle Reg	79 Officer, 1450 men
4th North Rifle Reg	48 Officer, 1502 men
5th North Rifle reg	53 Officer,1286 men
6th North Rifle	Being formed
7th North Rifle	29 officer,1200 men
8th North Rifle	83 officer, 2300 men
1st and 2nd Cavalry	12 Officer, 268 men
1st artillery Brigade	26 Officer, 526 men 1st Btty: four 18 pdrs 2nd Btty: three 60 pdrs. 3rd Btty: two 155mm, two 4.5"How, two 3" naval guns
2nd Artillery Brigade	26 officer, 537 men 1st Btty: six 75mm guns 2nd Btty: four 74mm guns 3rd Btty: two 6" How, two 155mm plus: nine 75mm, three 155mm attached.
1st Eng.Co.	7 officer, 250 men
2nd Eng.Co.	11 officer, 300 men
1st and 2nd Trench Mortar batty	60 men each.

Part of the RAF's problem was keeping the machines sent in a flyable condition. A good example of this was the RAF located near Troitsa along the Dvina in mid-July.

In his report, Capt. Altham clearly begs for the additional 12 planes he requested in the previous month (these arrived aboard the world's first aircraft carrier, CV *Argus* on July 31st) and then cites his problem:

> " the present situation is this regarding aircraft:
> In action: 3 FaireyIIIC and 2 Short 184
> In repair: 3 FaireyIIIC and 2 Short 184
> Fitting out: 4 Fairey and 1 Short
> Lost: 2 Fairey and 1 short
> Three of these are new machines with no floats."

Thus, out of 18 planes only 5 were flyable!

The RAF River Seaplane Force consisted of the following by mid-July:

Base unit: HMS *Pegasus* (Seaplane CV)
SSB1, B Flight under Capt. Freser at Troitsa
SSB2, A Flight under Capt. Trace at Chamova Bar in the Dvina
SSB3, S Flight under Capt. MacDougall at Beresnik
Kite Balloon 1 and 2, Capt. Hunter

The RAF ground based aircraft were mostly based at Beresnik (No.3 Squadron) and Archangel (No1. SBAC Squadron) and mainly composed of DH9 and DH9A bombers, some RE 8, or Avro. The ground based forces, in theory, were to only support the troops along the Dvina, while the Seaplanes, only to support the monitors and gunships. Naturally, this distinction evaporated during offensives.

On July 7th, the SBAC Dyers battalion (Cos. 1and 2) mutinied resulting in the murder of four Russian and five British Officers at 0230. Some 200 men then fled to the Red lines.

The *HMS Monitor 29* used along the Dvina River in 1919. The monitors and gunboats provided artillery support. Photo: John Maber

This incident occurred during the switch over period when the Grogan Brigade (still in the Troitsa area to some extent) was being replaced by the newly arrived Sadlier-Jackson brigade. The Reds knew of the mutiny and opened up with fierce volleys of shells. To counter this, the few seaplanes made repeated sorties all during the 7th and 8th. The *Cricket, Monitor 33* and *Humber* were brought up to counter. So critical the situation was that 50 seamen and a detachment of Marines landed nearby to prevent a total panic. The Dyer incident was a severe blow to Ironside, as this was thought to be a loyal unit and there had been no indication of problems. After the officers were murdered, the eight mutineers ripped out the dead men's intestines and spattered them on their faces. To counter, Ironside ordered 13 of the mutineers that had been caught executed. The rest of the unit was converted to a labor force. Such a blow to Ironside was the mutiny, he wrote the following to the War Office:

> " They are not worth fighting for...."

But this was not all. On the 20th, another North Russian unit of 4000 men (the 8th NRR) handed over the Onega area to the Reds! This shattered Ironside. He again wrote the War Office:

> "...my efforts to consolidate the Russian Army are definitely a failure. As early evacuation as possible essential now...."

In the first week of July, the 2nd Bn/Hampshires moved from the Troitsa area to Ust-Pinega, a village where the Pinega and Dvina Rivers meet. Eventually by the 12th, Company W moved upstream to Leunovo, and Company X was at Nizhni-Palenga. Company Y and Z, were rushed to Obozerskaya after the Onega mutiny. Defending the Railway area now consisted of two Russian battalions and two field batteries with two more in reserve. Rounding this out was a Polish machine gun company and a newly arrived Australian 150 man MG company.

Besides the newly arrived Australians, the minesweepers *Swordance, Morrisdance,* and *Stepdance* also arrived. Arriving near the end of the month was the aircraft carrier *Argus* carrying 10 Short 184, 5 FaireyIII C, and 5 Avro.

The minesweepers were a critical part for the upcoming offensive. These boats would be in the lead to remove the many mines floating down the Dvina. A very dangerous job. Eventually, a net was used to span the river where the base camp was. This net caught the floating mines, which were then disarmed.

On July 8th, the Reds attacked the right bank of the Dvina in strength with the support of several gunboats. The RAF went into action flying numerous bombing and strafing missions. By 1200, the order was given to withdraw the flotilla further down stream. The Reds advanced past Trotisa. On this day alone, the RAF seaplanes had dropped over one ton of bombs. During one of the flights, a Fairey IIIC was hit flown by Lt. Hilton. With it's gas tank pierced, the engine cut out over the enemy flotilla. The Observer, Lt. Ross, plugged the hole with his foot and both men pumped the hand pressure pumps. The plane returned to base. The North Russians were ordered to conduct a counterattack with the support of three monitors. They refused. On the 18th, three DH9A bombers flown by Lts. Scott, Scramlin and Mitchell bombed Borok, dropping 1350 lbs of bombs. The town was hit hard and the

Reds fired a heavy volley of AA fire. On the 19th, these same bombers hit Gorodok, dropping 1400 lbs of bombs and then conducted a photo reconnaissance of Selmanga. Earlier, four DH9A bombers flew attacking Red gunboats on the 14th. One of the planes dropped to 200 feet to conduct a bombing run on a gunboat. The bombs made a direct hit in the amidships sinking it. As they did so, intense HMG fire was directed at them. The other bombers opened up with their Lewis guns and some 300 rounds of ammo. A total of 1344 lbs had been dropped.

Colonel Kazakov acted boldly as did other White Russian pilots. The British pilots were perplexed as how he handled his fighter, totally disregarding dense machine-gun fire from the Bolshevik trenches at a height of 30 to 60 ft! Again and again, he strafed the Reds buzzing just above the enemy heads as though playing with death. After several passes, the Reds could bear no more and with their morale broken turned to escape straight into the machine-guns of British units that had encircled them from the rear. The defeat was full. On the abandoned Red positions, hundreds of corpses laid and more than 500 men surrendered into captivity. The staff of the 6th Army nearly was caught but steered clear of this fate and hid in the forest. Kazakov would be killed on August 18th, when his aircraft after taking off went up in an almost vertical position and then suddenly overturned and at full power slammed back into the airfield. For a few minutes all pilots were stunned. The destruction of the best pilot in the Tsar's army was dead. Colonel Shebalin was then appointed the commander of the 1st Squadron.

On August 19th, there was another group of desertions of Red pilots to the White side. Naval pilot, Znamenski (Commander of North aerial battalion) and Matve, in a M-20 seaplane, naval pilot Yakovitsk (Commander of 1st Naval Fighter Detachment) in a "Nieuport-10" took off in the morning on a recon mission and flew their aircraft to a nearby White airbase.

While the M33 et.al. were brought up, the M31 and Cicala gunboats were pounding Selmenga and Seltso. These too, ran into heavy opposition of the long range Red guns. M27 then fired it's triple 4" guns on the Red infantry advancing, pulverizing them. But the Red gunboats were relentless and their shots grew closer and closer.

During the last two weeks of July, the RAF sorties amounted to 48 hours, 3 tons of bombs had been dropped and 16000 rounds of ammo fired.

By mid-July, Capt. Altham, the commander of the Royal Navy flotilla reported that of his six gunboats, two were refitting at Archangel, two recent arrivals were not able to move up river due to the river's depth, one fell victim to a Red direct hit and stranded on a sandbar and the last one was limping around after it had been hit by a mine. According to Altham:

> "...the whole general aspect had changed. Kolchak was retreating, the North Russian Army was unreliable, and the whole objective to attack towards Kotlas was gone."

While the British reinforced their units, at Archangel, the required shipping was gathered for the coming evacuation in September.

On July 29th, the Reds conducted a very strong attack hoping to break the 6th North Russian Regiment along the railroad. The usual intense artillery barrage began at 0200 and the Reds charged the front lines following the barrage. The nearby Allied troops, rather nervous about what to expect from the NNR were stunned. The regiment held their positions and mowed down the advancing Reds with a fierce concentrated machine gun fire. The attack was repelled.

When the new Sadlier-Jackson brigade arrived, GHQ issued order #5 on July 3rd. The new brigade was ordered to relieve the Grogan brigade, moving from Ossinova to Troitsa, arrivng on the 7th. The Grogan Brigade would then move to Ust Pinega. Once the Jackson brigade arrived, it also took control of Morusi's brigade (located at Kuliga), consisting of:

8th MG Bn
1st Bn SBAL
1st Russian brigade (minus two batteries)
1st Russian Hvy battery
55th Mountain battery,RFA (six 3.7" guns)
Three Cavalry companies.

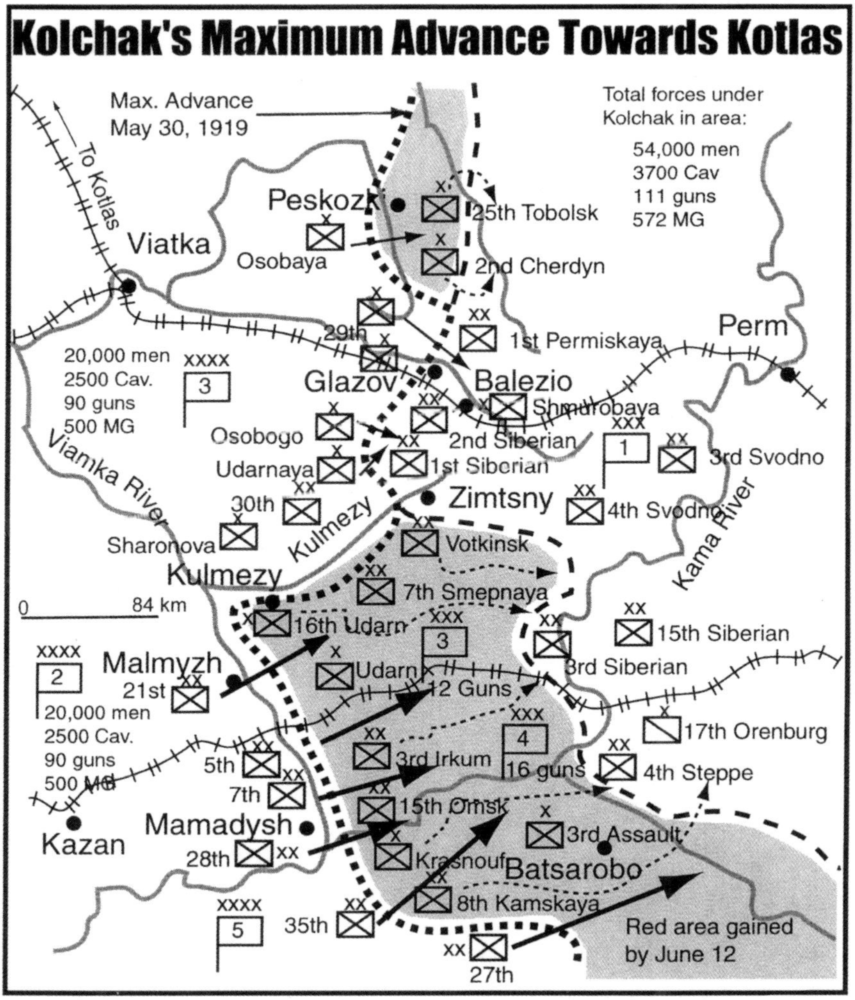

Kolchak's Maximum Advance Towards Kotlas

The Order of Battle and unit location of all the Allied forces on July 4, 1919, was as follows:

OBOZERSKAYA	6th NNR	471
	3rd MG Co/1stNRR	140
	Russian Eng.Co.	65
	Polish Legion	176
	1st btty/2nd Brigade (2 75mm)	44
	3rd btty (2 75mm)	44
	2nd Btty (2 155mm)	47
	No.4 Armor train (1 155mm, 2 75mm, 1 77mm)	24
	Arty btty (4 75mm)	43
VOLCHINETZ	1 pla/6th NRR	49
BOLSHOI-OZERKE	1 Co/6th bn/Yorks	124
	1 sec/3rd MG Co/1stNRR	72
NEAR VERST 445	HQ	63
	6th NRR MG	766
	Det/French Foreign	24
	1sec/1st Co Eng	54
	1st Russ.Trench Mtr Btty	32
	1sec/1stBtty/2nd NRR (2 75mm)	15
	3rd Btty/2nd NRR art.x (4 75mm)	61
	2nd Btty/Heavy Gun (2 6" gun, 2 155mm, 1 60pdr)	95
	Arm.Train #1 (1 18pdr, 2 77mm How)	46
	Arm.Train #2 (2 6" guns)	32
KLESTEVO	5th NRR, 2 MG Cos	1557
	1sec/1st Btty	54
	Partisans	273
	1 troop of Cavalry	18
	2nd Bttty/2nd Arty Brig.	150
SHRED MEKRENGA	7th NRR	1250
	1st,2nd Cos/French F.L	195
	Russ.Eng.Sec.	54
	1 troop of Cavalry	25
	1 co/13th Bn/Yorks	124
	1 sec/252MG Co	44
	1 sec/17th Bn/Liverpools	17
	420 Btty (2 4.5," 2 18pdr)	40
	1st Btty SBAL (2 2.75mm)	173

YAKOYSLEYSKOE- SELMENGA (Grogan x)	2nd Bn/Hampshires 8th MG Bn 55th btty (6 3.7")	384th Eng Co 238th Signal Co 239 Trench Mtr btty 1152 Transport Co.
KULIGA (Moroussi x)	3rd and 4th NRR	2nd Trench Mtr btty 2nd Eng.Co.
KURGOMIN RU.S.SIAN ARTILLERY	1 SBAL Cavalry Co. 2nd btty/1st x 4th btty/1st x 1st btty/Heavy	1st and 2nd N. Dragoons 4 18pdrs. 4 4.5" howitzers, 2 155mm 3 3" gun, 2 60 pdr.
NINJI KITSA-MALA BERESNIK (Vaga R)	1st Bn/Ox and Bucks reg 1 sec/384th Eng.Co	239th Trench Mtr Btty 2 sec/8th MG Bn 1st btty/Hvy x
TOMOMSK (Pinega)	8th NRR 2 18 pdr	Sec/17th bn/Liverpool 3rd btty/1st arty x on rafts: 2 6" how.
RESERVES – BERESNIK OSSINOVA (Jackson x)	1 PLA/1ST Bn/Ox and Buck reg, 9 18 pdr guns, 45th and 46th bns/Royal Fusilier; 240 Trench Mtr btty	2 3.7mm 441st Trench Mtr batty 201 MG Bn 385th Eng.co. 1st Bn SBAL (1039)
Defending the Line of Communications to Archangel	Railroad 1 pla/Co.A/17th Bn/Kings 2nd SBAL Bn (575) Russ.Penal unit (175) Chinese Co.(209) No.2 Arm.Train (1 6 pdr, 1 75mm) No.3 Arm.Train (2 47mm)	Other Kholmogory: 125 men 1 pla/2nd bn/Hampshire at Siskoe; 1 Cavlary sec. 2nd btty SBAL
ARCHANGEL BASE	2/ 7th bn/Durham Lt.Inf 17th bn/Kings Liverpool 6th Bn/Yorks 13th Bn/Yorks 252 MG Co 280 MG Co. 1st Bn SBAL, depot 3rd Mtn Btty SBAL 3rd Co.French Foreign Juvenile Bn 12Co/7th NNR	232 456 280 328 90 134 117

The last U.S. battalion departed in late July; this officially ended American involvement.

On August 1st, Monitor 26 went up to Onega and began a bombardment. This began the allied attack for the town held by 800 Reds. The attacking forces consisted of *Danilof's* force, which landed nearby at 1415, August 2nd. In what was described as a "small amphibious assault," the Reds put up strong resisting to the landing. Danilof's force consisted of 120 men and 21 officers, all Russian with elements of British Co.D/ Ox & Bucks. The battle lasted nine hours by which time part of Onega was secured. The total Red force came to six companies with a MG company and infantry company fleeing to Nijmozero. Another company retreated to Chekuevo. But the Reds returned with additional men and several 5" guns. They counterattacked and a bloody fight for Onega began in earnest. The White Russian troops fought a tenacious defense but were overwhelmed and by 2300, the Reds had retaken the town. Danilof's force fell back and evacuated it at 2350, seeking refuge aboard the *Walton Belle and Kerret*. They returned to Archangel. The assault had cost the Allies some 23 men (three British) and 55 wounded.. For this price, some 5 POW and one MG was captured.

The attack only proved that without the British, the North Russian Army was inferior to the Reds much like the ARVN was to the NVA in Vietnam 45 years later.

As the British prepped for their upcoming "spoiling" offensive, the Reds also prepared. Their positions astride the Dvina were strong, held by 6000 men, 18 artillery guns and many mortars. This defensive line was complete with trenches and wire from the south bank of the Selmenga River and in front of Nizhni Seltso. The defenses reached to the forests edge on both sides, about two miles on each side. The total front was six miles long and had a depth of 10 miles. Further augmenting were numerous gunboats and rafts. The Reds morale was high. They were ready for the "big British show."

It was clear from the recent actions, the Red force was not the same force which had opposed the Allies a year earlier. During the first week of August, the gunboat *Cicala* was hit on the 5th, damaging it. Then on the 7th, the M33, commanded by Kenneth Michell, was hit three times, causing only minor damage. Each time, the RAF seaplanes swooped down as the British returned fire. Odder still, the seldom use of the Red airforce. On July 19th, the Depot ship *Borodino* was attacked, Red bombs narrowly missing. On the 27th, the *Hyderabad* was attacked, and on the 28th, the Depot Barge on the Dvina received a direct hit.

British intelligence had an accurate picture of the Red's Northern Aerial Division based in Kotlas:

One A-8 Albatross, Nieuport 25
SS Pobeda, Dedronov,Koltsov
Two Spad w/MG, one Nieuport 10
100 poods of fuel, 20 poods of oil
M20 seaplane, 2 launching barges
10 inductive phones w/ 6 miles of wire
8000 rds of British ammo, 20 rifles
SS Victor Hugo, Volodarsky

The land based aircraft were located at Vereny Toimoe, along the Dvina. Two airplanes existed. The White Sea detachment, with 3 M20 seaplanes armed with 2 Lewis Guns w/ 10,000 rds defended by 25 men, was two miles further up the river. It's base had 100 40 lb bombs, 20 25 lb bombs, 60 poods of fuel. Another 2 miles up the river was the Kama Section, with 3 M20 planes (all unflyable), 3 Lewis Guns with 4000 rds, 12 rifles and 3500 rds. At Onega, one M9 and M15 seaplane.

As the British prepared, units were issued their weapons and ammuniton according to the standard set in North Russia. The unit breakdowns were as follows:

INFANTRY BATTALION

16 platoons armed 32 Lewis Guns and 4 carts.
Four companies, one Lewis Gun company with 16 Lewis Guns and 4 carts
Two Stokes Mortar batteries, each with 4 mortars and 4 carts. Each contained 66 boxes of ammunition and 4 carts.

MACHINE GUN BATTALION (2 companies)

16 Machine Guns, 128 MG ammo belts, 5 carts PER company.

RATIONS

The following were issued per soldier daily:

Biscuits	15oz
P.M.	1 tin
Tea	.5 oz
Milk	1 oz
Sugar	3 oz
Jam	2 oz
Rum	.5 oz
Pickles	.5 oz

It was expected to forage for 5 lbs of oats for each of the 138 animals needed to carry the weapons etc.

The attack plan called for the British objectives being the capture of Gorodok and Seltso. The plan called for the simultaneous movement and attack on sector 1 and 3, while sector 2, was bombarded by the flotilla and artillery. Sector 1 had the objective of Seltso, Sector 3, Gorodok. The time of the attack was set at 0600, August 10th.

The British Tank Detachment with two Whippet, Type B in Archangel, 1919.

The Order of Battle attacking in Sector One was:

NIJNY-SELTSO	2 Russian platoons
SELTSO	Co A/45th Bn/RF (191 men)
	1 Stoke Mortar Batty
	1 pla/ MG Co/45th Bn/RF
	2 Russian companies
LIPOVETS	2 Companies/45th Bn/RF
	1 section Stokes Mtr
	1 pla. MG
	2 sec/ 55th arty btty
	2 sec/201st MG Bn
	1 Russian company
CHUDINOVA	5 Cavalry troops
	2 Russian companies
PURSUIT TROOPS	1 Cos. of cavalry
	1 Russian company
RESERVE	1 Lewis Gun Co/45th Bn
	1 Russian Company
	1 Co/45th Bn

Attacking sector 3 was:

SELMENGA	2 lewis Guns Pla/46th RF
	1 Russian Company/3rd NRR
GORODOK	Cos C and D/46th Bn/RF
	2 Lewis Gun pla/46th
	241st Stokes batty
	1 sec/55th arty
	2 Russian Companies/1st bn/3rdNRR
BOROK	Co A/46th Bn
	1 sec/Stokes Btty
RESERVE	2 pla./46th RF
	1 sec/201 MG 1 sec/Engineers
	1 Co/46th Bn
ARTILLERY SUPPORT	32 British guns and 42 Russian
All guns fired for one hour before and after	(13) 18 pdr
the attack. ROF was 50 rds per minute.	(4) 4.5" How
At the end of hour 2, the artillery would	(2) 15.5 How,
redeploy.	60 pdr
NIJNY-SELTSO	12 guns
SELTSO	8 guns
GORODOK	20 guns
As Needed	22 guns
Naval transport on river	28 guns

As far as transport, the following amounts were allocated:
FOR EACH INFANTRY ATTACK:

One Pony per gun and tripod; 2 ponies to carry 12 ammo boxes containing 3000 rds. For each group: 15 Ponies. Unlike the Mules, the Ponies would enter and cross bogs and marshes.

Deployments for the coming offensive began on the 9th. The Selmenga column was to move through the forests to positions behind the Selmenga defenses and to block the enemy retreat line cutting the Selmenga-Gorodok road. The going was slow, reaching the Selmenga defenses at 1730 on the 10th. It was finally in their last position at 1400, the 11th. The Borok column was behind the Selmenga column with Co.A/46th RF. This movement had the force cross the Selmenga river and then march down the Teed river for two miles and take positions north east of Borok. The going was tough with the ankle deep mud causing the pack mules to fall. Only a few small firefights had occurred to this group and by 1800 of the 10th, it had taken Borok and killed 60 Reds. The Gorodok column with Cos C and D/46th Bn also met slow going taking some two hours to reach Selmenga due to the mud. By 01515 on the 10th, it was near the town ready to attack. This force had to attack a well defended ridge containing wire and machine guns. However, when the British mortars laid down a solid barrage and the men advanced, the defending Reds fled. Form this point, the town was 500 yards from the forests edge and the companies rushed the town. Company D reached the west part of the town and immediately became pinned from fierce Red gun fire and intense house to house fighting. A mortar unit opened up on the Red positions and by 1300, Gorodok had fallen and the 300 Reds fled. A platoon was sent to seize a battery of Red 3" guns just outside the town, they immediately came under heavy point blank fire. Three attempts were made all had failed (later in the day, it was taken and several German soldiers were found manning the battery). With the road cut, the trapped Reds around Selmenga began to attempt to break out but all attempts failed. Soon the British had killed

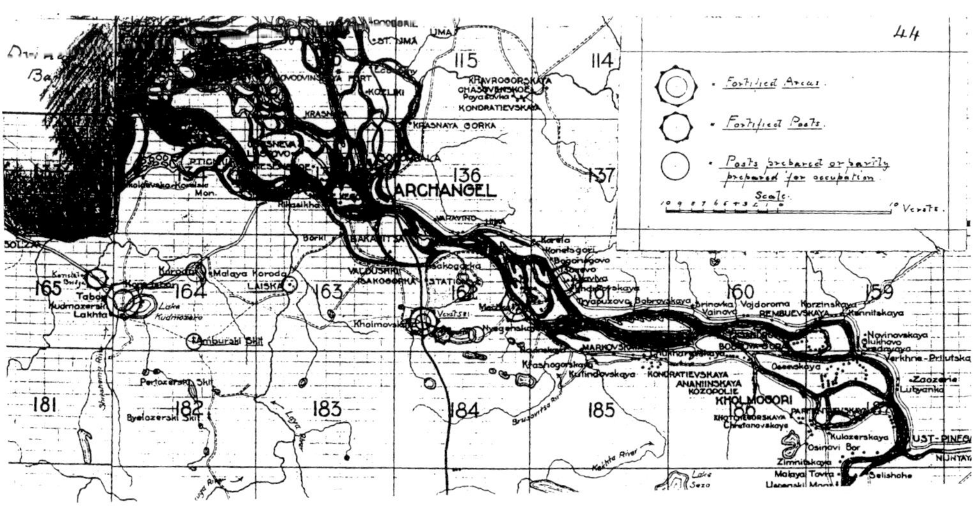

Archangel defense map. Map: Univ. of Michigan

750. The war booty was impressive: 9 field guns, 5 mortars, 900 rifles, 70000 rds. Success was high for the column of the right bank of the Dvina. This would NOT be the case for the column on the left bank.

The Left Column objective was Seltso and on August 9th, a company of 45th Bn RF trekked for miles until the path became impassable to mules. This was bad as the mules carried the 3.7" guns, MGs. Wireless contact had also been lost and the men were fatigued. Also marching some 25 miles was the Cavalry and 2nd Bn/4thNRR, these too, were totally exhausted. The mules were then unloaded and the men carried the various heavy weapons over the worst part of the track. Both the Cavalry and artillery were sent back being unable to cross the deep mud. By 1100 on the 10th, this column force was in their starting positions. The Seltso column was 500 yards south of the town, the other force some 400 yards west of Kockamikha and the Chudinova column, 600 yards east of it.

As soon as the attack began, it was pinned dowe. The commanding officer killed. The two companies of the 45th Bn/RF fell back to regroup. The column attacking Seltso was ordered to pull back to Yakovlevskoe. Not all was bad, the Lipovets force had taken Kochmikha and checked any further advance by intense Red artillery and gunboat fire. It managed to advance later taking Sludkha. Now, the Reds made a surprise move and landed 100 Marines with four MG's behind the Lipovets force, retaking Kochmikha. The Reds penetrated through the forests and conducted an attack on the British flank while, at the same time, another Red force attacked them from Seltso. These attacks were beaten back and the column took Lipovets at 1630. By this time, the British force had 588 POWs to guard! This was the furthest the column was able to advance on Seltso and it, too, was ordered to pullback with its POWs.

The Red force opposing the Sadlier-Jackson Brigade was the 3rd brigade/ 18th division commanded by Gen. Philipovski. His 162nd Regiment (1700 men, 29 MG) and Marine detachment (300 men) were in the Troitsa area. The 161st regiment (1300 men, 32 MG, 50 Cavalry and 300 others) blocked the way to Seltso, where the Brigade HQ was located. The 161st was located near Tulgas. Supporting the 161st were four 3" guns, two 6" How, one 6" Naval. Supporting the 162nd reg were eight 3" guns, two 6" How. Each group of artillery also contained about 275 men.

Typical transportation during the winter months in North Russia. Photo: Univ. of Michigan

The offensive was supported by the flotilla: *HMS Humber* (Lt. Johnstone); *Monitor 27* (Lt.Parker); *Monitor 31* (Lt.Back); and *Monitor 33* (Lt.Michell). These took their positions at 1120 on the 10th and began their bombardment:

> *Humber* and *M33* to bombard Terekovskaya and lewushinskaya
> *M31* to bombard Gorodok
> *M27* to bombard Seltso

Spotting was done by seaplane and the two Kite Balloons. The flotilla began its barrages at 1120, firing 72 rounds in 3 minutes. The barrage halted at noon. The Red flotilla returned fire, but no hits were secured. Because the weather was so bad for visibility, the *HMS Cicala* crept up with her 6" gun. The ship was marginally operational due to damage suffered when hitting a mine. The monitors could not advance too far up the river. By this date the water level had dropped to 4 feet, making running aground a common affair. The coordination between the naval flotilla and the ground troops advancing along the river proved to be perfect.

In the air, the RAF ground based lanes at Beresnik provided their support despite the horrible weather and rain. This bad weather hampered what would've been a very satisfactory show of force. Bombing Gorodok on the 9th was six DH9's and five DH9A bombers. This force dropped over 3 tons of bombs, returned to base, reloaded and flew again providing support to the troops. On the 10th, seven DH9's and two DH9A's took off carrying Phosphorous and HE bombs. On their return home, the fog was thick and four of the sortie became lost: two landed at Pinega, 200 miles away; one at Kholmogori and one in enemy territory. This particular raid was not a success, two planes had only found their targets. The weather cleared at Noon, and four DH9'a and one DH9A took off to bomb Puchega. This group did considerable damage and on their return ran into thunderstorms. Only three planes landed, one crashed and one blew up due to an unreleased bomb. Two Snipes took off to strafe, only to be forced down due to the weather. At 1400, two DH9's took off and were overtaken by rain. One crashed and the other one returned. One of the bigger raids against Puchega occurred on the 12th by six DH9's, one DH9A, four Snipe and one Avro. Five machines carried Phosphorous bombs and lit up the town. Another attack was attempted with five DH9, one DH9A, but turned back because of bad weather. Additional attacks were conducted on the 13th, and when British troops attacked the town on the 14th, little opposition existed.

The RAF had dropped some 14 tons of bombs causing major damage to Seltso, Gorodok, Borok and Puchega. In the first two weeks of August, 86 hours of flight had been conducted. From mid August to September another 40 hours of flight time occurred. Kite Balloons 1 and 2 had also spent 123 hours in operations.

The seaplane situation for Capt.Altham remained the same, that is, out of some 18 planes, only 5-6 could fly. These carried mostly recon,strafing and spotting missions. Although, because of low visibility their impact was less than normal.

The big offensive that had begun on the 10th, ended on the 14th. It resulted in a 20 mile advance along the Dvina, ending short of Seltso. The defending Red 3rd Brigade of the 18th division had suffered greatly losing 500 Kia, 800 Wia and 300 subjected to 600 rounds of Mustard gas. Some 2164 POWs, including 63 officers. Total losses reached 3964 men, some 2000 others fleeing to other defenses along the Dvina. In material, 18 3" guns were captured. The British had lost 20 KIA.

Leaving England aboard the *SS Kildonan Castel* were the 1st Bn/East Surreys, 19th MG Bn, the 86th and 135th artillery batteries. More curiously aboard was the British North Russian Tank detachment of 9 officers and 60 men commanded by Major Bryan. Aboard were four Mark V and two Whippet, Type B tanks. These were sent without the knowledge of Ironside to help cover the evacuation in September. Once completed, the tanks would be handed over to the North Russians. These tanks and detachment arrived at Archangel on the 29th.

The British were not quite done and on the 27th began offensive operations along the Railroad Front toward Emtsa. A few Snipes raked the enemy lines with smoke bombs producing a panic in the Reds who thought it was gas. In a secret memo, a new weapon had been created allowing for gas bombs to be dropped from airplanes was noted. An officer was sent on the 9th to discuss about the possibilities. The memo clearly stated that the allied countries already know of this new innovation and it is at best, only a few years before the enemy knows of the innovation.. The basic question of the memo states:

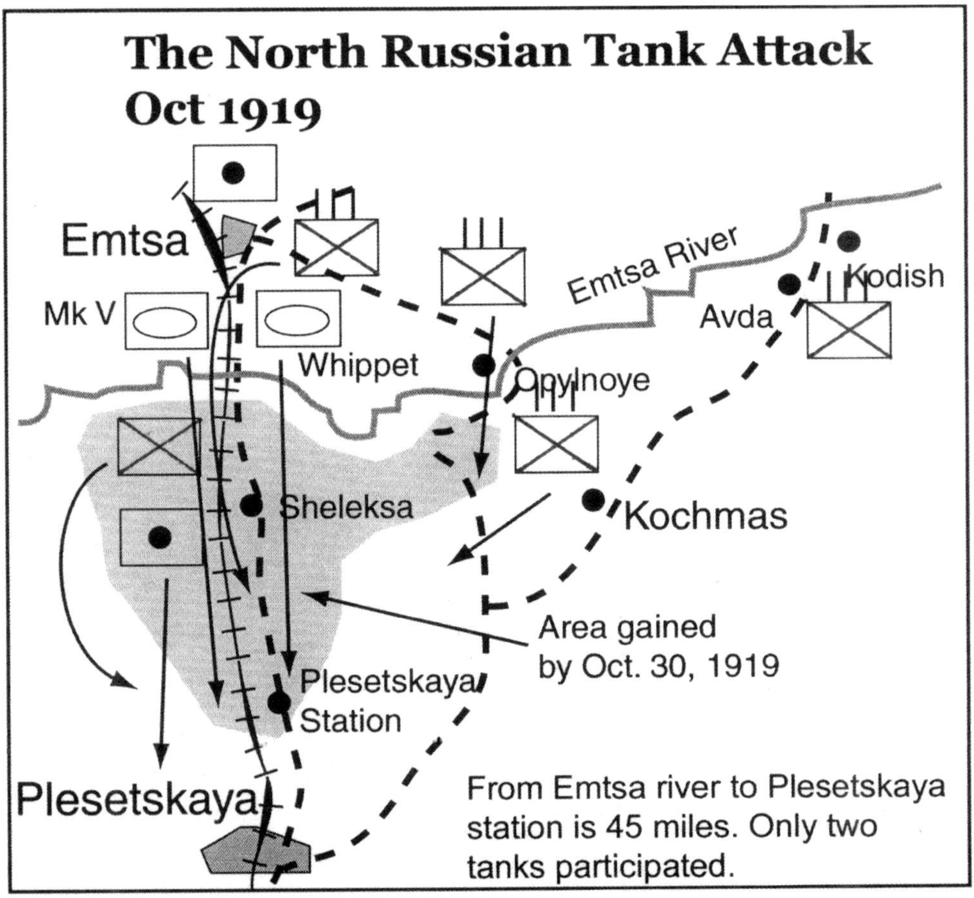

> "...whether are we likely to have any use for this gas within the next few years, if we are, it is a pity to use in Russia, if not, then use it."

In the Chunova and Eusolia area, Squadron No.4 based at Oberzskaya, dropped an average of 80 lbs of bombs daily. By the end of the week, some 600 lbs were dropped on Red positions. More important, the new innovation was used, the aerial gas bomb. Between Noon and 1400 hrs., planes dropped 53 gas bombs on Emtsa creating a large gas cloud. The pilots witnessed a total panic and chaos in the Red lines, many fleeing into the woods. Thus, for the first time in history, aerial gas bombs were used and regarded as a complete success.

In another attack, between 1830 and 2000, No.4 squadron dropped another 63 gas bombs on Emsta. The planes then raked the streets in strafing runs. By the end of the 27th, Emtsa had been hit with 115 gas bombs. On the 28th, the Squadron returned, dropping another 45 gas bombs. One Snipe chased a Red armor train, which fled in panic.

On the 29th, the 6th NRR and some British troops began their ground attack easily taking the Red positions all the way up to Emtsa gathering some 550 POWs. However, the town of Emtsa remained stoutly defended and the town changed hands several times with troops and armored trains. Attacking the Red artillery batteries were 3 Snipes, which dropped smoke bombs, while another two Snipes strafed the battery. Always over the front was at least two Snipes providing ground support.

According to the Intelligence reports examining the impacts of the gas bombs were as follows:

> "...the bombs dropped at Emtsa exploded making a cloud of thick about 16 yards in diameter and remained stationary for some time due to no wind. As soon as the airplanes were spotted on subsequent flights, the enemy scattered into the forests or dugouts. At least 20 men from the 115th Labor Company are reported casualties. The symptoms are said to have been Coughing, Vomiting and Eyes watery. In some reports, it is said the gas is stronger than normally used, yet in others, some men having no masks were not affected. These effects are to have lasted three hours. One victim had eyes and mouth turned yellow and died."
> Enemy losses directly from the gas bombs are as follows:

Emtsa :	30 men
Plesetskaya:	20 men
Chunova:	8 men
Front lines:	22 men

The RAF and Seaplanes used were frequently in conducting reconnaissance missions. During August 1919, some 160 flights were made over the Dvina and Vaga from Beresnik, 62 were made over the Railroad front and Onega by Squadron No.4 at Obozerskaya. The total RAF now consisted of the following numbers: One Strutter, seven DH9, four Avro, 10 DH9A, 8 Snipe and one Re8. At Murmansk, the RAF had: Three Re8, Six Fairey IIIC, six Short 184 and six Camel. There was also a large base at Kem.

On the 28th, additional British reinforcements arrived, the 2nd Bn/ Highland Light Infantry (733 men)The unit was sent for security reasons in the Archangel area.

On the 29th, the tank detachment arrived. When Major Bryan reported in, Ironside gave them a warm welcome and then added, " why was it seen fit by the powers to send tanks in a country with bogs and forests?" It was pointed out that the unit will see little combat but that it would raise the morale. It was later planned that one tank would remain in Archangel, another one assigned to Solombala, one was sent to Bakaritza to guard the storage areas. The others for training the North Russians. The Russian tank detachment being trained was under Colonel Kenotkenitch and 15 other officers.

The British continued with offensive operations with the amphibious assault on Lake Onega on the 29th. This was a combined operation with naval and air support. The objective was to seize the village of Rimskaya. The flotilla comprised of the steamers *Silny* carrying Russian and Serb troops, the *Azod and the Svietlana*. For an escort, several British manned torpedo boats were used. The flotilla sailed and anchored about 500 yards away from the village at 0100. The "invasion" force had 37 British, 25 Russian and 25 Serbs. No MG's were carried only rifles and six Lewis guns. The MG fire and bombs would be provided by the RAF. At 0500, the RAF attacked and then the troops assaulted. The torpedo boats silently arrived at the piers and unloaded a backup squad consisting of 60 men and 8 Lewis Guns. These men quickly followed the others holding the center position with the Russian and Serbs to the right and left. The *Silny* provided artillery supported with their 75mm guns. The various weapons aboard the others (two 3 pdr, 5 MG's and 12 lewis guns also opened up. The British caught a platoon of Reds napping in the woods, disarming them. The Russian, Serb and British linked up and advanced through the wooded area to the town. Little opposition was encountered until about 500 yards from the village. The 200 Reds armed with six MG and 300 rifles opened up with token resistance, their aim being not good. The British sections took parts of the village one by one and by 1100, it was a done deal. Captured were all 200 men, six MG, 300 rifles, 17 cases of ammo, 17 sets of entrenching tools, a box of handgrenades, 14 MG belts of ammo.

The Airbase at Lumbushi contained land airplanes consisting of five Camels, four Re 8 and two Avros. These did a considerable amount of strafing and bombing.

Between August and September these planes flew 130 hours, dropping 20 tons of bombs and firing 8600 rds of ammo.

Ussuna airfield, operated by the Reds, came under attack from four Fairey IIIC, one Camel and one Re 8. These remained strafing and bombing for about an hour.

Air operations in the Syren Force were equally large. Some 775 hours in flying time, dropping 30 tons of bombs, 280 gas bombs, expending 60000 rds of MG fire. The effective-

Officers of the North Russian Tank Detachment, Archangel 1919.

ness is shown by the number of direct hits: 44 buildings; 3 ships; 19 trains; 4 bridges; and 6 on enemy trenches.

But like the maintenance problem that Capt. Altham had, the following figures show the average numbers of aircraft in flyable condition:

June and July:	3 aircraft
August:	5 airplanes
September:	10 airplanes

On Aug. 31, after a two day bombardment, the British also attacked along the RR and at Seleskole with two companies of the Royal Fusiliers which succeeded in retaking Onega by Sept. 10.

During the first two weeks of September there was little fighting. The British were pulling back front their front lines without any interference. Whether this was intentional on the part of the Reds or due to lack of intelligence, by the 16th, the British had evacuated the Toitsa area and destroyed several bridges across the Dvina. Assisting in the withdrawal the *Monitors 25 and 27* remained on the Upper Dvina, despite the river level falling. Unable to move past Khorobritsky, they were dismantled and then destroyed. On the 11th, during the withdrawal, the rearguard came under attack from the woods west of Kurgomin. The attacking force was the former *4th NRR*, which had defected to the Reds. Elements of the British 46th Bn were sent to create a defensive line and supported by two gun barges. On the 12th, air recon noted about 1000 men entering Kurgomin. The 46th Bn repelled the attack. Oddly, the 9th Co/161st regiment of the Red 3rd brigade then defected to the British!

On the 14th, the British 45th attacked Nevonskaya using about 80 men supported by a Lewis gun platoon and trench mortars. The Reds retreated and the 45th advanced up to Bulanovskaya. The Reds then counterattacked and retook both towns.

During the first two weeks, the port was busy as numerous transports entered, loaded up and left with men under such colorful names as *La Plata, Menominee, Ulua, Czaritza, Toloa and Kildonam Castle.* During these two weeks some 4500 allied forces had left including the bulk being the Slavo-British force, French and British.

On the Syren front, the last gas bombings occurred at Chorga, some 40 bombs were dropped and 30 bombs dropped on Mikeeva Selga. Additional gas bombings occurred on enemy gun positions near Lijma, where 30 more were dropped. At Lake Onega, another landing occurred on the 14th, supported by the RAF. An all White Russian force landed at Vate Navolok. Gas bombs were also dropped on Konchozero.

While most of the withdrawals were harmless, Co.Bs/45th Bn was not. It was aboard a barge being escorted down the Vaga when it fell under withering MG fire. The company replied but not until 3 men were killed and 11 were wounded. The convoy finally reached Archangel on the 22nd.

By the 24th, the RAF had flown 126 hours in support missions. Soon, the weapons and ammo depots along with the airplanes and few tanks would be turned over to the North Russian Army to carry on their own war.

By the end of September, another 7500 soldiers were back in the U.K. These were primarily British. The evacuations continued until October 12th, when the last transports arrived, *Kalyan, Santa Elena, St.Giles and Welshman.* They loaded up with mostly Serbs and Russians and 200 or so British and the "big show" was over. The total evacuated amounted to 2491 British officers, and 26,485 men. The total of the Allied forces came to 562 officers, 12,902 men, 6535 civilians. The grand total came to 48, 975. From September, some 25 transports arrived and left at Archangel.

The amount of air support provided to the Syren and Archangel theatres was extensive. In the Comprehensive Summary for Units (seaplanes and land planes) of the Forward Wing of the RAF, SYREN force the following air sorties are noted:

Reconnaissance flights:	361
Hours flown:	660
Communication Flights:	38
Hours flown:	54
Instructional Flying Hours:	38
Test Flight Hours:	65
Total hours flown:	820
No. Of Bombs dropper:	1103
Tons:	29
MG Rounds fired:	58,540
Gas Bombs dropped:	241
No. Of photographic plates exposed:	13,910
Approx. Area photographed:	250 miles
Russian pilots trained:	6

The above figures are from June through Sept.17th. The Losses to the Americans amounted to 222 men, and for the British, 321 men.

What was left behind was the 25,000 man North Russian Army now led by Generals Kveitsinsky and Miller. This army was divided and morally weak, despite extensive training and supplies. It held a fortified line from Emetskoe on the Dvina-Seletskoe-Obozerskaya-Bolshiozerki. Their deployment was as follows:

6th NRR at Oberzerkaya area
7th NRR at Seletskoe area
3rd and 4th NRR at Ivanovskaya area
8th NRR at Pinega area
1st NRR at Nijmoero and Archangel

The Reds wasted little time and attacked on the 29th, taking Emsta. The Reds then advanced on Seletskoe. The only bright spot in the North Russian army history and the only tank action in North Russia occurred on October 29th. The North Russian tank corps attacked along the railway with infantry. The attack, led by Colonel Kenotkenitch, used the MK V and Whippet tanks the British had left behind. The Reds ran as usual at the sight of tanks and the NRR seized five fortified areas including the Plesetskaya rail station. This had been something the allied forces had been unable to do! The rail station was a major win and indicates the tanks had advanced from Emtsa to the station, some 15 miles! The use of tanks was possible only along the railroad. Obviously, the British were totally wrong in their assumptions regarding the use of tanks.

After the English departure, the remaining white Russian pilots were taken into the Murmansk Air Division, which was led by Colonel Barbas, and included the hydro-detachment under the command of Lieutenant Kraevsk. In this battalion also served lieutenant Tumanov, Junior Lieutenant Klembovski, Lieutenant Melnitski, non-commissioned officers Vershinin and Dushutin, and recent new pilots Yakovitsk, Znamenski and Matve. From Berlin arrived Ensign Anikin.

The Matchast air-battalion and seaplane detachments put together three old Grigorovich flying boats, three Shorts, two Fairies, three Camels, eight Avro-504, D_.9, Sopwith and RE.8s. In all,22 machines or more aircraft than pilots. Fuel and bombs continued to exist in large quantities. General Miller attempted to recruit pilot volunteers in England and France. But despite the generous salaries none were. White Russian desertions sharply increased with the news that both Kholchak and Denikin had failed.. On October 6th, Pilot Anikin, took off on a recon mission and touched down in Red territory. The Avro's observer Staff-captain Filippov was shot. Anikin upon interrogation declared that the desertion was intentional and this may be the only case in the Civil war when a regular pilot of the White Army voluntarily flew over to the Bolsheviks.

In December, Lieutenants Yakovitsk and Tumanov conducted six air sorties of observation and air bombardment But even if more was conducted the outcome was unlikely to have been changed. In March, the Bolsheviks began to revolt with sailors and occupied Murmansk. The North front was now totally liquidated. All of the pilots of White Murmansk air battalion evacuated on a steamer to Norway.

On Dec.15th, the 7th and 4th NRR regiments (some 2000 men) attacked to retake Shenkursk. This failed. On February 4th, 1920, the Red 4th Regiment attacked the 7th NRR forcing it to retreat recklessly back along the Dvina (many went over to the Reds) By the 17th, most of the army along the RR and elsewhere ceased to exist. This turned into a rout and the Red 154 regiment was able to enter Archangel on the 21st.

The 1700 men under Gen. Valichevich retreated toward Onega and upon arriving advanced to Soroka on the Murmansk RR hoping to join other allied forces. On the 23rd, the fled across Finland to Virma, 20miles east of Soroka. Reds were waiting here. A bloody

The port of Murmansk in 1919.

butchering battle followed, and 1500 White Russians were able to escape after walking on foot through ice and snow to Lahti.

*****

U.S. Troops in Siberia

Farther to the east, at Vladivostock, President Wilson dispatched the 27th and 31st regiments of the 85th division from Manila to Eastern Siberia. These troops were once again ordered to defend the stockpiled ammunitions and protect the lines of communications from Vladiostock , westward to the rear of Kolchak's army. Combat was prohibited. Leading the American force was General Graves. The American force was subordinated to the Japanese, General Otani, who also commanded some 72,000 Japanese troops. However, Graves refused to follow the orders of Otani.

The American force amounted 338 Officers, 8,050 men, 17 nurses and 17 clerks. Upon their arrival, the 31st regiment was deployed and strung out along the Trans-Siberian railroad to protect it and make safe for supplies heading for Kolchak and the Czech Legion trying to escape eastward. Units were also posted to protect the coal mines in the Suchan area. Coal was vital to run the locomotives. Most of the workers in this area were Bolsheviks under White control.

June 1919

The American garrison duties were fairly mundane. Little combat had occurred until June 21st. On this day, three US soldiers (from Company H)went fishing on their day off in the Suchan River. The men waded into the water. Soon, locals surrounded them and took them into custody at Novitskaya. Two additional men were also captured. When the soldiers were missed the next day, Company H (110 men) deployed and surrounded the town demanding their release. Then, the battle erupted lasting all day. A few soldiers were killed but the American POWs had been taken away to Frolovka. The Americans did not pursue and returned to their camp some six miles away.

When General Graves had heard about this, he ordered Companies C and D, and a MG company towards Suchon from Shtova. These traveled by train and all along their transit came under fire from Reds. At Sitsa, some 200 Reds blasted the train. A brief firefight ensued but the train continued. At Romanovka, a US detail of 72 men from Company A was ordered to protect the railroad. Its 3rd platoon (51 men)was reinforced with 21 men. This group was ambushed by 100 Reds early in the morning as most Americans were sleeping. One soldier was hit 17 times. The surviving US troops fled to a nearby wooden cabin.

The survivors sent a few men to locate and get Company E, some six miles away. They stopped a nearby passing train and boarded. However, the train took off in the opposite direction that Company E was in!

Eventually, Company E was found and a detachment of 30 men were sent to join Company A's battle. Upon their arrival, most of the Reds had vanished. The battle proved to be bloody, some 19 Kia, 25 Wia of the 72 man US platoon.

The Reds attacked in similar fashion on June 26th upon US troops located in Novo-Nezhino. This failed. The Reds continued to harrass and cut communication lines and by July 1, General Graves planned to attack one Red base at Novitskaya.

For this offensive, Cos. C and D.of the 31st were used. Company C was commanded by Grave's son, Major Graves and armed with two MGs. Company attacked from the north and Company D, one Japanese company, 2 MGs and one 37mm, from the south. At 0500, July 2, the attack commenced, and by 1000 hrs the town was secured. On July 3rd, the town of Kazanka was attacked. After about one hour, the town was taken.

The men of the 31st regiment left Russia on August 19th, 1919, the remaining US troops would remain until into 1920.

*****

The midnight war, like its sister in the south, was Churchill's private war. For some time, it was an unknown war with Russia using a forgotten army and for the Reds, it became a victor's dilemma afterwards. For the allies, it was, for sometime, a secret war following on the heels of World War 1. Afterwards, many referred to it as Churchill's Archangel fiasco, which it was. The ignorant armies used were second rate, filled with untrained and unprepared troops. It was a stillborn crusade, but one that would repeated nearly a half century later by the French (1946-54) and Americans (1963-73) in Vietnam. How ironic, their foe would be under a more modern name called Communism, the son of Bolshevism. Unlike most of the allies that forgot this debacle as time went on, the Russians never have.

Finally, the Russian Civil war saw a young, twenty-something, Joseph Stalin in Tsaritsyn, fighting the Whites. Years later, he renamed the city Stalingrad (now you know why) a name infamous for the beginning of the end for German army in World War Two. The allies had missed the perfect chance to crush the communist virus in its embryonic state. It would prove to be a very heavy price in human life and hardship for simply lacking the will to do it right.

Sources:

1 ADM 173/1695, WO 95/5487, WO 95/1955, WO 158/735, WO 106/1164, WO/32/5705, WO 158/736, WO 106/1148, WO 73/111, WO32/5705, ADM 137/1695, ADM 137/1613, AIR 1/435/15/274, AIR 1/472/15/312, AIR 1/438/15/301, WO 106/1153, WO 161/5, WO 158/735, WO 106/1164+1155, WO95/5419, WO95/5419, WO 158/735+739, WO 158/715, AIR 1/438/15/301/4. Public Record Office, London, U.K.

2 Bradley, John. *Allied Intervention in Russia*. 1984

3 Halliday, E. *The Ignorant Armies*. 1960

4 *Red Armies of the Russian Civil War*. Osprey, 1998.

5 Kondratev,C. *Aircraft of the Russian Civil War*. Moscow Press, 2000.

6 Kettle, Michael. *Churchill and the Archangel Fiasco*. 1992.

7 Fogelsong, David. *America's Secret War Against Russia*. 1995

8 Carey, Donald. *Fighting the Bolsheviks*. 1997

9 Weekly Tank Reports 40-52, North Russia, August 1919.

10 Microfilm 924, Reels 1 and 2. American North Russia Exp. Force, U.S. National Archives

11 *The Russian Civil War Encyclopedia*. Moscow Press, 1982.

12 Butt, V.P. *The Russian Civil War: Documents from the Soviet Archives*. 1990

13 Strakhovsky, Leonid. *Intervention in Archangel*. 1971.

14 Adams, Samual. *The Fogotten Army*. 1970

15 Goldhurst, Richard. *The Midnight War*, 1978.

8

The End Analysis

In monetary terms, the British paid some 100,000,000 pounds for this intervention. In casualties, 41 officers and 286 KIA, 1100 WIA.

The North Russia intervention was the first modern war conducted in the Arctic regions. In late 1919, General Ironsides and others put together a comprehensive report on about everything, how the climate affected weapons, men etc. Many of these lessons were subsequently forgotten as the years went by, only to be learned once again by the Russian when they attacked into Finland in 1939.

The following excepts provide an inside view into the opinions of Ironside on the variety of troops sent:

> On the British officers: " I have never been more struck in my life as I have been by the superiority of the British officer...he has succeeded in imbuing a great many Russian officers."
>
> On the Slavo British Legion: " We tried to enlist a motley crowd of various nationalities totaling 3000, but only 500 were combatants. The Russian is totally adverse to any voluntary action on his own part, he has no initiative."
>
> On the French Foreign Legion: " a purely French unit...commands are in French. French officers make no attempt to arrange sanitation matters for their troops. Their billets are filthy adn ill-kept.
>
> On the Polish Legion: "a force of 300 men of great value. The men are smart and fought exceedingly well. They despise the Russian and refuse to serve under them.

The men use French weapons and conflicts exist between the French and Polish. Altogether they are the most useful and dependable troops."

French and American troops: "They are not a success.The French and American are jealous to a certain degree of the British command, sowed propaganda amongst the Russians (meaning, derogatory remarks) stating it was they who were saving Russia. The French refuse to fight and generally ill-disciplined and slovenliness. The American officers are incompetent and their men worthless (history has shown this not to be the case). The Americans sold their rations to obtain money.

Air forces: They have been the greatest value.

Sanitation: " this has been peculiarly difficult, neither the French or Russians have the most rudimentary ideas of its necessity and the incompetence of the American officers result in their men having bad sanitation."

Combat: " the heavy fighting devolved chiefly on the Russians and British troops. The French troops collapsed completely and the Americans have never been good fighting troops [this is certainly untrue]. When heavy fighting occurred, British troops provided a fine example to the Russian. There never was a comparison between British troops and the allies. Offensive actions were carried out invariably by British or Russian troops. Neither the American nor French troops could be prevailed on [obviously, Ironside was unfair in his assessment. To say that the French or Americans were worse than their White Russians does not ring true and if they were that bad, why did he send them to hold the front?]

Weapons

It was reported that the Russian 3-inch field gun was an extremely useful weapon, equal to the British 18-pdr. Several experiments bearing on artillery matters were carried out during the winter battles.

(1) Endless experiments on various types of gun wheel runners for transporting vehicles over the snow were made. No one seemed to have a clear conception of what was required, and runners of all shapes and sizes were manufactured. It was thought that a suitable design for field guns had been arrived at based on a drawing for runners for a wagon. In actual practice, because the wheel track of the guns were greater than the track, made by the ordinary Russian sleigh, it was found that the runners were unsatisfactory, and that the best method was to discard the runners and to load the gun on the Russian sleigh. A 60-pdr. was in this manner transported from Archangel to Kurgomin.

A suitable sleigh used as a firing platform was built for the 2.75 inch guns.

(2) Because the British non-freezing buffer oil froze frequently, Major Barratt mixed ordinary non-freezing buffer oil with turpentine, which produced a mixture which did not freeze at -60° C. The above-mentioned mixture gave excellent results during the winter months.

Ammunition in North Russia

Very little information was available regarding the behavior of ammunition of various natures at such low temperatures as are experienced during the six or seven months' winter of Northern Russia. Temperature coefficient had never been practically tested at such low temperatures as -40° F, which is quite an ordinary figure, especially at night, in Archangel and district.

> Cordite in Extreme Cold: The effect of extreme cold on the behavior of cordite was very marked. A gunner officer of the C.F.A. at Ust Padenga stated that he had to range at 3,750 yards to obtain 3,000. At Tulgas and at Seletskoe similar results were reported.

The gun employed was an 18-pdr., and the propellant cordite at temperatures in the region of -10° F., and the results do not agree at all with the range table variations.The British investigated and some tests were carried out on a measured range at Isaka Gorka (near Archangel), a new 18-pr. gun being employed.

The tests consisted of warming up 12 rounds of 18-pdr. ammunition with cordite propellant in a room at about 60°F. The warming was continued for about a week, the rounds being occasionally turned over to allow of uniform absorption of the nitro-glycerine, which is known to be squeezed out of the cordite if stored at temperatures below -45° F.

The rounds were brought out of the room, allowed to cool, and then fired alternately with the same number of exactly similar rounds that had been stored for some months in this country and not warmed previously to firing.

The results showed a difference on the average of 158 yards in a range of 2,000 yards, i.e., about 8 percent increase of range in the case of the warmed up cordite.

The figures obtained might have been expected, as the squeezing out of the nitro-glycerine must have the effect of nullifying the mixture of nitro-cellulose and nitroglycerine that is necessary for the rapid burning of the cordite in the sun.

> Cordite V., N.C.T.: As a sequel to the above experimental results it. was recommended —at any rate for 18-pdr. ammunition—that N.C.T. should, if possible, be employed (during the winter months, say from December to March inclusive).
>
> This propellant had the additional advantage of having a much smaller temperature co-efficient. On the other hand N.C.T. was very susceptible to damp, and it swells and suffers in its ballistic properties when it becomes wet.

The atmosphere in the summer months in Northern Russia are very humid, and in many parts is more or less a huge swamp for the greater part of the time. Consequently the storage of N.C.T. in dumps near gun positions would present difficulties. The British experiments on cordite recommended it for use at all times other than in the winter months in spite of its comparatively high temperature co-efficient.

> Tests on Serviceability of Propellants: Many heat tests were carried out on cordite that had been stored at very low temperatures for several months. It was found that the cordite had not deteriorated in quality.

The Russian" propellant generally used is " Besdimnie Porokh," or " smokeless powder," a type of nitro-cellulose not containing any nitro-glycerine. This did not suffer from the effect mentioned above in the case of cordite, and it appears to withstand the extreme cold without perceptible deterioration for many years. It is usually tested here by methods very similar to our heat tests.

One method was to maintain a sample at 115° C. for some hours in contact with blue litmus paper. The number of hours that elapse before the litmus becomes red is observed and sentence given accordingly.

Another method was to warm at 75° C. for several days and weigh the sample once a day. The stability of the powder is expressed in the number of days that elapse before decomposition sets in, this being accompanied by rapid loss of weight.

Fuses: For H.E. shell, the fuses that appear to give most general satisfaction were "direct action," e.g., No. 106 British and "I.A." French.

Because of the presence of deep snow in winter and soft swamp in summer the " Graze" type of fuse was unsatisfactory, as the time required by the fuse to function after striking, though exceedingly small, was enough to smother the effect.

Trench Mortar Ammunition: The 3-inch trench mortar ammunition did not prove satisfactory. Reports of large percentages of " duds." An examination of over 20 duds at the trench mortar school in Archangel showed that failures were due to various causes, e.g :

1. Fuse 146 or pistol head had functioned and also cap of igniter set, but either safety fuse or detonator had not fired 13
2. Fuse functioned, but cap at not fired 2
3. Fuse, cap, and safety fuse correct, but detonator had not fired 2
4. Pistol head had functioned, but not fired cap 2
5. Always fuse had functioned, but not fired cap 5
6. Pistol head lever not released 7
7. Igniting set (apparently) not inserted in bomb 1

The firing tests took place in deep snow, but this did not seem to have any effect on the functioning of the 146 fuse. Several experiments were made. The procedure being to attach the fuse and igniter set to the head of a Stokes bomb and drop them from a height on the ground. In practically every case the fuse itself fired, and usually also the detonator, but there was generally too. great an interval (up to two or three seconds} between the firing of the fuse and that of the detonator.

This may have been due to the effect of the extreme cold on the instantaneous fuse connecting cap and detonator. Some of them may also at some time or other have been damp, though external examination did not reveal any traces of this.

Rifle Grenades: Rifle Grenades No. 35 frequently failed to explode in deep snow. This was found to be due to the fact that the needle did not strike the detonator with sufficient force to fire it. In any case these grenades were unsuitable when fired into snow, their effect being practically nil at a few yards distance from the burst. On this account these grenades were not recommended for use at the front. No other rifle grenades were available during the winter.

Buffer Oils: In November 1918, at the request of G.R.A., various samples of supposed non-freezing buffer oils were tested with results as follows:

Oil became very viscous at:	
French non-freezing oil	-24°C (-11°F)
Russian	-20°C (-4°)
British oil (mineral, non-freezing)	-24°C (-11°F)

The British oil, mineral, non-freezing, when stored for some weeks in a shed near Archangel, was found to contain lumps of frozen oil.

These observations indicated that at the temperatures experienced during the winter the freezing of the oils would involve damage to the gun. Experiments were undertaken with the object of discovering an oil which would be really non-freezing at very low temperatures.

With the help of solid carbon dioxide and ether a freezing temperature of about -80° C (-112° F) was obtained.

It was found that a mixture of one part turpentine, white, with two parts oil, mineral, non-freezing, did not become appreciably more viscous at - 40° C (-40° F), nor freeze at -60° C (-76° F). The turpentine employed was obtained locally and was very pure. It gave no acid reaction, and mixed well with the oil.

Its freezing point alone was about -8° C (+14° F), but mixed as above with the oil it does not freeze even at -76° F! Fifty rounds of rapid fire in an 18-pdr gun did not raise its temperature more than about 25° F, so that its boiling point (313° F) was sufficiently high for absolute safety, especially as it is not a volatile liquid.

Experiments in the gun itself gave satisfactory results at a temperature of -13° F, and its use was recommended during the winter months.

Further experiments in warmer weather showed that it is not suitable for use in the summer.

Lubricating Oils: The "oil, lubricating, G.S., special," sent to North Russia was also tested at low temperatures. It was found to become very viscous at about -10° G, and to contain lumps of frozen oil when stored for some time there in the winter. A mixture of two parts of this oil with one of turpentine, white, however, did not become very viscous at -40° G., nor freeze at -60° C.

The Russian oil "Oleonapthe" mixed with an equal quantity of turpentine was also found to be satisfactory.

Either of these oils can be used for lubricating parts of guns, machine guns, or rifles. For the barrel casing of machine guns a mixture of two parts of pure glycerin to one part of water gives a suitable non-freezing mixture. Its freezing point is about -40° C.

It was found that a mixture of spirit (e.g., vodka) was occasionally used in the Russian machine guns, but that it frequently disappeared. The mixture is also, of course, very volatile.

> Nature of Fighting: Both sides were unaccustomed to fighting in forest country, and this campaign in Northern Russia differed in this respect from other small wars, where the native of the country derives such great advantage from local knowledge as to how to fight.

During the winter in Northern Russia the Russian peasant did not move about in the woods. They kept to the roads, using his sleighs and pony, but skis and snow-shoes are practically unknown. The Bolshevik, the workman, and communist of the big towns and the political agitator, were less hardy than the Allies, and had no conception of rough fighting.

The few Russian officers present with the Allies knew nothing of fighting in the forests. Both sides were very badly equipped as regards mobility in the snow in or out of woods. Neither had much knowledge of the fighting required.

The Allies made plans to turn out hundreds of men on skis and snow-shoes, but *none* of the winter equipment arrived until after it was impossible to employ it, and then only succeeded in making a very moderate company of 150 snow-shoers.

Had the Allies been opposed to bodies of good skiers of even one quarter their strength, the Allies would have found much more difficult.

Mobility, when shown by either side, met with instant success.

The Bolsheviks were curiously inert in the matter of cutting and harassing lines of communications. Only on very few occasions were telephone wires cut, and then in no systematic manner.

Allied troops were uniformly bad and two of the Allied contingents would hardly defend themselves, but the Bolsheviks were badly led and failed utterly in the task of turning us out of Archangel, which should have been an easy one.

> Defensive: Thrown upon the defensive, from the beginning of the winter the Allies found themselves in the worst possible state of morale. The announcement of an armistice, the horrors of a long winter, and the moral effect of the port of Archangel being closed to navigation for eight months, had a bad effect upon the weaker members of the command.

Practically all the Governments were being pestered with questions about North Russia. All demands for withdrawal were printed with big headlines in the papers and came back to the men in Russia to add fuel to their discontent.

Insidious Bolshevik propaganda was sown broadcast and renegade journalists on the other side. Archangel and the whole Northern Region was swamped with printed pamphlets in French and English. It is curious to note that the French were more easily affected than the Americans, and though commanded by French regular officers, these latter proved of no value and did not seem to mind if their men disobeyed an order or not.

Gunfire: Russian troops on both sides were much affected by gunfire. They did not stand bombardment like the Allies did.

Climate: It was difficult to form any idea of what could or could not be done in a severe northern climate, and literature on the subject was almost nonexistent.

The fault of the equipment, as far as Northern Russia was concerned, was that it was all designed far too much for a mighty mobile effort such as a dash to the Pole and back, carried out with chosen men, and lasting for a definite and determinable period. The windproof kit, the sleeping bags, and special underclothes were the best that could be provided, but continuous winter operations on the pattern of a polar dash were, of course, impossible. Troops could not remain out for long, and had of necessity, to return. In the forest country there is practically never any wind, and snow-shoes in forest are preferable to skis, and are much more easily learned.

The peasant houses were well built, supplied with good stoves and double windows, so that the severe winter can be borne without much hardship. It was easy to erect in & few days good warm blockhouses to defy the very coldest weather. As a whole the men were much better housed and more comfortable than they ever were in France. It is true sanitary conditions were difficult, but there was no danger of epidemic during winter.

As the campaign progressed it became more and more evident that the fighting was one of accommodation. If your accommodation was destroyed, even to the extent of breaking your windows, you had to evacuate your position. Prolonged operations in the open were impossible.

Defensive Positions in Winter in Northern Russia

Moat villages consist of substantial wooden houses, clustered closely together on either side of a long street, or close to the bank of a river.

The clearing which surrounds the village depends in size upon the age of the village and the number of its inhabitants.

For some hundreds of yards around each village are the special small grass paddocks, fenced in with good stiff posts and rails, each of about an acre. These can very easily be entangled as an obstacle to the "keep," or inner defense.

The temperature being so low, operations cannot be carried out for any length of time without accommodation. The location of defensive positions is bound up with the available accommodation for troops in support and reserve to these positions.

If your accommodation is destroyed, you must necessarily evacuate your position through physical exhaustion.

Accommodation must be kept out of gun range from the enemy or it cannot be considered safe, for the breaking of even one of the double panes of glass in a window may lead to serious consequences in really cold weather.

The defense of this kind nearly always settles down to a perimeter defense of his accommodation, with a continuous obstacle. The following points should be followed:

(a) Keep the enemy out of gun range of your windows. (b) Enemy must have observation to enable him to bombard with success. Keep him back in woods.
(c) Guns can only be moved along roads except after an operation of several days cutting trees and making snow track.
(d) A perimeter defense is not economical and can easily be broken. *(e)* Parties which break through your defense can be dealt with by the keep and its obstacle.

Each position was self-contained, even though it consists of a single blockhouse. It was prepared for all-round defense, and should be a definite defensive unit, under one commander.

The usual defense in forest country was a blockhouse. Several patterns were employed, the most useful being the one of logs cut and piled up from the surrounding forest. The following points should be borne in mind:

(a) A blockhouse to be efficient must be built *in* the forest and not in the clearing, so as to be free from artillery observation. In the open a blockhouse merely becomes a deathtrap. Trenches can and should be used in areas which are not marshy. Trenches are the only defense possible in the open, but cannot be occupied for long periods.
(b) Only very little clearing, that of undergrowth, should be done for 30 yards round the blockhouse. The tendency is for the men to cut down everything close to the blockhouse to give them a smaller distance to haul the logs. The result is an unmistakable blockhouse standing in a clearing, a good target for anyone who can reach the end of the clearing.

Each blockhouse should contain an automatic weapon, but the steady continuous firing ones like the Vickers should not be in the front line blockhouses.

Every position devolves into a line of blockhouses with its flanks thrown back as a front line and some sort of second line behind.

It is practically impossible to prevent an enemy, even unprovided with aerial photography, from locating the position of front line blockhouses, but it is possible to prevent him reconnoitering the inner defenses, and these should come as a surprise to him.

Winter conditions commenced in North Russia about October 1st.

At first snowstorms, low clouds, and ground mists were experienced. The days became shorter and shorter, and the cold spells colder and more frequent.

In November the lowest temperature recorded was -10° F

December:	- 5° F
January:	-40° F (the average +8° F)
February:	-33° F (the average was +3° F)
March:	+12° F (average)
April:	+31° F (average)
May :	+41° F (average)

In spite of the great difficulties due to the extreme cold, constant endeavor and ever increasing experience made flying possible, and certain machines carried out reconnaissance's with comparative regularity during the entire winter; many flights being made when the thermometer recorded -60° or more of frost.

The intervening mild spells were almost invariably accompanied by severe snowstorms which made flying impossible. The average snow depth was 18 inches.

Trouble was constantly experienced with radiator honeycombs of airplanes which would crack while standing empty, though every effort was made to keep them warm with flameless lamps and covers.

Boiling water poured into the radiators would often become cold before the engine could be started. Heated oil would re-thicken so rapidly as to cease to lubricate effectively. Wires were liable to snap owing to crystallization.

Aircraft hangars were a constant source of trouble. The snow had continually to be cleared off the roofs, and this work, when performed in very low temperature, is extremely arduous. Curtains and ropes would freeze, causing great; difficulty and delay in opening the hangars.

Great hardships were experienced by the personnel whenever work had to be done in the open. The conditions often made it almost impossible to handle metal or tools. While minor adjustments to machines or engines, which under ordinary conditions would take but a few minuets, frequently occupied a party of men a very considerable time.

Bombing in the extreme cold presented many difficulties. Trouble was continually caused by the release gear freezing during flight, and in most cases 20-lb. bombs had to be carried in the observer's seat and dropped over the side by hand.

All machines had to be fitted with skis, the size and weight of the ski, of course, varying with different machines. It is not possible for any type of machine, no matter how light it may be, to take off in 2 feet of snow unless fitted with skis, nor can any machine make a safe landing without these. In certain cases the added head resistance and weight proved too great to allow the machine to carry bombs. The dimensions of skis for:

Sopwith 1^ strutters were	7 feet 7 inches by 8 inches.
Sopwith Camel	8 feet 1 inch by 8 inches
D.H. 4	10 feet 3.5 inches by 10 inches
R.E. 8	10 feet 6 inches by 8 inches
D.H. 9A	12 feet 10 inches by 1 foot 3 inches.

Electrically-heated clothing was found to be absolutely necessary when flying in extreme cold, and much benefit was derived from its use. Nevertheless, cases of frostbite were not infrequent, usually affecting the face or feet.

The fact must be emphasized that both water-cooled and air-cooled stationary engines are useless for winter flying North Russia. It was found practically impossible to get these to function at all.

On the other hand, rotary engines proved serviceable even in the extremes cold, though many precautions had to be taken, such as keeping the engine always warm by means of six or eight flameless lamps and thick padded engine covers, and heating the oil before use.

The North Russian country is of a very difficult nature, and few natural landing grounds exist. These were found along the banks of the Dvina river. A forced landing when flying across country is almost certain to mean a bad crash and, at the best, the loss of a machine. Even if the crash should not be very serious, extreme difficulty is experienced in rendering assistance, owing to inaccessibility. Any machine forced to land in swamp or forest was seldom, if at all, be salved.

Even with a compass it is extremely difficult to keep direction in these forests, and going was very slow. Should both pilot and observer be injured on crashing in the forest, the chances of their being saved were nil. Even if only one of the occupants was injured, the chances of rescuing him in time, during the winter, were exceedingly small, as the temperature at night frequently exceeds -60° (Fahr.) of frost. Apart from. this, the relief party would, in all probability, be unable to find the machine. The lack of daylight was extreme. Out of 24 hours, the following was the number of hours that it was possible to read with natural light:

December:	4 hrs
January:	7 hrs
February:	10 hrs
March:	13 hrs

In May and June, the natural lighting was 21-24 hours!

A very dispersed distribution of artillery was necessary for the defense of flanks and rear communications.

Any artillery heavier than field guns was transported only by rail or river. The howitzer was the principal weapon for this country, and longer range field guns than the old pattern 18-pdr.

Very special attention to cooperation of artillery with R.A.F. and infantry was necessary. Circumstances for the employment of particular natures of ammunition were carefully considered.

Distribution: On all fronts it was frequently found necessary to have guns in action at selected places on the lines of communication to deal with enemy raids, which have sometimes penetrated as far as 60 versts behind the front positions.

Employment of Artillery: For defensive warfare 4.5-inch howitzers, using 106 fuses, were of the greatest service, and in conjunction with a few Mark IV. 18-pdrs. were all that was required. The older patterns of 18-pdr. have been outranged throughout the winter. For offensive columns operating on the flank or in rear of the enemy the ideal weapon was the 3.7-inch mountain howitzer.

Guns *v.* Howitzers: On all fronts howitzers proved themselves invaluable, while guns have frequently been useless, particularly when the only positions available were on roads. At times the guns had to be withdrawn as much as 2,000 yards to enable them to fire in order to clear the woods in front. The three types of howitzers required are:

3.7-inch Q.F. mountain howitzer. 4.5-inch Q.F. howitzer. 6-inch 26-cwt. howitzer.

Positions: In selecting defensive positions infantry commanders must bear in mind the possibility of observation for artillery, and if necessary arrange for an escort for forward observation officers and for the protection of the observation post. Villages were selected frequently for defensive localities, and are unsuitable for artillery positions owing to the amount of fire they draw and the limited field of fire they allow.

The provision of an escort for the guns was often neglected.

Infantry commanders should be exactly acquainted with the fire capacity of their defense guns, so that they may arrange to cover dead ground with machine gun fire. Where infantry hold isolated posts their moral was greatly increased by their witnessing artillery registration.

The position of artillery in action automatically provides a secondary position for the infantry.

On occasion special defensive measures must be taken for the protection of horses.

Observation: Observation was very difficult owing to the flatness of the country and to its being heavily wooded, and also to the breadth of front to be covered. Hence it was essential that the infantry should have the training and facilities to enable them to assist in observation and to communicate promptly with the artillery, and also that every possible means should be employed to perfect co-operation between R.A.F. and artillery. Ground observers, either infantry or artillery, must also co-operate with the Royal Navy, whose experience of land shooting is limited, particularly from under cover.

Communications and Ammunition Reserves: The formidable difficulties of transport during the spring thaw and at the commencement of winter necessitate the maintenance at points near the front of very large reserves of guns and ammunition compared with the amount of actual shooting done.

Ammunition:

Gas: Gas shell was used only as a weapon of retaliation, and only employed with good effect during the summer.

Smoke: Smoke shell is valuable for all guns, especially for the 18-pdr. when shooting for airplane registration, as the burst of other types is difficult to observe against snow backgrounds or in woods.

Incendiary: The value of incendiary shell is in defensive action, as it forces the enemy to retire and deprives him of jumping-off places, since it destroys the only accommodation for personnel.

Organization. The battery must have such organization and establishment as will permit each of its sections to act as an independent fighting unit and to provide itself with a small escort. It requires, therefore, a proportionately large number of officers, signalers, and other specialists, and at least two Lewis guns per section.

The following are the principal factors, which affect the technical side of Artillery:—
Cold.—Its effect on a) Gunnery, (b) Ammunition, (c) Mechanism.

British

13-pdr. of 9-cwt. A.A.-	This gun was mounted on railway mountings. It can only be used from a boat or from a railway truck.
18-pdr. Q.F.-	This gun was thoroughly reliable. Its main disadvantages lie in its being too heavy for easy transport and its limited range in the absence of air recuperators, 7,200 yards being the maximum ever obtained during really cold weather. The springs worked well.
60-pdr. B.L.-	On land or railway mountings, the long range of this gun made it of great value; but on the river front, where extreme elevations were required, it was found that even comparatively new springs failed to return the gun to its correct firing position.
2. 75-inch B.L.-	One section, armed with this equipment, was in action throughout the winter, and did excellent work; but the gun suffers from the disadvantages of low trajectory, already alluded to. Draught attachments and a large reserve of spare breech blocks are required.
3. 7-inch Q.F. Howitzer-	This was ideal for the country.
4.5-inch QF. Howitzer-	The most useful defensive gun in use in North Russia. Its value was enormously increased by the addition of an extra charge, giving a further 1,500 yards range. This bears out the experience gained on the front in France.
6-inch 26-cwt.- Howitzer	Four of these howitzers were satisfactorily employed, two of them mounted on railway truck and two on barges. The guns were kept on their own wheels.

French

75-mm. Field- 155-mm. Howitzer	The 75-mm. field gun and the 155-mm. St. Chamond howitzer have been continually employed North Russia.

The use of French material presented very serious administrative difficulties, which were never satisfactorily overcome, and which point to the inadvisability of employing this armament in a country where ordnance services are under British control alone. These difficulties fall under the following main headings: the supply of ammunition, buffer oil, and spare parts, the repair of guns.

In any case, the 75-mm. field gun was quite unsuited for work in this climate owing to the inability of the buffers' to stand the cold weather. Seven buffers out of twenty became unserviceable during a period of two months. In addition it may be remarked that no French officer or N.C.O. was able or was authorized to repair these buffers. Apart from the disadvantages mentioned above, the 155-mm. howitzer proved satisfactory.

Russian

3-inch Naval Howitzer- This weapon, on pivot mountings, with a range of 5,000 yards, did excellent work, being employed for all-round fire from boats and armored trucks.

3-mch Field Gun- This equipment was used with good results, and but for lack of ammunition and spare parts, could have been permanently employed. It is a lighter gun than the British 18-pdr., which it has outranged here.

The guns mentioned below, although of no great value and meriting no special comment, were made use of during the winter months, when the situation was at times serious and no other armament was available. All were on pedestal mountings, except the British 8-inch howitzer and the Italian 4.2-line gun, and like other naval guns, were unsuitable for land work, in spite their long range, owing to the effect of their shell-bursts being minimized by the nature of the fuse and target.

8-inch Howitzer- (British) No ammunition was available. In any case the gun is too heavy for use in this type of country.

6-inch Naval Gun-

47mm Naval, 57mm Naval, and 75mm Naval all used on armor trains.

76 • 5-mm. Naval- (Austrian) This gun worked well itself, but the ammunition found here proved very inferior.

42-line (105-mm.)- (Italian) Four complete batteries in cases, consigned to Roumania, were salved here. These were extremely well equipped and fitted, but were never used, as no ammunition was available. The employment of these guns, in spite of their range of 13,000 yards, was not recommended owing to the weight and size of the piece and carriage and the smallness of the projectile.

Lewis guns- These, with trained detachments, were essential. At least two are required for each section, operating as a separate unit.

Shell Proportions-	For each 18-pdr. Q.F: 50 percent. H.E., 50 percent shrapnel. For each 60-pdr. B.L.: 60 percent. H.E., 40 percent shrapnel. For each 2.75-inch. B.L., 50 percent H.E., 50 percent shrapnel.
Smoke-	This was supplied for all guns for ranging purposes. Chemical.—This was only of use in summer. The proportion of supply should be: 50 percent persistent, such as B.B. 50 percent non-persistent, such as C.Gr.

The French guns, the long I.A. (itnstantanee allongee), corresponding to the British 106, were found satisfactory, if kept free from damp. The " Fusee courte sans retard" has also proved satisfactory. The French artillery authorities recommended that the 24/31 LD 1917 model should be supplied for use with the 155 mm. howitzer, and the 24/31 1916 model for use with the 75-mm. field gun. These are both T and P fuses.

E- Gun Pits
These were built on the same plan as in France with slightly larger accommodation for ammunition. They were constructed on the same principle as Russian houses, which were warm and free from draughts. They were shell proof against Russian 3-inch field gun. They were also provided with a large stove.
Five hundred rounds of ammunition were kept in the pit or in some warm store close by.
Outside each pit was a wooden platform with a circular trail-arc, from which the gun can fire in all directions, with a wooden ramp to run the gun out from the pit.
Three hundred yards clear field of fire and barbed wire entanglements were necessary around all positions.
Rifles, bombs, reserve rations, and water were also kept in each position, together with Lewis guns and ammunition.

Shooting

18-pdr. Q.F.-	After all weather conditions had been allowed for during the cold season, a further average addition of 300 to 400 yards had to be made at ranges of from 3,500 to 4,500 yards. With T and P fuse 80 (Iron), an extra 8 to 10 points was deducted from the corrector.
French Guns-	The French artillery reported that during the winter the guns were shooting 20 per cent. short of range. Of this loss the muzzle velocity, one half could only be accounted for by the abnormal climatic conditions, range-table corrections accounting for the other half.
Telephones-	D I11 telephones proved satisfactory. Four were issued per section.
Wireless-	A special allotment of wireless masts for artillery was not found to be necessary.

Transport

Guns were moved on their wheels on ordinary roads, until the snow was very heavy, i.e., halfway through December.

Ammunition wagons were not required.

Twenty 18-pdr. shells or 400 Ibs. could be carried on the local carts in summer) and forty 18-pdr. shells or 800 Ibs. on the local sleighs in winter.

No other transport was available throughout the winter for the carriage of ammunition, baggage, and rations, but local transport.

It may be taken as a general rule that guns can in winter keep up an average rate of movement of 20 versts (12 miles) per day.

Movement of Guns

Field Guns- The following were the methods used:

The gun was moved on its own wheels until about halfway through December, when the snow became too deep.

The limber was allowed to run on its own wheels with ordinary pole-draught, while the gun wheels were placed upon broad steel runners, 5 feet 6 inches in length and 9 inches in breadth.

The disadvantages of this method lay in the fact that the track made was much broader than that of the ordinary convoy sleigh, with the result that the gun was very heavy to.pull.

The gun was run muzzle first on to a sleigh, with the wheels resting on two strong boards laid transversely across it, while the spade was supported on a bob-sleigli behind.

The local pattern of sleigh is suitable for this method, but requires strengthening.

Machine Guns

Technical- Four guns have been used as follows:

(1) Vickers
(2) Colt
(3) Lewis
(4) Chouchat

The first three are the Russian 7 '62 pattern, and the last is the ordinary French bore.

1. The Vickers Guns.—Similar to the '303 gun, except for the bore, which necessitates alteration in the extractor and feed block; the barrel; the muzzle attachment; attachment of steam tube.

(a) The efficiency of the gun is considerably detracted from by the alteration to the extractor owing to its weakened condition and the large number of breakage resulting. The same lock is used in both the 7 ' 62-mm. and the ' 303 gun, though the 7 '62 bullet is smaller than the '303, though its case is larger, and in order to take the base on the face of the extractor the extractor guide grooves have had to be made thinner and to a dangerous degree. A slight fault in the feed from any cause is apt to break off the top half inch of the right extractor guide groove, and a very large number have been broken in this way.
The steam tube in the '303 gun is screwed on, whereas the 7'62 gun's tube is attached by a clip. The former is the best.

> The gun is made in America, and is generally of inferior make to the '303 gun made by Vickers, Ltd., in England. It becomes unserviceable far quicker than the '303 gun, and is subject to numerous breakage of parts owing to indifferent manufacture.

2. The Colt Gun- The 1914 pattern gun was used. The gun worked satisfactorily, but has one very great fault in extreme cold, and that is the impossibility to remedy a bad stoppage should one occur. The openings in the gun are very small, and in the case of a stoppage, in most cases it is necessary to strip the gun as there is not room. To put in one's fingers or an implement to get at the cause of the stoppage. This is impossible to do in a reasonable time in the intense cold, when men cannot touch the metal without gloves.

3. The Lewis Gun- Except for the bore, identical with the '303 gun, and has been very satisfactory.

4. The Chouchat Gun- An automatic rifle, which cannot be compared with the Lewis gun, though it has done good work.

(b) One of the greatest' difficulties with the use of machine guns in the winter in Northern Russia has been the extreme cold. The difficulty was met with in four ways:
 (1) Slowness in handling the guns owing to the necessity of always using very thick gloves—two or more pairs at times.
 (2) Freezing of lubricating oil.
 (3) Freezing of water.
 (4) Brittleness of springs.

The first difficulty could only be met with by continual practice in repairs and adjustments while using thick groves.

The second—freezing of the lubricating oil—was eventually overcome by the use of the following mixture:

Half turpentine. Half lubricating nil *G.S.* (special non-freezing oil.)

This mixture, after a long series of tests in other proportions and with different mixtures was found to withstand the greatest cold experienced, i.e., between -75 and -80 Fahrenheit. The ordinary oil froze immediately. On one occasion the Lewis gun was being fired, and the order to cease fire and advance was given; the firer ran about 50 yards and then, on trying to fire, found his gun was frozen. On another, a Vickers gun being kept in all oil in order to prevent freezing was brought into action. Very shortly, owing to friction, it became necessary to oil slightly and fire was ceased soon after. On testing the gun a few minutes later it was immovable and quite frozen up. It eventually had to be thawed with boiling water before being stripped!

The third difficulty—freezing of the water—only affected the Vickers gun. Several different experiments and tests were carried out in the endeavor to discover a satisfactory solution to this difficulty. The ordinary mixtures of water and glycerin were useless and froze at once; boiling water put in the gun under cover froze solid in a few minutes. Other mixtures were tried. A hole was cut in the barrel casing through which to put snow.Eventually, a mixture of two parts glycerin, one part water was found to be satisfactory and never froze. Only five pints were used in the barrel casing.

Heavy Guns-	1. Heavy artillery can only be moved by road in winter; in summer it is impossible 2. In winter the following methods were employed:
155-mm. Howitzer-	One of these guns was moved with difficulty, over a good road, with a IO-horse team
60-pr. B.L.-	Three 60-prs. covered a distance of 120 miles in from 10 to 12 days, over bad roads with many inclines, under the following con ditions: The guns were each dismounted, and the parts transported on separate vehicles variously horsed: The piece on one IO-horsed sleigh. The trail and carriage, one IO-horsed sleigh. The buffer on one 6-horsed sleigh. Each wheel on one 4-horsed sleigh.

In the case of each of the first two guns to be moved a special type of steel sleigh was constructed for the transportation of the piece. In this the front and rear runners constituted separate vehicles, which were connected by crossed chains, and between which the piece was slung from the superstructure. The sleighs, upon which the trails were carried, were of the same type, with front and rear runners connected by chains; in this case, however, wood reinforced with steel was -used for their construction.

6-inch Russian- Naval Gun	Three of these guns, removed from their coast defense mountings, were transported by local civilian transport without military assistance over a distance of 30 miles in winter ; the weight of each piece was 6 tons. They were subsequently put on railway mountings, iron-sided coal wagons being used. Satisfactory pedestal mountings were made in the Russian shipyards under Russian naval supervision. In order to employ the guns against Emtsa, for which a range of 13,000 yards was necessary, the mountings were constructed on an inclined plane to allow of the necessary elevation.
47-mm. Naval Gun-	For a special operation, where forest trails alone were available, one of these guns was mounted on a narrow steel sleigh, from which it could fire without moving appreciably. The sleigh was transported by two horses, harnessed in tandem, and could be moved at a trot. This constituted the only horse artillery in the country.

Bullet Penetrations

Experimentation provided the following results of various defensive positions using a Russian rifle:

Cut Timber	4ft.4 inches penetration
Poles (4-6 inches dia)	2 ft 8 inches
Logs (8-12 inches dia)	1 ft 8 inches
Sand between one inch planking	8 inches

Trains

Archangel seemed to be a hub for the railroad. Upon the arrival of the Allies, the engineers found some 60 engines. Of the 60, 48 were built between 1896 and 1907. Ten were built in 1868, two others, were modern. Eighteen engines could not be repaired.

Transport

What supplies could not go up river, would be carried by hired peasants.The general scheme was that convoys were found by villagers which reported to the issuing depot and under a lead man, they selected, were loaded and dispatched. The head man was given a convoy card showing what was in the convoy. Once the convoy reached the destination, the head man was then paid at the rate of seven kopecks per verst per pood or 2s.7d. per ton per mile. The losses were minimal and the system worked. The convoys moved at their own pace, usually stopping every 10 to 27 miles at a rest house for five hours. Thus, on average a convoy could cover 25-40 miles in 24 hours. During the thaw which begins in April, what normally takes a convoy to travel 60-75 miles in 5 days, would now take 12 days.

Between Dec 1918 and April 1919, the following tonnage was carried:

Bakharitsa-Onega	120 mile	220 ton
" " -Kholmogory	40 mile	1500 ton
Kholmogory –Beresnik	50 mile	1000 ton
Sleighs used:	28,209	
Transport cost:	£82,200	
Beresnik –Shenkurk	60 miles	2600 ton
Sleighs used:	7209	
Cost:	£5500	
Oberskaya-Seletskoe	45 miles	1100 ton
" " Chekuevo	45 miles	500 ton
Sleighs used:	7139	
Cost:	£14000	

Artillery employed in North Russia comprised the following types of guns:

British:	60 pdr., 18 pdr., 13 pdr. AA, 2.75", 6 pdr, 8," 6," 4.5," 3.7."
French:	105mm (no ammo,never used) 75mm,155mm
Italian:	105mm (no ammo, never used)
Russian:	120mm, 3," 75mm, 47mm,37mm
Austrian:	76.5mm

Medical Conditions

Fighting in the North Russian environment was harsh. Death came quickly during the winter. There was only one hospital in Archangel, this was No.53 and contained 633 beds. To augment this, the French hospital ship, KALYAN arrived, adding another 756 beds. Near the front to cope with emergencies and wounds, small units were created. These contained between 5 to 100 beds. There was also a 100 bed hospital at Yemetskoe.

The common diseases found there were Scurvy among the POWs, Typhus and Typhoid. Both reached epidemic proportions. Diarrhea was common due to Flexner's bacteria among the U.S. troops or others that neglected sanitary precautions. Small pox was a constant, sporadic problem.

Sanitation and health always go hand and hand, and due to the raw sewage that polluted the Dvina River, health was always at risk. Water is obtained from the well or river directly. The Allies set up 135 gallon drums of water each used for chlorinating and storing good water.

Minor Matters

Archangel had no banks, thus, everyone and soldiers was paid in cash. There were four types of Russian:

1. The old Czarist money
2. The new money
3. The old roubles that had varied exchange rates
4. The new roubles that a fixed rate.

To further complicate matters, the new roubles looked very similar to the old ones. Allied troops were paid with roubles.

Women

Women were used as laborers extensively due to a shortage of men. They outperformed the men in the light duties but also in coaling, heavy lifting, etc.

Mail

Rain, shine or snow, the mail was received and sent on a regular basis. The average times between the arrival of a ship in port and delivery of mail at the railroad front was 30 hours, on the Dvina and Vaga River areas, 60 hours. During the winter, mail dispatched from Archangel to the railroad front took one day, to the Dvina/Vaga river, 5 days.

The British view of the North Russian was amazingly low. This attitude permeates all their writings and reports, insinuating that they were superior to all, including their allies. To illustrate, here is a typical opinion included in a report written by Major Leslie Bunce:

"As far as the Russian element is concerned, they are lazy, stupid, indolent, pleasure loving and seeking, and if it was not for the large number of Finns and Letts, no work where even the least amount of brain is required could be undertaken owing to their lack of education and want of intellect."

It was little wonder that the Russians hated the British and preferred the French and Americans, who developed a true friendship with the Russian peasant.

Military Lessons

The war in North Russia was the first battle conducted in the Arctic environment. It was also a war with scattered fronts, long lines of communications and advances using river flotillas. The lessons of the 1918 Dvina River expedition were as follows:

1. Very great importance on the close cooperation between the Naval and Military commands.
2. The need for an adequate Naval Staff owing to the peculiar conditions of the expedition.
3. The necessity of clearly defined orders for the strategic employment and allocation of aircraft. No independent air command unless sufficient airplanes exist.
4. A highly organized communications system and defined military and naval procedures in signaling.
5. The need to properly organize water transport service so that the fighting commands are free of this worry and concern.
6. Define responsibilities in the evacuation of personnel.

The following signaling equipment were sent to Archangel:

Flotilla River Command to Archangel:	600 spark wavelength
Brigade HQ to Archangel:	1600 or 2100 CW
Battalion HQ to Brigade HQ:	200-300 CW
Flotilla and spotting aircraft to HQ:	220 spark
Seaplane Barges:	600 spark

All ships in the flotilla had a receiving set for aerial spotting. Certain ships had sending and receiving CW. Telephones were used wherever possible.

Order of Battle for the North Russian Expeditionary Force

Syren Force (Murmansk)
Elope Force (Archangel)
Royal Artillery HQ (Seletskoe)
- 6th Artillery Brigade
- 420th Artillery Battery
- 434th Artillery Battery
- 435th Artillery Battery
- 1203rd Artillery Battery

252nd Machine Gun Company
HQ Vaga Column
HQ River Column (Dvina)
2nd Line/10th Battalion/Royal Scottish Regiment
17th Bn/The Kings Liverpool Regiment
9th Bn/Gurkha Rifles
2nd Line/7th Battalion/Durham Light Infantry Regiment.
1st Battalion/East Surrey Regiment
No.1 Special Company/Middlesex regiment
No.1 Special Company/60th Rifles

236th Infantry Brigade
- 11th Bn/Royal Sussex Regiment
- 6th Bn/ Yorkshire Regiment
- 236th Trench Mortar Battery
- 280th Machine Gun Company
- 492nd Engineer Company

237th Infantry Brigade
- 13th Bn/Yorkshire Regiment
- 237th Trench Mortar Battery
- 253rd Machine Gun Company

General Grogan's Brigade(238th Brigade)
- 2nd Bn/Hampshire Regiment
- 1st Bn/Oxs & Bucks Light Infantry Regiment
- 55th Artillery Battery
- 238th Lt. Trench Mortar Battery
- 239th Lt. Trench Mortar Battery
- 238th Signal Company
- 384th Engineer Company
- 8th Machine Gun Battalion
- 1152nd Supply Company

Campion Battery
Royal Engineers
548th Engineer Company
Garrisons
Kola
Petchanga
Kem
Soroka

Sadlier-Jackson's Brigade

45th Bn/Royal Fusiliers Regiment
46th Bn/Royal Fusiliers Regiment
385th Engineer Company
1153rd Supply Company
201st Special Machine Gun Company

393rd Supply Depot Unit
394th Supply Depot Unit
400th Supply Depot Unit

Naval

HMS Glory (BB)
HMS Cyclops
HMS Fox
HMS Humber (Gunboat)
HMS Cicala (Gunboat)
HMSLadybird (Gunboat)
HMS Cricket (Gunboat)
HMS Cockshafer (Gunboat)
HMS Glow-worm (Gunboat)
HMS Argus (CV)
HMS Pegasus (CV)
HMS Nairana (CV)
HMS Wargrange
HMS Monitor 33,25,31, 27,29
HMS MorrisDance (minesweeper)
HMS Swordance (minesweeper)
HMS Fandango (minesweeper)
HMS Stepdance (minesweeper)

Canadian

16th Artillery brigade (67th and 68th batteries)

French

21st Colonial Bn
French Foreign Legion
CA Amiral Gueyon
63rd Artillery battery

American

339th Regiment/85th Division
310th Engineer Bn
337th Medical Company

Endnote:

In a secret memo written in May 1919, the following observations were made:

> "Since the withdrawal of German troops from Finland, there is no serious threat. Any danger of attack has been greatly exagerrated. Having commited ourselves to the policy of intervention and the prop of the Provisional Government against Bolshevik aggression, a premature withdrawal would mean disaster to those we have befriended."

The rest is the history of the Communist era until its collapse in 1991.

South Russia

9

The Volunteer Army Rises from the Ashes of Imperialism in South Russia

In South Russia, the only allied influence came from the British and French. Both had their own interests at stake. For France, the general position was economic recovery from millions lost when the Bolshevik revolution took over their interests. For England, it was a more lofty embryonic notion of destroying Bolshevism (i.e., communisim), and securing the economic riches of the oil fields in the Trans Caucasus. However, like in North Russia, the War Cabinet in London and Parliment were both determined to remain indecisive. The support ran hot and cold, depending on the success of the forces opposing the Red Armies. Ultimately, this is how policy and military plans were determined and actions restricted. This similar situation would occur to the Americans in Vietnam some 45 years later.

In December 1917, a decision was made between Lord Milner and Clemenceau to secure South Russia from the turmoil. In the agreement, the British were to defend the Cossack territories and Caucasus, while the French were to do the same over Bessarabia, Crimea and Ukraine. This agreement was to prevent the German seizure of the grain and oil there, to protect the Naval bases at Batum, and allow the Allies to blockade the Black Sea. The impetus for this Allied intervention was the infamous treaty of Brest-Litovsk between Russia and Germany. This treaty gave the German forces a position of overwhelming economic control in the Ukraine.

In January 1918, the British issued a very secret request for volunteers to serve in an "unnamed" theatre of operations. The request went out to units on the Western front. The appeal would be cryptic, never indicating what or where the duty was. All selected volunteers were told virtually nothing except they would be taken to London. To the surprise of the British generals, the response was higher than needed. By mid January, some 300 officers and NCO's had been selected and waiting. The purpose of this force was to insure that the Turkish/German forces would not threaten the Indian border or seize the rich oil fields. This was indeed a real threat, as German authorities were negotiating with Transcaucasian authorities for the oil, cotton and maganese.

These troops left London on January, 29th, and arrived at Basra, Iraq, on March 2nd. From there, they moved up river to Baghdad. By Summer, it was designated as "Dunsterforce." Without waiting for the 300 additional volunteers marching to join Dunsterforce, the British moved to take Enzeli. While enroute, at Kasvin, the former Imperial Army Russian units under Bicherakov joined with his 1200 men (which were still an effective fighting unit) for a price in British pounds. By June 15th, Dunsterforce and the 300 men sent to reinforce it had finally united at Enzeli. While the British had reached Enzeli, a small German force reached Tiflis. Armed with the success, the British 39th Brigade comprised of :

7th bn/Gloucestershire (568 men), 9th bn/Worcestshire (678 men), 7th bn/North Staffordshire (526 men), 39th Machine Gun Company (140 men), 39th Supply Company.

The brigade had around 2000 men, attached to the unit was the 15th Light Armor Mobile battery, 1 section of the 8th artillery battery, and 2 sections of the 44th artillery battery.

As this intervention moved further and further into the Russian Civil War, far to the west, the German 45th division entered Kharkov on April 10th, 1918. The French press went into an uproar concerning the French inaction to oppose the Germans. The Germans were seizing vast amounts of territory without any opposition. The French were paralyzed as to what to do and what could be done. It was all a political "hot tomato" and this froze any military action. Thus, the Germans continued thier march and by May, 12th, had begun to occupy the Don River basin area with the 7th and 16th divisions, while the 2nd Cavalry division arrived at Rostov and Millerovo. Soon, it was rightfully feared, the Germans would be sending home the coal, iron, and grains the from the area. Yet, the French continued to be indecisive and unresponsive in supporting initiatives to oppose this. Developing at this time

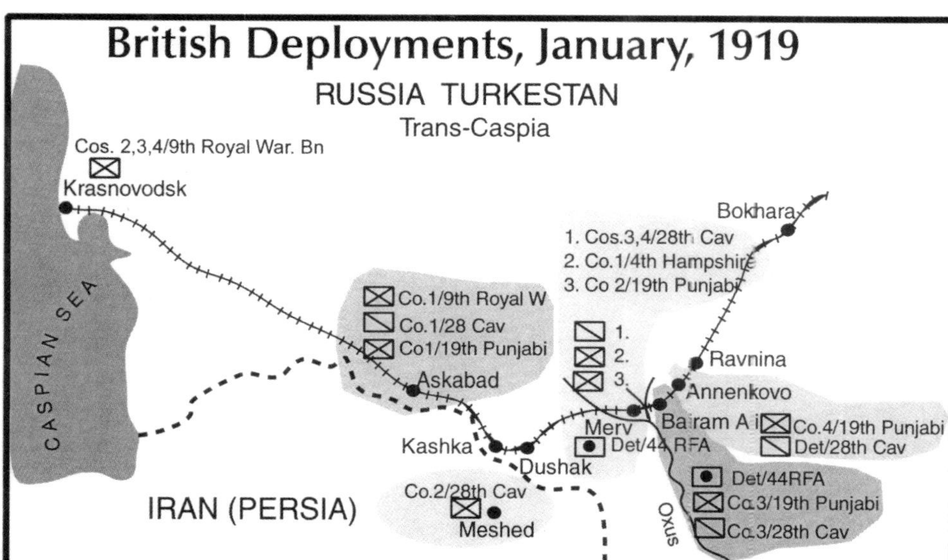

was the embryonic Volunteer army, created by former Imperial Russian General Alekseev in February, 1918. He and many officers opposed the Bolshevik revolution. The French balked at giving aid to the fledging army for some time, but finally sent 10 million roubles (funding for six weeks). The Volunteer Army in February, 1918, consisted of:

The Officers' Regiment (800 men, Gen. Markov)
Kornilovsky Shock Regiment
Partisan Regiment
Special Training Battalion
1st and 2nd Cavalry Detachments
Two artillery batteries

The best troops of the Volunteer Army were its shock troops. The shock units recruited from a pool of experienced combat veterans before they were reassigned to the front or released from duty. Shock units were based on the German Stormtrooper units methodology (i.e., units trained in assault tactics with extra assault weapons). Kornilov initiated their use in the Russia's Army. The common denominators in all the battles occurring in South Russia were the following units. These would be his "SS"—Denikin's most loyal and ardent followers. One British advisor noted that they were equal in all qualities to the British soldier, first class.

*****

Denikin's Shock Troops

- The most famous of the shock units was the *Kornilov division*, starting its history in May 1917 by order of the Commander of the 8th Army of the South-West Front, Lieutenant-General L.G. Kornilov, to General Staff Captain M.O. Nezhentsev, for the creation of the 1st Shock Detachment in the 8th Army (renamed later the Kornilov Shock Detachment) made from volunteers - nationalistic and patriotic officers, non-commissioned officers and soldiers. This detachment took action at the front in the June offensive and rushed to prove themselves to the Russian Army as one of the most elite military units. By August, the detachment was re-formed into a three-battalion Kornilov Shock Regiment. On September 10, the regiment was renamed to the 1st Russian Shock, and then on the 30th to the Slavic Shock. In August, 1919, the regiment reformed into two, 1st and 2nd Officer General Markov Regiments and in October the 3rd Regiment was formed.

- The *Alekseev* division was in honor of the patron name General of Infantry M.V. Alekseev. At first it was a Partisan Foot Cossack Regiment, formed in Stanitsa Olginskoy in February 1918, from Don foot partisan unit. Its first commander was Brigadier-General A.P. Bogaevsky. The Regiment participated in the "1st Kuban Ice Campaign and after joined the Volunteer Army with the forces of the Kuban Rada (Government). The regiment by now was under the command Brigadier-General B.I. Kazanov. It was placed in the 2nd Independent Infantry Brigade of General Bogaevsky. They actively participated in battles. After Ekaterindar, they returned to the Don. The Volunteers reorganized before the 2nd Kuban Campaign at the end of May. In June, the regiment then commanded by Colonel P.K. Pisarev, went into the composition of the 2nd Infantry Division of General A.A. Borovsky. In the second half of October it was temporarily commanded by Colonel E.I. Emelyanovs, then after December 1918, Colonel P.K. Pisarev, and in January 1919 by Colonel Duke Gagarin.

Following the death of General M.V. Alekseev in September 1918, the Regiment in November was renamed the *General Alekseev Partisan Infantry* and in November because of heavy losses it withdrew to Novorossik. About this time (December) the Alekseev artillery unit made its first appearance. The 2nd battery of the 2nd of Light Artillery battalion (two batteries) was renamed in 2nd General Alekseev Battery.

In January 1919, the regiment was transferred over to the Donets Basin, where it conducted battles to April, whereupon it participated in the Volunteer's offensive Northward. In October 1919, the command was issued for the development of the regiment into the 1st and 2nd General Alekseev Partisan Infantry Regiments. The order was issued to form the Partisan General Alekseev Infantry (Alekseev Infantry) Division with the following composition:

Headquarters, 1st and 2nd Partisan General Alekseev Infantry Regiments (3rd Regiment was to be formed afterwards on special order, but this remained a project). The Alekseev Artillery Brigade had a Headquarters, 1st (1st General Alekseev Light and 2nd Batteries), 2nd (3rd and 4th batteries) and 4th (7th and 8th Batteries) artillery battalions, one company of engineers and a reserve battalion, also attached was the Samorsk Infantry Regiment plus a division from the 5th Cavalry Corps.

The commander of the Armed Forces of South Russia, General Denikin, 1919.

This is one of five postage stamps created in 1919 under General Denikin's control of South Russia. What is amazing is that Denikin even bothered with this minor matter. Of course, it was only required for mail within his controlled territory.

- The *Markov* unit was another elite unit composite-officers regiment formed on February 12, 1918, in stanitsa Olginskoy with the 1st, 2nd and 3rd Officer battalions, naval company and a Demi-regiment from the Death Division of Caucasian Cavalry. The regiment was put together by the officers-volunteers arriving in Novocherkassk and to Rostov-to the-Don. The Commander appointed from his General Staff the Lieutenant-General S.L. Markov. In the time of the 1st Kuban Campaign the regiment began to be called Officer Regiment; following the campaign it was commanded by Brigadier-General A.A. Borovski. During the reorganization of the Volunteer Army in May 17 the regiment was named 1st Officer and went into General Markov's 1st Division. Thus, by September, 1919, The Markov division consisted of:
  divisional HQ, 1st, 2ndand 3rd General Markov Infantry Regiments, Markov Artillery Brigade (Headquarters, 1st, 2nd, 3rd and 4th(howitzer) battalions), separate General Markov Engineers Company, Independent General Markov Cavalry Demi-regiment and a reserve battalion.

- The *Drozdovsky* division was the name for the officers and other ranks of a diverse military unit accorded the honor of Brigadier-General M.G. Drozdovsky. Toward the end of 1917, in the Romanian lines, he started forming three detachments of Russian volunteer brigades to fight against the Bolsheviks. Its first Commander was General Staff Colonel M.G. Drozdovsky. In February 1918, following a command to disband the volunteer units, Drozdovsky refused and in February, 1918, at the head of this brigade, with some other small units trailing with it, came forward from Town of Yassas to the Don, to join the Volunteer army. Detachment Drozdovsky brought over units of all of armies (except of aviation) elements and counted 667 officers, 370 soldiers, 14 doctors, priests and officials and 12 nurses. After a 61-day march, walking for 1200 verst (600 mile) detachments of M.G. Drozdovsky arrived to the Don where they gave essential help to Don Cossacks in rebelling against the Bolsheviks.
  The Drozdovsky joined the Volunteer Army and became its 3rd Division, to be commanded by the then Colonel Drozdovsky. The division participated in 2nd Kuban March and in battles for Stavrpol and Armavip in the fall of 1918, where Drozdovsky was killed. The 2nd Officer Rifle Regiment appeared first in the main body of the 3rd Division of M.G. Drozdovsky when it transferred in December 1918 to the Don Basin. In

January 1919, it was under the command of the HQ Armed Forces of South Russia and was renamed the 2nd Officer General Drozdovsky Rifle Regiment.
After completion of operations in Don basin, they went out on the Ukraine and Kharkov region in August 1919, and the regiment was divided into two units, the 2nd and 4th Officer General Drozdovsky Rifle Regiments. These were both formed into the Officer General Drozdovsky Rifle Brigade commanded by Brigadier-General K. Kelner. In September, the 4th Officer General Drozdovsky Rifle Regiment was renamed to the 2nd, and former 2nd to the 1st. After Kharkov fell the 3rd Officer General Drozdovsky Rifle Regiment was formed and was included in the composition of the AFSR's 3rd Infantry Division. In October, the division was renamed to the *Officer General Drozdovsky Rifle Division.*

- The *2nd General Drozdovsky Horse Regiment*, which started its beginning as a squadron, was formed by Rotmister B.A. Gaevsk in Yassa. After joining with the Horse-pioneer Squadron of Rotmister Dvoychenko in March 1918 at Dobossarakh, it was formed into a Horse Demi-regiment (2 squadrons) under Gaevsk's command. In late April at Novocherkassk this Demi-regiment expanded to a Horse Regiment (4 squadron, HQ, horse machine-gun company and field engineers). By June, it was under Denikin's command and renamed to the *2nd Horse Regiment*, participating in 2nd Kuban march. The number of squadrons permanently grew and by August the unit had nine companies. By June, 1919, the regiment became an Independent Cavalry-brigade of the 4th Infantry Division and was under the command of Colonel I.G. Barbov, participating in the liquidation of Red Partisan in the Kerch Quarries. After going to the

A typical White Cossack soldier, Gen. Balakhovich, in 1919. Photo: Museum of Russian Army, Moscow

Crimea, the brigade was re-formed into the *2nd Cavalry Division* by adding a Compos ite 2nd Brigade and 2nd Horse Regiment. In July, the regiment was transferred to Colonel A.G. Shapron Du Larre, and under his command he captured the Station of Bakhmach and after moved in the direction Cheringov to Kiev. In October, the regiment was granted the honor of patronage to Brigadier-General Drozdovsky, and it was named the *2nd General Drozdovsky Horse Regiment.*

In February 1918 white forces in the Kuban area were under pressure from superior Bolshevik forces moving into the city of Ekaterindar. These forces came forward to join the Volunteer Army under General L.G. Kornilov. All of the Kuban Horse Cossack units were formed into a *Kuban Cossack Regiment* (800 men).

During March in the Stanitsa of Novo-Dmitriev, the Military Government and Commander of the Volunteer army reached an agreement allowing some of the Kuban units to join. A large cavalry force in March was subsequently put together with a reformed Kuban Horse Demi-regiment (horse detachments of General Staff Colonels Koznetsov and Demyannika and a cavalry detachment from Colonel S.G. Olaga), which was to be commanded by Colonel G.Y. Kosinov. This Demi-regiment was expanded into the *1st Kuban Horse Regiment* of the *Independent Horse Brigade* under the General of Cavalry I.G. Erdeli. This was the first to be formed in the Volunteer army but created with Cossacks of diverse detachments of Kuban Cossacks.

- *The 1st Kuban Horse Regiment* participated in the 1st Kuban Ice march. After this was finished the army was reorganized. In June, Order No 313 was issued and *the Independent Cavalry brigade*, who then was commanded by Cavalry General A.M. Dragomirov, was expanded into the *1st Horse Division.* The *1st Kuban Cossacks Regiment* was part of the *1st brigade.* At that time, the regiment had 510 sabers and 20 non-combatants with an attached 4 machine-guns.

In June, the Volunteers drove forward and in the 2nd Kuban march occupied in August, the city of Ekaterindar. The first to enter were hundreds from the 1st Kuban Cossack Regiment under the command General Staff Colonel V.G. Naomenko.. After Stavorpol's capture by the partisan Colonel A.G. Shkuro, they began to reform in the territory of the Labinsky area. (Note: There was also the 1st Kuban Regiment under command of Lieutenant Colonel M.A. Fostikov also in the Volunteer army, they both had two identical named and numbered regiments).

On August 4th, Colonel Naomenko requested from Volunteers Commander, Lieutenant-General A.N. Denkin:

"For merited service to the Mother Country, after all labors, deprivations and excellent battle work, the 1st Kuban Regiment entrusted to me to be renamed to the KORNILOVS, in honor of the Russian national hero General Lavr Georgiev Kornilov."

General Denkin affirmed and from now on it was the *Kornilov Horse* regiment. By 1919, it contained about 200 cavalrymen and another 200 in support personel.

The *Kornilov Horse Regiment* participated and *1st Horse division* fought at Zakoban in the autumn of 1918. Later, at Petropavlovsk, in the Maykopsk region.

*****

The regular soldier in the Volunteer army carried the following in the field:

One haversack containing two shirts, one pair of pants, two pairs of foot clothes (sock wraps), towel, pair of mitts, 4 1/2 lbs of army biscuits in two bags, bag of salt, rifle cleaning kit, sewing kit, and a drinking cup. A greatcoat was rolled and worn bandolier style; tied to it was one-sixth of a shelter tent (sheet, pegs, poles and rope), a spare pair of boots, and a mess-tin.

The "army" totalled a mere 3000 men, 400 cavalry, 8 guns, 6000 rifles with 200 cartridges per rifle, 50 MG, 100 Horses, 650 carts. Short in weapons and manpower, they all had devout devotion to overthrow the Bolsheviks. They often found themselves against overwhelming odds, but it was the morale and fighting spirit that saved them in battles from 1918-20..

Opposing this force was a Soviet group led by Sievers, which had arrived in the area direct from Petrograd. It contained 10, 000 men, 16 squadrons of cavalry, 42 artillery guns and two armor trains. This Red unit chased the small Volunteer Army out of Rostov. At this point, the Reds were more concerned with the anti-bolshevik revolution movement in the Don basin.

General Denikin became the new commander on April 13th, when General Kornilov was killed. Denikin was not Russian, but Polish. He was born on Dec. 4th, 1874, at Wloclawek, near Warsaw. He was the son of a poor family of serfs and his father had been a Major in the Russian army earning 18 dollars a month. Denikin entered into the army as a private, but by 1890, he went to Officer Candidate School becoming a 2nd Lt. with the 2nd artillery brigade. He was stationed at Warsaw. By 1904, he commanded a Cossack regiment and fought in the Russo-Japanese war at Tsinchentchen. It was here that his superiors noticed him. He was promoted to Colonel. At the start of WW1, he was a Major General stationed at Kiev and was a staff officer of the 8th Corps, commanding the 4th "Iron" brigade. In 1915, the unit became a division and considered one of Russia's best units. Being the daring commander as he was, his success got him promoted to Lt. General and by September, 1916, commanded the 8th Corps. In 1917, he was appointed Chief of Staff. By May 1917, he commanded the Western Front. This led to the catastrophic attack of July, 7th, which ended in total failure. By September, he became one of many generals imprisioned and labeled as a "counter-revolutionary" (most of the known White Generals were this). In October, the daring Denikin escaped incognito with other former generals to the Don basin at Novotcherkask. Denikin's false papers indicated he was "Alexander Dombrowsky" attached to the 73rd Polish First Aid unit. He arrived by late November, 1917, and then fled to the Kuban area to hide.

In April, the Volunteer Army concentrated in the vicinity of Metchetinskaya with only 7000 infantry, 4500 cavalry and 20 guns. The Army marched eastward and was opposed by 30,000 Bolsheviks and another 40,000 on the flank in the Bataisk District. This marked the beginning of his advance into the Kuban. A campaign that lasted into October.

In June, the army had grown to 9000 men and 3000 cavalry. It comprised of :

1st Infantry division (Gen. Markov)
2nd Infantry division (Gen Borovsky)
3rd Infantry division (Col. Drodovsky)***
1st and 2nd Plastoons battalions
1st Cavalry division (Gen Erdeli, and then Wrangel)
1st Kuban Cavalry brigade
2nd Kuban Cossack Division
Kuban Cossack Brigade

The 3rd Infantry division (1010 men) under Col. Drodovsky fled Rumania on March 3rd, 1918, at Doubossar. For the next six weeks, the force walked towards Rostov to rejoin the Volunteer army. On the 13th, at Birgonka and Jimerinka, the Austrians attacked them and were repelled. They continued to march and by the 28th, had reached the Dneipr River. At the only river crossing, two German battalions stood. After some intense negotiations, the Germans allowed them to pass with gun barrels aimed. They arrived at Rostov on April 21st. It was a most welcome reinforcement.

The following German divisions continued to move into the Ukraine: the 212th division entered the Crimea by April 30th; the 1st Cavalry Brigade at Kerch; the 59th and 34th divisions in the Ekaterinoslav area; the 92nd and 19th Cav. Brigade at Kiev on March 3rd; the 11th division at Kherson; the 54th division near Odessa on March 13th; the 14th, 46th, and 85th divisions east of Minsk; and the 155th division at Kamenets-Podolsk. The 72nd, 61st, and 63rd divisions moved south of the Pruth river near Iassy. By the time the Germans

A typical Bolshevik poster used to stir up support. This one is to stimulate feelings for Petrograd.

were done, some 26 German/Austrian divisions occupied the Ukraine, spanning some 500,000 km in nine provinces!

The German presence actually divided the White cause, as many of the Don Cossack leaders favored ties with them and accepted weapons from them. One of the largest groups was led by Ataman Krasnov, comprising of 40,000 men, 56 guns and 180 MG's. This group was respected by the Red army in the area of Tsaritsyn (Stalingrad). It was independant of both the White's and Red's, although, it favored the Whites and Germans.

The Volunteer army continued to occupy areas where the Red forces were weak or totally absent. For the most part, this was in the Kuban. By September, many of the main cities were in White control. By the Fall, 1918, the army contained 11,000 men. It enabled the Rada(local government) to be established in Ekaterinodar, which also was the headquarters for the Army. General Wrangel's division held this area and contained 5500 men and 3 artillery guns.

*****

The German Activities on the Eastern Front

No book on the events taking place in Russia during the Russian Civil war would be complete without some mention of the Germans.

On November 11, 1918, Marshal Foch's staff signed the instrument of Germany's surrender. By November 13, the Soviet Government declared the Brest Peace Agreement with Germany was no longer valid.

German and Austrian troops then retreated hastily from the territory of the former Russian Empire over a two-day period. On November 15, a Ukrainian Insurgent Division was created and moved on the retreating German units. The German puppet in the Ukraine, Hetman Skoropadsky, handed down power to a new Nationalist-Democratic Government proclaiming the creation of an independent Ukrainian People's Republic. This caught the Bolshevik leaders by complete surprise.

On the 30th, a Ukrainian Soviet Army was created. In December, it also advanced on the heels of the German Armies and occupied Novozybkovs, Shostky, Belgorod, Chotoevs and the outskirts of Kharkov. At the close of November the allied powers suddenly occupied Novorossik, Odessa, Sevastopol and in December, Nikolaev, Feodosiya and Kherson. From the Macedonian Front, the French 504th and 509th Escadrilles (Br-14) flew into Odessa. The Allies declared their backing of the White Movement of the General Denikin's Volun-

A German Fokker DVII landing in 1918. Photo: Grosz

teer Army. Within the first days of 1919 Denikin's airmen arrived in Odessa from Novorossik and started to form the 3rd Air Division of the Volunteer army. The Air Division was under the command of Captain Gartman and comprised three detachments, 7th, 8th and 9th(*1st and 2nd Divisions already existed with Dets. 1-6*). On January 25, the 7th Detachment (commander is Lieutenant Legat) had six Kodronovs with 80-hp motors and a Nieuport-23. In the 8th and 9th detachments (the commanders were Junior Lieutenant Zhovnep and Rotmister Shirkovs) they had time only to hand down a few Nieuports, two Anades and three Anasals.

On January 1919, Soviet troops with minimum losses occupied half of the Ukraine and by February 5th, was assaulting Kiev. The Petlyurov group fled in disorder retreating in all directions. Units of the 1st, 2nd and 3rd Ukrainian Soviet Armies, united on the Ukrainian Front and forced the Dnieper and went on with the offensive.

Much further north, the Reds occupied almost all Latvia and eastern parts of Lithuania and Byelorussia. Their goal was Riga, which was defended by the "White Latvians" (detachments of Ulmanis' Latvian National Government) and units of the so called "Baltic Landesver" volunteer formations made up mainly from local Germans and former soldiers of the German Army. They quickly created a covering force, but the Reds were able to take Riga.

At the end of January 1919, the Latvians and Germans were able to establish a foothold on the Venty river (Vindavy). The Landesver was made up of former units from the German army and volunteers. The German 1st Guard's Reserve Division had an aviation unit attached to it called the Kampfgeschwader Sachsenberg. This regiment was formed on the

German troops on patrol somewhere in Russia, 1918.

basis of a demobilized field regiment of marine aviation (Marinefeldjagdgeschwader). It contained three squadrons: FA 413 (reconnaissance), FA 416 (fighter) and FA 417 (assault).

Lieutenant Gottshard Sachenburg, was a former naval pilot of the Kaiser's army and had shot down in 1917-1918 more than 30 British aircraft, this regiment also had such celebrated aces as Joseph Jacobs (47 aerial victories) and Teodor Osterkamp. The "Sachenburg" command counted upwards of 50 experienced pilots and observers. Its 30 crews flew the newest all-metal monoplanes of the Junkers D-1 and CL-1 types. These machines were produced for the German Air Force at the close of the World War . The regiment also had the very well proven wooden biplanes, like the "Halberstadt," "DFW," "LVG," "Rumpler" "Fokker" D-VII and D-VIII types!

Sachenberg later wrote, "that thanks to the endurance of the phenomenal "Junkers" his regiment worked without interruption or breakdowns during their few months in the Baltic. The all metal "Junkers" were exclusive to the Germans, the Reds, Whites or even the Anglo-French Interventionist force had nothing comparable. The Sachenburg regiment contained the best pilots and aircraft in the Civil war. Because of this,they had no rivals to confront. After eight months on the front, February to September 1919, they had not been in one air battle! By March 1919, their central base was an airfield in Vaynode (more west of Libau), where during the WW1 the enormous hangars for zeppelins were built. Sachenburg made use of them as airplane hangars. From there the German air unit moved to Alt-Auts and Petersfeld (more south river Dobel). Here, the Germans flew reconnaissance and bombardment sorties on the Red forces. As far as it is known, they lost at least two "Junkers," one of which force landed in a village behind enemy lines due to engine trouble and the other (faulty and worn) was simply abandoned during the retreat to the airfield at Alt-Auts. The Reds took both aircraft to Moscow for careful study.

Other than the Sachenburg regiment during the winter of 1918, there were based other German air units: Squadrons FA 408, FA 409, FA 424, FA 425, FA 426, FA 427, FA 429 and air-detachments of the Memel's* Volunteer Corps. These squadrons counted more than 150 aircraft. At close of 1918, German volunteer air-detachments defended the eastern borders of the former empire. Attempting to regulate this process, the German command founded official numeration for the field detachments (Flieger Abteilung - FA) from No.400 to 433. Flying artillery detachments started with No.100. A staffel (Abteilung) during the last year of the war counted 9 aircraft. In the post-war period they included 20 aircraft in a Staffel of three six aircraft flights. These reinforced squadrons (equal to a Red air-division) could be formed into a three squadron or Staffel air regiment (Geschwader), which was a powerful air combination and mass application which could influence strategic ground operations. The majority of them were based on Lithuanian airfields at Kovno (Kaunas), Shavli (Shyaul) and Mariyampol. In the air, the Germans battled the Red Latvian Air Division formed in April 1918, near Moscow above the village of Podosinki.

This air division contained three detachments under the Command of Rudolf Stukalis and arrived on the front in January 1919. After three months, the 1st Detachment equipped with "Nieuports" flew 14 combat sorties, the 2nd less than 10, and 3rd did only three reconnaissance flights. German aircraft also regularly appeared over Riga, but did not bomb the city, limiting flights to reconnaissance only. The pilots of the 1st Latvian Detachment, commanded by flier Veynberg, were on duty to fly aerial cover over the city, however they failed to intercept the enemy reconnaissance patrols. The Germans, in turn, did not attempt to attack the Latvian's airfield. How odd. This continued until May 9th, when a reconnaissance "Rumpler," was intercepted by three Red "Nieuports." The fighters pursued the German to his airfield, but did not fire on it.

On May 22nd, the Germans suddenly captured Riga. The Red Latvians were forced to quickly evacuate the staff of the 1st Latvian detachment. In June, the 1st, 2nd and 3rd the Latvian Air Detachments were renamed to the 44th, 45th and 46th Reconnaissance. By August, 1919, the Air Regiment Veinshenk (FA424 and FA 426) had 32 aircraft and was based in Radzvilishkakh, Lithuania. The Air Regiment Sachenburg with 32 aircraft in Petersfeld. Aviation of the German Iron Division (FA427, FA429 and artillery detachment 101) were 28 aircraft located in Elgave were manned almost completely by Germans. Thus, the Bermont-Avalova Air Fleet counted 140 aircraft. Due to lack of benzene and the little desire to fight, the crews mainly sat around the airfields. The Western Army, which was created to oppose the Bolsheviks fought not against the Red army but the Lithuanians, Latvians and Estonians, who saw them as a tool of German Baltic colonization.

The pro-German Bermont-Avalov air group made an effort to improve relations with Denikin. To do so, a two-engine "Fridrikhskhafen" G.llla with a military delegation flew to the Ukraine near the end of October. A 1200-kilometer flight from Mitau to Kiev., but the aircraft was forced to land just outside Kiev in a nearby village. The "Fridrikhskafen" landed in a field and the aircraft was instantaneously attacked ransacked then burned by one of the local bandit groups. The fliers and the delegation members by a miracle were able to escape. However, the mission totally failed.

By May 1919, Denikin had received Camel "RE8s" and "DH9s" in Novorossiisk. This total came to 50 aircraft: 18 DH9s, 16 Camels, and 16 RE8s. They were distributed in the following manner: six DH9s to the 1st, 2nd, and 5th Detachments; eight Camels to the 6th and 3rd Don air force detachments; and 16 RE8s to training.

*****

Part of the German 52nd Corps occupying Kiev in the sping of 1918.

The Volunteer Army had fought a series of battles with the Reds since June. The rise and fall of manpower within a army changed from victory or loss. In one case, Denikin's men fought the Red "Iron" division (Denikin's old unit) of 10,000 men. Denikin outnumbered, divided his units into three 3000 man brigades and enveloped the attacking Reds. Almost immediately, 5000 of the Iron division defected to Denikin, which turned and fought against the Reds! The reason for this was the Red forces were more militia quality with bad morale. Men in the Red army fought to get food or money not for the Bolshevik cause. In Contrast, the Whites fought for the ideal of a New Russia.

By July 15th, Denikin now had 20,000 men, 3 armor trains, 70 artillery guns, 1 airplane and 20 armor cars. The Red army under Sorokin had been near Rostov and battling both the Germans and Don Cossacks. He retreated to Tsaritsyn. This conceded the most important prize to Denikin: the port of Novorossisk. This port would become the main conduit of British supplies in the months to come. However, Denikin could not occupy it until August 28th, after the Germans left.

Clearly, the French were concerned and alarmed by the German presence. But while the French remained undecided, at least the British did act, albeit, in a small way with the force at Enzeli. During this time, the Dunsterforce had been supplemented with a large contingent of Austin Armor cars at the request and advice of General Locker Lampson. It was his letter on December 10th, 1917, which requested an Armor Car unit be sent immediately to Basra. The force was to be a self-contained unit and destined for Northern Persia (Iran). Once landing at Basra, the force would be supplied with fuel and ammo. In his letter, Locker Lampson requested the following:

> A force of 400 men, 25 officers, 500 tons of stores, and 38 twin turret Austin Armor cars.

However, only 8 Austin ACs were available, and the remaining 30 still had to be manufactured. This was part of an order placed by the Russians for a total of 70. The 30 cars would be sent within a month, with the balance being sent to Basra and to the Caucasus. These would form the Anglo-Russian Armor Car squadron in the Caucasus and manned with 450 Belgian mechanics then at Kiev. It consisted of:

> 16 Touring cars
> 18 Heavy 3 ton trucks with double drive
> 50 Ford trucks
> 4 Workshop Cars
> 5 Wireless Cars each with one 1.5-2 KW set
> 4 Water and Gasoline trucks
> 16 Light Trucks
> 200 Maxim Heavy MG and 30 Lewis Guns

Lampson noted that the force would be created from volunteers consisting of 300 men and another 100 drivers and mechanics were needed, and suggested recruiting efforts be placed in North Ireland (oddly, the 300 men he notes is clearly the force slated for Dunsterforce). He requested that the Treasury set aside some £100,000 for the needs of the special unit, of which, £6500 be placed at the disposal of the Officer in Charge of the Armor car unit to purchase incidentals.

The most curious item in the request was contained in the postscript where he writes," *The British force now at Kursk is sufficient to transfer the material from there to the Caucasus.*" Clearly, this must be a mistake, as the British were not in Kursk on December 1917 (unless, it was a secret unit with 450 Belgians!).

This special armor car unit, clearly to support Dunsterforce, was approved by the War Office on December 13th. Again, with some cryptic langauge: *"to dispatch to Armenia armor cars and men now in Russia to Resht, forcasting the departure of Locker Lampson for Basra. ...Locker Lampson should take out with him to Basra a force capable of acting in Northern Persia and possibly of joining up with the force from Russia."* This statement implies a force of some sort existed at Kursk and Kiev containing at least some British troops. The War Office granted Locker Lampson some £ 6171 to outfit the men in the unit, and that all men are of a rank of Petty Officer or higher . It is clear that the British had intervened in the Russian civil war as early as December, 1917.

France continued its indecisiveness despite a policy of economic encirclement, and the overthrow of Bolshevism. This policy was stated in October 1917. This policy was then given to General Berthelot, the French commander in Rumania, for execution. Even before the first French forces actually landed in South Russia, the French commanders had warned their political cohorts that, *"at best, we could hold Odessa and other nearby ports. But*

The father of Communism, VI Lenin, in Moscow, 1919. He is third from the right. Note how well dressed he is in his so-called "classless society."

prolongation of the war in the Ukraine and Russia would be taken badly and risk unfortunate consequences."

These warnings fell on deaf ears. The French continued to meander in indecision as to what actually should be done. At one point, Clemenceau, stated that the French position was only to keep the Bolshevik away from the Ukraine and Caucasus. The French foreign minister, Pichon, stated that no military mission was at all envisaged. At the tactical level, General d"Esperey wrote General Denikin stating that the Volunteer Army would not be abandoned by France and that France will ship munitons. Clearly, the signals were crossed at all levels in French circles. Despite this, the goal continued to be "*France must do something.*"

While France waivered with indecision and contradictory movements, the British special force advanced from Enzeli towards Baku. Baku, in July, was defended by motley and poorly armed Red units incapable of attacking or defending. Opposing this was a strong Turkish force (some 12,000 men, 5th and 6th Divisions), which by the end of July, had surrounded the city and within 2 miles of it. Then a series of oddities happened: first, the Turkish force stopped and withdrew but still surrounded Baku, and, the local government of Baku voted to seek the help of the British! This resulted in the Bolsheviks leaving Baku, which greatly angered Lenin and Trotsky in Moscow.

So, when the Baku and the Trans-Caspian governments both send SOS messages to the British 39th and 38th Brigades, which were in Persia or close by, the first steps into allied intervention began in Trans-Caspia, while to the west, the British were simply fighting a continuation WW1.

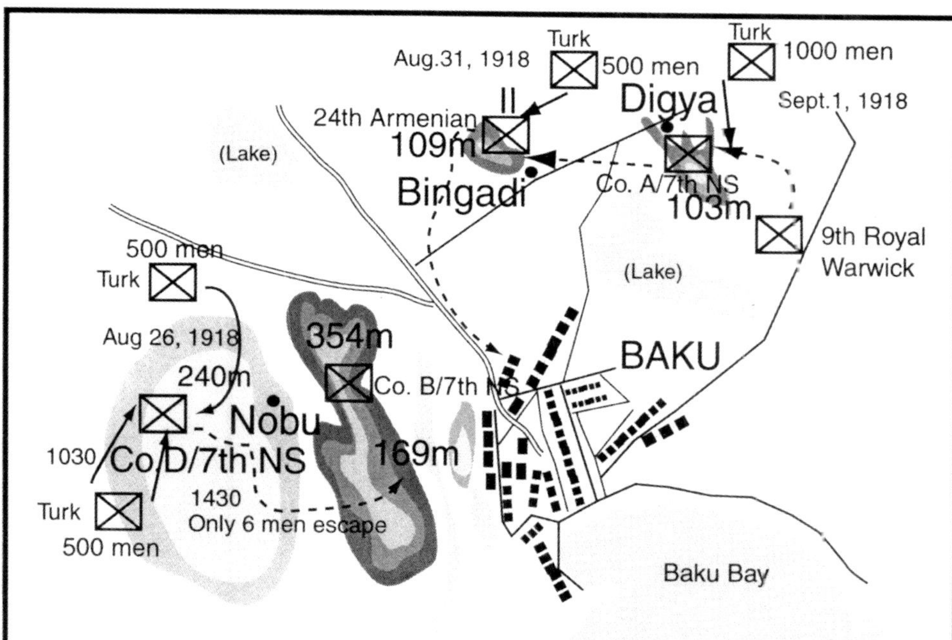

LAST STAND AT BAKU, Sept. 1918

On July 1st, the 39th Bde received orders to move to north Persia. The men began moving on July 4th northward to. Khaniqin(July 25th), Kermanshah (27th) and Hamadan (29th). On Aug. 1, the troops moved towards Kazvin and Enzeli and on the 8th, the 7th N Stafford battalion reached Baku. Initially, the only men Dunsterforce could send were 44 soldiers of the 7th Bn/North Staffordshires. This was a token force, but it proved to be enough to prevent the Turkish troops from taking Baku. This platoon arrived aboard the steamer President Kruger, supported by gunboats Kursk and Abo. By the end of August, the following units had also made the grueling 300 mile voyage from Enzeli to Baku:

7th Bn/ North Staffordshires, 1st Line/4th Bn/ North Hampshire,
9th Bn/Warwickshire
9th Bn/Worchestershire, 39th Brigade HQ, 39th Brigade MG Company,
2 sections/44th artillery Btty, 2 sections/8th artillery btty

Upon their arrival, the British began to build 12 miles of defensive lines around the beautiful, european styled city of 200,000 people. Aiding with the defense was the 24th Armenian battalion and others, totaling 6000 men. This group proved to be totally unreliable and untrained.

The 39th Brigade was grossly outnumbered by the 9th Turk Army, which by now, had advanced close to Baku. The brigade held part of the defensive line north and west of Baku from Digya-Bingadi-Mud Volcano. The fighting at Baku was divided into four phases:

(1) Turkish Attack on Mud Volcano (held by D Coy 7th N Staffs on Aug. 26th).
(2) Turkish Attack on Bingadi Hill, Aug 31st.
(3) Turkish Attack on Digya, Sept. 1st
(4) Turkish General Attack on Baku, Sept 14th.

On the 26th, the Turk attack on Mud Volcano, west of Baku, opened at 1030 am. The company of men were facing 1000 Turks attacking and encircling them. By 1430 Capt Sparrow and the last of D Company were seen surrounded and engaged in ferocious bloody hand to hand fighting. Little could be done about the Turk frenzy. Only six unwounded men got away and the company lost 3 officers and 80 other ranks killed, wounded and missing.

The Turks then moved against Bingadi Hill and defended by the 24th Armenian battalion who hurriedly evacuated it. Company A/ 7th N Staffs was deployed to their right at Dinya and hurried from Digya to Binagadi to fill the gap. It arrived at 1515, just in time to save the situation by occupying the empty trenches and surprising a party of 250 Turks who were moving up the western slope to occupy the hill. The Turks were driven back with heavy loss. At 0630 on the 31st, the Turks attacked Bingadi Hill again with 1000 men and at 0830 after severe fighting, Company A was ordered to withdraw to the Oil Derricks (south of the hill). During this defense, the company lost the commander and one other officer as well as 34 other ranks killed, wounded or missing.

On Sept. 1st, the Turks attacked Digya. The Armenians and Russians defending Digya broke and fled. The 9th Royal Warwicks quickly replaced them and after hours of close combat had lost 4 officers and 67 other ranks either taken prisoner or missing. .Meanwhile, another Turkish division began to move towards Hamadan in Iran, which threatened to cut

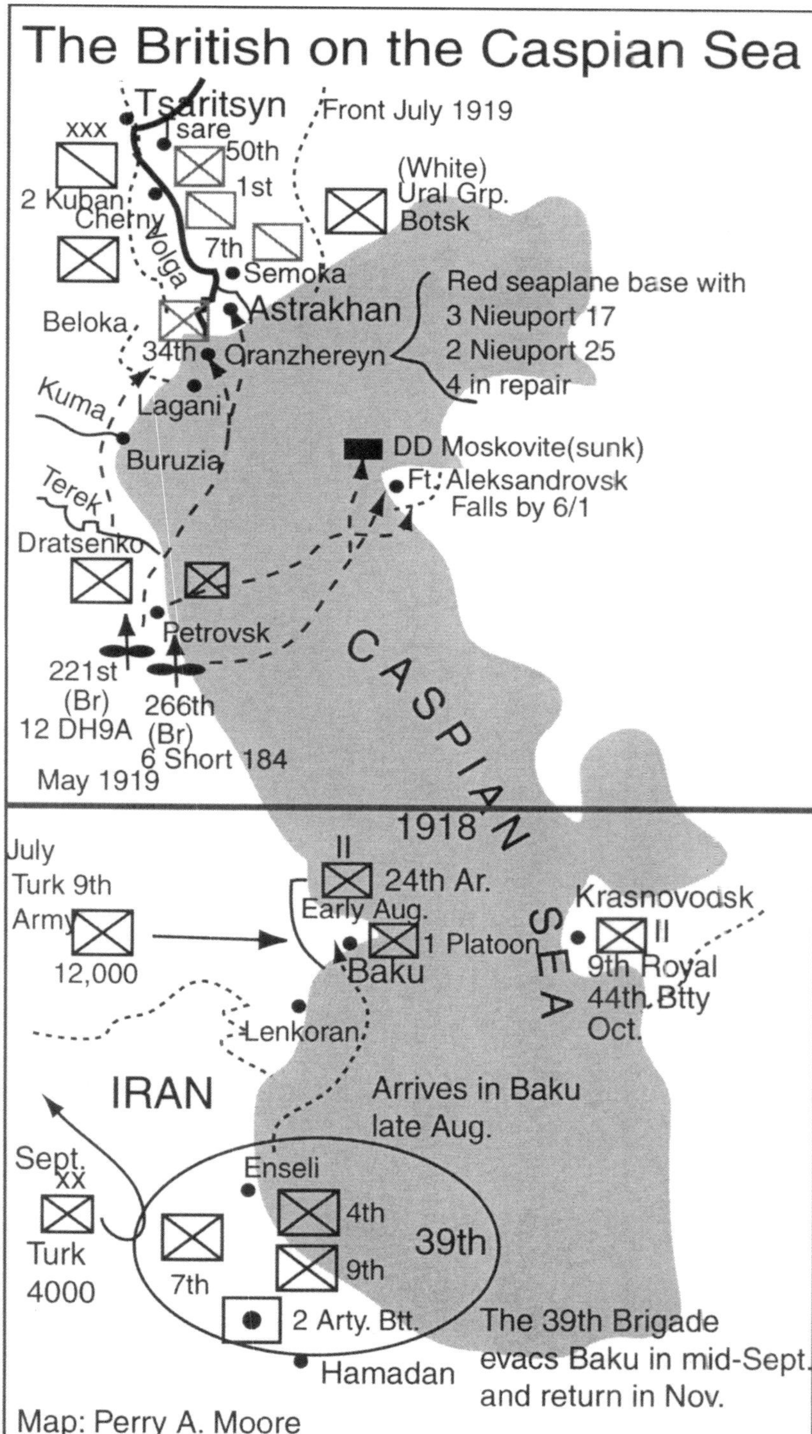
The British on the Caspian Sea
Tsaritsyn
Front July 1919
XXX
Tsare
50th
1st
(White)
Ural Grp.
Botsk
2 Kuban
Cherny
Volga
7th
Semoka
Red seaplane base with
3 Nieuport 17
2 Nieuport 25
4 in repair
Astrakhan
Beloka
34th
Oranzhereyn
Kuma
Lagani
Buruzia
DD Moskovite(sunk)
Ft. Aleksandrovsk
Falls by 6/1
Terek
Dratsenko
Petrovsk
221st
(Br)
12 DH9A
266th
(Br)
6 Short 184
May 1919
CASPIAN SEA
1918
July
Turk 9th
Army
12,000
II
24th Ar.
Early Aug.
1 Platoon
Baku
Krasnovodsk
II
9th Royal
44th Btty
Oct.
Lenkoran
IRAN
Arrives in Baku
late Aug.
Sept.
XX
Turk
4000
Enseli
4th
9th
39th
7th
2 Arty. Btt.
Hamadan
The 39th Brigade
evacs Baku in mid-Sept.
and return in Nov.
Map: Perry A. Moore

off Dunsterforce's only supply route and within Baku, the local government tried to prevent the British from evacuating and considered surrendering to the Turks while the British troops were there. Luckily, this did not occur.

On Sept 14th, the Turks launched a general attack against local troops who still occupied part of the Baku defences. These local troops broke at once and exposed the flanks of the British troops,

Baku was quickly evacuated and the situation seemed so serious that all documents were destroyed. Eventually the Turks were held back; but owing to lack of reserves, the situation could not be restored and the British troops re-embarked. With no chance of stopping the Turks, the British force had to evacuate in small groups at pre-arranged docking sites. By Dusk, the British troops were dogged tired after 14 hours of battle, loaded onto the steamer and two gunboats. The steamer sailed at midnight with 870 men. Baku fell to the Turks on the 15th. The Turks lost approximately 2000 men.

On the 19th, 9th Worcester moved to Resht. On the 29th, 9th Royal Warwicks sailed from Enzil to Krasnovodsk to join Maj-Gen Malleson's Force.

On Oct 1st, the 7th Gloucester Bn was moving up from Bijar-Zenjan, and by the end of the month 7th Gloucesters concentrated at Kazvin; the other Bns were then at Enzeli, Resht, and Krasnovodsk. At noon on Thursday, Oct 31st, 1918, hostilities ceased with Turkey. On Nov 15th, 7th Gloucesters concentrated at Enzeli (Persia); and on the same day, 39th Bde HQ, 7th Gloucesters, (less 1 coy), 9th Worcesters, 7th N Staffs, 39th Bde MG coy (less 1 sec at Krasnovodsk), and 39th Bde S and T coy embarked at Enzeli and disembarked at Baku on the 17th.. On the 30th, the strength of the 39th brigade was 1,480 all ranks. On Dec. 9th, the remaining coy of 7th Gloucesters reached Baku, and on 12th, 39th Bde S.A.A. section and part of the 72nd Field artillery also arrived. At the end of the year the effective strength of the brigade was 2,027 all ranks.When the Turks captured Baku on September 14th, the British and Russians fell back to Petrovsk. The key port of Astrakhan remained in Red hands. When the Turks surrendered, the British re-entered Baku with the Russians on November, 17th, along with 30 transports escorted by British armed vessels.Baku had cost Dunsterforce 125 men. The Turks held the city for a month and evacuated the city . The British returned to Baku on November 17th.

From January 1919, all troops in Baku came under the orders of GHQ Constantinople, and on March 27th, the 39th Brigade at Baku was placed directly under 27th Divison at Tiflis. Demobilization proceeded slowly and parties left for UK via Batum.

On April 7th, the 9th Royal Warwicks left Krasnovodsk and rejoined the 39th Bde at Baku.

On June 13th, 72nd Field Coy RE left for Batum. On the 14th, the 7th North Staffords were disbanded and the personnel left Baku and joined the 7th Royal Berkshire at Tiflis. By July 8th, the 9th Royal Warwicks left by train for Tiflis.

Orders were issued to evacuate Baku in August. All animals, saddlery and Harnesses were sold. The move by train to Batum began on the 15th, and the evacuation of Baku was completed by 1800 on the 24th. The 39th Brigade embarked at Batum for Constantinople on the 29th. It was demobilized on the 31st at Constantinople.

The 9th Royal Warwicks reached Haidar Pasha (Constantinople) from Batum on Sept. 2nd, and moved to Tuzla (20 miles SE of Constantinople). On the 24th, the unit was disbanded and the personnel was transferred to 9th Worcesters. The 7th Gloucesters reached

Haidar Pashar on the 2nd and absorbed by 8th Oxs and Bucks LI. The 9th Worcesters moved on Aug. 13th, 1 Coy was sent by sea from Baku to Petrovsk and then by rail to Novorossisk (on Black Sea) to escort stores On Sept 3rd, the batalion entrained for Tuzla. The 39th MG Company arrived at Constantinople and its personnel absorbed by the 82st Bde MG Coy. The 39th Sanitary Section reached Baku on April 14th, and joined 39th Bde. The section left Baku on Aug. 20th, embarking at Batum on sept 1st, and landed at Haidar Pasha on the 6th.

The British had also decided to intevene directly in the Caspian Sea, and in August, 1918, sent a party of officers and men with 4.7" guns and 4" guns from Basra, Iraq, to the Caspian. The objective of this intervention was to control the Caspian and stop any German-Turkish advances toward India. To do this, orders were given to arm captured ships, halt enemy sea transporting, control all shipping lanes, and deny their use to the enemy. Captured ships were armed in the ports of Enzeli and Krasnovodsk. Eventually, the British obtained eight ships from the Russians,which were partially manned by British/Russian crews. The Russian crews were all paid handsome allowances.

The Blending of Two Wars

The British had the unfortunate position of dealing with two separate, yet, dangerous situations during the summer of 1918. The first was WW1, which had not ended and at that time and there was no end in sight. The second was the Bolshevik revolution. It was in the Caspian sea and Trans-Caspia areas that the two wars blended and sucked the British military into intervention.

The general situation was that the Germans remained on the east front and in parts of the Ukraine. The Germans had considerable influence there and with their Turkish allies, which had recently created a new 9th Army consisting of 12,000 men. It was this army that was now advancing towards Baku, Russia in July 1918. The Germans remained in Tiflis.

Further east, the Bolshviks in Trans-Caspia Russia (northeast of Persia) also were advancing along the only railroad line that ran through Annenkovo and Merv near the Persian border. The Bolsheviks were poorly trained but had sufficient arms. In reality, there was nothing to halt them except their own fears of the British. The local Trans-Caspian Russian government sought the help of the British, which was nearly bankrupt. The British Mission was formed at Meshed in June. The Reds were forced out of this area on July 14th and had retreated back across the Oxus river. It was now the White Trans-Caspian army was created. On the 24th, the Reds attacked at Charjui routing the Whites and retook the strategic bridge over the Oxus river. The Reds continued in their advance reaching the Merv area by August 10th. On the 11th, the White government sent their SOS to the British and the first of many British troops were sent. The British now had directly intervened in the Russian Civil war. The British machine detachment from the 19th Punjabi Bn, helped, but could halt the Red advance that had pushed into Merv by the 14th.

The British own fears played quite well here. First, they feared the German presence in the area and the thousands of Austro-Hungarian POWs interned in Russia now under Red control. The British correctly feared the Turks, which were clearly advancing towards Baku. If this was taken, British plans to control the Caspian Sea and the oil pipelines and rail system would be threatened. The British were also aware of the Bolsheviks and their plans to control Trans-Caspia and threaten Persia and they were already on the border!

In Trans-Caspia, the British detachment sent to Merv and to bolster the Whites felt their position was dangerous and left Merv on August 14th, allowing the Reds to enter. The Whites and British fell back to Dushak, where on the 19th, one company from the 19th Punjabis battalion reinforced them. Even this reinforcement was slacking. Dushak was indefensible with the given troops so the British et. al., retreated to Kakha where the remaining companies of the 19th Punjabis stood. Kahka was reached on the 26th.

In the Trans-Caspia, the local government had requested from the British 1,000,000 roubles to help pay for the army and a monthly maintenance sum of 16,000,000 roubles! The exchange rate then was 1 English pound to 133 roubles. Britain could not afford this and instead decided to use military forces to bolster the Trans-Caspian army, which so far had proved to be worthless.

On the 28th August the Bolsheviks attacked Kakhka, a small village grouped around a railway station. The railway line went through the village from southeast to northwest. A mile to the east of the station the line was crossed by a stream at right angles to the line, which was carried by an iron girder bridge. To the east of the stream, and south of the railway line, there was a low ridge running north and south. The railway line curved around this ridge providing shelter for the trains. The ridge was overlooked by an extensive plateau to the north of the railway line.

The Bolshevik positions were at Arman Sagad, nine miles to the east of Kakhka. The Trans-Caspian troops had been deployed expecting an attack from the south flank with the bulk of their troops on the ridge to the south and their guns behind the ridge. Their armored train was on the track to the west of the ridge, but their troop trains were in Kakha. The only troops north of the line were 200-400 Turkoman cavalry in an old fort. The 19th Punjabis noticed that the left flank was the most exposed and deployed troops accordingly. Co. 1 of

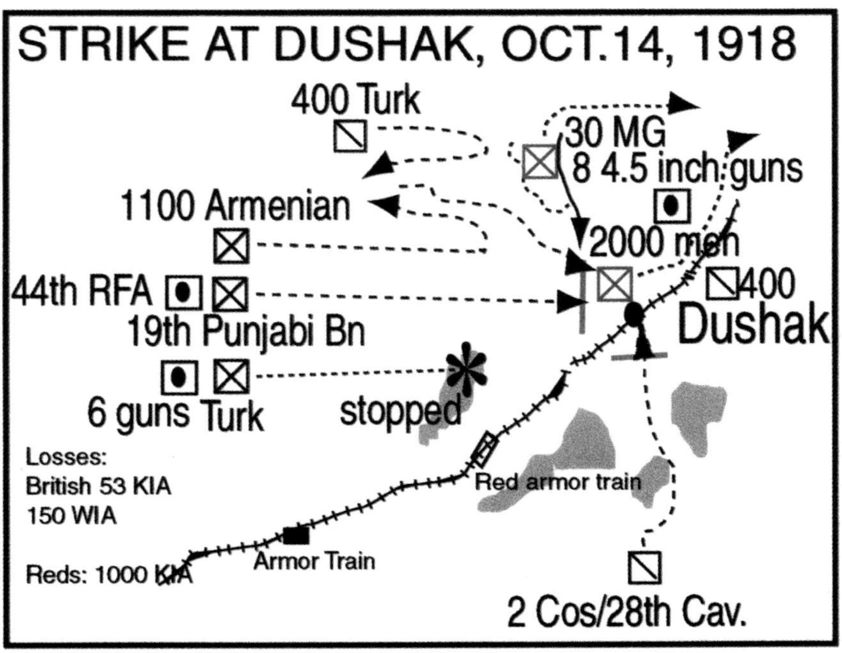

the 19th with a machine gun section was positioned north of the railway, on the western edge of Kakha. The other two companies were held in reserve between the village and the stream.

At 0700 on the 28th, the Bolshevik artillery opened fire from the plateau to the north, where it had been positioned overnight. At 0730 their infantry attacked the old fort and easily caused the Turkoman cavalry to panic and flee. The Reds continued their advance towards the village through the enclosed fields, but were slowed down by the fire from the Punjabi infantry and machine guns positioned north of the railway line and the few Trans-Caspian troops left in Kakha.

As the Bolsheviks reached the edge of the village, one of the two companies of Punjabis held in reserve charged the Bolsheviks at bayonet point. The Bolsheviks were completely taken by surprise and horrified and were driven out of Kakha after hand to hand fighting in the fields and orchards. The British had won this first clash.. On August 29th, the position was reinforced by the arrival of one company 1/4th Hampshire Regiment, and on Sept. 5th, a section (2 guns) 44th Battery Royal Field Artillery had also arrived.

In Trans-Caspia, the second clash between the British and Bolshevik forces occurred when the British attacked on October 14th. The 28th Light Cavalry advanced through the hills to the south of the railway to outflank the Bolsheviks, and a force of Turkoman cavalry

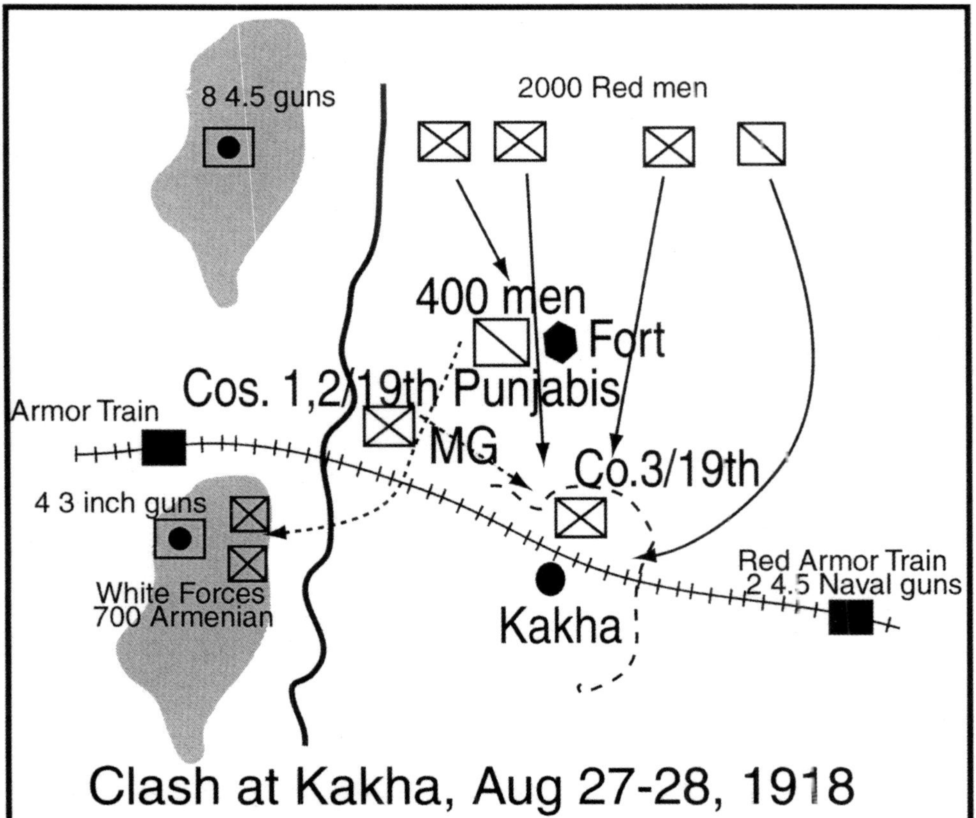

Clash at Kakha, Aug 27-28, 1918

made a wide swing north to the rear of the Bolshevik position with the intention of cutting the railway track and preventing their retreat. The company of 1/4th Hants was left at Arman Sagad as a reserve.

The night march went well until the 19th Punjabis reached a small hamlet just north of Dushak, when two of their own patrols clashed in the darkness, each mistaking the other for the enemy! The sound of gunfire alerted the enemy to the British presence. Daylight broke before the march could be resumed, so the force deployed roughly a mile from Dushak, with the Trans-Caspian infantry on the right, the Punjabis in the center, and Turkoman infantry on the left. The 28th Light Cavalry had deployed approximately a mile south of Dushak, and were to make a dismounted attack from this direction.

The Bolshevik infantry defended from irrigation channels and hidden by a fringe of trees on the outskirts of Dushak supported by thirty machine guns, according to the official British report. Their artillery deployed on the higher ground to the east. The Bolshevik armored train was in a cutting to the west of Dushak, still facing Arman Sagad.

The dismounted attack by the 28th Light Cavalry was a success. They then remounted and charged through the Bolsheviks on the south of the town, killing at least thirty and dispersing the rest. The 28th cleared the area south of the railway and redeployed to the east to defend against any counter-attack from this direction.

The infantry attack launched at 0700 did not proceed well since the Trans-Caspian infantry went prone as soon as the Bolshevik artillery and machine guns opened fire and the Turkomans disappearing altogether! The Punjabis, despite incurring heavy casualties (all their British officers being killed or wounded) fought their way into the town by 1000, capturing 16 machine guns and six artillery pieces. The Trans-Caspian and Turkoman troops regained their bravery and arrived in the town to indulge in an orgy of massacre and looting. The few British officers left with the Punjabis were unable stop them and all semblance of order was lost. It was chaos after the battle.

The Bolsheviks now took advantage of this and attacked at 1130 from west and east since the Turkomans had failed to cut the railway to the east as planned. By this time, the only cohesive forces left to defend Dushak were the Punjabis, the 28th Light Cavalry, and a company of about 80 ex-Tsarist regulars who remained with them. In view of the strength of the Bolshevik counterattack, the British and the allies fell back to Arman Sagad. The Reds due to lack of ammunition retreated to Merv. The British 28th Cavalry followed the retreating Bolos and by the 28th and moved to cut them off east of Merv. The Reds were so shocked by this event they fled Merv and retreated to Charjui. The British now walked into Merv!

The British now wished to limit their advance and consolidated at Bairum Ali. On Novemeber 14th, at Uch Aji, a gun on one of the Trans-Caspian armored trains exploded, which alerted the Red artillery which opened up. This caused panic in the ranks and the Trans-Caspian forces retreated rapidly to Annenkovo, some 100 miles to the south and 30 miles from Bairam Ali.

In this desperate situation and in spite of his orders, the commanding officer, Colonel Knollys, sent two troops of the 28th Light Cavalry to the front to support the Trans-Caspian army. On November 17th, the expected Bolshevik attack was launched, but despite heavy casualties over a two day period, the Trans-Caspian army managed to stand its ground!

The Trans-Caspian forces remained at Annenkovo and the Bolsheviks at Ravnina, with advanced positions at some sand dunes midway between the two stations.

On December 7th, the Trans-Caspian forces attacked trying to evict the Bolsheviks from their positions at Ravnina.. A frontal assault was successful on the station and despite taking it for a while, they failed to hold it, both sides then returned to their original positions.

1919

On January 16th, 1919, the last major battle between the British and the Bolsheviks occurred at Annenokovo. The morning fog concealed the Reds as and Trans-Caspian patrols returned to their positions at 0830. Suddenly, the Red artillery opened up and shells rained in from the sky. Soon, communications had been cut on both sides of Annenkovo station. By 1000, all communications had been restored, and Co. 2 of 19th Punjabis was entrained at Bairam Ali and sent to the front.

The Trans-Caspian positions were on sand dunes to the north-west of, and parallel to, the railway, which curved northward. The two troops of the 28th Light Cavalry were deployed on the right flank together with the Turkoman Horse. In the center was the Co.1 of Punjabi infantry, and on the left flank, the Trans-Caspian Infantry.

At 1230, the Trans-Caspian infantry were ordered to advance and soon met with the Bolsheviks who were supported by artillery fire. Despite fighting well, the Trans-Caspian infantry were pushed back and greatly outnumbered they broke and ran.

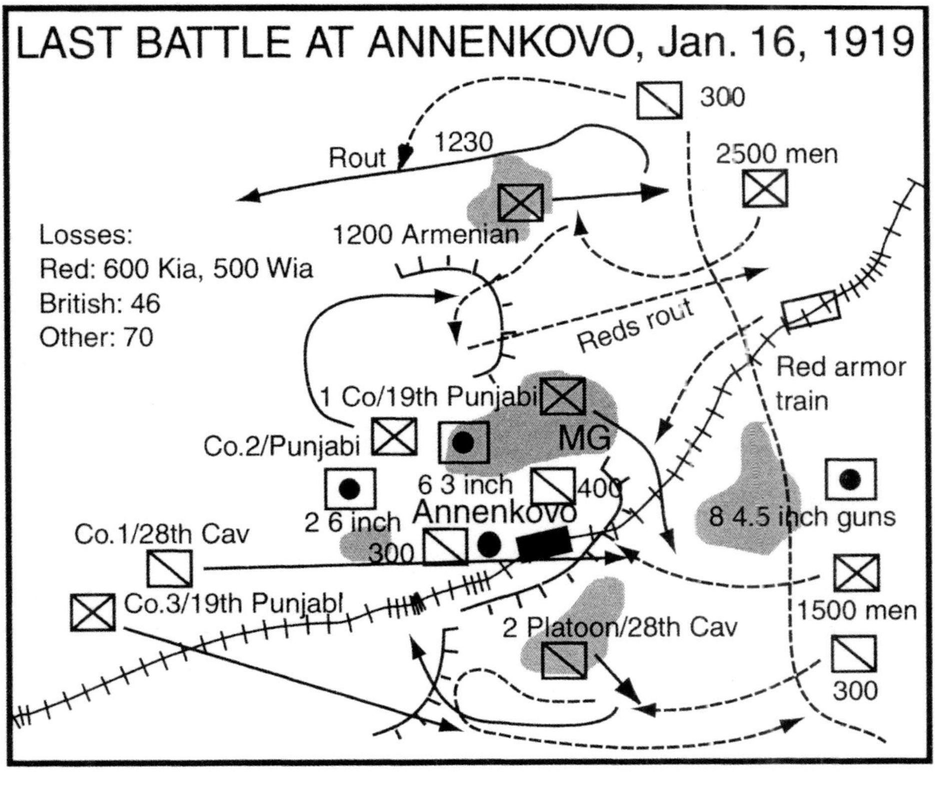

At this point, the whole position was being outflanked, but fortunately the British train arrived from Bairam Ali carrying Co.2 / Punjabis. They immediately detrained, formed line, and advanced through the fog into the Bolshevik right flank. The Bolsheviks broke and fled across the front of Co.1/ Punjabi company.

Meanwhile, the right flank had also been under attack from some 1500 infantry and 450 cavalry supported by an armored train and heavy artillery. This attack was repulsed by the 19th Punjabis and Turkoman cavalry and supported by the Trans-Caspian armored trains. Several sources indicate the Bolsheviks used large numbers of Austro-Hungarian POWs in their forces at Annenkovo, (which is true) but they were not any more effective than the rest of the Bolshevik infantry.

Annenkovo was the last large scale assault by the Bolsheviks upon the British troops as they bolstered the Trans-Caspian forces. On March 2nd, a patrol of 14 men from the 28th Light Cavalry charged twice through over 100 Bolshevik cavalry men. At least 21 were killed at at a loss of only two Indian cavalry taken prisoner.

The British Government decided on January 21st, 1919, to withdraw all forces from Trans-Caspia area, and the last troops actually left for Persia on April 5th. After this it was only a matter of time before the Bolsheviks regained control of Trans-Caspia. Their conquest was completed by the autumn of 1919.

According to General Greenley of the British South Russian Mission, the German forces during the Summer of 1918 were actively engaged in thier policy of " Drang nach Osten" (Push to the East) using Atamen Kraznov and his Don army. Kraznov admitted that because of the British successes in Persia and Mesopotamina (Iran/Iraq) he cooperated with the Germans. The German plan called for uniting the Don Cossacks, Kalmucks, Astrakhan Cossacks and Ural Cossacks. This would allow the Germans to secure a channel for their influence to Central Asia. Key to this was Ataman Kranzov, who was pro-German. Another important figure was Prince Tundutov, the head of the Klamucks. The Prince was captured and sent to Germany to be persuaded. When he returned, he was loaded with a large supply of forged rouble notes. This helped to create the Astrakhan Army, which then joined the Don Army under Kranzov. Both were well armed with German weapons (Kraznov received 11,600 rifles, 88 MG and 460 artillery guns) . In return, these two armies (in reality, weak divisions) fought against the Bolsheviks. These White forces only fought against the Whites when they had to in 1918. The Germans also tried to persuade the Volunteer Army by sending them arms and ammunition. However, while Denikin gladly accepted needed weapons and ammunition, he resisted all German attempts of persuasion.

The Volunteer Army, by September, 1918, contained some 35,000 men, 86 artillery guns, 256 MG, 8 armor cars, 7 airplanes and 4 armor trains. France provided Denikin with weapons and ammunition amounting to 5500 rifles, 47 MG and 1600 km of telegraph cable.

By Fall, 1918, with WW1 ending, the German presence in South Russia had a lesser impact on both the Allies (who feared the Drang Nach Osten), and the Reds and Whites. For the Reds, the German presence had been a kind of halting presence. The Red forces avoided German held areas. For the Whites, some independent groups and armies (like the Don Army) had to decide on which side to fall. For the most part, these tended to fall on the White side. But nothing was black and white. In battle, both sides lost men through defections based upon the winner or loser . This was true for both the Reds and Whites. An exception to this belonged to the true believers in either Bolshevism(Red) or a free

Russia(White). These units formed the cadre, but were always too small. In the Volunteer Army, one such unit was the Markov Division (named after their 29 yr old. Leader). These men were the "elite" infantry forces for Denikin.

As we have seen, the French and British governments and military agreed to intervene in the Bolshevik Revolution of 1917. That, each country had their own agenda. France, simply wanted to recover the millions lost, while the British viewed Bolshevism as a threatening virus that needed to be stopped. For the British, direct military intervention occurred by December, 1917, on the fringe of Russia. For France, they waffled with indecision for most of 1918. For Denikin and his Volunteer army, it was a means to create a "Free Russia."

Weapons Synopsis

For the most part, the weapons used during the Civil war were those of WW1. It was an odd mixture of some 60 artillery gun types and 35 types of rifle models. Some of the standard weapons used were:

Small Arms

Russian 7.62mm Mosin-Nagant Model 1891
Moisin Model 1908
German 7.92mm Mauser Model 1898
Austrian 8mm Mannlicher Model 1895
American Winchester Model 1895 and modified for 7.62mm shells in America.
Nagant 7.62mm Revolver Model 1895
German Mauser revolver
Smith and Wesson Model 1893 revolver

Machine Guns

Russian Maxim Heavy Machine Gun Model 1910
French Hotchkiss MG Model 1914
American Colt MG
British Vickers MkI MG
British LMG Lewis Gun Model 1915
German Model 1908 MG

Mortars

Russian Likhonin 47mm, 58mm (range of 500m)
Russian 90mm mortar
Russian 240mm mortar
British Stokes Mortars

Artillery

Russian 3" (76mm) field gun, Model 1902
Russian Mountain Gun, 3," Model 1908
Russian Howitzer, Model 1910
Russian 107mm field gun, Model 1910
Russian 6" (152mm)howitzer, model 1910
French 120 mm, Model 1878
British 6" Model 1904 Howitzer

British 8" Howitzer
French 11" Model 1914 Schneider Howitzer
Model 1915 37mm trench gun
Russian Model 1910, 107mm
Russian Model 1900, 122mm

Aircraft

British Sopwith Strutter
British BE2e
British Vickers FB19
French Nieuport 17, 23, 10, 11,21
Spad A2, VII
British DH9, DH9A (1919 only)
British Snipe
Russian Grigorovich M5, M9
Lebed XII

Armor Cars

British Austin twin turret car w/ 2 MG
Various German Armor Cars
Tanks (1919 only)
French Renault FT17
British Whippet, Type A/B
British Mark V male

Armor Trains

These units were critical as Russia had few good all-weather roads and the supplies were usually brought to the front by train. Thus, the advance of a army would be astride of a railroad line on either side for several miles. This was where the front line actually existed. In the areas where there was no access via a railroad, the front either was manned very lightly (thus, very porous) or none existed. The trains also provided the advancing armies their artillery support to a large extent and usually stayed a few miles behind the front.

There were three types of armor trains used by either side. These were as follows:

1. The shock or first line armor train consisted of 76mm guns and MGs.
2. The Support Fire train consisted of 107mm and 122mm guns, plus MG.
These were assigned to the front commander.
3. The heavy support trains consisted of 152mm and 203mm guns.
This was under the direct control of the Army General.

In all of the above, the armor train was usually protected by at least .50" or more armor plating and contained anywhere from 4-8 artillery guns, and up to 20 heavy Machine guns. Some guns were mounted in revolving turrets.

The armor train, while well armed, was in a fragile position. If the frontline troops fled, the train could easily be trapped simply by cutting the rail line miles away. Once isolated, it became prey for the hunter.

Sources:

1. WO 158/751, Public Record Office (PRO), London.
2. WO 106/1206, PRO, London.
3. WO 95/4955, PRO London.
4. ADM 137/3943, PRO, London.
5. WO 32/5752, PRO, London.
6. CAB 45/105, PRO, London.
7. 158/715, PRO, London.
8. 95/5430, PRO, London.
9. The Vrangel Collection, Standord University.
10. Deryabin, A. *The White Armies.* Moscow Press. 2000
12. *The Encyclopedia of the Russian Civil War.* Moscow Press. 1982
13. Roberts, C. *In Denikin's Russia and Caucasus 1919-20.* 1921.
14. Erickson, E. *Ordered to Die, History of the Turkish Army in WWI.*

10

The Estimated Organization and Cost of the Volunteer Army

As the Volunteer army grew, it was estimated that ten divisions could be formed, each consisting of nine regiments and one artillery brigade. However, due to other external problems and security matters it was decided to create only five divisions in February, 1919.

At this time, the currency exchange rate was about 100 roubles to 1 franc. The price of 410 grams of bread at Novororissk cost 20 roubles. The same loaf in Paris was 1 franc.

The Volunteer army organizational plan was as follows:

Five infantry divisions
One Cavalry regiment
Five light Artillery batteries
Four Mountain artillery batteries
Nine heavy artillery batteries
Three anti-aircraft batteries
Three armor car batteries
Four tank batteries
Two airplane squadrons
Five Engineer battalions
Five March Battalions
Three Medical transports

Each Infantry division would ideally contain: 27 battalions (9 regiments), one artillery brigade, divisional staff. Each division, in theory, would contain 888 Officiers, 19,866 men, 4625 horses, 16 light batteries and 8 howitzers. Had this plan been achieved, the Volunteer Army would have been a potent force. This would not be the case.

The estimated montly cost to sustain these five divisions was estimated at 6, 057,490 francs or 1,211,498 francs per division for salaries alone. This figure also assumed that each soldier cost about three Francs daily for ammunition, the costs for ammunition alone ran 1,787,940 Francs per division, or 8,930.790 Francs for five divisions. It was assumed that for one horse, the cost was three francs daily, so the monthly cost to maintain the horses ran 416,250 Francs per division. In the end, Denikin's accountants calculated that to operate one division for one month would cost 3,415,688 francs. These monthly costs did not include the listed armament costs:

To operate one artillery battery (3 guns) cost 153,160 Francs.
A Heavy artillery battery (4 guns, 8 Howitzer) cost 150,283 Francs.
A Armor Car battery (16 cars) cost 36,156 Francs.
An airplane Battery (27 airplanes, 9 of which are fighter.) cost 53,834 francs.
(A Battery consisted of 3 squadrons, each with 9 planes)
One Truck Park (100 trucks) cost 50,389 Francs.
One Medical Park (100 carriages) cost 36, 382 Francs.
One Infantry March battalion (9 companies) cost 312,903 Francs.
One Tank battery (4 tanks) cost 60,834.

Denikin was informed that to operate his planned army for one month would cost 21, 864,091 francs. This figure did not include the purchase of medical supplies, office supplies and other miscellaneous non-war material also required. This "miscellaneous" cost ran another 2,000,000 francs a month! The total cost was 23,864,091 francs per month!

All of the previous provides an "accountants" view for creating an army. Denikin was heavily supplemented with funds from the French and British. But as the above costs re-

French troops in Odessa, 1919. These men are from the 129th Senegalais Bn. Photo: Museum of Russian Army, Moscow

veal, these were quickly consumed forcing Denikin to pursue a quick resolution of the Civil War in 1919. For the Reds, the prolongation of the war was in their best interest for obvious reasons.

For example, here is the breakdown of the monthly payroll for the Administrative part of a single division:

Division Commander	X 1	1,665 Francs
Brigade Commander	X 3 (1200 ea)	3,600 Francs
Staff Head	X1	990 Francs
Senior Staff	X3 (575 ea)	1725 Francs
Division Doctor	X1	990 Francs
Quartermaster	X1	750 Francs
Asst. Officers	X3 (407 ea)	1221 Francs
Communications Officer	X1	575 Francs
Commandant	X1	575 Francs
Total		12,091 Francs
Soldiers attached to HQ	40 Communications, 50 Security, 12 Writers, 21 Horsekeeper	3690 Francs
Horses	34	
Carriages	7	
Cars	2	
Motorcycles	4	
50 km of phone wire		

The cost for nine infantry regiments (27 battalions) to maintain for one month was:

389,916 Francs for Officers and Staff
718, 200 Francs for infantry
3115 Francs for Horses
Total cost: 1,108,116 francs per month.

In comparison, the divisional artillery brigade was a bargain:

22,924 Francs for Officers and staff
49, 730 Francs for all others
1108 for Horses
Total cost: 73,654 francs.

When the divisional transport costs were added (15,000 francs), the total cost for one division amounted to 1,211,500 francs.

The monthly pay for officers was as follows:

Brigade commander: 990 francs
Regimental Commander: 750 francs
Battalion Commander: 675 francs
Company Commander: 574 francs

Denikin's (Denikin himself earned 2000 Fr. per month) regiments contained 91 officers, their monthly salary was 43,324 francs.

The 1,920 soldiers each were paid 40 francs a month, or 76,800 Fr. Note the disparity between officer and the rank and file. Also included were 206 carts, 52 machine guns and 4 mortars. Each Regiment would have three battalions, each with three companies. The battalion would have 20 officers and 600 men. The Cavalry regiment contained 46 officers, 960 men in six squadrons, 24 carts, 32 MG. The monthly cost ran 63,338 Fr. The artillery battery contained 5 officers, 213 men, 263 horses, 4 guns,. The cost to operate monthly was only 11,500 Fr. The artillery brigade had 44 officers, 1139 men, 263 horses, 16 lt. Guns and 8 Howitzers. The cost to operate the brigade came to 50,000 Fr. monthly.

The Automobile division contained some 27 officers, 80 men, 24 cars, and 20 trucks. The cost to maintain was 20,000 Fr. monthly. The unit had only 4 mechanics, each being paid 407 fr. monthly. Oddly, the Automobile column consisted of 7 officers, 370 soldiers, 102 trucks, 3 cars and motorcycles. The monthly cost to operate was 17,000 Fr.

More interestingly was the medical unit/hospital for the army. It consisted of 4 officers, of which only 2 were doctors. A doctor was paid only 575 Fr. a month. The 124 soldiers attached received 30 Fr. a month since they were not on the front lines (those soldiers received 40 fr. per month). The medical unit cost 6000 Fr a month.

Denikin's staff detailed the actual costs to arm and supply a single corps in amazingly detail. The following show the costs for one corps:

504 MG @5000 Fr. each = 2,520,000 Fr.
37,800,000 MG roounds for MG= 9,828,000 Fr.
162 mortars @ 5,000 Fr. each = 810,000 Fr.
500 cases of shells for the mortars = 10,854,000 Fr.
Ammunition for 1500 rifles (35,000,000 rounds)= 9,080,340 Fr.
For 23,306 rifles @ 200 Fr. each = 4,661,200 Fr.
16,200 Shells for 100 90mm mortars @ 350 fr. ea. = 5,751,000 Fr.
3000 automatic revolvers @ 39 Fr ea.= 117,000 fr.
2114 Horses@ 1,800-2500 Fr ea. = 6,000,000+ fr.
1,500,000 automatic revolver cartridges = 165,000 fr.

The total cost to arm a single corps was 57,445,736 Fr. Other costs are listed below:

48 3" guns @ 31,000fr. ea. = 1, 488,000 fr.
24 48mm guns @ 55,000 ea. = 1,320,000 fr.
24 6" guns @ 93,000 ea. = 2,232,000 fr.
12 3" mountain guns @ 22,000 fr ea = 264,000 fr.

8 42mm guns @ 69,000 fr ea. = 552,000 fr.
4 Tanks @ 65,000 fr. ea. = 260,000 fr.
8 Armor Cars@ 40,000 ea. = 320,000 fr.
124 Machine guns @ 5,000 fr ea. = 620,000 fr.
9,300,000 rounds for MG= 2,418,000 fr.
7000 horses @ 2,000-2500 fr ea. = 15,250,000 fr.
560 Harnesses for horses = 28,000,000 dr.
540 carts @ 1800 fr ea. = 972,000 fr.
Ammunition for 96 howitzers= 864,000 fr.
Ammuniton for 144 3" guns= 1,872,000 fr.

These "other" costs amounted 34,750, 230 fr.

A divisons' depot of arms cost 8,577,542 Fr. The two most expensive items were horses, some 2330 of them, costing 4,056,000 Fr. The cost of 120 mortars ran 1,560,000 fr. Some 2000 cases of 3" shells (96,000 shells) ran 7,680.000 Fr; 500 cases of 6" shells (12,000 shells) cost 3,600,000 Fr; 2000 cases of 37mm (8000 shells) for the tanks 320,000 fr.

The total cost of ammunition in the depot alone cost 18,049,200 Fr. The cavalry regiment's largest expense were 1,150 horses amounting to 2,800,000 Fr. The regiment total came to 4,222,356 Fr. The automobile section contained 102 trucks, each costing 15,000 Fr, for a total of 1,530,000.

The total cost to arm and to provide ammunition to a single corps was 143,677,250 Francs. The total number of horses in a corps was 15,723, plus 3,891 carts. Thus, the estimated cost to operate a single corps unit in Denikins Volunteer army was as follows:

Equipment	Infantry 57,445,735 Fr. Artillery 61, 376,972 Fr. Engineer 8,903, 350 Fr. Cavalry 4,222,356 Fr Automobile Column 1,771,500 Fr Division transport 3, 149,096 Fr Medical Units 1,903, 536 Fr Misc costs 4,904,704 Fr **Total: 143,677,250 Fr.**
Salaries	Infantry 1, 358, 776 Fr. Artillery 600,000 Fr. Engineer 113,516 Fr. Cavalry 83,836 Fr. Medical 17, 856 Fr. Automobile Col. 51, 261 Fr. Divisional transport 44, 841 Fr. Misc expenses 73,400 Fr. **Total: 2,341,440 Fr.**

The food and upkeep of the horses alone in a corps cost 1,415.070 Fr. To operate five corps sized units, the total cost resulted in a whopping 700,000,000 francs.

The Composition of the Volunteer Army

A corps sized unit in Denikin's Army, in theory, was suppose to contain the following:

Three Infantry divisions
Twelve 3" gun batteries
Six 48mm gun batteries
Three 6" gun batteries
Four gun carrier
Twelve tanks and armor cars (four of each per division)
One Cavalry regiment
Three medical units
Three Automobile columns
Three Engineer battalions

The composition of the Denikin army, as planned, followed the conventional triangular line:

The Infantry Division

Four companies to a battalion (each company contained 4 infantry and 1 MG platoon) totaling 225 men, 8 officers,4 MG. The actual combat strength was 160 men. Three battalions to a regiment (each battalion had 850 soldiers, 15 officers,12 MG). The actual combat strength was 640 men.

Three regiments to a division (each regiment had 4274 men, 56 MG, 8 mortars,8 90mm mortars). There were 149 officers, 60 wirers, 559 horses, 4 motorcycles, 3 sapper platoons. The actual combat strength was 1920 men 12 companies.

Three divisions to a Corps (each division had 9 battalions,some 12,800 men, 160 MG, 54 mortars and 54 90mm mortars). The actual combat strength was 5780 men.

Other attached units:

288 Cavalry with 8 MG, one artillery brigade of 4 battalions totaling 32 guns and 16 MG. It was further subdivided into batteries, of which, one battery consisted of 4 guns and 2 MG. There was two 3" gun battalions, one 48mm gun battalion, one 6" gun battalion. There was one Armor Car battery consisting of 8 Austin Armor cars, 4 MG. The divisional staff contained 2 cars and 2 motorcycles. One engineer battalion with one Sapper and Road company (each with 4 platoons).

Cavalry Units

The Cavalry units contained squadrons. Each squadron had 4 platoons, each with 36 men. The squadron consisted of 220 men, 6 officers and 4 Lewis Guns. The combat strength was 144 men. The Cavalry regiment contained six squadrons, 66 officers, 1737 men, 32 MG and 24 Lewis Guns. Effective combat strength was 960 men. Included were 2020 horses, 93 carts.

The Cavalry division had three brigades. The Horse brigade contained six horse regiments (36 squadrons) totaling 5760 men,144 Lewis Guns. The Infantry Brigade had one infantry regiment. The infantry regiment had a total of 960 men, 232 MG. The artillery brigade contained eight batteries with a total of 32 guns.

The Corps

A Corps contained three infantry divisions. In addition to these units, the Corps had one Cavalry brigade and artillery brigade. The artillery brigade contained three batteries, each with two 42mm guns and one 6 " gun, four armor car batteries, each with eight Austin ACs, and one tank battery with eight tanks (Whippet or MkV male). The Corps also contained an Engineer regiment containing four battalions: One Sapper battalion (3 Cos.), one road battalion (3 Cos.), one engineer battalion and one telegraph battalion. The Corps also had an aviation division attached containing a reconnaissance battery, ground attack battery and one fighter battery, and one reserve regiment containing nine companies.

In total, a Corps (including the three divisions) contained 17,280 men, 480 MG, 36 mortars, 12 cavalry squadrons (totaling 1780 men), 48 Lewis guns, 31 artillery batteries (124 guns of which 84 were 3," 36 were howitzer, 4 anti-aircraft), 32 Austin Armor Cars, and eight tanks.

The Army

An Army contained four corps, one cavalry group, one heavy artillery brigade (containing two artillery battalions with 8, 9 10, 11 and 12" guns). These two battalions had a total of 12 batteries with a total of 24 guns. The Engineer regiment contained a road battalion, a telegraph battalion, and a Sapper battalion. Also attached was another aviation group with 24 fighter airplanes, 18 ground support airplanes, 12 reconnaissance airplanes. There was also a railroad repair battalion with three companies. The army also contained a reserve brigade containing four regiments, each with three battalions.

The **Divisional artillery** consisted of the following:

Four 3" batteries, each battery with 4 guns.
Two 48mm batteries, each battery with 4 guns.
One 3" Mountain battery with 4 guns
One 6" howitzer battery with 4 guns
A mortar battery with 32 mortars
Three tanks, Six Armor Cars

Thus, the division had (48) 3" guns, (24) 48mm guns, (12) 3" mountain guns, (12) 6 " guns, and (96) mortars.

The **Corps Artillery** consisted of:

Four 6" batteries each with 4 guns
Two 42mm batteries each with 4 guns
28 Mortars
One Tank battery
Two Armor Car batteries

When including the divisional and corps artillery totals, a single corps contained:

(12) 3" batteries = 48 guns
(6) 48mm batteries = 24 guns
(3) 3" mountain batteries = 12 guns
(7) 6" batteries = 24 guns
(2) 42mm batteries = 8 guns
124 mortars
Four tanks = 8 guns
Eight Armor Cars
Totaling 31 batteries with 124 guns and 124 mortars.

The final tally for a Corps in the Volunteer Army amounted to around 18,000 combat men, 124 guns, 4-8 tanks, 8-32 Armor cars, 500+ mortars. In reality, this varied considerably.

The armor car battalion consisted of 27 officers, 80 soldiers, 4 mechanics, 16 Austin Armor cars, 20 heavy trucks and eight light trucks. The salaries per month ran 20,000 francs.

The cost of the Volunteer Army alone demanded that Denikin receive funds from England and France. Worse, the costs noted previously does NOT include the cost of the Don Army, or any others that were also under the leadership of Denikin under the the banner of the " Armed Forces of South Russia"(AFSR). Another matter becomes quite clear, and remains true in the 21st Century, that a short war is mandatory due to the unusual high cost of weapons and support. In Denikin's case, he knew he could only prevail for a short time. Denikin knew the allied nations would not continue to "bankroll" this effort for long (and he was right) and that a prolong war would defeat for him.

Soldiers of Denikin's Army, 1919.

The Don Army

Another independent army that would come under Denikin's authority was the Don Army. It was led by General Krasnov and Kaldedine. Kaldeine was a 56 year old former commander of the 12th Cavalry division in 1916, under General Brusilov. He later became the Corps commander of the 8th Corps on the Southwest Front.

The Don region had become the berthing area for the White movement to a large extent, over 200 former officers of the Imperial Army fled from the purges in the North. The Don army held an area south of Voronezh (including Rostov) and south of Saratov passing west of Tsaritsyn (Stalingrad) to Manich Lake. Krasnov, while pro-German, made plans to move on Moscow and wished to remain an independent state until Russia became a great power.

The Don Army, as of June, 1918, consisted of the following:

- 1st Division
  - 1st Black Sea Infantry Reg.
  - 1st Kuban Rifle Reg.
  - 1st Black Sea Horse Reg.
  - 1st Artillery Battery (3 guns)
  - 1st Engineer Company
- 2nd Division
  - 4th Kuban Horse regiment
  - 2nd Artillery battery (3 guns)
  - 2nd Engineer regiment
  - 1st Strike regiment
  - 1st Infantry regiment
- 3rd Division
  - 2nd Infantry regiment
  - 2nd Horse Regiment
  - 3rd Artillery battery (6 guns)
  - Heavy Artillery battery (4 guns)
  - Naval platoon (2 guns)
  - 3rd Engineer Company
- 1st Cavalry Division
  - 1st Kuban Cavalry regiment
  - 1st Caucasus Cavalry regiment
  - 1st Ukrainian Cavalry regiment
- 1st Kuban Cavalry Brigade
  - 2nd Kuban Cavalry regiment
  - 3rd Kuban Cavalry regiment
  - Artillery section (2 guns)

Armor Trains "Vernyi," "Kornilvosky," and "Don."

The Don Army totaled five infantry regiments, eight Cavalry regiments, five batteries, some 8,500 to 9, 000 men, 21 guns. Besides the Don army, Denikin would also command other smaller bands of anti-bolshevik forces by the end of 1918:

The Crimean-Azov Army
The North Caucasus Army
The Army of Turkestan
The Molodaya Army (20,000 18 yr.old recruits)

By January 1919, all these independent armies would fall under the Armed Forces of South Russia banner. It was this group that had the best shot of ending communism before it had become rooted. Despite the assorted armies, only one could be called elite, that was the Volunteer Army, which comprised of mostly experienced and professional soldiers. Most of the Volunteer Army uniforms were not the dull khaki worn by most others, but black with white piping or other colors.

The situation continued to remained unclear by mid-1918. The first area to claim independence was the Ukraine, which did so near the end of 1917. This group of nationalists were led by Vladmir Vinnichencho, a writer, and Simon Petlyura, a journalist. Together, they rallied enough men to create a small army. This army was squashed in January, 1918, by the Soviet forces. By March, the Soviets gave the region to the Germans. The Germans appointed their own puppet, Pavel Skoropadsky. The Ukrainian army was not a formal army, as witnessed in this German report to General Hoffman, who was in charge of operations on the East Front:

> "May, 1918. The Ukrainian Army consists of mercenaries, former soldiers and officers, adventurers and unemployed men. There is no rank system. A commander of a post earn 400 roubles a month and receives little respect from subordinates. The food,quarters and uniforms are free. The force consists of 2,000 men. The uniforms are mostly old Russian, and fur hats with long flammes of many colors. A soldier's weapon is anything that he can carry. There is no standard issue."

As with the Ukraine, the Caucasus region also declared independence from Russia, namely Georgia, Armenia and Azerbaijan. Georgia and Armenia welcomed all allied aid, while Azerbaijan cooperated with Turkey and the Germans. Georgia was occupied by elements of the British 13th and 39th divisions, almost 30,000 men. In the Black Sea, the British kept two battleships, six cruisers, and eight destroyers. In eastern Georgia, the Turk 7th division with 25,000 men opposed the allies, which included 30,000 Germans led by General Von Kressenstein. By June, 1918, the Germans had taken Tiflis. During this time, the Turks created a " Caucasian Muslim Army" consisting of 13,000 men and 40 guns.

It is clear that "chaos" reigned decisively in Southern Russia. The Nationalists were independent and pro-Russian but anti Soviet. The Anarchists wanted to destroy everything. The Soviets or Reds wanted communism. The Whites despised the Soviets and pro Russians. Finally, there were those who simply wanted independence.

As 1918 continued, it was clear these anti-Soviet forces under Denikin had the full support of the allies in terms of money and weapons. Thus, for the time being, these adverse bedfellows, each having their own agenda, collasced towards the end of that year into the AFSR. The problem was their own prejudices and rivalries remained separate and intact. This caused serious problems as Denikin attempted to move north toward Moscow. Denikins problems were not only the Soviet forces opposing him, but the internal political differences amongst the many small armies that joined the cause.

General chaos continued through the summer and into the fall. The general pattern followed the same line: the allies talked intervention, but took no action until intervening in North Russia in August,1918, at Archangel. In South Russia, it remained talk and discussion, except for the British intervention in the Baku region via Iran. The main reason for this was of course, WW1, which continued and despite the foreseeable end, remained in the allies uppermost minds.

The allied intervention took the first concrete form during November, 1918, in Jassy, Rumania. This meeting, organized by the British and French, was to solve problems of the German withdrawal from the Ukraine and how to overthrow Bolshevism (aka communism). The Russian delegates present were undecided as to what type of government they wanted. The only matter they, the Russians, agreed on was that a government under Petlyura was impossible. Denikin's interest was served by his representitive, Prince Kakurine, who requested aid from the allies. The French offered a division.

To Denikin, this offer was lacking, he had expected an allied expeditionary force of 150,00 men. The Jassy conference ended with the allies promising to send arms and extensive financial support in the sum of 1,500,000 roubles. Further, Denikin had been promised that the the French and Greeks would occupy Odessa, Sebastopol, Kiev and Kharkov, and that all supplies left by the Germans including those in Rumania were for the AFSR.

On Novemeber 10th, two British light cruisers, the Liverpool and Renan arrived at Novorissk. The Russians greeted them wildly. On November 15th, the French proposed that Bulgaria ship to Novorossisk 20,000 rifles and 50 million cartridges. On the 16th, the French offered to send 12 divisions (Greek and French) and all surplus arms and ammuni-

Artillery of the Don Army, 1919.

tion in the Southeast Front. On the 23rd, a French naval squadron appeared at Novorossisk, and on the 28th, French and British representitives met with Denikin at Ekaterinodor.

During this meeting, it was discussed that five French, two British, two Italian and three Greek divisions would arrive in the Ukraine. A week later, this had changed and only the 56th, 30th, and 16th French divisions would be sent along with the 1st Greek Corps (1st, 2nd and 13th divisions) under General Borius. Oddly, France's General Berthelot warned that if intervention is going to take place, it should be done with sufficient force, not token units because the French soldier was sick of war. These would be famous last words as the French sent troops into the quagmire of the Ukraine.

In September, 1918, the Volunteer army comprised of 35,000 men, 86 guns, 256 MG, 5 armor trains, 8 armor cars and 7 airplanes. Because the Kuban forces had joined the White movement, by November, his army had increased to 90,000 men and was composed of:

1st Corps (Kutepov)
2nd Corps (Borovsky)
3rd Corps (Schilling)
1st Cavalry Corps (Wrangel)

In addition to this, he also had several independent battalions and brigades.

French Intervention Debacle

The French plan was to seize Odessa, Sevastopol, Nikolale, Tararrog, Kiev and Kharkov. The orders were issued on Dec. 5th, 1918. In Odessa, Denikin had 1500 men and 10 guns under Grishin. They held Odessa until Ukrainian patriots under Petylura took It. Petylura allowed the first French to land, some 400 Marines, landed at Odessa, led by General Borius who was aboard the Cruiser Mirabeau. Odessa was occupied. The first French forces to land were 2400 men from the 176th regiment/56th division on December, 17th. These men were not well equlpped and shared ownership of Odessa with 3000 Ukrainians (the Germans had left the week before). In addition to these, 1800 French Colonial troops arrived from the 1st African Regiment (the 241st artillery battalion) and one Greek regiment (2000 men). These were to be used to occupy the Ukraine in order fill the void left behind by the Germans. Since outside of Odessa was in Ukrainian hands, the French troops were not allowed to leave Odessa until January, 1919. Meanwhile, another French unit, the 175th Regiment/56th division occupied Sebastopol. When the French arrived, their purpose was not to conquer but to provide security and to support all White forces. However, upon their arrival they found two or three separate groups, each opposing not only Soviet forces but against one another. This was an unexpected dilemma, causing confusion to which side the French should support?

French troops advanced occupying the towns of Otchokov, Nicolaiev, and Kherson by Jan 31st. The French attempted to create a Ukrainian Armiy with 30,000 nfles and 42 million rounds of ammo brought with them. However, the Ukrainians did not like the French at all, although, they liked them more than the Germans encroaching at Kiev. In Odessa, some 100,000 men were available for military service out of the one million residents. As France tried to bring the anti-Bolshevik forces together, the more alienating it became. Few enlisted in the French Ukrainian army.

Odessa was without electricity due to a lack of coal and wood, soon, telephone poles began to disappear! The city Itself had few police and abounded with hoodlums and gangs. To control this situation, the French introduced draconian methods to maintain law and order. This had the opposite effect. The lawlessness increased.

The first inkling of disaster for the French began on Feb 4, 1919, when French troops were ordered to attack Tiraspol held by the Reds. The attack failed due to poor execution. On the 6th, the 58th regiment/30th division was ordered to re-attack. This regiment refused. This was followed by the 19th battery/2nd Lt. Artillery regiment on the 7th, which refused. Eventually, the artillery did barrage, but the 467 men from the 1st and 2nd Bns/531h continued to refused. They stated that four years of war was enough. The division commander. Gan. Antoine Novel, had heard the same reasons before and understood. The French decided to call off the attack and ordered other allied units which did capture the city. Reports from the 56th division also revealed that some French troops were covertly attending some Red rallies and meetings and that the propaganda was effectively argued. Red propaganda argued that, "the war *was* over and Germany was defeated, so why are you here?" French soldiers began to ask "what do we have against the Reds?"

The French also managed to irritate even their friend, General Denikin, as one of his subordinate units in Odessa grew to 5000 men under General Tumanovsky. The French proposed to Denikin that mixed brigades should be created from the Russian soldiers and led by French officers. This proved to be insulting to Denikin and he ordered his subordinate not to cooperate in this matter.

The French continued their advance and arrived in Birzula and Tiraspol disregarding Russian dignity and patriotism. This caused nearly all of their allies to oppose them. Meanwhile, the Soviets occupied Kiev and Kharkov.

By March, the French Occupation forces consisted of:

> 56th French division, 13th and 1st Greek division, a Polish brigade, 1st bn/144th regiment, 103rd Tank Company (Renault tanks), 1 btty/345th Heavy Art. Regiment, 10 th reg/4th Algerian division, 1st Bn/66the Regiment, 125th, 123rd, 129th, 144th, 130th Sengalese Bns, 241st art. Regiment. This totaled 40-45,000 men.

At Kherson, three Greek battalions (under Col. Tsalakopoulos) and 4 French Bns stood. These forces were dispersed to surrounding areas until the Kherson Garrison had 1000 men (700 Greek and 300 French under Col. Clavieres), two artillery guns and several gunboats. On March 8th, a former ally, Grigorev, with 1700 men and 3 guns, attacked. The Greek/French held Kherson whose population was pro Red, and when attacked, the Greeks and French held for a short time. By the end of the 9th, the Reds had nearly surrounded the town and two companies of the French 176th regiment refused to continue to fight. Red tanks, FT-17's, appeared while the promised Greek reinforcements failed to appear.Col. Clavieres then issued an evacuation order, which caused heavy civilain losses. These losses amounted to 400 killed, 131wounded, 51 missing. By the l0th, the storm was approachIng the Greek garrison at Nikolaev (held by 100 French and 1500 Greek) the base of the 15th Landwehr German division (10,000 men). The Germans had been cut off and by terms of the agreement, were subject to French orders (this division was commanded by General Zak, who was under Rear Adm. Von Kessler). The French ordered the Germans to defend the city with 50 guns and 100 MG. The Reds attacked and were repulsed. The defending French and Greek troops were losing men at a high rate, some companies had only 30 men! The total force of 2000 men had only 1200 rifles. The commander of the French forces requested permission to withdraw French troops, to be replaced by colonial troops who are willing fight. In one day alone, there were four instances where French troops refused to fight. At Beriezovka, held by one Greek regiment, the Red 15th regiment attacked sending an armor train into the town with guns blazing creating a panic. The Red force numbered only a few hundered. Then the Reds attacked using aircraft and tanks supported by artillery forcing the French and Greeks to fall back to Odessa (defended by two French, two Greek, part of a Rumanian division, some 35,000 men) which fell under siege on March 15th.

The French morale plummeted and the local population became the enemy. The French tried to reassure the population of Odessa that France would defend this to the end. On March 20th, France declared the city under seige and that all emergency measures would be taken. But the French continued to be bewildered, and thus, sent out the same contradictory signals to the Russians. This gave the feeling to the Russians that France would not oppose the Soviet bolsheviks.

In Sevastopol, only 6000 troops defended. The situation here was somewhat better for the French held off the Reds until the city was evacuated on April 12th. This was mainly due to the 20 French warships in the harbor that lended support. However, even the 10,000 naval personnel were not exempt from the Red propaganda. On March 17th, a series of rebellions occurred within the French Navy on the Black Sea. These had been stirred up when French naval personnel went ashore on leave and attended pro – Red rallies. When the French shore police intervened, gunfire erupted and 20 French sailors were killed. The source of the rebellion nested with some of the crew aboard the Battleship *France*. This spread to the crews of the *Jean Bart, Mirabeau, Vergniaud, Briux, Rousseau*. It became so bad that the Admiral of BB France scuttled away from the others. By the 22nd, the rebellion was over.

The French issued orders to evacuate Odessa on April 2nd. Due to a lack of transport, some 30,000 Colonial troops of France were forced to march to Bessarabia. They arrived there on April 15th. The 5000 man brigade under Denikin's control escaped to Rumania where it was interned by the French! The evacuation of Odessa amounted to 16,000 French Colonials, including five Algerian battalions and 15,000 Greeks. The evacuation was completed by the 8th. By May, the French had evacuated Sevastopol.

This short intervention had cost France 1.19 Billion francs!

In June, the French created a commission to look into the debacle. The Minister of the Navy attributed the rebellion to poor food, poor mail service and lack of sufficient leave. Privately, the reasons voiced were poor political objectives and goals of the intervention not any lack of supplies or men.

The French connection with Denikin had left a bitter taste with Denikin but he had no choice except to continue to plead with the French Military Mission (led by Captain Fouquet) for men and material. Denikin openly complained that the French troops were wasted in the Odessa area and should have been used with his forces along the Don river.

By early March 1919, both the British and French had tried military intervention, albeit, half-hearted and misdirected. Both had failed miserably. For France, from April onward, any help given would only be in money or weapons. The British,too, were willing to sending huge stocks of weapons and establish training schools in the Taganrog area with their Military Mission under Gen. Holman. They would refuse to send combat units and only volunteers could go to South Russia.

The main staging area for any military units being sent to South Russia was at Istanbul, Turkey. Once Turkey surrendered, the following units were stationed there and available for military intervention in 1919. Out of all the units available, only one would be used to land in South Russia.

Army of the Black Sea (British)

83rd and 85th Infantry brigade HQ
84th Punjabis Reg
1st Hants Reg
2nd bn/Royal Scots Fusiliers
31st Punjabis Reg
2nd Bn/39th Gharwals
Thracian Reg
28th Division HQ
84th Infantry Brigade HQ
1st Bn/54th Sikhs reg.
1st Bn/24th Pubjabis Reg.
1st Bn/21st Punjabis Reg.
2nd Bn/128th Engineer reg.
242nd Infantry brigade
1st bn/ Gordon Highlanders
1st bn/110Jats
30th Brigade
2 Bn /4th Gurhkas
1st Bn/89th Punjabis Reg.
28th Artillery Brigade
2nd Bn/Dublin Fusiliers
1st Bn / 25th Panjubis
1st Bn/2nd Rajputs
2nd bn/Durham Lt Infantry
39th Artillery Brigade
21st Panjubi Reg.
10th Artillery Brigade
20th Hussars

Bulgarian Troops (2400 Officers, 34,000 men)

4th Division (Sumen, Varna, Pleven)
3rd Division (Silven, Burgas)
6th Division (Sofia)
1st Division (Sofia)
2nd Division (Philippopel)
10th Division (Haskov)

Greek Troops

14th Division (9th,29th regs) (Seres)
Seres Division
9th Division (Adrianople)
Xanthi division (Kirk Killissa)
Smyrna Division (Turkey)
Archipelago Division (Turkey)
Manissa Division (Turkey)
Chatalja, Stefano, Makrikeui, Gallipoli, Heraclee reg.(Istanbul)

Italian

2nd Bn/313th Reg (Istanbul)

Rumanian (230,000 men)

15th Corps
- 15th Division (Constanta)
- 9th Division
- 10th Division

2nd Corps (Bucharest)
- 12th Division
- 13th Division
- 6th Division
- 2nd Cavalry Division
- 1st Corps
- 11th Division

7th Corps
- 21st Division
- 18th Division
- 1st Cavalry Divison

18th, 19th, 21st, 9th,10th, 15th, 5th, 6th,13th Artillery Brigades.

In adfition to these forces, the British had the 27th Division HQ and 87th brigade in Batum, two artillery batteries of the 81st Brigade and the Brigade HQ in Tiflis.

One of the major forces opposing the bolsheviks was the Polish Army. This had the effect of drawing off many of the Red armies and strengths since both viewed one another with increased animosity. Denikin sought to have some of Poles fight with his men and under General Zogligouski, some 1000 men and 400 officers created the 4th Polish Light Infantry Division. Another 10,000 Polish soldiers, formerly under German control, volunteered and created a special legion. In France, 25,000 Poles and 434 officers had completed training and simply needed transportation to Denikin.

It was clear that the French and British possessed the troops to send to Denikin. Of all the troops mentioned, only those in the Istanbul area were earmarked for such possible use. The political will was simply lacking to the commitment and the chance to kill communism was missed and has been since regretted. Even sending one token allied unit to fight along side of Denikin's men would have had huge morale enhancements for the White troops..

While the French were unwilling to have direct intervention, they did enjoy a steady business from Denikin. Denikin had Russian officers in France (General Svidersky of 94, Avenue d' Iena, Paris, was one) wheeling and dealing for military supplies beginning in November, 1918. There was nothing secretive about this and it was purely business.The French were always more than willing to sell most military supplies to Denikin for a price. As for the British, their military aid was a grant from Churchill for the goal of stopping Bolshevism. It was "Churchill's War."

By June 1919, Denikin had received 4500 syringes, 80 tons of medicene, and 1000 cases of Iodine. Other material purchased were 80 French 76.2mm artillery guns, 22000 sabers, 18000 rifles (Model 1886), 240,000 76.2mm shells, 75 Vicker Machine Guns with belts, and 72,000 bombs. This material was shipped to the French Military Mission, South Russia. Once the material arrived, payment was due to the Military mission.

France did make money, for example, they sold 24 Renault FT-17 tanks to Denikin for 1,500,000 Francs; 470 Berdan Rifles ran 64,000 Fr.; 17,400 cartridges for the old rifles cost 48,000 Fr; 50 Lewis Guns cost 30,000 Fr; and 25 airplanes ran 1,750,000 Fr. Denikin received 30 Sopwith, 60 Salsom, 30 Spad 13, 18 Levy Seaplanes for his upstart airforce.

In August, Denikin received 11,000 Mauser rifles, 46 artillery guns and 88 Machine guns in trade with the Germans for harvested grain. He also bought weapons from the Germans: One Mauser rifle = 1 DM, 1 artillery gun = 150 DM, telegraph machine= 500 DM.

Arms sales to the White armies was a quite profitable business.

By October 1918, the Red airforce counted 88 detachments. However, a majority of them were incomplete and some existed only on paper for Lenin and others to see. A total of 27 detachments were dismantled. These were combined with others creating 61 full detachments each with six aircraft.

This was to provide each rifle or cavalry division an air reconnaissance air-detachment (called PAO). Each front (composed of several armies) was assigned a fighter division made up of three detachments (called IAO). Of the 61 detachments created, 46 were designated air reconnaissance (40 divisional and 6 reserve detachments) and 12 fighter detachments (4 divizions (battalion), one for the East, North, South and Western Fronts). The detachment's geographic names were done away with (with the exception of special honorable names) and replaced by a simple number type designation : 1st reconnaissance, 2nd fighter, etc. The detachment's number normally conformed to the division's number it was assigned to.

In practice, this was a slender and fragile air system and the small air strength made it practically impossible for the Reds to launch large independent operations. In such a situation, the Red airforce rapidly found itself without air assets. Instead of planning large scale air-strikes, the staff officers were required to stitch together circulars, put together educational manuals and go about their routine handling complaints on the distribution to detachments of scarce leather jackets!

The aviation workers settled down in their swank and comfortable private residences along the Garden-Samotechnoy Street. Before long, the Red Airforce staff officers occupied even better accomdations: a former manor-house farmstead near Serpukhov.

In time, many pilots made their way to the White Armies. In 1918, on the Eastern and Southern fronts no less than 30 pilots flew their aircraft over to the enemy. Such flights were and have been carefully concealed by official Soviet historians and written off as aircraft losses in the Red airforce. In September 1918, there was 266 aircraft in good condition and 59 needing repair. In storage, 169 in good condition. Thus, excluding aircraft production and flying schools the Red Air force some 435 combat ready aircraft existed.

In October, the Red aviation counted only 269 pilots and 59 fliers/observers. And most were not to be trusted by the Bolshevik. Almost 80% of the pilots (of which 60% were detachment commanders) and 100% of the observers were former officers of the Tsar's Army. Only a handful preferred the Red to the White.

It was in the West, where after the establishment in May 1918, of a line of demarcation between Soviet and German armies, there was no air combat activity. Along this front were 10 air-detachments (1st Vitebsky, 3rd and 4th Smolensk, 3rd and 4th Orlovsk, 1st Tolsky, 1st and 2nd Kalizhsky, 1st and 12th Moscow Fighter). In fact, in all of these detachments, by September, only 19 operational aircraft existed.

The Siberian Republic also possessed some military aviation consisting of four aircraft (two Voisins and two Morane) found in the village of Inokkentevsk near Irkutsk, and two Lebedevs from the Germans in Krasnoyarsk. These formed the White 1st Siberian Air Detachment. Besides those already mentioned it also had a Farmen-16 and even a rare Bleriot-I_ 1909.

In the Trans-Causcasus, on June 23rd, in Baku arrived from Saratov the Red 1st Kuban Air Division under the command of Flying Officer Develya with 13 brand new and still packed in box "Nieuports." Moscow had ordered this unit to the area with British interest increasing. On the June 25th, these aircraft gathered on Bakinsk race rack and re-equipped on the Armenikend airfield. The division was divided into three detachments, which were commanded by the pilots Lokyashko, Manocharov and Torosov. Two of them at once were sent to the front near Kyurdamir. Here they performed various recons and bombardment of hostile positions. Also, the Reds had a seaplane squadron based on the Caspian Sea formed from pilots of the Bakinsk flying school and some arriving from Petrograd. These pilots of the Baltic Fleet were made up of Russian and Armenian nationalities (H.Sakharov, G.Eryandyan, F.Ocheretyan, A.Yuzbashyan and others). The seaplane squadron was under the command of A.A.Stepanov and broke down to two detachments. The 1st detachment was commanded by Kropotov and the second by Ervandyan..

The Whites' aircraft units were created in May-June 1918. At Rostov the 1st Air Detachment of the Volunteer Army was formed.

At the close of August their aviation comprised two detachments with nine pilots and several airplanes. By October, 1918, the number of detachments increased to 5, 22 pilots and 27 aircraft.. Some of these machines were taken from the Reds and others were bartered from the Don army. In the fall of 1918, the first air battles between the Volunteer Airforce and the Red Army and air detachments occurred over Caucasus foothills, Chechnya and Daghestan.

Sources

1. WO 153/795, Public Record Office, London
2. WO 153/1208, PRO, London
3. The Vrangel Collection, Stanford University
4. WO 106/1206, PRO,London
5. WO 95/4955.PRO, London
6. CAB 45/105, PRO, London
7. WO 33/971. PRO, London.
8. Kondratev, C. *Aircraft of the Russian Civl War*. Moscow Press. 2000
9. *The Encyclopedia of the Russian Civil War*. Moscow Press. 1982
10. Marty, Andre. *The Glorious Hours on the Black Sea*. 1972
11. Grey, Marina. *Les Armees Blanches*. Paris. 1968
12. Carley, Michael. *The French Government and the Russian Civil War*. 1980
13. Xydia, Jean. *The French Intervention in Russia*. 1927
14. Warth, Rober. *The Allies and the Russian Revolution*. 1973
15. Iakushikin, E. *English Intervention in 1918-19*. Moscow Press. 1928
16. Quainton, Antony. *The French in South Russia*. 1959
17. "Armor in the Russian Civil War." Armada Magazine h#14. Moscow Press. 2000

11

Military Actions

The Soviet forces that opposed Denikin were led by a former friend of Denikin, Sorokin. He had served with Denikin before the revolution of 1917 and chose to support the Bolshevik revolution. Sorokin had 100,000 men, greatly outnumbering Denikin's small army in the Rostov area.

In late June, 1918, an irony occurred to Denikin's small army. After his army had seized the town of Torgorvaya on the 25th, the Volunteer army advanced on the the town of Belaya Glina defended by Denikin's old division, the "Iron" division (10,000 men). Denikin decided to divide his small force into three groups, each about 3000 men and advanced on the town from three opposite directions. With no way to retreat, 5000 men of the Red "Iron" division surrendered to Denikin. His army instantly grew to 14,000 men. Denikin would use the same tactic at Tikhonetskaya on July 15th. This battle is a prime example of how the combat units suddenly loss or grew in size. Defections were common on both sides when a unit became surrounded or success had been achieved. Denikin knew that the key was to set a momentum and keep it moving successfully.

After the collapse of Tikhonestskaya, Denikin's army increased to 20,000 men, 3 armor trains, 70 artillery guns, one airplane and 20 armor cars. Sorokin was now in a precarious situation as he was along the Yeya River at Kuschkeva, near Rostov and was battling the Germans and Don Cossacks. He decided to retreat to the Ekaterinodar railroad line to defend the approaches to Tsaritsyn (Stalingrad) on the Volga. Denikin quickly seized Ekaterinodar causing his army to swell with volunteers. It was a serious blow to Sorokin.

On August 26th, the key port of Novorossisk fell to Denikin after the Reds evacuated it and the Germans left. This was critical for it was where all the British war material would enter in 1919. By now, Denikin's army had grown to 50,000. In Ekaterindor, General Wrangel had his division of 5,500 men and 3 artillery guns.

Another key battle occurred on October 26th. Sorokin's army suddenly seized the town of Stavropol. Denikin ordered his units to surround the town. Then on November 15th,

Denikin ordered Wrangel's division to charge into it. This lightening thrust caught the Reds by total surprise causing a total breakdown and panic. The remainder of Sorokin's men fled towards Tsaritysn.

Most of the battles occuring in the fall of 1918 can be characterized by fleeting moments of victory, defections of men from either side to the victor, a general lack of real military operations, and Soviet morale was generally lower than that of Denikin's forces. This would be generally true until mid-October, 1919. The quality of men can also be generalized by saying the quality of the Soviet bolshevik forces were of militia quality and quite unreliable. The forces of Denikin were average for most, and in the officer's units, elite. The men under Sorokin were there for self preservation (i.e., food, money, subsistence). Under Denikin, these were secondary (at least those in the Volunteer army) to the notion of having a united, democratic Russia. This in itself raised their moral.

By late October, the Red army under Sorokin, which had up to now occupied some of the Kuban, evacuated the region. In effect, the White armies of Denikin and the Don had succeeded in creating a bridgehead free of Red forces. This was the Kuban region, flanked by the Sea of Azov to the south of Rostov. This area consisted of several hundred of miles. The first serious British attention that Denikin received was after General Greenly had visited the Volunteer Army in December, 1918. Greenly's mission was to obtain information for the British Military Mission at Novorissk.

The purpose of the Voluntary Army was to complete the following objectives:

1. Destroy Bolshevik forces in the North Caucasus
2. Defend the area which they are operating.
3. Extend the sphere of influence and control to the Crimea and Southern Districts, and to use this as a base for future operations.

To carry out #1, Denikin would use five cavalry divisions, one Infantry division and three Cossack Brigades. These were formed into three Corps under Generals Liakhoff, Kazanovitch and Wrangel. These three corps would drive both the Red 11th and 12th Armies out of the province containing Stavropol. The ultimate objective was the town of Sviati Kresti. The Red operations base was at Astrakhan and the only road leading from there ran through Sviati Kresti and then by rail. The other objective was the Grozyni oilfields, which would also cut the rail line west of Kisliar. These objectives would also bring in the agricultural bounties and allow Denikin to have direct communication with the Admiral Kolchak at Omsk.

The 2nd objective would use another infantry division and various garrisons from Novorissisk, Tuapse, Ekaterinodar, Armavir, and Temruk. Part of this force would be used to defend against the Georgians on their right flank.. The Georgians were neither a friend nor foe to the Volunteer Army. However, their actions had been hostile in the past by cutting the telegraph wires leading from Novorissisk.

The last objective would use another infantry division that operated with the Don army forces in the Southern Donets Basin. These units would gradually enlarge their operational areas toward Berdiansk. New recruits would be raised. Other small groups would act as garrisions in such places as Yalta, Kerch, Simferopol, Militopol and had the task of holding the country to south of the Dneiper River from Kherson to Alexandrovsk. By January 21st,

1919, the Volunteer Army held the following postions:

> **Stavropol Front**: Lake Manystch southwards to Dialga, Derebetovskow, Ovoshtchi, Kresta, Novogrigorievskoe, Georgievsk, Mineralaiya, Essentuki and Kislobodvsk.
>
> **Dneiper Front**: From west to east, Dneiper to Balka, then to Fedorovka, Tokmak, Karlovka. The Don Cossacks held the Donetz basin as far north as Bachmut.

This part of Russia is a vast, open rolling countryside with virtually no obstacles. Ideal for cavalry. The roads were all unpaved and turned quickly into a liquid mass of mud during rainy periods. Movement across the open fields was slow for cavalry units and very difficult for infantry and towing artillery guns. The Maxim and Vickers HMG's were skillfully handled by both sides and both transported these heavy weapons on a small four wheeled cart drawn by 2-4 horses. This allowed them to keep with cavalry movements.

Cavalry was used as a breakthrough unit for exploitation while artillery and infantry reserved for attacking strongpoints and towns. Advances usually moved along rail lines not the road network. The main line of resistance usually ran for a few miles on either side of the railroad line, afterwhich, the line was very lightly held and very porous. It was not uncommon for either side to gain or lose a depth of up to 30 miles in one day. Tanks and aircraft were usually sent in at critical moments.

General Greenly was taken to the front line area to witness combat, in his report, he stated the following:

> " The formation used by the cavalry is the old Larva formation brought up to date and combined with machine guns....fighting is fierce, no quarter is given to either side...captured enemy soldiers are drafted into the other sides forces or killed. I inspected one Bolshevik unit fighting with the Whites, they fought extremely well. There is practically no use of airplanes. The Whites send up a few and they drop a few incendiary bombs from great altitudes....artillery fire was so scant, it is practically useless."

More importantly, Greenly was the first to suggest to the British government to send tanks and airplanes:

> "If the Volunteer army were given airplanes and tanks, it would create such a panic amongst the Bolshevik troops that after a few days fighting they would be absolutely demoralised. The moral effect on the word "tank" is elation or depression for either side. Everywhere I went, I was bombarded with requests for tanks and there is no doubt whatsoever that the sight of them would create an unheard enthusiasm amongst Denikin's troops. If supplied, they should be of the "Whippet" type. These tanks could easily move with the cavalry."

This was indeed the case. When the first tanks were used in battle in May, 1919, the Soviet troops fled in panic. In some cases, the mere "word" that tanks were approaching sent the enemy into a retreat. Oddly, although more tanks were sent, only a handful ever were used at any particular time. In most cases, they were parceled out and kept in reserve. Thus, instead of using them as a breakthrough weapon, once again, they were used as infantry support. The times they were used offensively, the Red defenses fell apart.

Regardling the Staff of the Army, Greenly made the following observations:

> " As far as operations, the staff is well organized and efficient. The Administrative services are not efficient and the Medical service is deplorable. General Denikin does not stand out as a brilliant soldier or administrator, but reliable and honest, full of determiniation and patriotism. He has full support of his men. General Romanovsky, the Chief of Staff, is hard working. He is not a brilliant soldier. General Dragomirov, the assitant to Romanovsky, is an extremely capable officer and a very successful commander of the Northern Army in WW1. General Wrangel, is a very fine, dashing cavalry officer and very successful."

The British Caspian Sea Adventure

By December, 1918, the British still sought to control the large Caspian Sea. To their minds, at that time, the Reds posed a real menace that could not be ignored. It was also in concert with the plans of the Volunteer Army. Denikin's Chief of Staff, General Romanovski, presented several objectives to the Allies at the Jassy conference:

1. Occupy Baku and Grozyni
2. Occupy Petrovsk to come in communication with British troops
3. To be the masters of the Caspian Sea
4. To occupy Astrakhan and the estuary of the Volga.

The Caspian sea was important, as the Soviets were arming many of their ships and had several torpedo boats and submarines, which had arrived from the Baltic via the Volga River to Astrakhan (which was one of Denikin's objectives). Both Lenin and Trotsky openly announced that the objective for the Reds was Baku. At that time, the British had only eight ships there and to reinforce they sent a squadron of airplanes and twelve 40 foot motor boats from Batum using the railroad. Four of the armed merchant ships patrolled the northern part of the sea.

The first surface to surface action occurred on Dec.8th, 1918. Three Red ships approached the British ships Zoraster and Allaverdi and opened salvoes. The Reds fired a large amount of ammunition and never achieved a single hit even though both British ships were anchored! The British pulled anchor and began a pursuit, chasing the Reds through the fog. By the end of December, the Soviet ships were now frozen in their port. This posed a ripe target for the RAF based at Petrovsk. However, it was found that the squadron sent did not have the range to reach Astrakhan. On the 29th, the British sent four ships to the new Red base at Staro Terechnaya, bombardment commenced destroying military stores and capturing one ship. The siituation deteriorated politically due to Soviet propaganda and the White Russian Caspian Fleet considered defecting to the Reds.

Denikin's role in the British plans called for him to seize Astrakhan, so to deny the Reds a line of communication using the Volga. At first, Denikin's army was successful in moving eastwards and by February had made serious advances. During these advances, the British airplanes conducted bombing runs on Grosnyi from Petrovsk. This advance was stopped by the Reds at Kisliar. Denikin's forces were being hard pressed in the Donetz region and his advance halted along the Kuma River for lack of supplies and men.

The Naval situation for the British continued to worsen. The Caspian Sea Flotilla had planned to sortie from Baku, sailing for the Terek region. The British could not permit this force to join with the Red fleet frozen in at Astrakhan. General Denikin was informed and he immediately gave orders to the crews of the Caspian flotilla to demobilize. They would be paid off instead. The amount of the payoff would amount to £40,000. Luckily, the British Naval and Military at Baku convinced the Russian crews to remain. While the British presence in the Caspian Sea appears unecessary, the fact was that if there had been no British presence, the Reds would have threatened Baku. This could have occurred by landing a force at Lenkoran and Astara (captured documents revealed the Reds had planned an amphibious assault). Denikin's Caucasus army's right flank was protected by the British flotilla on the Caspian. Bolshevik forces considered attackiing across the Caucasus mountain range at Dariel Pass through Petrovsk and along the coast or a Red landing south of Baku. Advancing from Petrovsk to Baku was subject to British naval bombarment. The Reds decided to do neither.

The Possession of Krasnovsk may also appear wasteful, however, the British were greatly concerned about the four Red submarines based at Astrakhan. It was found out that about 100 miles south of this port, the water was too shallow for submarines to dive. This made them second class torpedo boats as they had to remain on the surface. The deep water port at Kransovsk is 150 miles from Baku. If the British did not defend this, Red ships operating nearby would be a worthy menace. The port at Petrovsk was in the ideal position allowing the British to keep the Red fleet "corralled" and remain in the northern part of the Caspian Sea.

Another purpose of the British presence in the Caspian was to provide assistance to the Ural Cossacks. At the entrance of the Ural River, some 15,000 Cossacks had gathered from their retreat near Orenburg. What they lacked were munitions. The British flotilla sailed

A British Re 8 in South Russia. Neither the British or Russian pilots like this aircraft, as it was very dangerous and hard to control.

from Baku to Guriev to bring the needed munitions to them. It would also test the Red Fleet's desire to take on the British flotilla.

The morale of the Red fleet was poor. Usually the Red ships would turn and run once the British began chase. Their fleet appeared to be serious threat with some 10 armed mechant cruisers, 9 torpedo boat destroyers, 8 small torpedo boats, 18 airplanes and 4 submarines. Many of these ships had their guns removed and for some, the draught was too deep for the channel of six to eight feet.

The British Caspian Naval Flotilla consisted of:

Name	Armament	Speed	Crew
Kruger	2 x 4," 1 x 12pdr	9	37 RN, 44 Russ
Venture	2 x 4" B.L.	12	46 RN, 28 Russ
Slava	1 x 4.7," 1x12pdr	11	53RN, 25 Russ
Zoraster	2 x 4.7"	9	42 RN, 27Russ
Bibi Ahat	4 x12pdr	9	42RN, 21Russ
Alla Vardi	2x4"	9	49 RN,25 Russ
Asia	2X4"	10	47 RN, 18 Russ
Emile Noble	1x 4.7," 2x4"	10	71 RN, 21 Russ
Volga	2x4.7," 1x4"	7	All russ.
Aladav Yusanoff	2x4.7,"1x4"	10	All russ
Piralagi	1x75mm,1x47mm	9	4 RN
Seaplane Carrier	1x4.7"		
Tula Depot ship		11	50 RN
Two tankers	12 40ft. CMB	1 Squadron of airplanes	1 Squadron of seaplanes

The following Russian ships were docked at Baku. These lacked crews:

Kara (four 4 " guns, spd of 14, crew 45)
Ardagan (three 4" guns, one 3 " gun, spd 14, crew 50)
Astrabad (two 3" guns, spf 13,crew 35)
Centro Caspie (two 4"guns)
Lt. Schmidt (five 4.7" guns, spd 15, 65 crew)
Geok Tepe (two 4," two 3")
Orlionok (thre 3"guns)
Jupiter (one 12 pdr)
Paddy (two 4," two 3")

The *Lt. Schmidt* was in the process of being activated.

The Soviet/Bolshevik Fleet in the Caspian

Torpedo boat Destroyer Finnadmon	1x3," 1x2"	
TBD Moskviatyan	1x3," 1x2"	At Simbirsk
TBD Kviatinal	1x3," 1x2"	
TBD Reshitelny	Four guns	
TBD Novik type		
TBD Emir Bukhaiskil	2x4," 1x3pdr	At Simbrisk
TBD Dyeini	2x4"	Astrakhan
TBD Turkhmenetz	3x4"	Nigni Novogrod
TBD Retive Ryani	2x 11pdrs	Pruitki type
Two TBs	2x42mm	
Six TBs	1x3"	Spd 20knts, may be dismantled
Makrel Submarine	2 tubes	100-150ft long
Minorga Submarine	2 tubes	
Okun submarine	2 tubes	
Ketr Submarine	2 tubes	
12 Motor launches	2 x2" ea, 2 MG ea.	22 knts spd
2 Minesweepers	1x47mm,1x37mm ea	
6 Minesweepers	1x37mm ea.	
CL Kolomno	4x120mm	
CL Dyele	8x120mm	
CL Bombak	2x120mm,2x75mm	
CL Aalekhar	1x3"	
CL Aga Selim	1x3,"1x47mm	
CL Mehta	1x3"	
CL Horrosan	1x75mm	Seaplane carrier
CL Sevan	1x3"	
CL Alesger	1x3"	
CL Baku	1x3"	
TR Rachael		
IceBreaker Kaspy	2x4,"2x3"	
Tug Vega	1x47mm	
Communist	2 small guns	
Volsdovski	1x47mm	
Sevsk	2x47mm	
Latish	?	
Astrakhan	1x47mm,1x37mm	
14 airplanes, 4 Seaplanes		

At this time, the British air units arrived: the 221st and 266th Squadrons of the RAF. Previously these units had fought against the Austrians in Northern Greece, and in December 1918 they unloaded off steamers in Batum. They became part of the composition of British forces that occupied the Transcaucasian, and afterwards in Baku. Eventually, their base was at the newly captured port of Petrovsk (Makhachkal today). By the end of April 1919 their six "Short 184" seaplanes and 12 DH-9 bombers were based there.

The seaplanes belonged to the 266th, and the De Havillands to the 221st Squadron. The DH-9s in Petrovsk were commanded by Colonel Bookhill, and the 266th Squadron was commanded by Captain Seydler.

In Petrovsk three "Shorts" were loaded onto the former oil tanker *Aldar Oseyn*, which was re-equipped by the British to carry seaplanes. The British planned to attack the Bolshevik-occupied city of Fort-Aleksandrovsk, on the northeastern Caspian seacoast, at the close of April. On May 12th, the English floatilla went out to sea.

On May 20th, two seaplanes dropped the first bombs on the urban port and ships standing in the harbor. Upon their return, one of the aircraft was not able to make the carrier and made an emergency landing. The remaining two seaplanes took off to bombard Fort-Aleksandrovsk, dropping 15 bombs. In their last flight on May 23rd, another "Short" crashed while landing. The British bombardments damaged a few ships and destroyed port buildings. However, unbeknownst to them, on May 22nd a direct hit had sunk the Red destroyer *Moskvite*, the largest fighting ship to be sunk by aviation in the Civil War.

For the Reds, the nearest Soviet airfield was almost two hundred kilometers from Aleksandrovsk, therefore, no interceptions against the British could be made. The commander of the Astrakhsk region sent reinforcements on May 22 to the rescue of the defenders of Fort-Aleksandrovsk. The "Shorts" reappeared over Aleksandrovsk, providing aerial cover for a naval landing. The Whites landed on the seacoast using cutters and barges. After a few minutes it was all over, and the small Soviet garrison capitulated. After this operation Denikin found himself in control of all the seacoast of the Caspian Sea, with the exclusion of the Volga Delta, where the Bolsheviks erected a powerful Astrakhansk perimeter defended by the 11th Army.

The 221st Squadron went into action by mid-May. Its first task was to bomb Astrakhan. These raids were accomplished from Petrovsk with an intermediate landing for refueling at

Red airmen in their French Nieuports armed with a 37 mm gun. Photo: V. Kulikov

a field on the island of Chechen. The flight distance was 600 kilometers total, with most of it over sea. The crews were in the air for about 4 hours. The first attack ocurred over the village of Oranzhereyn, some 60 kilometers to the southwest of Astrakhan, where the Astrakhsk Red seaplane division was based. The effectiveness of the British raids on the seaplane division can be seen in the following telegraph exchanges between Air-Director Spokesman Gorchkov and Superior of Astrakhsk Aviation Vmiokurenko:

> VINOKURENO: May 14th, perfect raid on Oranzhereyn. The British dropped 8 bombs perfectly, destroying the barge for the detachment's seaplanes. The enemy strafed with machine-guns. There were losses.
>
> GORSHKOV: You are to dispatch two pilots from the Moscow Flying School, 2 aircraft, and I with a German pilot.
>
> VINOKURENO: The seaplane division is at no more than half of its necessary amount of nine aircraft. There are only five aircraft, and all are at full disintegration. The seaplane division's land detachment has three Russian Nieuport-17, two Nieuport-25, and the rest are in repair. I sent one to be repaired by the 4th aviation train, and the other to Saratovsk. The two Russian SPADs are in repair. The unit will not be, by my thinking, efficient by this summer—and I can only get acknowledgment from the detachment commander and former division commander Demchenko. The rest of the fliers are ready for departure, and the hydro-aviation's relation to me is not subordinate....

Obviously. the British did not need to focus on the Astrakhsk Hydrodivision, as its military efficiency was nil. On May 31st, the British aircraft flew over Astrakhan for the first time. The raid was propaganda in nature. Three DH9s quietly circled round and round over the city dropping leaflets, and went away out to sea!

On June 5th, the British made a repeat visit. This time they dropped HE bombs without causing much damage. The British were intercepted by the 47th Red detachment to no avail; they had no chance of gaining speed on the De Havillands.

On June 16th, the British attempted to bomb the Baldinsk Railway Bridge over the Volga, thus cutting the Astrakhan supply link to central Russian. On that day Red pilots Shchekin and Korotkov caught sight of four approaching De Havillands from the south over the Caspian. The DH9s' altitude was 2100 meters. The Red fliers signaled each other by rocking their wings and dived down on the enemy. Shchekin, flying first, caught in his sight the leading bomber, pressed the trigger, and the MG rattled. A bullet from the synchronous machie-gun made a hole in the DH9's radiator and motor cooling shirt. After 30 seconds, the bomber engine stopped. The DH9 gracefully went nose down, crashing into the ground. Lieutenants Ingram and Mentel both survived the crash but became POWs. Their further fate is unknown. Red Army pilot Daniel Shchekin was awarded five thousand roubles after this success. The loss of two British aircraft caused them to change tactics. The DH9s now approached at an altitude of 4 km and from different directions. The worn motors of the Soviet Nieuports working on lousy substitute fuel could not reach that altitude. From the end of June to the beginning of July, the British repeatedly bombed Astrakhan in groups of 4-5 aircraft. The Red 47th detachment had only one Nieuport 23 in good order, while another three badly needed repairs. By the end of June, the 266th squadron flew raids on the port of Astrakhan and ships of the Red Caspian Flotilla. They were operating from their new floating base, the re-equipped former aircraft carrier *Eagle*.

In Petrovsk during the summer of 1919 the White 5th Air Detachment of the Volunteer Army also operated, under the command of Lieutenant Zavodsk. They arrived in May from Chechnya. The detachment had 10 aircraft: three Nieuports (remaining in Gromy); Morane 4; SPAD-7; and five newly received DH9s. This detachment also participated in raids on Astrakhan and the boats of the Bolshevik Caspian flotilla, refueling on Berezyak Island's airfield. The 221st squadron RAF was in Petrovsk until the end of August. On 1 September, in conjunction with the decision of the British Parliament to withdraw combat forces from Russia, it was broken up. The 266th squadron RAF left Russia at the end October, leaving their aircraft and aircraft carrier to the Whites.

The Volunteer Army as of January, 1919

The Volunteer army had a total of 56 battalions, 360 squadrons, 294 MG and 110 artillery guns. Of these guns, 100 are field and mountain guns, mostly 3"; ten 4.8" and 6." The combat strength came to 36,800 men with 14,400 in reserves. When counting the men in the artillery, signal, transport units (and all others) the total strength in manpower was 80,000.

The composition of the combat units (in reality)came to six cavalry and four infantry divisions plus three Cossack infantry Brigades. These units were then formed into one Cavalry and three Infantry Corps. The **1st Infantry Corps** consisted of the 1st Infantry division with nine battalions, 10 Cavalry companies, 10 artillery guns and the 1st Kuban Cossack Division with 36 Cavalry companies and 10 artillery guns. The **2nd Infantry Corps** contained the 3rd infantry division containing six battalions, six Cavalry companies and 13 artillery guns. **The 3rd Infantry Corps** consisted of the 1st and 2nd Cossack infantry brigade. The 1st Brigade had four battalions and 4 artillery guns, while the 2nd Brigade contained two battalions and two artillery guns. The 1st Caucasus Cossack cavalry division had two battalions, 36 Cavalry companies and 12 artillery guns. The Circassian Cavalry division contained 32 Cavalry companies and two artillery guns. The Terek Cossack unit amounted to one infantry battalion, 27 cavalry companies and 14 artillery guns.

The **1st Cavalry Corps** contained the 1st Cavalry division with 32 Cavalry companies, four infantry companies and 11 artillery guns. The 2nd Kuban Cossack cavalry division with 24 companies and nine guns. The 3rd Cossack brigade had three infantry battalions. Also attached was a detachment of two infantry battalions, 18 Cavalry companies and four guns under General Stankevitch. The Corps also contained an additonal cavalry regiment.

The army had some 19 infantry battalions, 25 cavalry companies, and 31 guns in various garrisons along the Georgian front.

A cavalry regiment consisted of six cavalry companies with up to six machine guns. The average sabre strength was between 150 to 800. The regiment had 1200 men. An Infantry regiment consisted of four battalions. The regiment had up to 29 machine guns. The average strength came to 1200 men, however, some had 3000. A Cossack infantry battalion contained 1000 men. Each infantry division had three light field artillery batteries. The

Cavalry division had two to three artillery batteries. Some formations contained three howitzer batteries and one heavy battery.

For communication, the normal method was the telegraph between Army, Corps and Divisional headquarters using permanent lines when available; and by telephone between divisions, brigades and regiments. Each infantry Corps had one wireless set capable of transmitting up to 133 miles (200 versts). The Cavalry corps had a wireless set with a transmission range of 100 miles.

Artillery ammunition sources were from captured enemy stocks. Most of the White guns (also captured) were in poor condition with no spare parts. Most of the artillery batteries even lacked binoculars and telephones. The men manning the batteries entirely consisted of former officers and when the artillery did fire, accuracy was good. The equipment of the Don Army was, in general, better at this time. Most of their weapons had come from the Germans.

The Air corps (commanded by Col. Kravtsevitch) of the Volunteer Army comprised of four squadrons. The 1st, 2nd and 5th squadrons supported the 3rd Infantry corps. The 6th squadron remained in reserve. Thus, three air squadrons would support the active corps on a front. Each squadron (a detachment) contains 4-5 airplanes. The Air corps had 38 airplanes. Of these, only 10 were in fair operating status. The airplanes were old and in a bad state of repair.

A Red armor train and observation balloon in South Russia.

The airplane types were as follows:

24 Nieuport 17
5 Morgan
1 Spad
3 Sonougatch
3 German
2 Bouazen

The number pilots amounted to 142 trained, 78 trained observers, 7 mechanics and 90 untrained mechanics. The army had also started a pilot school in the Sevastopol area. It was expected to train 280 pilots by October, 1919. The Don Army had between 20-30 airplanes, in the same condition, 60 trained pilots and observers.

In Greenly's report, the condition of the troops was stated as follows:

> "...the appearance of the troops leaves little to be desired. The officers are keen...morale is good...the horses are in poor condition....the weapons are as a rule badly cared for....all ranks are badly clothed and there is a need for practically everything....men are sent to the front after receiving 4-6 months of drill....."

The personnel and mobilzation of men for the Volunteer army came from three classes:

1. The patriotic and self sacrificing men from the Old Russian Army that had been Allies in WW1
2. The Kuban and Terek Cossacks who joined
3. Compulsory drafts of young men under the control of the army, ages 17-18 years old. By January, 1919, some 20,000 had already been drafted from various provinces.

Captured aircraft, lewis guns, and bombs left by retreating White forces on display. Photo: ZKM

Order of Battle for the Volunteer Army, January 1919

1st Kuban Cossack Cavalry Division (Gen. Pokrovsky)
- (2900 Cavalry, 10 guns)

2nd and 3rd Kuban Cossack Regiments
- 2nd Uman Cossack Regiment
- 2nd Zaporoshski Cossack Regiment
- 2nd Black Sea Cossack Regiment
- 2nd Line Cossack Regiment
- Kuban Guard Cossack Regiment (Ekaterinodar garrison)

2nd Kuban Cossack Cavalry Division (Gen. Ulagai, 1500 cavalry, 9 guns)
- 1st Labinski Cossack cavalry regiment
- 2nd Labinski Cossack cavalry regiment (Armavir garrison)
- 1st Kuban Cossack cavalry regiment
- 2nd Kuban Cossack cavalry regiment
- 1st Poltava Cossack cavalry regiment

1st Kuban Horse Artillery Division
- 1st and 4th Kuban Horse Batteries

2nd Kuban Artillery division
- 1st and 3rd Kuban Mountain batteries

1st Cavalry Division (2700 cavalry, 11 guns)
- Korniloff Kuban Cossack regiment
- 1st Ekaterinodar Cossack regiment
- 1st Uman Cossack regiment
- 1st Zapovozhski regiment
- 1st line regiment
- Ingerman and Hussar regiment (2 squadrons)
- Rifle Cavalry regiment (dismounted)
- 1st, 2nd 3rd Horse artillery batteries

1st Caucasus Cossack Cavalry Division (Gen. Shkuro)
- 2500 Cavalry, 1000 men, 12 guns.

1st and 2nd Kuban Partisan Cavalry regiments
- 1st and 2nd Khoper Cossack Cavalry regiments
- 1st and 2nd Volga Cossack Cavalry regiments
- 1st Volga infantry battalion
- 1st Terek partisan infantry battalion
- 1st and 2nd Kuban Horse artillery batteries
- Special Kuban battery

Circassian Cavalry Division (Gen. Girei, 3000 men, 2 guns)
- 1st, 2nd, 3rd, 4th Circassian Cavalry Regiments
- Karalaevski cavalry regiment
- Osetin cavalry regiment
- Daghestan, Suverovskaya, Bekeeshevskaya, Abasuiskaya cavalry companies
- One artillery section (2 guns)

3rd Kuban Cossack Cavalry division
- 1st Taman Cossack Cavalry regiment
- 1st Caucasus Cossack Cavalry Regiment
- 2nd Poltava Cossack Cavalry Regiment
- 1st Black Sea Cossack Cavalry Regiment
- 5th Kuban Artillery Battery

1st Infantry Division (Gen. Stankevitch, 1200 men,800 cav,4 guns)
- Composite Guard regiment
- 1st Officers Regiment (later, the Markoff)
- 1st Kuban Rifle Regiment
- Grenadier Regiment
- 1st Cavalry regiment
- 1st Izyum Hussars (2 cavalry Cos)
- Scouting company
- One Cavalry detachment (2 cos)
- 1st,2nd,3rd artillery batteries
- 1st Howitzer battery
- Guards battery
- One engineer detachment
- One reserve infantry battalion
- One wireless station

2nd Infantry Division (Gen. Tcherepoff, 3900 men, 4 guns)
- Partisan Infantry regiment
- Caucasus officers regiment
- Czech-Slovak battalion
- Korniloff regiment
- 4th Kuban Cossack Cavalry regiment
- 1st, 2nd 3rd light artillery batteries
- 2nd Reserve battalion

3rd Infantry Division (Gen. Drozdovski, Gen. Mai-Maevski)
- 1350 men, 700 cavalry, 13 guns.
- Samurski regiment
- 2nd Stavropol Rifle regiment
- 2nd Officers regiment
- 2nd Cavalry regiment
- 1st,2nd light artillery batteries
- 3rd Howitzer battery
- One mountain battery
- One engineer detachment
- 3rd reserve regiment

1st Cossack Infantry Brigade (Col. Sviashtcheff. 1600 men,4 guns)
- Elite Infantry battalion
- 6th, 7th,12th Infantry battalions
- Scout detachment
- 1st artillery battery

2nd Cossack Infantry Brigade (Gen. Geyman)(1350 men,2 guns)
- 2nd, 8th, 4th, 3rd, 11th Infantry battalions

3rd Cossack Infantry Brigade (2900 men)
- 1st, 5th, 9th Infantry battalions

Crimean Infantry Division(Gen. De Bode)
- Simferpol Officers Battalion
- Misc. Infantry regiment
- Petrenko detachment
- 2nd Taman Cavalry regiment
- Simferopol Howitzer artillery battery
- Eupatoria light artillery battery

Independent Units
- 1st and 2nd Karbardinski cavalry regiments (2000 cavalry)
- 1st Terek Cavalry regiment (1500 cavalry)
- 3rd Khoper Cavalry regiment (1500 cavalry)
- Terek Osetin Cavalry regiment (1000 cavalry)
- Terek Officer infantry battalion
- Taman Cossack infantry battalion
- Syndstron infantry battalion
- Terek Horse mountain battery
- Terek Officers battery
- 1st Heavy field battery
- Kerch heavy battery
- 2nd and 4th Howitzer batteries

Armor Trains
- Officer
- United Russia
- Gen. Alexioff
- Forward for Fatherland
- General Korniloff
- Vityaz

Support
- Medical company
- Railway repair company
- Armor car division
- Airplane repair
- Automobile division
- Wireless/Telegraph division

Independant Reserve units
- 4th Infantry battalion
- Kuban Cossack Reserve regiment
- Cossack Infantry Battalion
- Batalpashuisk Cossack battalion
- Warsaw Arsenal

General Wrangel
6000 Cavalry (84 squadrons) 4100 infantry (5 battalions) 24 guns.
General Liakhoff
4700 Infantry (9 battalions) 8750 Cavalry (97 squadrons) 34 guns.
Garrisons
Ekaterinodar: Kuban Guard Regiment/1st Kuban Cossack Cav. Div.
Armavir: 2nd Labinski Cossack Reg/2nd Kuban Cossack Cav.Div..
Bysk: One Elite Company
Temruk: Taman Cossack Battalion
Crimea: Crimean Division

Order of Battle, The Don Army, January 1919

Much of the fighting at this time was carried out by the Don Army, which consisted of Cossacks from the Astrakhan area and the Southern army (comprising of the Saratov and Voronejh Corps). The front began at the western frontier of the Don River, north of the railway from Lysky to Novokopersk, southeast to near Tsaritsyn, and southwest to Lake Manich where the boundary met the Volunteer Army.

According to General Greenly, the Don Army was of a higher standard than any other army he had seen. He noted that the men were smart and soldierly, instruction was excellant and the horses were in good condition. He noted that cavalry units were well cared for and given extra clothing and equipement, while the infantry, lacked everything and were in a bad state.

While Greenly said it was the best army he had seen, he questioned the loyalty of its leaders. Speaking of Krasnov, he stated that he "stands out both in ability and capacity far above any Russian Officer....ambitious....his past actions make him unreliable and his actions will always be guided by self interest." Of General Denisov, " a most capable soldier....very pro-German." Of General Poloakov, " A fine soldier....really brillant staff officer." Of General Mamontov, " A most gallant soldier and fine Cossack leader. He led the uprising against the Bolsheviks....used to keep a pack of hounds at Moscow." Of General Zikov, "Commands the Astrakhan Cossacks who rescued Korniloff." Of General Ibanov, "Commands the Southern Army....well respected, but is too old."

The Don Army was organized into seven groups:

Western Front (Gen Filimonov)
96th Cavalry Regiment
96th Infantry Regiment
97th Infantry Regiment
Partisan Detachments
Two guns
(This division was comprised of young Cossack men and defended the Donets Basin, assisted by the 3rd Infantry division of the Volunteer Army).
Northwestern Front (Gen Fitzkelaurov)
28th, 29th,30th Cavalry regiments
23rd,24th Infantry regiments
9 guns

- Khoper Detachment (Col Avromov)
- 4th Khoper Cav. Regiment
- 21st, 22nd, 23rd Cav. Regs.
- 6 guns
- Special Detachment (Col. Popov)
- 35th, 36th Cav. Regs.

Sitnikov Corps (Gen Sitnikov)

- At Buzuluski:
  - 24th,25th,26th Cav. Regs.
  - 22nd Infantry reg.
  - 5 guns
- At Don:
  - 32nd,33rd,34th Cav regs.
  - 31st infantry reg
  - 3 guns
- At Kumilzhenski (Col. Morgunov)
  - 3rd Infantry reg
  - 27th Cav reg.
  - 1 gun, 1 airplane, 1 armor train

Ust Medvednie Force (Gen. Yakovliev)

- 18th,19th Cav. Regs.

Tatarkin Corps (Gen Tatarkin)

- 1st,2nd,3rd,4th Cav Regs
- 2nd,3rd, 4th, 17th Infantry regs
- 7 guns

Golubenchev Detachment

- 13th,14th,15th,16th Cav.Regs.
- 1st Independent Cav.Reg

Starikov Detachment

- 9th,10th,11th,12th Infantry regs.
- 6th Cavalry Reg.
- 4 guns.

Rikovsko Detachment

- 42nd,44th Infantry regiments
- guns, 1 airplane.

Tsaritsyn Front (Gen. Mamontov)

- 1st, 4th Sotni Regs.
- 43rd,44th Cavalry regs
- 45th Infantry regs
- 8 guns

Donskov Detachment

- 41st,42nd Infantry regs. 10 guns
- 46th,47th,48th,49th,52nd,92nd Infantry regs.
- Popov Cavalry Detachment
- 45th,46th,47th,48th Cavalry reg. 6 guns.

Popov Infantry Detachment
- 1st,2nd Cossack Infantry Reg.
- 5th,6th,7th,8th Infantry regs.
- 1st Engineer Bn
- 9 guns

Zudilin Detachment
- 41st,42nd, 49th Cavalry regs.
- 43rd,44th Infantry regs.
- boats and armor trains.

Trans-Don Detachment (Gen.Alexandrin)
- 61st 62nd 63rd Cavalry regs.
- Baklan Cavalry reg.
- 61st, 62nd, 63rd, 80th Infantry regs.
- 8 guns

Zikov Corps (Gen. Zikov)
- 76th,77th Cavalry reg.
- 76th, 77th, 80th, Infantry reg.
- Salski Infantry division
- 78th,79th, 82nd Cavalry reg.
- 3 armor trains, 2 airplanes, 17 guns

The total strength of the Don army at this time came to 40,000 men, 193 guns, 621 MGs, 8 armor trains, 8 armor cars, and 16 airplanes. Opposing the Don Army were the 8th, 9th, 10th, and 11th Red Armies. These totaled 108,000 infantry, 20,000 cavalry, 1468 MGs, 34 Armor Cars, 14 Armor Trains, and 67 airplanes.

The Don Army was made up from three main classes: young men between 18-21 yrs. Old and anti-Bolshevik. Those men returning from the front many of which were tainted with communism. These were remobilzed and mixed with more elderly men. The last group were more elderly men up to 67 yrs.old.

While the Don Army was strong, its morale had been impaired by the propaganda of the Reds. In one case, three regiments simply resigned and returned home. The effective force of the mobilized Don Army deployment by fronts was as follows:

Northern Front:
- 23 cavalry regiments (12,000 men), 13 Infantry regiments (10,800 men), 70 guns, 300 MG, 3 Armor Trains, 4 airplanes.

North Eastern Front:
- 12 Cav. Regs (7000 men) 10 Infantry regs (6,500 men), 38 guns, 161 MG, 1 Armor Train, 1 airplane.

Eastern Front:
- 15 Cav. Regs (8000 men) 10 infantry regs(6500 men), 68 MG, 3 Armor trains, 4 armor cars, 6 airplanes.

South Eastern Front:
- 5 Cav. Regs (2700 men), 4 Infantry regs (2200 men), 11 guns, 43 MG.

The effective force of the Regular Don Army was as follows:

1st Don Cossack Brigade 3230 men, 8 guns, 46 MG	2 Infantry regs
2nd Don Rifle Brigade 3000 men, 6 guns, 38 MG	2 Infantry regs
1st Don Cavalry Division 5460 men, 8 guns, 28 MG	4 Cav. Regs.
2nd Don Cavalry Division 3500 men, 8 guns, 32 MG	4 Cav.Regs.
3rd Don Cavalry Division 3650 men, 8 guns,29 MG	4 Cav.Regs.
4th Don Frontier Division Regs 2000/2000 men	2 Cav regs, 2 Inf. 7 guns
1st Cossack Heavy Division 480 men, 5 airplanes	
Don Flying Division	495 men
Armed Railway Div. 4 guns, 88MG, 2 Armor Train	202 Men
Don Instructional Regiment	1171 men 2 guns, 10 MG
Don Sapper Bn	400 men
Don Chemical Detachment	60 men
Cycle Company	75 men
Convoy	125 men
Drafted Cossacks	11,000 men

The Caucasion Army consisted of:
1st and 3rd Infantry Corps, 1st and 2nd Kuban Cavalry Corps, totaling 25,000 men and 75 guns. At this time, its mission was to clear the Northern Caucasus and the west coast of the Caspian sea and to reach the Volga. It was hoped to establish communications with the British and to cut off the Reds at Baku. Protecting the the Coal mines and Rostov were 3500 men and 13 guns. Protecting the Black Sea Fleet, some 2000 men with 3-10 guns. The Novorissk port was defended by 3000 men and 4 guns.

The opposing Red 11th and 12th Armies had a combined strength of 72,000 men and 100 guns.

One can see the division in the Russian civil war was seldom that, but more likely a regiment in actual combat strength. In fact, the name Army was often deceptive. Many times it was only comprised of 10,000 men or more.

In General Poole's report written at the same time, he noted that the administrative and supply organization was terrible. He went on to state, " they lack material in all descriptions, I do not think that the best use is being made of what they have. There is a lack of grip and method throughout ". Poole suggested that British officers be attached to make sure that the stores and supplies sent are handled ecomincally and improve the Russian administration. Interestingly enough, Poole objected to further shipments of supplies to Denikin and those that Denikin wanted. He stated, "I consider them excessive in every way and should be ignored."

The Russian civil war relied totally on railroads. Roads were used, but the bulk of the fighting and shipment of supplies rested entirely on the railroads. In South Russia, there was one good such rail line, the Vladikavkaz line. Prior to the war, it was the best line, by 1919, it was in fair condition. The Volunteer Army was absolutely dependent on it. However, Denikin only controlled some of the line and had to rely on other lesser rail lines.

For Denikin, his engines all ran on oil fuel. They required 90,000 lbs of oil per day and he had only 36,000 lbs available daily. To ease this shortage, British engineers went to Baku and Batum to get as much oil as possible. Because the lack of oil was never overcome, the engines were then converted to coal. The coal was mined in the Donetz Basin. The locomotives consumed 4,320,000 lbs of coal per month. Only 2,520,000 lbs. were available due to the terrible state of the railways. Located at the pitheads, some 3,600,000,000 lbs of coal sat. Thus, the source for coal was plentiful but getting to the storage facitlies was the problem. Of the 400 engines in the Volunteer Army's possession, 160 were under repair because of the use of coal and engine deterioration. The situation for raw materials was also a problem. The workshops could not supply the trains with material until the trains carried the raw material to them. The trains could not do this until they received the needed spare parts from the workshops. Thus, the only solution was to get the supplies from the outside.

The Red or Bolshevik forces in January, 1919, appeared to be surrounded by either British,French and White forces. It was decided to create 16 armies from their 47 infantry and 4 cavalry divisions totaling 430,000 men, 25,000 cavalry and 1120 guns. Opposing the Volunteer Army's men were the Red 8th, 9th, 10th, 11th and 12th armies totaling eight divisions (21st, 22nd,23rd, 24th, 25th, 26th, 27th, 28th). Totaling some 300,000 men, 21,000 cavalry and 600 guns.

The Reds quickly created new infantry and artillery divisions. Each infantry division consisted of three brigades, each with two regiments. A regiment contained three battalions. Each Battalion had four companies. Each division would have three batteries for a total of 12 guns, and three mountain and heavy batteries (24 guns).

The Reds feared the growth of the Volunteer and Don Armies, so much, that six million roubles were spent on propaganda stating the motto: "Remember the fate of the world wide social revolution will be decided on the Southern Front." Much of this money went to pay agitators who went to the rear areas of the Volunteer army. The Reds also drafted all men born from 1885 to 1900, and all citizens up to age 40. All officers up to age 40 were drafted in the areas controlled by the Reds and those who served in the Imperial Russian army. In addition, all Generals and Officers up age 60 were ordered to register. Up to July, 1918, the Red Army was all volunteer. In July, the first draft was begun as well as voluntary enlistments. All males were given compulsory instruction in the art of war, which created the Red Army reserve. This training lasted eight weeks and not less than 12 hours per week to all 16 to 40 year olds. Once drafted or volunteered, the length of service was a minimum of six months. Only those men who were pro-Bolshevik and recommended by a Bolshevik organization would be drafted. Once in the army, every company had a "communist member" for a source of socilistic ideals. Every Section also contained an agitator to continue the idealism and was paid 500-700 roubles a month. Those unfit for military service were publicly announced.

In January, 1919, Denikin's Chief of Staff, Lt. General Romanovski, presented a plan using Allied military forces. He noted that the Germans had occupied the Ukraine region with 28 Infantry and 8 Cavalry divisions. In other parts, another 21 German divisions occupied Russia totaling 49 divisions. The reason for such a high amount was due to hostility of the populace. Denikin suggested that an Allied force of 16 Infantry and 4 Cavalry divisions would be sufficient since these allied forces would be used as a shield for the Volunteer and Don Armies. Five of these divisions would cover the Moscow to Petrograd area. The Baltic would have two divisions.The balance would be spread out among the following districts/ cities:

> Bahmut, Ekaterinoslav, Tchnerigov, Kiev, Kharkov, Zitomir, Bessarabia, Minsk, Vilna One Cavalry division would be at Kiev, Kharkov, Minsk, and the Baltic. To defend the Black Sea ports and Transcaucasus area, a single infantry division each. Nothing ever came of this plan.

When the first British Military Mission arrived at Novorissk at 1500 November 23rd, 1918, the officers of the mission (Capt. Blake and Craig, Lt. Gen. Blackwood) were greeted with an outpouring of enthusiasm. The French Military Mission sailed and arrived at the same time, thus, the little port had docked the HMS Liverpool, Superb, French cruiser Ernest Renan and two destroyers. The reception at the port lasted two hours, then, both missions boarded the train to Ekaterinodar. The time it took to travel from Novorissk to Ekaterinodar illustrates the railwway problem: The train left at 1900 on Nov 24th and arrived on Nov.25th at 0930. Ekaterinodar is only 60-70 miles This equates to an average speed of 5 mph.

The Mission spent the rest of the time gathering information for reports to their respective governments. They did not meet with Denikin until noon, the 25th. The British mission seemed to have meetings with everyone including British businessmen who represented British Oil firms in the Maikop district on the 28th. The mission left on Dec 3rd, carrying many maps and other documents.

One issue of concern to the Mission was the continued German support of the Trans-Caucasia area called Georgia. This region declared itself independent but a protectorate of Germany. The government was powerless and the Germans dictated all issues. The Georgians did not mind, as the Germans were helping them create their own army of two divisions, a brigade of artillery and cavalry, plus a frontier brigade. These forces were enemies with the Volunteer Army. The forces clashed in the Tuapse area

All the military missions came to the same conclusion about halting Bolshevism and to support the Volunteer and Don armies with General Denikin the Supreme Commander. They all agreed that the supply system was haphazard to non-existant. The weapons, for the most part, consisted of such a variety that supplying them was a nightmare. The weapons in White possession were in poor condition since there were no spare parts and were always in action. General Blackwood went on to say the following:

"...the ammunition supply is at disastrous levels. There have been periods where the whole army has not more than a few thousand rounds and if at the start of a battle a machine gun had two or three belts of ammuntion it was thought to be in an extremely good position. A private in the army never has enough rounds, as rifle ammunitions is considered to be "gold" and its distribution is always arranged by high commanders in order to ensure that the distribution corresponded most nearly to the strategic situation. In mid-November,the Army had only 1,870,000 rounds and a division was issued only 10,000 rounds for three days of fighting. Artillery shells are so limited that fire of normal intensity is impossible. The reserve artillery shell depot at times had 100 rounds. In December, it had the following:

7200 rds of field artillery
1520 rds of mountain artillery
2770 rds for howitzer
200 for heavy artillery

The aviation equipment of the army consists of 24 airplanes (in six detachments), mostly Voisin and Nieuport fighters. Half of these were in such a condition that they could not perform even the smallest part of the tasks allotted to them. Only one was operational. The uniforms of the army are an assorted collection of odds and ends. The areas of occupation have no clothing, even the dead are stripped and their clothing is used. Medical stores are non-existant. There are no bandages, linen, only doctors with a little medicene. The pay for the officers and foot soldiers is low. The only repect in which the Volunteer army is rich is in the unfailingly high spirit and their faith in their cause. This morale that sustains them is remarkable."

Denikin quickly attacked on 20 January between Starvopol and the Caspian Sea. The Reds fell into disarray leaving over 30,000 POWs. The Reds then counterattacked along the Don River, at Rostov and Novocherkassk.

From the East, the other White army under Kolchak began its offensive on March 13th. The Northern and Central armies seized Ufa and defeated the Red 5th Army. The Northern Army seized Glazov but could not advance farther due to poor supplies and Red flanking attacks. The Southern Army failed to take Orenburg. By the end of March, a British platoon had advanced over 400 miles southeast of Archangel and met with a reconnaissance patrol from Kolchak's Northern Army!

The spring of 1919 was a period of see-saw battles between the Whites and Reds. The Volunteer and Don Armies were not able to hold what gains they had achieved and neither could the Reds. On April 14th, Denikin proposed Operation Manytsch (a river that is parallel with the Black Sea about 400 km north), which was the first of several operations directed at seizing Tsaritsyn (Stalingrad). General Wrangel opposed the operation due to the condition of the Cossack Army. On April 22nd, Denikin ordered the operation to begin and attacked the Red 10th Army. The operation quickly bogged down and by the 25th, Denikin ordered a reassembling of five cavalry divisions. This proved its worth, as by May 5th,

Wrangel had taken Vielikoknia. The operation ended on the 8th. It had been a huge success, bagging 15,000 POWs, 55 artillery guns and it had forced 10th Army to retreat further towards Tsaritsyn. However, as they did, the Reds destroyed all bridges and ferries. As this operation occurred, the Don Army attacked and took Slaviansk, reaching the Donetz River and threatened Kharkov. This city fell on June 11th. By this time, the Red 8th, 9th, 13th,and 14th armies were all retreating. To celebrate, Denikin and his men celebrated at Novorissk on the 16th. Because the city of Tsaritsyn was a military and political symbol of major importance, the British now directly intervened.

One of the most interesting histories, is the RAF 47th squadron. The unit was formed in May, 1916, and contained 60 officers, 2000 men and 600 horses. It and the 17th Squadron formed part of the 16th Air Wing commanded by General Small. Once formed in England, it sailed to the Middle East becoming part of the Mideast forces there and later was shipped to Salonika arriving there on September 19, 1916. There, the 47th joined the 17th, which had arrived from Egypt in July. These two squadrons, each with about 12 planes, proved to be an invaluable spotting and bombing force for the British 16th and 12th Corps. The Bulgarians had little air opposition and the two squadrons covered some 90 miles of front. The Bulgarians only real airforce comprised of the German 1st Kampf Geschwader, which contained 18 Halberstadts and AEG fighters, two giant Friedrichshafner bombers and one Gotha Bomber. It was based at Bucharest on Feb.26th and immediately flew from Hudora on many bombing raids. On one such raid, the 47th intercepted with three Be 12s, four Sopwiths and two DH2s. The interception failed. The 47th was successful in photo recon and artillery spotting since the Be 12's carried a wireless, which allowed for instant gun adjustments for the 13th, 18th, 186th,190, 201st heavy batteries. When the German Cruiser Goeben ran aground on January 22, 1918, the 47th was called upon to conduct dive bombing attacks. These attacks were conducted in relays of nine Be 12s for two consecutive days. All together, the squadron flew 270 sorties against the ship and dropped 15 tons of bombs. On the humorous side, only one 65 lb. or 112 lb. bomb hit the ship! The Germans fired heavy AA barrages and missed everytime.

The squadron first receive its DH 9s in August, 1918. When the Bulgarians began to retreat through the Kosturino Pass, the 47th attacked the fleeing columns along the road with 25 planes, dropping 5,096 lbs of HE. This totally disrupted any organized retreat of the Bulgarians. Altogether, the 47th dropped 54 tons of bombs on the Bulgarians since its arrival.

After the war, the 47th was moved to Amberkoi on February 19, 1919. When the British decided to intervene in the Russian Civil war, the 47th was sent to support to the White Army under Denikin. Flight A sailed for Novorossisk on April 16, 1919. Four days later, Flight B sailed aboard the SS Warpointer. By May, 28th, the whole squadron was in South Russia under Maj. Collishaw. It contained 12 planes and 186 men and based at Ekaterindor by July 11. C flight then moved to Beketovka to support Gen. Wrangels advance on Stalingrad. The flight contained five DH9s at Velikojeskaya (180 miles from Ekaterindor) however, one crashed. The four planes then leaped to Ramontraya (another 140 miles). The support train for the C flight took 12 hrs to advance 55 miles due to the deplorable situation. By late June, C flight was stationed 60 miles from Stalingrad at Gniloaksaiskaya. By now, C flight was down to three DH9s. The first raid on the Reds occurred on June, 23rd, carrying 16 20 lb. bombs and two 112 lb. bombs. The flight bombed the railway in the city, dropping their bombs from 5000 ft. While returning, they straffed the enemy cavalry routing them. On July, 15, B Flight was diverted from Kharkov to replace C flight. Upon arrival, B flight became C flight and commenced bombing on the 23rd. These attacks occurred daily until the end of August. C flight returned by September and together both flights played havoc on the Reds. C flight alone dropped 67 bombs in one day. The only opposing aircraft the Reds threw up were some French Nieuports. Another British squadron, the 221st, was based at Petrovsk on the Caspian Sea and provided support to the flotilla. This unit flew DH9A bombers. In September, both B and C flights attacked numerous Red positions. On the 17th, a Red barge carrying eight planes up the Volga received a direct hit. Flight A joined the others by October.

The British air units and the White cavalry devised an excellent attack method: First, the aircraft would attack and create a disruption in the Red unit, while in this state, the White cavalry would charge, which totally routed the Red forces over and over. However, the White capture of Stalingrad only lasted for a short time and by late October, a Red cavalry division under Dumenko broke through 40 miles west of Stalingrad (then Tsaritsyn). Dumenko's men raced towards the city with nothing to stop them except B flight. Flight B straffed the division until the unit was so dispersed and disrupted, Dumenko recalled the unit from its advance to regroup. This allowed the Whites to fall back. The 47th squadron was officially dissolved and called "A" squadron in November, 1919. Many of the pilots volunteered to continue flying but Denikan's army was now recklessly falling back and routing to Novorossisk.

The 47th squadron continued to have a decisive impact on the Reds. The bombers continued dropping their bombs on the gunboat flotilla moving up the Volga. The planes bombed the railways on a frequent basis, disrupting the ability of the Reds to move troops and supplies. The planes bombed the trenches on a continuous basis until the Reds fled. Because there was no enemy aircraft to speak of, and weak AA fire, the squadron acted with impunity. The flights also bombed Kamychin and Tcherniyar. The bombing continued throughout August,September and October. On one occassion, the unit attacked as dive bombers upon moored Red destroyers and gunboats that had arrived from the Baltic. The planes swooped down, and when the target appeared in the Aldus sights, the bombs dropped. In this manner, 17 vessels were sunk with anti-submarine bombs. The RAF presence was a morale boost to the Russian soldier under Denikin and a detriment to the Reds. When the squadron was recalled, General Maund, advised against the withdrawal, citing a serious blow to the Russian morale. The pilots were given a choice to go home or volunteer for service under Denikin. Many chose to fly in this manner until March 1920.

Perhaps the only American involved in combat in the South Russian forces was Captain Marion Aten. He went to Canada to join the RAF but never saw action in WW1. He volunteered to go South Russia. He became an ace pilot shooting down three Nieuports, one Spad and one Fokker DVIII over the Tsaritsyn area from April to August.

On June 16th, Wrangels army of 20,000 men (30 cavalry regiments, one infantry division) was supported by the British 47th Squadron and three Mark V and three Whippet tanks. The Red 10th Army contained 33,000 men. This battle was the culmination of a 300 km march through barren steppe along both sides of the only line of communication: the Velikokniageskia-Tsaritsyn railway. Upon arrival at Tsaritsyn, Wrangel found that the city had several lines of trenches and 4-5 lines of barb wire surrounding it. All avenues of approach were covered by artillery fire. On June 1st, Wrangel's first attack was a bloodbath for the already fatigued soldiers. A few penetrations occurred with high loss. By June 3rd, the attack was called off and a withdrawal occurred. Wrangel had lost eight Generals and 11 Captains and enormous other losses. The Reds counterattacked on the 4th, and Wrangel had no choice but to pull back some 20 km from the city. Wrangel telegraphed Denikin asking where the promised reinforcements were and if they did not arrive he could not go on. On the same day, Denikin informed him that one infantry division, five artillery batteries, three armor cars and six tanks were enroute via the railway. The crucial reinforcements arrive on the 16th. Despite orders from the War Department for all British members not to participate in combat, at least one tank was a British crew under Captain Walsh. Wrangel's third attack began on June 17th, with the tanks in the advance. Two broke down, leaving four that burst through the wire and across the trenches with guns blazing. The Reds fled in panic. The British manned tank quickly moved along the trenches firing it's guns, while the other three tanks with mixed crews advanced. Wrangel's cavalry exploited the gap in classic charges and the advance was significant. The tanks however now ran out of fuel. Luckily, the opposing forces had bolted for miles and on June,19th, enough fuel had been received to fill up only the British manned tank. With the British DH9s supporting the single tank, the British were the first to enter Tsaritsyn on June 19th (some sources indicate 29th or 30th. Wrangel states the 19th).

The Revolutionary War Soviet Chairman of the North-Caucasus district was I.V.Stalin, in whose authority was Tsaritsyn (today, Volgograd). On June 10th, he telegraphed the Council of People's Commissars: "If you will not give me aeroplanes with fliers, armored cars, six inch artillery pieces, the Tsaritsyn front will not be held." Nothing came. After waiting five days, Stalin dashed away a repeated telegram: "Tsaritsyn requires from you urgently 1000 disciplined soldier, 4 aeroplanes with experienced fliers, six inch projectiles. Here the fliers are not able to do what is needed.Send, while it is not too late." Finally, an air detachment arrived comprising of 11 "Sopwiths" under the command of V.V.Karpov. The basic red pilot's task was reconnaissance mission,each flying a square block of 50 km. By July, the air units of the 9th and 10th Armies holding defenses along Volga from Astrakhan to Kamishin, counted the following six Red air detachments:

> Tsaritsynsky, Astrakhansk, 1st Kuban, 1st South, 1st Mogilevsky (and the Ryzansky) and the Airgroup Nizhegorodsk. In all, 41 aircraft and 43 pilots, not counting hydroplanes.

By this date, Denikin had began receiving substantial amounts of new aircraft from England. Almost two thirds all of 120 aircraft delivered (more than 80 machines) were RAF R_-8s (one reference states 130 RE-8s were delivered to Russia with 100+ going to the AFSR. This number does not include DH-9, SE-5 or Camels, which account for another 100+/-. Created in the spring of 1916, the two-seater R_-8 was a light bomber with very good speed and air armament. It was well regarded in its class by Great Britain. The RE-8 had some other unpleasant qualities, such as, complicated to steer and instability, which led one into a tailspin rapidly and it was a firetrap. They failed many times while in flight. Due to its poor reputation, many British pilots refused to fly the RE-8t they put together the basis of British military help to Denikin.

All supplies landed in Novorossiysk. After these initial deliveries of Camels and DH 4s and 9s, the first two types arrived more slowly, and receipt of the RE 8s continued up to November 1919. Denikin would receive at least 36 or more DH 9 bombers. Some sources say 160 DH-9s were shipped to South Russia.

By the middle of May, the 1st General Alekseev Air-Detachment (A/O) of the Volunteer Army received six DH 9s. Prior to that the Alekseev detachment was armed with a collection of rare aircraft. Literally after a month of studying the new machines they took off for the front on 26 June. In the beginning of July, the 6th air-detachment similarly had mastered the "Sopwith Camel" fighter. The 3rd, 4th and 9th detachments were also planning to be armed with the RE 8s. Training on the R_-8, even for experienced pilots, was a protracted and complicated process. The training of the flying and ground personnel by the English RAF was directed in Ekaterindar by the RAF Mission, which started work in June 1919. In the beginning of July, the RAF began the retraining of Denikin's pilots. Their retraining covered almost two months.

On the 19th, 21st, and 24th of August three English instructors, Lieutenants Smit, Ritchies and Khed crashed their RE8s. The first RE8 pilot loss were three Don pilots (Lieutenant Ostashevsk, Ensign Bobrov and Esaul Zhmet), who all crashed in August. And on September 2nd, another two RE-8 with Russian crews crashed killing Colnel Lyaskovsk, Junior Lieutenant Mashorko, mechanics Panoenko and Ploskolovs. The trust in the RE 8 was almost nil.

In July 1919, the Volunteer Army counted 106 battle aircraft in 9 air-detachments. Each had 6-12 RE 8 aircraft. The 6th Fighter det. was trained using 8 "Sopwith Camels," but had at one time an additional two "Nieuport-23." The detachment operated four other aircraft for communication, reconnaissance or liaison use. Russian detachments were assigned to support a Corps and were required to perform varied missions. The detachment numbers go down quickly, not from combat, but from wear and tear. It was common for a detachment to have three aircraft flyable, three for major repair, and six under minor repair or for liaison use.

But these solid numbers do not reflect a real situation. Three detachments contained RE 8s and for a long time were not used. Still two, the 7th and 8th, continued to be active in air combat.

Red air forces in the south contained 32 air detachments, and by August their number had grown to 36! The Soviet command understood where the main threat was. So, against Denikin more than half of all of the Red air-fleet was positioned. Even with an average detachment quantity of four aircraft and to deduct detachments fighting in the Volga area, the Reds possessed in the Moscow region a four-fold superiority in the air (this assumes all were operational and pilots could be found who could be trusted!).

During July, 1919, the 1st Volunteer Air-battalion was assigned to General Bredov's Army Corps. The battalion was formed with the 1st and 6th air detachments and commanded by Colonel Konovalov. In dispatches from the front on July 22nd, the unit had 6 DH9s and 8 Camels. The1st detachment flew 36 sorties of bombardment, dropping more 180 kilos. In following month, air-battalion pilots had performed 129 flights totaling 349 hours and dropped on 720 kilos of bombs.

Russian cavalry followed and quickly began to surrounded the POWs, numbering some 40,000. The fall of this key city was due to the British and the modern weapons of war that

Denikin's army did not possess. The 47th squadron continued attacking the Red gunboats on the Volga and battled an Albatross DV in a rare air to air combat. Flight B, with Sopwith Camels, strafed the Reds from 50-100 feet, which caused a disruption. Wrangel's cavalry charged the distracted enemy. This tactic worked many times.

Tsaritsyn was a turning point for Denikin's army. The loss to the Reds was staggering in both supplies, men and political propaganda. Wrangel had succeeded in punching though the prepared Red defenses capturing two armor trains, 131 locomotives, 10000 trucks, 2085 cases of ammunition, 70 artillery guns, 300 machine guns.

Among the POWs were 18 Generals and Colonels. However, as the Red Army fled the city, they murdered 12,000 civilians, 400 horses.

When Denikin arrived and the celebration ended, a debate occurred. Denikin now proposed "Operation Moscow," to which Wrangel was opposed. Wrangel's opposition was valid:

> "I stressed the danger of increasing the length of the front without having necessary reserves and a well organized rear. I proposed that we should entrench on the Tsaritsyn-Ekaterinoslav front for now so the the volga and the Dniepr would cover our flank. We could detach troops to attack toward Astrakhan."

On the 20th, Denikin gave his famous "Moscow Directive." Wrangel was ordered to march to Saratov, then Nijni-Novgorod and on to Moscow! The Don Army, now under Gen. Sidorin, was to advance to Voronege, Riazan then Moscow. The Volunteer Army, under Gen. Mai-Maievsky, from Kharkov to Kursk, then Orel and Tula. Wrangel was dumbfounded. Denikin was giddy: "Yes, we are going to advance on big lines now. I shall have to use a lage scale map for this campaign!"

Wrangel lost many of the reinforcements he was given,which returned to the Volunteer army. Wrangel requested a few days rest for his exhausted troops and was granted two weeks. Then,on the 22nd, Wrangel received orders to advance! Wrangel sent his least tired troops, the 1st Kuban Cossack Cavalry Corps towards Saratov. Upon reaching the town of Kamychin, they were stopped by the remnants of the Red 10th Army, which had now received Siberian divisions, strong artillery and gunboat support. Wrangel then sent his 4th Cavalry Corps. Wrangel's regiments were weak each had 500-600 men. Wrangel, again pleaded for reinforcements from Denikin, Denikin told him to talk to the Kubans. When a meeting was set up with the Kuban leaders, they complained about the broken promises of Denikin for not creating a Kuban Army. The Kubans indicated that if the promise was kept, Wrangel would receive all the reinforcements he needed. Wrangel began to lose his temper about all these "politcal" matters.

Wrangel resumed the offensive for Kamychin on July 12th, and after four days, took the town including 13,000 POWs, 43 guns, 12 locomotives, 1000 trucks and large stocks of ammunition. Denikin continued to siphon troops away from Wrangel including the Terek division. The promised 7th infantry division still had not arrived. As Wrangel advanced, both the enemy and Denikin sapped his strength. The advance toward Saratov ended some 90 km from it.

Military operations now developed in an atmosphere of serious discord between the army commanders. Though small in numbers, the lack of supplies created a situation of continual shortage. Each commander thought his advance and troops should get the supplies available. Troop transfers became a sore issue, most notably with Wrangel. As Denikin later wrote:

> "...not a single day went by without a telegram from General Wrangel...sharp, exacting and at times insulting messages. Sometimes we received from him whole pamphlets in the form of letters, copies that he had circulated among commanding officers. All of this was to prove that his strategy was the best way."

The internal bickering continued and created a most unpleasant atmosphere and mutual antagonism between all leaders. This impacted the dealings with the British, the public and the troops in more subtle ways.

Another contingent under Wrangel, some 5000 men, were ordered to seize Astrakhan, but this unit was able to only come within 55 km. Oddly, the British Caspian Flotilla withheld it's support until mid July. Denikin's men came under the thunder of the Red flotilla. Enemy uprisings began to occur in the Whites rear making any advance very difficult. Both Tsaritysn and Astrakhan were very important objectives.

Wrangel's force now amounted to only 400 combat effectives, many of the horses had foot disease and there was a lack of saddles. Meanwhile, the Reds at Saratov had received large amounts of reinforcements. Wrangel's protests were all ignored. Denikin issued the order for the advance on Saratov. As Wrangel advanced, in his rear, at Tsaritsyn, the city life became one of excesses of all kinds. Wrangel's advance met with only minor success, each time sapping more men he could not afford to lose. The Reds continually shifted forces to the area. On July 26th, the Reds conducted their offensive from Saratov. Wrangel issued orders to resist and delay and then retreat to the next position. Wrangel issued orders to fortify Tsaritsyn. The Reds could not be stopped and the Caucasian Army of Wrangel evacuated the city using eight trains. When the Reds arrived most of the city had been evacuated. Wrangel finally received reinforcements on August 20th: one brigade of Cossack infantry from Denikin. This unit occupied parts outside of Tsaritsyn and further reinforced with one cavalry division (which also had arrived). These were the last fresh troops he had, his other troops had been marching and fighting for 20 days.

The force dispositions were:

> North of Tsaritsyn, left bank of Volga, the Reds had 8000 infantry, 2800 cavalry and 65 guns. The Red 58th division (4000 men) and 28th division (4800 men). Red forces on the right bank had 2000 men, 15 guns, 500 cavalry.
>
> South of the city, the Reds had 2700 infantry, 1650 Cavalry (300,301,304,37th Cav, 39th regiments). In addition, 2500 infantry, 2500 Cavalry, 13 guns (309, 313, 38th Cav, 28th, 13th regiments).

Wrangel estimated the opposing forces amounted to 21,000 infantry, 7000 Cavalry and 70 guns. For several days, the opposing forces clashed outside of the city. In one battle, the first line was defended by former Red soldiers (now White) who bolted back to the Reds when attacked. Wrangel's 4th Kuban Cossack division was in reserve and without waiting for orders galloped into battle charging the enemy (this unit had just marched 250 km). Along the river bank, the Red marines supported by gunboats held a portion of the city. The 4th Kuban was ordered to attack their flank forcing the marines to fall back. During the three day battle, the 10th and 11th Red armies had lost some 18,000 POWs, 31 guns and 160 MG. The Reds were so beaten that further attempts to seize Tsaritsyn ceased. It is also worthy to note that a young man fought with the Reds during this time, his name was Stalin.

On the economic side of the ledger, Denikin needed from the Allies one million roubles per week and in May and June he only received 55,000! His accountants noted that 10 million roubles would keep his army in operation for only six weeks. By the end of July, the British had spent 26 million pounds on supplies to support Denikin's army.

Red Air Unit Strengths

REDS (Tsaritsyn area)	F1918	*R1919	S1919	F1919	
1 Oth Army (14,16,40th PAO)	13	10	10	9	Recon only
7th Fighter	5	5	1	4	Recon only, unit retreats to Saratov, Fighters go to 4th A/D
4th Fighter		4	1	5	Retreats to Kamyshin and ineffective til reorg.
Vol-Cas Naval					
seaplane			12	5	M-5,9 or 20 reconn only
fighter			3	0	
Total:	18	19	27	23	

*F= Fall, R= Spring, S= Summer

During the summer the Whites knocked the 4th and 7th out of the air, then pounded the naval.

During the summer the Reds only had 3 navy fighters before they were lost.

During the fall the Reds gave back the fighters from the 40th, 2nd and 7th to the 4th.

	F1918	*R1919	S1919	F1919	
British	12	10	8	12	
C 47th			6	6	DH4 then RE8
B 47th				6	Camels
A 47th				6	DH.9 and DH.9a
Total:	12	10	14	30	

DH.9 and DH.9A totals to Russia

Issued to the 47th Squadron	47 (15 were 9As) needing only 12 at a time, they went through four sets as they turned them over to the Whites
North Russia	22 (5 were 9A)
Issued to 221st	9 (6 are 9A of Flt 552, 9 under 'A' Detachment) all turned over the White Russians.
To RAF Depot or Training	82
Total number to Russia	157 (135 to the South Front)

Some 31-50 of these came into Novorossisk at the last minute and were destroyed in their shipping crates, captured or sent to the Crimea in March 1919. About 80 went to the Whites in addition to the 130+ RE.8 that they used at first.

By March 1919 the following DH9s were in the following units:

The 47th Squadron	2
Vol. 5th Det had received	16
2nd Kuban Detachment had received	16
2nd Don Detachment had received	16
RAF Depot, repair or lost	20
Total:	80

The following RE8s were in:

47th and Z flt	12
Vol. Dets. 2,3,4,9	32
RAF trainers	14
RAF Depot and repair	36
Training loss	12
3rd Don Det.	24
Total:	130

For Sopwith Camels:

47th Sqd.	18
6th Vol. det	8
3rd Don det	7
1st Kuban det	8
RAF Depot	9
Total:	50

Sources

1) WO 32/5752, WO 153/1208, WO 153/795, PRO, London.
2) The Vrangel Collection, Stanford University, Palo Alto, CA.
3) WO 106/1206, WO 106/1205, PRO, London.
4) WO 95/4955 and 4757, PRO London.
5) WO 106/1164,1153, PRO London.
6) Kondratev, C. *Aircraft of the Russian Civil War*. Moscow Press. 2000
7) Kerybin, *White Armies*. Moscow Press. 1999
8) Stewart, George. *The White Armies of Russia*. 1970.
9) Krasnov, Peter. *The Don and Volunteer Armies*. Moscow Press 1991
10) Moberly, F. *Operations in Persia 1914-19*. HMSO, London. 1987
11) Sareen, Tilak. *The British Intevention in Central Asia/Trans-Caucasia*. India, 1989.
12) Quainton, Antony. *The French in South Russia*. 1919. 1959
13) Lehovich, Dmitry. *White Against Red*. 1973.
14) Krychencko,T. *Imperialism Intervention on the Don*. Moscow Press. 1988
15) Denikin, Anton. *The White Armies*. Hyperion Press. 1973
16) Wrangel, Peter. *Memoirs of General Wrangel*. 1930
17) Brinkly, George. *The Volunteer Army and Allied Intervention in S. Russia*. 1966

12

The Nuts and Bolts of War

The first massive amount of supplies began to arrive to Denikin in April, 1919. Everything an army required was sent during the Summer of 1919. Not only did the British send material, so did the French. A typical invoice from France would read as follows:

Two Million cartridges	520,000 Fr.
2000 Automatic pistols and ammunition	206,000 Fr.
One tank company of FT 17 tanks	2, 400,000 Fr.
25 airplanes	1,750,000 Fr.
Optical equipment	150,000 Fr.
Medical supplies	60,000 Fr.
1736 cases of ammo (42mm guns)	173,500 Fr.
3026 Syringes	
500 cases of Iodine	
230 wagons	
Total:	6,955,000 Fr.

The influx of military supplies helped the British get rid of huge amounts of overstocked war supplies left over from WW1. Many of the supplies were in the form of a grant, unlike from the French, who demanded payment before the supplies were given out.

But even the large amounts of supplies the British sent *gratis* never made it to the troops at the front. Plundering was so common in Denikin's rear depots that he issued a penalty of death for anyone caught stealing from them. Many times, even when the supplies did reach the front, they mysteriously disappeared or were not distributed.

The British sent some 558 artillery guns, 1,685,522 artillery shells, 160 million rifle cartridges and 250 complete uniform sets. Not everything sent by either the British or French was in perfect shape or arrived in its original manner.

General Holman (a main advocate for providing aid in the British Mission) noted in his July 1919 report the following:

> "Guns, Machine Guns and Lewis guns were deficient of spare parts and of buffer and lubricating oil, shortage of belts and drums. A great quantity of supplies needed at the front remains lying in the storehouses at the base and at depots. The effect on the frontline troops is disillusionment and loss of faith in our material and our efficacy of assistance. Enemy agents quickly spread propaganda that we were supplying defective and worn out articles at exorbitant prices. The fault is partly on the Russian Administrative services which are incompetent and partly ourselves because we do not have the staff to guarantee correct distribution. In Ekaterinodar, I visited an ordinance depot which had received 4400 complete sets of clothing and equipment (for 4400 men), out of which, not one has been issued according their books. However, these had been broken up piecemeal handouts. The entrenching tool was separated and not one was found. The books show that 150,000 sets of British uniforms were issued, however, I have yet to see a single soldier with a complete set of uniform. I have found large quantities of medical supplies and equipment for battalions which have been lying there for months."

Of all the reports submitted to the War Cabinet concerning South Russia by various members of the British Military Mission, General Holman's reports were keen and insightful. Unlike others, Holman literally traveled all over the Ukraine to see for himself the situation at hand. His job and the British Mission was to ensure the delivery of British war material to Denikin's fighting troops.

In Holman's report he continues:

> "...the units operating along the Taganrog to Kharkov railway are completely equipped with British weapons and uniforms, but the front is 600 miles long and much of our supplies are not being delivered. It was not until I visited other areas of the front did I realize that none of the supplies are getting through. Even the elite units of the Volunteer Army, composed of all officers were in rags and without boots."

Holman, who took over the duties of the Mission, eventually had 283 British Officers and 1200 other ranks, not including the air or tank detachments. Holman was blunt with Denikin about the problems and conceded he would try to correct the matter.

The supply problem Holman found never would be resolved. Even when special orders and arrangements were made allowing only British soldiers in issuing the material, the problem persisted. However, by October, 1919, Holman was able to report the following portion had actually been issued to Denikin's men:

Caps	271,891
Greatcoats	232,990
Jackets	264, 920
Pants	265,905 pairs
Boots	329,881 pairs
Shirts	858,422
Drawers	505,332 pair
Socks	660,967 pair
Towels	389.116
Belts	217,711
Packs	211, 563
Water Bottles	207,658
Mess tins	241, 284
Helmets	74,733
Respirators	35,482

2 field Hospitals
26 Field Ambulances
342 3 ton trucks
25 Workshop Trucks
31 Supply trucks
19 Sunbeam Touring cars
31 American Ford cars
Motor Ambulances (Sunbeam, Ford, Studebaker)
25 Douglas motorcycles
Austin Armor Cars
26 Holt Tractors
40 Caterpillar
1,925 miles of Signal cable
16,859 Cells
368 Fullerphones
20 Heliographs
750 17ft wooden poles
89 Switchboards
872 telephones
315 magneto telephones
260 Telegraph sets
1,078 miles of insulated wire
1,333 Electric Torches

As Holman found out by visiting the front, the British artillery sent were only used to 25% of it's effectiveness. This was because the guns were sent to crews with little training and had no spare parts. Minor problems or repairs put the guns out of use because the spare parts were at a depot miles away. The 36 batteries of the Volunteer army were spread out along 200 miles of front and no lateral communications, some 60 hours away from the nearest rail.

The actual number of artillery guns sent by August, 1919 was:

331 18 Pdr (450 were promised)
4.5 Howitzer (120 were promised)
60 Pdr.
6" Howitzer
8" Howitzer

However, because of expansion in Denikin's army, he needed guns for (31) 18 Pdr. Batteries and (27) 4.5" Howitzer batteries. Thus, Holman requested another (150) 18 Pdr and (120) 4.5" guns.

Holman noted that the ammunition requirements for artillery under Denikin's armies was hard to calculate. The needs were not based on the actual state of the artillery guns or the operations, and in reality, no one in the Russian army knew what the requirements were. According to Holman, the Ordnance section of the British Mission stated the following numbers had been issued to the Russians by August, 1919:

18 Pdr guns	1,338, 540 rounds
4.5 "Howitzer	203, 783 rounds
60 Pdr guns	91, 277 rounds
6 "Howitzer	34,540 rounds
8" Howitzer	8, 412 rounds

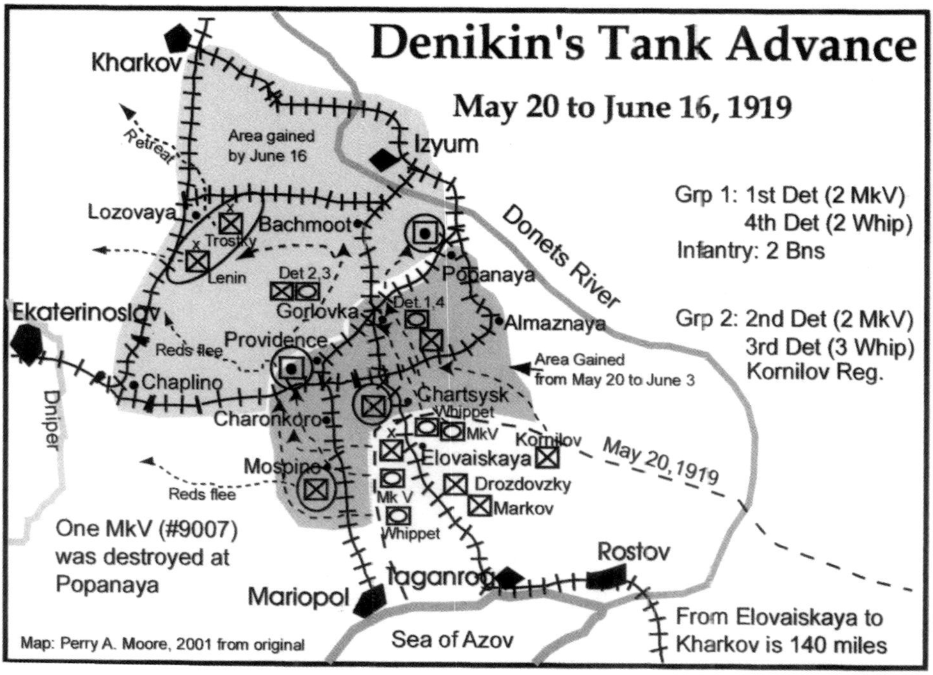

The Russians preferred the 4.5 "Howitzer for it's effectiveness and simplicity, thus, another 100,000 rounds were requested (all HE types). In addition, another 80,000 primers were needed due to the high number of misfires due to faulty parts.

As with the Vickers machine gun and Lewis guns, this proved to be more satisfactory. The training in their use was easier since it was handled at the Corps level. However, the Russian depots were issuing such weapons to anyone requesting them, whether they had been trained or not. In one case, a Terek Cossack division received 36 Lewis Guns even though nobody had even seen one before! The reason why the unit had received them was due to a complaint from the Ataman of the Terek Cossacks stating they were being "neglected." To prevent such poor distribution, all MG's and Lewis guns were issued by British soldiers in Rostov to Russian units. Units that required training went through the Russian Central Training School which could produce a completely outfitted MG company. This British mission trained some 5,825 men in the use of MG and Lewis Guns by September, 1919. The number of guns issued by September was:

Vickers MG	1,270
Lewis Guns	.2,743

Once the Russians were trained in their use, British officers accompanied the units to the front, acting as advisors in combat operations, and at times, becoming involved. Their presence alone, according to Holman, greatly increased the morale of the Russian soldiers.

As the front increased in size, additional Machine Gun schools were created at Kiev, Tsaritsyn, Kharkov, Anapa and Odessa.

The situation regarding the rifle and ammunition situation was, as Holman noted, "there is no system of returns on which to base accurate appreciation of the situation." However, the Russians conducted experiments on using the British .303 cartridge in a Russian .300 rifle. This was done by pinching the casing. However, this lead to split casings and other problems. It appears that as Summer and Autumn arrived, the Russians were more inclined to use the British weapons and ammunition supplied.

The British sent to Denikin:

200,000 British .303 rifles,
174,872 Russian Rifles
40,000 SMLE/Ross
Pistols

The following ammunition had also been sent and distributed:

British.303	180,000,000 rounds
Armor Piercing	90,000 rounds
Russian ammo	221, 697,000 rounds
Mauser ammo	22, 457,000 rounds

Holman requested an additional 200,000,000 rounds of.303 ammo and another 300,000,000 rounds of Russian ammo for the coming Winter campaign of 1919.

In charge of developing the South Russian Air Force was Lt. Col. Maund, who arrived on March 20th at Ekaterinodar. He began to lay the ground work for the 100 RE 8 airplanes and 12 officers and 70 men which would arrive in May, 1919. Once the aircraft and men arrived, the development and training began in June.

The Russians, of course, were not new to flying, and their 62nd Wing supplemented the 100 RE 8s. In April, some 15 Camels and 6 DH9 bombers arrived. These were old and arrived from Mudros and Malta with very incomplete equipment. Some training began and four 4 plane batteries were created and by June, these were operating on the front.

The training proved to be difficult for Russian pilots. The Russian pilot was casual and over confident. A "rift" occurred between the Inspector-General of the Russian Air Force and the British, it reached the point to where the Russian pilots were ordered to ignore the advice of the British instructors.

In any case, the training continued and by August, one "air division" containing 33 planes, 41 motors, 6 cars was sent to the front. The division was armed exclusively with RE 8 planes, however, on their way to the front, four machines crashed with a loss of 8 members. The causes were all due to poor British instruction. As a result, such a serious loss of confidence in the RE8 came about that two of the three squadrons demanded different aircraft. Eventually, the Russian pilots regained confidence in the RE8. This was accomplished by British pilots demostrating various maneuvers not normally or forbidden using a RE 8. Of course, part of the fault also was on the British. Four out of five original instructors had not flown in years, none of them had even flown an RE 8 airplane and only two were recent seaplane pilots. One of the instructors was reluctant to fly the airplane!

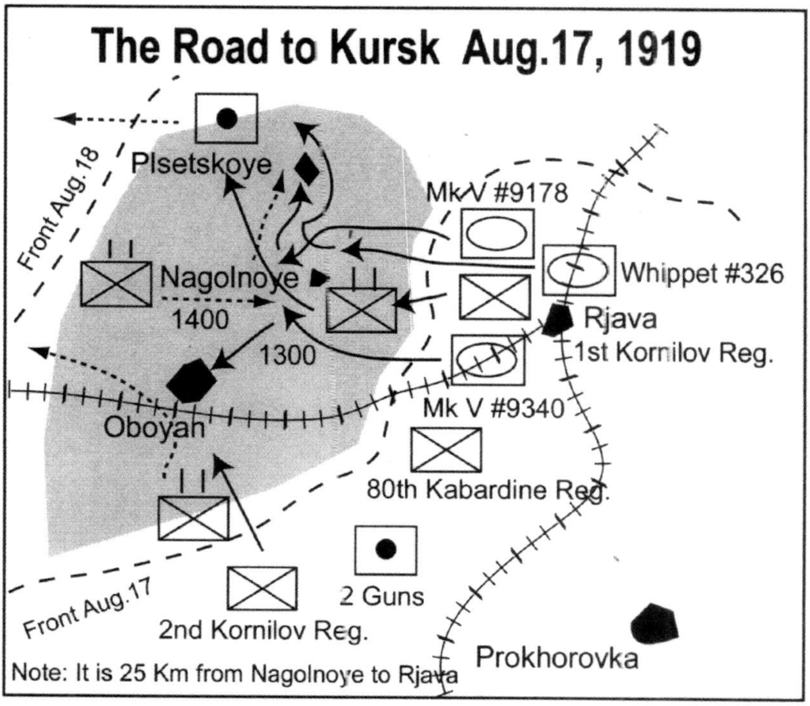

By September, the 2nd Aviation division was ready. Squadron 1 of the 1st Division was based at Ekaterinodar and Kiev.

By August, the following airplanes had been issued to the Russians under Denikin:

36 RE-8
21 DH9
21 Camels
9 DH9A
Total: 87 planes

Aircraft sitting at Novorossisk, not issued:
64 RE8
11 DH9 (need parts)
6 SE5

Grand total of airplanes: 168

When Wrangel seized Tsaritsyn, a Volga Flotilla was created. Its purpose was to defend and harass the Reds at Saratov and Astrakhan. This small force consisted of:

Four motor boats armed with 1 MG and 1 37mm.
Two motor boats armed with 1 37mm, 1 17mm and 1 MG.
Four mortar boats armed with 1 47mm, 4 MGs
Four motor boats armed with 1 37mm, 4 MGs.

To supply the numerous armor trains in use under Denikin, the British provided the following naval guns for the trains' armament. These were actually guns taken off the various interned Russian Naval ships lying about on the Black sea and Caspian.

Eleven 6" guns with 3777 rounds
Thirty 12 pdr guns with 15,959 rounds
Sixteen 6pdr guns with 9,886 rounds
Sixteen 3 pdr guns with 8000 rounds

British Mk V tanks at Taganrog, May 1919.

Denikin requested an additional 35 6" guns,75 4" guns, 40 4.7" guns and 37 12 pdr guns by September. Not all of these guns would be used on the armor trains but many formed batteries and placed in key areas, for example, the 6" battery at Tsaritsyn (Stalingrad) kept the Red flotilla in check and away. There was another such battery in Kiev and Petrovsk.

It was the British Naval Mission that advised and trained the Russians in their use of these special batteries. This mission consisted of 103 men. Their distribution in part, is as follows:

22 men at the armor train bases located at Tsaritsyn, Kharkov, Kiev.
5 men with the 6" gun batteries
10 men with the Dnepr and Volga River Flotillas
13 men at Kharkov

Trains played a vital part in the Russian Civil war, not only for the advance of military operations but for supply of those forces.

Denikin had 1720 operational locomotives and 1684 locomotives requiring some repair. To carry stock, his rail services had a total of 58,591 rail cars in working order and another 20,000 needing repair. These trains not only carried military goods but civilian as well. Certain districts, like north of Kharkov, were restricted to military trains.

To supplement the situation, America sent the following in August:

10 broad gage locomotives
21 narrow gage locomotives
300 broad gage cargo cars

As if the numbers were not enough, Holman requested another 1000 new locomotives in July. The coal situation became more acute with the lack of miners and this caused a monthly transporting of 50,000 tons of oil from Grozni. This was compounded by an acute lack of oil tanks to ship the oil in. The 400 oil tanks lended to the South Caucasian Railway lines were never returned and a fire consumed over 50,000 tons. Adding to all this was the fact the local governments demanded 28,000,000 roubles from one British Oil company for taxes or the permission to drill would be denied.

To say the Capitalists were the only ones making money is untrue. The Locals and foreigners all fed upon one another like barracudas. Even Holman, in his report, takes notice:

> "The trains are loaded with a human freight of speculators.....workman leave their work for days to travel the country buying flour which they sell in their home towns for a profit of 500%. In Kiev, a pound of beef costs 180 roubles. Foreign competition exists between the Americans, Italians, Slovak and Poles. It is Russia that Britain can look for markets amounting to 180,000, 000 pounds a year. The British firms travel to Rostov and Kharkov to sell their business up to a 30% profit. The train operators receive low pay and are neutral in their duties and subject to corruption. The rail situation is serious. The cargo cars carry only 10% of military

> supplies and 90% unnecessary human freight. Because of a lack of system and control, railway employees trade rather than doing their duty.
>
> The railways of South Russia are in a state of decay, many locomotives are in decrepit condition and it is not unusual for an engine to halt for 30 minutes in order to build up steam. Coal is very difficult to obtain, many run on logs or wood. The train stations gather literally thousands of peasants, most have a diet of bread, melons and sunflower seeds. When the train begins to move, there is wild dash to secure places and it will leave will all cars full to suffocation and hundreds clinging to the roof, buffers and running boards. "

The monetary problem occurred due to the descent of the rouble. In January, 1919, one pound equaled 26 roubles. This was an artificially allowed fixed rate of exchange. However, in Moscow, the rate was 42 roubles to a pound. In reality, it should have been 80 roubles to a pound. Compounding this problem was the fact that country three to four varieties of roubles including German imitations of the Romanov rouble existed. Various districts, likewise, created their own rouble. By July, 1919, the exchange rate had skyrocketed to 200 roubles to one pound. By October, it was 400 roubles to a pound. In Rostov, it was 700 roubles to a pound.

One of the least known aspects of the Civil war was the Jewish question. General Holman addresses this by stating that in England, it was believed that Denikin was allowing the mass executions of the Jews. Yet, in Russia, many thought Denikin had been "bought" by the Jew.

Holman points out that a large number of the Bolsheviks were actually Jewish. One of their top leaders, Trotski, had the birth name of Braunstein. Most of the generals in the Red armies were Jewish by origin. Oddly, it was the Jewish owned newspapers, which were always hostile to Denikin and his army, yet, when his forces entered an area the mass executions stopped. Holman states the following, "it was almost exclusively Jewish brains and money, which turned the amiable anarchy of the original revolution into this terrible war of annihilation."

Very few Jews actually lived in the Kuban area and only a small portion lived in Rostov. When the city fell to the Bolsheviks, all the comminsaars appointed were Jewish. The resentment toward the Jew began to grow. When the Volunteer army advanced past Kharkov, it was reported that Bolshevik troops were executing Jews. In the Don area, some 27,000 Jews had been executed.

Tanks

One of the most neglected aspects of all published materials on the Civil War were the use of tanks. Whether it has been simply overlooked, or deemed not important, I do not know. But the use of the tanks in combat proved over and over to be a decisive factor. At best, and in a few books only, there is a brief mention of tanks concerning the battle at Tsaritsyn and the British manned tanks. Suffice to say, the use of tanks is spotlighted here for the first time in any military history book on the Russian Civil War in 1919-20.

The first tanks arriving from the Allies were not British. They were French Renault FT-17 type tanks. These arrived on December 12, 1918, at Odessa. Company Three of the 303rd Assault Artillery regiment had 20 FT-17 tanks. These would not be used until February 7th, when the French attacked the town of Tiraspol (30,000), about 100 km north of Odessa.

The plan called for two French battalions attacking the town from the west, while one Polish battalion and one French company from Rasdielnaia attacked from the east. A tank detachment of five FT 17 tanks commanded by Lt. Marchal would also support. The detachment contained two sections of HQ, 3 mechanics and one truck carrying 500 gallons of fuel.

At 0900, the tank detachment arrived from Odessa and detrained. It gathered with the infantry and by 0930, the three tanks led the infantry into battle. The other two tanks were held in reserve. However, as the attacked progressed some 300 Reds counterattacked forcing the two FT17's in reserve to be committed. The tanks continued moving on the enemy's flank and opened up forcing the Reds to take flight. The other three tanks continued into Tiraspol along with the infantry. By 1300, the French had taken the town. Losses were almost nil to the French, and the tanks did not experience any tank breakdowns while consuming 97 37mm shells and 5 machine gun belts. The Poles lost 3 men, 10 Wia.

In a subsequent tank action on March 18th, 1919, the unit provided rearguard action for the French and Greek infantry disorderly retreat near Odessa. In this action, the Red 2nd Ukrainian army captured 100 MG, four artillery guns, 7 locomotives and four FT-17s. These four tanks were immediately sent to Moscow and Kharkov for examination.

The first British tank detachment commanded by Major McMickering, 10 officers and 55 enlisted men arrived on April 13th, 1919 (Russian sources indicate March 22, 1919). Also arriving with them were six Whippet, type A, and six Mark V tanks. The tanks were unloaded from the steamships, "Sacred Heart" onto the wharfs and took a week to prepare.

British tankers with their Whippet type B, in Archangel 1919.

In the following week, the tanks were paraded (at the request of Denikin) through the town of Novorossisk. The locals were in awe. For demostrating purposes, the Mk V tanks moved through brick walls and climbed nearby hills. The Mk V was called "Ricardo" by the Reds. Each had one six pdr.gun and 4-5 machine guns. The training began on the 22nd in Ekaterinodar. The Russian crews were all officers and each man was crossed trained in tank operations. The official tank school opened in June, at Taganrog. Originally, the British intended a tank crew to be trained within six months but necessity demanded training be reduced to one month. On April 14th (Russian sources) General Denikin issued Order #674, authorizing the creation of the 1st White Russian Tank battalion. This order would create four tank groups:

> Group One (three MkV), Group Two (two Mk V), Group Three (two Whippet) and Group Four (three Whippet), two tanks for training. Each group also had one American Colt tractor, one tank workshop with three-ton Thorneycroft trucks, a few motorcycles and three Ford cars.

The British Tank School would produce 200 cross-trained tankers, which was enough to man 15 tanks by November.The training was rushed because the tanks were needed on the Poltava front by May 8th.

The Reds were also keen in using their captured tanks and did so in May at Kremenchug. This armor formation contained one Austin armor car, two Ft-17 tanks, two Fiat trucks and two motorcycles armed with one MG each. The unit contained 52 men.

The newly trained Russian tankers would make their debut in supporting an infantry attack. For this action, the 1st Tank group with three Mk Vs were loaded onto four railroad cars, for the soldiers and officers, another two rail cars were loaded, and for tank supplies and fuel, another two rail cars were loaded. Thus, a tank group usually had 8-10 rail cars in the tank support train. This unit arrived near the front and a plan of attack was determined. The opposing forces were equal in terms of strength. When the tanks appeared hundreds of

Whippets loaded aboard a train heading to the front in 1919.

yards away, many of the Red infantry simply fled. Others, armed with machine guns, fired continuously. The bullets simply bounced off the armor. The tanks fired their guns and MGs. Soon, the whole Red force began to panic and flee. When the tank group reached a hill crest Red artillery fired. Shells landed close by but missed. The Red artillerymen realizing that even their fire was ineffective abandoned their guns. The rail station was seized.

The Chief of Staff (General Agapeev) from the 2nd Volunteer Corps filed this after action report:

> "In the May 8th action in the Voskrossensky area, a part of the 1st Tank division consisting of 3 MkV and 2 Whippet supported by infantry attacked the Reds at a distance of 1.5 to 2 miles. The enemy opened with heavy rifle fire and machine gun fire, but did no harm to the tanks as bullets could not pierce the armor. The MkV tanks could not keep up with the fast moving infantry and had only a chance to fire a few shots at advancing reserves. The Whippet tanks took an active part also in the pursuit of the enemy despite the heavy artillery fire of the enemy. On the 9th, the tanks rested due to crew exhaustion and technical repairs. On the 10th, the tanks were ready, but the enemy had fled. Thus, the tanks were loaded put on trucks and sent to Tchoumakevo Station to entrain. According to reports the tanks accomplished their task. The enemy on seeing them fled panic stricken. POWs say that the Bolsheviks on seeing the tanks left their positions and went to the rear shouting they would not fight unless they had tanks. The arrival of our tanks had a great impact on the local inhabitants.
>
> On the Khartisissk sector on May 10th, our troops attacked with three tanks. The enemy fought well with much artillery support and one tank received up to 20 indirect hits from shrapnel and one direct hit. No serious damage occurred. The tanks in this fight had a strong impression on the Reds, the mere sight of tanks threw the enemy into a panic. While the tanks impact was great, their impact would have been greater had their fewer tactical and technical faults. These were: insufficient crew training, crew lack of initiative, slow speed of the MkV and the large consumption of petrol which required a refilling every 6 miles! A few cavalry units should be attached."

The Russian Tank Corps was commanded by Col. Khaletski. He had commanded the Russian Armor Cars (when they first appeared in Russia in 1916) in WW1 and was a man of great energy.

With the help of the British, the Baltic Works in Taganrog became the South Russian Tank maintenance and training ground. It was here that about 1000 men worked in making artillery shells. The Russians were taught by taking apart the MKV and Whippet tanks and putting together again. The school taught driving, Hotchkiss machine gun and Six pounder gunnery. About 15 miles from the base was a "battle practice ground." The instructions were originally done via translators, but once the first class graduated, Russian officers became the trainers with British supervision. The entire training course ran for five weeks. The Russians looked at the 'tank" as a sort of magical item especially upon the Reds. In several cases, the mere knowledge of the enemy that tanks were enroute caused an immediate withdrawal of positions.

The British staff at Taganrog had a wonderful time. No work was done in the afternoon and soccer games between the British and Russians were popular. Other activities included swimming, boxing and boating on the Sea of Azov. The local yacht club was a popular spot. At night, British troops could go to one of several cinemas, or listen to Denikin's own string orchestra.

The Russians, up to this point, were only familiar with the Austin and White armor cars, which had arrived in 1916. Many of these remained with Denikin's forces. Using spare parts, Denikin created an armor car group in February 1919. This 3rd Caucasian group was unique, for it contained the first fully tracked armor personnel carrier. The APCs each had five MGs and were built on American made tractors. The two APCs created were fully protected in armor, like an armor car, and had a single turret. The APC could carry up to five men. These experimental machines were built in Taganrog and proved successful in combat against the Red 2nd Kuban Corps. These two early APCs were subsequently captured in December 1919 by the Red forces.

In addition to these APCs, the White forces created two experimental armored self-propelled guns. Each of the 120mm naval gun units were enclosed in an armor hull, mounted on one tractor. These two guns were assigned to the Naval gun section of the Caucasian army. In essence, these were assault tanks (since there was no turret). They were very slow. In the Spring of 1920, both were captured by the Reds. They became part of the 34th Heavy gun battery of 9th army. Subsequently, one of the SP guns was recaptured by the Whites on August 18th.

The South Russian First Tank Division (Battalion)

The division (battalion) was organized in Ekaterinodar and composed of four armor sections for a total of 10 tanks (5 MkV and 5 Whippet, Type A). Group one consisted of 2 Mk V and 2 Whippet, while Group 2 contained 3 Mk V and 3 Whippet. These were further divided into sections, with Group 1 consisting of the 1st and 4th sections and Group 2, the 2nd and 3rd Sections. One Mk V and Whippet remained at the Tank School. The division was then placed at the disposal of the 2nd Army Corps commanded by Mai-Maievsky whose staff was located at Ilovaiskaya Station. Between May 6th and 19th, the tanks were then

One of the two experimental armor personnel carriers created in Taganrog by the Whites in 1919.

divided into two groups. Group 1 deployed at Mospino Station and Group 2 at Chartsysk Station.

The general situation at this time on the Azov-Don Front was as follows:

> The Reds had the initiative advancing and attacked toward the White command center of 2nd Corps at Ilovaiskaya from the north. From the west, Red forces were pressuring the line some 50-60 west of Taganrog. The White forces consisted of one Cossack infantry brigade led by General Gamin and the elite officer regiments named Kornilov, Markov, Drozdov and Samoor. However, these forces were not strong enough to halt the Red advance.Taganrog was being threatened and defenses had been built a few miles from the city consisting of trenches and barb wire. White morale was dropping (even in the elite units) because the Reds continued to gain and had numerical superiority.

On May 20th, the tanks commenced operations on both sectors and almost immediately their appearance produced a panic amongst the Red troops who fled in disorder. This rout occurred while the tanks, themselves, were still some 1-2 miles away! Likewise, the dropping White morale suddenly sky rocketed and these troops marched about 800 yards from the tanks' rear. Thus, Group 1, supported by two infantry battalions captured several railway stations from Providence to Yaskinovatya, and Group 2, cleared the stations of Stat, Chartsysk, Chanshokoro and Gorlovka. Everywhere the tanks went, little resistance was

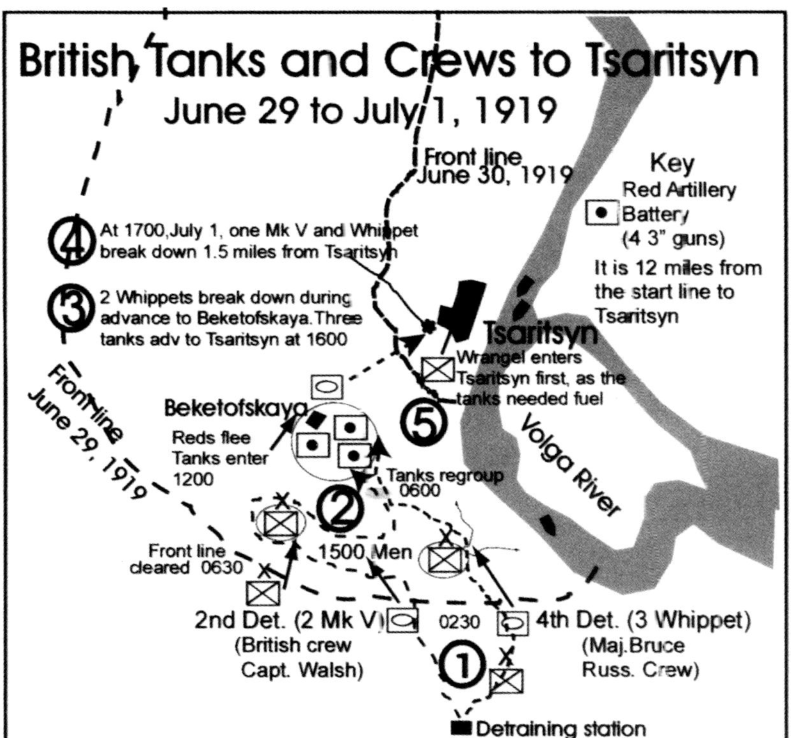

felt, only at Providence did the tanks encounter artillery fire from a Red battery slowing the advance.

Attached to Group 2 was a British officer who wrote this after action report:

> "During the night of Tuesday, May 20th, three Whippets and two Mark V's left the railhead and approached their target about 2 miles away. Our railway had been cut by the Reds some 3-4 miles south. The Whippets went off in fine style, steering a zig-zag course. The Reds fired about six rounds and fled. Their infantry and cavalry fled so quickly that the Mark V's could not compete with them. The Whippets advanced again the next, the 21st, since the grease, petrol and oil had been brought up by Holt tractors. Please agitate for many more tanks. Everyday Russians come to us desiring to transfer to the Tanks!"

More tank action occurred on June 3rd, when Group 1 moved from Yasinovataya Station to the right flank of the Corps and with the Kornilov Regiment cleared the Reds from Debagtsavo and Almaznaya Stations. Meanwhile, the Group 2 moved north to from Gorlavka advancing on Popasnaya station. In this battle, the Reds had an armor train which presented the only danger to the tanks. One Mk V tank was lost after being hit, Tank no. 9007, commanded by Col. Iagobov and four other officer killed and two wounded. However, the rail station and armor train were captured.

All remaining nine tanks were now sent to the Corps reserve at Bachmoot for refitting and overhauling. These small tank actions seemingly appear insignificant when compared to other tank battles in history, but the fact was, because of these few tanks, Denikin's men were able to advance 50 miles in this two week period. It must also be said, that in all these small battles, the Reds as a whole had no inclination to fight when tanks appeared or when word got out they were coming. Their retreat was so hasty they left their weapons and the tanks seldom had any targets to fire at. It was the "magic" of the Tank.

By June 15th, Sections 2 and 6 returned to the tank school at Taganrog. The 3rd Section (Whippet) was sent to Iyzum and the 1st section (Mk V) to Chaplino. However, because the Reds had destroyed all the bridges as they retreated north, the tanks could not move into battle. Section 3 of the division was in action and supported by the Drozdov regiment which succeeded in taking Lozovaya Station. Section 1 attacked westward towards the towns of Basan and Petropavlovka. This battle was by far the most difficult due to the Red regiments "Lenin" and "Trotsky." These units fought extremely well at point blank range inflicting high casualties to the Whites. However, the appearance of the Mark V tanks totally changed the original complexion of the Reds. As the tanks approached with their guns blazing, the communist broke and routed. The tanks continued their pursuit for another two miles.

On June 16th, the 2nd and 4th tank sections were sent to General Wrangel from Taganrog to his positions near Tsaritsyn (Stalingrad). These sections were supplemented by one Whippet and one Mk V from Ekaterinodar. Four tanks would actually be used in the battle to breakthrough to Tsaritsyn: 2 Whippets from 4th Section, 1 MkV from 2nd Section and 1 MkV from Ekaterinodar (manned with an all British crew) commanded by Captain Walsh. The two remaining tanks developed mechanical problems and could not be used.

The Reds had built up the surrounding Tsaritsyn area with rows of trenches and wire. It had the rare look of a WW1 battlefield. The Reds also had massed their artillery and MG units.

The offensive was directed against the front southwest of the city. The tanks approached during the night at intervals of 100-150 paces and before dawn had destroyed much of the wire by crushing and dragging a grapnel by the British manned tank. The Red artillery began their barrages at dawn and heavily shelled the tanks to no effect. Their own shells fell on their own men who remained in their trenches! This penetration was in the center of the line and once again, the Reds panicked. The Mark V's pursued towards the town, while the Whippets routed other Reds in their trenches. By 1700 hours, the tanks rallied at Voroponovo Station and moved in force towards the town from the south in order to help Wrangel's right flank hold (which was under strong pressure). The tanks and the few ships of the Volga Flotilla combined their artillery fire on the Reds which retreated into the town.

On the 30th, the Whippets continued their advance across some very difficult terrain and steep ditches but entered the town. Because of the lack of bridges, the Mk V tanks had to trek 2 miles from the town to entrain.

According to Captain McElvaine, who wrote an after action report on the British crew there (he was also a crew member), the following is his eyewitness account:

> "A detachment of tanks consisting of 2 Mk V and 3 Whippets manned by Russians and one Mark V manned by a British crew left Taganrog on June 25th. One of the two Russian Mk V tanks broke down. On the 26th, we reached the Corps HQ where General Wrangel requested that Major Bruce assume command of the tanks. The Russian section commanders were under Major Bruce. The British MkV was commanded by Captain Walsh. The British officers conducted reconnaissance of the area from the ground and from airplane. While in the air, an enemy balloon was attacked and forced to descend. The enemy defense line ran in a circle around the town at an average of 15 miles from it.

Officers of the South Russian Tank Detachment, Taganrog 1919.

The plan of attack was as follows:

1. The 2 MkV were to break the line 8 miles north of Tsaritsyn and then swing to the left, running along the enemy front line cutting the wire and clearing the enemy infantry and machine gunners. They were to proceed up to 5 miles along the front line if required.

2. The Whippets were to cross the line in the same area and advance to Beketofskaya to cut off the artillery guns located there. Then they were to rally up with the MkV's and await further orders from Major Bruce.

3. The RAF would supply one airplane for cooperation with the tanks and a code of signals arranged. Supplies for fuel, oil, grease and food would be brought up by truck and tractor. One large cart was allocated per tank which followed the tanks closely. These also carried fuel, oil and grease.

On June 28th, the tanks reached their assembly points. The attack began at 0200 on the 29th. The tanks advanced towards the enemy lines and crossed them at 0230. The tanks came under heavy rifle and MG fire for about 10- 15 minutes, then, the enemy bolted when the tanks moved very close. The British Mk V turned to the left and proceeded along the enemy line, pulling wire. The other MkV assisted a Whippet which had got caught in the wire!

The tanks continued moving up and down the trenches blasting their guns and coming under heavy artillery fire. None of the tanks received any hits. Once this had been completed the tanks returned to the starting points and at 0600 Major Bruce ordered the tanks to advance to Beketofskaya. The British tank continued to rip apart the wire using a grapple. No infantry was seen as the tank moved northward but it did encounter four artillery batteries which suddenly opened up. Captain Walsh was injured from a shell fragment and the tank was then commanded by myself. Thus, by 0630, the Reds manning the front line had fled to the rear areas and the forces under Wrangel advanced in several places. By Noon, all the tanks were at Beketofskaya and refueled and oiled. We awaited further orders. Major Bruce did not issue orders until 1500. These were to advance onto Tsaritsyn. The tanks began their movement and by 1700 reached the town. At this time, the Reds counterattack and pushed back the right flank of the Volunteer Army. Our tanks, two MkV and one Whippet (the other Whippet had broken down near the starting point) turned to oppose this. As soon as the Reds saw the tanks coming, they retreated and the Volunteer infantry advanced again! Our tanks continued the chase moving along a ridge towards the town when suddenly about 12 artillery guns barraged us. These guns were 4" guns firing over open sights. One Whippet received fragments from a shell which broke two engine holding bolts, one Mk V developed ignition trouble. Major Bruce ordered the tanks to take cover in a nearby ravine 1.5 miles from Tsaritsyn. The Volunteer infantry advance towards the town and suffered heavy losses as the Reds were firing rifles and machines guns from buildings. Major Bruce than arranged with the infantry commander to enter the town with two MkV 's provided fuel arrived by 0200 on July 1st. None arrived by this time. A truck finally did arrive with enough fuel for one tank. It was arranged to have the British tank to advance to the town at 1900. However, the Reds commenced to evacuate the town by river to our surprise. Wrangel's men entered at 1700 and 1500 Reds surrendered along with 10 guns in this section. No shots were fired."

This eyewitness account is odd in one respect, the date that Tsaritsyn fell is a one or two days later. And also, it was Wrangel's infantry that first entered the town, not the British tank as cited in the The Tanks by Liddell Hart.

To say that the British War Cabinet did not know about the magical effect tanks on the enemy would be a lie. Not only did they receive the reports, all saying the same things, but on June 28th, a London Times Special Correspondent reported from South Russia the following:

"The rout of the Bolsheviks on this front is complete and is due to their own internal decomposition.......and the great moral stimulus given to the Volunteer Army by the British of which Tanks are the most vivid evidence. It is incontrovertible now, that if it is desired to stop the civil war in Russian at minimum sacrifice of human life, the most effective policy is to send a copious supply of tanks and aeroplanes......If in January,1919, tanks had been sent instead of Prinkipo proposals, Denikin would have long met with Koltchak on the Volga."

The British Garford armor car was the only anti-tank weapon available to the Red forces. It carried a 57 mm gun.

The War Cabinet and others, perhaps, felt that this was too easy or just not so, but for whatever reason, the number of tanks sent to South Russia were only a token measure when it could have been decisive. They did send a tank specialist, a Major Sayer of the Tank Corps to study the prospects about the use of tanks. But he would not arrive in England until October with his report. Time was not on the side of Denikin. General Holman always advocated "send more tanks" in his telegrams to the War Cabinet. Holman also stated in his report the following:

> "Tanks invariably produce success when used against the Bolsheviks. A Russian Colonel from the 8th Red Army who was captured stated that his troops were completely demoralized by the appearance of our tanks which they will not face."

Perhaps, part of the reluctance to send more tanks was also addressed by Holman:

> "The first reports that the Russians mis-used the tanks and that they would soon be out of action were too hasty. Subsequently, it was feared that a single tank would come under the authority of three different departments. Luckily, these fears are unfounded. Russian engineers have proved their capacity of repairing a Mark V engine which received five direct hits."

Far to the West, the French 505th tank regiment was in Warsaw, Poland, with 120 FT-17s. These tanks were given to the Polish army, which created the 1st Polish tank regiment. They would be used against the Reds during the Russian-Polish war of 1920.

In July, the tanks were refitted and repaired. The 1st and 3rd sections were located at Poltava and unable to enter combat due to the unsuitable ground that the friendly troops were advancing on. The Kuban Cossacks were only supported by the tanks' "presence" which had the same worthy effect on the Reds.

Not all operations went well, a tank detachment was sent to support the Don Army in their attack. The attack went awry when the Don Cossacks failed to support the tanks at a critical moment. The Reds began to surround the tanks which became sitting ducks. Luckily, an airplane appeared and thwarted the enemy danger.

On August 5th, the 1st and 3rd Tank sections moved from Poltava to Povarino on the Don Front, the 2nd and 4th Tank sections returned to Taganrog. The 4th section was then sent to Filonovo Station on the Don Front while the 2nd Tank Section moved to the Kursk area on August 10th.

The 1st Tank Division had been in combat for one month. During this time the tanks clocked some 60-100 miles. More importantly, the front lines had increased greatly. When the tanks first appeared (May 10) the Volunteer Army had territory under it's control no more than a 60 mile radius from Rostov. By June 20th, this had extended 200 miles west to the Dniepr River, but northward to Kharkov, some 300+ miles. One of the main reasons for this rapid advance was due to the tanks.

Another part of the Tank problem was with the British control of the school at Taganrog and with the British Mission itself. Holman again states the following:

"The number of tanks which have been issued to the Russians as of September, 1919 is as follows:

11 Mk V and 5 Whippet, Type A.

However, 13 Whippet and 31 Mark V tanks remain in control of the British Tank Corps, ten are being used in the school (Taganrog) and eight are in workshops. These tanks will be issued when there are crews ready."

During this time, the Red leaders had decided to manufacture their own FT-17 tank. Official orders were issued in August, 1919. On September 29, 1919. the first disassembled FT-17 tank arrived. The parts were measured and four men created manufacturing specifications. The lead engineer was Comrade Artemsheva and under him, another five engineers. The unit and parted out tank was located in Moscow. Included in the engineering group were two Frenchmen, Messrs. Deir and Roshe. These men worked as independent contractors and given the task to create the drawings.

By October, another four Mk V tanks were issued to the Russians. The Tank School's students had to pass all of the following classes:

Mark V and Whippet driving and maintenance
Hotchkiss MG operations
Hotchkiss 6 pdr. Gun operations
Signalling

There would be one British instructor to every four students.

In the first week of August, the 1st, 3rd and 4th Tank sections wee involved in several engagements in the environs of Balashov starting August 2nd. The commander of the Don Independent Corps planned for part of his infantry to deploy along the Povorino-Balashov railway. The remaining part of his force would surround the Red flanks secretly by moving along the backs of the Kardail River. This would cut off the retreat path by blocking it at Nagrov-Baichnorovo.

A Red FT-17 tank in defensive mode, 1920. Photo: RWM

The commander of the tanks, Col. Teminkoff, carried a reconnaissance finding that a key bridge across the river had been destroyed. It was decided that a bridge had to be built and a road from Samodurovka to the ridge leading to the next objective, Peski. However, the ridge was so narrow, all six tanks could not operate there at the same time. Because of this, it was decided the tanks should attack on the right of the Corps.

The 1st Tank section, commanded by Capt. Veremeyey consisted of 2 Mk V. This was to attack along the railway to assist the 5th Don Cossack Infantry brigade to capture Peski and Mazurka.

The 3rd Tank section, commanded by Capt. Mironovitch, had 2 Whippets and the 4th Tank section under Col. Anitov, also with 2 Whippets were to attack together, along with the 5th Cavalry Brigade along the ridge which followed the Kardail River to cut the railway line near Nagorov-Baichurovo. This would hamper the Red retreat towards Balashov.

The Don forces had the support of an armor train but could not move past the bridge at Rodnichki station.

The 1st section arrived at Samodurovka station to detrain at 1800 on August 1st. This was accomplished. The ground on which the tanks were to operate on was muddy, and the trucks and tractors used to bring supplies for the tanks could not be used, so carts were. At 0300, the 5th Cossack Infantry brigade began to deploy with the tanks along the eastern slope of a cutting east of Samodurovka. At 0400 the attack began against Peski. The tanks moved north of the railway to avoid the swampy ground and drew further ahead of the infantry lagging. The Reds were so startled, they abandoned the town with no resistance. As the Reds fled over the nearby Choper River, the tanks MG's opened up. As the tanks approached the village center, Red artillery fired at the tanks from a mill at Kardail station. The Tanks now returned to nearby houses for cover. It was there that Tank No. 9079 oil pump malfunctioned. The crew frantically tried to repair it. Luckily, the infantry arrived and the remaining tanks with the infantry continued their advance toward Mazurka. Mazurka was taken by 1300, resistance was light. This advance was about 17 miles.

The 3rd and 4th Tank sections detrained at Aleksikovo at 0600. The tanks then proceeded to Skvortsov which was reached by 0900. The tanks remained there until 2000, when they moved to their starting positions some 5 miles northeast of Skvortsov. Tank No. 294, a Whippet, failed to reached the starting position due to the faulty Autovac. Another Whippet, No.356, operated on one engine due to a broken clutch spring. That left only Tanks 268 and 360 to operate on the right flank of the Corps. At 0500, the tanks advanced along the ridge reaching Kardail station and stumbling upon a Red formation in open order. The Reds fled quickly out of the Tank's weapon range. Another Red formation did not notice the tanks and continued to march. The tanks moved full throttle and cut into their lines causing a chaos. The Reds were retreating in all directions. Acting as a spotter, the tank section commander, Capt. Mironovitch directed artillery fire into the Reds and the 50th Don cavalry was tossed in.

The Russian tankers continued their pursuit too far and by 0830, both tanks had developed engine problem a few miles northwest of Kardail. As the crews tried to repair, the tanks were ordered to assist the 23rd Cavalry Regiment which was operating on their right flank. The tanks were to seize the hills near the rail station at Baichurovo. At 1130, the tanks continued to rumble and moved a few miles north stopping to rest on a hill a mile from

Baichurovo. There the tanks halted and the crews got out. The commander wrote the following in his report:

> "...from this hill we could see the whole of the surrounding country. Nowhere within a radius of 6 versts (about 4 miles) could we see any of our own troops! On the hills at the railway line near Baichurovo-Nagorovo there was nobody! At Baichurovo we saw strong enemy cavalry units. We were suddenly under a heavy enemy artillery barrage from a battery in the open."

Luckily none of the shells hit the tanks and the crew remounted and returned to wherever there troops were.

By 1400, it was obvious the Reds were pressuring the right flank. The Reds were counterattacking and by 2100 had taken Nicolayerka along the Kardail River and the tail end of the wagon train for the 7th Division was captured.. This division was ordered to hold Kardail station and the railway bridge at Samodurovka. On the 4th, the Reds continued to make solid advances on the flank, while the 7th division repelled all attacks at the station. Soon, the Reds were threatening Alexikovo. Thus, the tanks were ordered there but they could only reach the station at Yarzensyaya. Now the tank commander received ordered to send two tanks back to Kardail! Whippets Nos. 268 and 360 returned to Kardail arriving by August 5th.

By the 6th, the Reds had advanced to occupy a line from Nicolayerka – Kardail-Mazurka- Treated. The station at Kardail remained in control of the tanks and 7th division, while the town of Kardail was in Red control. A plan, led by Capt. Mironovitch called for advancing on the town from south of Mazurka, driving the Reds back to Baichurovo – Nagarov.

However, at 0730, the Reds attacked advancing for about two miles. The two Whippets counterattacked at 0900 by following the railway line despite the very heavy artillery bar-

War booty: Red forces show off their captured Mk-V tank somewhere in South Russia.

rages around them. Upon arriving at the railway crossing, they came out behind the Red infantry which had taken refuge in a hollow south of the crossing. The Whippets charged with their machine guns blazing and were supported by the artillery from a nearby armor train. The Reds fell back into the open. The tanks continued east and shortly thereafter, the Red attack turned into a full retreat. The 7th division advanced timidly and their cavalry arrived too late to do any good. So angry was the division's commander, he personally went to the 5th Cavalry Brigade and ordered them to attack. Even this did not cause the order to be followed!

At 1300, the tanks were a few miles west of Kardail and Whippet 268 began to have engine problem. At 1400, the Reds attacked the 21st and 22nd Cossack Infantry regiments forcing them to retreat. Enemy columns were also crossing at Tretyaky and reports arrived stating both the 21st and 22nd regiments had been broken. The tanks were now in serious trouble and orders were given to quietly recover the tanks. As the tanks were being loaded at Kardail station, the Reds began to shell it. Luckily, the train and the tanks left for Povorino just in time.

On the 7th, the Reds retook Kardail station. The 5th Infantry Brigade and two MkV tanks (Nos. 9358, 9079) detrained at Samodurovka and ordered to retake Peski and Ma-

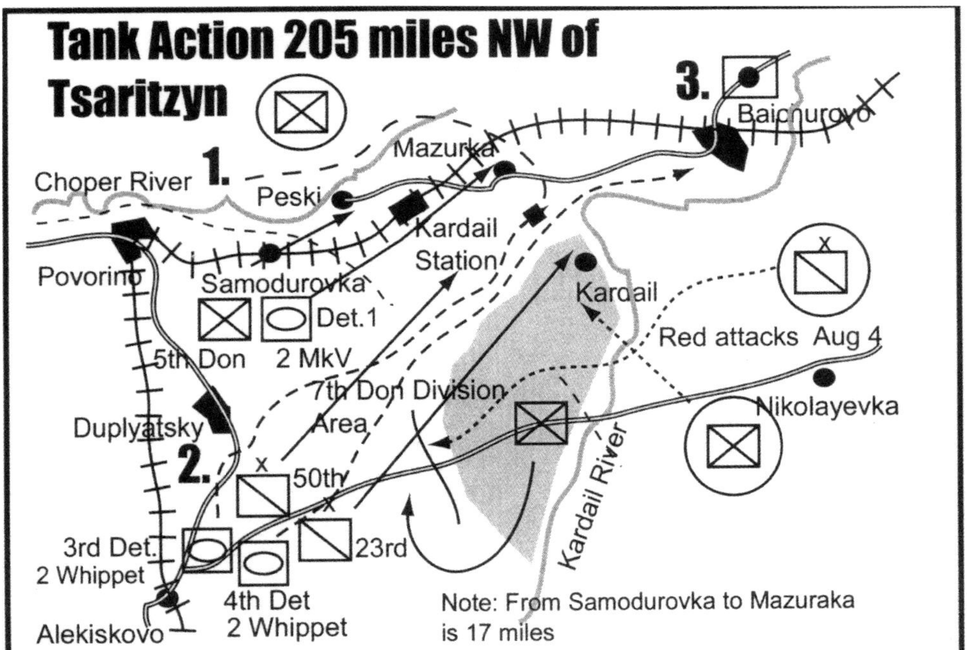

1. 1st Det attacks Peski and Mazurka at 0400 Aug 1. Mazurka falls at 1300
2. 3rd and 4th Det. detrain at Alekiskovo 0600. Move to Duply by 0900,deploy to front at 2000 and attacks with cavalry. Whippets # 294, 356 breakdown.
3. At 1130, Aug 3, the 4th Det (#268,360) arrives 1 mile from Baichurovo alone. Cavalry had stopped at Kardail station. Red artillery bombards. Tanks return to Kardail.
4. By the 7th, the Reds had taken Povorino, Duply. The tanks barely escaped.

zurka. For support, several armor trains positioned themselves close by. Tank 9079 became engulfed in a cloud of smoke and the faulty oil pump could not be repaired. The other tank remained ready. Both tanks were not entrained as it was felt that their own Cossacks would retreat!

The attack was cancelled and the Don Army abandoned Samodurovka and the Reds entered the same day. Another dangerous position found the tanks in, for they were enroute to Povorino. Reports arrived stating the Reds were close to cutting this line. Now the tanks were diverted to Alexikovo and then to safety at Taganrog.

On August 17th, the 2nd Tank section (commanded by Capt. Borschov) received orders to move to Rjava station and to be at the disposal of the 1st Kornilov Regiment. The tank train arrived at 0600 and two Mk V machines (Nos. 9340, 9178) were unloaded and joined the Kornilov regiment. This regiment's first objective was to seize Nagolynaye and then Troytskoye. This maneuver would turn the flank of the Reds, which were defending Oboyan, which was under attack by the 2nd Kornilov regiment. Included in this column was the 80th Kabardin regiment (3 Coys) one company from the 1st Kornikov and 2 artillery guns. The troops left Rjava station at 1000 with the tanks acting as a rearguard.

The advance continued for about 3 miles, at which time, the lead infantrymen fell under artillery shrapnel attacks causing them to disperse. The tanks moved out to the flank. All the forces continued advancing on Nagolnoye. The battle for the town erupted around 1300, held by a Red brigade. The Reds resisted but were then forced out of the town into a

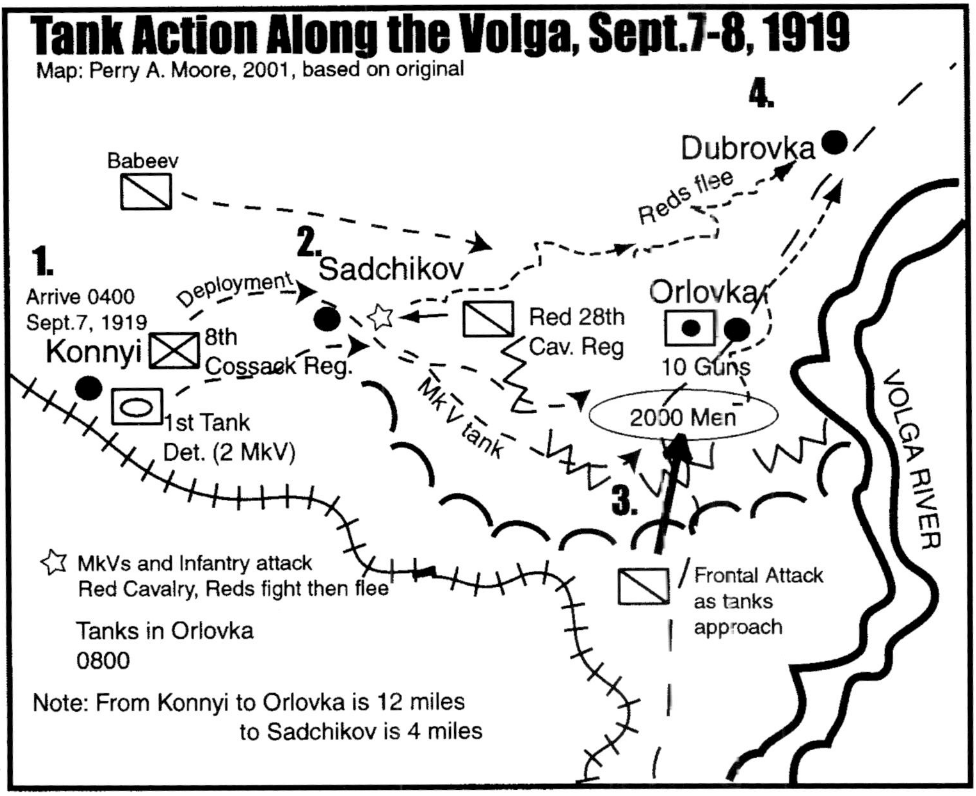

gully. The Kabardin regiment occupied the town. At 1400, after receiving reinforcements, the Reds counterattack and forced the center company back. As this occurred, the tanks attacked. Tank 9148 moved along the northern side and completely routed the Red infantry and cavalry that had been attempting to flank one of the companies. Tank 9340, at the southern end, the Mk V attacked Red infantry in the open causing a fast retreat far to the west of the town. The advance towards Troytskoye was halted not because of enemy troops but the Reds had fled there and also at Krivtsovo. The Reds fell back to Oboyan and concentrated there. The 2nd Kornilov regiment advanced on the town but were repulsed south of it.

The tanks during this battle fired 40 six pounder shells and 1000 rounds of MG. The tanks did not receive any damage. Tank # 9340 had received 5 bullet hits.

On the 18th, the tanks were placed on trucks and sent to Belgorod for the Corps reserve. By the 20th, the town of Oboyan had become very important and Denikin ordered it to be taken. The initial efforts had failed and now additional forces gathered, besides artillery, the two Mk V and a Whippet (No.326) were to be used. The tanks left Rjava Station at Midnight and reached their assembly area at 0300 (this assembly area was only 4 miles distant!) between the station and Oboyan. The 1st Kornilov Regiment consisting of two battalions and two light batteries also deployed for the attack. In Reserve was 1st battalion of the 80th Kabardin regiment. The 3rd battalion of the Kornilov regiment was to attack and retake Nagolnoya (this town was abandoned by the Whites on the 19th when six Red regiments attacked it) The 1st and 2nd battalions would attack the town from the west and north.

The attack began at 0400 and all three tanks advanced along the right of the front in order to turn the Red flank and attack him from the rear. The tanks led the way in front of the 2nd Battalion. By 0500, the attack had advanced so well that the Reds were taken by surprise and retreated eastwards without any resistance. This retreat developed into a panic when the tanks opened up with their 6 pdr guns from 1500 yards. The MG fire from the tanks riddled the ground.

By 0530, Nagolnoye was taken. The advance now turned towards the town of Pseletskoye. The Red artillery fire now opened up upon the tanks and infantry advancing across the steppes. The barrages were rapid and intense, but very poorly aimed. As the infantry advanced, by 0900, the orders were issued for a bayonet charge. The men of the Kornilov Regiment charged, screaming. Gunfire erupted, then hand to hand combat. The Whites had taken Pseletskoye. By Noon, the Reds had evacuated the whole front.

The 2nd battalion responsible for taking Oboyan, did so, that afternoon and drove the Reds in the direction of Kursk. Two Austin Armor cars were used as support in this operation.

These battles had captured 1500 men, 100 MG's.The tanks fired 50 six pounder rounds and 1500 rounds of MG. Now plans were drawn up to advance towards Kharkov.

The tanks that had captured Tsaritsyn in late June, were once again needed in the first week of September,1919. This time to keep the city in Wrangel's control. As a result of Wrangels retreat from Kamyshin forced upon him by the sudden retreat of the Don Army. Wrangel's left flank was dangerously exposed. Enemy forces, greatly superior in numbers were pressuring Wrangel and forced him to fall back to his fortified position north of Tsaritsyn.

On September 7th, the 1st Kuban Corps under General Pisarev held the positions with cavalry on the right. General Ulagay's cavalry concentrated near Kotlucan station while General Saraliens men were east of Sarepta. The 1st section (4 tanks) of tanks sat at Sarepta Station.

The Reds had shot their counterattack a day earlier in desperate bid to retake the city. This attack was well assisted by at least 10 gunboats on the Volga. The attack was repulsed.

Because of enemy dispositions, Wrangel planned to attack from two directions. One attack would be directed at the road to Saratov and one from the left flank towards Sadchikov and Orlouka. Most of the Red artillery was located on the right flank near Orlouka. Thus, tanks detrained at Konnyi several miles away from the Volga. The tanks would then reach the assembly area near Sadchikov. The tanks would advance due east and drive the Reds toward the Volga. Directly behind the tanks stood the 8th Cossack Infantry battalion. Cavalry units (the 1st Cavalry Brigade) would also move eastward. Conducting a frontal attack were men led by General Pisarev and protecting the left flank, General Udagay's cavalry at Kotlucan. Enemy forces were about 1 miles away from the assembly areas.

The tanks had arrived at the assembly areas by midnight, followed by fuel and oil carried on Camels and in carts. The tanks then moved closer arriving at 0400 northeast of Sadchikov. They were surprised to find out that only 800 yards away, the Red 28th Cavalry regiment camped. The tanks were ordered to immediately attack. The Red unit had heard them coming but did not fire until the tanks moved within 500 paces. At that distance, the MG and artillery opened up. The tanks stopped and fired their six pounders and MGs, dispersing the Soviet unit in disorder to the north. Much of the unit was captured by 1st Horse Brigade, which had been advancing from Besrodenensky. The tanks halted and refueled then continued southeast into the flank of the Reds.The 8th Cossack infantry regiment followed along with cavalry units. It was now 0520. The right Red flank resisted but when the frontal attacks began, it began to fold, retreating east and north. The tanks and infantry continued advancing turning the Red flank even more and by 0800 the town of Orlovka was taken. Because of the poor ground conditions, the tanks halted there. The cavalry and infantry continued their pursuit to Dubovko.

This battle saved Tsaritsyn for several weeks as the Reds fell back toward Saratov to regroup. Some 10 guns were captured and 100 MG. A total of 2000 POWs.

The Reds did fire AP bullets at the tanks but did so at such a far distance, none penetrated. Several were found imbedded in the tanks armor.

By October (according to Holman) the British had sent 13 Whippet and 31 Mk V tanks to Denikin. However, only 20 had been issued to the Russians by this time, and worse, only 12 had been used in combat. Part of the problem was that there had been insufficient crews trained, lack of parts, and tanks were needed for training but once the tanks were issued to the Russian, the British had no role in their tactical use. This was the other problem. According to Russian sources, British tanks arrived in South Russia on the following dates:

March 22, 1919	12 tanks
July 24, 1919	16 tanks
Sept.6, 1919	10 tanks
Oct. 10, 1919	33 tanks
Oct. 13, 1919	2 tanks

The Russian use of the tank, as magical as it seemed to be, was in small dribbles. It was seldom for any attack to have any more than four machines. This seems to have been a wasteful use of a weapon that did have a proven, profound, impact on the enemy. Why the Russians did use all 12 tanks in an attack for a blow out will never be known.

By November, Denikin had 57 MkV and 17 Whippets.

The question of not enough crews for the tanks at first seems plausible and logical. However, a report sent to the War Cabinet in mid-October stated that since April, 425 officers had been trained in all the gunnery, maintenance and driving courses. This number translates into crews sufficient to man 53 tanks. This clearly contradicts the "lack of crew" argument and leads one to be suspicious. Why, then, were not the tanks issued to the Russians? Why did the British Mission not issue another 33 tanks or at least another 15 tanks? In October, the British only released four Mk V tanks to the Whites on October 7th. By this date, a total of 20 tanks had been released to the Russians since April.

Denikin continued to use his tanks in driblets. As his troops approached Kursk in September, No.2 Tank section went into action three times. Each time the enemy fled without the tanks even firing a shot. Again, reports had a familiar sound:

> "...as the Bolsheviks heard the tanks approach, they rapidly evacuated their positions. The battle near Kursk called for tanks.The train carrying the tanks found it unnecessary to unload the tanks, as the Reds fled at seeing them."

As the Denikin spearhead approached it zenith at Orel, a detachment of tanks was used to capture the town.

By late October, Denikin's success was reversed and on November 1st, the Reds captured their first British tank at Liski. This tank would be recaptured a month later. Also, Denikins 2nd Tank Division had been formed and was being deployed. The division's deployment had been delayed by the guerilla Mahknov and his followers, which had been disrupting Denikin's rear area 60 miles from Taganrog. This division was ordered to stand by in case it was needed.

A rare photo showing the Red forces in action with a captured Mk V tank, 1920.

Denikin's Tank Order of Battle as of November 18, 1919, was as follows:

1st Russian Tank battalion

1st Grp (three tanks) at Taganrog
2nd Grp (three tanks) attached to Volunteer army
3rd Grp (four tanks) in Kiev area
4th Grp (four tanks) attached 1st Cavalry Corps and Volunteer army

2nd Russian Tank Battalion

5th Grp (three tanks)
6th Grp (four tanks) attached to Caucasian army
7th Grp (four tanks) attached to Don army
8th Grp (forming)
9th Grp (forming)
10th Grp (four tanks)
11th Grp (forming)
At Taganrog (11 tanks)
In repair (16 tanks)
At Novorossisk (11 tanks)

In Early December, 10 MkV tanks, while waiting on the pier to be transported at Novorossisk, washed into the sea. The cause issued by the British Mission stated it was a heavy gale. The tanks toppled into 16 feet of water. Later explanations stated that part of the pier collapsed since it was hard to believe a gale could blow 10 tanks into the water!

Tank sections continued to operate with success even in December, 1919, enabling Denikin to conduct counterattacks. One tank section was deployed in the Tsaritsyn area, two sections in the Kharkov area and one near Kiev. On December 15th, a tank section took part in a counterattack supported by infantry caused the Reds to flee and retreat when the tanks charged the lines. Despite the major reverses Denikin was having at this time, the British Tank School continued to turn out tank crews.

By the end of November the school had turned out:

47 men trained on the MkV	66 men trained on the MG
15 men trained on the Whippet	35 men trained on the 6 pdr guns

Winter conditions arrived in South Russian in 1919 by mid November. This caused additional problems for the tanks, namely snow, freezing and problems in withdrawing them as Denikin retreated. As the Reds, the taking apart and drawing manufacturing specifications of their FT-17 tank proved to be painfully a slow process. By December 19, the Reds had disassembled a FT-17 and now began to put it back to together. Each piece of the tank was became a specification on paper. A complete set of manufacturing drawings was completed. Now, the task of rebuilding the tank had begun.

The greatest danger to the tanks during Denikin's withdrawal was the lack of rail transport.

By January10th, 1920, the Reds had captured the Tank school at Taganrog (some 19 tanks were captured) including the key city of Rostov. At Rostov, the Reds captured nine tanks and when Novotcherkask fell they captured 100 guns and 8 tanks. Another 4 tanks were lost during the rapid withdrawal making a total of 36 tanks falling into enemy hands. When Novorossisk fell on March 27th, another 18 tanks were captured.

In the case of Taganrog, as the Reds approached, orders went out for all trains to carry off the tank equipment and tanks. All these requests fell on deaf ears. Finally, a train was commandeered by the British personnel there. During the retreat from Taganrog, another 25 tanks, 50 tons of stores and 15 trucks were lost to the enemy. Most of this equipment was rendered unserviceable. At least the British had hoped.

Denikin still had 45 tanks on February 10th, 1920, (by some accounts) but 28 of these were in need of major repair in order to operate. These tanks were quickly transported by sea to Sevastopol.

The tactical use of the British tanks by the Russians was wasteful. Granted, they had limited crews, supplies, spare parts and tank trains for transport but the ability was there to mass all 10-12 tanks at anytime in the Summer of 1919.

There is no question had they done so, the effect would have been a huge blow out in the Red defenses. If followed by cavalry, as was done at times, the advance could be sustained. Instead, they made the error the British themselves made in WW1 of using tanks in small numbers. Granted, in South Russia, the tank was a shock weapon of unbelievable proportions. Other methods were also obvious, such as, attacking at night or sunrise. Russian crews had become well trained but the infantry continued to lag far behind. For the tanks, the operational radius for a day could reach 100 miles.

German soldiers posing in 1941 with an Mk V. Photo: Schmul

The only weapons the Reds had against the tank were AP ammunition in limited quantities, Garford armor cars (which had a gun), artillery, and captured tanks. However, Red morale was so shakened by the appearance of a tank, that they always fired their AP ammo from such a far distance it failed to penetrate the tank's thin armor. The artillery when firing direct fire seldom hit a tank, and at best, shell fragments would splinter into the tank, engine compartment or vision slits. The few Garfords that the Reds had proved to be quite cumbersome and stayed tied to the few roads.There is no mention anywhere of any anti-tank guns in the records.

The London Times reporter was right. The tank was Denikin's secret weapon but it was used too sparingly to do much good.

When the Volunteer Army evacuated Novorossisk in late March, 1920, the tanks saved were sent to the Crimea and fought under General Wrangel for the rest of the year. The total evacuated came to 24 tanks. However, only 12 were fit for action in May (six Mk V and nine Whippet). Three were held in reserve. Another 3 tanks would be ready in the near future and another nine tanks by June. The British Tank detachment under Wrangel contained 4 officers and 15 enlisted.

And what did the famed tank expert and promoter Colonel Fuller have to say about the tanks sent to Russia? In his memo, dated March 25, 1919, he stated:

> "...for tanks to be employed against the Bolsheviks in a guerilla war will prove to be little good. They are too slow and their radius of action too limited. The tanks must be manned and fought by British personnel. It takes 4 months, at least, to turn a trained infantry man into an efficient Tank driver or gunner "

Recall, that the tank training in South Russia took only one month. All tanks were manned by Russian crews,and at times, there was guerilla warfare. The best example of tank skill is the single British manned tank at Tsaritsyn. Also, it was curious that General Wrangel appointed a British Tank officer to command the tanks at Tsaritsyn. Obviously, Fuller and Wrangel knew the tanks were best in the hands of the British. Yet, this short advice by the Tank master, Col. Fuller, was totally ignored.

Many of the arguments for not supplying Denikin with more tanks state a lack of surplus tanks. It must be remembered Britain occupied large portions of France with numerous tanks in 1919. However, the truth of the matter is there was an overabundance of tanks that could be sent to South Russia, North Russia or the Far East to support any determined attacks on Bolshevism.

The position of the British Tank Corps by March, 1919, was that of the 26 tank battalions existing on Nov.11th, 1918, only eight were due for demobilization. Five of these were in France and three in the UK. The three in the UK were not fit for action. The British Tank Training Center had been so reduced that it was almost inoperative. Recruiting for the Tank Corps amounted to only 20 new men, although, 500 had re-enlisted. The existing tank types were not suitable for guerilla warfare or a war that had few trench lines. Excluding the tanks in the battalions, some 300 remained parked in the open, rapidly deteriorating for lack of supervision and maintenance.

The tanks in Germany with the Army of the Rhine consisted of 156 MkV and 30 MkV*. In France, 82 MkV, 116 Mk V*, 58 Whippet, Type A. Scheduled for repair were an additional 89 MkV. The tanks laying out in the open, deteriorating, consisted of 24 MkV, 50 MkV* and 58 Whippet, a total of 132 tanks. The total tanks in France came 351 MkV, 196 Mk* and 116 Whippet. These figures do not include the hundreds of obsolete tanks (any Mk IV or less). The total tank strength in France therefore is 663 tanks! Thus, Britain had plenty of tanks but no will to send them.

The operational tank strengths in England during 1920 were as follows:

> 84 MkV*, 24 Whippet, Type C. The non-operational tanks requiring extensive repair were: 200 MkV*, 6 Whippet Type C, 2 Whippet Type A, 3 MkV. The tanks needing repaired and considered surplus and not needed were: 6 Mk VIII, 39 Mk IX troop carriers, 50 Whippet, Type B.

As one can see, the British had plenty of surplus tanks to send. Even the older Mk IV tanks amounting to the hundreds (which are not included here) could have had an impact in South Russia.

In Colonel Fuller's memo, he proposed to create a force of nine tank battalions (432 tanks) using the new Whippet, Type D. This Tank Expeditionary force could be ready by May, 1920. Fuller wanted the aim of the force to fight a guerilla war by employing tanks, airplanes, armor cars. The TYPE D tank placed emphasis on speed, a large action radius and using long life parts. Only one such tank existed in March, 1919. Fuller hoped that an average of 100 could be produced starting in December, 1919, and at the end of four years, some 500 Medium D tanks would exist. The Medium D tank had a crew of 4 men, speed of 25 m.p.h., armed with 3 MG. It had a radius of 200 miles and 30 ft. long. Only two were ever built in production, the programme was cancelled in 1921.

From a psychological view, the Russian soldier attached to the White tank units considered the tank to be very valuable. To lose such a weapon in battle was considered to be insulting to those entrusted with the tank. Because of this, tanks were deliberately held back and only committed in battle to obtain important objectives or to turn a battle. The Russian crews found the tank to be a large, formidable, yet slow weapon. These crews suffered the same inhospitable environment that their British counterparts did. One Russian officer and part of the crew wrote the following:

> "The men inside choked from the fumes after the tank had been operated for one hour. This caused men to faint during combat. The greatest threat to our tank was enemy artillery fire which easily destroyed any tank if hit. Many tanks were lost because of shell splinters piercing petrol containers and igniting. When this happened, the tank lit up like a candle along with the crew. Temperatures inside easily surpassed 50C. After several hours of operation, the crew had to have rest."

In all honesty, the tanks the British sent were in poor shape. Most had been sitting around in France, rusting with little or no maintenance. Therefore, a Mk V tank usually moved at less than 4 m.p.h. and the fast Whippet, much less than 8 m.p.h.

The transportation of tanks to the front was almost always done by the railroad. The tanks would be dropped off some 5-10 miles from the front line and this caused the tanks to take several days to reach a starting position. Many times, the tanks would unload, travel for days to reach the front, only to be ordered back to a train depot to embark again for another front. Tanks were at their best when attacking fixed positions or objectives or trenches. However, since the Russian Civil war was a more guerilla war, the tanks impact were less. As time went on, it was found that the Mk V was useless unless attacking in close combat or a defined defense. Because of this, many Russians preferred the Whippet tank, which they called the cavalry tank. The Whites also began to question the tanks' value in their war because armor cars and horses were much faster. This was a fluid war and not WW1.

As previously stated, the remaining tanks Denikin had in March,1920, had been withdrawn to Sevastopol, Crimea. This is where Wrangel took over the Volunteer army from Denikin on April 4, 1920. He reorganized the remnants into the 1st and 2nd Corps. He issued order # 2858 disbanding tank groups 1,2,7,8 and 11, the British Tank school and tank support units. Most of the personnel from these units returned to non-tank duties. Wrangel reformed his tank force into the 3,4,5, and 10 groups and created the 1st and 2nd tank battalions. Although not completely formed, Wrangel committed his 1st and 3rd tank groups in April to repeal and halt the Red 13th army attacking. These tank groups came under fierce antitank fire from the numerous artillery guns along the Red front. On the 14th, the tanks were able to counterattack with artillery support and force the Red defenses to be rolled up. This advance continued until the artillery fire had become so intense they were forced to halt. By the beginning of May, 1920, Wrangel's tank forces consisted of the following:

1st Tank group (six Mk V. Tank nos. 9381, 9040, 9186, 9335, 9003, 9300). The unit had 52 officers, 26 enlisted, six 57mm guns, 26 machine guns, four armor cars, 650 shells and 40,000 MG rds.
2nd Tank group (four Whippletree A. Tank nos. 358, 328,371, 388.) The unit had to officers, 15 soldiers, one 37mm AT gun, 14 MGs, 40,000 rds. of MG ammunition, no shells. Some of the tanks names were: Tiger, Sphinx, Crocodile).
3rd Tank group (six Mk Vs. Tank nos. 9007,9074, 9159,9034, 9358, 9141. The group had six 57mm guns, 27 MGs, one Garford armor car with a 57mm gun.
4th Tank group (four Whippet, Type A. Tank nos. 261, 242,346,315; and two FT-17s named Grey and Modest). This group had 13 officers, 19 enlisted, 12 MGs.

Because of the withering artillery fire from Red artillery during the April battles, Wrangel created a tank support group. Wrangel took time to look at the tactical situation tanks were in and noticed that the MkV gun, a 57mm, had a very short range and therefore could not engage Red artillery. To counter this, he created a suppression unit consisting of 76mm guns with crew to suppress the Red artillery. This unique unit was first put into action on June 7, when the 1st Tank group entered in to combat. The unit followed the tanks into action and deployed while under enemy fire. The suppression unit worked and kept the Red artillery at bay successfully. Wrangel also ordered mufflers to be installed on all tanks to achieve a better "element of surprise" effect. Each tank group also carried a steel cable with attached anchor to rip apart the Red use of barb wire.

During this same time frame, the Red 9th army had created its own 1st tank group from the captured tanks. This group had 50-100 men and up to three Mk Vs. The problem for the Reds was the lack of knowledge of tank operations and use, most were not familiar with the

MkV. To offset this lack of knowledge, engineers created "tank manuals" and "combat tactics manuals." Roles were assigned to each member. A volunteer for a tank crew member was rewarded with a daily ration of 200 gms of 30% proof vodka. As tank groups were created, it was decided to have three MkVs per platoon and an attached train for logistics. Oddly, the Reds first tank use was not against the White army, but against the Polish army on June 4th, 1920. This debut had not been planned but forced upon them when a Polish regiment with artillery support had penetrated into the rear of the 30th brigade (10th division) in the 9th army area. The Red 7th and 35th Tank groups were committed (a total of five Mk Vs) to cover the 30th brigade's withdrawal. Due to mud and enemy fire, two were immediately knocked out, one overturned. The 1st Tank group was then sent in. Both failed to reach their assigned objectives due to enemy fire, and one tank was knocked out by a bomb dropped from an airplane. The remaining tanks retreated back to Mogilyov leaving the brigade to be cutoff. On July 4th, the Reds, in another attack, sent in their 2nd group (3 Mk V) to support the attack of its 33rd Kuban division of 15th army. The group had been given orders to breakthrough Polish positions with the 14th Armor car group (three Austin ACs) and the 293rd Infantry regiment. The path of advance was the highway leading to Polotsk. The Poles had created two defense lines with trenches and four rows of barb wire. The Reds deployed at night and with camouflage. The Red artillery failed to suppress the Polish resistance, and in consequence, the Polish artillery saturated the attacking MkVs. The barrage forced the tanks to scatter and because of very muddy conditions, the tanks regrouped and moved single file along the only road. One tank became stuck in the mud when it veered off the road, another broke down. The remaining tank continued and broke through the first Polish row of wire. The Poles seeing this, counterattack further north breaking through. Red cavalry and the 98th Infantry regiment now conducted a delaying action to halt the Poles.

After the battle, the Reds changed their tank organization from three to four tanks in a platoon and decided that all tanks of a platoon must be of the same type. Due to the lack of infantry support for the tanks, a platoon of 30 men armed with two MGs was also created and became part of a tank platoon.

During this time, the Reds not only battled with Wrangel attempting to bust out of the Crimea, but also the Polish army. The Poles were well supplied with French equipment and now wanted to claim some of the area left by the Germans. This evolved into the Russian-Polish war. In July, the Reds had captured seven FT-17s at Grodno (Nos. 1661, 1806,3239 and others). These were sent to Minsk on August 23rd.

Recall that the Reds had decided to manufacture their own FT-17 tanks. After one year of making detailed drawings, the first manufactured FT-17 (named, "The Fighter for Freedom") was produced by August, 1920. The process continued each month with a production of one tank per month. In November, 1920, three had been produced. The Russian FT-17 was the same as the French version in most cases. In a few variants, the tank also had two MGs and a 37mm gun. In all cases, the Russians installed the 37mm gun. By June, 1921, the Reds had manufactured 15 FT-17s. Eight of the tanks had a 37mm gun and one MG, three had a 37mm gun and 2 MGs, the balanced were unarmed. None of the FT-17s produced in Russia were used in combat. According to Russian custom, tanks were given names. Some of the FT-17 names were: "Red Fighter," "Red Star," "Free Russia," "Kerches," and "Victories."

Unlike General Denikin, Wrangel (a cavalry soldier) had mixed and a more realistic views of using tanks during his tenure as the leader of the Volunteer army in 1920. He knew their limitations and weakness. Accordingly, he would use the tanks on fixed defenses, which became much more prevalent during this time of the civil war. One reason for this was because Wrangel's men were in the Crimea and were forced to break out from the narrows. The Reds attempted to seal this off and contain the enemy.

On between May 25-April 8, Wrangel sent his 1st and 4th Tank groups towards the narrow isthmus of the Crimea to support the 1st Corps attempting to break out.The 3rd Tank group supported the 2nd Corps. Already, the use of the tanks can be seen: Wrangel used 16 tanks on fixed defenses across a relatively narrow front. This had never been done under Denikin. Also, it was the first time Mk Vs, Whippets and FT-17s were used in the same attack.

Wrangel's attempt to bust out began at 0425. By 0500, the tanks were assaulting the fixed Red defenses with wire. Naturally, the tanks quickly pierced the line under a shield of well placed artillery fire. By 0510, the tanks and infantry had broken through the 2nd Red defensive line. The infantry became bogged down, but the tanks rumbled into Red rear areas creating considerable havoc and panic. The Reds, desperate, brought in their few Garford armor cars and a previously captured tank. This held the White tanks for some time. The Red Latvian division counterattacked the 1st Tank group using metal rods and bayonets, poking them into the vision slits. Tanks 9040, 9186 (Mk V) and 261 (Whippet) became disabled because of this. Tanks 9381, 346, 342 also received considerable damage, but managed to return to safety. The battle now centered around the disabled tanks as the Whites attempted to extradite them while under fire. This proved to be a deadly affair and difficult due to a lack of tractors. The 3rd Tank group received numerous awards for its heroic courage when facing enemy gun fire. The unit persisted in its attack and caused the Reds to retreat. This attack also marked the last time the Whites used their two FT-17 tanks. The condition of the FTs was horrible. Their condition was even worse than the British Mk Vs and Whippets. One FT-17 tank, "Grey," was in battle from 1400 to 0030. The engine overheated causing the piston rings to knock, the clutch jammed and the radiator cracked. The sister tank, "Modest," broke the front springs and a core valve. These were never repaired due to no replacement parts.

From July-August, 1920, Wrangel continued to use tanks. The 1st Tank group supported the 1st Corps during this time. On August 20, 1920, the 3rd Tank group counterattacked a Red attack at 0930. The Red advances were checked with tanks and infantry support. During this battle, the Red resistance proved to be so stiff that the tanks refueled and reloaded ammunition three times. It was on the third time the Reds had enough and retreated. The tanks pursued them for one mile. However, this overconfidence in the tank's abilities caused one of the tank's engine to seize during the pursuit. This forced another tank to be used as a tow. While this happened, the Reds began to fire their Garford armor cars (armed with a 76mm gun) destroying another tank! The tank was abandoned. As night fell, the two tanks managed to evacuate for rêpairs.

As already noted, Wrangel was quite sympathetic for crew members of a tank:

> "The crews suffer inhuman conditions, constant jolts, jerks, and gases from the engine exhaust and fuel inside their compartments. This concentration is ex-

> treme and causes the crews to become sick and incapacitated over time. The endurance of a tank crew is eight hours or less before they are exhausted and must be replaced. Crew members suffer from headaches, nausea, and heart palpitations. Inside the compartment, temperatures reach 50C or more, and the Mk V exhaust after only one hour of operation was quite noxious to the crew. During the summer, a tank crew could not be inside for more than three hours."

The White forces under Wrangel continued to battle with the Reds near the Dniepr River into the fall of 1920. The climax was at a town called Kahovka. In the early hours of August 7th, 1920, the Red 13th army made a forced crossing establishing a bridgehead with the 15th, 51st and Latvian rifle divisions. Here the units dug in. Wrangel was no shape to attack, and therefore, the Reds began to create a WW1 style battlefield consisting of three defense lines complete with trenches. This front ran 40 km long, 12 km deep. Eventually, the Reds created three defense lines: an advanced line, the main line and rear. The advanced line had huge gaps and lightly occupied with independent platoons or companies. The main line was a continuous line of trenches stretching 10 km. This line was reinforced with 150 machine gun nests and 27 small bunkers. These were protected by six rows of barb wire. The rear line surrounded the town itself and was only 2 km in length consisting of only a trench. In this his area, the Reds placed 15 artillery observation posts. The total amount of barb wire used amounted to 10,000 m.

Wrangel had decided to breakthrough using his 2nd Corps and the 2nd Tank group (this tank unit had deployed 100km from the nearest railway station to reach this front!). Wrangel, if successful, could cause the collapse of the Red Southern army front.

His first attack began on September 1st. The 2nd Tank group was in action for 10 hours and had reloaded twice. Its "Tiger" named MkV tank had broken through the main line and immediately subjected to withering direct artillery gun fire from 500m. All fire missed, however, a Garford armor car, armed with a 76mm gun opened up securing a disabling hit. Another tank approached to rescue it, but was also hit. White infantry finally arrived saving both tanks. In end, the Whites had captured five small villages near the main line and one Garford.

On the 5th, Wrangel conducted his second attack. This began at 0200 and heavy fighting occurred along the Kahovka-Chaplinka road. The 2nd Tank group, again, endured a grueling 10 hour battle reloading four times. Wrangel's 2nd Corps were supported by four MkV tanks (the Tiger, Sphinx, Artless, Sibiryak) and two Austin armor cars (the Stereguschi and Kavalerist) quickly busted through the first line of trenches. As soon as they entered into the zone, two Red Garford ACs began to fire their main guns. The Red infantry MG and rifle fire suppressed the White supporting infantry units and they were forced to take cover. The tanks continued moving and firing and routed the Red 45th rifle brigade (15th division) and some of their supporting artillery units. Commanders of the 15th division, Kuliikovski and Riltsevitch, personally took two of the artillery guns and together with their crews began to fire knocking out two of the tanks, Sphinx and Sibiryak. This forced the other two tanks and ACs to retreat back to their starting positions.

Wrangel's third attack was on October 11th. This time, the tanks, "General Skobelov and Field Marshal Kutuzov" encountered and dueled with two Red Garford armor cars, the "Uragan Revolution and Chort." The exchange of fire continued for sometime until the

"Chort" was hit, immobilizing it. The Whites succeeded in capturing it and using it in the upcoming battle.

The finale began with the fourth battle on the 14th. Because of the continuous use of tanks by the Whites, the Red commanders on the 8th, issued orders to create the first anti-tank defenses of the Russian Civil war. These AT ditches dug were 3.6 m long and 3.1 m deep and placed in staggered rows. Between the staggered rows and gaps the area was mined. All of the roads leading to the town were also mined. Special AT units, using artillery guns, were created to deal with any tank breaking through the main line. All gun units were also trained in night fighting. However, this was not all. The Reds also had created a "mobile reserve" unit, the 42nd Combined Heavy Infantry detachment consisting of six Garford ACs (each with a 76mm gun) named: "Antichrist," Moscow, Krasny Bogatyr, Pugachev, and two others with no names. Also attached were two Austin armor cars and two FT-17s.

By this date, only the 51st Red division commanded by V. Bluher defended the established bridgehead. The other two divisions had been diverted to other fronts. The 51st division contained the 151, 152, 153 rifle brigades, 9th Shock brigade, 51st Cavalry regiment and the 44th brigade of 15th division. Total men: 10,000, 500 cavalry, 250 machine guns. The 9th Shock brigade contained mortars and flamethrowers. The division was supported by the 4th light and 2nd Heavy battalions (Divizion) and two Special Purpose Heavy battalions. The following were the artillery strengths:

45 guns in the bridgehead (37 three inch guns, model 1902; one three inch Lender AA gun;
Two six inch howitzer, model 1909; two 122mm howitzers; one 107mm gun, model 1910 gun
Two French 120mm guns, model 1878
Ten guns on the right bank of the Dniepr (four 120mm, six 155mm guns, model 1877).

Also in the bridgehead, the 3rd, 23rd, 24th, 42nd, and 47th Armor Car detachments totaling:

Six Garfords with 76mm guns
One British White with a gun
Seven Italian Fiat ACs with MGs
Six British Austin ACs with MGs
One Jeffrey AC

Wrangel's opposing forces consisted of the Cherepov Group (Combined Rifle regiment, Terkso-Astrakistan infantry battalion) totaling 1200 men, 150 cavalry and eight guns. The 2nd Corps under General Vitkovski contained the 13th and 34th infantry divisions, the Vilenski and Simferopolski cavalry battalions and Czech infantry regiment) totaling 5000 men, 500 cavalry and 60 guns. The 1st Tank group was attached and the 1st Armor Car battalion, totaling 12 tanks and 11 armor cars. The odds were not in Wrangel's favor.

It would be Wrangel's "Kursk."

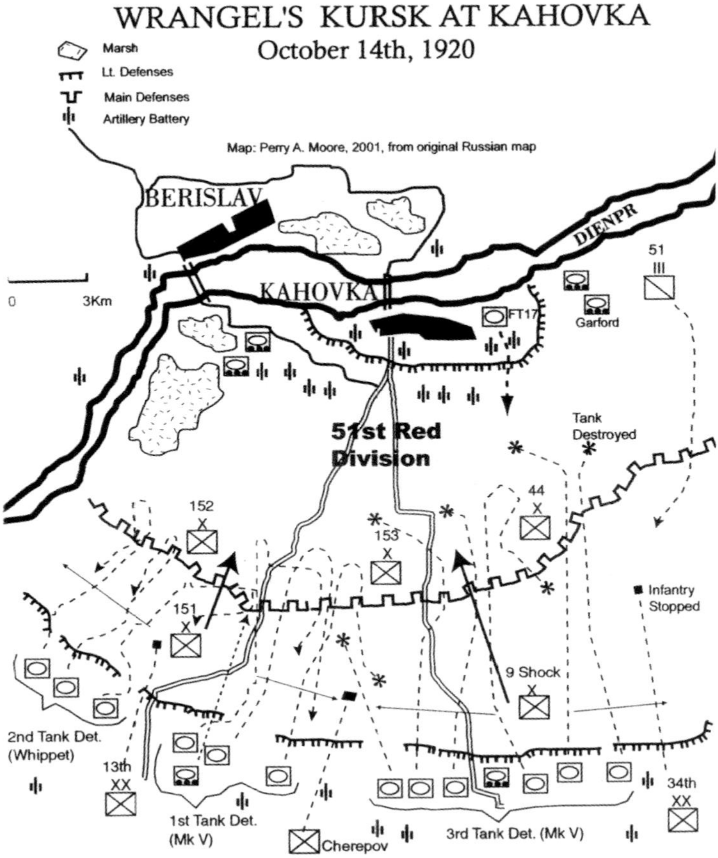
WRANGEL'S KURSK AT KAHOVKA
October 14th, 1920
Marsh
Lt. Defenses
Main Defenses
Artillery Battery
Map: Perry A. Moore, 2001, from original Russian map
BERISLAV
DIENPR
KAHOVKA
0
3Km
FT17
Garford
51
III
51st Red Division
Tank Destroyed
152
X
153
X
44
X
151
X
Infantry Stopped
9 Shock
X
2nd Tank Det. (Whippet)
13th
XX
1st Tank Det. (Mk V)
Cherepov
3rd Tank Det. (Mk V)
34th
XX

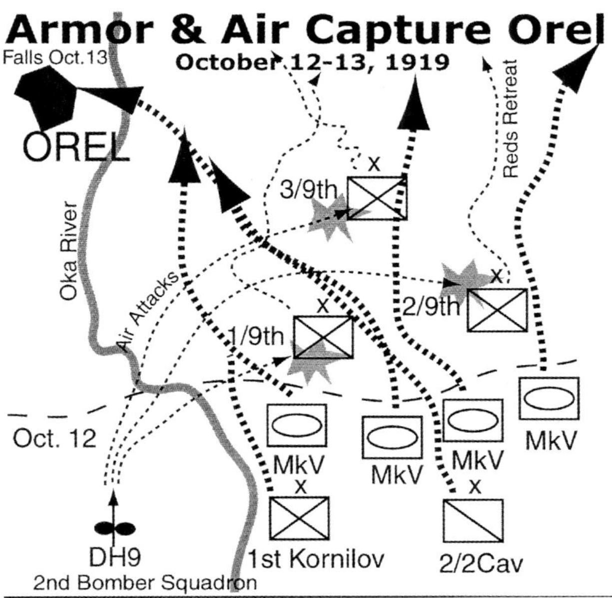
Armor & Air Capture Orel
October 12-13, 1919
Falls Oct.13
OREL
Oka River
Reds Retreat
3/9th
2/9th
1/9th
Air Attacks
Oct. 12
MkV
MkV
MkV
MkV
1st Kornilov
2/2Cav
DH9
2nd Bomber Squadron

The attack began at 0400, on the 14th, with the Whites heavily bombarding the Red defensive lines. In particular, the bulk of the artillery focused on the 151st brigade (451,452,453 regiments) and the 9th Shock brigade (1st and 2nd regiments). These held the southern portion of the line. The tanks, all 12 of them, attacked as one group (this was an unique use of tanks) and reached the advance defensive line at 0430. This line was quickly penetrated and the tanks approached the main line. Meanwhile, units of the 151st and 9th Shock failed to repel the White infantrymen and began a disorderly withdrawal. Oddly, the victorious White 13th and 34th divisions suddenly halted! Thus, both Red units reached the main line in good order. However, the White massive tank assault (nine MkV, three Whippet) broke through the 451st regiment's sector and crossed the trenches, broke through the 453rd regiment's sector and the 452nd regiments sector. However, the morale of the tank crews were not concrete and when they realized there infantry was several hundred of yards to their rear or when one tank was hit with artillery fire, many chose to withdraw to safer areas. However, five tanks braved the hail of artillery fire (the Ataman Yermak, FM Kutuzov, Surorov, Skobelev and Velikaya Rossia) and immediately met the Red Garfords with 76mm guns of the 42nd Armor detachment. A gun duel immobilized the Suvorov and damaged the Antichrist (Garford). The tanks, Kutuzov, Rossia and Skobelev, which had broke through the 2nd Regiment of the 9th Shock and crossed the main defense line, all fell prey to the Red AT defenses. These were either destroyed or immobilized. The tanks, Kutepov and Yermak, also crossed the main line. The Yermak rattled the HQ of the 1st regiment/9th Shock with direct hits, but they too, fell prey to the AT defenses. Both were destroyed.

By now, the time was 0600, and the main threat to the Red main line was at its height. However, the White infantry and cavalry were nowhere to be seen. They were far behind the tanks they were suppose to be supporting, pinned by MG and rifle fire. The tank assault became a Red hunting ground for guns and brave infantry assaulting immobilized tanks. By 1100, it had become obvious to both sides that the White attack had failed. The fighting continued and by 1300, the Red 51st division was ordered to counterattack. The Red counterattack quickly stalled as they tried to advance over the same deadly ground. The infantry tried to capture several of the White tanks, failing each time. The Whites counterattacked with two tanks and infantry with the same nowhere result. By sunset, both sides had enough and the front lines were where they had been when it had begun.

The Red 51st division had lost 28 KIA, 289 WIA, 65 MIA. It had captured 60 POWs, damaged seven tanks. Wrangel's 2nd Corps had attacked over a 13 km front and had committed over half of it's strength in the attack. His tanks had been spread out over 10 km. Wrangel had paid a dear price. His tankers had not been bold enough when not supported by infantry. His tanks did not act as a cohesive unit, but independent tanks and failed to support other tanks when attacking. They lost their nerve when faced with the Red AT defenses.

The Reds attacked on the 15th at 1130 with the 51st division and by 1600 had been halted. To tip the scales, the Reds tossed in another division along with three captured Mk Vs and two Garfords. By 1800, the whole affair had been grinded to a halt. This time, the White artillery had destroyed all of their former tanks. On the 16th, the Reds attacked again and was quickly repulsed.

The Reds attacked until the 17th, to no avail. Nothing more was to be gained. A stalemate set in. By now, the Whites had lost over 400 men, nine tanks. The Reds lost five

Garfords and managed to capture five tanks, the remaining were evacuated by the Whites. It was the last use of tanks by Wrangel.

Wrangel had little time remaining and when the Crimea fell in November, the Reds captured an additional five MkVs (nos. 9381, 9301,9034, 9309 and 9040).

By now (October 20), the Reds had the following tank groups:

1st Group (3 MkV, nos. 9185,9085,9153)
2nd Group (4 MkV, nos. 9050, 9387)
3rd Group (3 MkV, 1 Whippet, nos.9418, 9283, 9192, 371)
4th Group (4 MkVs, nos. 9336, 9066, 9113, 9028) at Kharkov.

A month later, the following were added:

5th Group (two Whippets, nos. 268, 294) in Moscow.
8th Group (three MkV, nos. 9137, 9152, 9302) with 9th army.

The last tank use of the Russian Civil war occurred on February 24, 1921. The last White opposing force was the Georgian army, in Georgia. Opposing them was the Red 11th army consisting of the 20th division, 12th division,one artillery regiment and four brigades. Supporting the attack was the 2nd Tank group and 55th Armor car (4 Garfords). The Gerogians had two MkVs.

The attack began at 1400 and Red forces advanced along the road toward Baku in the snow and mud. The tank crews fought freezing temperatures and poor visibility. The battle moved quickly as the tanks supported the attacking infantry and the Georgians provided little resistance. Only when one tank get stuck in the mud did the Georgians attack it. By now, the condition of the Mk Vs was horrendous. The Red tank crew members suffered severely from toxic petrol and exhaust fumes causing many to bleed externally. Baku fell on the 25th. The condition of the two MkVs that the Georgians possessed was found out when the Reds discovered them inside a warehouse in parts.

By 1922, the Soviets had 29 Mk Vs in 13 tank groups in operation. In 1923, this decreased to 16 MkVs, six Whippets and 12 FT-17s. In 1924, the Soviets adopted the regimental unit for tanks. Two were created, each with 356 men and 18 tanks. The British MkVs remained in Soviet use until 1931.

The following list is the most complete list of the tanks sent by the British to Denikin and subsequently captured by the Bolsheviks. The numbers are British designations, not Russian.

Whippet Nos. 242,361, 268, 938, 288,294, 315, 323, 326, 328, 345, 346, 356, 358, 360, 283, 388,371.
Mk V: 9003, 9007,9020.9024, 9028, 9033, 9034, 9038, 9040, 9050, 9056, 9066, 9074, 9075, 9079, 9085, 9113, 9118, 9122, 9137, 9139, 9141, 9146, 9148, 9152, 9153, 9159, 9185, 9186, 9192,9195, 9199, 9274, 9275, 9277, 9283, 9300, 9301, 9302, 9303, 9324, 9330,9335, 9336, 9340, 9344, 9353, 9358, 9373, 9374, 9376, 9366, 9387,9416,9417, 9418, 9431, 9439, 1613 (Whippet, type B).

While the South Russia adventure was dieing a slow death in March, 1920, far to the east, the Americans delivered, incognito, ten FT-17s at Vladiostock. These tanks were hidden from public view in covered rail cars and labeled, "American Red Cross." While they were awaiting delivery, the Reds stole the train at gunpoint and took off for Blagoveshchensk. Since none of the tanks had any 37mm guns or MGs, the Reds armed them and by Summer of 1920 five platoons had been created. The tanks were given additional armor plating around the turret and in some cases, two MGs in addition to a 37mm. These ten tanks created the Red 1st Amur tank division. The division consisted of the following:

1st Platoon (tank nos. 9254,9141)
2nd Platoon (tank nos.4320,9108)
3rd Platoon (tank no. 9446)
4th Platoon (tank nos. 9092, 1871)
5th Platoon (tank nos. 1930,9096)

The division had only 350 37mm shells and 5000 rounds of MG. In reality, the tanks were in very poor condition: two tanks were not armed, two were armed but lacked springs, two tanks had only MGs. Eventually, more of the tanks were ready for combat and used effectively in battles during Autumn of 1920. The unique thing about the division was in the manner they deployed. Unlike the Whites, the Reds used all the tanks at once during the same battle instead of piecemeal. In one battle on Oct. 19, 1920, the Whites who were manning artillery guns, ran when all 10 tanks approached. Due to a lack of spare parts, none of the tanks were operational in 1921.

Elsewhere in Russia, the British sent driblets of tanks to support the White uprising. At Archangel, where over 10,000 British, French and American troops battled the Reds, three Mk V and three Whippet, Type B, arrived in July 1919. The British intended to use the tanks for the defense of Archangel. These tanks had limited abilities due to the nature of the terrain consisting of forest and marsh. The only practical employment for the tanks here was use along the railroad. The tanks sent were never used in combat by the British. They were used with after the Allies withdrew in October, 1919, with success as the Whites advanced along the railroad. This attack involved one MkV and one Whippet (the other four had already been shipped elsewhere) Success was fleeing, and the Reds advanced toward the city from many directions. The tanks were eventually withdrawn and sunk in the Dvina river just before the Reds captured the town on February 20, 1920.

The remaining four tanks were then retrieved by the British and sent to Tallin with 48 British officers to train the Whites Estonian army in their use. By September, 1919, the tanks arrived at Narva with 30 trained Russian tank personnel. At the same time, two additional Mk Vs had arrived from England. The British then applied pressure to the Finns for tanks resulting in the Finns sending three FT-17s. These were used until November, after which, they were returned. The British created a tank support unit consisting of 200 men. On September 11, the six tanks and support unit went into action. Three tanks immediately broke down and by October, all tanks were under repair. The six tanks, armed with British and Russian crews, again entered into combat on October 12, making spectacular advances toward St. Petersburg. The Red army fell back blowing the bridges over major rivers. This halted the tanks until October 17. From October 19-25, the tanks advanced with near impunity until reaching the outskirts of St. Petersburg. The Reds were in near panic. Red artillery had only caused two of the tanks damage. Trotsky went to the front to encourage the Reds to not fear a tank and created mock tanks for morale purposes. The battle was lost when the tanks required repairs and the Reds counterattacked. By January, 1920, two of the MkVs were transferred to Latvia and the remaining four MkVs stayed in Estonia.

In 1941, when the Germans approached Tallin, the Soviet forces used the same four Mk Vs (which had been warehoused since 1930) to oppose the Panzers. However, none of the tanks were much threat, and the Germans knocked out one and were more interested in capturing the others. After their capture, German soldiers posed for the camera with the MkVs in the background.

Sources

1) WO 106/377 PRO London
2) WO32/5685 PRO London
3) RH 86TC Establishment of South Russian Tank Det. PRO London
4) ADM 137/3943 PRO London
5) *Organization of South Russian Forces*, Vrangel Collection, Hoover Institution, Stanford University, Palo Alto, CA.
6) WO 106/1198 PRO London
7) WO32/5732 PRO London
8) "Tanks in the Russian Revolution (Russian)," Armada Magazine # 14, Moscow Press, Feb. 1999
9) Russian documents: # 39664 "Tank Deliveries to Novorossisk 1919." #39540 "Structure of the Armed Forces of South Russia"
10) *Civil War in the Ukraine*, 1918-20 (a collection of documents) Kiev, 1967.
11) *The Russian Civil War Encyclopedia.* Moscow Press, 1985
12) Denikin, Anton. *March on Moscow.* Moscow Press, 1921
13) *The White Armies.* Hyperion Press, 1973
14) Wrangel, Peter. *Memoirs of General Wrangel.* 1930.
15) Krasnov, Peter. *The Don Army.* Moscow Press, 1992.
16) Lehovich, Dimitry. *White Against Red.* 1970
17) Iakushkin, Everginei. *English Intervention.* Moscow Press. 1928
18) *The Pavel Kusonskii papers (Wrangel's Volunteer Army)*, Hoover Institution, Stanford University, Palo Alto, CA.
19) *Over South Russia.* Author(?). 1925.
20) Schmid, Alex. *Churchill's Private War.* 1974 (German)
21) Agureev, K. *Defeating Denikin's Army.* Moscow Press. 1961.
22) *The Mikhail Girs Papers (Wrangel's diplomat)*, Hoover Institution, Stanford University, Palo Alto. CA.
23) WO 106/1198 , PRO London.
24) WO 158/746, PRO London.

13

Eyewitness Accounts

For the most part, many of the reports originating from the British Mission were devoid of any accounts concerning the conditions in South Russia. Naturally, most of the reports were not in a "novel" format but in a factual, non-descriptive account. Few members of the British Mission went on afterwards to publish any books regarding their experiences and personal insights. An exception to this was a then, young officer, a Major H. Williamson who had volunteered for yet another war after the "War to end all Wars." His diary was published in 1970 under the title, "Farewell to the Don" with some incredible descriptions of what life was like for the British officers. He later became a Brigadier in the British artillery. Born in 1886, he married in 1923, got divorced and remarried in 1926. He had one daughter, Mary, born in 1934. He died in 1971. The following are vivid and unbelievable:

Trains:

"Everytime we stopped at a station to take fuel there was this concerted rush of 3rd class passengers to collect water for washing, drinking or making tea. Everyone else went outside to stretch into a sea of vendors selling roasted foul, chickens, vegetables from peasants Train rides took a long time. On train ride to inspect a a battery, the engine simply quit. The steppe was lifeless and bare. Eerie. The train conductor told us we would wait for another. We stared across the vast empty steppes looking at grass and flowers for hours, finally, another ancient train arrived."

Ekaterinodar (the British Military Mission base):

"...we were driven to the Mission Headquarters, which was an abandoned girl's school. Nobody expected us and we slept on a wooden bed with a blanket. The building was filled with cockroaches, no water, no furniture. We had to fetch water in pales for washing and shaving. The food situation was no better, the only restaurant was about 400 yards. The restaurant was extremely dirty and the meal consisted of a cold, gritty omelette. The coffee was cold and poured from a chipped container into a tumbler that had been already used. The streets were filled with uniforms form various units, the streets muddy, buildings filled with bullet or shell holes from the fighting, outside the town, houses were burned down."

The British attitude:

"Headquarters showed the rankest intolerance to the Don Cossacks. When the soldiers under Denikin freed their villages, they had the habit of leaving the ranks to cultivate the land. The officers for the most part knew nothing at all about what was going on. If they did, they would only give vague answers and when pressed, took refuge behind the language barrier. They were lazy, arrogant, ignorant and often cowardly. No one at Mission HQ had a very high opinion of them and no attempts had been made to organize any supply system. It was pathetic to see people who had suffered so much and lost everything vying with one another to do us honour ". Their cry upon seeing us was, "The British have come, now all will be well. The commanders rarely so imagination, no unity of command. They could have held out for years if they retreated to strong points or coordinated their efforts. The generals were always plagued by ambition or laziness which persuaded them to do too much or not enough.

Weapons:

"The Don Army had only about 200 artillery rounds allotted to them daily. None of the artillery units had been trained an any training was "at the front," due to the necessity. The 18 pdrs supplied by us had deficient sights, spanners and buffer springs. The Russians preferred to guess the angle of sight rather than calculate it and fired their ranging bracket at one second intervals which was wasteful. To our surprise, they requested telescopic sights (long discarded by the British Army). Over 60% of their shells fired failed to explode. In June, British supplies finally arrived including six 18 pdr batteries, 2 4.5" Howitzer batteries, a good number of Vickers and Lewis Guns."

Women:

"We were introduced to the Nursing sisters attached to the brigade. These women seemed to be a combined secretary, dispatch carrier, medical officer, wives, girlfriends, mistresses, and prostitutes for the men of the brigade. They always followed their unit into action. They endured tremendous hardships and worked harder than many men. They were always treated with extreme courtesy and dog-like devotion by the men. Many staffs had too many women on them."

Medical Facilities (near 3rd Don Corps):

"...full of patients all with typhus, lying on straw in bare rooms. The dark reddish rash covered their bodies. Many were in comas and raving. There were no beds or mattresses and the sick and wounded lay side by side. The air was stifling and the rooms overcrowded. Swarms of huge flies perpetually settled in the eyes and noses of men who were gasping for air or wounded soldiers groaning with pain. None were washed and remained in their infected clothes. No anaesthetics were available for most operations. Surgical instruments were blunt and dirty. Gangrene was common and there were no bandages, in their place, straw or cloth was used. They were losing five men daily to Typhus."

Williamson went on to state he had witnessed many workers with communist sympathies, which welcomed a chance to throw matters into confusion. Many of the junior members of the staff were skilled and conducted a great deal of thieving at depots and dumps. He observed that the railway personnel remained on the side who controlled the railroad. There was no real loyalty to either side. Even members of the British Mission resented him for being so enthusiastic about helping the Whites, many preferred the old easy way. Williamson managed to get to the 1st Don Corps Front, in June, 1919, unlike most descriptions, this one provides contrast:

"As we halted outside of Surovikina, barefooted girls harvested the sunflower seeds, many stopping to watch us. Along our carriage, vendors appeared with enormous green melons. Bearded men worked in little patches of soil along the sandy, clay ground of the village orchards. The wind had scorched the grass that had shrivelled in yellow and in the road alongside the track there were huge cracks across the dried ruts that stretched across a rolling prairie empty of everything but tawny grass and clumps of birch and alder."

Williamson felt guilty about little he had accomplished:

"How had I helped up to then, I thought bitterly. Principally by attending banquets notable only for the orgy of food and speeches. Not a creditable record. I had shame and rage."

On one trip to visit the 2nd Don Corps, Williamson and others were packed into an American Packard car and traveled over 180 miles of potfilled, dusty roads with no protection from the sun. Upon their arrival, "more than alive," they were fed eggs, black bread and tea. So exhausted, all of the British officers fell asleep.

Finally, Williamson did meet troops that had come from a recent battle:

"The troops I saw at Borisoglybsk had been fighting the day before. They were all very badly equipped. Only 30% had boots and none had machine guns. The faces of men were blank and haggard and you could see their knees and elbows through their threadbare uniforms. Many had no shirts at all. I did not see any British equipment or uniforms. Some of the men actually wore spiked pickelhaube helmets left by the Germans! There was a fatalism about them. It was clear just then they hadn't much interest in who was winning the war. I was growing more disgusted every day...."

When the 1st Corps of the Volunteer Army advanced towards Poltava, Williamson and Holman were both present observing. The attack was typical of many consisting of three columns: The Guards Corps led by Gen. Stackelberg with the 8th Cossack Infantry Brigade. The 2nd column consisted of the 7th division and the Ossetine Infantry; the 3rd column consisted of Skouro's savage cavalry division. The 7th division was to advance along the railway line through Karlovka and supported by two armor trains.

The standard armor train configuration consisted of a light repair truck, followed by a car of MG's. The train itself would follow, armed with a light field gun, more machine guns, and heavily armored cars carrying infantry ready to reinforce the leading elements. The tail usually contained a large 6" naval gun. Along the flanks of the train, bodies of infantry advanced in carts, while cavalry units covered the train's flank much further out over the steppes. It was rare that opposing trains had face to face encounters, usually, they would simply barrage the other train. Encirclement tactics were used universally by both sides. Every commanding officer had their own train consisting of four to five cars comprising of a kitchen, dining room, offices and sleeping quarters.

In this type of war, the active front where the combat was heaviest was 10 to 15 miles of both sides of the railway along which groups moved. Outside of this range, the spaces were occupied and watched by small cavalry forces entirely living off the land. These forces seldom had contact with the enemy.

While the British military is known for its customs and "spit and polish" Williamson and Holman experienced a situation, which signified how stratified the Russian White Army remained. In this particular situation, the Whites had been firing their newly arrived 18 pdrs in rapid fashion. After ten minutes, the guns jammed because of sand in the breech. The Russian gunners suddenly looked at their officers with blank stares, cursed and waved their hands. The rest Williamson describes:

> "Holman looked at me and asked if we can fix this? I replied, I think so.
>
> We both took off our coats and began to work at cleaning and repairing the guns whilst all ranks of the Russians looked on from behind in amazement. Comments were heard, 'A General! A General who knows how to put a gun right himself and doesn't mind doing it!' As we worked, the Battery Commander appeared protesting violently at our undignified conduct."

Unlike with World War I, which had just ended, the typical advances of either side took on the look of a bygone period. It was typical for both sides to open an attack with an artillery bombardment, the unit's colors would be displayed using large flags, the men would be drawn up to the sound of marching music and bugles rang out. Then, swords would flash and a roar of many was heard as the attack unfolded. When Williamson saw this, he jotted down:

> "War, before the advent of the aeroplane, motor car, tank, and barbed wire, must have been like this. This is what it must have been like even as far back as Napoleon...."

Williamson continues:

> "...the whole body of troops was mobile and a number of carts had been commandeered. In them, infantry, about eight men to a cart in addition to a battery of 3" Russian guns, two batteries of 18 pdrs, and one battery of 4.5 howitzer."

Then another oddity:

> "...It was blazing hot and soon I took off my coat and rode in my shirt. I immediately became aware of stares from the men of all ranks. One Russian officer explained that taking off my coat struck the Russians curious as they considered it to be improper for an officer to be in this state of dishabille."

In one case, Williamson was at the front attempting to inspire the Russian gunners to fire at a Red train approaching some 2000 yards away. Williamson had been the observer and wondered why the gun was not firing. In rage, he ran back to the battery. The gunners were all sleeping! He kicked the men, stirring them up. After several minutes, the guns opened up and hit the train, disabling it. Suddenly, Williamson noticed the gunners were switching from HE to shrapnel, which was useless against armor. Williamson shouted, "For God sakes, not shrapnel." The gunner replied, "we prefer shrapnel."

This was typical of the Russian method and their resistance to being commanded by British advisors.

On a few occasions, both Williamson and Holman became directly involved in combat despite orders they were only to advise. In one instance, they joined the advance guard attacking Seleschina. Here, they joined in riding in the middle of the firing line driving the Reds out. It was here a Red commissar was captured and another horrific event had to be witnessed:

> "...the trembling commissar was beaten across the face and head until blood flowed and he was abused and reviled. I remonstrated with one of the officers and finally drew my revolver and said I will no longer witness this kind of brutality. A Russian officer turned angrily on me beating, my hand down. He then said, 'you do not appreciate the circumstances from the Russian point of view.'"

Besides the usual problems of getting the British supplies from the depots to the front, many times, what did arrive was as follows:

> "On going over the equipment of 18 pounders recently received, we found them in a parlous state. They had lost or never received spare springs, they had no buffer oil, the top of the director was missing."

The word "division" and other titles of unit designations were never what they normally would be in other armies. For example, the 3rd Don Corps consisted of the 5th and

3rd divisions. The 5th division was located at Saprina and had only 2,000 men. The 3rd division was at Pavlovsk, which had the same amount. The ultimate goal of this "Corps" was to seize Bobrov, some sixty miles south of Voronezh in August. The 3rd division had no uniforms or machine guns. Though the Don army, now claimed to have 100,000 men, Williamson questioned this:

> "I visited all the fronts and there were never more than 3-4000 men in any forward area and always badly equipped."

When Holman demanded to see combat units, a platoon of 12 men from the 12th Regiment arrived:

> "I have never seen such a miserable sight in my life. They had five boots among the lot, one had no rifle, another was clogged with dirt. Their clothes were rags, one man had no trousers and wore woolen underpants. They looked starved."

This incident made Holman furious and his staff returned to Taganrog and Novorossisk to personally collect all the supplies they could. The collected 2000 sets of uniforms and equipment, weapons, medical supplies and food.

Williamson and Holman arrived a little after Wrangel had taken Tsaritsyn on the Volga. Many of the inhabitants had been murdered, houses and stores looted. Thousands of corpses were found in a gully. It took one week to bury them and clear the streets of some 400 dead horses. The town was dirty and dusty, garbage was all over. In their discussions with Wrangel, Wrangel in hindsight seemed to be a prophet. He told Holman that Denikin's armies rear areas were much too big and is fast becoming a collection of tradesman and profiteers. There was too much drinking and gambling in the rear, while troops were neglected at the front.

Perhaps the most important thing that Williamson did, which if it had been used, would have blown away the Red front lines just north of Tsaritsyn. At a conference with Wrangel and Holman, he suggested that the artillery should use mustard gas. No book has ever mentioned this, and in his own hand he writes:

> "A large number of these and other gas shells had been dumped at the various railheads, but for political reasons had not been used not only because the Whites wanted to avoid harmless peasants but they were nervous about handling gas."

At this stage, the Reds were threatening the capture of the town again (which had it occurred would have been a severe blow to Denikin). Wrangel accepted the gas idea with keenness, as did Holman, who was enthusiastic. Holman instructed Williamson to go at once and gather the shells. He and Holman immediately drove to the airfield of the British 47th Squadron at Beketovka, got into a DH9 and flew off. Williamson had no clue where the shells might be and they flew 250 miles to Novotcherkask, near Rostov. Finding none there, they flew to Taganrog. There they found several cases of gas shells. These were flown back to Wrangel. Williamson had clocked 900 air miles gathering a few cases of gas shells. When he returned, General Maievsky, who controlled the artillery stated:

> "Although the gas shells have arrived, it will take so long to distribute them it is hardly worth having them."

Fate now intervened and the Reds suddenly conducted an attack forcing much of Wrangel's artillery to retreat. The promise of gas quickly took a "back seat" and as time went on, simply forgotten.

At times, despite repeated orders to British Officers from the War Office not to become directly involved, the opposite was true. Part of this was national pride. One such occasion, Williamson, was getting tired of the Russians not appreciating all the British aid being received. During one of the train rides back to the 3rd Don Corps, he had enough:

> "...whether it was correct or not, I hung a large Union Jack over the door of our coach as a sign the British Mission was in the offing! I felt it was time someone became aware of us."

On Armor Cars in use:

> "...the lack of artillery by either side made armor trains and armor cars of considerable strength and seemed to be just as frightful to the Russian infantry and cavalry as British tanks did to the Germans on their first appearance. Many armor cars were made from old tank turrets were especially mobile on the open steppes and could round up large bodies of infantry."

On airplanes use:

> "Two airplanes were above us, dropping bombs on Liski station, but they never came below 5000 feet, which considering a lack of antiaircraft fire, was excessively high. The Reds did fire with an elevated gun."

Most of the airplanes in the war were flown very cautiously by either side, each side protecting a valuable asset with very limited spare parts. For the Reds, they were afraid of defections (what easier way than to fly across).

Another weapon that the British sent in large amounts was the Lewis Gun, a light machine gun. But again, upon inspection of units on the Don, Williamson noted the following:

> "Lewis guns had been issued to the men, however, only six spare drums for each weapon existed and no tools. They were never a popular weapon with the Russians who always clamored for Vickers."

One common element in the Civil war were defections from one side to another. The usual practice was that the officers would be tortured and killed, while the infantry given a choice to fight or be killed. Thus, for either side, when POW's were seized, this option was available. Both sides needed the infantry soldiers.

Williamson, while at Yvestratovka, encountered a recently captured Red brigade:

> "This was the Tulsk brigade, which had come over en mass from the Bolsheviks to join Mamentov's cavalry. They were well seasoned and well equipped troops, formerly of the old Imperial Russian Army that was forced into service by the Bolsheviks for fear their families being massacred. Over 400 ex-Imperial officers were included."

The Russian Generals expected instant supplies from the British Mission. A typical request made to Williamson from General Ivanov was as follows:

> "15000 sets of uniforms, eight cars, 20 motorcycles, 5 stokes mortars, unlimited Vickers MGs, airplanes, 1000 cavalry saddles, 48 18 pdrs."

Williamson was expected to provide this within a few days. He promised "something would be sent."

Another oddity of the Russian Civil War in the south was a sort of casualness in war operations by both sides. In one case, Williamson and a Russian battery commander moved the observation post about 300 yards from the friendly trenches into no man's land. It was a high mound, about 70 yards square. Also accompanying them were 20 mounted cossacks, 12 horse holders, which promptly made two large bonfires. In normal wars, this would've invited the enemy's artillery to plaster the area. Williamson describes the rest:

> "We all stood on the top with our glasses and had a magnificent view of the country and we were left quite untroubled. About 6000 yards from us was the Red cavalry wandering in the village. A few patrols came toward us and the White forces fired their rifles and machine guns which could not have been less than 3000 yards. Meanwhile, two artillery guns of ours fired one round every 3-4 minutes. The shots were accurate and scattered the Reds. The enemy artillery now deployed in full view. Our artillery did not fire at them and after waiting 30 minutes, the enemy artillery fired. Their shells dropped some 1000 yards from us. The Red artillery fired about 40 rounds, only 15 shells exploded."

One can only imagine the following classic scene witnessed by Williamson when the Reds attacked:

> "The main attack appeared in the form of 400 Red infantry in three lines emerging from a fold in the ground about 4000 yards away. They carried large red banners and were urged forward by officers waving swords. They did not seem very eager to forge ahead...the lines came closer, straggling and ballooning......we could hear shouts of officers....we opened fired with our howitzers with instant fuses....the

infantry became pinned.....another three salvoes sent them back.....a horde of running figures.....behind them scatterings of equipment, flags and riderless horses. The General said the battle was now over and that we should go to the headquarters and some tea."

It is doubtful if the War Cabinet or Holman's superiors knew exactly what he was doing. Most assumed he remained at the Mission headquarters at Taganrog or elsewhere. It is quite obvious Holman was a man who liked to be in the "thick "of things as he and Williamson travelled extensively to the front and at times, became a participant. Williamson notes the following:

> "Holman appeared to spend more time on the wrong side of the Bolshevik lines than his exalted rank demanded, but he knew he was in good hands with the 47th RAF squadron."

As the hot summer and the high hopes of reaching Moscow faded into fall and then winter, conditions complicated matters:

> "The streets are covered with snow and thick black ice. It hurts to breath and fur hats are thick with rime. Every window has a crust of frozen snow and it was so cold that the Cossacks had taken to wrapping cloth round their stirrup irons to avoid frostbite. Morale declined in the lower ranks."

As with all military matters, there is a chaotic retreat of armies and civilians, each trying to survive. The following descriptions from Williamson have since occurred many times over in WW2, Korea (1950), Vietnam (1975) and Kosovo (1999). The time is December, 1919 to March 1920:

> "All the railways running from the forward areas had rapidly become crowded with stock and broken down engines. The stations were full of abandoned, snow plastered trains, their engines burnt out. Even the movement of troops was coming to a stop and thousands of passengers trudged southwards, desperate and glancing back nervously as the crack of enemy rifles were heard. The whole front had collapsed and in chaos. At Novotcherkask, Headquarters was a waste of torn paper and full of smoke as documents were destroyed."

As the retreat continued the differences between the officers and other ranks became more pronounced.

> "The officers seemed surprisingly indifferent to the condition of their troops or the state of the front. The old, lazy, indifferent attitude of the Russian Imperial high command showed in their casualness and how they managed to live in comfort on their trains while the troops starved or froze...."

Williamson, during the retreat, suddenly had a revelation about the political realities of the British Mission and the position of the British government:

> "As a British officer I wasn't a bit afraid of what might happen. Always I felt that even if things didn't go according to plan, I'd be rescued. I was quite wrong, of course, and I learned later, the British government was as quick to repudiate its servants as any other. All day long, stragglers of the 2nd division had been pouring through the Novotcherkask (near Rostov) on Christmas, the only troops ready to fight were the cavalry units under Pavlov who conducted a delaying action ten miles away. Refugees and armed/unarmed soldiers jammed the rail stations. Panic set in and wildly driven military cars kept tearing past. Demoralized and disordered troops, the men in rags and reluctant to obey their officers, kept appearing. These were followed by terror stricken women, children, old men and women, peasants on shaggy ponies. The station was an inferno of noise and we kept seeing outbreaks of violence. Everyone fought to get aboard the train, within seconds, it was filled, every inch inside and on the roof. The melee crushed the children and elderly as the doors were torn off. I started off again for the front, the few locomotives ran at their lowest ebb. The journey was an exercise in patience as the train crept forward only a few miles at a time, each one jammed hard up against the one in front. We crawled at barely 10 m.p.h. dragging some 80 cars starting and stopping over and over. There was no medical service and lice swarmed in the woodwork, on clothes spreading Typhus like wildfire. Whole truckloads of people perished. Their bodies frozen stiff like logs were dumped along the side of the track, stripped of boots and clothing, which only passed the disease to the healthy who removed them."

The officers of the Mission were by no means safe. One of Williamson's fellow advisor, Frecheville, went to the front to assist with the building of trenches and other fortifications outside of Novotcherkask. The force he was assisting, left him and his interpreter in the village and subsequently was captured by the Reds. They murdered the British officer and his body tied to a saddle and dragged around the streets. Oddly, when the Reds attacked across the ice of the Don river into Rostov, a Commissar was captured wearing Frecheville's tunic. The commissar told his captors that Frecheville had been beaten with steel ramrods before being killed.

In this state, the Russians accused the British for the failure and that the "real" troops promised never were sent. Whites accused other Whites for the collapse, the Kuban soldiers turned out to be utterly untrustworthy and appeared ready to explode in a mutiny. They refused any orders given them. The British officers regarded the whole thing fatalistically, knowing how hopeless the Russians were in adversity and how useless it would be to ask for action.

Williamson on atrocities:

> "...an ambulance train towing forty cars or more of dead bodies had been seen with not one living soul aboard. The men pushed the dead bodies out onto hand carts as though they were coals and throwing them into sandpits. The bodies of women, children and men were stripped of any clothes worth taking. These awful heaps, grey white, stiff, and stacked like piles of timber for the engines, increased as each train passed through and disgorged the dead."

By February 1920, even the trains moving south were in danger not only from the Reds, but the Greens. These were bandits and took whatever they wanted from the Reds or Whites. These roving bands boarded many trains murdering and robbing those trying to escape.

The railways, at times, were so clogged with debris, created an obstruction that was 15 miles in length. During the long retreat, 200,000 people died from typhus and exposure. Whole trainloads died from fever or cold. When Krymsk fell on March 19th, hordes of humans moved into Novorossisk, the only vital port left to Denikin:

> "It was freezing cold, snow and a fierce high wind piercing the clothes of the starving....ships were covered in ice, bodies lay in all sorts of corners while hospitals were under siege by sick people whom nothing could be done....typhus was reaping a dreadful harvest. British warships hurled shells towards the roads where the Reds were approaching the town. Every street store had boarded up windows and full of carts, troops, civilians. White officers ripped off their epaulets because the Reds would nail these to the shoulders of the wearer should they be captured. Young girls desperately wanted to marry a British soldier to gain passage, or prostituted themselves. It was a sick, desperate, terrified city with mobs of people surging for safety. On the wharves were rows of field guns and piles of ammunition, tanks, aeroplanes and other piles of equipment being pushed into the sea. Refugees were in their last stage of panic."

Williamson, himself, caught Typhus, while in the port. Up to the retreat (mid-November 1919) Britain has spent £100,000,000 and France another 35,000,000. Little was evacuated, most of it was lost.

The visual images of this civil war have been repeated many times over during other wars. Hudleston's diary allows those living today look through a window of time and experience life and war over 80 years ago.

The Cherezvichaykas

Durng the South Russian intervention, the British publiation "The Tank Corps Journal" published many issues regarding the events occurring there. One such discovery made public in order to gain further support from the government and public was from a reporter visiting the British tank corps in the fall of 1919. It should be pointed out that both the White and Reds frequently commited inhuman atrocities against one another. However, the Reds had set up a system, which literally translated means, "Extraordinary Commision". Locally, it was called the Cherezvichaya. The general public in England knew little about these. What the reporter for the journal saw follows:

> "When I left England, I had the vaguest ideas as the actual meaning of Bolshevism...I regarded it as nothing wose than a bitter conflict between workers and employers. Now, it is a depotism which condones and encourages organizations for the performance of horrors and results I have witnessed myself."

Th reporter arrived in Kharkov to inspect the tank detachment under Captain Thompson. He immediately was told of the numerous Red atrocities so recently discovered in local torture houses called Cherezvichaya:

> "I was shown a group of three houses known as slaughter houses. In one of these houses, a large and pretentious mansion,lived the Commandant named Stephan Saenko, a carpenter before the war. The Second house was used as a barracks for the guards. The third, a caprious block of flats converted into a jail for suspects. The building which formed the prison and execution yard was L shaped. The prisoners had been forced to dig a vast trench into which the corpses had been thrown, hundreds of them before Denikin had liberated the city. Eyewitness's indicated

A few of the thousands the Reds hanged when those who opposed them were captured.

that captured White officers had nails driven into their shoulders for each star they had in rank, strips of flesh were cut from their chest and thighs to correspond with any decorations the victim had worn. Bolling water and nails under the fingernails were also other forms of torture. Many photos were taken of the mutilated bodies."

The reporter was then taken to the recent liberated city of Kiev on September 16th:

" The city is bordering on complete famine. Shops and restaurants had practically nothing to offer in the way of edibles. I was charged the equivilent of 12 shillings for four cups of black coffee. There was no surgar or milk. There was absolutely nothing to eat by noon. We were approached by many seeking bread or biscuits.

There were five Cherezvichaykas in Kiev. Even passing them one had to hold their breath and nose using a hankerchief. Outside one of the houses, a queue of over 100 people awaited to identify the bodies. This house was, from the outside, a charming private house with a charming garden. The garden revealed twnety seven nude corpses. One of the muitlated corpses was a son of a man whose only crime had been too much money. Nearby a hole contained over fifty bodies and decompostion was far too advanced. In each case, their heads had been smashed in with hammers. Nearby was a garage where the massacres took place. This place was a veritable butcher's shambles, its walls were stained nearly to the ceiling with blood and were absolutely pock-marked with bullet holes, whilst the concrete floor was literally carpeted with dried blood and human debris. It has been estimated that just prior to the Whites liberating the city, some 400 persons were slaughtered here and no less than 40,000 since the Revolution in 1917. Most of the victims falling to Red tortures were those who refused to go along with Bolshevism or had been well to do before the Revolution. The Reds were jealous of those who had been well to do. While waiting for a mock trial, the prisoners were kept in cellars beneath the houses. There was no light provided and prisoners were never allowed to leave the cell. These cells were deliberatly overcrowded.They wallowed in their own excrements."

The femme fatale "Rosa," who enjoyed torturing men in a Kiev prison.

The reporter then met a woman named "Rosa":

"...the most notorious of these prisoners was Rosa, whom I had heard of before while in Poltava. She seemed to have had special relationship with the Red Commissaires, she could call for a prisoner at any time. One of her barbarous habits before killing a prisoner was to commence by shooting a revolver in the victim's knee, followed by a shot to the thigh and on up the body until the wretched subject was in utter collapse, whereupon she would dispatch a bullet in the vital part (groin). She had killed hundreds of White officers in this manner. Another woman was 'Schwartz' who had been an informer for the Reds as to who were the wealthy. Other witnesses said that prior to the Whites liberation, the prosperous people had been obliged to break their fingernails, grime their hands and to wear only their shabbiest clothes, in order to escape molestation by posing as manual workers."

Also in South Russia, attached to the tanks was Captain Shaw. Some of his insights are also enlightening and appeared in The Tank Corps Journal:

"I left London on July 17th, 1919, and arrived at Novorassisk on the morning of August 13th. By truck we went to Ekaterinodar and by evening at Taganrog. A Colonel Miroshinichenko was assigned to me as an interpretor. The Russian Tank Corps is commanded by Col. Khaletski who commanded the Russian armor cars in the Great War. He came to England in 1916 to study tanks. At the Baltic Works in Taganrog, I found the Central Workshop and Tank School rolled into one and employs nearly 1000 workers. It was erected by Austrian POWs in six months. The Russian Tank Corps comprises of 100 officers covered in dirt and grease and enjoying it. The school teaches driving, Hotchkiss and 6 pdr gunnery, whilst about 20 versts away from Taganrog is a battle practice ground. Originally, the training was done through interpreters by British officers, however, now there are many qualified Russian instructors. Five weeks is allotted for the entire course, the results are extremely good. It is of interest that the Reds themselves had captured six Renault tanks in Odessa. At this time, I had my first experience with Vodka, a noisome fluid resembling nothing more than methylated spirit. While visiting Tzaritsan, our motor-car nearly caused a casulty thanks to the utter and complete failure of all its brakes whilst descending a hill.. The railroads are in a state of almost absolute decay. All locomotives are in decrepit condition and it is common for it to halt for half-an-hour to gather steam. Coal is very difficult to obtain and many trains run on logs. The complete lack of any attempt to control leads to an appalling congestion on the entire railway system. At the main stations, literally thousands wait. When the train starts, there ensues a wild dash to board the train.. A very large portion of South Russian consists of Steppe country and one travels thousands of versts for days seeing an expanse of dead flat land used for grazing. Just occasionally, a village appears looking like a little cardboard model dumped in the middle of a football field. Large towns are very few. In all my travels I looked in vain for signs of the conflict, for nowhere could I find any trace of devastated towns. I had to hunt for shell holes. But for downed bridges and wires, there was no visible evidence of battle. Practically the whole of the fighting takes place along the railways and the two large rivers, the Volga and Dneipr, and there is no attemept at any form of consolidated line. The trenches around some towns are feeble attempts and little better than rifle pits. Fighting on a wide front is unknown with objectives the capture of industrial or strategic vantage points. Cavalry forces penetrate to a depth of several hundred versts behind the enemy lines conducting guerilla warfare, cut communications, destroy supplies and return."

North Russia

Luckily, for the reader, far to the north in Archangel, a Major J. Bryan wrote extensively about this area for theTank Journal in several issues. Major Byran was attached to the British Tank detachment sent to North Russia in August 1919.

On the port of Murmansk:

"The estimated population of Murmansk is between 3500-4000 people. The entire town is built of wood and consists of 350 buildings in three main districts. There appear to be no shops and open spaces are few but on a level stretch of sandy soil above the town there was a soccer game between army and navy personnel. The houses are mostly one story built of pine logs pieced together and stuffed with moss. The use of nails is rare. Most houses are like army huts used by troops in France. If there is a two story house, the entrance point to the bedroom is by way of a ladder into a small hole in the cornice of the roof. The town has the British, French and American consulates. The local iunhabitants do not attend picture shows as in more civilized parts but seems to be taking pot shots at British soldiers. Most officers going ashore carry their revolver. The streets are sand with ditches along the side for drainage. The inhabitants appear to be on a whole very tall and very dirty. Women look no cleaner than men. The fauna resembles those of lower latitudes. Murmansk appears as a temporary town, erected by a cinematograph company for some Wild West drama. Four years ago it did not exist and was entirely British built."

On money:

'The Russian rouble has dropped in value to about twopence halfpenny in English currency. Consequently, a new issue was made call the British North Russian rouble and backed by the Bank of England. A rouble was made equal to sixpence and two Russian roubles were equal to one British. The Russian rouble has a value of threepence. The lowest Russian money is 10 Kopeks, which roughly equals a farthing and the size of a postage stamp, the highest is 100 kopeks, which is one rouble. The average Russian has no real use for money. He much prefers to barter his stuff for something else."

On Russians:

"The Russian laborer is born bone lazy. Regularity and efficiency are words unknown in his vocabulary. If weather is bad, workers do not show up, the trams may stop functioning. Along the Dvina, running boats by a time table was one utterly repugnant to native character. The lower class does not really understand kindness. It savours to him too much weakness. They only seem to understand brute force and coercion"

On the North Russian Tank Corps:

"The tank corps consisted of 10 officers and 24 other ranks, most were former cavalrymen and all were motorists and very keen about tanks..After careful inspection, it was decided upon in Solombala for the training area. The G.O.C. was Col. Kenotkenitch, an excellent officer who was a pre-war staff officer. He had spent time in England and a keen admirer of the British and invited to a tank demostration at Bovington. Long before tanks were sent, he had request them from his government. Training was brisk and the Russians learned quickly. He spoke fluent English. Only officers could drive a tank. On September 24th, two tanks, a Mk V and Whippet, type B was handed over and left to the Russians. The North Russian Tank corps had brief glorious career. Shortly after our departure in late September, I received the following cable from Archangel dispatched on October 29th: Proud keep traditions. Tank Corps took in glorious fight five fortified points and Plesetskaya Station, Colonel Kenotkenitch."

On the British Tank Expeditionary force:

" It was an amazing fact that quite a large number of the personnel had never seen a tank in their lives! For many, this was their first theatre of operations. For others, many had been wounded early on in the war and had been on light duty at home prior to joining, and had missed the actions in France in which tanks played a part. The actual billeting arrangements were excellent for all ranks. Empty houses for the most past accommodated the troops. I had a delightful two room billet with a grand piano and emormous palms and ferns."

On tank deployments:

" According to the original plan, one tank would remain in Archangel to cover the final embarkation of the troops and to parade down Troitsky and Petrogradski streets for morale purposes. Another detachment was assigned to Solombala across the Kuzneckika river. This was a chief danger spot due to the local inhabitants. The third was to proceed up river to Bakaritza, some 40 minutes by steamboat. This was the central storehouse for the whole force. The tank would be used along the railway line to bolster defenses. The fourth tank would be at Economia, a settlement near the mouth of the river."

On Economia:

"The settlement is situated on the Dvina two hours run towards the mouth of the river from Archangel. It was used as a huge port and along side its wide expanse of quay were stacked thousands of tons of ammunition.The roads were all made entirely of wood, running in regualr streets at right angles to the main camp road. The whole town was made of wood. Life in Economia for the British Mission resembled life on a volcanoe. No one knew from hour to hour what alarms would occur. The locals disliked the British. The armament consisted of one 18 pdr aboard an armor train. It would've required one half hour to bring the gun into action, if required."

On Solombala:

"Solombala is like Economia. The chief advantage is that it is close to Archangel's gay and giddy cosmopolitan life. It is reached by crossing the one half mile bridge spanning the Kuznechika river just north of Archangel. The bridge is the only flat area of the roadway in which one can drive at top gear for 30 seconds. In this area, the riff-raff live. Murders occur nightly without notice, even police are in danger."

On Bakaritza:

"This lies directly south of Archangel on the island of Borislovskoi and is the railway terminus from Vologda. It is reached by river, taking about 40 minutes from Archangel. It is a vital area for the British."

On the Dvina river:

"The run up the Dvina river was extraordinary because of its rugged beauty. It is one of the finest rivers of the world for scenary and sport... the forest clad sloped stretch for miles... the river shallows and channels narrow in most intricate curves...guide posts along the shore help with navigation... there are few landing places... the only traffic are long low barges of very shallow draft looking lilke sampans with a single oar. The female elements seemed to be very friendly who hailed us in a mixed French and English jargon."

Sources:

1) Hudleston, Williamson, Brig. *Farewell to the Don*. John Day Publishing, NY 1971.
2) CAB 45/105; WO 33/971, PRO, London.
3) Capelotti, P. "Our Man in the Crimea: Commander Hugo Koehler Jones, T. Over the Balkans and South Russia: The 47th RAF Squadron." 1925
4) Tank Corps Journal, 1919.

14

Na Moskvu (To Moscow)

By the beginning of July 1919, Denikin's three armies had been strung out along a line which ran from Tsaritsyn to Bielgorod to Ekakterinoslav. The British equipment, by the tons, arrived in the ports, some amounts in the depots near the front. Denikin had issued his "Operation Moscow" directives, which became the glue for his forces as the morale soared. Simple in concept, his plan to take Moscow would prove difficult to execute. Denikin knew time would play against him and that his best equipped army, the Volunteers, would be the spearhead moving towards Kursk, Orel, Tula then Moscow. His other armies would suffer because of this. Wrangel, even at this early date, knew he could not complete the orders given, advancing from Tsaritsyn to Saratov, Nijni-Novogorod then Moscow. He had been lucky to take Kamyshin, 100 miles south of Saratov. The Don Army, under General Sidorin, was to advance to Voronezh then Riazan. The mission of General Schilling and Dobrovolsky was to take Kherson and Odessa. Kharkov fell on June 25th. The Bolsheviks were quite aware of the objective and since July had transferred the following to oppose Denikin: 47th,50th, 1st,11th, 5th,14th8th,122nd, 3rd, 94, 55th, 68, 36,56, 20th, 54th, 4th,5th,7th, 31st, 27th, 21st divisions. In Sept. and Oct. alone, 195,000 men had been transferred. Eventually 31 infantry divisions and 7 cavaly divisions were added!

The slogan, Na Moskvu, was on the lips of everyone from July to mid October. It was a wonderful slogan and everyone believed that it could be done. Even in local cafes, toasts between others would be made with this slogan. It was a euphoric state, which eventually played into a horrific tragedy.

The Don army continued to press towards Liski. The HQ of the their 5th division was at Saprina on the right bank of the Don and trying to keep in touch with the 3rd division whose HQ was at Pavlovsk. The Corps orders were to seize Losevo, cross the Bityug River and move towards Bobrov. The Reds had just taken Losevo. The British C Flight/47th RAF and the 1st Kuban flight (flying Nieuports) supported Wrangel's army.

Denikin issued the "Moscow Directive" on July 3rd. In July, the Volunteer army under Denikin took Poltava on July 21, while his 3rd Corps took Ochakov along the Don. Kamyshin also fell to Wrangel.

The Red 8th army opposed Denikin at this time. In June these forces consisted of:

2nd Soviet Division
2nd Partisan Rifle Division
5th Partisan Rifle Division
1st, 3rd, 4th Partisan Divisions
12th, 13th Rifle Divisions
1st Voronezh Division
Davidov Cavalry Brigade
1st Moscow Rifle Division

These units generally held a line about 125 miles north of Rostov. The frontline arc was about 150 miles in radius. The 8th Army had 30-50,000 men. The HQ was at Rubejnaya.

The Volunteer Army consisted of the 1st, 2nd Corps, 5th Cavalry Corps, 3rd Kuban Cavalry Corps and the Kiev group with a total of 45-50,000 men. Several old Tsarist Army units had sided with the Whites: 13th, 15t, 34th Infantry divisions, 80th Kabardinsky, 83rd Samursky, 13th Belozersky regiments.

The following Red 8th army units were held in the rear areas as reserves:

Kazan Division
1st Mixed Division
1st Nov. Division
3rd Ukrainian Division
Moscow Work Division

Red artillery guns being sighted somewhere on the Southern front, 1919.

To 8th army's right, was the 9th Army with 28-36,000 men, which also opposed part of the Volunteer and most of the Don Army. It consisted of:

11th, 14th, 16th, 23rd Rifle divisions
Inzinski and Saratov Rifle divisions
1st Cavalry division.
The HQ was at Cherraskdoff.

The Don army had 1282 officers, 31,300 other ranks, 80 guns, 267 MG, 3 Armor cars, 14 armor trains and 68 airplanes.

Facing Wrangel's Caucasian army was the Red 10th Army (24,000 men) its HQ was Tsaritsyn. It consisted of:

Morozov Rifle Division
Composite Rifle Division
Composite Cavalry Division
Steel Division
1st Don Cavalry Division
1st Don Rifle Division
1st Communist Division

The 11th army (15,000 men) held the southern Volga to Astrakhan and consisted of the 3rd Stavropol Rifle division, 1st Stavropol Cavalry Division. 1st Elizavetinski Rifle Division and Composite Moslem Division.

Wrangel's army of the Caucasus consisted of the 1st, 2nd, and 4th Kuban Corps with a total of 25,000 men, 250 MG and 60 artillery guns.

One might say that month of July was Denikin's buildup, the prelude to the offensive, which would begin with a bang in August. Except for the small gains mentioned, July was a relatively calm period. It was a time to set aside the political differences between the Don Cossacks, Kubans and those under the Volunteer Army, now united with the common cause of taking Moscow.

Part of this August offensive was the famous Mamentov's Raid, which was the opening salvo. The original plan had been an early "blitzkrieg" use of cavalry forces breaking into the enemy rear, penetrating deep to Tambov –Koslov-Orel to disrupt the rear areas of the 9th and 10th armies. This raid originally was to employ two cavalry corps, the Caucasians under Konovallov and the Don Cossacks led by Mamantov. But the recent successes of Denikin alarmed the Reds, which prompted them to attack first (which would divert the Caucasians). The 10th army attacked in early August from the Kursk- Voronezh area driving towards Kharkov, which had recently been captured. As this attack developed, the feared Red Cavalry leader, Budenny, attacked down the line along the Volga towards Wrangel from Balashov and Kamyshin to clear the lower Don. By the 23rd, Wrangel was desperately trying to hold onto Tsaritsyn, while the Whites continued to hold Kharkov with difficulty forcing them to use their reserves.

During July, the DH9s of the White 1st detachment flew 36 sorties of recon and bombardment dropping more 180 kilos of bombs. In August, air-divizion pilots had already performed 129 sorties totaling 349 hours and dropped on the enemy 720 kilos of bombs.

Once the Red attack had been contained, Denikin decided on a smaller scale raid for a shallow penetration of the enemy's front toward Koslov. This would use the 12th and 13th Don Cavalry divisions, the combined Cossack Division and one infantry brigade. It would be a tremendous and perhaps last major use of cavalry in the 20th century. In scope, it equalled those of the American Civil War (Major Williamson volunteered to accompany the Cossacks in this raid, but it was declined). Each of the cavalry divisions contained about 2000 cavalry and 1000 infantry, one horse drawn artillery battery and 2-3 Austin Armor cars. The total force was 6000 cavalry, 3000 infantry, 12 guns, 7 armor trains. The 18 pdr ammunition was carried in 20 rounds per one horse cart and driven by women.

The Last Large Scale Cavalry Raid of the 20th Century
The raid began August 10th, fording the Khoper River near Uryupinsk, which was the junction of the Red 8th and 9th armies. The Cossacks easily sliced through the Red 56th Rifle Division. The force rapidly moved to Tambov and captured the town on Aug.18th. The railways and depots destroyed and then the force moved onto Koslov, minus one regiment, which protected the rear facing Balashov. Koslov fell August 21-22 after stiff fighting (this had been where the HQ of the Southern Front was located) most Reds fell back to Orel. During this chaos, both HQ's of the 8th and 9th armies ceased to exist. At this point, Mamantov was 225 miles from Moscow! Naturally, the alarms went off all over the Red High Command. On the 23rd, Lenin issued orders to create an "airstike" detachment to track and destroy the Cossacks.

This Special Air group was created consisting of the 41st, 51st Recon, 8th fighter and two Ilya Muromets heavy bombers. The detachment had 15 aircraft: seven "Nieuports-17," three "Sopwith-1 _ strutters," "Farman-30," "Voisin," "LVG C-VI," fighter "Vickers FB-19" and a "Sopwith-Triplane."On August 27th, a special train with ground services for this detachment departed for the front. On the following day they unloaded the machines. On the 29th the detachment gathered in Zhdanka station near Bogoroditsk, where they prepared for battle.

On August 30th, Gerasimov with pilots Minin and Bratolubov flew the first sorties of the airgroup, killing 15 Cossacks by strafing with machine guns. Bratolubov, flying a "Triplane," attacked a small White wagon train. His firing synchronizer on his aircraft failed chewing up his propeller. The pilot made a forced landing in a nearby village and captured, then shot.

In September, the crews of the air group had time to fly only observation flights and failed to find any enemy units. It seemed that the Cossacks had vanished. In reality, General Mamontov worked hard in deceiving the enemy. The Reds thought that he would go west to Orel. Thinking this, the Reds urgently dispatched the heavy bombers "Ilya Muromets" and also the 8thand 51st air-detachments. However, Mamontov changed directions turning his regiments southeast. The Soviets patrolled in vain for days between Orel and Eltsom. As they did this, the white cavalry in the slipped through. On September 5th, Mamontov took

Zadonsk, on the 6th, Dirts, and on the 7th Osman. In seceding days, the forces of General Postovsk's column took Kastov, a hundred kilometers from Osman. This definitively bewildered the Bolsheviks intelligence unit. They could not guess in which direction Mamentov was headed.

They rapidly sent in the 21st brigade to restore the chaos Mamantov had created. The Reds created an "internal force" lead by Lashevitch consisting of 10,500 men, 1500 cavalry and assorted airplanes. But Mamantov was fast, moving 110 miles in ten days and despite resistance, he had liberated many areas and recruited men. The Cossacks were in a euphoric state killing all Red commissars and looting extensively. Now, the usual tendencies to not move far from their homes prevailed and the force began to return to their front with their war booty. On the 25th, the force advanced 60 miles west to Lebedyan, which fell on the 28th. He gathered his forces and attacked southwards to Voronezh and by the 31st, took Elets. For two days, the Cossacks drank and looted, loading their horses with anything that could be carried including furniture. Now, ready for more combat, on September 3rd, his forces attacked from Ismailkovo and on the 6th, Kastornay was taken. Voronezh fell on Sept. 11th. Meanwhile, the Soviets created internal forces in an attempt to contain this "blitzkrieg" in their rear. One group consisted in the Lipetsk, Elets areas with 2700 men, 900 cavalry, 36 MG and 4 guns. The Orlov forces consisted of 4100 men, 500 cavalry, 48 MG, 2 guns. At Ryasin, another 2500 men, 100 Cavalry and 25 MG.

These forces pressed hard on the Cossacks, who, as time went on, lost their cohesiveness as a fighting force. The Reds attacked and on the 12th, and Voronezh returned to Red control. The Cossacks had lost 2000 men by this time. Now, disaster struck the Reds, the

21st brigade, defected over to Mamantov! (It was typical in this war for either side to suddenly lose men).

By September 15th, the Red airstrike unit comprised of: 1st Soviet, 8th fighter, 13th Kazan, 41st and 51st Reconn, and Detachment _._.S. In Kshen, the heavy bomber "Ilya Muromets G-3" arrived. This heavy bomber prepared for the first time to participate in the civil war.

By now, not less than 40 experienced pilots were part of this elite unit. The only thing still remaining was to find the enemy, which still had eluded them!

The main forces of Mammontov easily evaded the Red aerial reconnaissance. Crews gave reports of small groups of only to 10-15 men. Soon, somebody offered to combine visual reports with interrogation of local habitants. The pilots would land near the village and asked the peasants about Cossacks. This was a new concept and method.

Certainly, it was much simpler and cheaper to send ground scouts into villages on horses or motorcycles. After each sighting report, the elusive Cossacks disappeared again. Crews and instructors of the detachment had many times landed in a village outskirts to share findings but everywhere no Cossacks were found. Akashev, the detachment's leader, was totally frustrated. Finally, Mamontov exposed himself. After Voronezh, they became sloppy in the cat and-mouse game, returning with their plunder instead. Greed and carelessness set in.

The Cossacks turned and retreated back to their front. Along the way came an enormous, stretching for miles, wagon train with trophies. Naturally, such a load would not be left behind and this deprived them of their main trump card- mobility. On the 17th ,Pilots Gerasimov and Gorelov found one of the wagon trains that stretched one and a half kilometers. They dropped eight bombs. The Cossacks did not panic and opened fire on aircraft with rifles.

On the following days, rain poured grounding the aircraft. It also sharply put on the brakes to Mamontov's movement. He was moving at a tortoise pace. On September 19th, four Red aircraft swooped down on Mamontov dropping 18 bombs and 15 pounds of metal darts. The Cossacks furiously fired back but missed. Akashev personally took off in a Ilya Muromets heavy bomber to bomb the White wagon train located in the village of Istobn. The aircraft was loaded 22 160-kilo bombs. While looking for targets two wagon trains, four miles in length, were spotted.

On September 20th, the Ilya Muromets bomber bombed the main forces of Mamontov along the Bobrov river. In this raid, Akashev and Zolotarev participated as observers with pilots Millers and Petrenko. This time the bomber contained 160 kilos of bombs and 20 kilos of leaflets. The crew reported:

> "...along river Bobrov stood the 5th cavalry on halt with up to 1500 horses and two batteries of eight guns. From the village of Stantisa Oskoli a cavalry column of about 150 horses and 50 vehicles. From Petrovsk to Oskoli came another wagon train of 30-40 vehicles. From Oskoli from the North on country roads moved more

Opposite; A superb photo of Red cavalry in charging formation and breaking through White lines. Note the troops surrendering near the bottom, while others are fleeing. Just how this photo was taken is quite odd—staged perhaps?

services and wagon trains. The aircraft dropped 18 bombs of 9 pood, let loose on them seven MG cartridge clips. The task was done."

Between the 12th and 15th, Mamantov regrouped his forces to return to the Don near Rojestvenski. On the 15th, Liski was attacked, and the Red forces, which had him trapped, melted. He safely returned as a White hero. This raid had gone 450 miles in 40 days. He had inflicted severe losses to four Red divisions, destroyed key depots and railways. When he returned, out of the 10000 men, he had only 4000 left. Most of these 6000 had left with their loot from Voronezh returning to their homes.

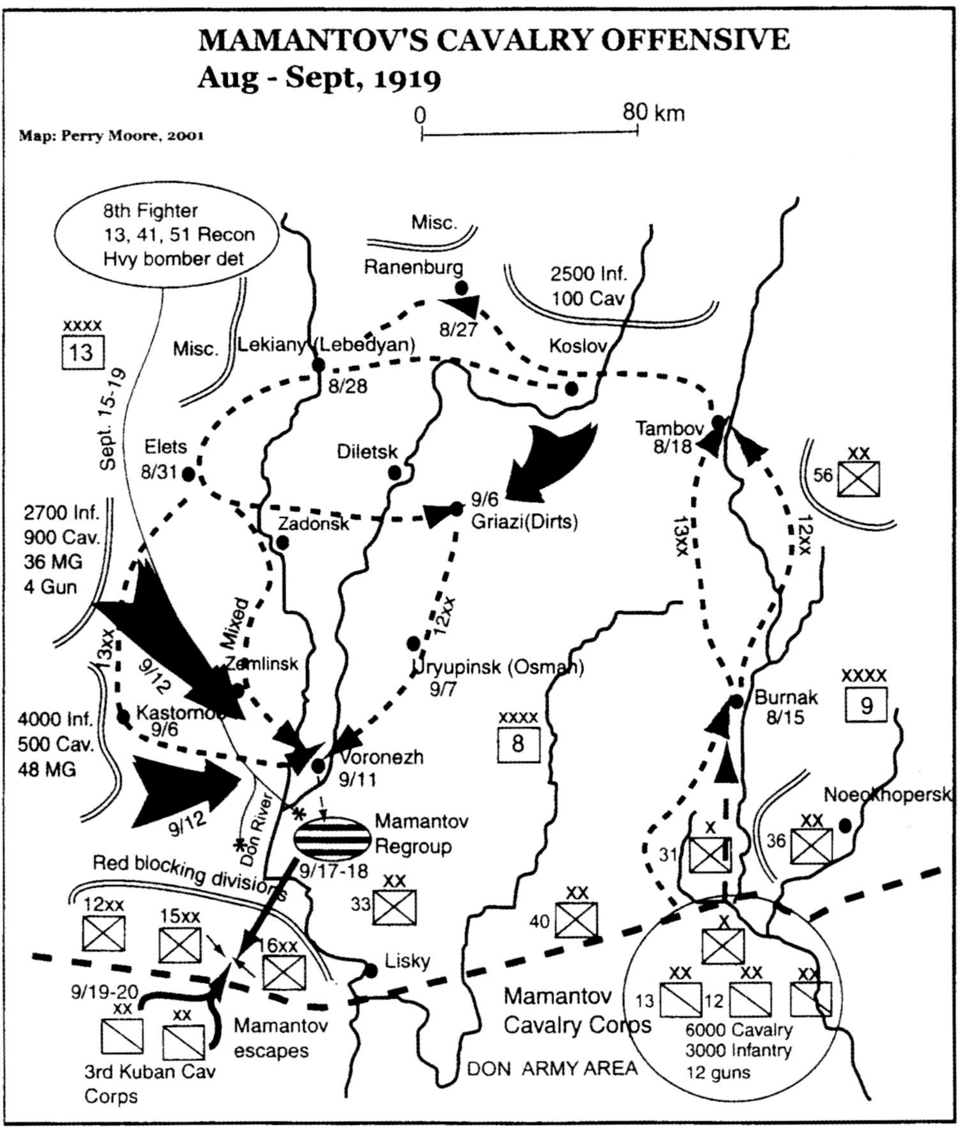

On September 22nd, the main battle group of Mammontov's cavalry broke through front to west from small town Korotoyak and united with oncoming Kuban Cavalry of General Shkuro. The wagon trains still took a few days. During this time, the red fliers continued to attack of the retiring enemy. The Ilya Muromets heavy bomber dropped 160 kilos of bombs and 8 kilo of leaflets on the White cavalry in the small town of Zhidov.

Mamantov rejoined the 3rd Kuban Corps which met them near the Don. For the Soviets, this raid showed them an immediate need to create at a fast pace, large cavalry striking force (this would be done by November and led by Budenny). The raid was a definite success and totally but temporarily prevented either the 8th or 9th army from conducting several planned actions. Oddly, it was almost a coup for the Denikin, as Mamantov's raid nearly captured Leon Trotsky, who was in the area as well as the headquarters of the 8th and 9th armies.

Meanwhile, on August 30th, the White forces of Generals Bredov and Yuzefovich occupied Kiev. The White 1st air-division of the Volunteer Army acted in the forefront of these advancing units. The flying was so frequent that by October 3rd, in the Alekseev detachment only two DH9s were flyable. The Camels of the 6th detachment found themselves the main White air unit in operation. The battalion by the end of September had only 10 aircraft that were flyable. During the months of battle, two planes were added both Nieuport-23. These arrived on September 7th, flown over from the Reds by Commander Fomagin from the 9th Air-Detachment.

In September, the Whites completed the agonizing re-training of crews on the RE8s of 3rd, 4th and 9th detachments. The fresh units departed for the front, but for some reason, they were not directed to main effort toward Moscow, but to the western flank, near Kiev. It is possible that the Whites hoped that the RE8s near Kiev would act to boost the defenses as did the British DH9s near Tsaritsyn.

The 16 RE8s of the 3rd and 4th detachments arrived in Kiev on October 6th. The aircraft arrived dismounted aboard train platforms. The coming Bolshevik offensive was not foreseen. On the 12th, a special train with the eight aircraft of the 9th detachment arrived. In that day, the Red attack commenced. The Whites had enough time to only unload and assemble five aircraft.

On the 13th, to the south of Kiev, advancing from the Ukraine were the Red Yakira and Kotovsk divisions. This sudden blow allowed the the Bolsheviks within minutes to occupy the right-bank of the city. Nearly all of the 9th air detachment was captured. The 3rd and 4th detachments narrowly escaped. Many were still on trucks.

After a few days of urban warfare, all the Reds were thrown out of the city. The White airmen returned to the airfield at Borispol and began again to assemble the aircraft. The use of aircraft in this area was a waste of resources. In a two month period, the RE8s flew seven times! None of the flights were bombing runs. Once or twice they changed airfields, flying over from Borispol to Brovar, from Brovar to Post-Bolynskoy, from Post-Bolynskoy back to Bovispol. By the end of October, the 3rd and 9th detachments had only three aircraft, and in 4th, , only four flyable aircraft. This is an example of the typical waste of military equipment and opportunity that existed in the White armies.

Other successes happened for other Denikin forces: Kherson fell on August 18, Odessa on 23rd, Kiev on the 30th.

On 17 September the Volunteers took Kursk, on October 1st, Shkuro's Cavalry Corps recaptured Voronezh. At this time Alekseev air-detachment had fully exhausted its aircraft and was transferred into more quiet area near Kiev and after directed to the Crimea to rest and re-form. The composition of the 1st Air-battalion was changed, adding the 2nd detachment, which had just received DH-9 bombers from the former 221st SQD RAF. Still, only eight aircraft were flyable: three are in 2nd and five in the 6th detachment.

The Don Army had only six bombers (not counting the recon types that carried little or no bombs).

Thus, on a 700 kilometer front the White airforce had only 14 aircraft with combat potential. In contrast, the Reds had based 13 air-detachments totaling 50-60 aircraft. However, they lacked the pilots.

One of the most misunderstood matters of the civil war deal with the numbers of men and weapons involved. The usual facts presented are that the Reds outnumbered the Whites two or three times in men and material. But the critical element, and one the Reds put a lot of effort into, was the morale factor. Generally, during the summer and fall of 1919, Denikins men were in a euphoric state as they marched on Moscow. Their morale had soared. Denikin seemed to be a serious threat and Moscow believed they were the ONLY real threat (of all the other White forces attacking elsewhere). Yet, to the Red soldiers fighting, unless they were party members, lacked the morale and consistently had lower morale. The forced conscription, harsh conditions, little pay were not attractive. Despite the deceptive numbers history gives the reader during this time, Red morale was unraveling in face of the continuous success's of Denikin.

The Southern Front, under Egoryev, in August, the Reds had 150,000 soldiers, 23,700 cavalry, 719 guns, 3197 MG. This does not include the various fortified areas that were built in September and October to stop Denikin. These areas amounted to 35,000 men, 129 guns, 185 MG. This front extended some 1400 km. When the Denikin forces had been halted by August 1st, the Reds planned their counterattack in hopes of retaking Rostov and Novercherkassk. The group to do this was the 9th and 10th Armies, and Budenny's cavalry totaling 52,500 infantry, 14,500 cavalry, 314 guns, 1227 MG.

A second Red group with 8th army, had the 3rd and 42nd divisions from the 13th army attacking towards Kupyansk. These forces added another 50,000 infantry, 4700 cavalry, 268 guns, 1381 MG. The length of this counterattack front was 780 km. The original date for the attack had been set for the first week in August, but troop and ammunition deployments delayed this. It was during this delay which lasted past August 10th, that Mamantov's 4th Don Cavalry Corps conducted it's raid. The raid totally disrupted the ability of the Reds to continue to prepare. By the 14th, the left group, with the 9th and 10th Armies, and Budenny cavalry attacked Wrangel (some accounts indicate he had 13,000 infantry, 22,000 cavalry, 93 guns, 349 MG).They were supported by the Volga flotilla (5 gunboats, 16 transport and one floating battery). The 10th Army and Budenny attacked Kamyshin and Tsaritsyn, while the 9th Army attacked towards Ust-Hoperskaya. By the end of August, the 10th Army was advancing on the Serebryakovo region capturing four armor trains. By Sept. 4th, it was closing in on Tsaritsyn.

Wrangel's 1st and 2nd Kuban Corps resisted in their prepared defenses. Another four White Kuban divisions under Gen. Ulagai were also nearby. From the 5th to 8th, Red forces tried to penetrate the defensive lines of consisting of trenches and wire. The Reds suffered heavily during these attacks and on the 9th, called off further attempts. Wrangel counterattack with 12 artillery batteries, a few tanks and pushed some of the 10th Army back. On the 11th, a stalemate set in and Budenny's Cavalry was withdrawn to Novohopersk. The 10th Army attack consisted of 28th, 32nd, 38th,39th divisions. The 9th Army only used the 23rd division which was opposed by strong Don Army units and it was not until the 21st, that a break in the line occurred forcing the Whites to the Khoper and Don rivers. The Khoper river was crossed on Sept. 12th, and the army advanced another 150 km, yet was unable to cross the Don.

On August 12th, Denikin's Kutepov Corps attacked towards Kursk and Rylask severing the communications between the 13th and 14th armies. On the 15th, the 8th and 13th Red Armies attacked the Don Army and the right flank of the Volunteer army (20,500 infantry, 9200 cavalry, 69 guns, 208 MG). This attack group consisted of the 12th, 15th, 16th, 13th Rifle divisions of 8th Army and the 3rd, 42nd Rifle divisions, 1st cavalry brigade of 13th army. The Volunteers were strong while the Don units had been stretched out. By the 27th, the Reds had seized some 60 km on the left flank reaching Novy Oskol, Birjuch, Vailuki. The right flank advanced on Belgorod and was 40 km from Kharkov. However, the Mamantov raid wrecked the communications between the 8th and 9th armies and the coordination and direction of the offensive went in unplanned directions.

The Whites concentrated huge forces on the 8th and 13th armies flanks (parts of 1st Corps, 3rd Kuban Cavalry Corps, 1st Terskaya cavalry division, 2nd Don Infantry division, 2nd Don Cavalry Division, 5th Don Infantry division, 8th Cossack division, 4 tanks). Denikin's forces attacked on the 26th from the Belgorod/Korocha areas and Karpenkov regions. The Reds were surrounded but the Red 12th and 42nd divisions held the flanks until the original attacking force and retreated back to the Seim River on Sept. 15th.

The Red failure was mainly due two matters: one, lack of cavalry to exploit,and two, Mamantov's raid, which added much confusion in the Red headquarters involved. The end positions of the Volunteer Army had them knocking on the Kursk door, only a few miles away.The 1st and 3rd Dons Corps held the west bank of the Don River, with 2nd Don Corps to their right, north and south of Pavlovsk after being pushed back by the Red 23rd division. The 2nd Don Rifle Brigade stood near Pukhova. The 17th battery and 3rd Don Division was at Liski, the 8th Cossack division was at Ostragozhsk, the 2nd Don Division was at Ribensdorf. The best unit of the Don Army, 1st Division was at Novoe Kalitva with Kalmuk Cavalry (400 men). The 1st division had two regiments, one of which was the Tsar's Imperial bodyguard. The whole unit was hand picked men and very well trained.

By September, both sides had acute problems. Both also knew that if the problems were not dealt with quickly, it could be their downfall. For Denikin, it was the horrendous state of his rear areas already addressed by Major Williamson and Holman. The rear depots and ports were all in a state of assorted mess and lawlessness. Numerous separatist groups had sprung up from the former Pelitura army that had controlled the Kiev area until Denikin's army removed them. Other groups in the Kuban area existed all with their own agenda. One of the worse group of bandits was under Makhano, numbering between 5000 – 10,000. These forces would raid Denikin's supply depots and cities, robbing and killing and creating terrorism. These bandits were neither pro Red or White, but took sides only when it benefited them. As these forces grew, Denikin was forced to commit his reserves not to the front but to keep the bandits in check.

Denikin's own troops seriously lacked military equipment and money. The rear area troops and officers freely took the law into their own hands to obtain items.

Even Denikin, in his book *The White Army*, acknowledges this:

> "War booty and requisition transgressed all legal limits and became bald plunder and violence. The Russian revolution had roused all the worst human passions lying dormant in normal times. Class egotism flourished everywhere. There was a great slackness in discharge of fiscal duties. Profiteering became appalling and involved people of all catagories. Embezzlement and bribery for items were the order of the day. Whole organizations became tainted. The troops in the rear had adopted the eat and drink, for tomorrow we die, outlook crippling out strategic efficiency and undermined our authority."

This was the main reason so much of the British supplies seldom or never reached the front. The other reasons were the inability to move them via the railways or the inability to move them from the depots and railheads. The rear troops represented Denikin's worse elements. He had little policing of the rear areas unless frontline forces were diverted to conduct this work.

The major problem for the Reds was the decline of their morale by the recent repeated successes of Denikin. This gave the peasant soldier the false impression the Volunteer army was unbeatable, when in reality, Denikin's army was built on muddy ground and slowly sinking.

The advances of Denikin sounded the alarms in Moscow. In September, morale was constantly being raised by the Central Committee through the use of new papers, leaflets and magazines. All with the sole purpose to mobilize the Russian peasants and Soviet followers. These newspapers were published in all cities and towns, distributed to troops on the front and in the rear. Nearly all of them spilled out the propaganda the Soviets are so well known for. From June to November, some 6,245,584 newspapers had been distributed. Besides newspapers, the Soviet line to defeat the "enemy of the state Denikin" could be seen in numerous colorful posters calling for the working class and laborers to defend. These were widely distributed wherever the Red army had been. For the more affluent Soviet, the propaganda could be seen and heard in the theatres, concerts, film, exhibitions of art and in the factories. Lenin and Trotsky were the "big" names in this public awareness, always drawing large crowds with their hot words. In the south, opposite Denikin, the Red propaganda was its most prevalent. There, the whole area was under military rule and the only thoughts were on war and defeating Denikin. Everything and everyone was subject to mobilization. The Central committee conducted some 166 local party sessions, held 220 meetings, 97 film sessions, attracting over 600,000 people combined. They spent 996,000 rubles in the propaganda effort on the Southern front alone. Over 180,000 copies of posters were given away.The usual argument was to defend the motherland from the coming invasion of Denikin, to sacrifice whatever the Soviet system demanded in order to rout the threat.

Another problem for the Reds was the question of arms supply, these needs greatly rose as the Red army grew. This crisis was due to the Volunteer army seizing the main armament factories in the south during their advance. There was a shortage of rifles, MG, artillery and shells. The factories the Reds continued to hold were at Simbirsk,Rybinsk and Podolsk. To remedy the situation, the method employed by the Reds was an old capitalist one: worker hours were lengthen to12 hours per day, and after four hours of work at normal pay, the balance was doubled their normal rate of pay. The worker would also receive bonuses if the normal monthly production level was surpassed. The worker would also receive overtime pay after 12 hours.

The incentives to meet and exceed arms production also carried over to those who distributed the weapons. On Sept. 27th, a bonus fee went into effect to increase the daily delivery trains. Apparently, all these incentives helped, but these were not enough as an order was issued calling for all foreign (US, Japanese and German) made rifles existing to be gathered. Some 33,310 of these were gathered and sent to the front. When the call for the public to give up their personal rifles, this yielded another 75,000. The production of other materials, such as army footwear yielded 2,096,500 pairs, and 2,568,129 overcoats.

It has been said that Denikin, was in fact, being dictated to by the British. While this may be true to some degree, the bottom line was that the Russians were very stubborn to use the British weapons according to how the British wanted them to be used. It was "the Russian way" or it was "no way" despite the pleas of the field advisors or instructors. In a secret memo from Major Torin, at the Intelligence headquarters in Constaninople, dated Sept. 15th, 1919, his observations are noted:

> "A conference took place at Taganrog with Gen.Holman and Denikin on Sept.5th to discuss the Tsaritsyn and Caspian Sea areas. It appeared Denikin was quite indifferent as to the fate of Wrangel and had nonconception of the condition in the Caspian Sea...it was pointed out that if Tsaritsyn fell, this would send another 16 ships from Tsaritsyn and the Bolsheviks would be able to command the Caspian and be able to obtain Baku oil. As a result of this discussion, Denikin ordered Admiral Gerasimoff to send 500 men from the Black Sea to the Caspian and said he would send reinforcements to Wrangel if needed. General Holman read his strongly worded "aide memoir" to Denikin and his entire staff of their incapability of utilizing the guns, equipment, supplies sent by us. The gist was equipment etc., seldom reached the front and usually remained at the base, given to garrison troops or is fraudulently disposed of. He added that we are nearing the end of our surplus stores and that this state of affairs must be instantly remedied or we might be compelled to cut off aid as we had done to Kolchak. This letter had the effect of causing the entire administrative staff of Denikin to tender their resignations. Gen.Denikin told them no to be children but to look the facts in the face and work to remedy this. As far as Romania, Gen. Denikin indicated that for the moment, he had issued orders to ignore any hostile acts of Romania and to cooperate with them, but stated as the moment was opportune it was his intention to declare war on Romania and reoccupy Bessarabia."

With regards to Romania, Romania stopped providing Russian ammunition to Denikin from their huge surplus because of the press and rumors that Denikin had planned to retake Bessarabia. The British wanted Denikin to make a statement stating that he had no intention of attack Romania. Denikin would never provide this.

In October, the "All Russia Extreme Commission" was created by the Reds. This unit had absolute power (Eminent Domain) to seize anything anyone owned if deemed necessary for the struggle against Denikin without compensation.

Unbeknownst to Denikin, the other item in preparation by the Soviet was the defense committee. With Denikin very near to Kursk, the Reds were very concerned and on Sept. 21st, the Committee began to organize defenses around Kaluga, Tula, Ryazan, Moscow and others. In other words, Kursk like defenses were being prepared. This little known fact has never been revealed in any book until now.

The order spoke of persistent defenses around Moscow, Vitebsk, Dniepr River, Chernigov, Voronezh, Tambov, Orel. It was decided to create four reserve divisions to man the various sectors. There would be four lines of defenses for the Volunteer army to punch through. Two lines would exist before Tula could be reached. Tula, itself, was a fortress. Assuming Tula was taken, another defense line existed after Tula. The strongest fortifications would exist at the railway stations. The fortifications consisted of barb wire, fences, foxholes, blockades, blockhouses, trenches. The fortified areas faced the most likely direction Denikin was going to advance and included observation posts, mines, strong telegraphic and telephone connections. Due to the lack of time, the Soviets concentrated on building defenses along the railway approaches, Moscow itself would be covered by two defense lines, one 12 km from the center and another one 18 km away.

From history, we know in hindsight, that Denikin's Volunteers avenue to Moscow would take him to Orel- Tula-Moscow axis. Wrangel had already failed. The Don Army remained strung out along the Don River. Therefore, for Denikin to reach Moscow, he would first have to take Orel (which he did). The first defense line would be 40-50 km north at Msensk, then Pomomarevo, some 80 km further. Tula was yet another 80 km. The city had two defensive lines around it before reaching the fortified area. To reach Serpukhov, was yet another 80 km. The next to last stop was at Podolsk, 40 km from Moscow and another defensive line.

The cost to build Tula into a fortified area was estimated at 118,677,500 rubles. To construct these defenses, the civilians and engineers were assigned to an internal army. At

A Red machine gun unit showing off their weapons, consisting of Maxim and French origin.

Kaluga, the 41st field construction reg, at Tula, the 4th, at Ryazan, the 14th, and in Moscow, the 48th and 49th. These were further strengthened by the following:

Ryazan:	71,72,73,74th groups
Tula:	82,85,87th groups
Kaluga;	83rd and 89th groups

Tula had been given a higher priority since it was on Denikins approach route and it contained vital armament factories. Thus, the fortified area of Tula was 85% completed by October 10th and the outer belt, 25% completed by October 22nd. By the 15th, 1400 meter of trenches, 450 meters of barb wire had been placed.

Apparently, the Soviets were quite concerned about the possibility that Denikin's airforce or the RAF may bomb Moscow. Thus, it was decided to create an air defense system for the city. The first elements consisted of observation posts and balloons positioned some 100-150 km from the city. These would act as an early warning system to allow the Soviet airplanes to ready and the anti-aircraft batteries to prepare. By October 27th, the observational items were in place at Ryazan, Tula, Vyazma, Serpukhov and manned by experts. The anti-aircraft guns were from the 3rd and 5th anti-aircraft regiment. There was also the 48th air group congesting of interceptor airplanes.

By October 28th, Tula had the 1st and 2nd regiments in place. There were 53,428 men total in the Moscow sector (Moscow, Ryazan, Kaluga and Tula) and 9,443 horses.

As Denikin drew closer to Moscow, the White's also used propaganda and small groups of followers to further disrupt the rear areas and towns under Soviet control. This effort was small in scale, but caused an even more acute paranoia in Central Committee. To combat this, the Committee urged all citizens to report any abnormal behavior of citizens that deviated from Soviet law.

The Denikin supporters tore up the tracks in the Soviet rear and the Soviets attempted to catch them. Persons caught in the act of doing this were shot on sight. Persons suspected of such activity were arrested and sent to trial within 24 hours.

The Soviet Extreme Committee raided the secret Denikin spy ring called "The National Center" in Moscow. This ring actually had officers inside three military schools in the area and a plan existed to cause a general revolt and military coup in Moscow in hopes of taking the city.

The Soviets, in turn, created several thousands of small groups consisting of 50-200 men in Denikin's rear causing havoc and disruption, which have been so well noted. Many of these groups contained much older men and completely invisible unless caught in the act. These underground units were deep in Denikin's rear area with only occasional contact with soviet armies for coordination purposes. Most were armed with only revolvers and rifles. Some had machine guns and artillery. By October some four brigades existed. These groups also existed along the path Denikin was expected to take. For example, in Tula, there was a guerilla group totaling 120 men which would surface after Denikin passed through.

On September 27th, it was decided by the Central Committee to divide the Southern Front to handle Denikin's Volunteer Army. The Southern Front would now comprise of the 13th, 14th and 8th armies, while the Southeastern front contained the 9th and 10th armies.

The Southeastern front would attack the Don and Kuban areas. The Southern Front's focus remained on Kharkov and Kursk.

By October 13th, the threat to Tula was real.Two days later, on the 15th, the Committee decided to make an all out effort to halt any further advance and for the Southern front to prepare for a counterattack while the Southeast Front went over to the defensive. With the main focus on the Southern Front for both sides, this allowed the Soviets to transfer several divisions from the Eastern and Western fronts, which by this time, were either stalled or retreating. The Latvian division (1st and 86th reg) from 12th Army on the western front was transferred and arrived on the Southern front on Oct. 15th. Not all units ordered for transferring were received well. When the Committee ordered a cavalry division from the Southeast Front to move to the Southern front, the commander of the Southeast Front refused. When the Committee cabled the commander 'threatening actions" about his motives, the division was released and arrived by October 8th in the 8th army zone.

By mid-October, the main avenues of attack had been decided upon and due to the poor road network, the offensive was based upon the railway system and dictated how the approach avenues would be directed. For these reasons, Kursk was selected as the main target since the main railway extended from there through Taganrog.

Trotsky wrote the following regarding strategy and the situation on the Southern/Eastern fronts in September 1919:

> "Attempts to put the blame on the state of the armies of the Southern front, the organisation of the apparatus, and so on, are utterly groundless. The armies of the

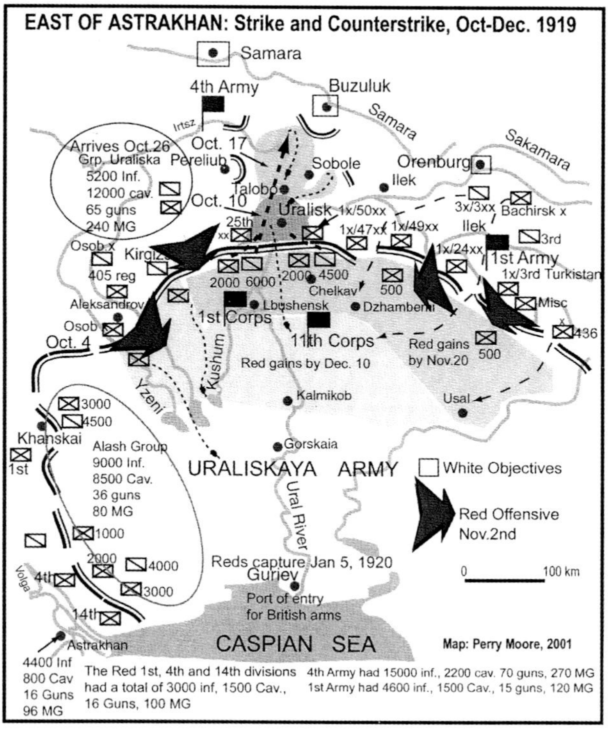

Southern front are in no way any worse than those of the Eastern front. The Eighth Army is fully as good as the Fifth. The weaker Thirteenth Army is in any case inferior to the Fourth. The Ninth Army is approximately on the same level as the Third. To a considerable extent these armies were built by the same group of workers, and, to anyone who has observed these armies during their periods of success and of failure, talk of some differences in organisation or combat-capacity between our armies of the Southern and Eastern fronts sounds utterly false.

What is true here is this alone, that Denikin is an incomparably more serious enemy than Kolchak. The divisions that were transferred from the Eastern to the Southern fronts proved to be in no way better than the Southern front divisions. This fully applies to the commanding personnel. On the contrary, indeed, in the initial period the divisions from the Eastern front showed themselves to be generally weaker, until they found their feet in the new conditions, facing a new enemy.

But if the enemy in the South was stronger, we too were incomparably stronger than we had ever been before, on any of our fronts. We must therefore seek the reasons for our failure entirely m the operational plan. We advanced along the line of most resistance, that is to say, units of average steadiness were sent into localities inhabited entirely by Cossacks, who were not attacking but defending their *stanitsas* and their homes. The atmosphere of a 'Don people's war' had a debilitating effect on our units. Under these conditions, Denikin's tanks, his skilful manoeuvnng, and so on, gave him a tremendous advantage.

In the region where smaller forces on our side could have achieved incomparably greater results, on the Donets and in the Ukraine, we left Denikin complete freedom of action, and thereby enabled him to obtain a huge reservoir for new formations.

All talk about Denikin not raising new forces in the Ukraine is rubbish. While there are in the Ukraine few politically- educated proletarians, a circumstance which hindered our attempts to raise new forces, the Ukraine has very many officers, sons of landlords and bourgeois, and brutal kulaks. Consequently, while we were pressing against the Don country, strengthening the Cossack barrier against us, Denikin was managing, almost unhindered, to raise new formations, especially of cavalry, throughout the whole territory he occupied.

The erroneousness of the plan is now so obvious that the question arises: how could this plan have been formed in the first place?

The Eastern front considered it impossible at that time to transfer any of its units. The then Commander-in-Chief accused the Eastern front of causing delay. The Eastern front stressed that the delay would not be too protracted or dangerous, as units would be brought up directly to the left flank (resting on the Volga) of the Southern front.

The echo of these old plans, plus secondary considerations about saving time in the transference of units from the Eastern front led to the creation of Shorn's special group. All the other considerations (about striking a decisive blow at the Don and Kuban bases, and so on) were thought up after the event, when the absurdity of the a-priori plan began to be revealed more and more harshly.

Order of Battle for the Armed Forces of South Russia (VSYuR) as of 15 of September 1919, and updated on 29 October 1919.

Staffs of the Supreme Commander and of the Army

Supreme Commander of the Armed Forces of South Russia	General-Lieutenant A.I. Denikin
Deputy Supreme Commander (Chief Of the Military Administration)	General-Lt A.S. Lukomskiy
Chief of Staff	Gen-Lt I.P. Romanovskiy
General Quartermaster	Gen-Maj Yu.N. Plyushchik-Plyushchevskiy
Duty General	Gen-Maj S.M. Trukhachev
Inspector of Artillery	Gen-Lt N.A. Il'kevich
Inspector of Formations	Gen-Lt N.M. Kiselevskiy
Chief of Aviation	Gen-Maj I. Kravtsevich
Chief of VSYuR Equipment	Gen-Lt A.S. Sannikov
Chief of VSYuR Tank Units	Col Khaletskiy

Military Administration of the VSYuR

Chief of Administration	Gen-Lt A.S. Lukomskiy
Chief of the Department of the General Staff	Gen-Lt V.E. Vyaz'mitinov
Chief of the Joint Department	Gen-Maj Firsov

Units belonging to the Supreme Command Staff

Special Officers of the Headquarters	
Company Commander	Captain Savel'ev
Security Company	Colonel Karpenko

Volunteer Army

Commander of the Army	Gen-Lt V.Z. Mae-Maevskiy
Chief of Staff	Gen-Lt N.P. Efimov
General Quartermaster	Colonel A.A. Von Goertz
Duty General	Gen-Maj Benson
Inspector of Artillery	Gen-Maj Lakhtinov
Chief of Military Transportation	Gen-Maj Messner
Chief of Equipment	Gen-Maj Deev

Army of the Caucasus

Commander of the Army	Gen-Lt Baron P.N. Wrangel
Chief of Staff	Gen-Lt P.N. Shatilov
General Quartermaster	Gen-Lt D.M. Von Ziegel
Duty General	Gen-Maj V.P. Petrov
Inspector of Artillery	Gen-Lt Makeev
Chief of Military Transportation	Gen-Lt P.S. Makhrov
Chief of Equipment	Gen-Maj P.A. Vil'chevskiy

Forces of the North Caucasus

Commander of the Forces	Cavalry General I.G. Erdeli
Deputy Commander	Gen-Lt P.A. Tomilov
Chief of Staff	Gen-Maj E.V. Maslovskiy
Ober-Quartermaster	Col K.G. Bulgakov
Duty General	Gen-Maj Maslennikov
Inspector of Artillery	Gen-Lt N.D. Nevodovskiy
Administrator of Force Movements	Gen-Maj Solov'ev
Chief of Equipment	Gen-Maj Artsishev

Forces of the Novorossiysk Oblast' (Region)

Army Commander	Gen-Lt N.N. Schilling
Chief of Staff	Gen-Maj V.V. Chernavin
General Quartermaster	Col Darovskiy
Duty General	Gen-Maj I.I. Vetvenitskiy
Inspector of Artillery	Gen-Maj Papa-Fedorov

Forces of the Kiev Oblast' (Region)

Army Commander	General of Cavalry A.M. Dragomirov
Deputy Commander	General of Infantry V.E. Flug
Chief of Staff	Gen-Lt M.N. Vakhrushev
General Quartermaster	Gen-Maj A.N. Shuberskiy
Chief of Equipment	Gen-Maj V.P. Bressler

Forces of the Trans-Caspian Oblast'

Commander of the Forces	Gen-Lt B.I. Kazanovich

*****

Administration of the Corps'

1st Army Corps (1st, 3rd, 9th Infantry Divisions) of the Volunteer Army

Corps Commander	Gen-Lt A.P. Kutepov
Chief of Staff	Gen-Lt V.P. Agapeev
Inspector of Artillery	Gen-Maj I.T. Belyaev

2nd Army Corps (5th and 7th Infantry Divisions) of the Volunteer Army

Corps Commander	Gen-Lt M.N. Promtov
Chief of Staff	Gen-Maj Abutkov
Inspector of Artillery	Gen-Maj Bodisko

1st Kuban Corps (1st Kuban Cossack Division) of the Caucasus Army

Corps Commander	Gen-Lt V.L. Pokrovskiy
Chief of Staff	Col I.A. Rebdev
Inspector of Artillery	Gen-Maj Stopchanskiy

2nd Kuban Corps (2nd, 3rd, and 4th Kuban Cossack Divisions) of the Caucasus Army

Corps Commander	Gen-Maj V.G. Naumenko (used to be Gen-Maj Ulagay)
Chief of Staff	unfilled - was Gen-Maj Shuberskiy
Inspector of Artillery	

3rd Kuban Corps (1st Caucasus & 1st Tersk Cossack Divisions) of the Volunteer Army

Corps Commander	Gen-Lt A.G. Shkuro
Chief of Staff	Gen-Maj A.M. Shifner-Markevich
Inspector of Artillery	Col Urchukin

4th Horse Corps (1st Composite Gorsk Horse Division) of the Caucasus Army

Corps Commander	Gen-Lt S.A. Toporkov
Chief of Staff	Gen-Maj M.M. Georgievich
Inspector of Artillery	Gen-Maj Mal'tsev

5th Cavalry Corps (1st & 2nd Cavalry Divisions) of the Volunteer Army

Corps Commander	Gen-Lt Ya.D. Yuzefovich
Chief of Staff	Gen-Maj P.A. Kusonskiy
Inspector of Artillery	Gen-Lt M.I. Rep'iev

1st Infantry Division (1st Army Corps)

Division Commander	Gen-Maj N.S. Timanovskiy
Chief of Staff	Col A. Bittenbinder
1st Brigade	Gen-Maj A.N. Tret'yakov
2nd Brigade	Col N.V. Skoblin
1st Officer's of General Markov Infantry Division	Col Blaish
2nd Officer's of General Markov Infantry Division	Col Morozov
1st Kornilov Shock Regiment	Col M.A. Peshnya
2nd Kornilov Shock Regiment	
3rd Kornilov Shock Regiment	
Reserve Battalion of the 1st Infantry Division	Col Konovalov
1st Artillery Brigade	
1st Battery	Col Mashin
2nd Battery	Col Mikhailov
3rd Battery	Col Rapponet
4th Battery	Col Ayvasov
1st Engineers of General Markov Company	Col Grottenhelm

Kornilov Division (1st Army Corps)

Division Commander	Col N.V. Skoblin (seems the same as the 1st Infantry Division's 2nd Brigade commander)
Chief of Staff	
1st Brigade	

2nd Brigade	
1st Kornilov Shock Regiment	Col M.A. Peshnya
2nd Kornilov Shock Regiment	Col Pashkevich
3rd Kornilov Shock Regiment	Cavalry Colonel (Esaul) Mileev
Kornilov Artillery Brigade	Col Erogin
Independent Engineer Company of the Kornilov Division	
Reserve Battalion of the Kornilov Division	

Markov Division (1st Army Corps)

Division Commander	Gen-Maj N.S. Timanovskiy
Chief of Staff	
1st Brigade	
2nd Brigade	
1st Officer's of General Markov Infantry Regiment	Col Blaish
2nd Officer's of General Markov Infantry Regiment	Col Morozov
3rd Officer's of General Markov Infantry Regiment	
Markov Artillery Brigade	
1st Battery	
2nd Battery	
3rd Battery	
4th Battery	
Independent Engineers of General Markov Company	
Reserve Battalion of Markov Division	

2nd Infantry Division (in the composition of the forces of the Black Sea Military Governate)

Division Commander	Gen-Maj A.N. Cherepov
Chief of Staff	unfilled - was Col Borodaevskiy
1st Brigade	
2nd Brigade	Col Borodaevskiy
Caucasus Officer's Regiment	unfilled - was Col Ushak
1st Kuban Rifle Regiment	Col Dmitriev
Black Sea Rifle Regiment	Col Nordashenko
Reserve Battalion of the 2nd Infantry Division	Col Semashko
2nd Artillery Brigade	Col Erogin
1st Battery	Col Pimenov
2nd Battery	Col Efremov
3rd Battery	Col S.D. Gegelashvili
4th Battery	Col Il'yashevich
2nd Independent Engineer Company	Col Bershov

Drozdovskiy (was the 3rd Infantry) Division (1st Army Corps)

Division Commander	Gen-Maj V.K. Vitkovskiy
Chief of Staff	Col F.E. Bredov
1st Brigade	Gen-Maj Kel'ner

2nd Brigade	
1st Officers of General Drozdovskiy Regiment	Col Rumel'
2nd Officers of General Drozdovskiy Regiment	unfilled - was Col M.A. Zvyagin
Reserve Battalion of the Drozdovskiy Division (was the Reserve Battalion of the 3rd Infantry Division)	Col En'kov
Drozdovskiy Artillery Brigade (was the 3rd Artillery Brigade)	Col M.N. Polzikov
1st Battery	Col V.A. Protasevich (the 1st Battery was called the 1st General Drozdovskiy Light Battery)
2nd Battery	Col Shane
3rd Battery	Col Sokolov
4th Battery	Col A.K. Medvedev
Independent Engineers of General Drozdovskiy Company (was the 3rd Engineers")	Col Borodin

4th Infantry Division (counted in the composition of the Novorossiysk Oblast' Forces)

Division Commander	Gen-Maj Ya.A. Slashchov
Chief of Staff	
1st Brigade	
2nd Brigade	
Simferopol' Officer's Regiment	Col Gvozdakov
1st Composite Regiment of the 13th Infantry Regiment	
2nd Composite Regiment of the 13th Infantry Regiment	
1st Composite Regiment of the 34th Infantry Regiment	
2nd Composite Regiment of the 34th Infantry Regiment	
Reserve Battalion of the 4th Infantry Division	Col Borisenko
4th Artillery Brigade	Gen-Maj Roslyakov
1st Battery	Col Gudima
2nd Battery	Col Zamfirov
3rd Battery	Gen-Maj Zhukov
4th Battery	Gen-Maj Sivitskiy
4th Independent Engineer Company	

Composite Guard Infantry Division (formerly the 5th Infantry Division) (2nd Army Corps)

Division Commander	Gen-Maj P.S. Ossovskiy
Chief of Staff	Col Akhatkin
1st Brigade	Gen-Maj Baron N.I. Shtackleberg
2nd Brigade	
Composite Regiment of the 1st Guard Division (formerly the Guard Composite Regiment)	Gen-Maj Moller
Composite Regiment of the 2nd Guard Division (formerly the Guard Composite Regiment)	Col Stessel

Composite Regiment of the Guard Rifle Division
Composite Regiment of the 19th Infantry Division (disbanded by 29 Oct (12 Nov))
Composite Regiment of the 20th Infantry Division (disbanded by 29 Oct (12 Nov))
80th Kabardino Infantry Regiment (disbanded by 29 Oct (12 Nov))
Reserve Battalion of the Composite Guard Division (formerly the Reserve Battalion of the 5th Infantry Division)

Composite Guard Artillery Brigade	Gen-Maj M. Bez-Kornilovich
1st Battery	Col
2nd Battery	Col Plyushchinskiy
3rd Battery	Col Abramovskiy
4th Battery	Col Sax
Independent Artillery Battery	Col Shpigel
Independent Guard Heavy Howitzer Battery	Col Kazachinskiy
Guard Independent Engineer Company	Col Beliy

Composite Grenadier Division (Caucasus Army)

Division Commander	Gen-Lt P.K. Pisarev
Chief of Staff	unfilled in Nov (was Col Skoblev)
1st Brigade	Gen-Maj M. Chichinadze
2nd Brigade	Col B.P.Kochkin (was Col B.K. Manakin)
Composite Regiment of the 1st Grenadier Division	unfilled in Nov (was Col B.K. Kochkin)
Composite Regiment of the 2nd Grenadier Division	Col Stavitskiy (was Col G.K. Pil'berg)
Composite Regiment of the 3rd Grenadier Division	Col Yakovlev
Composite Regiment of the Caucasus Grenadier Division	Col G.K. Pil'berg
Reserve Battalion of the Composite Grenadier Division	
Composite Grenadier Artillery Brigade	Gen-Maj S.M Ikishev
1st Battery	Col Ivanov
2nd Battery	Col Stolbin
3rd Battery	
4th Battery	Col Dzhizkaev
Grenadier Independent Engineer Company	

7th Infantry Division (2nd Army Corps)

Division Commander	Gen-Lt N.E. Bredov
Chief of Staff	Col Evert
1st Brigade	Gen-Maj P.P. Nepenin
2nd Brigade	
Composite Regiment of the 4th Rifle Division	Col Udovichenko
42nd Infantry Yakutsk Regiment	Gen-Maj T. Bernise
Composite Regiment of the 15th Infantry Division	
Reserve Battalion of the 7th Infantry Division	
7th Artillery Brigade	

1st Battery	Col Pashkov
2nd Battery	Col Krasovskiy
3rd Battery	Col Ostrovskiy
4th Battery	Col Dobrovol'skiy
7th Independent Engineer Company	Col Dobrovol'skiy

8th Infantry Division (in the Forces of North Caucasus)

Division Commander	Gen-Maj Rudnev
Chief of Staff	
1st Brigade	
2nd Brigade	Col Silin
81st Infantry Apsheronsk Regiment	Col Dubyago
82nd Infantry Dagestan Regiment	Col Timorenko-Krivitskiy
84th Infantry Shirvanskiy Regiment	Col Kamionko
1st Composite Regiment of the 52nd Infantry Division	Col Zhukovskiy
2nd Composite Regiment of the 52nd Infantry Division	Col Parkhomovich
Reserve Battalion of the 8th Infantry Division	Col Gurtikh
8th Artillery Brigade	Gen-Maj Milostanov
1st Battery	Col Zanfirov
2nd Battery	Col Menk (was Col Rzhevushkhin)
3rd Battery	Gen-Maj Erdman
4th Battery	Col D. Grigorovich
Caucasus Independent Artillery Battery	
8th Independent Engineer Company	

9th Infantry Division (1st Army Corps)

Division Commander	Gen-Maj Shevchenko
Chief of Staff	Col Lebedev
1st Brigade	
2nd Brigade	
*Partisans of General Alexeev Regiment	Col Gagarin - Note: this unit was disbanded by 29 Oct (12 Nov)
13th Belozersk Infantry Regiment	Col B.A. Steffan
14th Olen'ovka Infantry Regiment	Col Bykanov
Composite Rifle Regiment	Col G.K. Gravitskiy
Reserve Battalion of the 9th Infantry Division	
9th Artillery Brigade	
1st Battery	
2nd Battery	
4th Battery	
9th Independent Engineer Company	

Alexeev Infantry Division (5th Cavalry Corps)

Division Commander	Gen-Maj A.N. Tretyakov
Chief of Staff	

1st Brigade	
2nd Brigade	
1st Partisan's of General Alexeev Regiment	Col P.G. Buzun
2nd Partisan's of General Alexeev Regiment	Col Prince Gagarin
Samur Infantry Regiment	was commanded by Col M.A. Zvyagin
Alexeev Artillery Brigade	
Independent Engineers of General Alexeev Company	
Reserve Battalion of the Alexeev Infantry Division	

5th Infantry Division (2nd Army Corps)

Division Commander	
Chief of Staff	
1st Brigade	
2nd Brigade	
Composite Regiment of the 19th Infantry Division	
Composite Regiment of the 20th Infantry Division	
80th Infantry Kabardino Regiment	

1st Independent Infantry Brigade (of the Volunteer Army)

Brigade Commander	Gen-Maj Volkhovskiy
1st Regiment of the 31st Infantry Division	Col Smel'nitskiy
2nd Regiment of the 31st Infantry Division	Col Tkachev
Artillery Battery	
Engineer Company	

Reserve Units

Commander of the Reserve Units	Gen-Maj V.V. Kharlamov
Commander of the 1st Army Reserve Brigade	Gen-Maj Buyvid
3rd Army Reserve Battalion	Col Bulgakov
*4th Army Reserve Battalion	Col Stratonov Note: this unit was disbanded by 29 Oct (12 Nov)
5th Army Reserve Battalion	Col Yur'ev
6th Army Reserve Battalion	Col Yulatov (was Col Shekerov)
1st Army Reserve Battalion for Prisoners of War	Col Batalin
2nd Army Reserve Battalion for Prisoners of War	Note: this unit was disbanded by 29 Oct (12 Nov)
Commander of the 2nd Army Reserve Brigade	Col Sychev
1st Army Reserve Battalion	Col Esiv Note: disbanded by 29 Oct (12 Nov)
2nd Army Reserve Battalion	Col Koch
6th Army Reserve Battalion	Col Platonov Note: this unit was disbanded by 29 Oct (12 Nov)
7th Army Reserve Battalion	Col Bakeev
9th Army Reserve Battalion	Col Stupin

Reserve Machinegun Battalion	Col Glinskiy
Reserve Engineer Regiment	Col Levashev
Reserve Armored Car Division	
12th Army Reserve Battalion	
2nd Army Reserve Battalion for Prisoners of War	
Commander of the 3rd Army Reserve Brigade	
1st Army Reserve Battalion	
4th Army Reserve Battalion	Col Stratonov
8th Army Reserve Battalion	Col Shekerov
10th Army Reserve Battalion	
11th Army Reserve Battalion	

1st Cavalry Division (5th Cavalry Corps)

Division Commander	Gen-Maj I.I. Chekatovskiy
Chief of Staff	Col V.V. Crater
1st Brigade	Col I.G. Barbovich
2nd Brigade	Col Samsonov
3rd Brigade	Gen-Maj Zubov
1st Horse of General Alexeev Regiment	Col Saburov
10th Ingermanland Hussar Regiment	Cavalry Colonel (Rotmistr) Tikhonravov
Composite Regiment of the 9th Cavalry Division	Col V.N. Vygran
Composite Regiment of the 12th Cavalry Division of General Kaledin	Col Psiol
Composite Lancer Regiment	Col G.P. Aprelev
Composite Hussar Regiment	Col B. Gaevskiy
3rd Horse Artillery Battery	Capt Ermilov
Composite Battery of Caucasus Horse-Mountain Artillery	

2nd Cavalry Division (5th Cavalry Corps)

Division Commander	Col I.M. Miklashevskiy
Chief of Staff	Col B.M. Wordan
1st Brigade	Col Danilov
2nd Brigade	Col Baron Pritvits
3rd Brigade	
1st Guards Composite Cuirassier Regiment	Col Kossikovskiy
2nd Guards Composite Cavalry Regiment	Col Gryaznov
2nd Horse of General Drozdovskiy Regiment	Col A.G. Chapron du Lare
3rd Horse Regiment	
Composite Caucasus Cavalry Division	Col Popov
Composite Dragoon Regiment	Col Lermontov
Independent Division of Guards Horse Artillery	Col Perfil'ev (was Col Trepov)

Heavy Artillery

1st Independent Heavy Howitzer Battery (Caucasus Army)	Gen-Maj Podgoretskiy
2nd Independent Heavy Howitzer Battery (Volunteer Army)	Col Bek-Sofiev
3rd Independent Heavy Howitzer Battery (Volunteer Army)	
4th Independent Heavy Howitzer Battery (attached to the Forces of Novorossiysk Oblast')	Col Purzhinskiy
Independent Heavy Cannon-Tractor Division (Volunteer Army)	
Independent Heavy Howitzer Battery (attached to the Forces of Novorossiysk Oblast')	Col Saznevskiy
Independent Heavy Tractor-Howitzer Division	Col Rzhevutskiy
1st Battery	Col Koptev
2nd Battery	Col Tolmachev

Units not attached to the Divisions or Corps

Composite Regiment of the 31st Infantry Division (Volunteer Army)	Gen-Maj Volkhovskiy Note: disbanded by 29 Oct (12 Nov)
Slavyansk Rifle Regiment (attached to the Forces of Novorossiysk Oblast')	
Composite Siberian Rifle Regiment	Gen-Maj Vitsent'ev
Crimean Horse Regiment (attached to the Forces of Novorossiysk Oblast')	Gen-Maj Burnevich
Composite Regiment of the 1st Independent Cavalry Brigade (Volunteer Army)	Col Tugan-Mirza-Baranovskiy
5th Alexandriskiy Hussar Regiment (attached to the Forces of North Caucasus)	
Stavropol' Horse-Partisan Division (Caucasus Army)	Col Glebov
Composite Siberian Rifle Artillery Battery	
1st Independent Telegraph Company (General Command Staff)	
2nd Independent Telegraph Company (Command Staff of the Volunteer Army)	
3rd Independent Telegraph Company (attached to the Forces of Novorossiysk Oblast')	
4th Independent Telegraph Company (Command Staff of the Caucasus Army)	Capt Maevskiy
5th Independent Telegraph Company (Staff of the Volunteer Army)	Col Druzhinin
6th Independent Telegraph Company (Volunteer Army)	Lieutenant Chibirkov
7th Independent Telegraph Company (attached to the Forces of Novorossiysk Oblast')	
1st Radio-Telegraph Division (Caucasus Army)	
2nd Radio-Telegraph Division (Volunteer Army)	Col Rar
3rd Radio-Telegraph Division (attached to the Forces of Novorossiysk Oblast')	Col Schultz
8th Independent Telegraph Company (Command Staff of the Forces of Kiev Oblast')	Col Krasnopevtsev
10th Independent Telegraph Company (5th Cavalry Corps)	

1st Aviation Division	
2nd Aviation Division	
3rd Aviation Division	
10th Aviation Detachment	
1st Division of Tanks	Captain Hartman
2nd Division of Tanks (Volunteer Army)	
1st Railroad Battalion	
2nd Railroad Battalion	
3rd Railroad Battalion	Grossevich
4th Railroad Battalion	Col Safonov

2nd Independent Railroad Company Note: this unit was disbanded by 29 Oct (12 Nov)
Training Reserve Railroad Company
1st Worker's Railroad Battalion (was forming in Sep, formed by Oct)

2nd Worker's Railroad Battalion	
3rd Worker's Railroad Battalion	
4th Worker's Railroad Battalion	
Caucasus Engineer Battalion	
1st Caucasus Independent Engineer Company	
2nd Caucasus Independent Engineer Company	Col Vvedenskiy
1st Independent Pontoon Company	
2nd Independent Pontoon Company	
1st Automobile Battalion (Caucasus Army)	Captain Nyukhalov
2nd Automobile Battalion (attached to the Forces of North Caucasus)	Col Zakharov

3rd Automobile Battalion (attached to the Forces of Novorossiysk Oblast')
4th Automobile Battalion (attached to the Military Base)
5th Automobile Battalion (Volunteer Army)
6th Automobile Battalion (attached to the Forces of Kiev Oblast')
1st Reserve Automobile Battalion (attached to the General Command Staff)

Armored Trains

Chief of the Armored Train Divisions	Gen-Maj M. Ivanov
1st Armored Train Division	Col Skopin
Light Armored Train - "General Alekseev"	Col Shamov
Light Armored Train - "Forward for the Homeland"	Col Skoritovskiy
Heavy Armored Train - "Unified Russia"	Col Karpinskiy
2nd Armored Train Division	Col Gromyko
Light Armored Train - "General Kornilov"	Capt Lazarev
Light Armored Train - "Officer"	Col Lebedev
Heavy Armored Train - "Johann Kalita"	Col A.A. Zelenetskiy
3rd Armored Train Division	Col Gadd (or Hadd)
Light Armored Train - "Knight"	Col Gurskiy
Light Armored Train - "Dmitriy Donskoy"	Capt Pleskovskiy
Heavy Armored Train - "Prince Pozharskiy"	Col Morilin

4th Armored Train Division	Col Selikov
Light Armored Train - "Eagle"	Capt Muromets
Light Armored Train - "Glory to the Officer"	Capt Khar'kovtsev
Heavy Armored Train - "Terrible"	Col V. Barkalov
5th Armored Train Division	Gen-Maj Ivanov
Light Armored Train - "General Markov"	Capt Sipyagin
Light Armored Train - "Pounce"	Capt Magnitskiy
Heavy Armored Train - "Invincible"	Col Kuznetsov
6th Armored Train Division	
Light Armored Train - "General Drozdovskiy"	
Light Armored Train - "For Saint Rus'"	
Light Armored Train - "George the Victorious"	Col Mokritskiy
Light Armored Train - "Terets"	Col Loiko
Light Armored Train - "Caucasus Warrior"	
Heavy Armored Train - "To Moscow"	

Combat OOB for the VSYuR, October 1919

Forces of North Caucasus

8th Infantry Division - General of Cavalry Erdeli
1st Terek Cossack Infantry Brigade
2nd Terek Cossack Infantry Brigade (a Battalion and a Battery)
1st Kuban Cossack Infantry Brigade
3rd Terek Cossack Division
4th Terek Cossack Division
Kabardino Horse Division (part)
Ossetia Horse Division
Chechen Horse Division (part)
Dagestan Horse Division (part)
Units, not part of the Divisions or Brigades
Trans-Caspian Detachment

8th Infantry Division - Gen-Maj Rudnev
Apsheronskiy Infantry Regiment - 1286 Rifles, 16 machineguns
Dagestan Infantry Regiment - 738 Rifles, 9 machineguns
Shirvanskiy Infantry Regiment - 1011 Rifles, 9 machineguns

1st Composite Regiment of the 52nd Infantry Division - 1673 Rifles, 7 machineguns
2nd Composite Regiment of the 52nd Infantry Division - 538 Rifles, 6 machineguns
Supplemental Battalion - 411 Rifles
8th Artillery Brigade (4 Batteries) - 12 Light, 4 Mountain (cannons), & 3 howitzers
Total Numbers:
5657 Rifles, 47 machineguns, 12 Light, 4 Mountain (cannons), and 3 howitzers

1st Terek Cossack Infantry Brigade - Col Lesikov
9th Terek Cossack Infantry Battalion - 208 Rifles, 4 machineguns (there was a note in the original text stating that the 9th Terek had not yet become a part of the 1st Sunzhensko Battalion in view of operations).
1st Volga Cossack Infantry Battalion - 304 Rifles, 5 machineguns
2nd Volga Cossack Infantry Battalion - 85 Rifles, 1 machinegun
1st Sunzhensko-Vladikavkaz Cossack Infantry Battalion - 222 Rifles, 4 machineguns
2nd Sunzhensko-Vladikavkaz Cossack Infantry Battalion
1st Caucasus Artillery Division:
1st Caucasus Cossack Infantry Mountain Battery - 3 mountain cannons
1st Caucasus Howitzer Battery - 2 howitzers
Total: 819 Rifles, 14 machineguns, 3 mountain cannons, 2 howitzers

2nd Terek Cossack Infantry Brigade (brigade & army volunteers)
16th Terek Cossack Infantry Battalion - 111 Rifles, 4 machineguns
2nd Caucasus Cossack Infantry Mountain Battery - 4 light cannons

1st Kuban Cossack Infantry Brigade - Col Firsov
6th Kuban Cossack Infantry Battalion - 245 Rifles, 7 machineguns
7th Kuban Cossack Infantry Battalion - 562 Rifles, 12 machineguns
12th Kuban Cossack Infantry Battalion - 800 Rifles, 9 machineguns
Special Kuban Cossack Infantry Battalion
1st Kuban Cossack Infantry Battery
4th Kuban Cossack Infantry Battery - 4 light cannons
Total: 1607 Rifles, 28 machineguns, 4 light cannons

3rd Terek Cossack Division (there was a note in the original text stating that the 3rd Terek along with the 4th combined to later form the 2nd Terek Cossack Division)
1st Sunzhensko-Vladikavkaz Cossack Regiment - 212 sabers, 3 machineguns
2nd Sunzhensko-Vladikavkaz Cossack Regiment - 313 sabers, 7 machineguns
3rd Sunzhensko-Vladikavkaz Cossack Regiment - 240 sabers, 3 machineguns
3rd Terek Cossack Regiment - 380 sabers, 5 machineguns
4th Terek Cossack Battery - 3 light cannons
6th Terek Cossack Battery - 4 light cannons
Total: 1145 sabers, 18 machineguns, 7 light cannons

4th Terek Cossack Division - Gen-Maj Kolesnikov
1st Kizlyaro-Grebeni Horse Regiment - 235 sabers, 4 machineguns
2nd Kizlyaro-Grebeni Horse Regiment - 161 sabers, 6 machineguns
3rd Kizlyaro-Grebeni Horse Regiment - 253 sabers, 1 machinegun
4th Terek Cossack Regiment - 407 sabers
5th Terek Cossack Battery - 4 light cannons
Total: 1056 sabers, 11 machineguns, 4 light cannons

Kabardino Horse Division - Gen-Maj Anzorov
1st Kabardino Horse Regiment (in the Caucasus Army)
2nd Kabardino Horse Regiment (in the Caucasus Army)
3rd Kabardino Horse Regiment (in the Caucasus Army)
4th Kabardino Horse Regiment (in the Caucasus Army)
5th Kabardino Horse Regiment - 70 sabers, 2 machineguns
6th Kabardino Horse Regiment - 360 sabers
Training-Supplemental Command - 44 sabers
Machinegun Course - 7 machineguns
Total: 474 sabers, 9 machineguns

Ossetia Horse Division - Col Emmanuel
1st Ossetia Horse Regiment - 265 sabers, 5 machineguns
2nd Ossetia Horse Regiment - 244 sabers, 8 machineguns
3rd Ossetia Horse Regiment - in the Volunteer Army
4th Ossetia Horse Regiment - 93 sabers, 8 machineguns
1st Ossetia Rifle Battalion - in the Volunteer Army
2nd Ossetia Rifle Battalion - 308 rifles, 4 machineguns
3rd Ossetia Rifle Battalion - 384 rifles, 4 machineguns
Total: 692 Rifles, 8 machineguns; 602 sabers, 21 machineguns

Chechen Horse Division - Gen-Maj Revishin (the 4 Chechen Horse Regiments were sent to the rear area of the Volunteer Army)
1st Chechen Horse Regiment
2nd Chechen Horse Regiment
3rd Chechen Horse Regiment
4th Chechen Horse Regiment
Kumik Horse Regiment - 378 sabers, 4 machineguns
Total: 378 sabers, 4 machineguns

Dagestan Horse Brigade
1st Dagestan Horse Regiment - in the Caucasus Army, transferred to the Composite Gorsk (Horse) Division
2nd Dagestan Horse Regiment - in the Caucasus Army, transferred to the Composite Gorsk (Horse) Division

1st Dagestan Rifle Battalion - in the Caucasus Army, transferred to the Composite Gorsk (Horse) Division
2nd Dagestan Rifle Battalion - 36 rifles, 4 machineguns
3rd Dagestan Rifle Battalion - 177 rifles
4th Dagestan Rifle Battalion - 17 rifles
1st Detached Light Battery - 5 light cannons
Total: 230 rifles, 4 machineguns, 5 light cannons

Units not part of the Divisions or Brigades
Aleksandriyskiy Hussar Regiment - 861 sabers, 18 machineguns
Ossetia (Kuban) Division - 78 sabers
Ossetia Horse Division - 46 sabers, 1 machinegun
Partisan Detachment - 191 sabers, 1 machinegun
Astrakhan Detached Squadron (sotnya) - 120 sabers
Caucasus Engineer Battalion - 3 companies, 256 sappers
Supplemental Terek Battery - 6 light cannons
1st Independent Horse-Mountain Division (2 batteries) - 8 light cannons
Armored Trains: "Terets," "Caucasus Warrior," "George the Victorious"
Radio Stations numbers 18, 6, and 8
Air Detachment Number 5 - 2 airplanes
Total: 1296 sabers, 20 machineguns, 14 light cannons, 3 companies of 256 sappers, 2 airplanes and 3 armored trains.

Trans-Caspian Detachment

Trans-Caspian Division
1st Regiment - 923 rifles, 7 machineguns
Supplemental Battalion - 76 rifles
Turkestan Regiment - 952 rifles, 15 machineguns
Horse Dagestan Division - 297 sabers, 3 machineguns
Ossetia Horse Squadron (sotnya) - 68 sabers, 1 machinegun
Horse-Partisan Division - 107 sabers, 7 machineguns
Caucasus Artillery Battery - 2 light cannons
Trans-Caspian Artillery Battery- 4 light cannons
Sapper Company - 1 company, 72 sappers
Kizil-Arvat Railroad Militia - 144 rifles, 4 machineguns
Armored Trains: "Patrol," "General Kornilov," "Partisan," "Three Musketeers," and "Thunderstorm"
Total: 2051 rifles, 26 machineguns, 562 sabers, 11 machineguns, 8 cannons, 1 company of 72 sappers, 5 armored trains.

Total in the Forces of the North Caucasus
11,167 rifles, 131 machineguns
5513 sabers, 94 machineguns
58 light cannons, 7 mountain cannons, 5 howitzers

4 companies with a total of 328 sappers
2 airplanes
8 armored trains

Caucasus Army - Gen-Lt Baron Wrangel (also called the Cossack Army)

1st Kuban Corps
1st Kuban Cossack Division
4th Kuban Cossack Division (temporarily in the 4th Kuban Corps)
Attached to the Corps:
Composite Grenadier Division
3rd Kuban Cossack Infantry Brigade
2nd Kuban Cossack Infantry Brigade

2nd Kuban Corps
2nd Kuban Cossack Division
3rd Kuban Cossack Division
Attached to the Corps:
Composite Gorsk (Horse) Division (temporarily)

4th Horse Corps
1st Horse Division
Composite Gorsk (Horse) Division (temporarily attached to the 2nd Kuban Corps)
Kabardino (Horse) Division
Attached to the Corps:
4th Kuban Cossack Division (temporarily)
Attached to the Army:
Astrakhan Cossack Division
1st Independent Kuban Cossack Brigade
Naval Special Purpose (Spetsnaz) Detachment

1st Kuban Corps - Gen-Lt Pokrovskiy (temporarily was Gen-Lt Pisarev)

1st Kuban Cossack Division - Gen-Maj Kryzhnovskiy (temporarily - all the division without the 2nd Black Sea (Cossack) Regiment which was in the 2nd Corps)
2nd Line Cossack Regiment - 244 sabers, 6 machineguns
2nd Black Sea Cossack Regiment - 202 sabers, 6 machineguns
2nd Composite Kuban Cossack Regiment - 98 sabers, 7 machineguns
3rd Composite Kuban Cossack Regiment - 40 sabers, 1 machinegun
Guard Division - in Ekaterinburg
Rifle Regiment - 741 rifles, 20 machineguns
1st Kuban (Cossack) Horse-Artillery Division:
1st Kuban Cossack Horse Battery - 4 light cannons
4th Kuban Cossack Horse Battery - being brought up to strength in Zhutovo
Total: 741 rifles, 20 machineguns, 584 sabers, 20 machineguns, 4 light cannons

Attached to the Corps:
Composite Grenadier Division - Gen-Maj Pisarev (Gen-Maj Chichinadze temporarily assumed Pisarev's duties)
Composite Regiment 1st Grenadier Division
Composite Regiment 2nd Grenadier Division
Composite Regiment 3rd Grenadier Division
Composite Regiment Caucasus Grenadier Division
Grenadier Artillery Brigade (4 Batteries)
Grenadier Engineer Company
Total:
1149 rifles, 27 machineguns, 178 sabers, 3 machineguns, 13 light cannons, 4 howitzers

3rd Kuban Cossack Infantry Brigade - Gen-Maj Khodkevich
(Col Tsyganok temporarily assumed the duties)
1st Kuban Cossack Infantry Battalion - being brought up to strength in Otradniy
3rd Kuban Cossack Infantry Battalion - 721 rifles, 12 machinegun
5th Kuban Cossack Infantry Battalion - 508 rifles, 12 machinegun
11th Kuban Cossack Infantry Battalion - being brought up to strength in Otradniy
1st Kuban Cossack Infantry Howitzer Battery - being brought up to strength in Tikhoretskaya
3rd Kuban Cossack Infantry Battery - 3 light cannons
Total: 1229 rifles, 24 machineguns, 3 light cannons

2nd Kuban Cossack Infantry Brigade - Col Zapol'skiy
2nd Kuban Cossack Infantry Battalion - 1108 rifles, 20 machineguns
4th Kuban Cossack Infantry Battalion - 605 rifles, 26 machineguns, 2 light cannons
8th Kuban Cossack Infantry Battalion - 765 rifles, 21 machineguns
9th Kuban Cossack Infantry Battalion - 821 rifles, 11 machineguns
2nd (Cossack Infantry) Artillery Division:
2nd Light Cossack Infantry Battery - 3 light cannons
2nd Howitzer Cossack Infantry Battery - 3 howitzers
Total: 3289 rifles, 78 machineguns, 5 light cannons, 3 howitzers
(Note: Total should be 3299 rifles, but the official documents show 3289)

1st Independent Heavy Artillery Division:
1st Battery - 3 heavy cannons
2nd Battery (1 platoon) - 2 heavy cannons
4th Howitzer Division, 2nd Artillery Brigade:
7th Howitzer Battery - 2 howitzers
8th Howitzer Battery - 4 howitzers

Total in the Corps:
6408 rifles, 149 machineguns
862 sabers, 23 machinegun
25 light cannons
13 howitzers
5 heavy cannons

2nd Kuban Corps - Gen-Lt Ulagay

2nd Kuban Cossack Division - Gen-Maj Mamonov (temporarily was Col Shlyakhov)
1st Kuban Cossack Regiment - 150 sabers, 6 machineguns
1st Labin Cossack Regiment - 97 sabers, 7 machineguns
2nd Kuban Cossack Regiment - 96 sabers, 4 machineguns
1st Poltava Cossack Regiment - 210 sabers, 12 machineguns
Rifle Regiment - 157 rifles
2nd Cuban Cossack Horse-Artillery Division:
3rd Kuban Cossack Horse Battery - 2 light cannons
7th Kuban Cossack Horse Battery - 2 light cannons
1st Kuban Cossack Horse Howitzer Battery - 3 howitzers
Total: 157 rifles, 553 sabers, 29 machineguns, 4 light cannons, 3 howitzers

3rd Kuban Cossack Division
1st Black Sea Cossack Regiment - 190 sabers, 12 machineguns
1st Taman Cossack Regiment - 120 sabers, 8 machineguns
1st Caucasus Cossack Regiment - 364 sabers, 10 machineguns
2nd Poltava Cossack Regiment - 281 sabers, 12 machineguns
Rifle Regiment - 309 rifles, 14 machineguns, 31 sabers
Kornilov Cossack Regiment - 334 sabers, 21 machineguns
3rd Kuban Cossack Horse Artillery Division:
5th Kuban Cossack Horse Battery - 4 light cannons
1st Kuban Cossack Horse-Mountain Battery - 4 light cannons
Total: 309 rifles, 14 machineguns, 1320 sabers, 63 machineguns, 8 light cannons

Attached to the Corps:
Composite Gorsk (Horse) Division - Col Greaves (temporarily was Col Kotiev)
Ingushetia Horse Brigade:
1st Ingushetia Horse Regiment - 80 sabers
2nd Ingushetia Horse Regiment - 61 sabers, 3 machineguns
Karachaev Horse Regiment - being brought up to strength in Nevinnomyssk
Dagestan Horse Brigade:
1st Dagestan Horse Regiment - 249 sabers, 4 machineguns
2nd Dagestan Horse Regiment - 53 sabers
Total: 443 sabers, 7 machineguns

Attached to the Division:
1st Dagestan Rifle Battalion of Imam Shamil' - 230 rifles, 4 machineguns
Total in the Division: 230 rifles, 4 machineguns, 443 sabers, 7 machineguns
1st Independent Engineer Squadron of the Kuban Cossack Forces - 1 Company, 166 Sappers

Total in the Corps:
845 rifles, 18 machineguns (Note: total should be 843, number shown is in the official document)
2517 sabers, 99 machineguns
14 light cannons
3 howitzers
1 company of 166 sappers

4th Horse Corps - Gen-Lt Toporkov (Temporarily was Col Murav'ev)

1st Horse Division - Gen-Maj Uspenskiy (Temporarily was Gen-Maj Pavlichenko)
1st Ekaterinodar Cossack Regiment - 120 sabers, 1 machinegun
1st Line Cossack Regiment - 90 sabers, 6 machineguns
1st Uman Cossack Regiment - 151 sabers, 2 machineguns
1st Zaporozhye Cossack Regiment - 58 sabers, 2 machineguns
Rifle Regiment - 519 rifles, 12 machineguns
1st Horse Artillery Division:
2nd Horse Battery - under repair at Station Belaya Glina
3rd Horse Battery - 2 light cannons
4th Horse Battery - 1 light cannon
1st Horse Howitzer Battery - 4 howitzers
Total:
519 rifles, 12 machineguns, 419 sabers, 11 machineguns, 3 light cannons, 4 howitzers

Kabardino Horse Division - Gen-Maj Bekovich-Cherkasskiy
1st Kabardino Horse Regiment - 140 sabers
2nd Kabardino Horse Regiment - 35 sabers
3rd Kabardino Horse Regiment - 62 sabers, 3 machineguns
4th Kabardino Horse Regiment - 40 sabers
5th Kabardino Horse Regiment - in the forces of North Caucasus
6th Kabardino Horse Regiment - in the forces of North Caucasus
2nd Horse Artillery Division:
1st Horse Battery - 2 light cannons
2nd Horse Howitzer Battery - 1 howitzer
5th Horse Battery - 1 light cannon
Total: 277 sabers, 3 machineguns, 3 light cannons, 1 howitzer

Attached to the Corps:
4th Kuban Cossack Division - Col Buryak (Temporarily Col Zemtsev) (Note: a handwritten note in red on the original document states that this unit was sent to the rear area of the Volunteer Army).
2nd Zaporozhye Cossack Regiment - 105 sabers, 4 machineguns
2nd Uman Cossack Regiment - 109 sabers, 4 machineguns
2nd Ekaterinodar Cossack Regiment - 73 sabers, 3 machineguns

2nd Caucasus Cossack Regiment - 64 sabers, 1 machinegun
Rifle Regiment - 703 rifles, 9 machineguns
4th Kuban Cossack Horse Artillery Division:
6th Kuban Cossack Horse Battery - 2 light cannons
9th Kuban Cossack Horse Battery - 2 light cannons
Total: 703 rifles, 9 machineguns, 351 sabers, 12 machineguns, 4 light cannons

Total in the Corps:
1222 rifles, 21 machineguns
1047 sabers, 26 machineguns
10 light cannons
5 howitzers

Units not attached to the Corps

Astrakhan Cossack Division - Gen(-Maj) Kolossovskiy
1st Astrakhan Cossack Regiment - 546 sabers, 8 machineguns
2nd Astrakhan Cossack Regiment - 151 sabers, 6 machineguns
3rd Astrakhan-Manych Regiment - 425 sabers, 12 machineguns
4th Astrakhan-Kalmykia-Manych Regiment - 377 sabers, 11 machineguns
1st Inorodchesk Horse Regiment - 97 sabers, 3 machineguns
4th Horse Artillery Division:
1st Astrakhan Cossack Battery - 4 light cannons
9th Horse Battery - 5 light cannons
Total: 1595 sabers, 40 machineguns, 9 light cannons

1st Independent Kuban Cossack Brigade - Gen-Maj Kosinov
3rd Caucasus Cossack Regiment
3rd Black Sea Cossack Regiment - defending the railroad
16th (Kuban) Cossack Infantry Battalion
Total: unknown

Life Hussar Pavlograd Regiment - 94 sabers

Razdan Independent Squadron - defending the railroad

Independent Kuban Battery - 4 light cannons

1st Armored Train Division
"Unified Russia"
"Forward for the Homeland" - under repairs
"General Alexeev" - under repairs
The adapted armored train "Steppe" (Note: this entry was made in red pen on the original document)

Don Armored Trains
**"Steppe" (Note: this entry is lined out)
"Cossack Zemlyanukhin"
"Ataman Platov"
"Ilya Muromets"

2nd Armored Train Division
1st, 2nd, and 3rd Armored Detachments - under repairs

1st Tank Division
1st Tank Detachment
4th Tank Detachment - sent to Taganrog (Note: this is a major refit/repair facility for armor)

2nd Tank Division
6th Tank Detachment - sent to Tsaritsyn

Air Detachments
1st Kuban Cossacks - 3 airplanes
English 17-A - 5 airplanes
English 17 B - 4 airplanes
English 17 O - 3 airplanes

1st Railroad Battalion of the Volunteer Army

1st Caucasus Radio-Telegraph Division

1st Caucasus Independent Engineer Company - 1 company of 117 sappers

Naval Special Purpose (Spetsnaz) Detachment - Captain 1st Rank Zaev
Naval Independent Battalion - 165 rifles, 8 machineguns, 2 small caliber cannons

6th Division of River Cutters
cutters:
MK3, MK4, Mk7
MK5, SK1, SK2, MK10 - under repairs

7th Division of River Cutters
Armored Cutters:
"*Cossack*"
"*Cherkass*"
"*Cossack Infantryman*"
"*Line Infantryman*" - under repairs
"*Black Sea-man*"
"*Ataman Chipega*"
"*Anton Golovatiy*"

1st Division of Gunboats

Division of All Purpose Naval Heavy Artillery
1st Battery - under repairs
2nd Battery - 3 heavy guns

2nd Division of Naval Heavy Artillery
3rd Battery - 2 heavy guns

4th Division of Naval Heavy Artillery
7th Battery - 2 cannons
8th Battery - 1 cannon

6th Division of Naval Heavy Artillery
12th Battery - 2 cannons

Independent Howitzer Platoon - 2 howitzers

Total in the Cossack Army:
8640 rifles, 196 machineguns
6115 sabers, 188 machineguns
62 light cannons
21 howitzers
2 small caliber cannons
3 companies of 324 sappers
15 airplanes
7 armored trains

Armed Forces South Russia: General Anton Deniken. (98,000) July-Oct/November 1919

- 1st Tank detachment, 1st Division (three machines) – in minor repair at Taganrog
- 9th tank detachment (4 tanks) – forming
- 11th tank detachment (4 tanks) - forming.
- At the "English Tank School" at Taganrog - 11 tanks
- At the Baltic Oil Works at Taganrog - 16 tanks (in major repair)
- At Novorossisyk unloading - 11 tanks.
- 1st Armored Car Battalion (20 Lanchesters/Putilov/Garfords)
- 2nd Armored Car Battalion (20 same) both a/c BN were split up amongst the armies
- Don airpark in Ekaterinodar. Major repair and assembly depot.
- Navy: Cruiser Kornilov, 5 destroyers, 4 submarines and 20 gunboats. The Cruiser and some gunboats were operational. The rest were damaged for past battles or lacking fuel.

Volunteer Army (40,000 down to 24,500) General Mai-Maivsky. Western sector of the South Front. Against the 14th and 13th Red Armies.
- 1st Volunteer Air Division (supported the 1st Corps)
- 1st General Alekseev Volunteer A/O (6 DH.9, 6 mixed)
- 6th Vol. Fighter A/O (8 Sopwith Camels, 4 Nieuports)
- 8th tank detachment (four tanks) - to Volunteer Army
- 5th tank detachment (three tanks) - to Volunteer Army
- Several armored trains

1st Army Corps: General Kutepov. Near Orel against the ## Red Army
- 2nd Volunteer A/O (6 DH.9, 6 mixed)
- 2nd Tank detachment, 1st Division (3 MkV)
- Kornilov Division
- Drozdovsky Division
- Markov Division
- Composite Division (Alekseev Brigade, Samursky Regt.)
- Corps artillery (2 lt. batteries)

2nd Army Corps: General Slushov. South Caucasus and Crimea against rebels and Greens
- 7th Volunteer A/O (reforming w/ DH.9a in the Crimea after it was abandoned in the April 1919 rout from Odessa)
- 13th Division
- 34th Division

3rd Army Corps. General Shilling.
- 2 divisions

5th Cavalry Corps: General Yuzefovitch. Near Chernigov.
- 3rd Volunteer A/O (8 RE.8, arrived in Oct. from training)
- 4th tank detachment (4 MkA)
- 1st Cavalry Division
- 1st General Alekseev Cavalry Regiment
- 12th Akhtirsky Hussars Regt.
- 15th Tartars Lancers
- Cheringovski Hussars Demi-regiment
- Pskov Life-Dragoons Squadron
- 2nd Cavalry Division

3rd Kuban Cavalry Corps: General Shukov.
- 2 Kuban Cossack Divisions

Independent Kiev Army Group (9,000)
General Bredov. Near Kiev. Against the 12th Red Army
- few armored trains

- 4th, 9th Volunteer A/O (8 RE.8, 4 mixed, each) returned from the British Training Center on the RE.8 in October
- 3rd Tank detachment, 1st Division (4 tanks)
- 2nd Cavalry Division (w/ 2nd General Drozdovsky Horse Regiment)
- 15th Infantry Division

The Army of the Don (40,000)

General Sidorin, Six infantry and nine cavalry divisions
Organized into four corps. Divisions were under strength. Near the center of the South Front. Against the 8th and 9th Red Army.

- Don Aviation Division
- 1st Don A/O (12 mixed)
- 3rd Don Fighter A/O (8 camels, 4 Nieuports)
- 12 or so armored trains

1st Don Cossack Infantry Corps

- 2nd Aviation A/O (12 mixed)
- 3 infantry divisions

  2nd Don Cossack Corps
- 4th aviation A/O (12 mixed, late Oct. pulled to train on RE.8)
- 3 cavalry and 1 infantry divisions

  3rd Don Cossack Corps
- 5th aviation A/O (10 mixed, late Oct. pulled to train on RE.8)
- 3 cavalry divisions

4th Don Cossack Corps (Mammotov)

- 6th aviation A/O (10 mixed, late Oct. pulled to train on RE.8)
- 7th tank detachment (four MkV tanks)
- 3 cavalry divisions and 1 infantry divisions

The Army of Caucasus (14,500)

General Baron Wrangel. Near Tsaritsyn.
Against the 10th and 11th Red Armies

- 6th tank detachment (four tanks) - to Caucasian Army (Mk-A?)
- 10th tank detachment (four tanks) - directed to Tsaritsyn
- perhaps 6 armored trains
- 6th Mobile Battalion of Naval Heavy Artillery (120mm self-propelled tractors)
- 6th and 7th Division as reinforcements, formerly interned in Romania
- 47th Squadron RAF (12 DH.9, 6 camel, disbanded Oct.)
- 1st Kuban Air Division
- 1st Kuban fighter A/O (8 nieuports)
- 2nd Kuban A/O (8 mixed)

1st Kuban Horse Corps: General Pokrovsky

2nd Kuban Horse Corps (Oct. transferred to the Don then Vol. Army)
- 3rd Kuban Cossack Division (w/ General Kornilov Kuban Cossack Regt.)

4th Kuban Horse Corps

Trans-Volga Detachment
- 1st Caucasian Rifle Division (-).
- 3rd Astrakhan Cossack Regiment

Independent Lower Volga Detachment (4,000) (Gen. Erdeli)
- 221st Squadron RAF (12 DH.9, 6 DH.9a, disbanded Aug.)
- 226th RNAS short-184 seaplanes
- 5th Volunteer A/O (6 DH.9, 6 mixed)
- Astrakhan Cossack Division
- 3rd Kuban Cossack Division
- 5th Caucasian Rifle Regiment

The Crimea-Azov Army (4,000)
- 1 infantry division
- 7th Volunteer A/O (reforming w/ DH.9a in the Crimea after it and the 8th A/O were abandoned in the Apr. 1919 rout from Odessa).
- Crimea Airpark. Storage of old and assembly of new planes for a training school in Simerfol.

> Now, in order to gloss over the actual results, a fresh hypothesis has been advanced: if the principal forces had not been concentrated in the Tsaritsyn-Novocherkassk direction, Denikin would be in Saratov, and the Syzran bridge would have been blown up. [The special importance of the railway bridge over the Volga at Syzran was that this was the only rail link between Central Russia, on the one hand, and Siberia and Turkestan, on the other.] All these imagined terrors are meant to serve as our compensation for the real danger that threatens Orel and Tula, after our loss of Kursk. And the point is overlooked that it would have been as difficult for the Don Cossacks to get to Saratov as it is now for our forces to get to Novocherkassk."

A Critical Point in Time
September and October were critical months for both sides. Denikin knew his time for success shortened with every day. His forces were driving deeper into the heart of Russia, his rear areas were a mess and soaked away frontline troops, his ability to fund his men being was drained, and the last British donation of war material would arrive soon. His troop morale remained in a euphoric state flushed with recent victories. But Denikin's Don army had suffered several reverses from Red attacks since July. Wrangel barely could hold onto Tsaritsyn.

His front increased with the victories to 1400 km wide. For the Soviets, they were desperate in defeating this threat. Luckily for them, all the other White attempts by now had failed, allowing the shifting of troops to oppose Denikin. The infamous Soviet propaganda machine was created as well as guerilla warfare deep in the enemy's rear. To Lenin and Trotsky, they had to buy time. That was their greatest ally.

After the desperate battle to hold onto Kharkov in August, the Volunteer army remained quiet until mid- September. The army's 1st Corps then suddenly attacked catching the Soviet 13th and 14th armies off guard. Confusion reigned in on the Soviet and some 12 regiments defending the Kursk area broke and fled. On September 20th, Kursk fell to 1st Corps. It was a quick 50-60 mile advance. That was not all, on the 30th, the Soviets were again caught off balance when the Don Army's Shkuro Cavalry Corps and the 3rd Kuban Corps broke through the 8th army lines 30 miles south of Voronezh and quickly seized the town. Also, the 5th Cavalry Corps suddenly broke through the 14th Army lines west of Kursk and seized Bahmach and Konotop by October 6th, gaining another 80 miles. It appeared that the Soviet armies were falling apart. Red Panic was setting in as the 1st Corps was within 44 miles of Orel and 75 miles south of Bryansk.

The positions occupied at this time by the Volunteer army was as follows: 10 miles south of Kaloarchangelsk (44 miles SE of Orel then south of Dmitriev (located on the rail north of Lgov and 72miles SW of Orel, Glukov, Krolovets (23miles west of Glukhov , Makoshino (on the rail 30 miles NW of Bakhmach) and Svensk (25 miles west of Dmitriev).

The Reds occupied Kromy(25 miles SW of Orel), Kurachino (30 miles SE of Orel). West of Kiev, Denikin's forces advanced to the Irpen River (40 miles SW of Kiev) and west of Fastov (38 miles SW of Kiev). His forces were also at Slobedzkya, west of Balta.

Concern was growing in Denikin regarding Makhno whose bandits totaling 700 had taken Nikopol and was stirring up the locals. To deter this, Denikin created two groups, one at Kherson and called the Novorossisk district with 18,000 men, and the other, the Kiev group with 12,000 men. However, the Reds had forced the Don Army back behind the Don river from junction of the Ilovlya and Don Rivers to Lisky. Wrangel's attack toward Cheni Yar, 82 miles southeast of Tsaritsyn had also failed.

By October, Denikin's deployments covered 1130 km and were as follows:

Opposite Astrakhan:	The North Causcasus Grp with 4000 men
Tsaritsyn area:	Wrangel's Causcasus Army with 14,500 men.
From the Ilovl and Don river confluence to Zadonsk (85 km from Voronezh):	The Don Army with 50,000 (by far, the least reliable)
Between Voronezh and Chernigov:	the Volunteer army of 20,500 men. It was by far the best equipped and with tanks.
From Kiev and along the Desna River to Chernigov:	another 9,000 men.

TheWhite Russian Southern Armies by now had 72 combat aircraft, not including the 47th British SQD, Sevastopol Flying School and English Training Center in Ekaterindar. The Volunteers had their 1st Corps and the Don's one of their Corps. The 1st Corps had their 1st air detachment (3 aircraft) and their 6th Fighter det. (5). The Don's Corps had its combat effective detachment with 6-8 planes and their Armies 3rd Fighter detachment (6) for the total of 14 combat effective planes in 4 detachments. Denikin strengthen this sector with A and B flights of "A Group" from the Kuban Air-Divizion and Z Flight (put together by the English Training School, (mostly pilots of the 221st).

The Whites took Orel with air support from the 6th air-detachment, which distinguished themselves. Five pilots: Staff-Captain Botsyllo, Lieutenants Torenko and Tikhomirov, Junior Lieutenants Zarin and Pishvanov, did whatever was necessary to help the Volunteer Army. The Commander of the 1st Volunteer Corps, Lieutenant-General Kutepov said the following:

> "Fliers of the 6th detachment led by the temporarily command of Lieutenant Torenko, in operation at the time of the taking of Orel accomplished many flights. In the last 2 days, precedent to Orel's fall, these fliers, not concerned with bad weather and distance, tirelessly flew over Orel and the environs. These planes remained in the air 29 to 40 minutes. The enemies' armored trains, special trains and troops were spattered by bombs and thousands of rounds of bullets and poured into the ranks of shaking Reds.... Cordially I thank the valorous commander of the 6th A/O and all its composition for excellent and selfless service."

When used correctly, the White combined arms action proved victorious.

When Orel (100 miles north of Kursk) fell on October 13th, the spearhead force deployed was as follows:

Kornilov division/1st Corps was in and north of Orel.
The Markov division /1st Corps was at Elets
The Drozdovsky division/1st Corps was near Bryansk.

At the Don and Volunteer Army's boundary (right of 1st Corps) was Mamantov and Shkuro's Cavalry units

To the left of 1st Corps was the 5th Cavalry Corps which was scattered out along the Seim River.

Further to the left was General Bredov's force holding on at Kiev.

Further to the west, along the Desna River between Kiev and Chernigov were 9000 men under Gen. Dragomirov.

Denikin had 98,000 men (in all the forces under him) 2230 MG, 540 artillery guns, 20 tanks, 60 armor cars, two airplane squadrons. The men were tired, but with high morale especially in the 1st Corps. The morale in the cavalry units was fair to poor. With the capture of Orel, Moscow was within 200 miles!

The Soviet forces (in mid Sept.) opposite the Volunteer Army were comprised of the following:

8th Army

12th, 15th and 16th Rifle divisions

16th division: 1st brigade (700), 2nd Brigade(600), 3rd Brigade(1500)
The 2nd and 4th Cavalry regiments (1000 total)
Total: 3100 men, 1000 cav. 15 3" guns, 5 howitzer, 3 armor car

15th division: 1st brig.(500), 2nd and 3rd brig (400 ea.)
Total: 1300 men, 26 3" guns, 4 howitzer, 2 arm.car.
12th division: 1st brig(500), 2nd brig: 103 + 105 regiments
3rd brig(1000), 2 cav. Regs (300)
Total: 1500, 300 cav., 15 3" guns, 6 howitzer, 1 armor train.

Total 8th Army amount: 4100-5900 men, 1300 cavalry, 56 3" guns, 15 howitzer, 6 armor cars.

13th Army

42nd division, 3rd division, 9th division, Samursky brigade, Cavalry brigade.
42nd Division: 1st brig(1500), 2nd brig(1200), 2nd Cavalry bn (200)
Total: 2700 men, 200 cavalry, 8 3" guns, 4 howitzer
Samursky Brigade (1200) 1st,2nd 3rd regs.
3rd Division: 3rd brigade: 25th, 26th,27th regs (1200), 1st Cav.reg (300)
Total: 1200 men, 300 cav, 5 3" guns, 1 howitzer

Cavalry Brigade (1st, 3rd reg) (800)

9th Division: 1st Brig (700), 2nd brig (76,77,78 reg)(750), 3rd brig(600), 9th Cav.reg (300)
Total: 2100 men, 300 cav, 12 3" guns, 3 armor trains.

Dvina Brigade (1500)(604,606,605 reg) 4 armor cars.
Near Kursk: 1000 men, 100 cav, 5 3" guns.

7th division: 1st brig (55,56,57 regs)(900), 2nd brig (58,59,60 reg)(900), 3rd brig (61,62,63 regs)(500)
Total: 2000 men, 10 3 "guns.

1st brigade/5th division (1000)
Attached army units:
41st division: 1st brig (361,362,364 reg)(900) 8 guns
2nd brig (364,365,366 reg) (1200) 5 guns.
3rd brig (367,368,369 reg) (1200)
4th brig (6th,4th,2nd reg) (900) 10 guns
Total: 4200 men, 23 guns, 3 armor trains, 2 armor car.
1st Kuvanskia Cav Brig (300)
Total for Army: 14,900 men, 1900 cav, 69 guns, 6 armor trains, 8 armor cars.

14th Army

46th Division: 1st Brig (406,407,408 reg) (1000)
2nd Brig (409,410,411 reg) (600)
3rd Brig(1st,5th, 9th reg) (900)
Cavalry reg (300)
Total: 2500 men, 300 cavalry, 15 guns, 2 armor trains

51st, 31st regs/35th xx

57th Division: 1st Brigade(505,506,507 regs)(1000)
2nd Brigade(508,509,510 regs)
3rd Brigade(511,512,513) (1500)
Cavalry (300)

Total: 2500 men, 200 cav. 12 guns and 2 arm.trains

Total for Army: 4-5000 men, 500 cavalry, 27 guns, 4 arm.trains

12th Army

Kiev Brigade (4000, 4 guns)
2nd brigade (1250)
Soviet Brigade (1250, 12 guns)
1st and 3rd regs(1500)
Cavalry (200)
8 guns

60th Division: 1st brigade (538,539,540 reg) (1500)
1st Ind. Brigade(1000)
No.6 and 13 armor trains

6th Division (1800, 12 guns)

4th Division: 1st Brigade (2000, 8 guns)

Parts of 45th and 47th divisions

58th division: 1st Brigade (514,515,516) (2000)
2nd brigade (517,518,519 reg)(2500)
3rd brigade(520,521,522) (2000, 12 guns)

7th brigade (2000)
22nd Reg (500)
Cavalry (1000)

Other Independent units:

1st Tavosky reg, 2nd and 5th Ekaterinodar reg, 9th,10th,11th regs. 4th Novotcherkask MG reg.

Total 5000 men, 500 MG, 20 gun

Cavalry:

1st Kuban reg, 3rd Don reg, 6th Kursk reg,4th, 7th regs: Total 1500.

Total for Army: 22,300 men, 3700 Cav. 94 guns, 6 armor car,4 arm.trains

Garrisons:	Tula	3000 men
	Orel	20,000 men

Units arriving in Kursk area:	7th and 9th divisions, part of 3rd division.
Kiev area:	45th,47th divisions

10th Army

28th Division (3000), 245th reg, 28th Cav, 32 Division, 22 regiment
Total: 9000 men, 6700 cavalry, 80 guns

11th Army

301 brig, 305th brig, 34th brig, 304 brig, 7th Cav (3000, 640 Cav. 7 gun)

By October, the Red Southern Front (12th, 13th,14th, 8th armies) which faced the Volunteer and Don Armies had 104,000 men, 14,848 cavalry, 2765 MG and 607 artillery. The Southeastern Front (9th,10th 11th armies) had 51,579 men, 6367 cavalry, 1651 MG, 285 artillery.

Aircraft totals to South Russia were 130 RE.8, 160 DH.9 or 9a, 50 Camels and 15 SE.5a for use by the RAF and Russians. England deployed three squadrons to support the AFSR in combat operations. They drew their equipment from the stocks sent. The 221st SQD deployed in the Astrakhan region until disbanded August when their planes were handed over. The 226th SQD deployed with seaplanes to the Astrakhan region until pulled out in August. The 47th SQD deployed one DH.9 flight in July and another plus the Camel flight in September to the Tsaritsyn region. By October when all combat units were to be pulled from Russia they stayed on as "A" Group of the RAF mission, or the "Kuban Group," or Volunteer detachments 11, 12, and 13.

As Denikin's two main armies (the Volunteer and Don) advanced past Kursk to Orel, the Reds began a systematic transfer of units from more quiet fronts all destined to stop Denikin.

From the Baltic, the 10th division was ordered. The Siberian 21st, 20th, 25th, and 27th divisions were ordered. The 1st,2nd,8th Lettish division, 1st Esthosian Division, 44th, 47th, 52nd,53rd,55th divisions, 9th and 11th cavalry divisions. Most of these transfers were from the Polish front. These totalled 40,000 men. 3000 cavalry and 300 guns.

From the east came 48th division to Saratov, two brigades of 21st division and the 4th,24th and 54th divisions. In September, some 125,000 men had been diverted to oppose Denikin's armies. By the end of October, another 70,000 had been diverted. Most of the Siberian divisions now faced the Don Army. Most of the others, opposed the Volunteers.

From each of the armies that faced Denikin, the Soviet created a new army, the 17th, by taking one division from the armies opposite Denikin. This was held back and amounted to 30,000 men.

While these are impressive amounts, one must remember the key element for either side, morale. For the Reds, their most reliable troops were those of the communist party, the Letts and Siberians. Most of the others were formed from the peasant class where morale flickered like a candle and sometimes extinguished in battle.

Of course, Denikin, was in the same boat. His only reliable force was the 20, 000 men comprising the Volunteer Army, some Kuban units, and some Cossacks. But Denikin had to fight two wars: one against the Reds along the front and the other in his rear area in the Ukraine where the large groups under Pelitura and Makhano rampaged. The problem had become so acute, Denikin was forced to send a whole Corps to battle and chase Makhano.

In October, the Red morale was deteriorating to the point that brutal discipline was being invoked. The peasant Red soldier was well fed until they were sent to the front. The brutal methods of discipline often backfired forcing large scale defections. For instance, during Mamantov's raid, a whole cavalry division of 13,000 men defected with hardly any shots.

During this time, the Soviet Political Comminsaars came into being. Each unit down to company had a political commissar, who, besides being a spy on the unit, gave lectures twice a week on politics and propaganda to heighten morale.

In Gen. Holman's October report to the War Cabinet, he provided a forecast of the future in wishful thinking:

> "The Armed Forces of South Russia will win because they are fighting for a cause which is just, they have surviving officers of the old Imperial Army to lead the troops, they are greatly assisted by the war material by Great Britain."

As to why the Soviets will lose:

> "Their theories contain within themselves the germs of their own destruction, their armies are held together by lies and brutality, they are destructive not constructive."

Yet, even Holman sensed the key issues that would decide this war, despite his lofty observances:

> "Factors bearing on the final determination are:
> The morale, the strength of the opposing forces, the economic situation for each side."

From October 1st to 19th, the morale was very good in the Volunteer Army, fair in all other armies under Denikin. From the 19th onward, the morale of Denikins men slowly and then rapidly collapsed as the Reds attacked and won. As far as numbers go, it is clear it was in the Red favor, even if the men were unreliable, the numbers prevailed. The only reliable army Denikin had was his Volunteers. The Volunteers were Denikin's elite troops, retreating only when necessary or ordered. The Don army was average and retreated at will or when ordered.

The economics of Denikin continuing to pay his troops was also nearing the end. Denikin knew all of these critical elements were ripening quickly and he knew he could only win by taking Moscow ASAP. But the first two weeks of October continued to be "heady" times for Denikin's men and for the British government who provided all his support.

From The Times (London), leading article, October 14th:

> "Except by our fault or through some reversal of military fortune which no one can forecast, the Bolshevist Government is nearing its end, and it is quite conceivable that a continuance of the successes of Denikin may bring about in the next few weeks a sudden collapse."

The Daily Telegraph on the 16th, headlined SOVIET COLLAPSING:

> "Alarm at the irresistible advance of the Volunteers is spreading far and wide in Moscow.... Denikin's advance since May has been practically uninterrupted. He has pushed over 300 miles along the direct line to Moscow.....his armies are five times his former strength... at present, there seems no probability that the Bolsheviks will check this advance"

Meanwhile, the Reds had formulated a simple plan to rout the White forces. The plan called for severing the Volunteer army from the Don army. The 14th Army would attack from the northwest, left of the 1st Corps of the Volunteer army. Budenny's cavalry group consisting of four cavalry divisions, one armor car company, two armor trains (totaling 12,000 men, 48 guns, 300 MG, 1600 wagons) would attack from the east to Voronezh then to Kastonia (a rail station between Kursk and Voronezh) to prevent the Volunteer army retreating.

Denikin knew of the Red dispositions and reinforced the Don Army with Shkuro's cavalry. His plan was to sustain the blows, regroup and attack quickly. The reserves he counted on, however, would never arrive as they had been diverted to secure the rear. Areas. The units that did arrive were new and were not combined with veteran units, and under battle, they fell apart quickly.

Showdown at the Orel Corral

After seizing Kursk on September 20th, the Soviet 13th and 14th armies of the Southern front retreated. On the 29th, the 14th Don Cavalry brigade and the 3rd infantry brigade from the Don 1st Corps crossed the Don River and attacked the 417th reg/32nd division forcing it to retreat. According to the Soviet party directives, the transfer of the Latvian rifle division, two other brigades and a cavalry brigade were detached from the West. This group was to form the attack force concentrating at Navel and Dimitrovsk. Until their expected arrival on October 15th, these two armies conducted delaying actions as the Volunteer 1st Corps and 5th Cavalry Corps advanced toward Orel. Once these Red units arrived, it would augment the two main armies opposing the Denikin spearhead. Combined, they had 62,000 men, 1119 MG, 278 guns. The Volunteer army contained 22,300 men, 373 MG, 72 guns, 14 armor trains and 9 MkV and Whippet tanks.

By the 2nd of October, the 10th Army had tossed in their reserves, the 415th and 416th regiments to stabilize the area. This failed and the Don army units used the morning fog as cover and provided accurate artillery fire as troops ferried across the river.

By October 3rd, Denikin's spearhead was threatening the area where the reserves were to accumulate. On the Don Front, the 4th Don Cavalry Corps was battling the Soviet 13th and 16th divisions of 8th Army. The 4th Corps pushed the Soviets back seizing Voronezh. Two days later, a fierce battle developed when the 14th Army attacked the 5th cavalry and 1st Corps. In this battle, the 1st brigade/44th division, 46th division and 57th divisions fought a tenacious defense before falling back. Another soviet group containing the 3rd division, 4th brigade/41st division, 14th and 7th divisions attacked the 3rd division of the Volunteer 1st Corps. Meanwhile, in the Don area, 10th army received the 2nd brigade/20th division and 32nd division but these forces were unable to advance any further. The Red 56th division arrived and attacked the 3rd Don Corps. The 14th division, which was to have attacked also, never received the order to do so. By this time, the 2nd Don Corps had begun to arrive further reinforcing the 3rd Don Corps. The 56th divisions' attack was in vain.

In the 11th Army sector, the Soviets attacked with the 7th division, 449th reg/50th division, 37th and 38th regiments on Oct. 4th. The initial attacked easily overwhelmed the weak units. Wrangel, was well south of Tsaritsyn. On the 5th, the Wrangel counterattacked using the 1st Astrakhan reg., 5th Caucasian reg. and 3rd Kuban cavalry division. The attack was unique, as for the first time, the artillery fired a few gas shells into the Red lines. The defending 38th and 37th regiments continued to resist until compelled to fall back to their starting positions. It was the only time gas was used in minute quantities.

On the 6th, the 13th,16th divisions and 3rd brigade of 8th army conducted another attack on the 4th Don Cavalry Corps. The 4th Cavalry corps continued to repel and gain forcing the Soviets to toss part of the 21st division into the fray retaking some ground to the right of 8th Army. The battle continued and on the 7th, the 14th Army was growing tired and sluggish in their defenses and attacks. Their units had become spread out too far to hold the front. The communications with the 13th army were extremely bad, neither army commander had clear idea of what the other was doing or planning to do, and all coordination

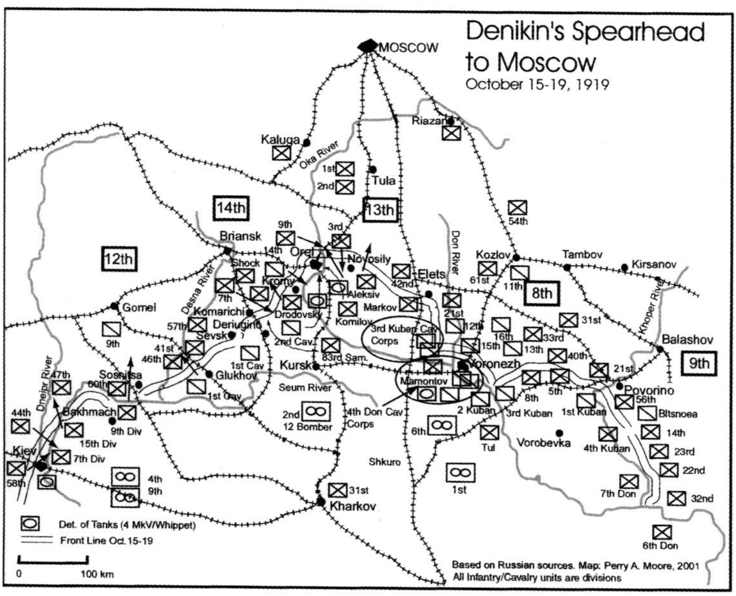

was lost in the planned united defense. The 9th and 55th divisions of the 13th Army attacked and seized a series of villages, but the Volunteers counterattack using tanks and armor cars. Unlike in previous times, the Reds did not run at the sight of the tanks approaching. For the next three days, these villages exchanged hands until finally the Soviets retreated. The tanks had turned the tide.

The 8th Army went over to an active defense with the 12th,15th,33rd and 40th divisions. The 13th and 16th divisions were in reserve near Top.

On the 8th, the 57th division attempted to counterattack, but this hit the stout resistance from the 3rd division of 1st Corps and it had failed by the 9th. The 57th then fell back towards the north and northwest. Additional confusion on the Soviet side continued that day as the 41st division was ordered to advance in the same direction that the 7th division was retreating in. These two units mingled and negated the attack of 41st division. The 13th Army failed to execute the issued order of concentrating their 9th and 55th divisions in a combined effort on the spearhead and instead, conducted a strung out frontal attack. The 42nd division was never committed and held in reserve as a shock unit. Since the 13th Army had failed to attack the Denikin spearhead the army was forced to fall back.

By the 9th, the front line boundary was as follows: Mikhailovsky-Sevsk-Dmitrowsk,Eropkino-Livny and Petrovskoye. The Commander in Chief, Kamenev, ordered Egorov, the Commander of the Southern Front and members of the Revolutionary Committee (a young Staling was among them) to attack without waiting for the reinforcements. The attack originated from the Kromy-Ponyri area and again directed at the 1st Corps of the Volunteers (now composed of the Kornilov division, Drozdovsky division, Composite division containing the Markov and Alekseev infantry brigades) to retake the Sevsk-Dmitriev-Fatezh-Livny boundary. Once this occurred, it was hoped to advance back to Kursk.

The Red attack group (9th, 55th and Composite divisions) contained 9700 men under Martusevitch and subordinated to 13th Army. This attack began in earnest on the 11th from the Turischevo area and directed southeast to cut the Kursk-Orel railway in the Ponyri area.

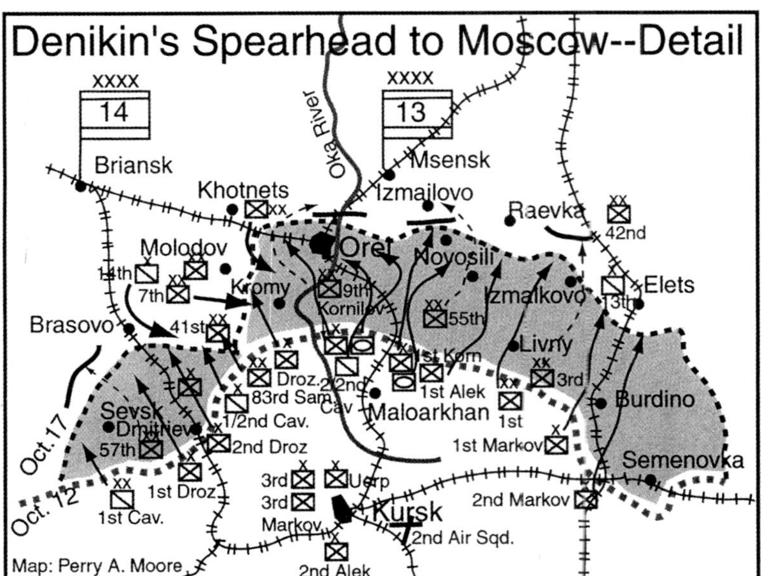

To attack the Kornilov division, another group consisting of the 3rd, 42nd divisions and 13th Cavalry brigade was to attack the Composite division at Livny. The 41st division was directed to take Mikhailovsky, while the 7th, 41st, 57th divisions, 11th and 14th Cavalry brigades would attack the Drozdov division at Dmitrovsk.

The Soviet plan was continually disrupted by rapid advances of the 1st Corps of the Volunteer army. The Reds had problems gathering their attack groups. It was during this time, when the 1st Corps forced the Red 9th, 55th, and Composite divisions to retreat and succeeded in taking Kromy on the 10th. The 1st Corps continued and on the 13th, Orel fell! The forces under 14th army never attacked and were forced to retreat over the Nerusa River. Once Orel fell, the Reds managed to counterattack making very small gains and by the 15th had retaken Kromy.

The resistance of the 1st and 2nd regiments/3rd division/1stCorps and parts of the 5th Cav.Corps repulsed all of the Red attacks. The 55th division attack hit a steel wall of fire and then retreated away from the scene. The battles were so costly that 13th Army (except for the 42nd division) had no attack capabilities remaining. Its staff had moved the headquarters, which resulted in losing communications with the other attacking groups. It was the retreat of the 55th division, and then 9th division that left Orel only defended by a small garrison on the 13th. The Red 3rd division still resisted along parts of the railway line.

An actual Troop disposition report dated October 9, 1919, at 1400 has the precise deployments of the 1st Army Corps (Volunteer Army) as follows:

The First Infantry Division

The 2nd Markovsky regiment and units of Chernnmorrsky (Black Sea) cavalry regiment are on the Lipovka- Galichya-Ivanaly-Kushkary-Golubovka front. The 1st Markovsky regiment is deployed Hmelevoe-Fedorovka-Ponomaryovka front.

The 1st Kornilov regiment at Zolotaryova front. The 3rd Kornilov regiment at Mikhailovka-Ljubanova. The 2nd Kornilov regiment and units of the Black Sea Cavalry at Dubovko-Golohvastova-Homuty-Ryshkova. The 3rd Markovsky regiment at Zakromokaya-Zmievka.

The Third Infantry Division

The Samursky regiment is on the Dubinka-Beloga-Popovka front. The 2nd Drozdov regiment at Brooding- Ljubenskaya to the south of Pogreby. No other information.

The Fifth Cavalry Corps

HQ at Belopolye. No information on the 1st or 2nd Cavalry divisions. The 3rd Cavalry division is crossing the Desna River and 2nd regiment at Gluhov. At Poltava area, a regiment of 31st division and a regiment 12 Cavalry division. Deployments of the General Revinsh Group are as follows:

> At Mariupol, the 6th reserve battalion, 3rd Reserve battalion, one artillery battery, 4th Chechen regiment, 3rd Ulan cavalry regiment of 9th Cavalry division.
> At Rozovka station, 1st Don engineer battalion, 1st Reserve battalion, 3rd Chechen Cavalry regiment, the armor train"Soldier."

The battles continued to rage just north, west and east of Orel. On the 14th, the 1st Army Corps of the Volunteer Army had its 1st Infantry division in the following disposition:

The 1st,2nd,3rd Markov regiments and Chernnmorrsky division a few kilometers from Elets some 100 km east of Orel. The 1st,2nd,3rd of the Alekseev and Partisan regiments holding onto Novosny, 60 km, east of Orel and just north or Orel. Its 3rd Infantry division (1st,2nd,3rd Drovsky regiments) was situated just west of Kromy and Sevsk. The 1st Cavalry division was further west at Lokov and spread out over 100 km. The 2nd Cavalry division was supporting the 3rd Infantry division.

The Soviet deployments had the 42nd division and 13th Cavalry brigade holding Elets opposite the Markov regiments. The 3rd division was battling the Alekseev regiments, the 9th cavalry division, 2nd brigade attacked Orel from the north. The Estonian division (1400 men) struck west. The 14th Cavalry brigade, 41st division,47th division was striking the 3rd Infantry division. The 3rd and 42nd divisions, 13th brigade struck for Livny.

The serious blow that halted any further advance of the 1st Corps towards Tula was the Soviet capture of Kromy, about 50km south Orel. This threatened the rear of the Corps and less than 40km to the only railway station at Kursk. This forced the Corps to change from it's original plan to one of encircling the Soviet units that had seized Kromy diverting the 3rd division and the Kornilov regiments. Forward movement for Denikin now stopped.

The Soviet 3rd Brigade/57th division and 365 reg/41st division were almost the victims of the encirclement at Sevsk. While the battle at Orel continued, the Red Cavalry Corps led by Budenny struck at Orlovka and bitter fighting between them and the White Shkuro Cavalry Corps lasted four hours. The Whites fell back leaving many dead horses and 100 dead men. The 8th Army then advanced with the 15th and 33rd divisions, which battled the 2nd Don Cavalry division, Tula regiment and 2nd Don Infantry brigade of 3rd Don Corps on the east bank of the Don river. It was not until the Reds tossed in their 16th division that the Don units retreated southwest to Sobakino.

Because the 8th Army intelligence did not know the whereabouts of the famed Mamantov Cavalry Corps, the army halted. The fierce battles waged all day on the 15th, mostly in the Orel area. These battles made few gains as villages exchanged hands numerous times. Despite the flank attack by the Soviets, the 1st Corps continued to attack and took Novosky in which the Red 56th division was able to halt. Between the 16th and 18th, Denikin's Kiev army attacked from the Chernigov area with infantry and cavalry forcing the Red 1st brigade/44th division to retreat. Parts of the Red 58th division was also compelled to retreat.

On the 16th, the Soviet High Command unfolded it's plan to retake Orel. The 13th,14th and 8th armies, plus Budenny's cavalry corps would attack the Volunteer Army units and the 4th Don Cavalry Corps to it's right. The objective was Kursk. The 12th and 9th armies on the Southeast front would regroup and redeploy and be used as needed. Specifically, the 57th and 46th divisions would strike for Sevsk, while the 1st and 2nd brigades/41st division would gather in the center of the 14th Army to attack the Volunteers and 5th Cavalry Corps. These two White units were now attempting to resume their offensive toward Bryansk. Because of this, the Reds ordered the 159th regiment, 14th Cavalry brigade and part of the 57th division on Sevsk to the Komarichi area from the 14th Army. On the left, the 7th division would attack and would threaten the right rear flank of the Volunteer 3rd Drozdovsky division. The 14th Army had also received the 45th division and the veteran Estonian infantry division, both were held in reserve at Moshenoe. The Estonian division and the 9th division were ordered to take Orel.

Denikin tried to maintain the initiative by attacking with several infantry regiments (the 3rd markov reg, 3rd Kornilov reg, 83rd Samursky and a cavalry brigade from the 5th Cav.Corps). However, these forces failed in their attempt to make any further gains. The Reds began their attack and almost immediately hit fierce resistance north of Orel, both sides winning ground in see-saw battles. About 50 km east of Sevsk, the Red 2nd Brig/7th division came under attack from Denikin. The 3rd Brigade/7th division and 3rd brigade/ 41st division all came under fire. The Red 2nd and 3rd Latvian Brigades (both recent arrivals from the West and veterans) began their attack on Orel with the other units. The 1st Corps of Denikin fought a brilliant defense giving up only small towns of Gorka and Ageevka after exchanging hands numerous times. But numbers began to prevail on the side of the Soviet.

The Battle for Orel began on the 19th and lasted all day and into the night, and on the 20th, the area was still engaged. Denikin's 4th Cavalry Corps surprised the Reds and attacked Budenny's Cav.Corps consisting of the 4th and 6th Cavalry divisions toward Khrenovoe. A bitter clash ensued and forced Budenny to defend with the 6th division while attacking with the 4th division from the north. The White attack was repelled and allowed Budenny to advance chasing the two divisions of Shkuro and one of Mamantov's. The 3rd Kuban Cavalry Corps also became involved and both Shkuro and the corps losses were high. Once this rout was achieved, the White 9th and 10th Don Cavalry divisions conducted an attack upon Budenny. Budenny continued to advance from Rogachevki to Voronezh.

Besides Budenny attacking, the Reds also tossed in the 12th and 15th infantry divisions for further exploitation. Holding the rear was the Red 16th and 33rd divisions, which had come under heavy attack from Don army units and had forced the Red 40th division to retreat. By 1100, part of the Don 3rd Corps attacked Khrenovoe and battled the Red 40th division all day for it. A break in the Red front lines occurred between the 13th Army and Budenny and then the South and Southeast Fronts. This was of grave concern to the Red High Command. The 54th division, 1st brigade/20th div, 1st reg and 611, 612 regiments of the Tambov Brigade were to be sent there along with the 11th Cavalry division, which had just arrived from Moscow. The Cavalry division gathered at Star, while the others at Kozlove. By the end of the 18th, the Soviets had been successful on with the 13th and 14th armies, Budenny's Corps and 8th Army, which captured Voronezh. It was only now that the High Command issued orders to strike for Kursk.

Parts of three armies now approached Orel and after a 12 hour battle on the 19th, the 1st division of the 1st Corps retreated. The propaganda value from the collapse of the Whites at Orel was enormous, which heightened the Soviet morale. It was exploited heavily. Denikin tried to conduct a flanking attack against 14th army, but failed. The Soviet 3rd Latvian brigade and 9th division entered Orel and continued to Stishch. The Soviets had been victorious and now the High Command issued orders to take Kursk. The 14th Army was to advance to Kursk. The 13th Army, with the 9th division would attack south from Orel, 3rd division to Verkhov, 42nd division to Livny. Budenny's corps to Kursk and cut off the White retreat southwards from Orel and seize Kastornoe and Marmyzhi. The 8th Army would continue to push back the Don Army and occupy the Don river line at Endovishe. All of the attacking units were ordered to not allow their forces to scatter and to attack in concentrated form on a narrow front. The Estonian division was held in reserve near Orel in case a Denikin counterattack occurred.

The Southern Front had the 46th and 47th attacking easterly to the railroad leading from Orel. The 1st brigade/ 57th division advanced on Komarichi and after a bitter struggle had the Whites retreating. Denikin tossed in the 3rd Drozdovsky regiment and 2nd cavalry division which had to withdrawn from the Bryansk advance at Nerusa. This allowed the 1st and 2nd brigades of 41st division to advance to Dmigrieba. During this time, 14th Army shorted it's front by 80 Km and because the Red 46th,57th and 41st divisions advanced to Havlia, Denikin was forced to toss in part of the 5th Cavalry Corps which had originally been targeted for Kromy. On the left flank, the 7th Red division and the Shock units hit a White wall of resistance from the 3rd markov reg and 2nd Kornilov reg. The White units had managed to turn the flank of the 1st Latvian brigade and even retook Kromy on the 22nd. Now, the Whites threatened to encircle the Red Shock group! Immediately, the 14th Army gathered the 3rd and 4th brigades of the 41st div and the 7th division on the right from Orel while the 3rd Latvian brigade filled in the gap between the 1st and 2nd Latvian brigades. By the 23rd, the Reds were close to Lmitorovsku.

As the Budenny Cavalry corps continued to advance, both them and the 8th army units hit Denikin's 3rd Don Corps. Budenny's 6th Cav. Division and 3rd brig/4th Cav. Division along with elements of the 12th division/8th Army attacked the suburbs of Voronezh from the east and southeast. Once the city fell, Budenny would advance to Podkletnoe on the Don river. The Soviets gathered all their artillery allocated and created artillery fronts (from the 40th and 13th divisions) of high concentrations focused on a narrow front for a breakthrough.

While this occurred, the Red 4th Cav.division and 21st brigade conducted a surprise night attack upon the Denikin's 1st Caucasian Cavalry division, which panicked and fled allowing the Reds to secure river crossings at Ramoni and Stunia. The advance of Budenny met with a surprise interception from Denikin's 13th Don Cavalry brig and 9th Cav. Division, which had barely begun it's attack when the Red 4th cav. Division swooped upon them scattering them north of Voronezh.

On the 24th, to the west, the 1st Latvian brig and the 8th Cav division (11th,14th brigades) were halted by the withering fire of Denikin's elite, the 3rd Drozdovsky regiment and 5th cavalry corps in the Kromy area. This situation was received when the 41st division attacked into the rear of Denikin's forces causing them to fall back. However, as parts of the Red 3rd Latvian brigade beat the elite Markov regiment there, Denikin quickly regrouped his forces and counterattacked retaking the town causing the Soviets to flee. Determined, the Soviet 3rd Latvian brigade tried four times in fierce battles, failing to retake the town. It finally fell on the 27th, when the Soviets conducted a surprise night attack causing the Whites to flee. The Markov regiment had been whittled down from 1000 men to 200.

To the east, the Soviet guerilla units within Voronezh conducted an uprising as Budenny attacked from the North, East and Southeast. Part of the town fell to the guerillas and parts fell to the Red 12th division entering from the south, followed by the 4th Cavalry division. Mamantov's 4th Cavalry corps continued to hold a portion but on the 25th, they too, fled. Budenny had defeated the once elite forces of Mamantov and Shkuro.

As the 26th dawned, the bitter fighting continued across the front. At Lisky rail station, the Whites fought a tenacious battle lasting 20 hours. The station was also a key river crossing containing a bridge that the Whites had not blown. The heroic defense ended with the Whites retreating in disorder. This allowed the Red 12th,15th,16th and 33rd divisions to advance to the Don with little opposition. The Red 40th division now became the target of a White counterattack with far superior forces near Mechetka, along the Don. In this attack, the 40th division sought the safety of the right bank of the Don to avoid destruction. The 9th Army also continued it's advance towards the Don River. However, the Red High command became very concern regarding a very large gap between the 8th and 9th armies. The 36th division was shattered and there were no strong forces on the right flank. The 1st Don Corps advanced into the gap toward Novochopersk pushing the weak Soviet forces aside. These fled from one town to another. The Red High Command issued orders to hold at all costs Borisoglenskia and the rail junction at Povorino. To do this, the 9th army shifted its 21st,36th and 14th divisions, but the 1st Don Corps had many Austin armor cars which out maneuvered the Red infantry that caused more problems in sealing the gaps. The situation was only remedied by using the army reserves, 32nd and 39th divisions.

On the 27th, the last day of the embattled Kromy area, saw more bitter blows by each side. This area had been contested since the 21st and now it was the pivotal time for Denikin. It was the last time Denikin tossed more precious reserves into battle. These units were his elite. All officers with an intense hatred of the Soviet political entity. After the collapse of Orel and Voronezh, this area was Denikin's last important battlefield. The men of the 1st and 3rd divisions/1st Corps fought to the end but fell back. Because of the success of the Soviet Southern Front offensive, orders were issued to advance to Orolovsko and Kursk direction with utmost speed by breaking off forces that opposed the Orel area and diverting them to the flanks.

Overhead in the air, the Red 3rd detachment had arrived and had been bombing and strafing. Likwise, the White 6th detachment somehow continued to operate as well, despite the reverses. Both provided air support to the units below.

The Southern Front, on the 28th, continued using the 14th Army, now only consisting of 46th and 57th divisions, attacked Denikin's 5th Cavalry Corps and the Drozdovsky division. The Whites were resistant but numbers prevailed and the Reds succeeded in capturing the Lgov to Byansk railway and threatened the Whites rear areas. It was now that Denikin created a Shock group consisting of the 1st and 2nd Drozdovsky regiments and two cavalry regiments west of Dmitriev with the intent of pushing the Red 46th division toward Sevsk. However, the Red Estonian division arrived at the scene and after more fierce battles the Kornilov division routed to Eropkino. Denikin conducted his counterattack and because he had force superiority began to surround the Estonians. The Denikin force retook nearby towns and the Drozdovsky regiments had regained the initiative forcing the Red 57th and 41st divisions back. Attacking Komarichi from the west and southwest, Denikin, despite suffering excessive loss, retook the town. This caused the 14th Army high command grave concerns and immediately began to rearrange it's forces: the 2nd brigade/41st xx was replaced with the 1st and 2nd brigade/46th division and ordered to retake it.

As this developed, the 3rd and 4th brigades of 41st division became embroiled in desperate battles with the Markov and Alekseev divisions at Cherni. Denikin continued and attacked parts of the 42nd division along the Livny-Orel railway using the 1st and 2nd

Markov regiments. This became a fierce battle as the Reds tossed in the 2nd brigade/42nd division and the 13th cavalry brigade, which decimated parts of the 1st Markov and the Black Sea Cavalry regiment. This defeat allowed Budenny cavalry to advance toward Kastornay. The Red 4th Cavalry division was chosen to cross the Don. The Whites had destroyed all the river crossings, and all approaches were exposed by White artillery and MG fire. However, the river was crossed at Zhivotiny with the 12th division and elements of the 6th Cavalry. The Whites who had been holding the town lost 300 men and 20 MG.

One of the British advisors attached to the Don Army, Major Williamson, wrote the following:

> "We arrived late night at Ust Medvyeditsa, the beams of the car lights yellow in the mist and jerking violently as it labored over the rutted road. The town was the home of the 6th Don Division which had been trying to advance northward. The snow and mud left the roads in appalling conditions, knee deep hollows where everything came to a stop. The officers remained snug in the car while the mud smeared soldiers attempted to free us. There was a huge jam of vehicles, all bogged down. The 3rd Don corps was holding a line from Podgornya to Vailuki. The mission of the 1st Corps appeared to be to hold the approaches to the Ust Medvyeditsa bridgehead and to keep in touch with Wrangel's left flank."

On the 28th, Denikin regrouped to create four new divisions from his existing 1st and 3rd divisions of 1st Corps and others. The new formation created comprised of: Konilov, Markov, Drozdovsky, Alekseev divisions, one artillery brigade and engineer regiment.

The last day of October had Denikin's 8th Don regiment, 1st and 3rd Don Cavalry divisions, and 7th Don Cavalry brigade attacking the Red 33rd and 40th divisions, which caused a break in the Soviet front lines at Bobrov. The Red 11th division was subsequently attached to Budenny to protect the right flank of his cavalry.

The battles continued into November, and on the 2nd, Denikins Mamantov Cavalry corps attacked the Red 6th Cavalry division left flank near Shyemiky, but was repelled. Because of the numerous counterattacks by Denikin's forces on the 8th Army, now comprising of the 12th, 15th, 16th,33rd and 40th Red divisions, part of the army was ordered to go on the defensive while units on the right flank attacked Bobrov, hopefully to close the gap. The 13th division was shifted to Kopla and the 31st to Makarovo. The 15th and 33rd would protect Budenny's rear.

After 20 days of battle, the Soviet forces had conducted an offensive that shattered Denikin's main forces of the Volunteer Army and the 4th and 3rd Don Corps of Don Army. These battles were hard fought, bitter and savage. Much of the Soviet military doctrine was formed here: shifting of forces, creating artillery fronts on a narrow front, breakthrough Shock troops, attacking the enemy rear using guerilla tactics and so on. They also revealed how rigid their command system was, that, until ordered, the next planned objective was not to be advanced upon. Denikin's 1st Corps showed an amazingly amount of elasticity when conducting offensive, and more particular, defensive actions. His tactics gave ground only when needed, battered groups regrouped creating new composite units that went on the offensive again.

The Long and Winding Road Back

Stage two of the Soviet offensive began November 3rd through the 20th. In this stage, the Red 12th Army and 9th armies would be activated, targeting the Cherigov area. Denikin knew of its strategic importance and sent additional troops from the Fastov-Kiev areas. Knowing this, the Reds activated the 58th division, the river flotilla, an artillery group and the 44th , 47th divisions.

On the 3rd, the Soviet High Command ordered the 14th army with 1st and 3rd Latvian brigades to attack and take Cherni. The Red Cavalry division was strengthened and now consisted of 1700 men, 32 MG, 6 guns. This unit would exploit the break in the front line and race to the rear to disorganize the White forces. Once completed, the unit was to strike for Diachu. Denikin's forces had blown the bridge at Svala but his forces had routed from Cherni. At Stydenka, the 3rd Drozdovsky regiment broke and the Reds captured their artillery battery. At Fatezh, the Red 60th Cavalry regiment blew up the railways in the White rear at Vaey. This cut off the retreat of a whole train.

On the 4th, in a blinding blizzard, the Red 12th army attacked from Repkina towards Chernigov. Because of the weather, not much was achieved, however, on the 5th, the weather subsided and the full weight of the Red attack overwhelmed the defending Whites after a fierce urban warfare battle. The first to enter Cherigov was the 532nd regiment and cavalry from the east, while from the north, elements of the 44th division. Once it was seized, Kiev was next.

Kiev was protected by a river and well defended by the Denikin forces consisting of 13th division, 42nd Yakut, Chechen Cav. Reg., an officer training battalion, many armor cars and artillery, which could conduct direct fire at the bridges near Desny. Bitter battles hovered all around the bridges costing heavy losses to both, but by the 6th, the Reds had captured the bridges; yet, were unable to cross due to weather and a lack of artillery support. On the 7th, the Red 58th divisions attacked the White 2nd Terskoi brigade with heavy artillery support. The 2nd brigade stood their ground until it could not absorb any more loss then it routed. The Reds took Fastov which threatened the rear and flank of Kiev.

At Sevsk, the Red 46th division battled the famed Mamantov Cavalry for 15 hours, after which, Mamantov retreated to Dmitry.

The Don Army of Denikin gathered its last remaining offensive strength on the 8th, in their bid to retake Voronezh. The forces gathered in the area of Livny and consisted of the 2nd brigade, Tula brigade, 2nd Don Cav division/3rd Don Corps, 8th Cav. Brigade/ Mamantov's 4th Cav corps, four armor trains, parts of the 5th and 8th Don divisions and 7th Don Cavalry brigade. The Red 8th and 9th army had lost all coordination between one another and all communications. Because of this, the 8th Army fell back towards Voronezh. The Don Army forces attacked and advanced with little resistance and by the 10th, the 8th Army commander sent an SOS to the Group HQ stating that the situation was very serious and he needed reinforcements. The GHQ scoured the reserves and sent the army a brigade of 10,000 men, two infantry regiments, another 5000 from spare units and a brigade from 61st division. These forces arrived just as the Don Army was approaching the area of Voronezh. A large, grand epic battle began. Both desperate to win, both suffering excessive losses. However, the Don Army had attacked with an iron fist, using all of the units and therefore, had no reserves. The 8th army counterattacked and Denikin on the 11th, called off the offensive.

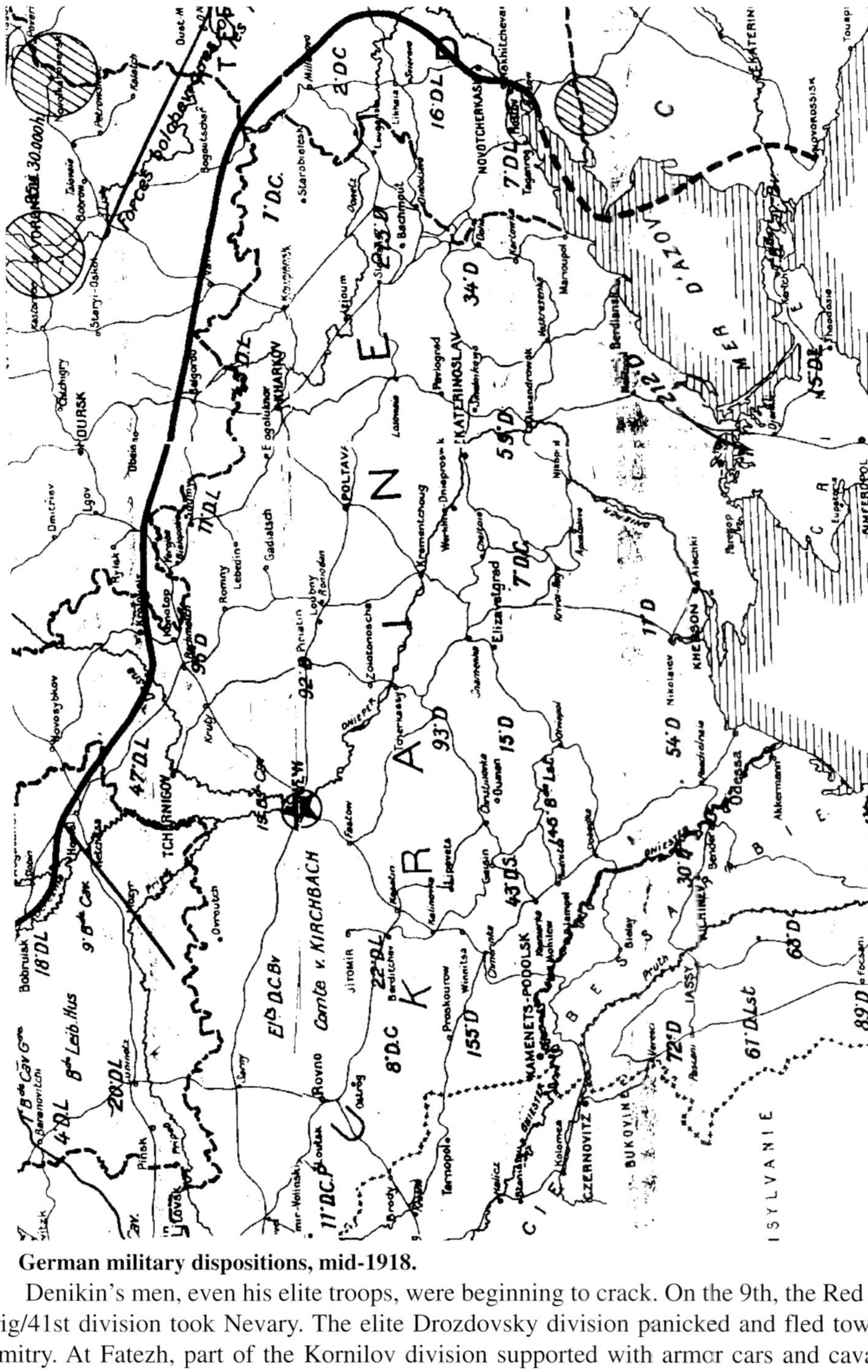

German military dispositions, mid-1918.

Denikin's men, even his elite troops, were beginning to crack. On the 9th, the Red 3rd brig/41st division took Nevary. The elite Drozdovsky division panicked and fled toward Dmitry. At Fatezh, part of the Kornilov division supported with armor cars and cavalry attacked along the road from Kromy forcing the 3rd Latvian brigade to retreat north. The

Reds continued to hammer with the 41st and 7th divisions. The defending Drozdovsky divisions' morale had dropped causing it to retreat. As it did, the retreat route was intercepted by the 46th Soviet division causing a rout. Luckily, Denikins 5th Cavalry corps rescued the rout by a surprise attack on the 46th division. All day the fierce back and forth battle raged around Dmitry. The town changed hands many times. Denikin was determined to halt the backward motion and held the town with the Drozdovsky division, a cavalry regiment, totaling 2500 men, 800 cavalry and 16 artillery guns. This time the Whites won.

On the 12th, the Red 47th,44th and 60th divisions assaulted Desny, but Denikin's defense held with the 7th, 9th and Guards divisions.

The Red 41st and 7th divisions now assaulted Dmitry on the 13th and after another bloodbath, the Whites retreat to Livny. By the 14th, the Soviet 14th Army had ravaged Denikins famed Drozdovsky and Kornilov divisions of 1st Corps. They had seriously damaged the 1st and 2nd regiments of 5th Cavalry Corps, which held an area around Glukov. The 8th Red cavalry division had wrecked many of the rear areas forcing the Whites to pull back to the Seim river. This division seized Livny cutting off a retreat route for the famed White units. Panic was setting in. As the Soviet forces seriously approached Kursk, the battles grew increasingly bloody and fierce. Denikin had few reserves in or around Kursk. His few armor trains were easily cut off. The Estonian division reached within 10 km of Kursk, the 9th division followed. These units conducted a sudden surprise attack on the city capturing it on the 18th. After it's capture, the divisions continued to advance south and the 3rd division secured the railway leading from Kursk northward.

By the 15th, Denikin had to pull use his last reserves from the North Caucasus army. As these forces gathered, bloody battles occurred around Tim giving Denikin additional losses as his troops attempted to fall back. The purpose of these last reserves was originally to retake Voronezh, and if achieved, this would cut the lines of communications to Budenny and 8th army. It was a daring move. His forces gathered amounting to eight infantry regiments (8-10,000 men), Shkuro Cavalry division, four MkV tanks and three armor trains. The infantry and tanks would attack from the Kastornay area, while the 4000 cavalry from Nishnedevnak. However, as the forces gathered, Budenny struck first, attacking the Shkuro cavalry and then using the 42nd division and 13th cavalry brigades attacking the infantry. Budenny attacked from the Sukoviina area and for two days a bloody battle ensued hovering around Kastornay. The White force conducted themselves as tenacious barracudas attacking and jabbing. Budenny's men found themselves embroiled in a fight, which endangered themselves! They had to fight their way out. The Red 4th and 6th divisions settled the issue when they attacked Denikin's rear seizing Kastornya. Denikin now ordered his troops to hastily fall back to prevent encirclement.

While the Volunteer Army was fighting 200 miles from Moscow, deep in their rear, the anarchist, Makhano, ravaged the Ukrainian areas. He was hated by both the Soviets and Whites for Makhano represented the people who hated any type of government (Anarchist). This campaign began on Sept. 26th, when he attacked the Whites at Peregonovka, which was midway between Kiev and Odessa. The White cordon was pierced and he seized 20 guns and 120 MG to arm his followers. Now armed, he attacked Krivi Rog, Nikopol and Alexandrovsk and took them. Then on Oct.11, he seized Berdiansk on the Sea of Azov, then Mariupol. Now he threatened the Denikin HQ at Taganrog. On the 20th, when Orel fell, he took Ekakterinoslav. Denikin sent most of his reserves to control Makhano (these units were: Chechen cavalry division, 1st Terskoi Cav. Division, 2nd Don Cavalry brigade, 9th division, Caucasian officer regiment, Nikolaev battalion, 1st Don Bn, a MG bn and 2 armor trains). The 1st Corps had only a few battalions in reserve. It may appear that Makhano was on the Soviet side, but the reality was, his force fell on any opportunities. He knew his quick advances would be much easier against the Whites than the Reds at this time (he would eventually die in the 1930's destitute and an a drunk).

The 13th and 14th armies now regrouped to prepare for another attack. However, by the 24th, the Soviet Budenny Cavalry Corps struck and retook Voronezh from the famed Mamantov and Shkuro Cavalry corps. By the 26th, the 1st Corps of the Volunteer army had conceded defeat from the Kromy area in hopes of holding the Sevsk-Dmitrovsk-Eropkino boundary. According to the Volunteer Intelligence reports, mainly from POW's, on the 14th, this is what the was Denikin's staff saw:

Kletsky area:

"After questioning the prisoner from the 371st regiment, we established that the regiment is near Shatavo and Baranovo. These are located 12 miles to the West of Elets. The 370th regiment is located in Petrovka, about 6 miles to the north, where the 1st Alat and 3rd Orlovsky cavalry regiments are. The 370th regiment has suffered excessive losses and is resting. POW's from the 2nd and 3rd Simbirsky regiments tell us of the new troops arriving.

Orolovsko Area:

On the 10th, the Plastunsky and Kievsky regiments were stationed in the Koslov village. These replaced the 6th and 7th Latvian regiments and the 1st Latvian cavalry regiment. The total numbers 1500 men and 500 cavalry and advancing toward Kromy.

Sevsk Area:

Near the village Supino, some 12 miles northeast of Sevsk, the following troops were active: 365th,366th,367th,369th regiments of the 41st division; 409th regiment of the 46th, 51st reg of the 57th division, 611th regiment of the 68th division and 463rd regent from the 52nd division. This strike group has the mission to advance on Dmitrovsk through Komariczi station.

Novogorod-Severski area:

According to testimonies of the POW's there is approximately 500 deserters who created a group. This is located near Lemeshovka, midway between Gluhov and Sevsk. The forest areas contain many Red groups. According to the people of the villages Polkovniczia and Krugalya, the Soviet 409th,410th, 411th and artillery passed through between the 6th and 9th, heading to Sevsk. Defectors indicate the Reds are falling back at Slauta,Tampol and Usok.

In our rear area:

On October 4th, Poltava was attacked by 2500 men. Mostly Red army men. Most of these had been born there. The group has three battalions, 12 companies (each with 50-100 men), two cavalry companies and two artillery guns. On the 13th, Makhno attacked Ekakterinoslav from Sursk and Litvosk. These included the 13th Rebel regiment and 1st Consolidated Soviet regiment. These companies have 80-100 men. Once attacked they quickly pulled south and crossed the Dnepr to the east bank."

The report shows how accurate and reliable the intelligence being gathered from the POW's was. The other item it shows is that despite Makhano's independence, at this period in time, he befriended the Soviets, who could also use his help since their newly created doctrine was to attack the flanks and rear areas of the enemy. Earlier, when Denikin was victorious, Makhano had been on the White side!

The balance of forces by mid-October was as follows:

Soviet	White
11th Army 19,000 men, 64 guns	N.Caucasus Gp. 21,500 men,82 guns
10th Army-28,000 men, 146 guns	Wrangel 20,000 men, 144 guns
9th Army-31,000 men,196 guns	Don army 71,000 men, 222 guns
8th Army 24,000 men, 180 guns	
13th Army 38,000 men, 135 guns	Volunteer Army 43.050 men 140 guns
14th Army 14,000 men, 42 guns	
12th Army 15,000 men, 53 guns	Kiev Army 14200 men 80 guns

The Armed Forces of South Russia under Denikin totaled 170,250 men of which 62,500 were cavalry, 107,750 rifles. The North Caucasus army that actually opposed the 11th Army was 10,000 men, the balance were in garrisons. The Kiev army, likewise, only fielded 7,000 men opposing the 12th Army. The balance were in the rear areas dealing with bandits. The bottom line reads that the Soviets had about 7000 more men and 230 more guns. These figures are deceptive for they are from the British and Denikin's intelligence, and fail to account for the thousands manning the defense lines in front of Moscow or the 17th Army or 18th Army which was being formed as a reserve.

The more interesting aspect of this report is the amount of forces in other areas other than the front. In the Novorossisk area 24,000 men and 82 guns were required, on the east coast of the Black Sea, another 11,000 men and 32 guns. Worse, the garrisons in the rear areas required 27,000 men and 162 guns! Clearly this shows the impact of Pelitura and Makhano's forces. Had Denikin had a secure rear area, he would have had at least another 20,000 men and 100 guns fighting the on the front. The total in the rear areas came to 51,000 infantry and 11,000 cavalry or 62,000 men and 276 guns!

Also in the rear was Denikin's long "tail" of the combat units, the technical, supply, rail, engineer auxiliaries, totaling 67,000. Total non-combatants came to 41,000. The sick and wounded, 30,000.

In machine guns, the Reds had a 2 to 1 ratio, 4000 to 2000 on the front, However, another 1000 MG's were used in the rear areas.

It would be a misconception if one believes that the Soviet forces opposing Denikin were akin to the "juggernauts" so famous in WW2. The counterattack groups which retook Orel and Voronezh struggled to do so. The objective was Kursk and this was not taken until

Nov.17th. A full 30 days had passed before the objective was seized. This indicates the stout resistance that both the Volunteer and Don Armies conducted. It also indicates that the Soviet troops were slow in attacking and planning, even their "fast" unit, Budenny's Cavalry Corps, was cautious. The Red military doctrine also reveals itself, one that remains true today incorporating flank and rear attacks, guerilla warfare in the enemy rear. It also reflects the rigidness of the High Command of not changing the objectives if the opportunity presents itself. For 30 days, all of the Red attacking forces focused on one objective in the end: Kursk.

On October 25th, the 1st Army Corps of the Volunteer Army was deployed as follows:

1st and 2nd regiments, Partisan reg, Chernnmorrsky Cav. Reg/Markov division
1st,2nd,3rd regiments, 12th Cav regiment/Kornilov Division
Severski, 1st,2nd 3rd regs/Drodvosky Division

These were on the frontline. The 3rd reg/Markov division had been withdrawn to Kursk.

The 5th Cavalry Corps:
1st Cav reg and Ulan reg/1st Cav division
1st,2nd,3rd Cavalry regs/2nd division
These continued to remain on the line.

General Revinsh's force in the Kursk and Ekaterinodar areas contained:

2nd and 3rd Chechen Cav. Regs, 2nd reserve bn, Tavorishky Cav. Division, elements of 9th Cav division and 5th division

The Garrisons comprised of:

1st Chechen Cav reg, 1st reserve bn, 7th reserve bn, 4th Chechen cav reg,6th reserve bn,6th Armenian bn.

General Denikin, from his command post in mid-October, wrote the following in his book *March on Moscow*:

> "Although we were aware of the troop concentrations of the enemy, our only response was to regroup accordingly, due to the lack of reserves. The offensive on the side of the Orel-Sevsk was not deemed as serious as the one from Voronezh side, which threatened the left flank of the Don army. Therefore, without stopping the army advancement towards the line bryansk-Orel-Elets, I ordered the Don Army to limit their defense at the center and right flank and shift forces facing Lisok and Voronezh. The Volunteer army was moderately successful at first, but the situation at Voronezh forced us to withdraw from Orel and Livny."

How wrong was Denikin's thinking?! As we have seen, Orel and the 1st Corps of the Volunteer Army were the targets. The Budenny attack at Voronezh was secondary. Only after Orel fell would the second counterattack strike there.

As to Makhno, Denikin reveals total frustration at dealing with real guerilla warfare tactics:

> "How numerous were his men no one knows, They have been estimated at both 10,000 and 40,000. Separate bands would gather, then disperse, obey orders or act independently of him. At Berdiansk, they blew one of our artillery depots. To deal with them we were obliged to withdraw forces from the Volunteer Army, two cavalry divisions. From the Pelitura front, we sent a whole corps under General Slastchev. His troops would attack, disseminate and reassemble again, scatter and disappear only to reappear. We steadily pushed them back towards the Dniepr by late November. This revolt had the effect of disorganizing our rear and weakening the front at the most critical period of its existence."

This kind of warfare was practised later in a more famous war called Vietnam from 1946-54 and 1964-1975, with the same sort of ending the Whites would have in the Civil war.

Also playing an important role in the fall of 1919, which would heavily impact Denikin was the Polish question. The Polish suspension of military operations against the Soviets did not help Denikin or the Kiev Army under General Dragomirov. Although, Denikin had met several times with the Polish Military Mission, where he was assured of friendship and that the Poles understood the military situation, the Poles did nothing. In the Ukraine area, the Soviet 12th Army was deployed to battle the Polish Army. Denikin requested several times for the Poles to begin offensive actions along the upper Dniepr. None came. The inactivity of the front and then armistice stunned Denikin. The Soviets then began to shift the 43,000 men from the Polish front to the Kiev and other areas Denikin controlled. Denikin played upon the fear element that if his army was defeated, Poland would be next on the Soviet aims. This increased pressure from the Soviets is spelled out in a Volunteer Intelligence Report, dated October 29th from the Kiev HQ:

> "Bolsheviks increase concentration of troops in Chytomyr-Radomysl-Chenilov regions with fresh troops. In this month agents have noticed the following new troops in the Kiev region:
>
> 1st Astrakhan reg, 1st and 2nd Moscow regs, 3rd and 4th Novogorod regs, 170th regiments, 58th Soviet reg.
>
> There are threatening signs of demoralization among our own troops. In the rear areas of the Kiev region there are 28 different groups totaling 12-15000 men."

The Reds sent to Marshal Pilusdsky, an envoy who persuaded the Marshal that the true enemy was Denikin. This secret agreement called for the Reds to stop all further operations against Poland in exchange for the Poles not attacking the 12th Army toward Kiev. Denikin did not know of this and none of the other allies were aware of it at that time. Poland did attack again, but only in December after the fall of Kiev to the Reds and Denikin's army was retreating. Of course, the Reds befriended Poland only until they defeated Denikin, for six months later in 1920, the Reds had invaded Poland and knocking on Warsaw's doorstep.

The Reds continued their internal campaign of propaganda on their own troops. Each regiment contained a comminsaars who was the political and moral chief. He was responsible for the morale and had considerable clout in charge of nearly all matters connected to military objectives. He had access to all meetings, all orders given and received, and took part in their formulation, but the regimental commanded would have the last say in matters. He was the watchdog.

The Southern Front developed extensive communist party propaganda to motivate it's troops and the local population. The 14th Army produced 741,300 newspapers and party membership rose to 11,153 men. The 12th Army had 5000 members. Together with the Southeast front, both had a combined membership of 55,881. This strengthened the armies capacity in the rear and on the front. The propaganda efforts went down to company level.

By mid-October, the Southern Front had been reinforced and contained 113,698 men, 2507 MG, 575 guns, 13 armor trains. According to Soviet sources, Denikin's Volunteer and Don Armies had a combined strength of 110,486 men, 1342 MG, 339 guns, 41 armor trains, 26 airplanes, 22 armor cars and 18 tanks.

Many Soviet methods of war were created during this counterattack phase. One example of this was a transition from the linear old ways of war seen in WW1 to those of maneuver in fast actions, shifting of forces to sectors and the extensive use of propaganda. One method created in the 8th army and then used extensively even today was the formation of the artillery breakthrough division. This formation was created by grouping the numerous artillery units of the army into one concentrated force directed at a narrow sector. The barrages intended to shatter the defender, which was subsequently attacked. The 8th army was the first to have an artillery breakthrough division. The 12th army would create two such divisions.

Guerilla warfare, as mentioned previously, also was used perhaps for the first time in a concerted action with the other military units. In short, the guerilla groups were led by party members who enlisted others against Denikin in his rear area. The sole purpose was to destroy the railways, wreck trains, cut the telephone and telegraph wires, attack and destroy depots, cause public uprisings. All this would deprive Denikin the ability to move supplies, shift troops, damage morale. When you add this to the normal problems that Denikin had have getting supplies to the front, the problem is compounded.

From October 1st to Nov.20th, the Soviets had advanced 165 km and had retaken some 50000 square km. They had captured Kursk, Orel, Voronezh and Chernigov, and 18 other towns. They had retaken 120 km of railway. The Southern Front armies had captured 300 officers, 7367 enlisted, 730 horses, 41 artillery guns, 280 MG, 12 trains and 37 armor cars.

Their next main goal was Kharkov and Rostov.

In a classified and secret intelligence report, dated Nov. 13th, Denikin's own intelligence assessed the situation:

> "Near Kursk, after conducting massive offensive operations along the front and taking Kursk, the Reds have advanced 45 km south from the railroad Kursk to Lgov. The Latvian division and 9th division are present. Cavalry is very effective. Using snowstorms and fog, their cavalry was able to break through deeply into our rear forcing our retreat. Latvian cavalry of the 1st division are approaching the Seim River, 20 versts from Lgov. The 2nd Latvian division HQ is located at Dmitrovsk. The enemy had taken Rylask. We have lost communication with units in the Grigorvka area. Based on our intelligence and agents the Red Command has in it's rear huge reserves obtained from taking the 7th, 41st and 57th divisions out from other fronts and arrival of new units, the 2nd Elite division from Tula to Tim

area, the 6th division from Nishny Novogorod, 2nd Latvian from West front plus 5000 other Latvians. On the internal front, the 4th Rebellious Corps of bandits are advancing toward the Dnepr."

From November 20th to January, 1920, it was all a rearward motion for the forces under General Denikin. The details are the same, the Red forces attacking and gaining, sporadic White units defending with what remaining forces they had, sometimes making gains only to be threatened in the rear.

On November 19th, the Reds decided to create a Cavalry Army on the Southern Front from Budenny's Cavalry Corps. It's main purpose was to destroy Denikin's forces. It's original composition was the 4th and 6th Cavalry divisions/1st Corps, and the 8th and 11th Cavalry divisions/2nd Corps. Attached were two infantry brigades. However, the 8th Cavalry Corps remained with the 14th army and there were no spare infantry units. Thus, the Cavalry army consisted of the 4th,6th and 11th Cavalry divisions.

The new Red offensive began on the 20th, heading towards Rostov and Kharkov. The White forces resisted strongly opposing the 14th Army. The Slogan for the effusive was, "Forward to Rostov."The 12th Army with the 44th and 47th divisions attacked towards Kiev along the railway, while the 60th division conducted a flanking action. Denikin sent in additional units to defend Kiev; the 5th division and a Caucasian Cavalry Regiment, to no avail. The only success Denikin had was opposite the 10th Army, which his 4th Kuban Cavalry Corps repulsed all of their attacks. In fact, the 4th Kubans attacked and forced the 1st brigade/39th division to retreat on December 1st. This Corps then made a surprise turn and joined the 1st Kuban Corps in a savage attack on the 38th,37th and 28th divisions of 10th Army forcing them to make wholesale withdrawals. But by December 4th, elements of the 39th division attacked into the rear of 4th Corps, which halted them. The 1st Kuban Corps continued it's attack on the 28th division and elements of the other shattered Red units causing further retreats along the Volga. The 4th Kuban corps continued to gain, but at a very high cost.

Elsewhere, the 14th Army south of Kursk, continued to face surprisingly stiff resistance. The 12th Army forced Denikin's Kiev army, 2nd Corps and Poltava forces to retreat. Finally on the 12th, the 12th and 14th Army closed and connected their flanks. Poltava fell. The 14th Army, with the 41st xx, 46th xx and Latvian xx on the front and the 7th and 57th divisions as reserves advanced towards Rostov. However, the next city in line was Kharkov. The 8th Cavalry division's spearhead had penetrated deep into Denikin's rear, which did not allow him much time to prepare any Kharkov defenses. Denikin's 5th Cavalry Corps confronted this incoming force and bitter cavalry battles ensued with much of the 5th Corps being decimated. Denikin's 1st Corps, still resisted near Rostov, but was weak and tired, it too, collapsed. The Red Latvian division also advanced toward Belgorod and Kharkov. The 13th Army, also advancing in the same direction, faced stiffer opposition despite it's Estonian, 3rd,9th and 42nd divisions heading south from Kursk.

Denikin had counterattacked on Nov.20th and threatened to retake Kursk from elements of the Red 3rd division. The 9th division was sent to reinforce. Between the 21st and 23rd, a bitter, savage battle raged near Kursk. In the end, Denikin's forces retreated. Budenny's cavalry out ran the infantry units and Denikin was quite concern as to Budenny's speed. Denikin then ordered his 3rd Kuban Cav. Corps to intercept them on Dec.1st. This time his units held and slowed down the advance buying him more time. Belgorod was taken on Dec. 7th by the Estonian and Latvian divisions.

As the Reds approached Kharkov, Denikin hoped to prevent it's capture using the 5th Cavalry Corps and 1st Corps. When the 14th Army began it's attack on the city, Denikin tossed the 1st Chechen Cavalry brigade into the flank of the army. In total, some seven regiments (between 4000-7000 men) were holding the Kharkov area. The Reds and Whites battled, the Reds surprised the Chechens when they were attacked by the 1st brigade/Latvian division on their flank. The Chechens fled in fear of being surrounded. The remaining parts of Denikins troops simply gave ground and on the night of the 11th, Kharkov was entered by the Reds and urban warfare began. By the end of the 12th, it was theirs. The Red 8th Cavalry division received the "Red Banner" award for it's heroic fight during this battle

To provide further punch to the Budenny cavalry army, on Dec.6th, the 9th and 12th divisions were assigned to the army. The army was then instructed to advanced to it's ultimate goal, Taganrog. On the very next day, the army charged into Denikin's 2nd Kuban Cav division and Black Sea cavalry regiment at Volokonovi and decimates both units. At Vailuki, it faced a tougher opponent, the 10th Don division and 4th Kuban Cavalry division, which conducted an elastic defense (led by Mamantov) until it suffered excessive losses forcing a retreat. The 8th Army (12th,16th,15th,40th, 31st divisions) continued to battle the 3rd Don Corps for three days at Moroeva. Here, the Red 40th division was shattered. A minor win, which again was negated by a Red flank attack into the Don Corps rear causing the all to familiar retreat.

The 13th Army's ultimate objective was Nikolaev on the coast of the Sea of Azov. It's spearhead unit was the 3rd division. As the unit approached the Nikolaev area, Denikin's 1st Caucasian cavalry division conducted a furious attack on the 23rd regiment/2nd brigade. Taken by surprise, the Reds routed, fleeing northward. On the following day (Dec. 16th), its 26th and 27th regiments are assaulted and the usual brutal battle is fought. The end this time had the 1st Caucasian fleeing in panic. The Red advance rolled some 280 km in one month from Nov.20 to Dec. 20th. Nearly all advances were along the railway system not along roads. By December 10th, to the right of the Volunteers, the Don Army held along the Don River line

From the West, the 12th Army had been assigned the objective of Kiev. Specifically, the 44th, 47th and 58th divisions. The rivers in the area proved to be obstacles due to their high water and thin ice. Many of the Red troops were ferried across or lead across by locals at fords. Despite the city's importance, Denikin did not contest it very much and by Dec. 16th and 1830 has, the Reds had it. By the 26th, they had pushed back the Whites to Uman, Gaisin, Enamenka, some 200 km south of Kiev.

The fighting with the Red 11th Army in the Tsaritsyn area had only mild successes against Wrangel. Wrangel was more concerned about his rear area and the events on the Don River, which forced him to pull back. To the left of the Red 11th Army was an independent force consisting of 1st brigade/ 34th Division and the Moriaky naval unit. These units prepared for an attack across the frozen sections of the Caspian Sea coastline with the 1st brigade while the Naval unit landed at Kasiskogo and moved south. Due to the low sea level, this amphibious assault did not occur. This left the attack up to 1st brigade. On Nov.18th, the 1st brigade attacked at Ganiushkino. The Whites defending the area and held for a staggering 10 days. Then on the 29th, the Reds stormed it. The result was a good size booty consisting of 117 officers, 128 MG, 23 guns, two million rounds of cartridges, thousands of artillery shells, a radio station, 6 steamers, 6000 rifles, and 5000 other ranks. This White force was the only force blocking the Reds' connection to Astrakhan. White resistance after December 21st, was noticeably less around Slaviansk, in fact, there was none for the Red 42nd division to face. At Khrestish, the Whites stood and fought well on Christmas until threatened with encirclement.

The Red Cavalry Army was now ordered to separate the Denikin Cavalry Corps and the Don Army near Svatova. After a brief bitter struggle with the 10th Don division for 13 hours, the division routed. To the Reds, the event was observed and noted:

> "...the division took flight. The sight is beyond description. The officers of the unit attempted in vain to stop the men who threw their rifles and machine guns to the ground. The crews of the artillery also ran leaving their guns. The rout and panic was uncontrollable southward."

Denikin decided to halt this Red cavalry army (now consisting of 4th, 11th Cavalry divisions, 9th and 12th infantry divisions) at Rubezh. It was there he had concentrated the 4th Don, 2nd and 3rd Kuban Cavalry corps, which had arrived from Sochi. A total of 10,000 men. From the 25th to 27th, the two forces fought the usual savage battles and despite the superiority of the Whites, the Reds won. The same forces continued to clash at Gorlovka, both supported by armor trains. But the Reds continued to push back Denikins force and by the 30th, Denikin sent in his Markov division from 1st Corps. Both the Chechen cavalry and Markov's men suffered heavily. On the 31st, the Reds were at Alekseeva, Ekakterinoslav and Likhaya.

By the 24th, Fastov was taken, on the 27th, Lugansk. Denikin's army had been cut in two and the Donetz coal basin was again in Red control.

Once again, the British advisor, Major Williamson, was present during this time:

> "There were far too few police about and far too many troops who appeared to have left from the front and seemed to be spending their time cursing the Allies and breaking into wine stores. The best, as usual, held the front, but so far as the Don Army was concerned, the fall of Kharkov, and later, Tsaritsyn, caused a general withdrawal towards Novercherkassk and Rostov. The 2nd Don Corps was rapidly falling back in face of Red cavalry. The protection of rivers was now negated since ice had formed and were strong enough to hold men,horses and artillery. There seemed no likelihood of holding any positions better than another. Wrangel's counterattack with tanks and bombers simply fizzled out as he commanded a very mixed lot of men. The main elements were Kubans who had already decided political separatism and were beginning to give up."

As the Reds approached the British Military Mission at Novercherkassk, he further writes a typical scene, which has been often repeated since 1919:

"The evacuation is imminent. HQ was a waste of torn paper and full of smoking fires as documents were destroyed. Every now and then, a rider appeared, or a car raced by driven wildly with the officers plastered with snow. The refugees were preparing another move and packing their few pathetic belongings into bundles and battered suitcases. The Russians watched every move the British made and always complaining to us about how we left them in this state. Beaten units walk through the town, trains loaded with wounded and cavalry passed trudging through the snow."

The Caucasian army was now commanded by Pokrovski and had fallen back from Tsaritsyn in early January, 1920, along the Tikhoryetsk railway and held positions along the Manytsch river. On the left was the 1st, 2nd and 3rd Don Corps from Torgorvya to Bataisk, while Pavlov's Cavalry Corps was held in reserve. Adjacent was the Borbovtich Guards cavalry brigade of the Volunteer Army, which occupied Bataisk and to the coast of the Azov Sea.The right bank of the Don was held by 1st Corps with remnants of Markov and Alekseev divisions.

The third act of the Russian Civil war was about to be played out.

Sources:

1) Denikin, Anton. *March on Moscow*. Moscow Press, 1921
2) Denikin, Anton. *The White Armies*. Hyperion Press, 1973.
3) Kondratev, C. *Aircraft of the Russian Civil war*. Moscow Press. 2000
4) Wrangel, Peter. *Memoirs of General Wrangel*. 1930.
5) Willimanson, Hudleston. *Farewell to the Don*. John Day Publishing, 1973
6) *Russian Civil War Encyclopedia*. Moscow Press. 1982
7) Krasnov, Peter. *The Don Army 1918-19*. Moscow Press 1992
8) Lehovich, Dmitry. *White Against Red*. 1973
9) Malet, Michael. *Nest Makhano in the Russian Civil War*. 1980
10) Somin, Illya. *Stillborn Crusade*. 1996
11) *White Armies of the Russian Civil War*. Osprey Publishing, 1998
12) *Red Armies of the Russian Civil War*. Osprey Publishing, 1998
13) Iakushkin, Evergenei. *English Intervention 1918-20*. Moscow Press. 1928
14) Schmid, Alex. *Churchills Private War*. 1974
15) Stewart, George. *The White Armies of Russia*. 1970
16) Brinkly, George. *The Volunteer Army and the Allied Intervention in South Russia*. 1966.
17) Roberts, C. *In Denikin's Russian and the Caucasus 1919-20*. 1921
18) The Vrangel Collection, Hoover Institution, Stanford University, Palo Alto, CA.
19) The Pavel Kusonskii Collection, Hoover Institution, Stanford University, Palo Alto, CA.
20) The Mikhail Girs Collection, Hoover Institution, Stanford University, Palo Alto, CA.
21) Agureev, K. *Defeating Denikin's Army*. Moscow Press, 1961.
22) WO 153/1208, WO 158/747, WO 106/1194, WO32/5752, WO158/746+747, WO 158/750) WO 106/1198, WO33/971, CAB45/105. Public Record Office, London.
23) *Armor in the Russian Civil War*. Armada #14, Moscow Press. 1999

15

The Backwater: The Orenburg Army

The British were also involved on the East front where they had assigned advisors and liaison officers to various White forces. One such liaison was attached to Dutov's Army also known as the "Orenburg" Army, which fought with the Kolchak forces advancing from the east. In the liaison's report, dated November, 1919, a detailed look covers this army located in the Petropavalosk area and the battles along the Ishim River. Dutov was important, for his advance might have connected with Wrangel (who was still at Tsaritsyn) had this been May/June, 1919. But, by time of the report, Dutov was positioned 200+ miles southeast of Chelyabinsk and in no position to alter the course of the civil war.

A motley army it was. Here, members of the Orenburg Army in 1919—nasty looking! Photo: Museum of Russian Army, Moscow

The Orenburg Army as of October 15th, 1919, consisted of the following:

1st Corps(Gen. Shilnikov)	Cavalry	Infantry	Artillery Guns
1st Orenburg Cossack Division	480		
2nd Orenburg Cossack Division	283		
1st Turkestan Brigade	451	700	1
2nd Corps (Gen. Bakich)			
3rd Orenburg Cossack Division	2030	225	4
4th Orenburg Cossack Division	589	659	5
2nd Rifle Division	1540	1477	7
Independent Brigade			
Jaeger Regiment		69	
1st Rifle Regiment	320	144	1
Misc.Units	200		1
Stepanov's Brigade			
1st,4th, 33rd Orenburg Cossack Reg.	1340		
HQ,Garrision	1036	215	3
Steppe Group		164	

Dutov had a total of 12,000 men of which 9000 were cavalry and 3000 were infantry. This includes other recruits and those in rear services and the wounded. Of this, at least 25% were unfit for duty due to Typhus. The actual net fighting force was between 8000-10000 men at the start of November. At this time, the army was scattered from Turgai, west of Atbasar to Kokchav, a distance 300 miles. As the Liaison noted, " the army was in such a state of disorganization that it is difficult to understand why Dutov ever accepted the command, unless he was ignorant of the situation in Siberia."

Obviously, Dutov was ignorant of such conditions. The retreat of the Orenburg Army followed the Tashkent railway leading to the Aral Sea and turned into a rout. Most of the army retreated from Kustanai. The odd thing was, that despite the retreat and pychological state of the men, they were actually in excellent condition and continued to believe in their cause, despite the terrible privations. Typhus had begun to spread even on the "fringe" of the civil war.

The Army was not in real danger as the Red's attention was focused on the Kolchak forces to the north and were also in retreat. Dutov halted their retreat in the Kokchetav-Akmolinsk-Atbasar region, which was triangle in shape. Kokchetav was located in the north. The area was the flat,barren, Russian steppe and the only road led south from Petropavlovsk with few other settlements. Since Winter was approaching, the only real avenue of attack was down this road. The country teamed with vast herds of cattle, sheep and horses. The Liaison noted:

> "Dutov could concentrate all his forces in any of the three towns, build defenses and defied anybody sent against him. He used his worst forces on the front and never used his best corps, the 2nd!"

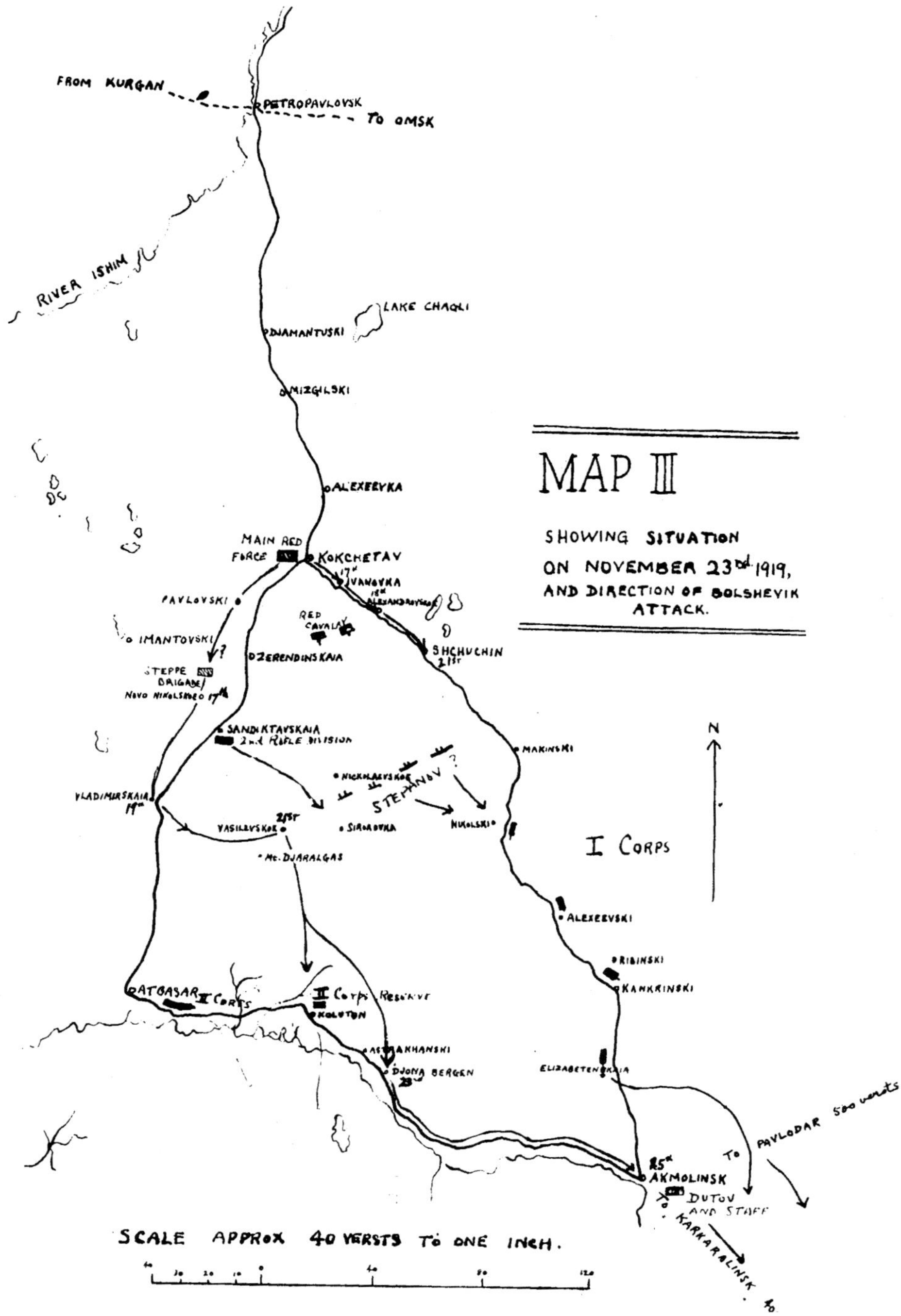
MAP III
SHOWING SITUATION ON NOVEMBER 23rd 1919, AND DIRECTION OF BOLSHEVIK ATTACK.
FROM KURGAN
PETROPAVLOVSK
TO OMSK
RIVER ISHIM
LAKE CHAQLI
DJAMANTUSKI
MIZGILSKI
ALEXEEVKA
MAIN RED FORCE
KOKCHETAV
IVANOVKA
PAVLOVSKI
IMANTOVSKI
RED CAVALRY
SHCHUCHIN
DZERENDINSKAIA
STEPPE BRIGADE
NOVO NIKOLSKOE
SANDIKTAVSKAIA
2nd RIFLE DIVISION
MAKINSKI
N
NICKOLAEVSKOE
STEPANOV
VLADIMIRSKAIA
VASILEVSKOE
SIRAOVKA
NIKOLSKI
I CORPS
ALEXEEVSKI
RIBINSKI
KANKRINSKI
ATBASAR
II CORPS
II Corps Reserve
KOLUTON
ASTRAKHANSKI
DJONA BERGEN
ELIZABETENSKAIA
TO PAVLODAR 500 versts
AKMOLINSK
DUTOV AND STAFF
To KARKARALINSK
SCALE APPROX 40 VERSTS TO ONE INCH.

The Soviet armies at this time were more interested in terrorizing the Cossack communities around Orenburg and contented with improving the line of communications to Tashkent. Thus, the only Red force that pursued the Orenburg Army was about 6000 men in November. About 5000 men occupied the Kokchetav area on November 15th and another 1000 men the road leading from Atbasar to Kokchetav. The Red plan, just prior to their attack, was to occupy Kokchevtev and to force Dutov to split up his army into small groups, which could be defeated, for as concentrated, he was a danger. Once Kokchetav fell, the Reds would attack on Shchuchin, Akmolinsk or Atbasar. The other important item was speed, as winter was setting in as most of the supplies were given to the fight against Kolchak.

Dutov's deployment was the opposite of what the British Liaison Officer recommended. The Stepanov brigade(1300) men had only reached Dnjlandi Adir (40 miles west of Atbasar) on November 2nd and the advance guard of 2nd Corps reached Atbasar. The remaining part of 2nd Corps was another 40 miles west. The 1st Corps was located around Eleninski (100+miles north of Atbasar) while Komarov's small force was near Mizgilski, another 50 miles north of 1st Corps. Red units were at Marinski, 60 miles west of Komarov and at Petropavlovsk,75 miles north of Komarov. Dutov had refused to obey the orders that arrived from Omsk directing his army to Lake Chagli (25 miles east of Mizgilski). Had Dutov obeyed the order, the Red attack would have failed.

Dutov basically strung out his units just as the Red's had hoped for trying to defend the road from Atbasar to Kokchetav. The garrison at Atbasar contained 500 men.

The Red force at Mariinski had 300 men, 2 guns and 4MG. Red patrols ventured out to Bug Altai, 50 miles south of Mariinski on the Ishim River. Red Cavalry were also located at Krivo Ozerni, 25 miles from elements of 1st Corps. By the 4th, a Soviet division was at Mariniiski. This was the start of the Red advance, for on the same day, the Red cavalry from Krivo attacked the Whites at Airtavski, which was repelled. Dutov's sense of security was over confidence. He was positive that there was no danger from the west or southwest. Dutov's intelligence had indicated that the Reds were not crossing the steppes between the Aral sea and Atbasar to pursue 2nd Corps or any pursuit from Kustanai. So, it appeared that the Reds were not going to bother with the Orenburg Army.

On the 6th, at 0800, the Reds attacked with 300 infantry, 200 cavalry and 2 guns, seizing Karlovka. The artillery tossed a few shells and Komarov's men retreated without any resistance. Dutov assumed that this was the start of the Red advance guard, then ordered the Stepanov brigade to Kokchetav. This order also went to 1st Corps which was ordered to Shchuchin. All the refugees were sent to Akmolinsk, and the Cossacks which had pledged to defend Kokchetav to the last, fled as well. Dutov also ordered the 2nd Corps to march across the Steppe to Shchuchin, while 1st Corps was ordered to Kokchetav.

On the 8th, the Reds advanced along the main road taking Akuiska. Red cavalry continued to push from a southeast direction while Dutov's Komarov detachment continued to retreat. The Orenburg Army was now made into an independent command, as Omsk was now being evacuated. Now Dutov ordered the 2nd Corps to march back to Atbasar with half his force, while 1st Corps was ordered back to Shchuchin! With the enemy pushing toward Kokchetav, Dutov's forces were marching and counter marching, strung out across the country. He had split them up into small units so distant from each other that any mutual support was impossible. On the 9th, Dutov's deployment was changed to the following:

1st Corps and Stepanov's Brigade at Kokchetav (2000 men) and
Shchuchin 3000 men.
2nd Corps at Atbasar (2500) and Sandiktavaskaia (3000).
Atameanski Regiment and others at Akmolinsk (1500).

The Red attackers used their cavalry units as flanking actions to induce additional fear on Dutov's men with encirclement. The Red units congesting of the 2nd Brigade/54th division, 1st,2nd,3rd Fortress Regiments and 1st Brigade/ 35th division totaled 5000 men and continued to advance with almost nil resistance. The Reds were poorly clothed,fed and their morale was bad.

The 1st Corps offered no resistance, nor did Stepanov's brigade, both retreated southeast. The reason given by General Shilnikov of 1st Corps was that it was too cold!

Kokchetav fell on the 15th. On the 17th, the Reds sent a force of 500 infantry and 200 cavalry attacking 1st Corps and took Ivanovka. On the 18th, Alexandrovskoe and by the 21st, Shchuchin had fallen. All of 1st Corps continued to flee to Akmolinsk. With the 1st Corps not willing to fight, the Reds focused on Backich's 2nd Corps.The 2nd Corps cavalry and HQ was now in Atbasar and it's infantry at Sandiktavaskia, some 80 miles north of the HQ.

The Red 1st Akmolinksi regiment took Novo Nickolskoe on the 17th with 250 men. On the 19th, the 2nd Kustanaiski regiment cut across the main Atbasar-Kokchetav road. This move now split the 2nd Corps and occupied Vladimirskaya and Vecelcia, some 60 miles north of Atbasar. On the 21st, it took Vasilevkoe, 30 miles east. This blocked the 2nd Rifle division/2nd Corps retreat route. All this critical information was not received in Akmolinsk until the 21st. The total Red force of the regiments involved came 2000 men.

Dutov's staff evinced no great panic with these moves and simply continued to prepare towards Karkaralinsk via Palovdar. The 2nd division was to withdraw towards Nickolaevskoe. On the 20th, Dutov ordered the 1st Corps to retreat to the Ribinski area, while Stepanov's brigade filled the gap between the two corps, some 60 miles apart. Stepanov would hold the door open from Nickolaevskoe to Sosnovka for 2nd Division to retreat through. The 2nd Corps moved to Koluton where the reserves (consisting of 1st infantry regiment and two Cavalry regiments) were under Captain Mogilov. On the 21st, Dutov received information that a large force was blocking the retreat of 2nd division. The Red armies were also 50 miles was of Omsk.

However, the Red force, after taking Vasilevskoe, headed southward to Kolution, some 55 miles. It was a bold cavalry move. However, Dutov thought the report was rubbish and disregarded it. He had no suspicion as to the danger his army was in.

The swift advances by the Reds on the 23rd, put White positions in danger. The 2nd Rifle division finally began to retreat across the steppes to Sirorovka, but the Cavalry force that headed south was now at Djona Bergen on the Atbasar to Akmolinsk road. This now blocked the retreat of 2nd Corps to Akmolinsk. This was a 60 mile advance in two days. Thus, 2nd corps was not only cut in two, it was isolated. It was at this time, Dutov and his staff decided that the main Red attack was against 2nd Corps. The odd thing was it offered no resistance! No orders arrived from Dutov or 2nd Corps HQ to stand and fight. As the Liaison wrote:

> "Everyone was thinking of his own safety and rather than risk with a handful of half hearted ill equipped men, each preferred to face the terrible hardships of a journey across the frozen Steppe in mid winter."

Dutov ordered each Corps commander to find their own ways to Karakaralink, some 250 miles further south. Most of 1st Corps by the 25th was within 25 miles of Akmolinsk. The Reds, by 0200, were right on the tail of 1st Corps. At Akmolinsk, panic set in and by noon the town was empty of soldiers except the sick and Cossacks pillaging. Captain Corrugate of the French Mission left at 1700 in his car. At 2100, the Reds occupied the town.

Nothing more was heard of 2nd Corps, Stepanov's brigade or the 2nd division! Thus, in 10 days, Dutov's army was routed by a force half it's size with almost nil resistance.

Dutov and his staff reached Karakaralinsk by Dec., 5th. The 2nd Corps managed to arrive with only a few hundred men marching via Spasski Zavod, while 1st Corps and Stepanov arrived via Baianaul. Karakaralinsk was evacuated on the 25th of December. In early January, 1920, Dutov handed over the command of the army to Annenkov of Serirechia. Stepanov was instructed to hold at Kour Bakanas, while General Bakich held Sergiopol. By this time, the remnants of the Orenburg Army was no more than 5000, mostly officers. When combined with the remnants of Ammenkov's 2nd Steppe Corps (which had held Semipalatinsk) totaled 15,000 men with shortages of artillery and ammunition.

Ataman Annenkov had commanded the Konvoy Partisan Regiment, a squadron from the Black Hussar Regiment, a Plastoon (dismounted Cossacks) Demi-Regiment, 1st and 2nd Partisan Rifle, Manchzhrsky Scouts, 1st Orenburg Cossacks, 1st, 2nd and 3rd Kirghiz-Horse Regiments, 1st Horse and 1st Cossack Batteries in July 1919. He was experienced.

Admiral Kolchak had now made Annenkov a Brigadier-General. In March 1920 the Reds broke up the army and the remains retreated into China at the close of May.

In April 1922,in Primov, western China, arrived the Annenkov Regiment containing guerrillas under the command Colonel Illarev (8 officers and 51 lower ranks). On September 1st, began the last battle for Primov. Annenkov's forces then consisted of: the Moscow Horse Regiment and the Annenkov Horse Demi-regiment (2+ squadrons) with a strength of 287 bayonets; They actively participated in these battles and then fled across over the border in October.

Returning, Ammenkov's front originally faced only south, but because of Dutov's rout and then the defection of most of the 2nd Steppe Corps at Semipalatinsk in early December, Annenkov now faced danger in all directions. Annenkov laid siege to Jarkent and his main body held Kopal with success. Stepanov with his remnants and those of the Atamanski regiment guarded the road from Karakaralinsk and 35 miles south of Semipalatinsk. Bakich and his ruminants were scattered along the Irtisk to Zaisan. Ammenkov's HQ was at Urdjar.

So the resistance continued, but the moral rot had set in from the Orenburg Army rout that infected Annenkov's men. On January 21st, 1920, Sergiopol was taken along with much of Dutov's old staff. By the end of the month, even Annenkov's army collapsed.

The Liaison makes the following humorous and insightful observations:

> "If Dutov had even concentrated half of his cavalry and secured one success, however temporary, it would have been invaluable. A cavalry charge against trained

infantry is not likely to succeed, but the Red troops were never in close formation and a victory would not have been hard to gain despite the low morale of the Cossacks. Dutov's inability to concentrate all available forces at the decisive point was necessary in order to gain even temporary success, caused Dutov's failure. This is not surprising when one learns that he spent his service during the Russo-Japanese War at the Staff College learning theory instead of gaining actual experience in the field."

Also:

"...so great was the terror inspired by the approach of the Reds, that the small Steppe Brigade marched straight on Akmolinsk while the Cossacks fled in terror in all directions. Dutov's men preferred to face the Steppe winter in face of facing a few conscript peasants whose only uniform was a red cockade in the cap and probably had never been in combat. When one remembers the success attained by Mamantov and cavalry corps on Denikin's front earlier in the year, it is possible to imagine what a different fate if Dutov's Cossacks had been promptly organized and led by a bold leader against the enemy communications in the north."

The Liaison on tactics & morale:

"Dutov had no tactics that I know of, he never got near enough to the enemy for that, his only tactic were to run away whenever a rumor of a Red Advance was heard....

...Their morale was not good. Like all half educated and ignorant peoples, the Cossacks would make good soldiers if decently fissured and disciplined. The officers usually ran away before anyone else and discipline in the real sense of the word was unknown. The Cossacks are good at charging through villages (where there is no enemy) and firing revolvers into the air or at old men,womena nd children. The Siberian troops were good except they hated the Cossacks almost more than the Bolsheviks. The non Cossack and Cossack forces refused to support one another in action and battle after battle was lost."

On Red Tactics and morale:

"It appears that the method employed by the Bolsheviks on entering a town was to conscript as many men as they needed, give each a rifle and a few rounds of ammunition, mix these new recruits with the older hands and send them off into action with no training. In the operations against Dutov, the Red infantry proceeded along the road towards the objective, all sitting in four wheeled carts. About six men to a cart or in big farm wagons, of a dozen. If these wee fired on, one would gallop back to the others. The carts were halted and the infantry clambered down to form a rough line. Night advances were common. Enemy morale was bad, most were peasants and sick of war, lacked food and clothes, Nearly all of them wanted to return to the days of the Tsar. Desertions were frequent and only the dreaded commissars kept them in order."

On elements/conditions:

"The weather was clear and cold during October,November and December. Usually the weather is in a blizzard condition. The ground was hard making for rapid movement in carts. The only road was the old post roads of the pre-revolutionary days. These are few in number and merely tracks across country. The telegraph line runs from Petropavlosk- Kokchetav-Atbasar-Akmolinsk-Karagandi-Semipalatinsk-Serigiopol-Verni. The country south of Petropavalosk is flat with small woods. South of the town, there are small hills of little height. The whole area is flat, with a few streams or woods."

On military intelligence:

"Both sides used the nomadic Kirghiz tribe to obtain information about the other. The Reds used women as spies. Marriage is of so little importance in Siberia in these days that a woman spy would have no compunction at going through a form of marriage with a white officer for purely political reasons. It is a notorious fact that the Russian officers could not keep secrets from their women."

On Propaganda:

"Little or nothing was done to enlighten the people as to the true state of affairs."

On Refugees:

"Russians wee selling their daughters and women to Chinese soldiers in order to get a little food and fuel. Each officer of the Cadre Brigade (200 Officers,400 men)had their own cart with his luggage, a woman, a servant and coachman. Women had extraordinary influence on the officers and it was always bad. Dutov had a mistress, a girl of seventeen. The Baron von Tisenhausen, one time Governor of Yakutsk and vice Governor of Orenburg stole four million roubles and employed it solely for his escape. The misappropriation of public money was very common, nearly every officer carried hundreds of thousands of roubles."

On Dutov and his Staff:

"However bad his generalship, it offered no excuse for the cowardice and disgraceful behavior of officers and men. The officers, and especially, the senior ones were chiefly to blame. Patriotism was an unknown quality, nearly all were dishonest and anxious only for personal safety. Their dislike of the Allies was ridiculous and many openly said that England and France had done nothing to help and Japan and America were secretly helping the Bolsheviks. Officers had not been on the front since July 1914 stated they were tired of war and that if the Allies sent troops to Siberia, they would retire and let the Allies fight. They were quite serious. Their admiration of Germany knew no bounds and most refused to believe that she was defeated! Their mental outlook was so childish that many wished for an alliance with Germany in order to punish the Allies. In my opinion, non interference by the Allies in Russian affairs is essential to peace in the world."

While this book's primary focus is not on the eastern front, it did play an important role up through the spring of 1919. The leader of the Siberian Army, as well as the others on this front was Admiral Kolchack. Even General Denikin was his subordinate. Kolchack's main thrust was simply along the Siberian railroad using the white forces, which included 30,000 Czech soldiers. Eventually, Kolchack would appoint a twenty-something year old Gadja the leader of the Northern army, to which, many Siberians were attached. A s mentioned before, Kolchack hoped to meet the allies near Kotlas in the north to create a solid front. It was also hoped the Dutov would meet with Wrangel near Tsaritysn. Neither would ever occur.

The Siberian army was formed on May 26,1918, in Novonikolaevsk after the overthrow of the Bolshevik authority of the Temporary Siberian Government using the base staff of the Western Siberia Military District. On June 13, 1918, it was named the Western Siberia Independent Army and renamed again on June 27, 1918, to the Siberian Army. The staff of the army coordinated the activity of all White Forces in Siberia and the Far East. At the beginning of June, the Army totaled 4000 men. By June 18, there were 6047 (4332 rifles, 1215 sabers, and 500 unarmed soldiers). At the end of June, 7600 men, 19 cannons, and 30 machineguns. By the middle of July, there were 23,400 men. By July 31, there were 6970 officers, 28,229 volunteers. By August, there were more than 40,000 men (nearly 10,000 officers and the remainder were volunteers). By September 20, 1918, the Army had called up about 166,000 men and was already larger than the Volunteer Army. The combat composition of the Army on September 1st, was 60,200 men (according to other data, there were only 37,600 men, 70 cannons, and 184 machineguns), and byOctober, there were 10,700 officers, 59,900 men, and 113,900 unarmed soldiers.

The Siberian Army was renamed back to the Siberian Independent Army by December 24, 1918. By the end of April, 1919, the Siberian Independent Army had approximately 40,000 soldiers (this is the combat component). By the end of spring 1919, the Army had liberated Okhansk, Osu, Sarapul, and Izhevsk. By June, the Army had split into Northern and Southern Groups, Composite Shock Siberian and 8th Kamsk Army Corps', and the 1st Cavalry Division. In July 1919, the Army totaled 350,000 men (56,600 rifles, 3900 sabers, 600 machineguns, 164 cannons, 4 armored trains, and 9 airplanes).

In Samara, all of the Red aircraft were concentrated in Kazan and when this fell to Kolchack, some 45-50 aircraft (the majority of them were unflyable were captured. This war booty created the 2nd White Air group composed of the 5th, 6th, 7th and 8th Air-Detachments. The Reds had the 23rd, 1st, 2nd and 4th air detachments.

The Siberian Army Order of Battle as of May, 1919

Ekaterinburg

Staff of the Siberian Army	Gen-Maj Bogoslavskiy
1st Immortal Shock Regiment	Col Vlasov
General Brigade of the Siberian Army	Forming
King of the Serbs Partisan Detachment	Voevoda (Governor) Voskar
Jaeger Company	Ensign Latynin
Independent Security Company of the Army Staff	Staff-Captain Zakharov
River Combat Flotilla	Counter-Admiral Smirnov
Independent Sapper Company	Lieutenant Urusov
3rd Battalion of the Railroad Security Detachment	LtCol Paritskiy
3rd Transportation Battalion	Col Lebedev
4th Railroad Battalion	
7th Battalion of the Railroad Security Detachment	LtCol Papin
8th Battalion of the Railroad Security Detachment	LtCol Nenashev
10th Battalion of the Railroad Security Detachment	
1st Independent Division of Armored Trains	Junior Lieutenant Shcherbakov
Personal Convoy of the Army Command	Cavalry Captain (Rotmistr) Time

1st Cavalry Division	
Division Commander	Gen-Lt Milovich
Chief of Staff	Col Semenov
Kazan' Dragoon Regiment	Forces Master Sergeant Vasil'ev
Tomsk Hussar Regiment	Col Klein
Ekaterinburg Lancer Regiment	Cavalry Captain (Rotmistr) Molostvov
Simbirskiy Lancer Regiment	Col Oshanin
1st Light Horse Artillery Division	LtCol Khaliletskiy
School for preparing Siberian Army Ensigns	Col Dybov
8th Kamskiy Army Corps	Gen-Lt Panov
Chief of the Corps Staff	LtCol Kononov

15th Votkinsk Rifle Division	Col Al'bokrinov
Chief of Staff	Cavalry Captain (Rotmistr) von Bach
57th Votkinsk Rifle Regiment of the 17 August Factory	Col Vol'skiy
58th Saigatskiy Rifle Regiment in the name of Czechoslovakia Col Crier	
59th Osinskiy Rifle Regiment in the name of Minin and Pozhar	Lieutenant Zhulanov
60th Votkinsk Rifle Regiment in the name of the Unity Powers	Col Otmar-Shtein

16th Sarapul' Rifle Division	
Chief of Staff	
1st Sarapul' Rifle Regiment	Forming
2nd Kazan Rifle Regiment	LtCol Ivanov
3rd Laishevo Rifle Regiment	LtCol Zaalov
4th Chistopol' Rifle Regiment	LtCol Rodzevich
Frontline Brigades	
15th Frontline Regiment	
16th Frontline Regiment	
Cavalry	
Votkinsk Horse Division	
Artillery	
15th Light Artillery Battery	Lieutenant Kurbalovskiy
16th Light Artillery Battery	Col Berens
Engineering Units	
15th Sapper Battalion	
16th Engineering Division	
Composite Shock Corps	
Corps Commander	Col Stepanov
Chief of Staff	Col Rybaltovskiy
1st Shock Division	
Division Commander	Col Labuntsev
Chief of Staff	
1st Siberian Shock Regiment	
2nd Siberian Shock Regiment	
3rd Siberian Shock Regiment	
2nd Shock Division	
Division Commander	Col Boronov
Chief of Staff	
5th Siberian Shock Regiment	
6th Siberian Shock Regiment	
7th Siberian Shock Regiment	
Cavalry	
Independent Hussar Shock Division	LtCol Matveev

Artillery

1st Light Artillery Shock Battery
2nd Light Artillery Shock Battery

Engineering Units

1st Engineering Shock Division
2nd Engineering Shock Division

The Group of General Lieutenant Pepelyaev

Chief of Staff	Gen-Maj Surnin
Non-Commissioned Officer Battalion	
Convoy Squadron	
Independent Telegraph Company	Staff Captain Aleksandrov
Sapper Battalion	LtCOl Zverev
Railroad Battalion	
2nd Siberian Aviation Detachment	Military Flight Staff Captain Il'ich
Air-Balloon Detachment	
Independent Automobile Company	Lieutenant Migai
Siberian Division of Armored Trains	
1st Siberian Dragoon Division	Rotmistr (Cavalry Captain) Yanert
11st Orenburg Cossack Regiment	Col Sukin
1st Siberian Spotlight Company	Junior Lieutenant Novozhilov

1st Mid-Siberian Army Corps

Corps Commander	Gen-Maj Zenevich
Chief of Staff	Col Turbin
Split-Squadron Convoy	
Telegraph Company	
Independent Heavy Battery	Lieutenant Bushuev
Independent Long-Range Battery	

1st Siberian Rifle Division

Division Commander	Gen-Maj Molchevskiy
Chief of Staff	LtCol Shtal'berg
1st Siberian Engineer Division	Staff Captain Kirenskiy
1st Composite Siberian Artillery Battery	LtCol Rekhov
1st Novonikolaevsk Siberian Rifle Regiment	Col Lastovskiy
2nd Barabinsk Siberian Rifle Regiment	Col Ivakin
3rd Barnaul Siberian Rifle Regiment	Col Yurmanov
4th Yenisey Siberian Rifle Regiment	LtCol Zhuravlev
1st Siberian Jaeger Regiment	Staff Captain Borzetsov

2nd Siberian Rifle Division

Division Commander	Gen-Maj Ukke-Ugovets
Chief of Staff	Col Ostroumov
2nd Siberian Engineer Division	
2nd Composite Artillery Battery	LtCol Popov
5th Tomsk Siberian Rifle Regiment	Gen-Maj Kuz'menskoy
6th Marinskiy Siberian Rifle Regiment	Capt Olifer
7th Kuznets Siberian Rifle Regiment	Col Shchetkin
8th Biysk Siberian Rifle Regiment	Capt Johanovich
2nd Siberian Jaeger Regiment	Col Nikolaev

16th Siberian Rifle Division

Division Commander	Gen-Maj Sharov
Chief of Staff	Col Sukharskiy
16th Siberian Engineer Division	Capt Razumov
16th Siberian Artillery Battery	LtCol Strizhov
61st Perm (Siberian) Rifle Regiment	LtCol Barmin
62nd Cherdyn' (Siberian) Rifle Regiment	Capt Reinhart
63rd Dobryanka (Siberian) Rifle Regiment	Col Polyakov
64th Solikamsk (Siberian) Rifle Regiment	LtCol Pravokhenskiy

17th Independent Siberian Rifle Brigade

Brigade Commander	
Chief of Staff	
17th Siberian Engineer Division	
17th Siberian Rifle Artillery Battery	
65th Obskiy Siberian Rifle Regiment	LtCol Serebryannikov
66th Altay Siberian Rifle Regiment	LtCol Verstak

17th Siberian Jaeger Division (as stated, I believe this should be Regiment)

1st Independent Siberian Assault Brigade

Brigade Commander	
Chief of Staff	
1st Siberian Assault Regiment	
2nd Siberian Assault Regiment	
1st Siberian Assault Cavalry Division	
1st Siberian Assault Artillery Battery	LtCol Strakhov
1st Siberian Assault Engineer Division	

1st Siberian Frontline Brigade

Brigade Commander	LtCol Schnaperman
Chief of Staff	
1st Siberian Frontline Regiment	LtCol Ignatyuk
2nd Siberian Frontline Regiment	Capt Erokhin
16th Siberian Frontline Regiment	Capt Pokrovskiy

The Group of General Lieutenant Verzhbitskiy

Group Commander	
Chief of Staff	Col Kruze

3rd Steppe Army Corps

Corps Commander	Gen-Maj Smolin
Chief of Staff	

4th Steppe Rifle Division

Division Commander	
Chief of Staff	
13th Omsk Siberian Rifle Regiment	Staff Captain Budilkin
14th Irtysh Siberian Rifle Regiment	LtCol Dombrovskiy
15th Kurgan Siberian Rifle Regiment	LtCol Verzhbolovich
16th Ishim Siberian Rifle Regiment	LtCol Kazagrandi

7th Steppe Rifle Division

Division Commander	Col Cherkasov
Chief of Staff	Capt Zuev
25th Tobol Siberian Rifle Regiment	Col Bordzilovskiy
26th Tyumen' Siberian Rifle Regiment	
27th Verkhnoturskiy Siberian Rifle Regiment	Capt Kurenskov
28th Yalutorovskiy Siberian Rifle Regiment	Capt Onushkevich

3rd Siberian Assault Brigade

Brigade Commander	
Chief of Staff	
5th Assault Regiment	
6th Assault Regiment	

Rear Cadre of the Brigade

Brigade Chief of Staff	
4th Rear Cadre Regiment	Col Gede
7th (50) Rear Cadre Regiment	Col Osipov

Krasnoufa Frontline Brigade

Brigade Commander	Col Pankov
Chief of Staff	
1st Kungur Frontline Regiment	Col Galileev
2nd Kungur Frontline Regiment	LtCol Parfenov

Cavalry

17th Orenburg Cossack Regiment	Col Kruchinin
Horse Half-Squadron	Lieutenant Neiman

Shtakor's Flying Detachment	Junior Lieutenant Bandzyak
Perm Cavalry Regiment	

Artillery

4th Light Artillery Battery	LtCol Plotnikov
4th Howitzer Artillery Battery	Col Cherepanov
7th Light Artillery Battery	
1st Siberian Independent Heavy Battery	Col Rozov

Engineering Units

3rd Sapper Battalion	LtCol Popov
3rd Siberian Aviation Detachment	Staff Captain Faddeev
7th Engineer Division	

4th Siberian Corps

Corps Commander	Gen-Maj Grivin
Chief of Staff	Col Shelavin

3rd Siberian Rifle Division

Division Commander	
Chief of Staff	LtCol Semenov
9th Irkutsk (Siberian) Rifle Regiment	LtCol Kaupin
10th Baikal (Siberian) Rifle Regiment	Col Kukharev
11th Nizheudinsk (Siberian) Rifle Regiment	Capt Boyarskov
12th Verkhneudinsk (Siberian) Rifle Regiment	Capt Popov

15th Siberian Rifle Division

Division Commander	Col Shul'kevich
Chief of Staff	
57th Pavlodar (Siberian) Rifle Regiment	
58th Akmolinsk (Celinograd) (Siberian) Rifle Regiment	Col Solov'ev
59th Sayan (Siberian) Rifle Regiment	Col Tonkoshkur
60th Siberia (Siberian) Rifle Regiment	LtCol Golovanenko

Zlatoust'-Krasnoufa Brigade

Brigade Commander	
Chief of Staff	
1st Krasnoufa Rifle Regiment	Junior Lieutenant Borshchaninov
2nd Kyshtim Rifle Regiment	Staff Captain Zhuk

Cavalry

General Tatar Squadron	Staff Captain Kurov
Achinsk Cavalry Division	

Artillery

3rd Light Artillery Battery	Staff Captain Smolyaninov
Krasnoufa Rifle Artillery Battery	
15th Siberian Light Artillery Battery	

Engineering Units

3rd Siberian Engineer Division	Staff Captain Bulygin

Cadre Units

Frontline Cadre Brigade:
3rd Frontline Cadre Regiment
15th Frontline Cadre Regiment

Sources:

1) Deryabin, A. White Armies. Moscow Press. 1999
2) The Encyclopedia of the Russian Civil War. Moscow Press. 1982
3) Kondratev, C. Aircraft of the Russian Civil War. Moscow Press. 1999
4) The White Guards. Moscow Press. 1999
5) WO106/1205, PRO, London.

16

The Script of the Defeated

In every war, in every battle, and in every fight there is defeat. Like so many times before the Russian Civil war and so many times since 1919, there is the usual script of the defeated that is followed. And so it went, the same course for General Denikin. The scene was the usual chaos, the spasms of defiant resistance from those defeated only to be overwhelmed by the basic mathematics of warfare. The once lofty goal of a "new Russia" was now "how do we remain alive." The discontent among the High Command and in the hapless Private in the field was irreparable. The usual nose dive in troop morale was rampant to which the civilians simply agitated even more. In a more modern time, the chaos of the end of the Vietnam War in April, 1975, is only a microcosim when compared to the horrors of the panic during this time. The Reds were coming and nothing could be done. Run for your life!

While the White soldiers in the field were losing faith and heart, those in Denikins High Command allowed their personal differences to cripple whatever chance they had. When Wrangel had been placed in command of the last Shock Group for offensive action, under him and in charge of the cavalry was the famed General Mamantov. He was admired and liked by his men, but not by Wrangel. General Wrangel, in spite of Denikin's objections (i.e., orders), Wrangel removed Mamantov and appointed the gallant Ulagai. This offended the Don Cossacks and Mamantov. Mamantov circulated this "disapproval" by wire to his superiors and regiments. When the cavalry attacked, the first to desert were the Cossacks. They were then followed by the Kuban Cossacks.

Denikin writes as to what followed:

> "For such an unprecedented breach of discipline I took Mamantov's command away, but the Ataman and General Sidorin of the Don Army, the persons controlling the Don Cossack territory, took his side because of his popularity and

thought he was the only man who could rally the Cossacks. The Cossacks were reincorporated and Mamantov was reinstated as commander."

On November 24th, General Denikin wrote to the British Secretary of War from Rostov, Armed Forces of South Russia HQ. This letter would arrive in London on December 16th:

> "Your Excellency, I take advantage of General Briggs departure to send you once more my deep gratitude for all the work you have been carrying on in the restoration of Russia, in spite of the hostility and misunderstanding which frequently surrounds you. At this moment my armies are passing through difficult times, but not for one moment has their faith in final victory wavered. In my opinion the following points are the most essential to hasten the termination of hostilities:
>
> 1. A more friendly attitude toward Russia on the part of the Allies as regarding the Caucasian and Baltic Political questions.
>
> 2. The energetic supply of material to armies and railways and the credit for the reconstruction of Russian industry.
>
> 3. Friendly neutrality on the part of Romania and hastening on her part of the supplies of Russian munitions.
>
> 4. A greater activity on the part of the Polish forces from whose front the Bolsheviks have transferred 43,000 sabres and bayonets against me.
>
> 5. The stringent blockading both materially and morally of Soviet Russia by the Allies.
>
> The day will come when the eyes of the blind shall be opened and when the actual fact of a powerful alliance born amidst the sufferings of the Russian people, and strengthened by the feelings of gratitude towards England, will recompense you for all your labours and will become a landmark in history."

Keep in mind when Denikin wrote this: Nov. 24th. His armies were in full reverse and the Red avalanche was in high gear. As to item 2, Denikin was not listening to General Holman when he was told that England was at the end of providing support. Most of the equipment seldom reached the front line troops. More alarming was Denikin expected England to rebuild the new Russia! As to item 3, as previously noted, Denikin planned to declare war on Romania at some point. Yet, he wanted England to apply political pressure on the country to release the needed Russian ammunition so he could defeat the Reds and then turn on Romania! As to item 4, Poland occupied a line from Kovno-Dvinsk-Jitomir-Proskurov. When Denikin took Kiev, the Poles stopped attacking the Reds and started negotiations to acquire land. Denikin hoped that England would impose upon Poland to attack.

Not much came of this letter, for on Dec. 29th, General Greenly ordered the letter not circulated at the request of the Secretary of State. The letter clearly shows Denikin was in denial as to his fate. A fate rapidly changing. By the time the letter reached the hands of the Secretary, the fate was sealed. Case closed, which is why the British were going to do as little as possible now.

General Holman had also written a letter to Winston Churchill on the 26th, which also was received about the same time. In it, Holman tries to justify the position of Denikin, as he was a staunch supporter of the Volunteer Army:

> "Dear Mr. Churchill, We have been working hard to get the necessary information from the Russian staff, but things are not as they are in ordinary armies. Returns are difficult to get, distances are enormous, communications are bad, and the situation changes sometimes with startling rapidity."

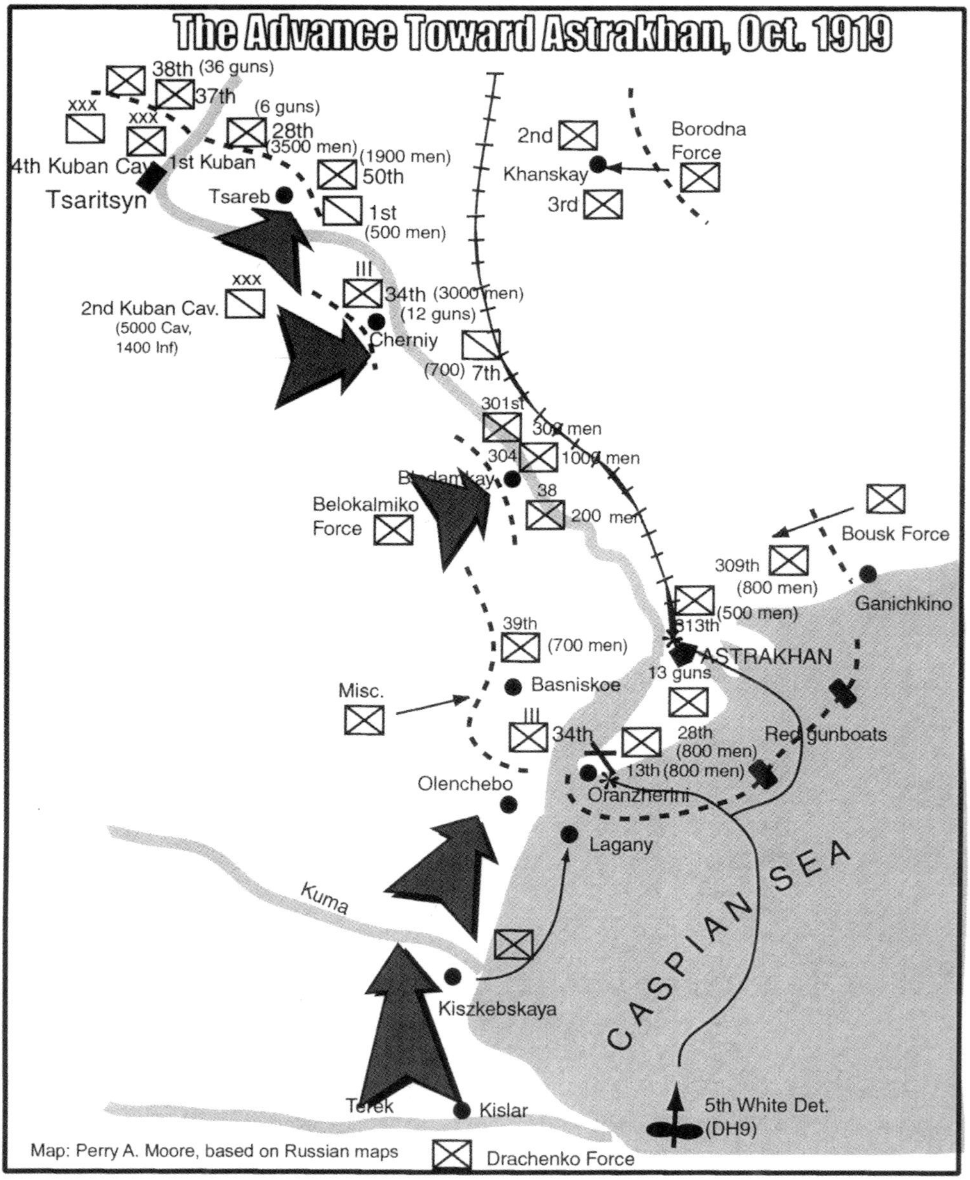

Holman continues:

> "The Bolshevik centres in western Europe are in Berne and Geneva. It is believed they are in touch with the German Government from whom they hope to obtain material. It is also believed that they are in touch with the United States of America. Since May, Red forces killed, wounded are 125,000, while 270,000 are prisoners. The forces opposite Denikin are estimated at 240,000."

The purpose of the Holman letter was to invoke additional support, which fell on deaf ears.

There was more political intrigue occurring in December unbeknownst to Denikin. General Wrangel had initiated a power play to have Denikin removed as Wrangel and many other Generals did not agree with Denikin's strategy. On December 11th, Wrangel and Sidorin (Commander of the Don Army) conducted a secret meeting without Denikin in Rostov. Gen.Shkuro was openly vocal about having Denikin removed due to the collapse of the Volunteer Army. Many of the Atamans and other officers from the Don and Kuban provinces also wanted a change. When Denikin found out, he summoned a staff meeting and demanded to know what was said. Wrangel explained that it was a meeting to study a list of problems. Denikin remained furious and called the secret meeting a violation of military protocol. On the 25th, Wrangel met with the Kuban province leaders on this matter only to find their support had now reversed and opposed Denikin's replacement! On the 31st, the British sent Wrangel a telegram stating that if there was a coup, Wrangel would be the designated successor. This undercurrent would continue to the very end.

In early December, Denikin concentrated another "Shock Group" to meet the Red threat, which he anticipated coming via Vailuki-Kupiansk-Lugansk. For this, he hand picked the best of what he had, a cavalry corps from the Caucasian Army, a cavalry division from the Don, and a Terek cavalry division from the internal front. He placed five divisions north of Vailuki and one in Vailuki. The unique thing about this force was the concentration of 40 tanks (by some accounts), mostly MkV, and all available aircraft. However, as Holman stated:

> "...the Russian commanders did not know how to employ tanks and were almost equally as bad as employing aeroplanes to the best advantage. Moreover, the weather was bad for either. The consequence was that both tanks and aeroplanes lost all opportunity to act effectively."

The end result when this force was confronted by Budenny's cavalry units were many bolted and the shock force which had looked awesome melted away. Later it was found out that Budenny had four German officers on his staff. That explained the "storm trooper" tactics the Red forces used at times with their lightening thrusts.

General Wrangel was given command of the Volunteer Army in December, which by now only contained 3600 Infantry and 4700 cavalry (Wrangel states it was 2600 infantry, 1000 cavalry). The Kuban corps was actually only 3000 men, the Kornilov division had only 800 men, the Markov division was a cadre only and the Drozdovsky division had only two companies remaining! Yes, the script was being followed here and in another 25 years

(1945) in Germany, and again in another 30 years(1975) in South Vietnam. The defeated grabbing for units that have been grinded down. Units with large sounding names to deceive the enemy and improve morale. However, this was the same for the Reds whose armies were composed of a few divisions, which in reality were equal to one division. Both sides were hurting, the Whites had some 42,723 men in hospitals. The Red 8th, 9th,10th and 11th armies were reduced to minimum levels of manpower due to Typhus epidemics by late December.

When Wrangel took over the Volunteer Army on November 24th, he imposed compulsory service and forced those in the army to continue to fight through use of harsh discipline. At principal points on the railroad he left a group of soliders with Generals and Colonels with plenary powers. They were to search all the trains going to the front, seize stolen objects, gather and send back deserters to their regiments, shoot recalcitrants and mauraders.

When Wrangel took over the Volunteer Army, he reported what he had found in a report to Denikin:

> " The units with tanks are not used because they are afraid of losing them. The artillery is no longer of use. The Alexeev division has only 300 men. The army has marched without rest for months and is utterly exhausted. The horses have developed foot disease forcing us to discard guns. The condition of the cavalry is lamentable. The horses have not been shod for a long while, and have nearly gone lame, others are ill from exhaustion. The bitter truth is that there is no longer an Army. We must look at the situation squarely in the face. I consider it indispensable:
>
> 1. Choose a single direction for the retreat to concentrate our forces.
> 2. Evacuate Rostov and Taganrog
> 3. Fortify rear bases
> 4. Reduce the over large General Staffs and send the surplus to the front.
> 5. Make arrangements to move the families of soldiers to the rear
> 6. Take ruthless measures to stop marauding, drunkeness, and every kind of abuse starting with the high ranks whose bad examples corrupt the troops
> 7. To re-equip the cavalry or this branch will be worthless
> 8. Put the railways under military control
>
> I have written many dispatches, but all in vain. Unless the measures are put into force, I must request you to transfer the command of the Volunteer Army to someone else."

Wrangel personally gave the dispatch to Denikin. Denikin opened it and read it, then looked at Wrangel desparingly, "All the same, we must go on with it."

Both men were clearly growing more frustrated with the hopeless situation. Wrangel tried in vain to get Denikin to retreat towards the Crimea. During the coming great retreat, some 25000 men and 10000 Don Cossacks retreated towards and into the Crimea. The Cavalry had few horses, weapons and completely demoralized. These men were shipped off to Eupatoria. The Volunteer Army was in complete disorganization. Cavalry with no horses, little artillery, and few machine guns.

Wrangel notes:

> "...the men were in rags and felt very bitter. For the most part they refused to obey their officers any longer. It was no longer an effective force. The front was held by the Crimean Corps under General Slachtchov. It was inumerable remnants totaling 3000 infantry and 2000 cavalry. The Red 13th Army opposite us had 6000 infantry and 3000 cavalry."

The Don Army under General Sidorin on Dec. 18th, was issued a "defend at all costs order." The order instructed the 1st Don Corps to hold when their retreat reached Tsimdianskyo and Konstantivovsku near the Kumshak River. The 2nd and 3rd Corps were to defend to the death the rail stations at Tarasovka Kamensku and Glubokia. Lugansk was defended by Dubrowsky.

When the Red 9th Army attacked using their encircling tactics on the 24th, instantly the orders Sidorin had issued were forgotten. However, on the 25th , when the Red 4th cavalry division conducted a flank attack at Alder Horn, they were met with the 2nd and 3rd Don Cavalry brigades. These two forces engaged in another six hour battle until the Whites retreated to Krivorozhe. When the 1st and 2nd Don Corps felt threatened by the 9th Army attacks, which were heading for the Don Army base at Novotcherkask, they retreated to the Donetz River line.

By the 19th, the Reds had successfully prevented Denkin from concentrating any forces by splitting up the Don Army into two parts.

The Red armies now began their approach to Rostov with the 8th Army (33rd,16th,15th divisions). On Dec.27th, the 33rd division was suddenly attacked by the 4th Don Cavalry Corps at Illiria. The attacked failed and the corps retreated to Novotcherkask. The 10th Army began it's offensive on the 29th, and this quickly routed the defending 1st Don Corps and Caucasian Army near Tsaritsyn(Stalingrad). The attack had used 8 divisions and one cavalry division against a combined White strength of 3 infantry divisions and 2 cavalry divisions, all depleted.

The New Year, 1920

The first week of January saw the Allies reviewing the question of continued aid to Denikin. Denikin had requested two army corps to bolster his collapsing situation and suggested they could be raised from Bulgarian volunteers. He also requested that the vast Bulgarian war stocks that had been promised to him in 1918, be sent to him. However, the French thought Denikin was not a good risk and sent nothing.

The following are troop dispositions for Denikin's men on January 8th:

> The Caucasian army under Porkrovski was mainly along the Sal river. The Don Army led by Sidorin and the Volunteer Corps led by Kutepov were ordered to hold the line from the Azov Sea near Khapri and Rostov/Novotcherkask, including from the Don River to the Sal River. The remaining parts of the Volunteer Army led by Schilling had the Crimean group led by Slastchev in the Crimea and Odessa. Nikolaev and Kherson was held by the Primotov Group. Lastly, the North

Caucasian Army led Erdeli, was ordered to hold Petrovsk-Grozny and Ekaterinodar railway.

The Denikin counterattacks continued to fail as the Red 13th Army, Budenny's cavalry army, and 8th Army easily pushed the remnants of the Volunteer Army, Udagai Cavalry Corps and the 3rd Don corps toward Taganrog - Rostov- Novotcherkask. Denikin reorganized the Volunteer Army creating a Volunteer Corps. The 2nd and 3rd Kuban Cavalry Corps were sent to the Kuban area. Meanwhile, the Red 21st and 16th divisions seized the railway station at Valiant held by 4500 men of the 5th Don division of 3rd Don Corps. There was no fight, only surrender. The 23rd,14th, 22nd divisions and 3rd cavalry brigade battled with Denikin's 7th Don division, which resisted for a few days. Once the 7th Don division gave way, the Reds advance some 95 km south of Moroevsay. The remnants of the 5th cavalry Corps, a cavalry brigade and parts of the Markov division were withdrawn to Kushevskaia. Denikin had hoped to halt the Reds along the Don and Tuedov Rivers with the remaining parts of the Volunteer, Don and Caucasian Armies.

The Soviets began to plan for Operation Novercherkassk-Rostov on January 2nd. The Southern front was instructed to take Berdiansk, Mariupol and Taganrog. The left wing of the South and Southeast Fronts were to seize Rostov and Novercherkassk. Rostov was of prime importance. The 14th and 13th armies would attack from Berdiansk to Taganrog, while Budenny's Cavalry army and 8th Army towards Rostov-Novercherkassk.

Denikin used his units to slow down the advance towards Rostov and Novercherkassk and instructed his engineers to fortify the Don river area using large amounts of artillery, tanks and armor trains for support. Accordingly, his defensive forces consisted of:

Tolorkova Corps:
1st Kazan Cavalry division
2nd Tersky Cavalry brigade
1st Regiment
Stavropol Training Schools

In charge of the overall defenses was General Sidorin. It was decided to defend this area using the Volunteer Army and 3rd Don Corps, while the 4th Don cavalry Corps, defended the bridge at Kuteinikov and Nesevtaisaki. The Mamantov cavalry corps would hold Darevskyi. These units would counterattack the 8th Army. The Red attack began on January 7th. The 1st and 2nd Don Corps along with the Caucasian army defended the Novotcherkask to Tsaritsyn approaches.

The Red Southeast Front also prepared to attack at a river crossing near Medvyeditsa and Idovdia. The Red main attack force would consist of the 21st,23rd, 36th divisions, Budenny's cavalry and the 2nd Cavalry Brigade attacking from Bychok-Leskovo to Boguchier-Meshkoviski.

Novotcherkask was the main Don Army base and the Soviet coming offensive would produce another morale blow to Denikin.

At Novotcherkask, the White defenses consisted of cavalry units from the Don Army and reinforced with the 4th Don cavalry, 7th Don cavalry brigade, 4th infantry regiment, 8th Don partisan division and 3rd Don cavalry division. At Mokrodogovsky, the 4th Don cavalry division and the 14th Don cavalry brigade concentrated. General Sidorin presumed that the Reds would advance along the railroad. He planned to attack when the spearhead reached Grusheveskomya using the 4th Don Cavalry Corps.

The 9th army was ordered to seize the base by the 7th,and to do this, the 2nd cavalry brigade, the Vilna division, 21st and 23rd divisions plus a Cavalry corps waited. The attack began at 0800 on the 5th. The attacked called for an advance of 90 km and the attacking units were instructed to advance 30 km per day. However, 9th Army advanced only 10-25 km daily. The 21st division attacked the 8th Don division while the cavalry of the 9th army attacked the 3rd Don cavalry division.The 8th Don division began to retreat by nightfall of the 6th. When General Sidorin heard of the loss of Grushevskogo he tossed in the 10th Cavalry Brigade and the 7th and 11th Tank battalions at Persianovki. The tank battalions, totaling 7-8 MkV tanks. These were about 8 km east of the town. This event was one of the last tank uses of the Civil war for the White forces under Denikin. Apparently, the Reds by now were not petrified of the tanks and simply bypassed them in their counterattacks. Between the 8th Don division and the 10th Cavalry Brigade was the 3rd Don Division which held. This force was a significant gathering of units and included two armor trains and several armor cars besides the tanks. Yet, this force, also, melted away.

The Soviet Southern Front was ordered to reach the Sea of Azov and Rostov. Mariupol fell on the 4th to the 37th regiment of the 42nd division. By the 7th, the Estonian division, 42nd and 43rd divisions left the coast to advance on Nikolaev, 80 kms away. Taganrog fell on the 6th.

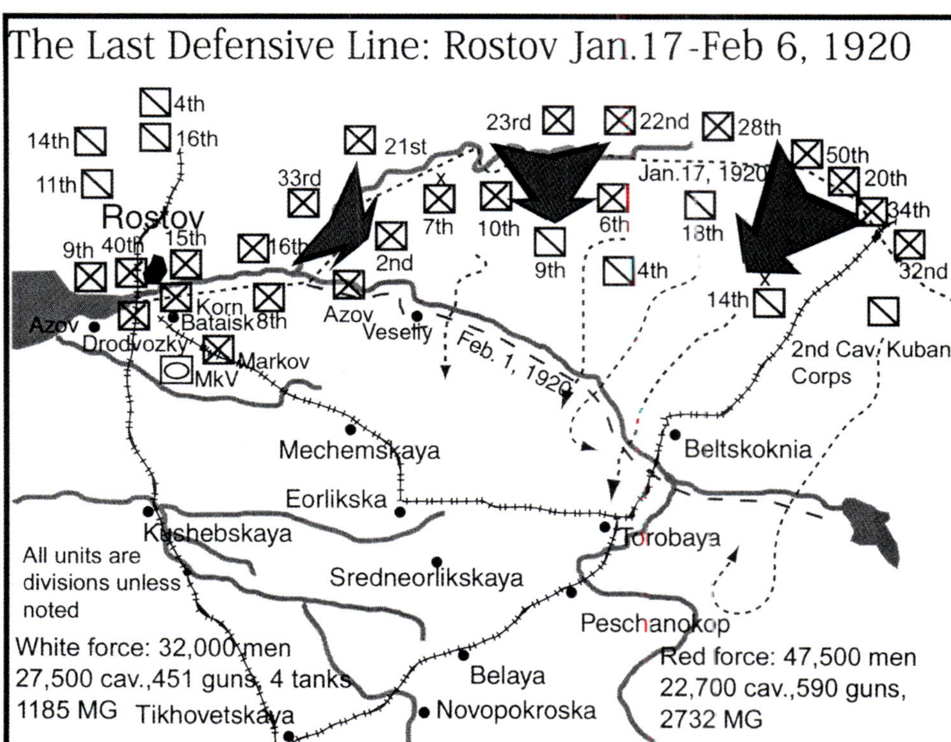

The bloody battle towards Rostov began on the 7th with the 21st and 16th divisions. As the Reds advanced, the rest of 8th Don Cavalry division and 10th Don Cavalry, 3rd Don Cavalry divisions attacked suffering huge losses. Red aircraft from the 3rd aircraft squadron attacked Novotcherkask. The White 9th air detachment escaped to Odessa and then subsequently its aircraft captured. Its sister, the 3rd air detachment was able to load up on the armor train "Muscovite" and fled to Rostov. Upon arrival there, the aircraft were unloaded and armor train was used for support. However, in the debacle, the aircraft of this detachment also were captured. Here are some lines from pilot S. Pokrovsk's recollections:

> "Going out of Ilovaysk station, the 2nd air detachment with their brand new 400 hp D_-9As aboard the train ran into a break in the railway. The train was diverted into Mariopol, where they were to abandoned the planes. The machines were burned and the personnel of the unit went through great labors to reach the Crimea."

In the Caucasus, upon departing the station at Karavanna, the 5th air-detachment had to abandoned their aircraft sitting on the platform cars. The only good condition steam engine was deemed necessary to pull the special train loaded with guns and projectiles of the 3rd battalion of heavy naval artillery. The Whites felt that artillery guns were more important than aircraft. Even the celebrated 6th Volunteer air-detachment during the retreat found itself in Grozny, where they were fighting the Tribal Chechen Insurgents and Red Army. To steer clear of captivity the surviving pilots, Pishvanov, Zarin and Tikhomivov in March 1920, flew their Camels to Georgia. There and without a penny in their pockets they worked in the service of the Georgian Army. They handed over their Camels to that country. They worked as chauffeurs in a Tiflis motor-car company.

But the major blow to White aviation was with the loss of Novocherkassk and Taganrog.

In storage at the port and at the Lebedev factory, where the assembling of the aircraft arriving from England took place, the Red Army took not less than 30 "DH9s," "RE8s, "Camels" and a few RAF S.E.5A fighters. This was last large batch of British aircraft shipped to Russia in November 1919, and almost all fell into the hands of the Reds. A majority of these vehicles were still in their packing containers. At the Lebedev factory, the Reds displayed four "Camel," five "RE8s," and 12 "Hispano-Suiza" motors.

The Red airforces on the Southern and Southeast fronts flew more than 1600 sorties, dropped 2560 kilos of bombs and logged 2600 hours of recon flights. Most of these during the last quarter of 1919.

With the Don army's base under attack, one would have thought that a bitter battle would've occurred, but that was not the case. By 2300 has on the 7th, the Soviets has taken it and reaped an enormous war booty: 167 artillery guns, 8- 9 Mk V tanks, 8 airplanes, 2 armor trains, 52 trucks and 60 tractors. The 7th Don division continued to fight a tough rearguard action before it, too, collapsed..

Williamson was at Novotcherkask when the Reds were there:

> "I started to the edge of town. Suddenly an exited Cossack captain galloped down the street. As he pulled his foamed mouth horse to a stop, it went down to it's

knees, exhausted. "It's all over" he yelled. "The counterattack failed, the Reds will soon be in the town!." He continues, "People started to run immediately, shouting the news, and the crowd scattered at top speed. I rode to the top of the hill looking over the plain towards Persianovki, which was covered with small bodies of troops black against the snow and groups of guns retiring in great disorder, their horses lashed to frenzy and pursued."

General Denikin wrote the following:

> "I concentrated my reserve, approximately two and a half divisions at Novotcherkask as the nearest jumping off ground to Rostov and there, if need be, I determined to fight the decisive battle. Our centre group was unable to hold the line allotted to them. By force of inertia, due to moral causes, the troops were drawn into retreating to some natural barrier the Don River. In the battle,the troops gave proofs alternately of marvellous valor and panic, of a stern sense of duty and loss of discipline."

The capture of Novotcherkask created a severe threat to Denikin and broke whatever other defenses he had. Both sides knew that the outcome had already been determined.

Meanwhile, Budenny and the 8th Soviet army now began their Operation Rostov using the 6th Cavalry division and 33rd division advancing for the bridges. However, the Cavalry Corps led by Topovkova of the Whites counterattack fiercely pushing back the startled Soviet units toward the northwest. This did not last long as the Soviet forces counterattack and returned the favor. The Red 4th Cavalry division gathered at Boloshino with their 12th division nearby at Sultan. The 8th Army with the 15th and 16th divisions continued towards Rostov with the 17th Cavalry brigade in the lead until it met Denikins 4th Don Cavalry corps. Both sides crossed their swords as in bygone wars, and in the end, the Whites prevailed destroying the Soviet unit. The 4th Don went on and attacked the 15th and 16th divisions. This was another bitterly fought battle, again, pushing the two Soviet units back. Then, the Soviet 40th division arrived in the nick of time and tipped the scales. Mamantov's 4th Cavalry Corps was stopped. Fixed, the Soviet 9th Army units tried to threaten Mamantov, but wisely, he fell back.

By the end of 8th, the Soviet 8th cavalry division was near Rostov. The 4th Cavalry division of Budenny's Cavalry Army was at Nakhichevan. The populace of Rostov was in panic.

Again, citing Williamson:

> "The town had been so chaotic that the military commander had hanged both men and women and left their bodies dangling from the lamp posts as a means of restoring order. All the shops had been shuttered and there had been no food for the refugees."

Rostov was first entered by the Red 33rd division during the night followed cavalry. There some White units conducted an urban warfare battle, but it did not last long.

Williamson:

> "The Reds charged into Rostov. Budenny's men were flushed with victory. There was an orgy of shooting and murder rampaging during the night. Everything was in turmoil, even the British officers there scrambled out, which infuriated Holman."

The war booty taken at Rostov was large, some 10000 POWs, 9 tanks,32 guns,200 MG and thousands of rifles.

While the Reds celebrated, the Whites dug in near Bataisk on a strong position located on hills south of the Don river. Just below them on the Red side was a marsh. Although the river was frozen, allowing for Soviet units to cross, the Denikin forces held for eight brutal frontal attacks.

By this time, the Caucasian Army, now commanded by Pokrovski, had fallen back from Tsaritsyn along the Tikhoryetsk railroad to the Manytch River. On their left was the 3rd Don Corps on the railway from Torgovaya to Bataisk. Pavlov's Cavalry Corps was in reserve. Adjacent to them was Borbovtich Guard Cavalry Brigade at Bataisk to the shore of the Azov Sea. The right bank of the Don River was held by 1st Corps of the Volunteers.

The total war booty the Reds had taken along the entire Southern Front consisted of: 40,500 POW, 12000 rifles, 4 armor cars, 1240 MG, 50 mortars, 780 artillery guns, 300000 shells, 216 cars, 25 armor trains, 11 tanks, 5 airplanes, 370 locomotives, 12289 railroad freight cars and 200 trucks.

During this time, little occurred along the Southeastern Front. The Soviets did activate the front, attacking on January 3rd at Tsaritsyn (Stalingrad). The 450th regiment of the 50th division crossed the Volga and seized the power station there. Then, the 449th regiment entered and captured the city. Actually, the city had been evacuated when Denikin had ordered a withdrawal of the Caucasian army on Dec.28th.

Since mid October to 1920, the SouthEastern Front had taken 20.550 POWs, 6000 rifles, 935 MG, 242 guns, 8 tanks, 15 planes, 65 cars, 29 locomotives. When the war booty is combined from all Soviet Fronts, the war booty is even more staggering: 61000 POW, 18000 rifles, 2169 MG, 50 mortars, 1022 guns, 19 tanks, 20 airplanes, 27 armor trains, 13280 rail freight cars.

In 51 days, the Soviets had advanced 100-550 km, much of it in deep snow.

The Kharkov operation was completed in 25 days and advanced 225 km, the average rate of movement was 12.5 km per day. The average rate of movement of the armies on a whole was 9 km per day. Some Soviet tactics were developed at this time, usually each front reserve had 2-3 divisions. When attacking, the division would use one and two echelons. Tactics were the same, surround and destroy.

After the capture of Rostov, the forces under Denikin did not simply wither away. While they were mere remnants of their former units, amazingly, they continued to fight. The Red 9th Army continued to pursue the 2nd and 3rd Don Corps while the 10th Army chased the 1st Don Corps and Caucasian armies. The weather now turned for the worse, this slowed down the Soviet units. The snow and rain played havoc on everything. On the 14th, Budenny and 8th Army were ordered to cross the Don at Eisk to Kushevskaya. The Don was now slush and frozen, but due to the weather becoming worse, the assault across the river was postponed until the 17th. On the 15th, the battle at Bataisk saw the Soviet Army defeated by forces led by Wrangel.

The defenses of Denikin's forces along the Don consisted of the Volunteer Corps near Pomanovskoi; the 1st, 2nd and 3rd Don Corps were at Bataisk, the 1st Kuban and 2nd Terskoi Cavalry divisions, the 2nd and 4th Don Cavalry Corps near Postovsko. This was where Budenny was expected to attack. On the 17th, the Soviet 1st brigade/12th division, 2nd Cav.Brigade/6th Cav.division, and 11th Cavalry division assaulted across the Don at Bataisk and Starocherkasskoi. Due to continued heavy resistance, the Soviet assault by Budenny failed. On the 18th, the 16th and 33rd divisions attempted to cross. The 16th division and 4th Cavalry division crossed on ferries and obtained a small bridgehead opposed by Denikin's 8th and 1st Partisan divisions, 2nd Don Cav. Division at Olginskoi. The White forces began to panic and the Reds pursued them to Khomutouskio. The Red 33rd division had also crossed the Don at Ksai and after a brief battle continued to advance. However, all other Soviet attempts to cross failed. This created two independent bridgeheads. The Don Troops incensed by the Reds occupying their country attacked the Reds at Karagalskaya taking 1000 POWs and many guns.

On the 19th, the Red 21st and 14th divisions crossed at Melekhovska and Orlovka, however, the 2nd Don Corps remained stead fast limiting the bridgehead. Denikin gathered his forces into Shock groups by combining his Cavalry brigade with the Toporkova Cavalry corps at Bataisk, his 4th Don Cavalry Corps at Pavlova and Zlodeiskola and the Volunteer Corps and 3rd Don Corps near both towns. The Soviet bridgeheads were near Bataisk and Olginskai. The Whites attacked the Soviets at noon on the 19th, and after several hours of raging battle, the Whites again prevailed, pushing back the Soviets to Nakhichevanskoi, where a ferry existed. But Denikin, because of losses pulled his forces back from Bataisk, leaving only the 3rd Don Corps near Olginskai.

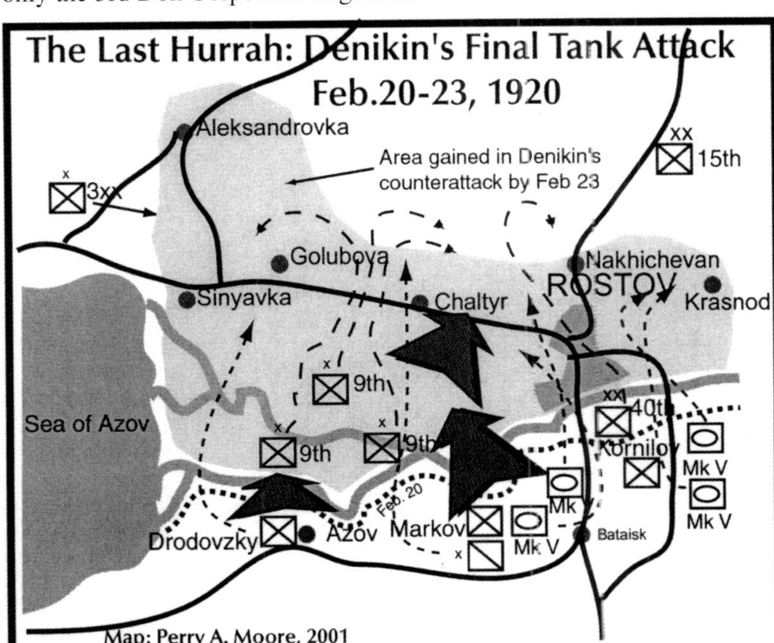

On the 20th, Denikin attacked with four MkV tanks and the Volunteer units along the railway from Bataisk including the 4th and 3rd Don cavalry corps. The Whites had superiority and despite the valiant Soviet resistance at the ferry crossing, by the end of the day, Denikin had forced the Reds to evacuate their bridgehead and return to right bank of the Don river!

The battles for the Don River crossings continued more violently on the 21st. This time, the Soviet front sent reinforcements consisting of the 4th, 6th and 11th Cavalry divisions, 9th, 12th, 31st,40th, and 21st divisions from the mouth of the Don to Manychskoi. Again, raging violent battles continued throughout the day, but in the end, the Soviets fell back across the river! Suffice to say, the fighting spirit seemed to have returned to Denikin's men. However, success here was not enough, as the Soviet 9th army continued to rip apart the 2nd Don Corps along the Manysch. Soviet forces from the 21st division crossed this river and advance threatening the flank and rear of Denikin's strong defensive position. This threat would increase and Denikin did little to halt it and by the 28th, the 2nd Don Corps had routed at Khut, Efremova. Some 5000 POW, 4 guns and hundreds of MG were taken.

Budenny now concentrated his army near Bagaevskaya and planned to hit Denikin on the flank and rear. This he did with a sudden shattering impact at Omutovskaya. The 9th and 10th armies now continued to advance taking Mechetinskoy by the 27th. The Reds now planned to have the 8th,9th, Budenny and 10th Armies attack Denikin simultaneously. However, the order for this was not conveyed correctly and the armies instead conducted piecemeal attacks in an uncoordinated manner. In one action, Budenny routed the whites at Efremova, after which, it continued to advance. Denikin's 2nd and 3rd Volunteer Brigades both surrendered.

The rout of the 2nd Don Corps further increased Denikin's anxiety about his tenuous position. Denikin decided to destroy the Soviet corps threatening from the 9th Army due west using the 7th Don division of 2nd Don Corps and the 4th Don cavalry corps from the east, while the 1st Don Corps attacked from the south. It was the perfect situation. For the attack, the 1st and 2nd Corps regrouped while the 4th cavalry corps gathered at Popov. The Volunteer corps and 3rd Don corps would continue to resist along the Don river at Pozdeeva.

Unbeknownst to Denikin, the Soviets also had planned to resume their offensive on the 28th. Thus, both sides began their offensive action on January 28th.

When the 28th dawned, the Red 15th,31st and 40th divisions of 8th Army approached the Don River at Star, the Whites repelled the attack. Budenny's cavalry units attacked with the 21st division of 9th army upon the 7th Don division. After a brief fight, the 7th Don retreated. The corps of the 9th Army and 23rd divisions were then attacked by Denikins forces and another bloodbath ensued forcing the 10th Army on the defensive. On the 29th, Budenny arrived and sent in the 6th Cavalry division smashing into the 4th Don cavalry division of 2nd Don corps and the 9th Don division of 4th Don corps. The Red 6th Cavalry division was nearly destroyed and forced to hastily retreat. This division was to have been supported by the remaining units of Budenny or the 9th Army, but support never came. The 11th cavalry and 4th Cavalry divisions of Budenny's Army now attacked the 10th Don cavalry division of the 4th Don Corps. The Reds were once again repelled and retreated to Kudinov and Elkin. On the 31st, the 1st Corps of the Volunteers attacked the Reds south of Rostov driving them back across the Don River. On February 1st, Budenny's army combined with 9th Army and attempted to cross the Manytsch River but were repelled. Their 10th Army battled with the 4th cavalry corps and the 1st Kuban cavalry corps. This battle last for three days near Zherebkova. Again, the whites forced the 10th Army to retreat.

The Caucasian Front also failed to breakthrough the White positions as ordered. This reason was because of the uncoordinated actions of the units.

The Soviet failures were a result of having insufficient intelligence on the enemy forces and their deployments. This resulted in a constant under estimation of their strength, especially from January 17th-21st and 28th -29th. To remedy this, the Soviet High Command ceased all further attacks on the 3rd. During this interlude, the Reds developed a coordinated plan, rearranged units and set common goals. Much of the time, communications were re-established from the Army to divisional levels, which had been lacking. It was also a time when the Soviets planned their upcoming Kuban-Novorossisk operation.

This operation was planned to destroy the Caucasian army and surround the forces just south of Rostov. The planned force would comprise of 13 divisions and involve 3 armies. The 9th army, with at least four divisions was deployed at Sadkovsky-Dalny; the 10th army, with at least six divisions at Kolodezh, and Budenny's cavalry army at Sharanbulu.

However, Denikin decided to continue his own attack. He could not wait for spring to retake Rostov and Novotcherkask and used his Volunteer Corps and Don Army towards Novotcherkask. The Kuban army, formerly the Caucasian, planned to attack along the railroad to Velikokriazeska to insure the line of communications of Stavropol. General Dubrowsky was ordered to retake the Sochi area and to clear the Black Sea coast area. Denikin planned to begin this offensive in mid-February.

The Soviet intelligence was informed of the details and on the 12th, stated their own plans and instructions to their armies. The 8th Army would attack toward Kalanichovy, 9th Army to Novorviski, Budenny would attack Latovvskoi to Tizcrekoi and force the flanks of the Don and Kuban armies by the 21st; 10th army was reinforced with the 34th, 39th and 50th divisions and ordered to cut off the retreat route of the Kuban army at Armavir then advance to Terinev by the 19th, finally, the 11th army was to take Stavropol with the 7th cavalry division. This offensive was to start on the 14th.

However, the Soviet front commander, once again, underestimated the strength of Denikin's opposing forces. He ordered his 9th Army to advance 15 km, his 10th Army, 18 km and Budenny's cavalry some 20 km.

Denikin's forces now covered a 800 km front manned by 53,165 infantry, 65,083 cavalry, 1984 MG, 453 Guns, 18 armor trains, 31 armor cars, 8 tanks and 96 airplanes. The Soviet forces had 48,554 infantry, 2063 cavalry, 2399 MG, 512 guns, 10 Armor trains and 10 airplanes.

These number are deceptive, as Denikin had many injured in hospitals and thousands in the rear and in garrisons. The Soviets had most of theirs on or near the Southern and Southeast Fronts.

Much of Denikin's strength was centered around Bataisk and near the mouth of the Manytch River. Crossing the Don and Manytsh Rivers would be phase one of the Soviet planned operation lasting from February 14 to March 2nd.

Because of the rigidness in the Red Command, Budenny's cavalry army was not in place when the Red offensive began. This was ironic because the High Command knew this and yet allowed the attack to begin. They took the risk and would pay for it. On the 14th, the

Red 8th, 9th,10th,11th armies simultaneously attacked along the whole Southern and Southeast fronts. The 8th Army attacked the Volunteer Corps and 3rd Don Corps and took Kulechovkoy but could not hold it against the Volunteer counterattacks. The staff of the 8th army was captured. On the 15th, the 3rd Don Corps and the Volunteers attacked the Soviets along the Don river. All day the battle raged until the 8th Army retreated after the army attempted a counterattack. The Don Army crossed the Don river and cut off the communication between Rostov and Novercherkassk. Likewise, 9th Army made repeated attacks, it's 21st division broke and fled. The Red 23rd division collided with the 4th and 2nd Don cavalry Corps and were stopped cold. By the 15th, 9th Army had expended most of it's artillery shells and their infantry was short of ammunition. This forced the army to fall back from the Manytsh River. Denikin's 1st and 3rd brigades attacked and made significant gains on the flank of 9th army also crossing the river.

During this time Denikin wrote:

> "The Volunteer Corps emerged from the Volunteer Army still preserved its discipline, energy and readiness to carry on the struggle. On the other hand, the Don Army not only the rank and file but the commanding staff had lost their morale.The process of the demoralization of the Kuban Cossacks developed more rapidly, only about five to eight thousand remained at the front. I strained every nerve to overcome the inert force of the retreat because in my opinion a prolongation of the operation might be an effective means of undermining the enemy's strength. The guerillas that had fought against us, now fought for us, such as Makhno."

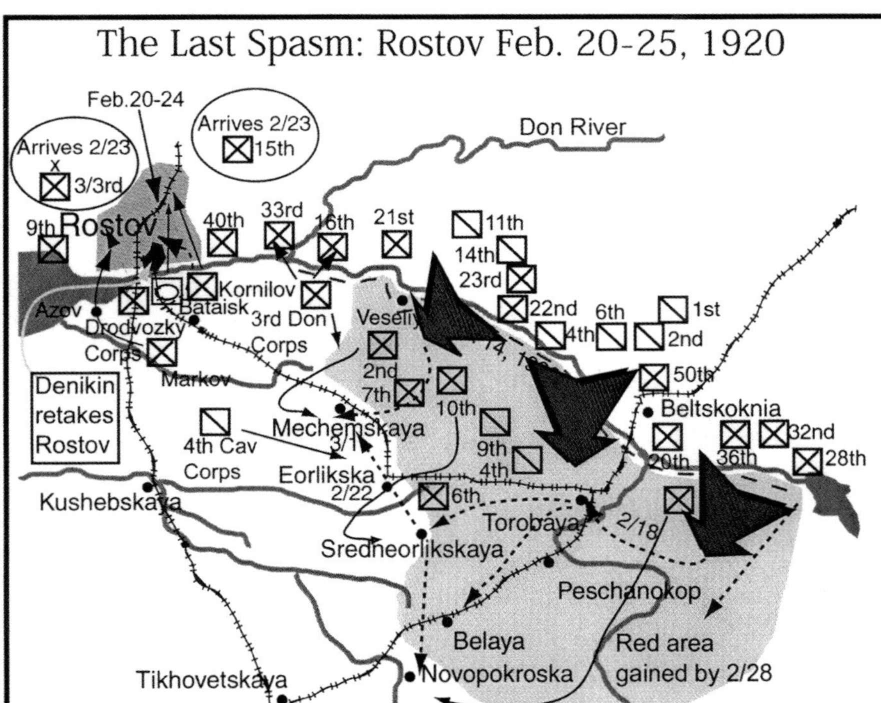

The Last Spasm: Rostov Feb. 20-25, 1920

Denikin was aware of the change in the attack of Budenny's First cavalry army and the 10th army, which was directed at the weak link—the Kuban Cossacks. Therefore, he sent 12,000 cavalry led by Pavlov up the Manytch River to strike at Budenny's flank and rear. Pavlov routed the Red cavalry led by Dumenko along the lower Manytch and toward Torgovaia, which the Kubans had also abandoned. Pavlov continued to advance along the left bank of the river in secrecy and because of the snow blizzards and intense cold, the elements wore his men out and he lost 6000 to sickness and frostbite. After three days, Pavlov reached Torgovaia. In their condition, they were unable to take it and fell back to Lezhanka.

During this time Major Williamson noted:

> "Things were actually beginning to look inexpediently brighter for Denikin's Army, as the Reds has suffered two successive defeats in their efforts to cross the Don and Manytch Rivers.....The Reds had lost many guns at Bataisk and Vieseli, unfortunately, these successes were more than counter balanced by the behavior of the Kuban Cossacks who were now wanting to stop the war Gradually, these forces drifted away to their villages, sometimes a whole regiment."

The only British advisors known to have been murdered by the Reds were made known to Williamson as he rushed through Rostov earlier. The advisor's name was Captain Frecheville and Lt. Couche who had been attached to the 1st Corps (he had assisted in the building of trenches and other defenses for the city). The 1st corps left him and his interpreter at Sultan Sala on the night of the 10th. There, the Reds captured him who killed him. His body had been tied to saddle and dragged through the streets. Later, when the Reds conducted a raid across the Don, a Soviet Commissar named Paichkin of the 136th Cavalry regiment was captured by the Volunteer Army wearing Frecheville's tunic! During the interrogation, the Commissar said that Frecheville had been beaten to death with steel ramrods.

Williamson's visit to the 3rd and 2nd Don Corps is revealing:

> "At Metchetinskaya was the advance base of the Don army. In quick succession the 3rd and 2nd Don Corps consisted of nothing but a few shattered remnant of the 4th and 7th Don divisions and only mustered 1000 men, and at the 1st Don Corps, the 6th division had 600 men and few groups of cavalry. On each section of front, there were only enough men to watch important crossings from the north side of the Manytch River...the position of the 1st Don Corps looked very dubious because of the wavering Kuban Army....Russian officers watched their men with worried eyes, wondering if they were ready to turn on them. As usual, there was no definite information, nobody was exercising any proper command and everyone accused everyone else for letting them down."

By February 17th, both the 8th and 9th Armies had been stopped cold. The only successes the Soviets were having hung with the 10th Army, which had forced a crossing across the Manytch River using a cavalry division. It attacked the 1st Don corps and pushed them back to Korolikova. The Don units fell back leaving the right flank of the Don river open and also exposed the left flank of the Kuban Army. The 6th Don division and the Red Caucasian cavalry division battled most of the day, while the Soviet 28th division joined in the battle and repelled the 14th Don Cavalry Brigade and 18th Cavalry regiment near Zimova. The 2nd and 1st Kuban corps fought a stout defense against the Soviet 50th, 20th,34th and 32nd divisions for Zablievsky, Ekaterinovku and Baranikoe. The Reds were forced to toss in the 4th Cavalry division, which sealed the fate of the Don units. Thus, the 10th Army had succeeded in breaking through the defenses and threatened the flank of the Don Army and the rear of the Volunteer Army.

The 1st and 3rd Red cavalry brigades now attacked the 4th Don Cavalry division near Shara in the Manytch River area. Pavlov's 9th and 10th Cavalry divisions reach the town of Korolikova. These units were suddenly attacked by the Caucasian cavalry and 28th Soviet division from the Northwest at the same time the 1st Don Corps had attacked from the Southwest. After a long battle, the two Soviet units suffered high losses yet continue to resist. At the last moment, the Soviet 50th and 20th divisions arrived. Pavlov retreated hastily from Torgorvaia, leaving most of his artillery. Later, Pavlov attempted to retake the town that night with his 3rd Cavalry division, but this also failed.

Budenny's First cavalry army was now determined to destroy Denikin's Pavlov cavalry corps. Besides the organic cavalry divisions of Budenny, the 20th, 34th and 50th infantry divisions were attached to pursue Pavlov and destroy it near Kruchenia.

On the 21st, the 1st Kuban corps attacked Budenny, while the Soviet 32nd and 39th divisions of 10th Army fought the 2nd and 3rd Kuban regiments of the 2nd Kuban Cavalry Corps. Neither side won. The 10th Army then attempted to surround and destroy the 1st Kuban corps at Belnia-Glina with the support of Budenny. This began on the 22nd. It did not take too much time as the 4th Cavalry division, 20th,34th and 50th Soviet divisions tightened their grip. In the end, 4500 Kubans and 3 armor trains surrendered.

Denikin writes:

> "Our massed cavalry, sometimes doubly superior in numbers to the enemy, hovered around their flank but avoided encounters, a prey to demoralization. Strategically, the armies must halt on the River Kuban which was a splendid natural defence. By the 20th, the Kuban River was lost. The remnants of the Kuban Cossack, utterly demoralized, were in full retreat."

The British 47th air squadron (officially, the unit did not exist.But many pilots continued to fly for the Whites) continued to fly support missions from their fields at Kuskchevska, flying bombing missions on Taganrog and Rostov.

During this same time, near the mouth of the Don and Manytch Rivers, the Volunteer corps and Don army attacked the 9th Army. The Soviets resisted and then counter attacked, but were forced to retreat back to Akasaiska, just as the Soviet 15th and 16th divisions arrived at Nakhichevau.

The last stroke of Denikin's armed forces before they plunged into the abyss began on the 20th. The last spasm of their strength and morale once again surged to the amazement of even the Soviets.

Major Williamson was present as the strength gathered one last time:

> " Here all was bustle and excitement as an attempt was to be made to recapture Rostov. Squadrons of cavalry, ill equipped still but no longer the wretched men we'd seen in the north, were jingling past, trainloads of infantry leaving for the front towards Bataisk."

Thus, on February 20th, the Volunteer corps with four Mk V tanks and parts of the Don army attacked the Soviet 9th Army and 40th division of 8th Army near the suburbs of Rostov and from the west. The Volunteers easily seized the towns of Khoper and Gnilovisku then penetrated into the fringe of the city. The Soviets fought bitterly. Their 33rd and 16th divisions stood along the banks of the Don being battered by the 3rd Don Corps. These units held. The break in the line came when the 9th Soviet division routed and a gap appeared. The division retreated from Sniavka and Semernikov. The Volunteers penetrated further now and the Soviet Front command was quite nervous about this reversal. So much so, he sent the following telegram to the Southwest Front commander:

> "The situation is serious. There is the possibility of losing Rostov and Novercherkassk and the opponent is also attempting a drive in the Donetz area. Start the acceleration of the 42nd division and Latvian Division and begin the reinforcement. I expect you will devote all your energies to this."

In the Taganrog area, the Red 3rd, 42nd and 52nd divisions stood. Part of the Soviet 3rd division was ordered into Rostov while a strong shock force consisting of the 10th,18th,19th and 56th divisions was gathered and formed in the Kharkov area.

Denikin had now used all of the available units worthy of combat for this last gasp. By the end of the 20th, Rostov was Denikin's again! On the 21st, the urban battle for the city

The End for Denikin, March 24-27, 1920

began in earnest. All day long the 16th Soviet division battled the Volunteers in Rostov and at Nakhichevan. However, by night, even that town fell to the Volunteers and units of the 3rd Don Corps. The Red command grew more concerned when the Volunteers also managed to advance towards Novotcherkask and Logovsky. Aleksandrova fell to the Volunteers that night. The Reds counterattacked retaking the towns of Leksandrovka and Krasnod. On the 23rd, the 9th division of 8th Army and the 3rd Brigade/3rd division attacked at Gnilovskyia and Zarechyiu taking both suburbs and continued their advance towards Rostov. Simultaneously from the north, the 15th and 16th Soviet divisions attacked the Volunteers. The remaining day and night consisted of street battles in the city. By the morning, the Soviets had reclaimed Rostov and Nakhichevan. Using the 33rd division, the soviets advanced and on the 24th retook Starocherkassku bagging some 1000 POWs. On the 25th, the Volunteer and 3rd Don Corps began their retreat back to their former starting positions. Now the Reds continued to push and took some ground on the left bank of the Manytch River.

That was Denikin's last hurrah.

Williamson on their return:

> "The news was heartbreaking. General Sidorin was even more reticent about their plans. Sidorin distributed large numbers of Don War Crosses for bravery. Things were going from bad to worse. The growing atmosphere of distaste for Denikin's command by the Don Cossacks. The same wretched scenes were being enacted all over again, the sluggish stream of humanity, cavalry reduced to a few men, gunners dragging dismantled guns on sledges, officers without any men. It seemed like the end was very near."

After the 1st Kuban cavalry corps had been destroyed by Budenny and the 10th army, the Soviets continued to Tikhoryetsk. Denikin knew he could do little because he had few troops in that area. On the 25th, Denikin ordered the Pavlov cavalry group again to that area in horrible weather to face Budenny and part of the 10th Army. The 11th cavalry division of that corps, this time, was wiped out. The Soviets then descended upon the remaining group (about 5000 men) at the town of Egorlikskoi. Budenny, with three cavalry divisions and one infantry division battled with Pavlov. This battle was short, as many of Pavlov's men were frozen and numb. Pavlov lost all his artillery (29 guns),100 MG, hundreds of men. Pavlov was no longer any threat and was not pursued any further.

The Soviets continued to attack the Volunteers and Don army. The 8th Army attacked from the north while the 9th Army from the east and Budenny from the south with 10th Army. A decisive battle was hoped. The attack began on the 26th from the mouth of the Don River and fierce battles prevailed. The 33rd Soviet division attack the Markov division pushing it back to Olginskai. By March 2nd, the 15th and 16th divisions had taken Bataisk and the frontlines of the Volunteer corps near the Don River mouth had been broken through. The 9th Army met a stiff defense from the 3rd Don Corps on the right flank against the Soviet 21st and 23rd divisions. The 8th Don division was destroyed at Turchaninov. The 14th and 22nd divisions advanced to Egorliksyi where the 6th Don division had finally had enough and routed. The Soviet 20th and 50th divisions now advanced with little resistance. Meanwhile, the 32nd,34th and 39th divisions and a cavalry brigade now threatened the railroad at Armavir. The Red 11th Army (7th cavalry division and 50th division) approached

Stavropol despite stout resistance. The city fell on the February 29th. These new developments threatened the rear of the Kuban Army.

Meanwhile, in a distant land, the British had prepared two battalions at Constantinople to be sent to Novorossisk to help Denikin retreat and to defend the port.

Denikin hastily withdrew his Volunteer Army and Don Army to avoid entrapment. Denikin wrote:

> "Numbers of Cossacks threw their arms down, and whole regiments deserted to the anarchists. General Sidorin was running a serious risk of being made prisoner."

On March 3rd, the Soviet High command prepared for the kill of Denikin's forces. The 18th Army was ordered to Novorossisk, 9th Army to Abinskaya, 10th Army to Ekaterinodar, 11th Army to Armavir. The 9th Army was responsible for pursing and further routing Denikin's Volunteers and Don armies. The 21st and 23rd divisions were on the right and the 14th,22nd and cavalry Corps were on the left. On the 5th, the 11th Army faced the White cavalry group led by Babieva in the Stavropol area and for 7 days it and the 7th Red Cavalry division fought. In the end, Babieva had been surrounded and destroyed. The Red 21st and 33rd divisions then attacked Denikin's retreating men, while the 8th Army freed the Taman Peninsula and now struck south to the last port of Novorossisk.

It was now, for the first time, the British sent their first and only combat battalion, the 2nd Royal Scot Fusiliers, about 1000 men, to hold the areas around Novorossisk. The date was March 10th.

Our friend Williamson was there:

> "At about 1800 on the 12th, we left Ekaterinodar and arrived at Krymsk on the 13th, which was to be the next rallying point for the final defence of the hills surrounding Novorossisk. Trenches were being dug and a few disorganized troops were being placed in position, not much more than a few sullen men thawing out frozen weapons. We were greeted with worse news. The whole country south of the railway down to the Georgian frontier was full of Green Guards, deserters

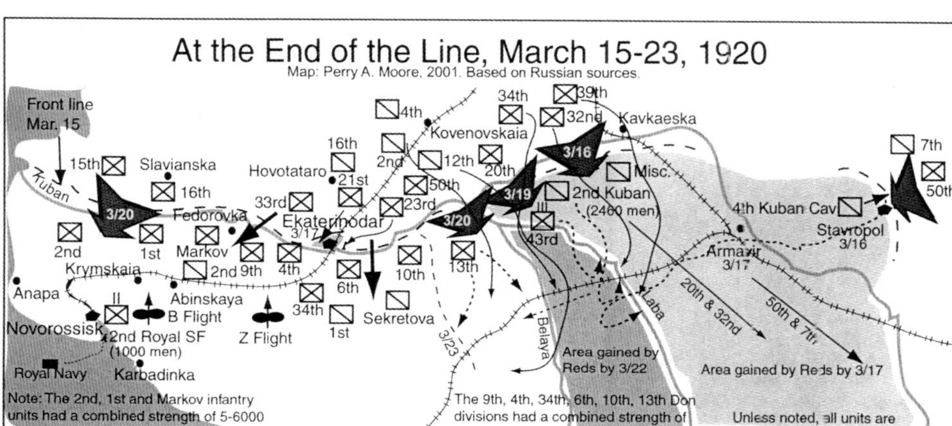

from both armies and raiding the vast stores located at Novorossisk. At one point, the line was obstructed for 15 miles by debris of rolling stock and piles of merchandise and no guards. Trucks full of ammunition which should have been on the front had been turned over and destroyed. More bands of Green Guards raided the trains moving toward Novorossisk. At the port, every hotel was full, people sleeping on the floor and food was running out, mobs attacked the shops and refugees. It was obvious that nothing could be done to save Denikin and it only remained to take all possible steps to cover the evacuation. The Royal Navy had been called in to help."

The resemblance of the scenes and fighting of Denikin's army and that of Hitter's Wehrmacht in April, 1945, are uncanny. It is a familiar script. The counterattacks, the brief success only for a breakthrough somewhere else, the faces of the defeated in face of enemy superiority. Oddly, in both times, the enemy was the Soviet forces!

At the start of March, Denikin's front lines ran from Ternovka-Novi Yergolik-Mechetinskaya-Kagalniskaya- along the Kagalnik river to the Sea of Azov. The port of Novorossisk had been the main port of entry for all British supplies. The supplies were stored in all kinds of manner and places. On March 3rd, 1920, they consisted of the following:

Clothing:	124,878 pairs of combat boots	
	109182 Greatcoats	
	158428 Pants	
	143488 Shirts	
	1,505,718 Socks	
Equipment:	57972 Packs	
	74060 Haversacks	
	30000 Shovels	
	34440 Water Bottle Carriers	
Munitions:	Vicker Machine Guns	584
	Lewis LMG	250
	Light Trench Mortars	87
	Rifles	3301
	Ammunition	8,000,000 rounds
	Gallons of oil	364,625
	Compasses	1740
	No.7 Dial Sights	86
	No 4 Directors	28
	Artillery range finders	12
	Field Plotters	34
	18 pdr guns	121
	4.5" Howitzer	110
	60 pdr guns	7

	6" Howitzer	6
	Running out springs for artillery	1200
	Ammo wagons	282
Saddlery	3000 Saddles	
Medical	130 Panniers	
	Poison	81 cases
	Sterilizing	214 cases
	Water bottles	284
Engineer	Barb wire	12738 coils
	Detonators	11202 boxes
	Safety Fuses	244 boxes
	Non Barb wire	408 coils
Transport	Cars	22
	Vans	6
	3 ton Trucks	10
	Motorcycles	17

Supplies: There was a bulk store of supplies of all kinds enough for 3000 men and 100 horses for up to 292 days.

On March 11th, a secret wire was sent from General Bridges in Novorossisk to the British Forces in Constantinople:

> "I reached the port at 0930 with the 2nd Royal Scot Fusiliers battalion. The Mission at Ekaterinodar is being reduced to 12 officers and 40 others. General Holman states that will leave him with 22 officers, 42 others and Z flight/47th Squadron of 11 officers and 33 others. Totaling 33 officers and 75 others. Ships are urgently needed for wounded: at Novorossisk there are 2000 in pitiable condition. Holman states that at Ekaterinodar, there are 1000 and another 3000 arriving. Holman states the situation is bad. The Kuban Cossacks are not fighting. There is no immediate reason for alarm here. The inhabitants are hostile and the surrounding countryside is not safe. The local ration strength including civilians and military will reach 400,000. The port has only a seven day supply for the inhabitants. Holman suggests evacuating the Volunteer Corps to the Crimea. There are emergency ships to evacuate 3000, and 4000 who want to go. Denikin has offered to hire ships upon payment to evacuate all women and children wanting to go. This money is reported to be in Constantinople. Holman states that 60000 refugees have left Ekaterinodar and that Budenny is not pressing. The surplus personnel of the British Mission and the tanks left Ekaterinodar. The RAF trains leave tomorrow from there. A Volunteer regiment has arrived here. Evacuations have not proceeded due to a lack of shipping."

The Royal Scots turned the port into a fortified area and occupied the Cement Works. It was a very effective force checking the anarchists (Greens) and a deterrent to the Reds.

By this time, the Soviet 34th and 37th divisions were in the Ekaterinodar area. On the 12th, Denikin attempted to regroup his Sekretova cavalry group and the 3rd Kuban cavalry corps for yet another counterattack on the 9th army flank near Marke and Vicha. However, the chaotic situation did not allow this regrouping and the counterattack failed to occur. Instead, the unravelling continued caused by 9th army's fast advance on Tizorechkoi. Denikin's Sekretova cavalry group astonishingly repelled eight Soviet attacks before it retreated to Korenovskoy.

The Soviet units were approaching the last defensive lines that Williamson had mentioned. The Kornilov division of the Volunteers Corps was largely responsible for holding the Soviet units back as others evacuated. In particular, the heroics of it's 3rd battalion continued to amaze friend and enemy. The Markov division was another unit holding the Reds. The British warships also contributed to the halting of the Soviets upon Novorossisk. Even a few MkV and Whippets driven by British crews got into the attack.

On the 15th, General Bridges in Novorossisk sends another secret wire to Constantinople:

> "Denikin has reached Novorossisk. He intends to remain here another week. From the point of view of administration, Denikin will always be a failure and, in my opinion, we ought to decline to support him. The transports Kherson and Hanover are evacuating. In a two hour interview, he stated that the Volunteer Corps has 6000 men and the Don Cavalry some 14,000 and are good troops. The Don infantry are not. He plans to fight a holding battle and then withdraw to the Crimea. According to French intelligence, the Volunteers have only 4000."

Williamson was also in Novorossisk:

> "On the wharves were rows of field guns and piles of ammunition and soldiers pushed them into the dark water of the bay. Large numbers of tanks and aeroplanes were pushed into the sea, together with mountains of equipment. The water was filled with cruisers, battleships and destroyers, most of them British, their guns trained on the route into town."

The combat ships in the harbor consisted of HMS Empress of India, Calypso, Stuart, Montrose, Steadfast, Seraph, Sikh, CV Pegasus, CV Ark Royal, Cardiff and Marlborough.

On the 17th, Ekaterinodar fell after a fierce 12 hour battle. The Soviet 21st and 23rd divisions entered. The British Mission with Holman had left only the day earlier. Denikin ordered the Volunteer corps to defend the left bank of the Kuban River up to Fedorovka, which covered the approaches to Novorossisk, while the Don Army held from Fedorovka to Maikop. Soviet artillery was now firing into the port town igniting the huge stockpiled ammunition dumps creating additional panic and huge columns of smoke. Soviet lead elements entered the town only be demolished by the British Navy. By now, the Volunteers had taken what weapons they could and had evacuated.

Weeks earlier, Denikin and the British worked out what was to be called the MacKinder Guarantee. The British would supply all the available shipping to evacuate the families of officers. Over 7000 had registered of which 5300 had evacuated. All those wanting to be evacuated had to be in Novorossisk by the 16th. There was no refugee shipping available.

The Greens or anarchists became bolder and infiltrated into Novorossisk seizing the only wireless station there. The Volunteers and the British infantry counterattacked retaking it with naval support. Some 50 RAF men were posted there as a garrison.

Denikin's train arrived in the town and parked alongside the quay and water. He was prepared for a fast exit when required. Holman's train reached Krimskaya on the 16th at 2000. He was on the last train into the port. The last evacuation of the Volunteer army was on the 15th, some 300 men under Col. Mannsheim of the 3rd Drozdovsky regiment and 600 others left near Karbindinka. The Markov regiment had only 200 remaining. This was a last minute rescue as the Soviets had surrounded the unit except along the coast. At this last minute, the British warships opened up and kept the Reds prone as the men boarded a torpedo boat under fire. Another British ship began to shell forcing the Reds to fall back.

The American Navy was also present for the evacuation, the TR Samogan, which could carry 2500, and was one of the largest transports present.

On the 19th, the Reds took Krymsk. On the 22nd, the 2nd Bn Royal Scot Fusiliers made a show of force, parading through the town of Novorossisk. Denikin was very pleased at the pipes playing Scottish music. The town also seem to calm down from it's panic.

The remnants of Denikin's army were now holding the Labar River line. But on the 23rd, a Don division surrendered to a company of Soviets! The Volunteer units that remained continued to hold the Kuban river near Krimskaya.

In one of the secret wireless messages from Lt. General Bridges in the port to Constantinople stated that Denikin's defense lines were about 10 miles out of the port and in nearby villages, and some 700 deserters from Denikin's army lurked about causing trouble. Then, a suicide by a British officer:

> "Lt Col. Bingham, 84th Punjabis, shot himself dead this morning. He was in charge of intelligence. I have not heard any satisfactory explanation but fancy something will come to light. I am told he was "queer.""

How odd, a homosexual man commits suicide in one of the worst times in history. Why?

On the 20th, Wrangel was aboard the HMS Ajax. He was told that Denikin had been informed of the British demands that the struggle should be ended and to negotiate with the Soviets or the British will not provide their support. Denikin refused. The British Military Mission had been dispersed with liaison groups attached to the Causcasian and Don Forces at Odessa and with the Ural Cossacks. Most of the staff remained at Novorossisk and a smaller contingent at Theodosia. The Intelligence staff remained near Ekaterinodar. Holman with communications was near Tikhorestskaya.

The RAF had moved to the following locations: A flight with DH9's was at Dnankoe in the Crimea; B flight remained at Novorossisk with Camels; C Flight, with RE 8's were aboard a train from Ekaterinodar; Z Flight with RE 8's was near Ekaterinodar. Much of the Russian Air Force can be summed up by Holman: "it was never much use and was scattered and had lost most of it's airplanes." Many of the Camels and DH9A's had been lost in the chaos at Taganrog as the Reds approached. Many were simply abandoned because the Russians had given priorities to all others first, leaving the RAF and the Tank trains stuck. During the Rostov evacuation, two RAF trains and one tank train with equipment had to be abandoned as the Reds had taken the last bridge across the Don. The British personnel fled through the countryside and across the Don reaching Bataisk.

Because the Green's were becoming bolder and stronger, Holman feared that the railways from Ekaterinodar area to Novorossisk might be cut preventing the evacuation. As a preventive measure, he composed a group of 200 British Officers and three tanks to act as a firebrigade to clear the line should this occur.

In the meantime, the defenses at Novorossisk were interfered with by the Kuban Cossacks. The British and Wrangel had decided upon a defense line many miles away from the port, out of enemy artillery range. This construction had already begun. The Kubans objected to further construction on the grounds that it should be built at Ekaterinodar for the defense of the Kuban area. The building of defenses stopped because the Kubans refused to supply the labor required. Soon, the Green's would be also creating chaos. Thus, the 2nd Royal Scot Fusiliers battalion dug trenches, put up barb wire around the Cement Works and various quays which constituted a complete sector of inner defenses of the port, which was away from the city.

Many miles away in the Crimea on the 21st, a military counsel convened in Sevastopol composed of the Corps, Brigade and Divisional leaders formerly with Denikin. They were there to elect a successor to Denikin. Wrangel had set up the meeting. On the 22nd, it was demanded of Denikin to name a successor. For Denikin it was over and Wrangel took over the evacuated soldiers in the Crimea.

On the 23rd, 400 British soldiers evacuated from the British Mission and sailed for the Crimea to assist General Wrangel. On the 26th, all others of the Mission left. The 2nd Royal Scots also embarked and sailed during the night.

Novorossisk fell on the morning of the 27th. It was a huge evacuation, some 30,000 men of Denikin's army had been transported to the Crimea to continue the fight. Budenny's HQ was now at Maikop with 15000 cavalry, 10000 infantry and 100 guns. General Denikin, his wife and child, were at sea now aboard the Hospital Ship Berbice and then MHS Marlborough heading to Malta. They eventually sailed on the SS Kursk to England, arriving at Southhampton on April 19th. Wrangel was in the Crimea, forming a new army to carry on the fight.

Holman left at 0500 aboard the DD HMS Steadfast for Theodesia. He reached Constantinople on April 5th, took a train on the 7th travelling through Belgrade, Trieste,Milan and Paris. By the 17th, he reported back to the War Office. On the 29th, General Percy assumed command of the British Military Mission in the Crimea with 175 officers and 450 enlisted.

Only the Volunteer corps consisting of remnants from the Markov, Drozdovsky and Alekseev regiments, the 2nd partisan division, 2nd x/52nd Partisan division, a Machine Gun group lead by Shevchenko and two Don divisions of the Don Army were evacuated to the Crimea or had crossed the Taman Peninsula. All others had been either killed or captured. Some 22,000 retreated into the Tuapse area, another 4000 fled to Georgia. The Allies evacuated some 8579 refugees from Novorossisk and 4558 from Odessa

From February 14th to May,1920, some 163,577 men had been captured, 32590 rifles, 723 MG, 537 guns, 17 tanks, 23 armor cars, 30 airplanes and 3.4 million shells had been seized by the Soviets.

This Soviet operation had lasted 42 days, advanced some 350 km and averaged 8.5 km per day. The Cavalry army of Budenny, at times, averaged 20 km per day. From January 13th to February 12th, the Southern front had taken in 19,314 POWs, captured 75000 rifles, 796 MG, 454 guns, 28 armor trains, 13 armor cars, 15 airplanes, 278 cars, 553 locomotives and 5.5 million shells.

According to Holman's "Final Report" on the South Russia episode, Denikin was seriously hindered by the Greens, who were further agitated by Soviet propaganda. During the last three months they greatly interfered with Denikin's rear lines of communication (mostly railroads) to the extent that he, once again, diverted a good Don division to deal with them. More interestingly, is Holman's comments on the British officers and other ranks, which had volunteered and paid in rubles:

> "The Mission included some of the best and included many from the following categories:
> A.Officers who went to merely continue their temporary employment in the Army.
> B.Officers who volunteered to further their own interests such good pay or making money
> C. Officers who had been prisoners of war and wanted to win distinctions
> D. Unfit Officers
> E. Officers who were appointed a commission solely on the account they knew Russian.
>
> Some of (A) are neither keen or capable. Some of (B) were most undesirable and brought discredit on the Mission from mischievous activities. Nearly all of (C) were of little use. In Category (D) these were totally out of place in South Russia as the environment could try the strongest constitution. Those in (E) as a rule were unfit to be appointed an officer. The other ranks of the Mission were a mixed lot, and except for the motor drivers of the Service Corps, as a rule, they were bad. They did learn Russian faster than the officers."

The number of British killed between August 1919 and March 1920 came to 45 (16 officer and 29 enlisted). The number in the hospitals during this time was as follows:

> 266 for Venereal Disease, 89 for Typhus, 43 for wounds, 29 for Pneumonia,26 for Dysentery, 18 for malaria, 150 for other diseases.

The British Mission did make improvements in the horrendous railway system they adopted. Formerly, the trains were loaded randomly and without escort. These could and were looted many times before reaching the intended depot. The British devised a new system where each army had it's own train and travelled under the supervision of British advisors These trains were loaded at Novorossisk using Soviet POWs and then headed to it's Army depot, reaching it in 4- 6 days instead of 3 weeks using the old method. For example, the first batch of machine gun equipment sent to the main equipping station in Rostov was 401 Vickers and 1240 Lewis Guns which arrived in 23 railway cars from the port at Novorossisk in 19 days! In another example, 80 Vickers and 220 Lewis guns arrived at Kkarkov from Rostov in a week. These were distributed to the front line. The units were astonished and delighted. Few supply trains brought any military supplies to Denikin in October. The reason being, all of the rail cars and trains were moving refugees and 4000 animals, which had arrived from Batum. The ships in the harbor could not be unloaded until the port area was clear.

From June through December 1919, the following total tonnage was unloaded at the port:

Ordnance Stores	26000 tons
Artillery	2300 tons
Ammunition	35000 tons

The British issued to the forces under Denikin from June 1919 to April 1920 the following:

18 pdr	491
"howitzer	181
60 pdr.	60
6" howitzer	61
8" howitzer	8
Stokes 3" mortars	106
Range finders	92
Directors	169
Plotters	111
Verey Pistols	10
Vicker HMG	1913
Lewis LMG	4264
Rifles: Russian, SMLE,Ross:	198,015
Webley Pistols	1257
Bayonets	70,524
Cavalry swords	13,094

The following ammunition had been sent:

6 pdr	20000 rds
7.62cm	904 rds
13pdr AA	2172
18pdr	1,463,210 rds
4.5 howitzer	261,861 rds
60 pdr.	97,934 rds
6" howitzer	70,490 rds
Mortar	16,142 rds

8" howitzer	8455 rds.
Armor piercing	89,766 rds
British Mk VII	212,258,509 rds.
Russian	262,155,801 rds
Mauser	22,784,000 rds
French	1,000,000 rds

In Clothing:

Around 500,000 Caps, Greatcoats, Jackets,Pants,Boots, Gloves, Packs, Towels. Almost 2,000,000 shirts, 1,000,000 underwear, 1,500,000 Socks. Over 100,000 steel helmets

Hospital Equipment:
Twelve General Hospitals of 500 beds.
Eight casualty stations of 200.
Over 800,000 field dressings
Eleven Stationary hospitals of 200 beds.
Some 28 field ambulances
One Stationary hospital with 1000 beds.
Three stationary hospitals with 100 beds.

Transport:

Of 3 ton trucks:	173 Thornycroft, 12 Peerless , 158 Albion
Workshops:	25
Store trucks:	31
Cars:	
Ford:	36 cars, 11 vans, 30 ambulances
Studebaker:	38 ambulances
Sunbeam:	19 cars, 42 ambulances
Talbot:	6 armor cars
Douglas:	187 motorcycles
Triumph:	92 motorcycles.

Also, 35 Caterpillar tractors and 63 caterpillar trucks.

Communications:
8,053 miles of cable, 4039 Cells, 616 Fullerphones, 1550 17ft telephone poles, 253 switchboards, 1740 telephones,170 Vibrator telegraph sets, 4466 electric torches, 2068 miles of enamelled electric wire, 44 miles of insulated wire, 1000 miles of electric permanent line, 14 wireless pack sets, Marconi, _ kilowatt, 1 1.5 kilowatt wagon set, 2 trucks with 2 kilowatt spark,Mark I set, 7 receiver boxes.

Wire:	10,550 coils of barb wire, 350 coils of plain wire.
Bridges:	84 Pontoons, 32 Trestles.

Naval Guns:	37 six inch guns
	102 four inch guns
	twelve pounders
	six pounders
	three pounders
	25 pom-pom

Denikin's great offensive from April to October had taken 250,000 POWs, 700 artillery guns and 35 armor trains. Now it was almost all gone. Denikin had failed because of several reasons:

1.Soviet propaganda which was vast, widespread and systematic.
2.The White army severe corruption of many of his officers and total administrative incapacity to improve the soldier's life with basic necessities.
3.Typhus Epidemics, which affected both sides and a lack of medical treatment. Typhus usually caused more casualties than a battle did.
4. Denikin had no conscriptions or draft to replace his losses, the Reds did.
5. The peasants did not like Denikin's land laws.
6. Looting by the soldiers under Denikin which set bad examples to those who might have allies.
7. The vaccillation of the Allies and failure to support Denikin economically. Liberated towns looked to the British to help and when it did not materialize, they became bitter.
8. The Policies of Poland and Romania
9. Profiteering by the men under Denikin which caused great discontent.
10.The British Economic Mission to Moscow headed by the High Commissioner of South Russia, Mr. Mackinder.

The British sent him there after the January 10th agreement, which stated that the wives and families of the Russian officers would be evacuated when the need arises. Before Mackinder was able to return to England, he was sent to Moscow. This was reported in the Russian newspapers. This destroyed any faith in the Allies, which the Whites needed to continue fighting. Holman was dumbfounded and could do nothing to contradict the effects.

17

The British Mission in South Russia

The British Mission had set up many schools to instruct in the use of British artillery and machines guns. At Armavir, one artillery school existed, the other was at Novercherkassk. From the start, it was a mess to sort out since both the instructors and equipment arrived at the same time. The Russians knew nothing of this equipment. The situation was made worse when parts failed to arrive. The Schools only had 4 men to instruct with in June 1919. In the end, the Russian soldier preferred the 4.5" howitzer because of it's simplicity. Even this gun was too heavy for the Russian ponies. The 18th pdr. proved to be too complicated for the Russian. By July, 1919, the British had also set up machine gun schools at Armavir for the Volunteer Army, Novercherkassk for the Don Army, at Anapa for the Kuban Cossacks and at Piatigorsk for the Terek Cossacks. Eventually, the school acted as a reserve machine gun battalion with one Company of each: Vickers, Maxim, Colt and Lewis machine guns. By the end of August, the machine gun schools had trained 402 officers and 600 enlisted in using the Vickers and Lewis. However, Holman states that the effectiveness was only 20% because the Russians failed to take care of their weapons for a variety of reasons and lack of supplies, grease etc.

A brigade sized unit would receive three Vicker gun companies totaling 24 guns on mounted carts and 36 Lewis Guns. By March, 1920, the British schools had trained some 9000 men in using the Vickers and Lewis guns. By that time, the only schools training were located at Djankow in the Crimea, Ekaterinodar and Novorojdesvenskaya. During the first week in March, the British Mission repacked for shipment to the Crimea some 361 Vickers, 182 Lewis Guns, 87 mortars and 3000 rifles. By July, 1919, the number of Stokes light mortar in each of Denikin's armies was as follows:

Volunteer Army 12, Don Army 4, Caucasian Army 5, Armor trains 4, schools 7.

By the end of August, two mortar batteries had been formed and discontinued themselves in the combat at Lisky. No more training could occur since no more mortars were sent until February, 1920. Some 87 mortars and 60,000 rounds arrived,but only 25% were any good. The remaining were rusty and /or missing parts to make operational. The fuses sent were the 1916 pattern, limiting the range to only 666 yards instead of the 900 yards using the Always fuze.

Holman made his opinions known regarding the forces. As to Mamantov's raid, Holman indicated it was a not a great military achievement because there was no opposition and he did not obey orders. But it did teach the Reds a lesson and led them raise their own cavalry army led by Budenny. Budenny, according to Holman, was the greatest cavalry leader of either side. He was a sergeant major in the old Imperial Army. As to the Cossacks, Holman thought they were great swordsman but would have been more formidable had they been skilled in rifle action and dismounting actions. With Armor trains, they usually operated in pairs. A light train armed with field and machine guns was well advance of the heavily armed train. The trains fought with great abilities and their use was made easier by the incomprehensible lack of ability by the other opposing arms dealing with them. Heavy artillery proved to be unsuitable because of the lack of horses required to pull them. Thus, in retreats, they were left behind. All field guns operating with infantry had a great morale effect. Engineers were used mostly for rail repair not as field troops armed with explosives to blow up railways.

As to infantry, the Volunteers were excellent and fought as well as any and were hard to beat. The Don Army infantry was useless. They disliked marching and only covered ground in retreats. The Kuban Cossacks were "more or less" reliable. The mobilized peasants were ignorant men who did not know what they were fighting for. One day it was with the Bolsheviks, after a capture, they would be with Denikin's forces. They had no idea of keeping their weapons in order.

Until June,1919, there was no communication by radio except by ships or through the Naval Station at Novorossisk. On June 3rd, 1920, a 5-kilowatt German Telefuken station was opened at Novorossisk. The set had 100 ft. masts and eventually a 500 watt set was erected in the Cement Works. The Cement Works had two 300 ft. chimneys and an 250 ft..aerial. At Taganrog, one 16 Poulsen arc set arrived in December and one at Theodesia. As far as telephones, only two telephones existed. One at Novorossisk and one at Ekaterinodar. This was never improved upon as it was simply too difficult during a civil war.

Of the various mechanical transport sent to Denikin, each army would receive a quota:

Volunteer Army received 1 workshop, 19 trucks, 15 motorcycles, 10 bikes
Wrangel's Caucasian Army received 1 workshop, 7 trucks, 1 car, 20 motorcycles and 10 bikes.
The North Caucasian Army received 1 workshop,16 trucks,15 cycles, 35 bikes.
The Don Army received 29 trucks and 15 cycles.
Denikin also had a transport battalion consisting of 2 workshops, 72 trucks, 12 ambulances, 1 car,3 cycles and 10 bikes.

As far as Armor Cars units, Denikin had 74 trucks, 12 workshops,1 Van,5 amublances,9 cars, 64 cycles, 100 bikes.
Artillery units each had 25 trucks,6 cycles,5 bikes. The units located on the front were supported by 67 trucks, 2 Vans, 8 ambulances, 18 cars, 35 cycles,90 bikes.

All told, Denikin had been issued 25 workshops, 374 trucks, 11 vans, 174 ambulances, 55 cars, 215 motorcycles and 378 bikes. These workshops were located in Ekakterinoslav, Stavropol,Rostov,Odessa,Kiev, Novorossisk and Novotcherkask. According to Holman, about 40% of the trucks were in need of repair and complete overall by December, 1919. Most were very well "used" trucks and the Thornycroft make was not well adapted on Russian roads. At <text>least 75% of the trucks sent, upon their arrival required repairs and spare parts were scarce. Nearly all American Studebaker makes had to be repaired upon their arrival. So, while the numbers are impressive, Denikin clearly was not mechanized. Most of the drivers were Russian, some 5000, were employed. Each received between 900 to 1500 rubles monthly plus rations and clothing. A skilled 1st class workman received 10 rubles and hour, or 40 rubles a day.

The medical staffing and care for those injured was simply horrendous. During the retreat in December, one hospital in Tcherkovo in the Don area housed 2,023 patients intended for 410! The patients in this hospital were huddled on the floor in rags, unwashed and packed. To nurse them was impossible and the medical staff itself suffered from various diseases. The senior doctor died, and when Holman visited it, three out of eight doctors were sick and even greater numbers of nurses had come down with Typhus! As Holman stated, it was a typical example. In another example Holman cites, near Tsaritsyn, there were four hospitals. One had 325 patients intended for 100 and one doctor; another for 165 patients was near empty with 4 doctors. The ambulances sent by Britain were found to be too heavy for off road movement, thus, those injured were carried in a springless cart from the field station near the front to the rear hospital. The injured were much worse by they time they arrived from the exposure to the harsh elements. This travel to the rear was usually around 70 miles! The hospitals in Novorossisk during the Spring of 1920, had the capacity of 4500 patients, yet 7000 were in them from the Typhus outbreak. The arrangements for cleaning and washing or disinfection were non-existent. The patients bedded on straw, nursing was nominal and there were no sanitary arrangements. Patients were dirty, filthy,many dying as vermin roamed on them. Of course, the British had their own hospital at Taganrog which opened August 19th. By October, it had 100 beds for British personnel only. The doctor in the Russian Army was not an officer and had no power, entirely subordinate to the orders of the combatant officers.Thus, many times, a doctor would defend the patient as being not ready to return, but the patient was forced to by his commander. The total numbered of sick evacuated from the port came to 7114. These were in addition to those under the Mackinder agreement.

The British supplied Denikin with 527 Horses and 4735 mules. These were nearly all used to haul artillery guns. The British also sent Denikin 42 locomotives and 500 railcars to help modernize the rail system.

Besides the sick and those under the Mackinder agreement, the Allies evacuated 8579 refugees from Novorossisk and 4558 from Odessa by March 28th. The equipment that fell into the Red hands amounted to mostly the clothing and engineering tools. Of the only significance were the 91 artillery guns, which were made unserviceable. Most of these were 18 pdrs. and French 45mm. The one item, which in numbers was the highest left behind were 1,035,936 pairs of socks.The number transport ships involved in the British Military Mission buildup and evacuation amount to 41 transports.

18

Wrangel's Turn to Carry On

As we now know, there was no love loss between Wrangel and Denikin. The rift had begun with Wrangel's approach to Tsaritsyn in June, 1919. Initially, it had been over the whereabouts of his reinforcements Wrangel desperately needed. Denikin made him wait. Then, once the city was taken, Denikin's Operation Moscow was announced, the rift widened because both thought their method of warfare and plans were correct. However, Wrangel was his subordinate and acted faithfully, if not, brilliantly in his tactics and military doctrine.

Denikin was now gone and Wrangel was now the appointed new Commander in Chief of the Army of South Russia relocated in the Crimea. The Reds did not let up, on March 31st, they attacked in Perekop area with 3000 cavalry only to be repelled by the remnants of the Volunteer Corps. Wrangels main foe at this time was the Red 13th Army consisting of 6000 infantry and 3000 cavalry (8th Cav. Division, 13th Cav. Brigade, 6th,46th divisions) But like everyone else, the Reds were in bad shape due to the Typhus epidemic. Wrangels army now consisted of Kutepov Corps (Volunteers), the Slachtchov Corps (the 13th and 34th divisions) and the Don Cavalry Corps (six regiments). The Reds first attempt to burst into the Crimea was over the Perekopsk isthmus beginning March. Their Estonian, Latvian and 46th Infantry Divisions possessing an overwhelming superiority in manpower started an offensive into Yushon. Slashchev (the White commander) sent into the battle all of his reserves, including the officers of his staff, but the chances to retain the position were nil. It was the 8th Volunteer Air Detachment with two "Anasals" and two "LVG C VI" and the 5th Detachment with five in good condition "DH9s" and also aircraft of the Kachinskoy Flying School with some out of date and unarmed "Anasals," "Nieuports" and "Morane-Parasol" that saved the White ground forces. All were urgently banded together on the front airfields near Dzhanko for the oncoming assault of the Reds.

At dawn, March 8, the White fliers flew repeated attacks on the massing Bolshevik troops and wagon trains near Yushon. The raids went on all day long. The resulting effect was that some of the poorer morale Red units in their exposed positions routed toward the north that evening. Those who stayed suffered continuous aerial bombardments on the following morning. They routed when a flanking blow by White cavalry arrived from Simferopol. Suffering big losses, the Reds on 10 March retreated beyond Perekopsk. This was one of the few times aircraft had been used in such concentrated form on specific targets. The Reds at this time in the Crimea had the 3rd Fighter Detachment, 13th 'Kazan' and 48th Reconnaissance Air Detachments, but these were in much worse state than even the Whites.

Wrangel attacked again on April 1st, this time, a landing of near Kirilovka, 20 miles NE of Guenitchesk. The Reds counterattacked and were repelled. Wrangel seized Guenitchesk on the 2nd and landed more troops at Khorly. The town was held by two Soviet regiments and 4 guns. After a bitter battle, Khorly fell. On the 3rd, the whole area erupted in attacks and counterattacks and Wrangels troops were running short of ammunition. However, Wrangels men, despite the previous months of retreat, were advancing and seized Djimbuluk station which had been fortified. Once taken, the Reds fled the Tchongar Peninsula in a panic.

Wrangel had been immensely helped by the actions of Poland, which now attacked the Soviets. The wish that Denikin had was finally true, but for him, too late. Now the Reds were forced to deal with Poland on their western front. Wrangel welcomed the respite of fighting. He ordered his men to dig in and fortify. It was because of Poland the Soviet attention had been diverted and this allowed Wrangel to gather forces. Had it not occurred, the Soviets could have forced their way into the Crimea with the 13th and 14th Armies. This is how the anticlimatic continuation of the Russian Civil war developed.

In the beginning of April on the Southern Ukrainian front area between Poland and Russia were two Polish air divisions comprised of five squadrons (2nd, 5th, 6th and 9th Reconnaissance and 7th Fighter). The reconnaissance squadrons were equipped with German and Austrian two-seater multipurpose aircraft of different types: "Albatrosses," "Halberstadts", "Rolands," "Brandenburg," "DFW," "LVG" and "AEG." The 7th Fighter Squadron was armed mainly with new "Albatross." These aircraft were flown by American volunteer pilots, veterans of the 1st World War. The Squadron bore the name Tadeush Kostiushko, after a Polish General. The commander of the squadron was Major Cedric E. Fauntleroy. In the middle of the month, the Polish air strength in the Ukraine was further replenished by the 3rd, 16th and 17th squadrons equipped with French "Breguet-14." Although these units were reconnaissance they carried bomb racks. The same was also true for a majority of the German aircraft.

Along the northern (Lithuanian-Byelorussian) front area, the Poles concentrated another three air divisions. In these were the 1st, 4th, 8th, 11th, 12th, 14th and 18th Reconnaissance and the 13th Fighter squadron. Later, they were joined by the 10th Reconnaissance and 19th Fighter. Many of these units, like in the south, were armed with different German biplanes. Only the 1st and 18th squadrons flew French "Salmsons" and the 19th fighter flew "SPADs." The composition of Polish aviation squadrons contained 10 aircraft. In practice, this was rarely met. The number of combat ready aircraft varied widely, but usually did not exceed 7-8. Poland had roughly 130-140 aircraft.

Near Borisov station, the Red 4th Fighter squadron arrived under the command of the reputed flier, winner of the "Order of the Red Banner," A.D.Shirihkin. The squadron contained 4 detachments, the 10th, 11th, 12th and 13th*, in which there were 29 fighters (17 "Nieuports-24bis," 2 "Nieuport-23," "Nieuport-11," "Nieuport-21" and 8 "SPAD-7"). However, of this number by the end of April amounted to 10 flyable aircraft. The rest were in various states of needed repair.

On April 11th, the squadron combined with the 38th and 44th Reconnaissance detachments, which also flew "Nieuports." On April 25th, units of the 2nd, 3rd and 6th Polish armies moved east. Ágainst these considerable armies the troops of the 12th Red Army were instantaneously squashed. The operation continued for 10 days, after this time the Poles occupied Korosten, Zhitomir, Vinnits and Kiev. The Reds without much resistance retreated to the Dnieper river.

This Polish "blitzkrieg" was supported by the 2nd, 3rd and 5th Squadrons bombed the Ukrainian cities, stormed the outgoing columns of soviets and railway compositions. The American 7th named Squadron Kostiushko accomplished many daily sorties displayed special activity.

In mid-late April, the Crimea was quiet due to the recent Polish successes, which had defeated the Soviet 12th,15th and 16th armies. Once again, the Red command was panicky and tossing all reserves in. They transferred their 1st Cavalry Army led by Budenny and weakened the 13th Army by sending the 8th cavalry division to the Polish area.

By May, the Soviets focused on Wrangel again by strengthening the 13th Army to 12000 infantry and 3000 cavalry. Wrangel,by now, had 10 operational tanks and 21 assorted airplanes. Wrangel had just acquired 4000 horses which allowed him to mount 400 cavalry. His troops by had rested and dug in, but Wrangel knew he would have to break out because of the horrible economic situation in the Crimea. The Reds reinforced with the 2nd Fighter squadron under command I.K. Spatarel. In its composition were the 5th and 6th detachments. In these detachments there were 10 efficient machines of mainly "Nieuport and SPADs." Before long the division received the 16th and 49th Reconnaissance Detachments.

While the British Military Mission had disappeared from Novorossisk, it surfaced again with the same purpose in the Crimea. The mission in the Crimea, was equally as large, some

Whippets (Type A) moving through Novorissk, 1919.

169 officers (2 Generals,4 Colonels,6 Lt.Colonels, 35 Majors, 89 Captains, 33 Lieutenants) and 459 men (28 warrant officers, 71 Seargents,82 Corporals, 243 Privates)

Wrangel had plenty of trains since his area of operations had shrunk. He possessed 106 engines in running order and an equal amount that needed repair and non-operational.

On May 16th, General Percy submitted his Secret General Staff Report on General Wrangel's Crimean Army. Percy made the following observations:

> "There is a great shortage of food and no effort to cultivate. It is essential that the army advance out of the Crimea into rich country beyond. Preparations for such advance have been made but lack of petrol for tanks and aeroplanes have postponed it. All units have rifles, there is still confusion and no proper plan for organization. Trains run as far as Voienka. Bolshevik aeroplanes have been very active over Kerch dropping bombs on the 14th,18th,20th,22nd and 25th near Yeni-kale and Kerch harbor. Several attempts have also been made to bomb the HMS Pegasus Seaplane Carrier while docked and in the Sea of Azov. The seaplanes of the Pegasus were unable to climb more than 3000 feet to fight the enemy, which two are DK 4's and 1 Nieuport. An aerodome was discovered on the 15th near Temriuk. On the 25th, a Bolshevik aeroplane was brought down by anti-aircraft fire. At Chongar, the 2nd Corps is being relieved by the 3rd Corps. When relieved, the 2nd Corps will go into the Theodesia-Kerch area."

Wrangel on the economics of war:

> "...we managed to cover our ordinary expenses with revenue, but the extraordinary budget showed a deficit of 250 milliards, which was still very large. The Crimea was poor and could not support a huge army. Including all types of personnel (POWs, schools, Navy, WIAs etc) we had 250-300,000 mouths to feed, although, our actual fighting strength was 30-35,000. Corn was our sole export and by September, nearly 1.5 million poods (1 pood = 40 lbs) were at our ports and 1 million had been exported. Some 275,000 poods were sent to France. Our financial situation grew steadily worse and our small foreign reserves were melting away. Corn ensured our only way of ensuring the re-equipment of the army with war material."

By the 25th, Wrangel's army had four corps: 1) The 1st Corps led by General Kutepov. These had the three Volunteer divisions, now rebuilt and still a formidable force. It also contained the 2000 man 2nd Cavalry division led by Morozov, and a mixed cavalry brigade of Terek and Astrakhan Cossacks.2) The 2nd Corps, led by Gen. Slachtchov and contained the 13th and 34th divisions. 3) The 3rd Corps, led by Pisarev, was a mixed lot of various troops and the Don Army Corps, led by Abramov, contained the 9th and 12th Don divisions. Each one of the 3rd and 4th Corps had a 200 man cavalry unit, all other cavalry units were used as infantry due to a lack of horses. All total, Wrangel only had 25,000 men.

His airforce consisted of the following:

At Djankoi: Squadron 4 (4 DH9)
Squadron 5 (7 DH9, 2 DH9A, 2 RE8)
Squadron 8 (3 Nieuports, 2 German Nassals, one German DFW)
At Saribash: Squadron 1 (3 Camels , 4 DH9)
At Simferpol: Squadron 2 (1 DH9, 1 RE8)
Squadron 7: (6 Monoplanes, 1 Farman, 2 Nieuport,1 DH9)
At Sevastopol: 1 Albatross
Total personnel is 390 officers, 1500 men.

Wrangel also had 15 fit tanks at the following locations:

3 MkV and 3 MkA (Whippet) at Armiansk with 1st Corps.
3 MkV at Djimboulovk with 13th division
6 MKA Whippet at Magazinka in reserve for 1st Corps.

There were another nine tanks that needed one month's work. The British support included 4 officers and 15 men.

Wrangel, the commander of the Caucasian Army under Denikin, and later the Russian Army in 1920. Photo: Russian Civil War Museum

The **Russian Army under General Peter Wrangel** was comprised of the following:

1st and 2nd Divisions of Volunteers (1st Corps)
4th and 6th Don Divisions (Don Corps)
13th and 34th divisions (2nd Corps)
2nd Cavalry division (1st Corps)
1st Cavalry division (580 men)
9th and 10th Don Divisions (each had 2000 men, 3 MG)
43rd Don Cossack Regiment (550 men)
Kalinin regiment (475 men)
Misc. Kuban Units (2460 men)
Caucasians regiment (910 men)
Misc. troops from Adler (8867 men, 29 MG,15 guns)

In Armor trains he had:

At Chongar the "Moscow" (w/2 8" guns), "John Kaelta" and "United Russia"(these last two had 2 60pdr each and 1 6" howitzer)

At Kerch, supporting the 4th division, the "Isgoi," "Dmitri Donskoi" and "Wolf." Each had 2-4 3" guns, 2 18 pdrs. At Sevastopol supporting the 6th division, the "Soldier," "Grozni" and "Sevetopoletz." At Theodesia, the "Drozdovetz" with 4 3" guns.

The Army artillery consisted of:

1st Corps:	Markov Brigade (8 18 pdrs, 4 4.5 Howitzer, 600 men)
	Kornilov Brigade (8 18 pdrs. 4 4.5 Howitzer, 450 men)
	Drozdovsky Brigade (4 18 pdrs, 4 3," 4 4.5 Howitzer, 900 men)
	1st Cav. Division (8 3" guns)
	Heavy Artillery (4 60pdr,4 6," 4 8" guns,300 men)
	Alekseev Brigade 2 4.5," 4 3" guns)

At Sevastopol: 16 18 pdrs, 4 8" guns, 4 4.5 howitzer, 1700 men.

2nd Corps:	13th Division (18 18 pdrs, 4 3" guns, 470 men)
	34th Division (18 3" guns, 2 4.8" guns, 837 men)
	4th heavy brigade (8 6," 4 18 pdr, 400 men)

Don Corps:	Eight 18 pdrs, 300 men.
Kuban Corps:	Eleven 3" guns, 600 men.
2nd Cav Division:	13 3" guns, 400 men.
In the Kerch area:	Four 6" guns.
Coastal Defense:	Six 3" guns, 11 3.4" guns, two 6" guns.

The only school for the training in the use of British weapons was at Theodesia, which had 700 men, 86 MG, 35 Stokes mortars. The Aviation School was at Kacha and at Sevastopol, the artillery school was with 2100 men, 20 heavy and 4 light guns.

On the 21st, Wrangel issued orders to prepare for his first offensive:

> The 2nd Corps were to embark at Feodossia and make a coastal attack in the Kirilovka area and cut off Slakovo-Melitopol railway and then cooperate with the 3rd Corps against the rear of the Red forces in the Perekop area. The 3rd Corps had been moved to the Salkovo front. Wrangel also ordered the 3rd and 1st Corps to attack on the 25th and drive towards the Dniepr River, while the Don Army Corps was held in reserve near Djankoie Station. A section of the river flotilla would support the attack at the mouth of the Dniepr. This first operation, unlike those under Denikin, was kept secret and disinformation was purposefully leaked out stating that a landing would be at Odessa or Novorossisk. The 2nd Corps commander was not to open the orders until he was at sea for the actual landing zone.

The 2nd Corps landed on the 24th disembarking during a storm near Kirilovka and on the 25th, the remaining units began the offensive. The 3rd Corps attacked with armor cars and tanks. The old familiar trends appeared as the Reds fled when the tanks appeared. The 3rd Corps took several hundreds of POWs. However, the Reds opposing the 1st Corps in trenches and behind barb wire fought tenaciously despite the Mk V tanks and Austin Armor Cars on the Perekop Front. The Red artillery now were used at antitank guns destroying several tanks but the positions were taken. The 2nd Corps by evening of the 26th had taken the railway and had taken 1000 POWs, while 3rd Corps continued to face stiff opposition along with 1st Corps. By the 28th, the attack had succeeded and 1st Corps had netted some 3500 POWs,25 guns and 3 armor cars. But a high price was paid as Wrangel noted:

The huge Russian bomber used by the Reds, the Ilya Mouromets Type G heavy bomber. Built in 1915, it could carry 1150 lbs of bombs. It was used against Wrangel in 1920 and Mamontov in 1919. Photo: G. Haddow

"Our own losses were very heavy especially in 1st Corps. In one of the regiments all the battalion and company officers had been killed."

On the 28th, Melitopol station had been taken by 2nd Corps despite furious Red counterattacks. The Reds were now retreating toward Kahovka that had been reinforced. The battle for Melitopol continued until the 30th, but 1st Corps held their positions. Part of the 13th army retreated back across the Dniepr blowing up the bridges. The Soviet 13th Army during the five day battle had suffered heavy losses:

8000 POWs, 30 guns, over a hundred MG. The army had lost 75% of it's effective.

The Soviets were focused on attacking the Poles on the 27th and had made good gains.By the 31st, the Poles had lost Kiev.

Overall, England had become hostile to the anti-Bolshevik cause and in June withdrew the British Military Mission. General Percy was so disgusted with this that when he returned to England, sometime later, he retired and moved to Canada to farm. However, France was moving toward recognition of Wrangel as the legitimate government of Russia! America remained neutral but increasingly anti-Bolshevik.

Wrangel launched his offensive on June 7th. The attack with ground forces was supported by practically all the White aviation. At Perekopsk were concentrated 25 aircraft out of 30 available. Immediately over the isthmus the 1st General Alekseev Volunteer Air Detachment, 3rd, 4th and 5th Detachments flew bombing and ground support missions. The 8th Detachment fought on the Chongarsk sector. Reconnaissance missions were flown without a break over the front exposing enemy forces and defensive. The aircraft made aerial bombardments in groups of 3 to 6 aircraft. Flights led by Tkachev bombarded the settlement of Chaplinko where the staff of the 13th Army was located. Tkachev reported: "The Red fliers took steps to intercept our aircraft by putting up 3 to 4 aircraft, but unsuccessfully." In reality, there were only 2-3 ineffectual skirmishes between Red and White airplanes. The Reds defenses were resilient and the ground battle turned to hand-to-hand fighting with both sides taking heavy losses. The Whites even sent in tanks for extra combat power. Soviet artillery bątteries engaged the tanks and armored cars with direct fire. By the evening, the Bolsheviks had retreated, however at night Red reinforcements were brought up and on the following morning the battle flamed up with fresh and new forces.

The furious attacks and counterattacks went on a few days. Reds and Whites fought to the death. Only June 12th, the lines finally broke. The exhausted and bloodied Soviet divisions fell back toward the northwest across the Dnieper and northeast to Aleksandrovky (Zaporozhia). But the Whites simply did not have the resources to exploit. The Losses were too high. Some regiments were left with half their personal. They lacked strong cavalry units. The cavalry's role was taken on by the aviation. Tkachev's aircraft overtook the retreating columns of Red Army soldiers and wagon trains and attacked them with machine-guns and shrapnel bombs. Stronger Red units under Kakhovk reached the ferry points over the Dnieper saving 10,000 soldier and more than 8,000 vehicles (carts mostly).

The Perekopsk operation had ended with a victory for the White. The White airforce proved to be a deciding factor and did their utmost to guarantee this victory. After the first two days, June 7-8, the airforce flew 150 sorties dropping 6.5 tons (13,000 lb.) of bombs on the Reds.

On June 15th, the Reds launched a strong offensive against the weaker Don cavalry corps containing one cavalry division with armor cars. The Don corps was unable to contain the Reds and fell back. On the 16th, the Reds attempted to cross the Dneipr but were repulsed at Kartachinkca.. The Don corps continued to be hammered by Red cavalry units and the Don corps fell back . The Red cavalry now avoided day time marches and advances in order to avoid the continuous and effective air attacks from Wrangel's air units, which had suffered heavy losses. The Don corps was exhausted and the nearby 2nd corps was in no position to lend assistance. By the 19th, Wrangel's frontline strength was 15,000 men, however, actual combat forces amounted to only 11,000 (infantry and cavalry). It's opposition, the 13th Army, had 25,000 infantry and 10,000 cavalry (according to Wrangel). By this time, the wear and tear on the airplanes and tanks was beginning to show. Some were in such bad shape that they would be unfit for use for 4-6 weeks. Fuel and oil also was at critically low levels. The lack of men had also become serious for Wrangel forcing him to resort to recruiting from the north and northwest fronts and in the Cossack territories.

Wrangel had extensively used his aircraft, some 30 assorted planes to strafe and bomb the enemy in the past month. Now his airforce was in such a state of disrepair, they had to be grounded for at least a month for repairs. Most of the tanks followed the similar path. Fuel and oil was in short supply and difficult to obtain. Wrangel bought these types of supplies from Rumania, Bulgaria and Georgia. However, according to Wrangel:

Wrangel's Armor Breakout Attack
May 25 to June 1, 1920

> "England put all kinds of obstacles in our way and held up our cargoes on a thousand and one pretexts. Our financial situation was growing steadily worse. Corn was out sole exportable commodity, and our only way to rearm the Army was to exchange corn for ammunition."

On the big May offensive to break out of the Crimea, Wrangel wrote:

> "By May 25th, the enemy had brought up 15-16,000 men and 3-4,000 cavalry against the Russian army. We had about 25,000 men in four Corps: 1st, 2nd, Mixed and Don. Only the 2nd cavalry division with 2000 men and a Terek/Astrakhan Cossack brigade had any horses. The Don corps had only 150-200 horses, the rest of the cavalry were on foot. The 1st and Mixed corps were to attack at dawn and beat the enemy back to the Dniepr. The 2nd corps would embark at Feodossia and make a coastal attack near the Salkovo-Melitopol area and cut the railroad. By the evening of the 24th, the 2nd corps had landed at Kirillovka without enemy notice. At dawn, the attack began supported by tanks, aircraft and armor cars, all going ahead of our troops. The enemy barb wire and defenses were wrecked. Enemy artillery fired from point blank range on our tanks. Many were wrecked. On the first day, we captured 15 artillery guns, The 2nd corps approached the railway and the enemy fled almost without resisting. Heavy fighting continued on the 26th, the 2nd corps had taken 1000 POWs and was nearly at the railway line. The 1st corps continued to face stiff resistance. The 1st corps had taken 3500 POWs, 25 guns. Our own losses were very heavy among the officers. In one regiment, all of the officers had bee killed. On the 28th, 2nd corps took Melitopol station and held the town against furious enemy attacks. The enemy forces (13th army) opposite 1st corps retreated towards Kahovka where reinforcements had arrived. Heavy fighting continued on the 29th and 30th for Melitopol. The 1st and Mixed corps consolidated their postions. By now, 13th army had lost 8000 and 30 artillery guns and huge stores of ammunition. They had lost 75% of their effectives."

The enemy forces opposing Wrangel grew as the Polish situation posed less danger to the Soviet, and by July, Wrangel was facing 11 infantry and 6 cavalry divisions, some 35000 infantry and 10000 cavalry. To keep the Reds from gathering, Wrangel attacked on July 15th, and in a series of spoiling attacks ending on the 20th, captured 5000 POWs, 30 guns and 150 MG. Despite their strength, the Reds fell back. On the 22nd, Wrangel and the Kuban area governments had signed a cooperation agreement to oppose the Soviet. Wrangel would have complete control of all the armed forces within the Kuban. The Bolsheviks still possessed a large numerical superiority and in course of time superiority this is only increased. In the middle of June to the South Front was transferred the 1st Zhloby Cavalry Corps (former Dumenko Corps) with 8000 men. Adding this replenishment the Reds now had 35,000 infantrymen and 10,000 riders against 22,000 soldier and 2,000 cavalrymen with Wrangel.

By June 28th, the Red Zhloby Corps was further reinforced by the 2nd Stavrpolsk Cavalry Division, artillery, armored cars and an armored train. It was able to break through the front and swifly on Melitopol. This operation broke up Wrangel's Army into two unequal parts and the main part was cut off from the Crimea where it eventually was doomed to a death on the steppes of North Taurida. In time Zhloby captured the defenseless Melitopol and marched seaward toward the Azov. Wrangel's last hope was his aviation. Tkachev's fliers on the night of the 28th and 29th were ordered in to stop the Red cavalry. Recon aircraft took off immediately to determine targets. By wireless, recon showed that the Zhloby Corps was encamped for the night in the village of Chernigov. Early in the morning, 12 "DH9s" from the 4th and 5th detachments, in series of sorties dove on the unsuspecting forward columns of the Red cavalry. At first the cavalry broke in panic, fleeing in all directions. The terrified horses tore straight over fences, threw down riders, tipped over carts and artillery vehicles. It was complete chaos. After dropping the bombs, the aircraft lowered and strafed with machineguns. The raid continued for an hour. The aircraft flew back to replenish ammunition and the Red commanders attempted to gather up their scattered units, but the DH9s returned not once, but twice. By evening, Zhloby Corps had lost about 400 men and 500 horses. The following morning, Zhloby Corps attempted to resume the offensive. But when the tired horsemen formed into their marching columns the DH9s swooped down on them again. The chaotic scene was repeated. On June 30th, Zhloby Corps ceased to exist as an organized force. The riders of Zhloby Corps were scattered in villages and farms. All contact with the command was lost. A large majority of them surrendered into captivity when Wrangels ground forces arrived in the area. Unlike in Denikin's time, Wrangel used his aircraft correctly as an air hammer to totally disorganized a much stronger enemy.

Wrangel was not finished yet, the White army now pulled up reserves and started to envelop the disorganized Zhloby Corps on the flanks. By July 3rd, the encirclement was complete. The Corps Commander with his staff and most of the Red cavalry squadrons fled to the northeast. The remaining were killed or surrendered into captivity. Of the total 12000 combatants in Zhloby Corps that had begun the raid, not more than 2000 had remained!. The White Guards reinforced their forces with almost 3000 horses found and left behind.

The defeat of Red Zhloby Cavalry Corps was the greatest and highest achievement of White aviation in the entire Civil war. Even Soviet military science accepted this fact and in the 1920's the students of Soviet flying academies studied the White aircraft tactics against

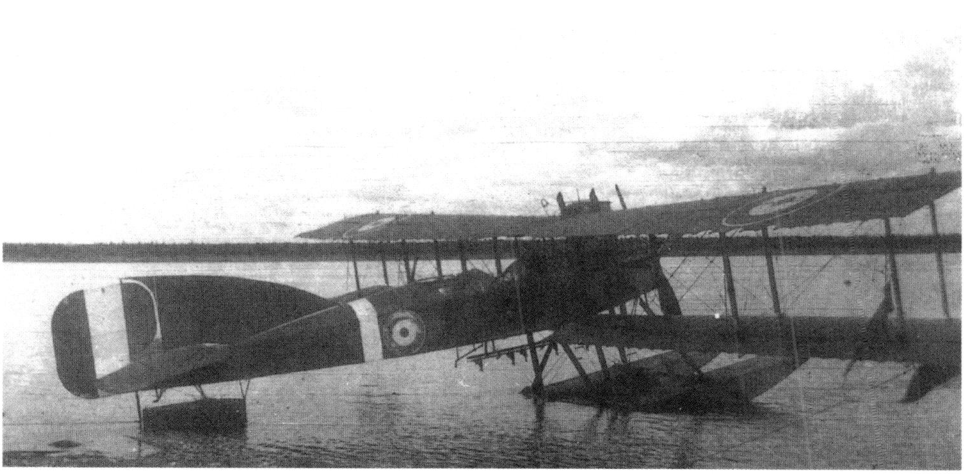

A RAF Fairey IIIC along the Dvina River in 1919. Photo; J. Bruce Collection

cavalry. Although examples previously occurred in the region of Velikokiyzhecky and near Tsaritsyn in 1919, and near Yushon in 1920, none were on this scale or as significant as in North Taurida.

Wrangel now amended his Kuban Campaign with troop landings from Feodossia and Kerch. These troops were to advance rapidly to Ekaterinodar and rally rebels. In other words, conduct guerilla warfare as the Reds had done to Denikin. Wrangel hoped that the combination of conventional and guerilla warfare would yield the Kuban areas to him. However, Wrangel knew he has to act, he later wrote:

> "The little Crimea cannot continue to feed us for much longer .Our base is too small, it is necessary to enlarge our base and seize new areas rich in natural wealth, we must increase the size of the army and this seems an impossible task in view of our lack of technical equipment, arms and ammunition. Thus, a vicious circle"

And then there was England, who had up to now been a staunch supporter and sole source of military support. Wrangel writes:

> "In June, the British government had declared that is was taking no further responsibility for the continuation of the struggle, the Mission had been recalled and nothing remain British but a little information bureau. When General Percy had heard that his government intended to negotiate with the Bolsheviks he telegraphed his superiors that he would not take part. He resigned and months later was in Canada on a farm. England put all kinds of obstacles in our way when trying to obtain necessaries, and held up our cargoes on a thousand and one pretexts. We managed to avoid them but we squandered a great of time and effort."

In July, the Reds began wholesale transfers of divisions from the now defunct fronts, mainly from the eastern and western areas where no White forces presented any further danger. By this time, the Reds opposed Wrangel with 11 infantry and 6 cavalry divisions totaling 35,000 infantry and 10,000 cavalry along the front lines (excluding the rear areas).

Wrangel writes:

> " I ordered my troops to attack to prevent them from concentrating and resuming the initiative. From July 12th to 20th, fighting erupted all along the front, by the 18th, we had the upper hand and by the 20th, the enemy was retreating, we had taken more than 5000 POWs, 30 guns, 150 MGs, and 4 armor trains."

Wrangel's Amphibious Assault

Unlike Denikin, who was an officer of the old school, Wrangel was progressive and innovative. Realizing that his small Crimea base was insufficient, he planned and executed a daring amphibious assault across the Sea of Azov on August 15, 1920.

This invasion of the Kuban peninsula was no small feat or force and consisted of over 11,000 men , 26 artillery guns and around 275 machine guns. Further, it was supported by 10 armor cars and 8 DH9 bombers. Wrangel planned for a three prong attack:

General Ulagai with 4000 infantry, 4000 cavalry, 17 guns, 10 armor cars, 243 MG (these were in the 1st and 2nd Kuban Cavalry, and Svodno Infantry divisions) would invade at Aktaria on the 15th. A smaller force under Gen. Cherepov consisting of 1500 men, 15 MG and 2 guns would land near Anapa on the 17th. The last force, under General Kharlamovaz, would cross from the Taman peninsula with 3000 men, 6 guns and 25 MGs on the 23rd.

The Red forces had heard about this invasion of the Kuban and knew Wrangel had wanted to re-establish his army in the Ekaterinodar region. The Reds, themselves, had had their hands full with White forces in this area under Gen. Maiora who commanded some 5550 men, 10 guns and 35 MG. The Red 9th Army was ineffective in dealing with them and Wrangel counted on Maiora to conduct guerilla warfare in the Red rear during the invasion.

Defending the invasion area were very weak Red forces consisting of two infantry companies at Aktaria, while the rest of 9th Army (some 30,000 men, 4000 Cav., 157 guns and 711 MG) covered a vast area from Novoroissk to Eiska. Since the 9th Army had received information regarding the invasion, it cancelled the transfer of the 9th and 2nd divisions.

On the 15th, Ulagai's forces steamed into Aktaria and easily pushed aside the opposing Red forces. Between the 15th and 18th, the Reds tossed in its 1st Cavalry division(1000 men, 2 guns) which suffered high losses and retreated. Becoming more concerned, the Reds

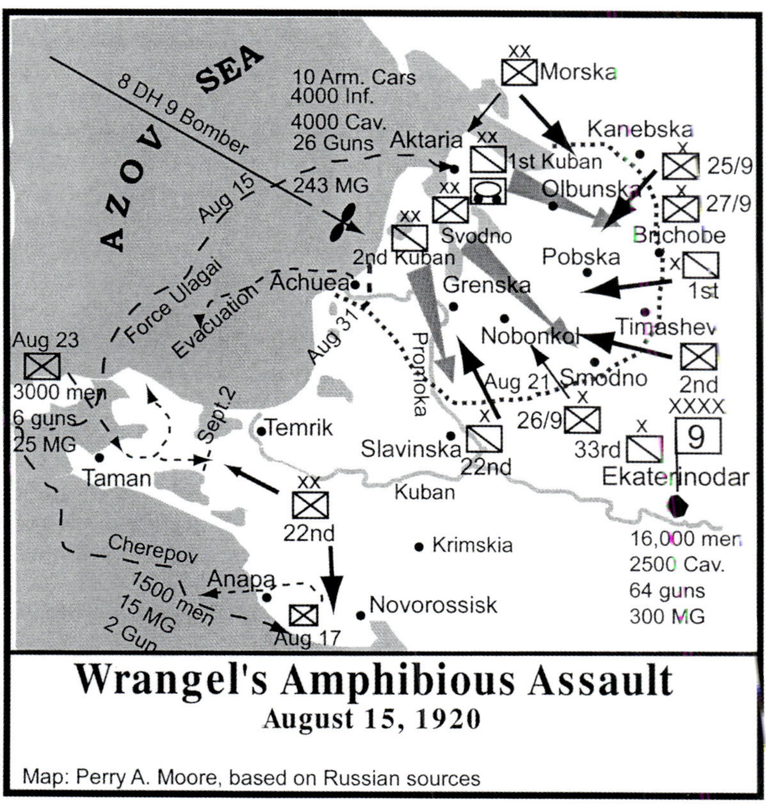

Wrangel's Amphibious Assault
August 15, 1920

Map: Perry A. Moore, based on Russian sources

then tossed in the 14th Cavalry brigade on the 18th, with the same results. Nothing seemed to be slowing the White advance. Thus, the Red 2nd brigade (some 3500 men) was thrown in. All these measures were defensive, trading lives for time while giving up the least amount of ground.

By the 18th, the situation was dangerous. Ulagai's forces had penetrated some 90 km deep and held a front that was 80 km wide. His forces that had landed at Anapa had caused the Red 22nd division to be diverted away from Ulagai, as Wrangel had planned. It looked as if the objective, Ekaterinodar, would be achieved.

The White forces had seized Timashev, Smodno, Brichobe and approached Slavinska.

On the 19th, for some unknown reason, General Ulagai suddenly halted the advance! Just when the White forces were on the verge of breaking through the thin delaying screeen the Reds had put up, the forces halt. Fot the next day, nothing happened and a lull set in. It was during this time the Reds rapidly gathered forces from the surrounding areas (which they had been trying to do since the 15th). On the 20th, nothing happened. The White forces seemed to have simply dug in awaiting for the order to continue the advance.

On the 21st, the Red Azov naval flotilla conducted a surprise attacked with shore bombardment upon the port at Aktaria. This was a coup and created a huge panic in the rear of Ulagai, which diverted his attention. This created a logistical problem for Ulagai since many had fled.

By the 22nd, the Reds had gathered the 9th and 2nd divisions, the 33rd Cav. Brigade and the Morska Cadet brigade, all total, some 16,000 infantry, 2500 cavalry and 64 guns. Preparations were being made to coordinate a counterattack.

The White forces resumed their attack but the tone had changed. Now, bitter fighting began and every foot of ground contested. The Cherepov force had been contained and many were now retreating to evacuate from Anapa.

On the 24th, the Reds conducted their own amphibious assault across the Azov. Some 1200 men, 15 MG and 4 guns aboard three steamers and four barges landed near Aktaria and again, created a huge panic in the White rear forces. All of the rearguard White units fled at the shock and the Reds walked into Aktaria. Now Ulagai had to change gears from offensive to a defensive withdrawal and evacuation from the only other port located at Achuea.

The Guerilla forces operating in the Red rear were squelched and executed. Wrangel's third prong now attacked across the Taman peninsula and easily took Taman. This forced the Red 22nd division to divert additional forces.

The grinding defensive withdrawal continued. The circle slowly grew smaller until by Aug. 31st, the area around Achuea was all that Ulagai controlled. The Reds did not press their attacks as the threat was gone. However, the third prong continued to advance and now approached Temrik and the Kuban river by Sept. 2nd.

The Ulagai and Cherepov forces completed their evacuation by Sept.7th. It was a daring operation and had it not been for the sudden, mysterious halt order, might have been a success. Wrangel noted that perhaps because of a lack of local support (as was hoped for) from the Kubans had convinced Ulagai that the effort had failed by the 19th. A local uprising did not occur on the scale that had been expected and counted on. But the failure of Maiora and his guerillas perhaps really had thrown water on the initial success, and when this was found out, Ulagai lost enthusiasm.

From Constantinople came only one steamer with two DH9s and five unarmed Avro-504k trainers sent by England for the Kachinskoy Flying School These machines formed the 2nd Air Detachment of the White Russian Army.

This invasion force was commanded by the well liked General Ulagai, whom the Cossacks liked. Wrangel was soon to find out that his chosen delegatee had further delegated the duties and planning to others. What was suppose to be a secret, was now public information and everywhere rumors existed. The invasion force ended up being some 16,400 men and 500 horses being embarked even though the actual number of combat troops totaled only 5000!

Elsewhere,on the 25th, the Soviet's conducted their own amphibious assault using three divisions at Kahovka under the cover of artillery fire from the right bank of the Dniepr. They immediately began to build a pontoon bridge. Another grouped crossed at Alechy and by nightfall had occupied the town with 2000 men including several batteries. The Whites were decimated from the artillery fire and forced to retreat losing 50%. The Reds continued on the 26th-27th and despite the resistance were able to create a bridgehead on a wide front. By the 28th, the 2nd Corps defended a fortified area along the main Perekop road.

While this happened the Red attacked the 1st Corps using the 2nd Cavalry Army, 1st,3rd,and 46th divisions, which made desperate efforts in breaking through. But the 1st Corps resisted all the attacks but with a huge rate of loss. The Reds continued to attack until August 1st, when suddenly they halted. Luck had been with 1st Corps.

In the Kuban, Wrangel had landed undetected at Akhtarsky and 2nd Corps had halted Red attacks at the Kahovka bridge, which had been fortified by the Reds.

On the 10th, France officially recognized Wrangel as the de facto government of Russia. Wrangel was elated and it was hoped that supplies would be sent. America, in a very carefully worded document also "supported "Wrangel and the crusade against Bolshevism. When Wrangel went to the front to inspect the troops he was shocked by their appearance. He wrote later:

> "The faces of the soldiers were tanned and weather beaten, their boots worn out, their shirts discolored and threadbare. Many men had no shirts and wore woolen vests instead. One soldier had no trousers and wore only a pair of woollen drawers. Another soldier wore a patterned cretonne shirt, old khaki trousers, and yellow English half boots. The terrible destitution of the troops simply leapt to the eyes."

Wrangels army now consisted of:

First Army

1st Corps (Kornilov,Markov,Drozdovsky divisions)

Don Corps (1st and 2nd Cavalry divisions, 3rd Don Infantry division)

Second Army

2nd Corps (13th and 34th divisions)

3rd Corps (6th, 7th, 2nd Kuban Cavalry divisions, Guards Bed.,
1st Kuban Cavalry division)

Cavalry Corps (1st and 2nd Cavalry divisions)

1000 MG, 26 Armor Cars, 19 tanks,249 artillery guns and 34 aircraft.

By this time, the Kuban invasion (previously noted) had turned into an evacuation!

A new Red army appeared in early September, the 6th Army. This was commanded by Gen. Eidemann and comprised of the 1st,3rd,13th,46th and 52nd divisions and Goff's cavalry brigade. This unit was located on the left bank of the Dniepr River. On the right bank was the Red 2nd Cavalry Army, under Mironov, and composed of the 2nd, 16th and 21st Cavalry divisions. When combined with the 7th Army, the combined strength of the 7th and 2nd cavalry was 15000 infantry and 6000 cavalry. The 13th army that faced the 1st Corps, numbered 30000 infantry and 7000 cavalry. In July soviet aviation was accorded new and considerable reinforcement. To the South Front the following air units arrived: 12th Fighter, 38th and 44th Reconnaissance Detachments, and also a section «aces» made up of experienced fighter pilots like Kozhevnikov, Melnikov and Sapozhnikov. These new forces were combined with the 3rd, 9th, 13th, 16th and 48th Detachments and became the Central Air Group in the Aleksandrovsk sector. In numbers, it equaled that of Wrangels. It contained 17 fighter and 11 observer pilots. The Red air detachments in the South Front amounted to 79 aircraft (of them 42 were in good condition). However, only 10, at most, were ever able to be used at the same time due to parts and pilots. This irritated Stalin, who demanded to know a mass bombing could not take place. Pavlov, its commander cited the usual reasons.

By September, the Red Central Air Group was replenished with two heavy bombers, the "Ilya Muromets." Their appearance over the lines shocked the Whites who for the first time felt the weight of the large bombers. Each such aircraft could lift 16 pood of bombs (256 kilo or 578 lbs.) and could inflict very serious losses.

On September 2nd, one of the «Muromets» under the command of Red Army pilot Shkodov dropped 11 pood of bombs on the village of Prishib, where the staff of Drozdovsky's Officer Division was located. On September 8th, another "Muromets" piloted by Timansk dropped 4 incindiary bombs and 2 HE bombs on the airfield containing the 2nd Detachment of the Russian Army near Fedorovk. Four White Guard airplanes were destroyed. On September 14th, the bombers bombed the German colony of Fridricksfeld, where about three thousand White Guards were camped This raid resulted in 27 killed. On September 16th, two «Muromets» made an appearance over the village of Prishib. But this raid posed danger as it was defended by an armored train armed with AA guns. The aircraft dueled with the flak resulting in small mutual damage. Shrapnel from the flak guns hit Timansk's wing and incapacitating one motor of Shkodov's aircraft. On return both bombers were in need of repair.

The Red bombers returned after repairs, bombing Wrangel's troops in Andrebirg, Geidelberg and Gogkheim. Some 16 pood of bombs and 6 pood darts were dropped. On their return journey, already over its own territory, the two bombers unexpectedly met four White DH9s that were also returning from a mission. The unique battle between single-engine bombers and multiengine bombers now commenced! The "DH9s" concentrated fire upon Timansk's aircraft. Three attacked from the rearl and one came in from below. The gunner Mikhailovsk on the type G-3 "Muromets" desperately beat off the rear attacks. In the battle, the gunner consumed 16 "Lewis" machine-gun pans. The DH9s had previously already used most of the MG rounds and were only able to hit a fuel pan. The encounter was unique and luckily for the Red heavy bombers, the White DH9s had little ammo remaining to attack with. This was the last combat flight of heavy bombers in the Civil war. Some 20 machines in September flew to rear airfields in Osier and then to Kharkov. It is possible that the Reds did not want run risks by a few expensive machines, and also that the "Muromets" were excessive in their use of fuel. One four-engine bomber burned 30 poods of benzene and one and a half pood of motor oil in one sortie.

Wrangel's total force amounted to 25,000 infantry and 8000 cavalry. Wrangel now began his last offensive which started on the 25th along the Dniepr River. The 2nd Army under General Dratzenko crossed at the Isle of Khoritsa and reached Alexandrovsk on the left bank. His men were up to their necks in water as the crossed while under MG and artillery fire. This created panic in the Reds, which fled. A critical pontoon bridge was placed at Uchkelkaon the night of the 26th allowing Wrangel to cross in pursuit. Taking 3000 POWs, 8 guns, 6 armor cars and one train. The 2nd Army continued the advance on the 27th and 28th as the Reds fell back. On the 29th, a brilliant cavalry raid led by General Babiev caught the Reds retreating and totally disorganized them. Meanwhile, Dratzenko was too cautious and indecisive in his advance and on the 30th, Wrangel sent him a telegram, demanding swift action. Wrangel's air reconnaissance indicated that the Reds were leaving the fortress at Kahovka. By Oct. 1st, Wrangel was at the Dniepr river and the Red 2nd Cavalry army raced to fortify the right bank. The 1st Army led by Kutepov had also arrived at the river, crossing it on the 8th with a shock force of three infantry and three cavalry divisions.

Now, the Red 6th army was facing destruction and only the 2nd cavalry army prevented this.

Wrangel's "Across the Dniepr"operation would be his last. He knew that once the 1st cavalry army arrived led by Budenny from the Polish front, any success would be harder. Wrangel and Poland could (he hoped) join in their attacks.

The only Red force that prevented Wrangel was the Red 2nd cavalry army commanded by Philip Mironov, a popular Don leader sentenced to death by Trotsky. The death sentence was commuted because of need. In 1920, Lenin greatly feared that Poland and Wrangel would link. Lenin appointed him the commander. The army had been held in reserve since September, which was only 2760 men,130 MG and 19 guns. By October, it was 8100 men, 400 MG and 60 guns.

On the 11th, Babiev's cavalry captured 3000 Reds by outflanking the Kahovka position while the 1st Army north of Melitpol cut elements of the 6th and 13th Soviet armies. On October 12th, the 1st Corps under Kutepov captured Mariupol and capturing 4000 Reds. The Alexandrovsk operation had only cost 1st corps 50 Kia and 300 Wia. The plan to take Kahovka, a fortified Red zone using three lines of trenches, wire, blockhouses and artillery on the hill behind the town at Berislav. To seize it, the 1st Army would strike from Alexandrovsk into the rear of Nikopol, while 2nd Army (minus Vitkovski's Corps) would cross at Nikopol using 3rd Corps and advance on Berislav. Vitkovski's 34th division would cross at the French Monastery, 15 miles south of Kahovka, using a large barge and entrusted to the newly create Guard Regiment of 16 companies. The 13th division would storm the town itself using tanks and air support. All this was to advance to the Donetz, which if a success, would be the end of the Reds. But Wrangel's air reconnaissance had provided very incorrect information about the Reds abandoning the town.

On the 12th, General Vitkorvsky's units attacked the fortress of Kahovka using tanks. The MkV's and Whippets rumbled across the barb wire allowing the Whites penetrate, but the infantry lagged, and five tanks were able to cross the main trench line. The five MkV tanks neared the town thinking the infantry was behind them. Subsequently. the crews were easily picked off by special anti-tank artillery guns until none were left. Apparently, the air recon information had been totally incorrect. Later, Wrangel found out that Gen. Babiev had been killed and then his replacement, Gen. Naoumenko, was also wounded. This left the cavalry leaderless, which is why they had become so disorganized. The battle raged from October 11th to 14th, and 1st army had taken Nikopol before Mironov had learned that Wrangel's Pisarev Corps also threatening him on the right.

The climax was reached on the 14th. Mironov knowing this, summoned his 2nd cavalry division and ordered a brigade to charge Wrangel's trenches in a series of delayed bunches of cavalry. This made his force appear much larger than it was. The White artillery honed in, but against charging cavalry had little effect. Company after company charged over a distance of 300 paces. The Whites began to lose nerve and abandoned Marinskoye once Grushevka fell. Wrangel's men retreated back across the Dnepr only to find out that the Markov and Kornilov divisions, Babiev's cavalry and the 6th and 7th divisions had been crushed and left behind on the right bank (Red side). It was over. Mironov later wrote:

> "...the time had come for rapidity, purposefulness and decisiveness. It was sheer hell, what with the thunder of artillery and the clatter of machine guns and rifles."

Wrangel withdrew and now was faced with feeding 250,000 inhabitants of the area he had recently won and with no means to do so. The Treasury showed a deficit of 250 milliards.

Earlier, on Oct. 6th, French General Brossaud visited Wrangel at Sevastopol and discussed the gloomy outlook of success.

On the 15th, the Reds attacked with 45000 men, 15000 cavalry(by some accounts). The 2nd Corps amazingly gave ground slowly and on the 16th, Budenny's 1st Cavalry Army arrived and tried to envelope the retreating 2nd Corps in very thick fog. The temperature was –14°F below zero. The only way out was now through Salkovo (this was only lightly manned). Wrangel on the 17th, ordered a division to Salkovo, but because the roads were clogged progress was slow. Salkovo was stormed by the Reds on the 18th. The door to the Crimea was open and Wrangel was helpless. The fighting withdrawal was difficult in freezing temperatures and by the 20th, half of the Corps had arrived there. On the 26th, The Reds had broken through near Perekop and encircled the 1st Corps. Wrangel planned for an evacuation and the Allies agreed to evacuate 13000 men. By October 31, it really was finally all over. The Russian Civil War had ended. By November 16th, the last massive evacuation occurred as 126 Allied ships carried 100,000 persons away.

The Soviets and Communist virus had been allowed to flourish until the system collapsed in 1991.

Flyable Aircraft in Wrangel's Air Detachments

Detachments	9/22/.20	10/7/20	10/23/20
1st	3	2	0
2nd	7	6	5
3rd fighter	1	3	2
4th	4	4	6
5th	6	4	7
6th	4	6	?*
8th	5	3	2
Total	30	28	22

The Red Airforce flew against 2100 sorties and dropped on 6400 kilos of bombs. The Whites flew 387 sorties and had dropped 12800 kilos of bombs.

The only Americans to see action in South Russia were Admiral McCully and Lt.Cmdr. Hugo Koehler, US Navy Intelligence. Like General Holman, Koehler went to the front and disregarded Admiral's McCully's direct orders not to intervene and only observe. McCully was never involved in combat, although, the Cruiser USS Galvestan did fire occassionally.

Koehler became personally involved on June 10th, 1920, the Reds had entered into combat with Wrangel's forces front line cavalry troops attacking Melitopol. During the attack, the troops became surrounded by a Red counterattack. Koehler and others fought their way out and the papers he had taken from the Red headquarters earlier were of great use to Wrangel. Thus, the only American in South Russia was awarded the Distinguished Service Medal by McCully. Wrangel awarded him the Order of St. Anne medal. The Americans were also at Novorossisk on March 26th, 1920. Lt. Cmdr. Koehler noted the following:

> "Friday morning broke calm and clear. Temperatures range from minus 5 degrees to 20 degrees. A chicken in the market cost 600 rubles, while Denikin himself received 6000 rubles per month. The Galveston laid just off the docks. Outside in the bay lay the mighty Battleship Emperor of India,Light Cruiser Calypso and the French Battleship Wedlock Rousseau. With powerful glasses we scanned the surrounding hills from crest down the winding roads, to the base......to the northeast where small cavalry units could be seen making their way down the slopes. These were the Volunteer forces. Early in forenoon, the BB Emperor of India opened up with 13.5 inch turret guns, firing directly over us toward the village perhaps seven miles up the valley. A scouting aeroplane flew back and forth to report the results. The naval fire did not seem effective. About noon, fires begin to break out in the area of the railway....soon an uncontrolled and vicious fire was raging,consuming everything in its path. By 1100 on Saturday, the Reds were in possession of the town."

There is little doubt in this author's mind that had the British been more committed and provided Denikin even one standard British, first line infantry division, Denikin may have been able to reach Moscow. The whole issue was morale, and if British troops were actually deployed in the beginning instead of the end, the outcome could have had been different. The "will" so far off in London, in the War Cabinet, simply was lacking. Granted, this is not to say that Communism would had never occurred, but had Moscow been reached in October, 1919, the repercussions would had been astounding. For that matter, even the 47th Squadron could have caused a panic if they had been allowed to bomb Moscow (as was proposed).

As in Kosovo, 1999, the politics dictated the military role. And in 1919, the British wanted to stamp out the communist virus and had the means, it lacked the will to allow it's military to be directly and knowingly involved in most cases. When the brave British men refuted the War Cabinets orders regarding participation, the results were astounding. Looked at what a British crew achieved with a single MkV tank at Tsaritsyn, look at the damage the 47th squadron did to the Volga flotilla and how Wrangel thanked them for their skillied air support.

This issue was repeated again with the French in Vietnam and then the Americans. They had the military strength but lacked the will.

The body count of the Russian Civil War is estimated at 25 million KIA.

The White Armies used a sort of Blitzkrieg in their attacks. The cavalry was lightening fast and maneuvered quickly outflanking and surrounding the enemy. But Denikin failed to listen to Wrangel's advice, to create a cavalry army; instead, Denikin parceled out these units across the vast front as he did with the tanks. Wrangel had suggested of creating this cavalry army in June, 1919, three months before the Reds would. The unit as far as Wrangel was concerned would be used as a breakthrough unit allowing the infantry to follow. To do so, Wrangel had proposed to use the Volunteer, Don, Kuban,and Terek cavalry corps. Denikin listened to this plan after the fall of Tsaritsyn. He rejected it as he felt it would weaken the front. Oddly, both men were right. But it was Mamentov's raid that allowed the Soviets to see the promise. A month later, the 1st Cavalry Army existed and caused considerable problems to Denikin's demise months later.

Epilogue

The costs are estimated at £100,000,000 for England and £35,000,000 for France. This intervention that did not have to fail. From January-February, 1920, £250,000 worth of equipment and supplies had been stolen from the docks at Novorossisk. It was a very costly failure.

The following are some of lesser known key participants:

General Peter Wrangel died in Brussels, Belgium in 1928 and buried in Belgrade

General Kuptepov, the commander of the 1st Corps, the best unit in the Volunteers, was murdered in Paris. On January 26th, 1930, he was kidnapped off the streets and Soviet agents took him back to a Russian trawler. In 1965, the KGB finally admitted they had executed him.

General Romanovski, Denikin's Chief of Staff, was murdered in Constantinople by a Soviet agent.

General Denikin, lived in France, raising his Daughter, Marina, born in February 1920. He wrote books and gardened. Later he moved to the United States of America and died in 1947. Oddly, he had seen how the failure of stamping out communism had piqued the world. In 1940, the Nazi's tried to persuade him to make radio broadcasts delivering anti-communist propaganda.

Hudleston Williamson, became a Lt. Col. in 1935,in 1939, he commanded the 50th division and became the 3rd Corps commander. He retired in 1945 as Brig. General. He died in 1970. He served in South Russia as an artillery advisor.

General Holman retired after he returned and died in the 1930's.

Lt. William Elliot, who was an low ranking officer in 1919 and who flew Williamson around the South Russia area looking for gas shells. He became Chief Air Marshal Sir William Elliot much later in WW2.

Major Collishaw, who was the commander of the famed 47th RAF Squadron, became Air Vice Marshal in WW2. He commanded the RAF at Alamein. He approved of direct intervention. He had shot down over 50 aircraft in his career.

General Budenny, the famed Soviet Cavalry leader, proved he was inept when he lost 500,000 Russians at Kiev in 1941 to an old enemy. He died in 1973 at age 90 yrs.

Nestor Makhano, the vicious guerilla fighter, escaped the Soviet Police in 1922, fleeing to Poland with his beautiful Polish girlfriend. Upon his arrival, he murdered her parents. The two got married. He died an alcoholic in the 30's.

Peter Krasnov, the Commander of the Don Army was hanged in 1947 by the Soviets after the British handed him over.

Ataman Shkuro, who was a fierce Cavalry Corps commander under Mamantov, was hanged with Krasnov. During the inter war period of the thirties, he performed in a circus. In 1941, fought along side with Germans when Russia was invaded.

The two most famous Comminsaars were **Stalin** and **Kruschev**, who in the fall of 1919, rallied the Soviet party members against Denikin. Both became the "President" of the Soviet Union. Stalin ordered millions murdered in the 30's. Stalin died in 1953. Kruschev, followed as "President" and never forgot the American intervention. He reminded president Kennedy of this "invasion" in 1961-2. Kennedy denied this ever happening and no knowledge of this event. Stalin renamed Tsaritsyn, Stalingrad, which was his area of responsibility in 1919.

Koniev, the most famous Generals of the WW2, was a young commander in the 2nd division under Semenov fighting Kolchak. By 1934, he was commanding an Army, and in WW2, a whole Front. He died in 1973.

Popov, another famous General of WW2, commanded the 96th battalion of the 11th division in Nov. 1919. He was Front Commander in WW2. He died in 1962.

Timoshenko, another well-known General in WW2, was part of the 2nd Cavalry brigade of 1st division in June 1919 and fought with 10th Army against Denikin in the Kuban and later the Crimea. He died in 1970.

Lt. Cmdr. Koehler, the only American in combat in South Russia. He became an attache for the US in Poland in the mid twenties. His son was born in 1929, then he became divorced. He died in 1941.

2nd Lieutenant Marion Hughes Aten - Order of St. Vladimir, 4th Class, with Swords and Bow - date uncertain - see Air 1/1957/204/260/12. American pilot (family owned a ranch near El Centro, California). Joined RFC in Toronto, November 1917; appointed Second Lieutenant, RAF, 24 April 1918; Flew with Collishaw in South Russia and wrote Last Train Over Rostov Bridge.

Lieutenant John Sharpe Griffith - Distinguished Flying Cross . Another American from Los Angeles, California, joined RFC and trained in Canada, going overseas in late 1917. Subsequently posted to the ELOPE Squadron which left Britain for Archangel, September 1918, although he did not join until spring of 1919. Seems to have flown Camels in Russia, sometimes with a camera. Served in American forces, Second World War, including a party that negotiated USAAF bombing bases in Russia. Died 14 October 1974 in Rivermead, California. For reports of balloon busting see Air 1/1552/204/79/58 in MG.40 D.1 Vol.27.

Flying Officer Lloyd Wesley Mason - Distinguished Flying Cross . Another American from Detroit, Michigan; appointed 2nd Lieutenant, RFC (Canada), 13 August 1917; with "D" Squadron, Upavon, 15 December 1917; No.2 AASD, 3-9 March, 1918 when hospitalized; invalided to UK, 30 March 1918; to No.95 Squadron, 1 October 1918; died in Phoenix, Arizona, 22 December 1971. Award won in Russia.

"This officer has shown great dash and courage whilst flying a Snipe at extremely low altitudes. He has taken part in operations throughout the summer both on the Dwina and Railway Fronts, and has attacked many targets with his machine guns, dispersing troops and breaking up counter-attacks. In an attack on Puchega Aerodrome he descended very near the ground in an endeavour to silence machine-guns which were concentrated on his Squadron Commander's machine"

Dmitry Lehovich, he was a young 19yr.old foot soldier in Denikin's Volunteer army and excellent eyewitness to these events. He survived and immigrated to America, got married, received his college degree in Banking. He wrote the fine book "White Against Red" published in 1970. Imagine what his eyes had seen.

Sources

1) Agureev, K.B. *Defeating Denikins Army*. Moscow Press. 1961
2) Denikin, Anton. *March on Moscow*. Moscow Press. 1921
3) Denikin, Anton. *The White Armies*. Hyperion Press. 1973
4) Wrangel, Peter. *Memoirs of General Wrangel*. 1930

5) *Civil War and Foreign Intervention in USSR Encylclopedia.* Moscow Press. 1983
6) Krasnov, Peter. *The Don Army 1918-19.* Moscow Press. 1992
7) Wrangel, Peter. The Peter Vrangel Collection. The Hoover Archives, Stanford University.
8) Lehovich, Dmity. *White Against Red.* 1970
9) Reed, John. *Ten Days That Shook the World.*
10) Butt, V.P. *The Russian Civil War: Documents from the Soviet Archives.* Moscow Press.
11) Malet, Michael. *Nestor Makhano in the Russian Civil War.*
12) Capelotti, P.J. *Our Man in the Crimea: Commander Hugo Koehler.*
13) Iakushkin, Everginei. *English Intervention 1918-20.* Moscow Press. 1928
14) *Imperialism and Intervention on the Don.* Moscow Press. 1988.
15) Dobson, Christopher. *The Day They Almost Bombed Moscow.* 1986
16) Krylenko, N. *Red and White Terror.* London. 1928
17) Stewart,George. *The White Armies of Russia.* 1970
18) Brinkly,George. *The Volunteer Army and the Allied Intervention in Russia in South Russia.* 1966
19) Weekly Tank Notes. Vols.40-52, British Army. August 1919.
20) Roberts, C. *In Denikin's Russia and the Caucasus, 1919-20.* 1921.
21) The Pavel Kusonskii Collection. Hoover Institution, Stanford University.
22) *Tanks in the Russian Revolution.* Armada No.14. Moscow Press. 1999
23) *Armor Cars of the Russian Civil War.* Moscow Press. 2000
24) *The First Russian Tanks.* Moscow Press. 2000.
25) *Aircraft of the Russian Civil War.* Moscow Press. 2000

The following are from the Public Records Office in London:

WO 106/1198
WO 158/746,747
WO 153/795
WO 33/971
CAB 45/5752
WO 153/1208
ADM 137/3943
WO 32/5685
WO 106/377
WO 106/1204, 1191
CAB 45/105
ADM 137/1613
WO 158/715, 751, 748
WO 106/1153,1155
WO 106/1206
WO 95/4955
WO 106/1205